REPUBLICA ARGENTINA
DIRECCION NACIONAL DE MIGRACIONES
19 OCT.
TURISTA 3 MESES
KU-244-595
24 MAY
UruguayNatural
JUL 2
BRASIL
●活字体で記入して下さい。
●折らないで下さい。
●カード②は出国時に入国審査官へ提出するものです。
＊Please type or print. ＊Do not fold.
＊CARD ② is to be submitted to the Immigration Inspector at the

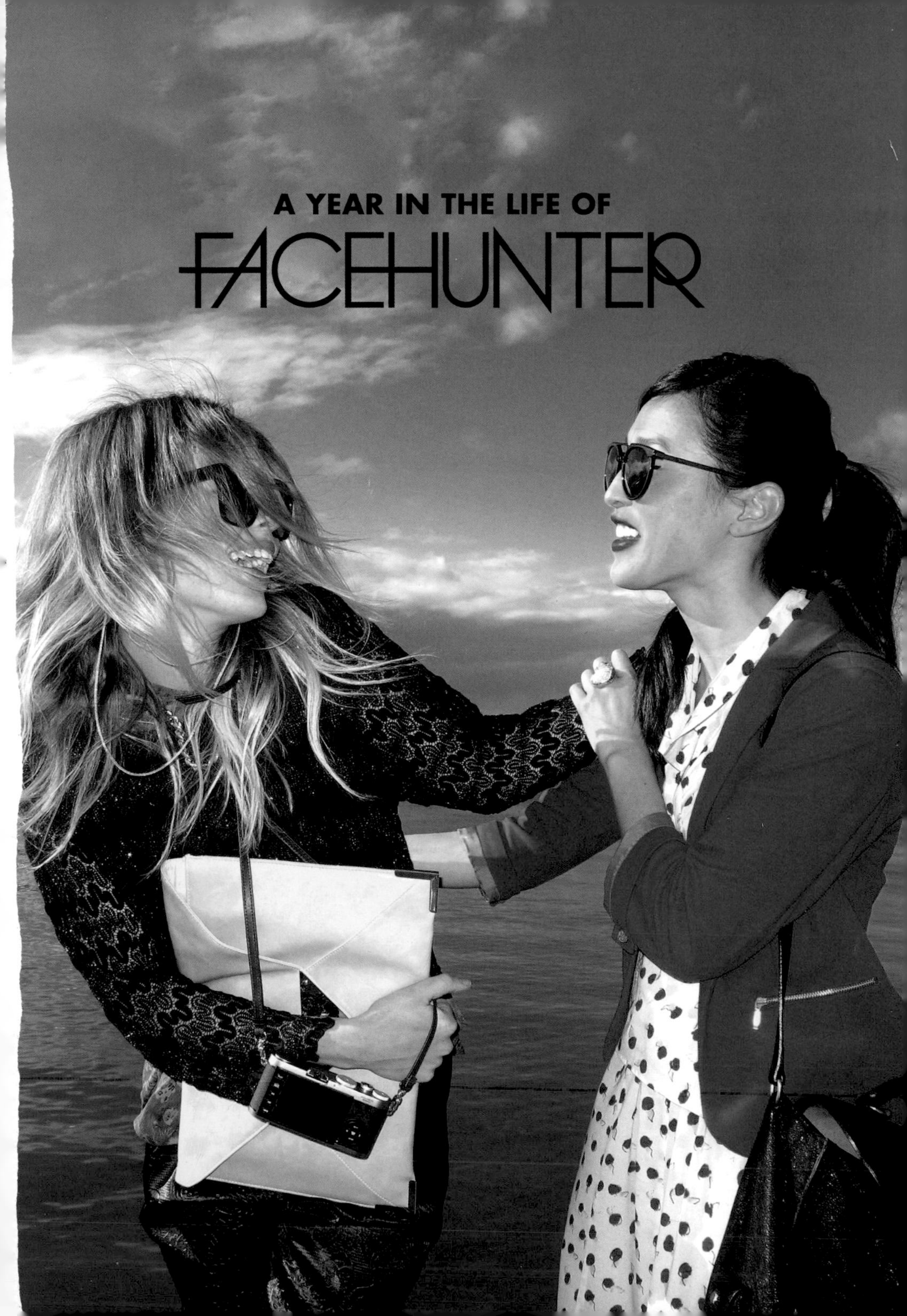

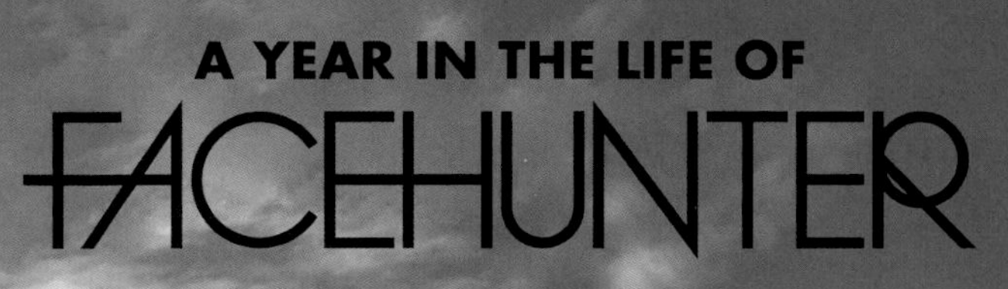
A YEAR IN THE LIFE OF
FACEHUNTER

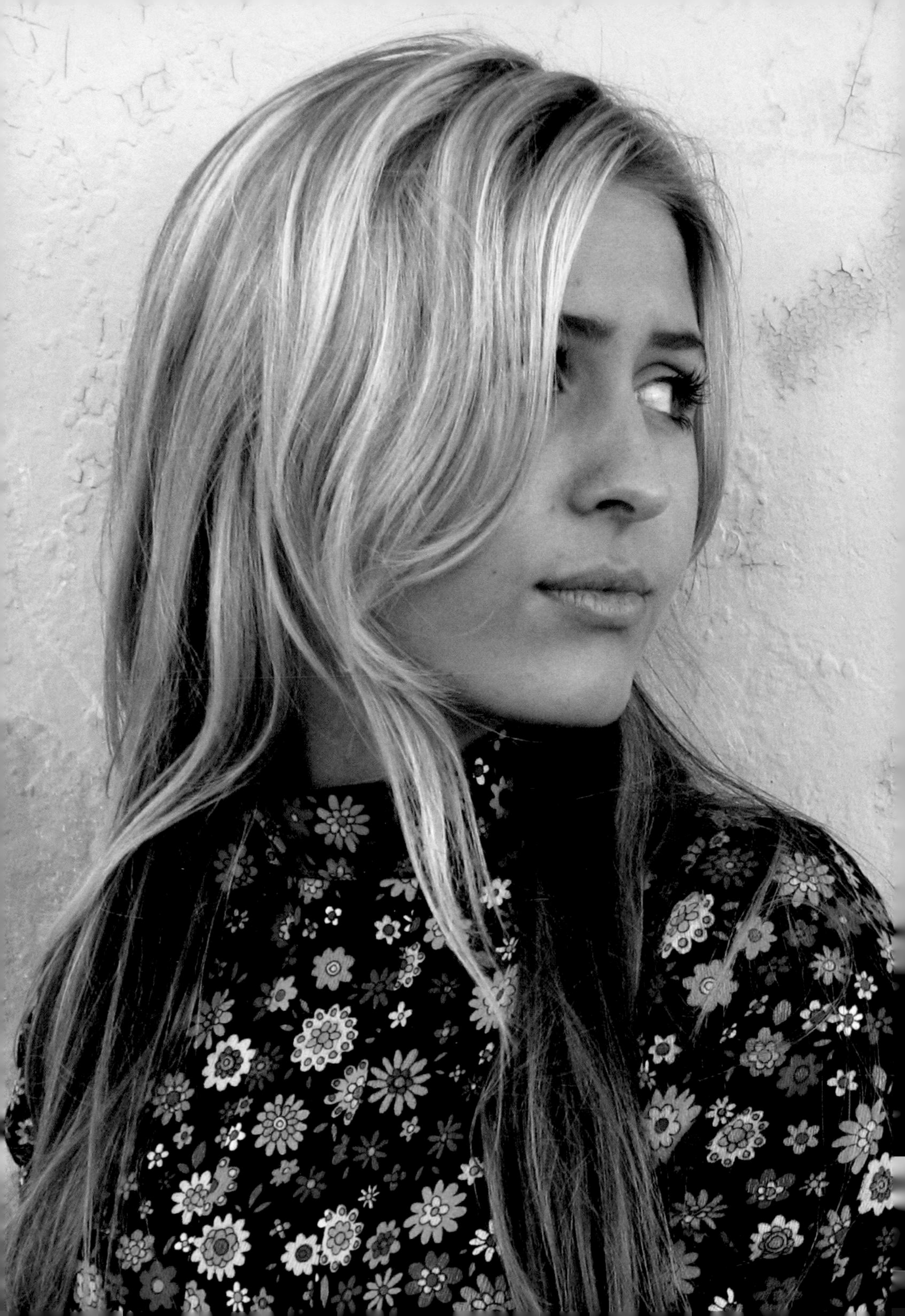

A YEAR IN THE LIFE OF
FACEHUNTER

YVAN RODIC

With 680 photographs, 656 in colour

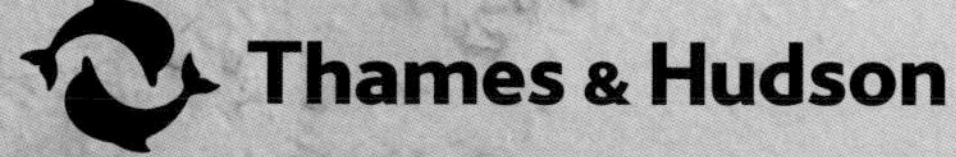

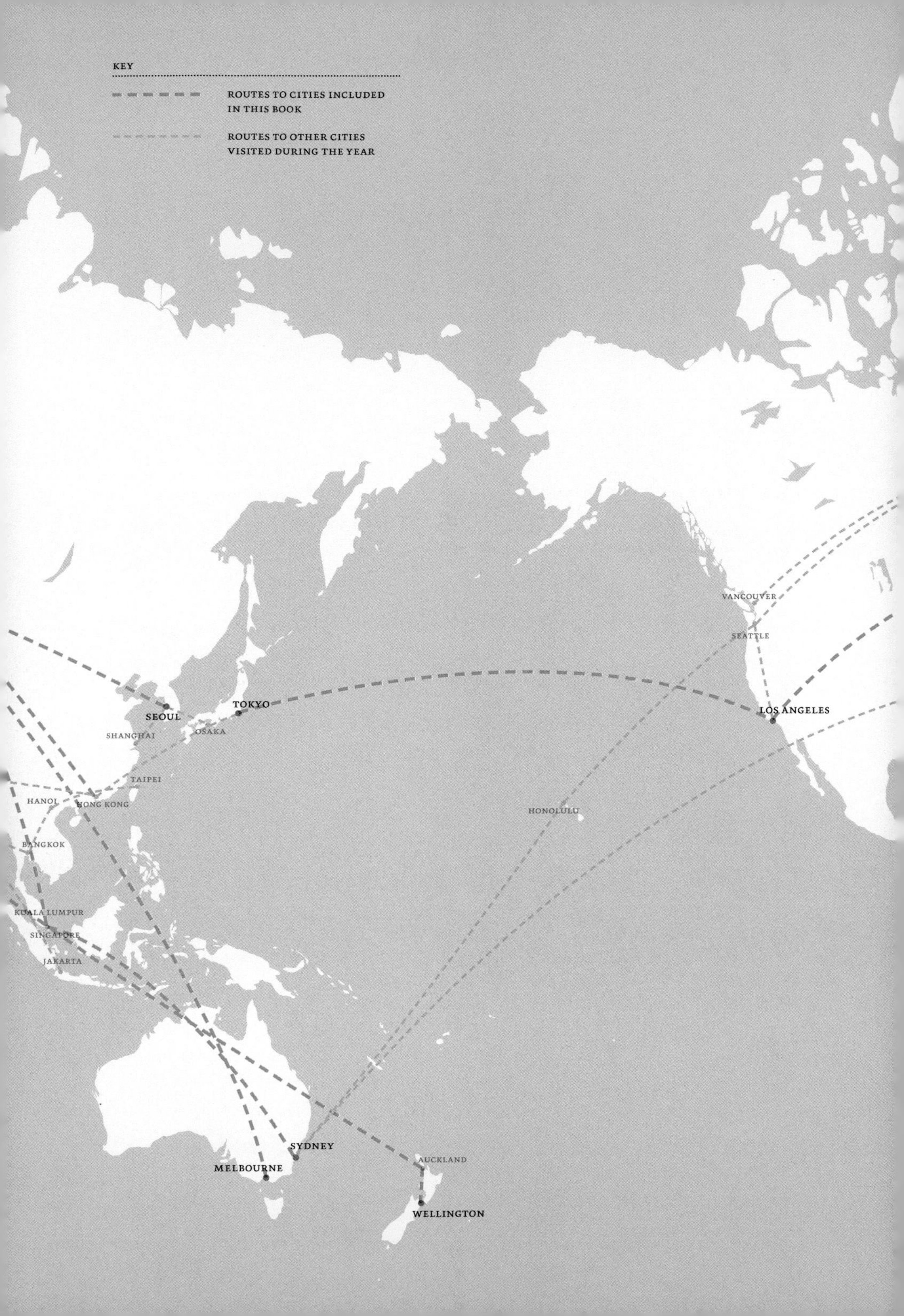

KEY

ROUTES TO CITIES INCLUDED IN THIS BOOK

ROUTES TO OTHER CITIES VISITED DURING THE YEAR

VANCOUVER
SEATTLE
LOS ANGELES
TOKYO
SEOUL
OSAKA
SHANGHAI
TAIPEI
HANOI
HONG KONG
HONOLULU
BANGKOK
KUALA LUMPUR
SINGAPORE
JAKARTA
SYDNEY
MELBOURNE
AUCKLAND
WELLINGTON

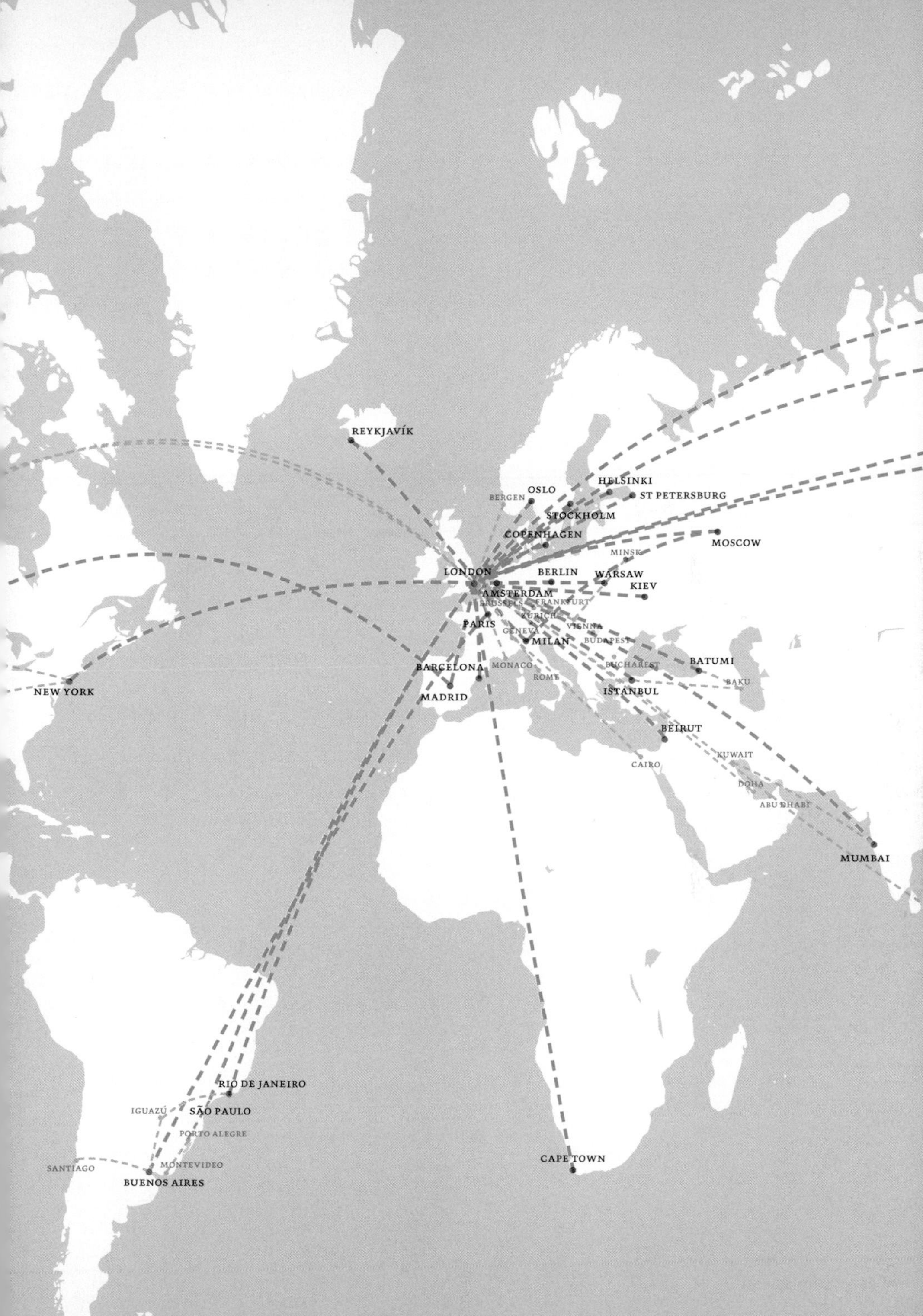

REYKJAVÍK
BERGEN
OSLO
HELSINKI
ST PETERSBURG
STOCKHOLM
COPENHAGEN
MOSCOW
MINSK
LONDON
BERLIN
WARSAW
KIEV
AMSTERDAM
BRUSSELS
FRANKFURT
ZURICH
PARIS
GENEVA
VIENNA
MILAN
BUDAPEST
BATUMI
BARCELONA
MONACO
BUCHAREST
ROME
BAKU
NEW YORK
ISTANBUL
MADRID
BEIRUT
KUWAIT
CAIRO
DOHA
ABU DHABI
MUMBAI
RIO DE JANEIRO
IGUAZÚ
SÃO PAULO
PORTO ALEGRE
CAPE TOWN
SANTIAGO
MONTEVIDEO
BUENOS AIRES

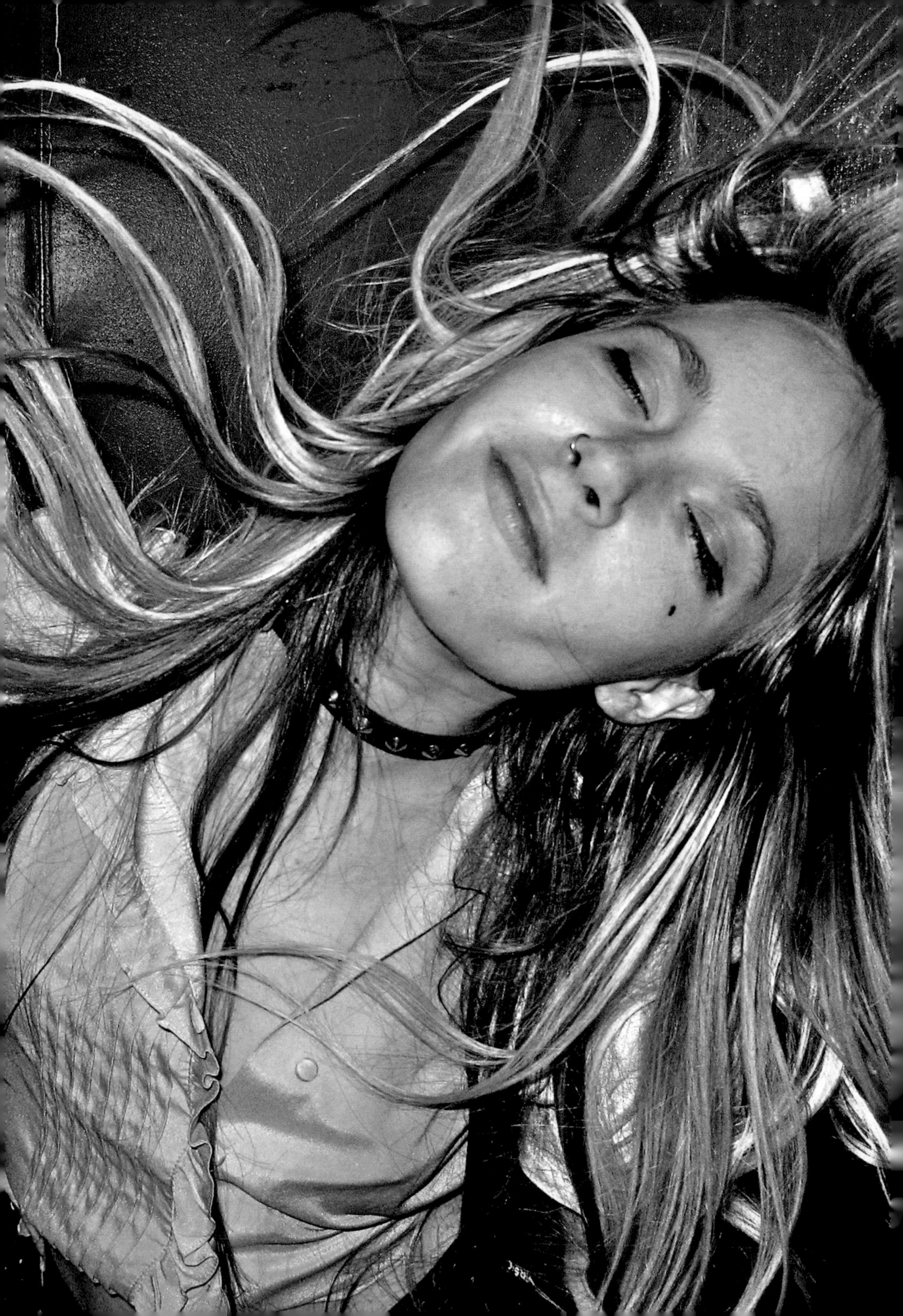

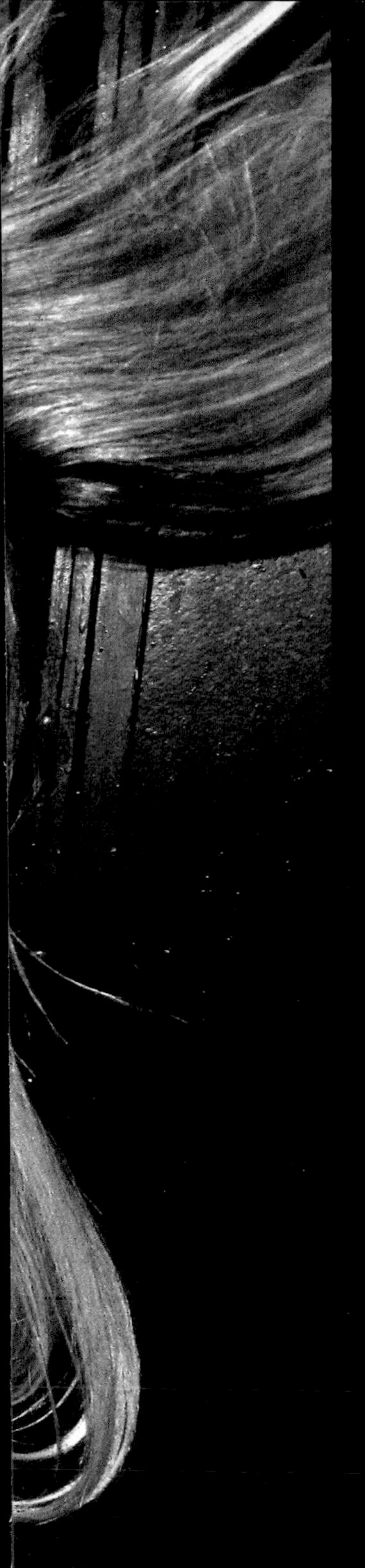

CONTENTS

INTRODUCTION 8

NEW YORK 12
MILAN 26
REYKJAVÍK 36
SÃO PAULO 48
BATUMI 58
BEIRUT 68
ISTANBUL 78
SEOUL 90
TOKYO 100
CAPE TOWN 112
BERLIN 122
MOSCOW 132
STOCKHOLM 142
HELSINKI 152
LONDON 162
LOS ANGELES 176
MADRID 184
WARSAW 192
ST PETERSBURG 202
WELLINGTON 212
SYDNEY 220
KIEV 230
RIO DE JANEIRO 238
OSLO 248
MUMBAI 256
COPENHAGEN 262
BARCELONA 272
AMSTERDAM 280
PARIS 286
BUENOS AIRES 298
MELBOURNE 306
STATISTICS 318

INTRODUCTION

The book you are holding is a miracle. Strictly speaking, it should not even exist! After I visited Rio, where everyone warned me to be careful and to watch out for thieves, I flew to Oslo, one of the safest and wealthiest cities in the world, and had my laptop stolen from my hotel room in broad daylight, in the middle of a Monday afternoon. I lost everything: years of photographs gone, including many of the images in this book. A few months later I got an email from the French border patrol, who had caught two guys who they suspected had a stolen laptop, and, thanks to Apple, Inc., had managed to trace me from the laptop's serial number. Six months later, when I finally went to Bayonne to pick up my computer from the police, I discovered that the thieves had wiped my hard drive and added their own photos. (Getting my computer back with a picture of the thief still set as the wallpaper has to be one of my most disturbing experiences ever.) Luckily I found a data-recovery expert in East London who for £100 recovered around half a million files. The bad news was that half of them were corrupted. But that still left about 250,000 good pictures. So, to finally be able to publish images that were in criminal hands for months – how magic is that?

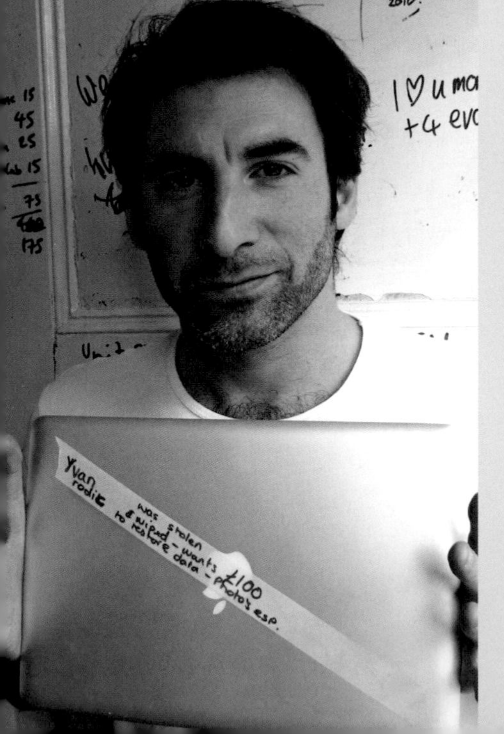

As I looked through all these old pictures, deciding what could be salvaged, I realized how much my work had been changing over the past few years – and how much street style itself had changed as well. In the romantic early days when I first started blogging as Face Hunter (http://www.facehunter.org/), the street-style photographer had to walk the streets for hours like a *flâneur* to find his subjects. Now, street-style photography – once a grass-roots alternative to the mainstream, commercial fashion media – has itself become commercialized, a change that is summed up by the hardcore competitive 'speed-dating' scene that you see outside the annual fashion shows, with hundreds of 'creatively' dressed people (some brands even send their latest designs to street-style darlings so they can wear them when they attend the show) vying for the attention of the 'street' photographers and fashion bloggers. Street style still interests me, but it's becoming an increasingly narrow field. So I felt that it was time to widen the spectrum and take inspiration not just from the people waiting outside the Chanel show, but from entire cities: the architecture, the food, the people.

This new book shows the evolution of my work as I've moved from being a street-style blogger to something more like a cultural explorer. It's no longer about fashion people inspiring fashion people – it's about real life inspiring people. My second website (http://yvanrodic.com/), from which the material for this book comes, takes travel as its theme, reflecting my current interests and lifestyle. It's about capturing sources of creative inspiration from people and cities around the world, which can be applied to any creative field, not just fashion.

This is also a book about travelling without a guidebook. I've never, ever bought a travel guide – it's against my entire philosophy. There's something depressingly unadventurous about trying to reproduce someone else's route and visit all the trendy places a writer has described a couple years before. I'm more interested in social travelling. I meet people – often via my website – who encourage me to visit their home countries or cities, and usually these people end up being my guides. They take me with them to their favourite places, restaurants and parties, introduce me to their friends, and in an organic way I get to discover new parts of the world without really thinking about it or doing much planning. I've flown over ten times around the earth this year, logging over 600 hours in a plane and visiting on average two or three countries a week. (I know all this because Kate, the book's designer, thought it would be fun to compile my complete annual travel statistics on p. 318.) This book chronicles some of my favourite trips in a typical year. To all the beautiful people I met in Shanghai, Taipei, Hong Kong, Hanoi, Bangkok, Kuala Lumpur, Singapore, Jakarta, Honolulu, Vancouver, Seattle, Chicago, Santiago, Iguazú, Montevideo, Porto Allegre, Bergen, Brussels, Monaco, Frankfurt, Zurich, Geneva, Rome, Vienna, Budapest, Bucharest, Cairo, Kuwait, Doha, Abu Dhabi, Minsk and Baku – it's not your fault that the pictures didn't come out as well as I wanted this time (or, in many cases, didn't survive the theft of my laptop)! We'll try again next year.

BISOUS, YVAN

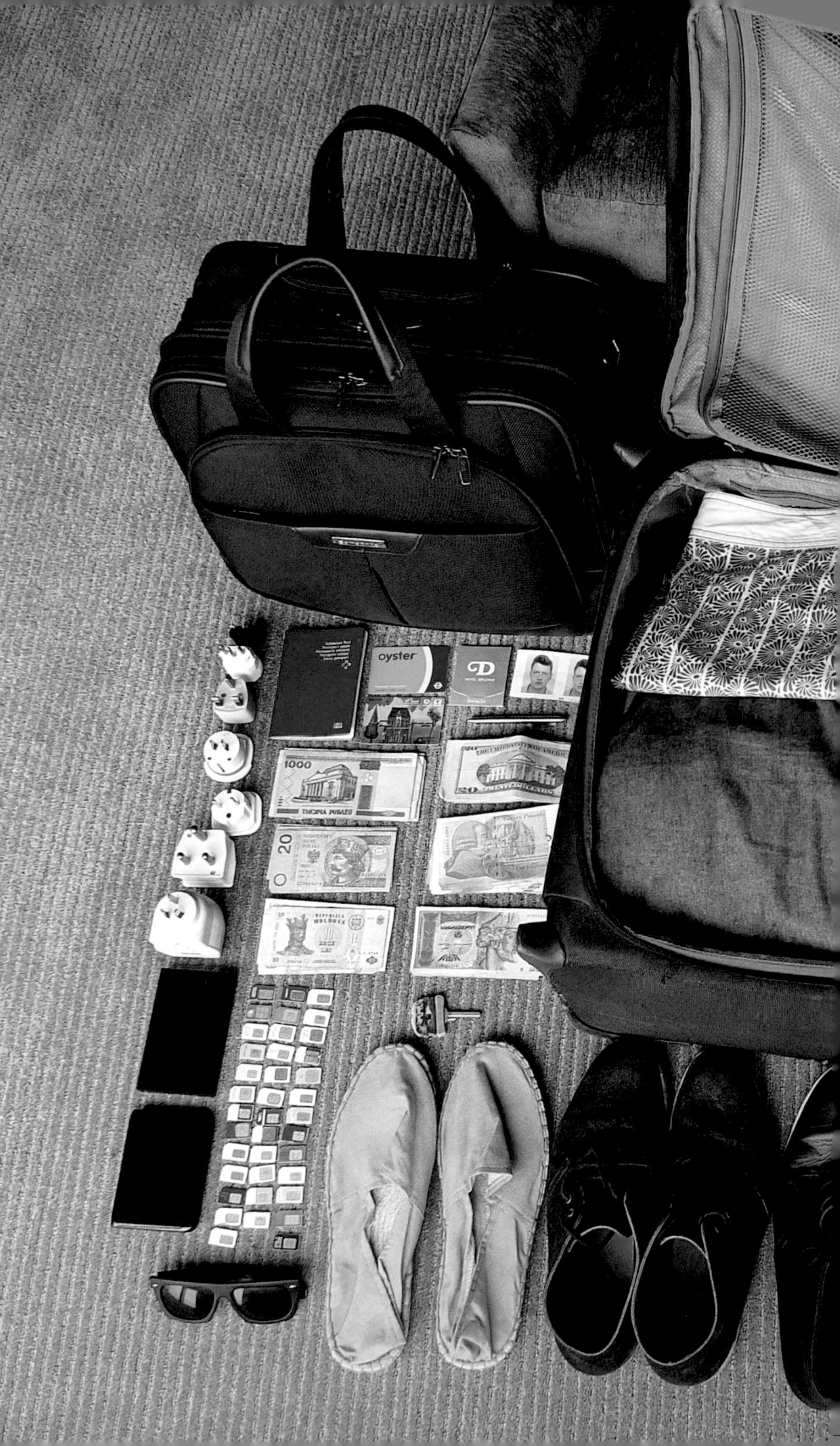
oyster

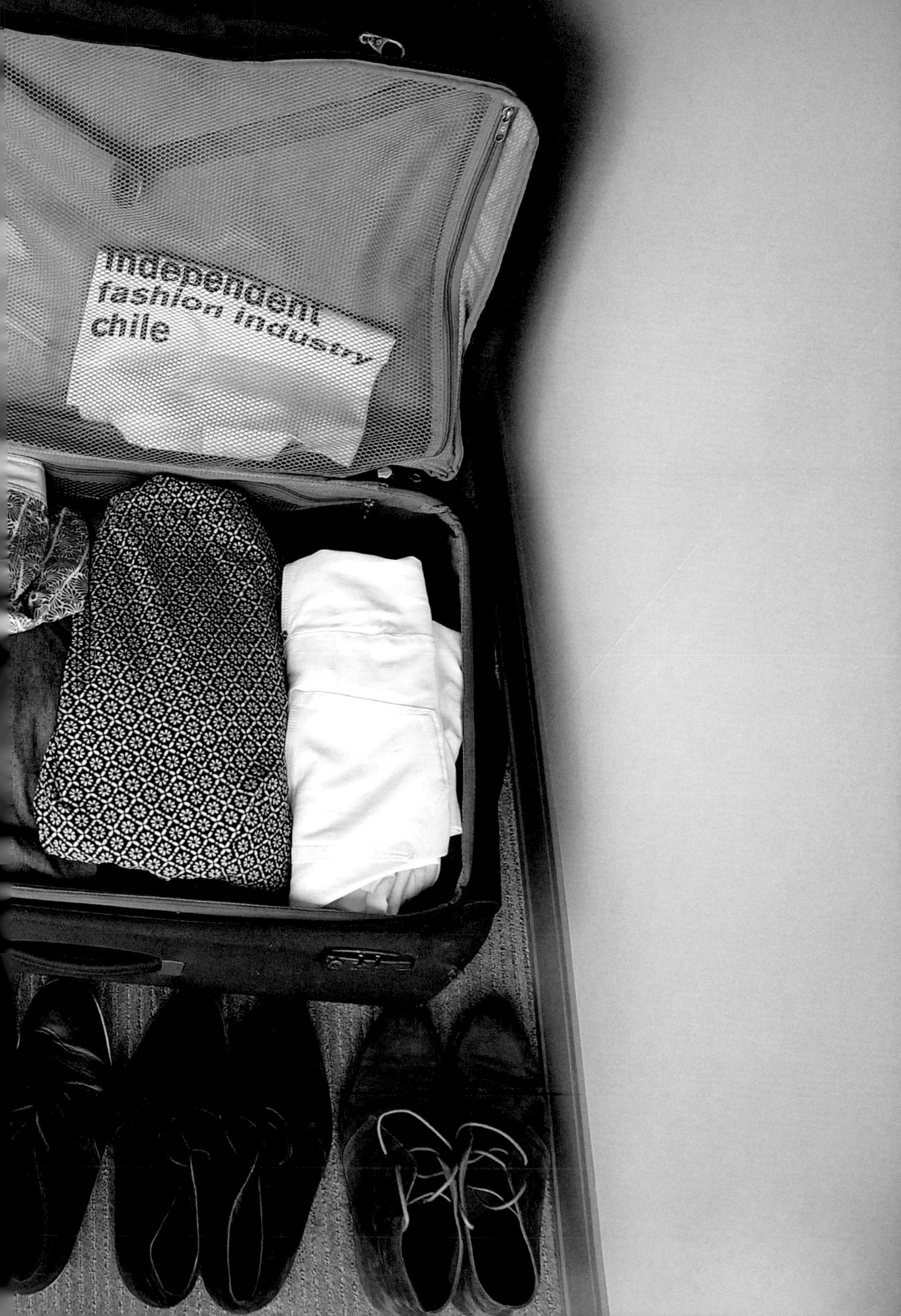
independent
fashion industry
chile

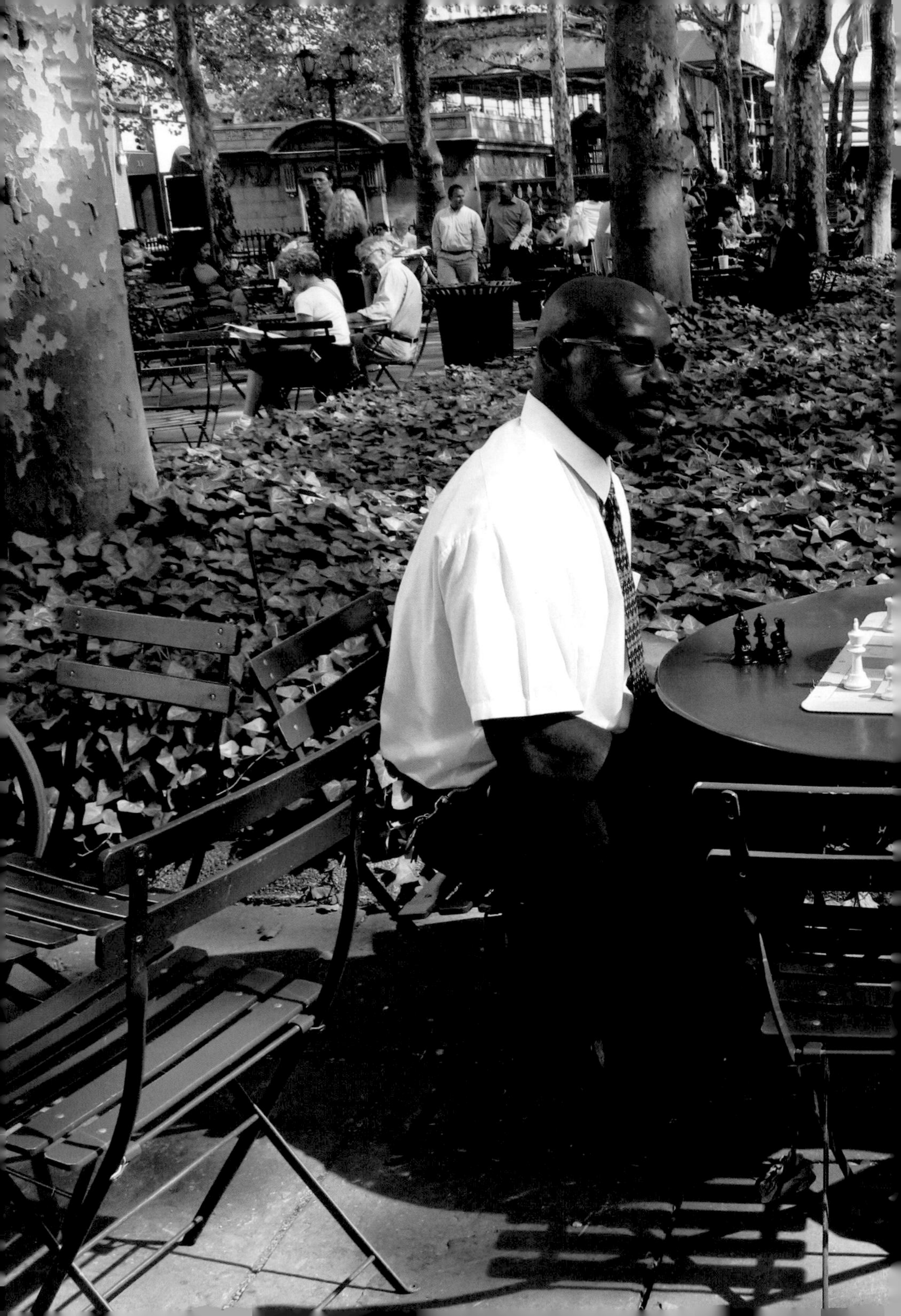

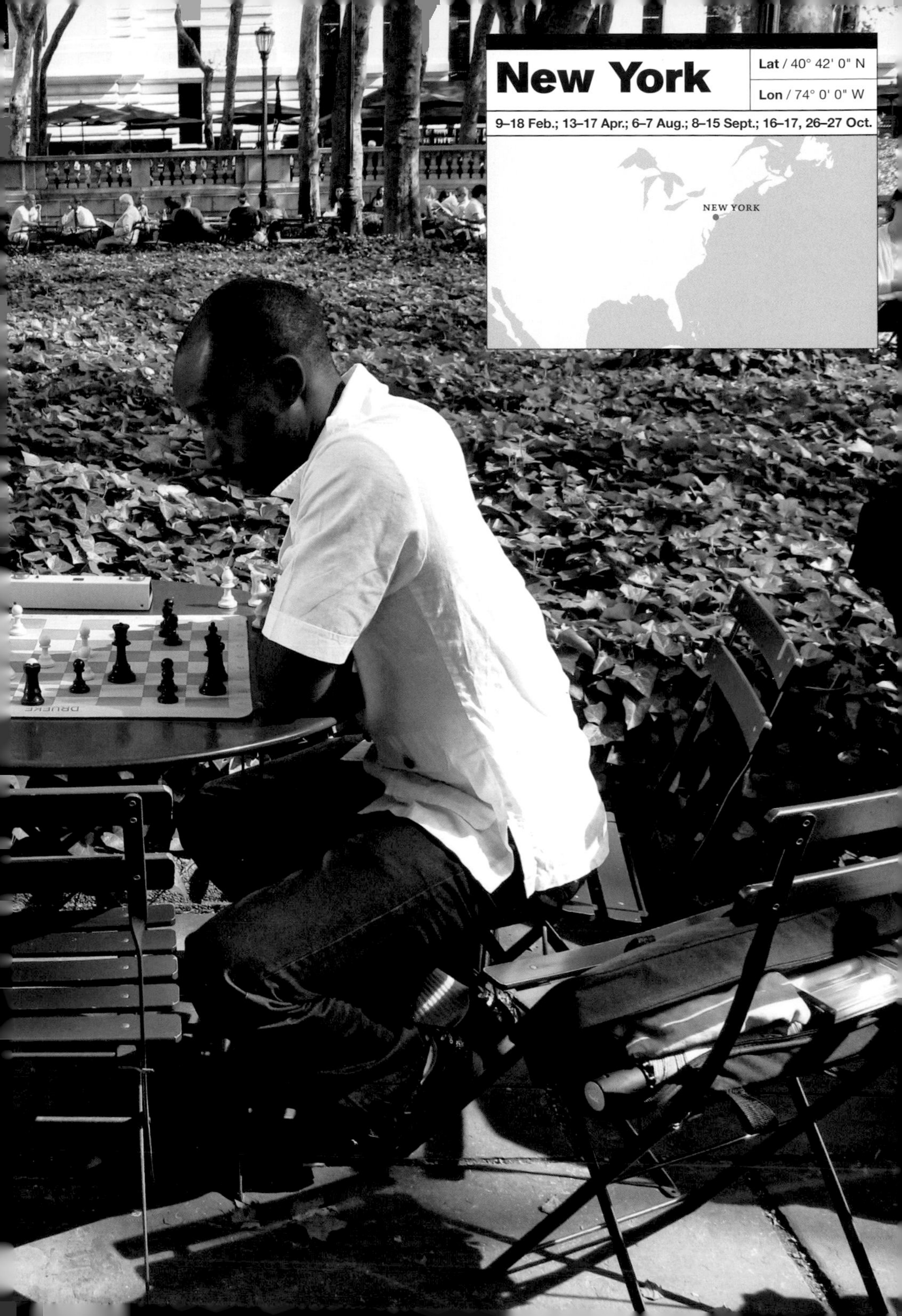
New York
Lat / 40° 42' 0" N
Lon / 74° 0' 0" W
9–18 Feb.; 13–17 Apr.; 6–7 Aug.; 8–15 Sept.; 16–17, 26–27 Oct.
NEW YORK

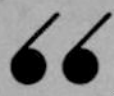

New York City is the world's capital of both loneliness and social excess. Why do people from all around the globe dream of moving to a place where you eat alone, think alone and talk alone? Maybe to flirt with the sensation of meeting a larger number of people than the average person can handle emotionally – there's something overwhelmingly sensual about the city's permanent, extreme crowdedness and hyper-multiethnicity, which on one hand cancels out individual differences and on the other hand celebrates them. New York also has a special visual chemistry that makes it unique. I think there's no other city that has such an instantly recognizable aesthetic signature. Even if you see just a glimpse of part of a street in a picture you instantly know it's in New York. The special light in the city, filtering down through the skyscrapers and store awnings, creates permanent drama. Down on the street, it seems like every day is Fashion Week. New York is one of the few places in the USA where you see so many well-dressed people everywhere – not just in little niche pockets in the trendiest parts of town. New York is such a public, competitive city, and it seems like everyone is engaged in a constant fashion war with everyone else. One of my favourite places in New York is this hidden cocktail bar in the East Village. You enter via an ordinary-looking hotdog joint. Inside, there is a phone booth. When you lift the receiver on the pay phone and speak to the hostess, the phone booth revolves to reveal the entrance to the cocktail bar. The bar itself is elegant and refined, and the whole thing feels like something out of a James Bond movie.

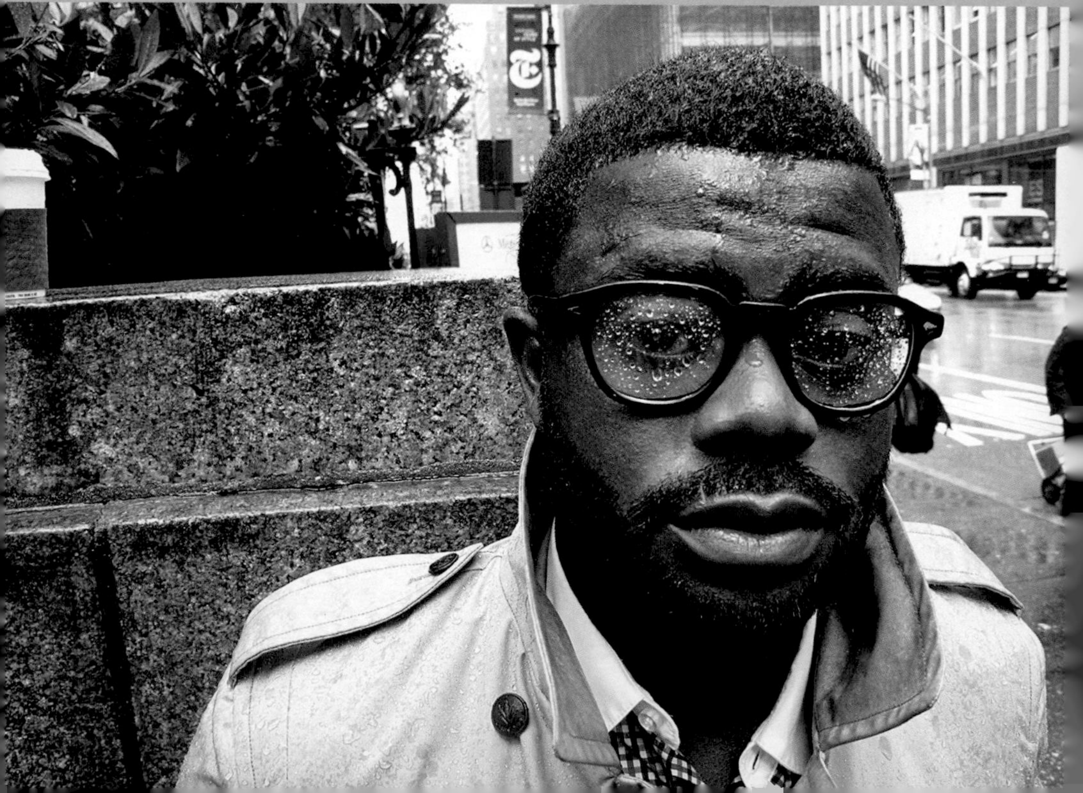

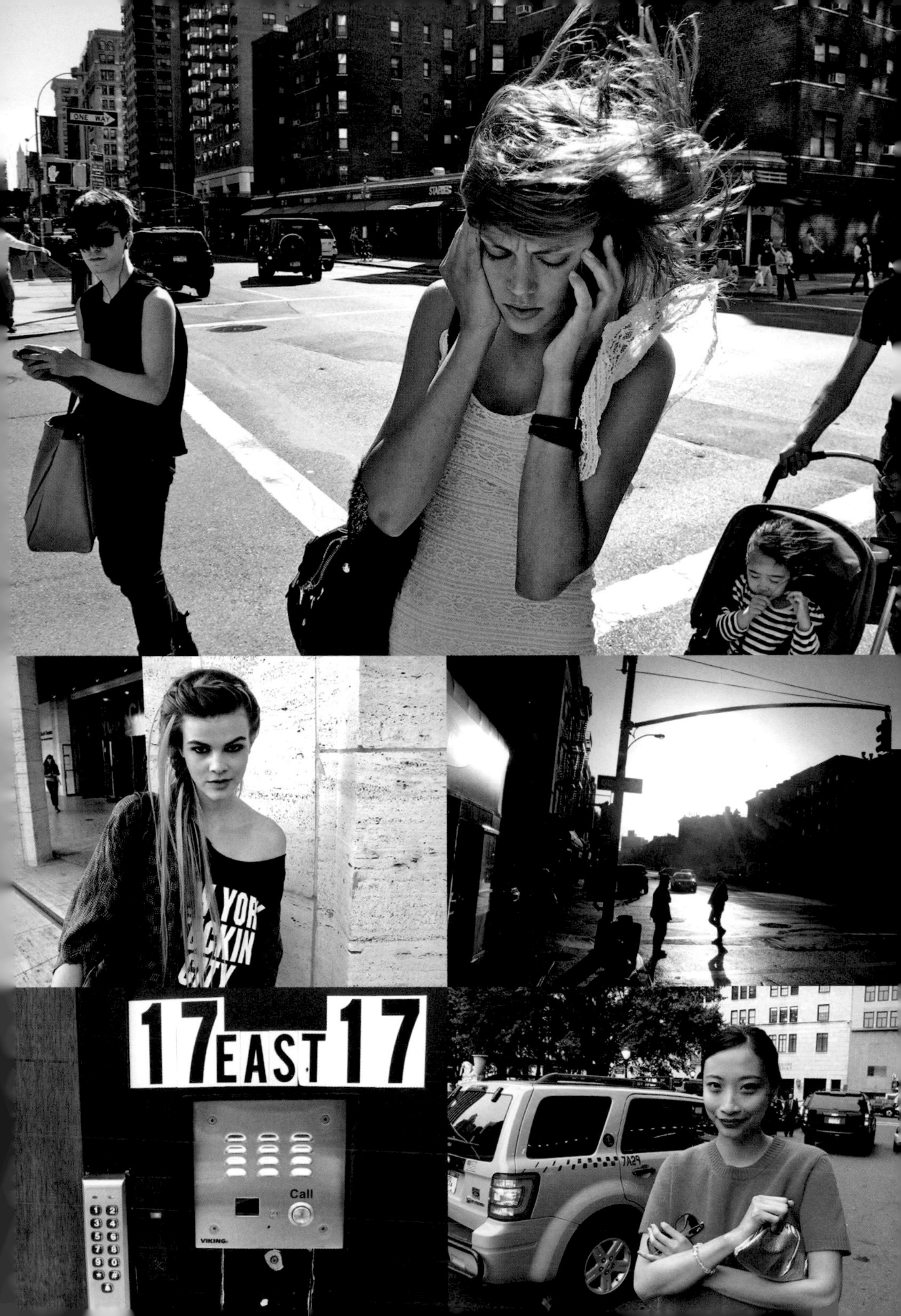
ONE WAY
17 EAST 17
Call
VIKING
7A29

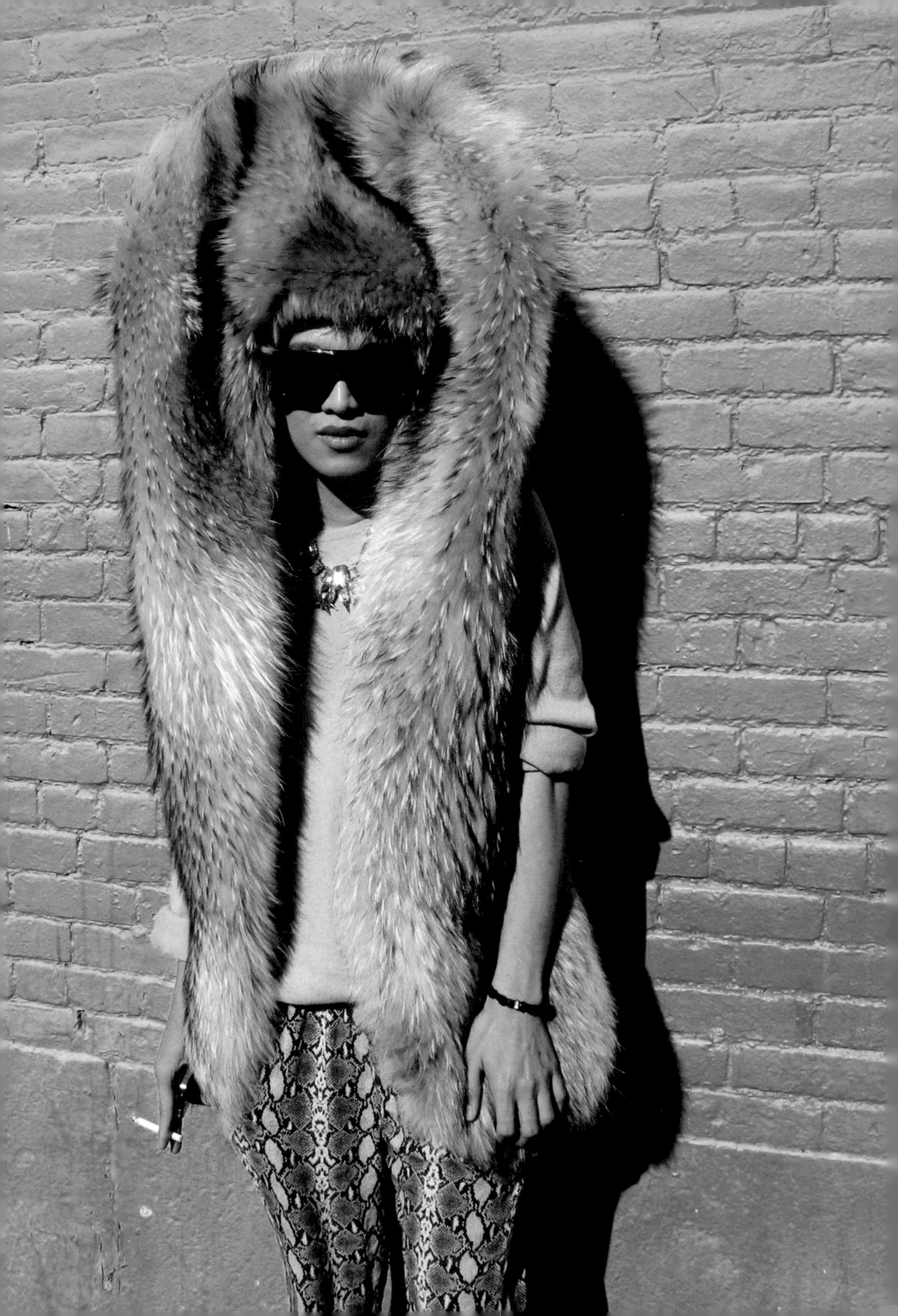

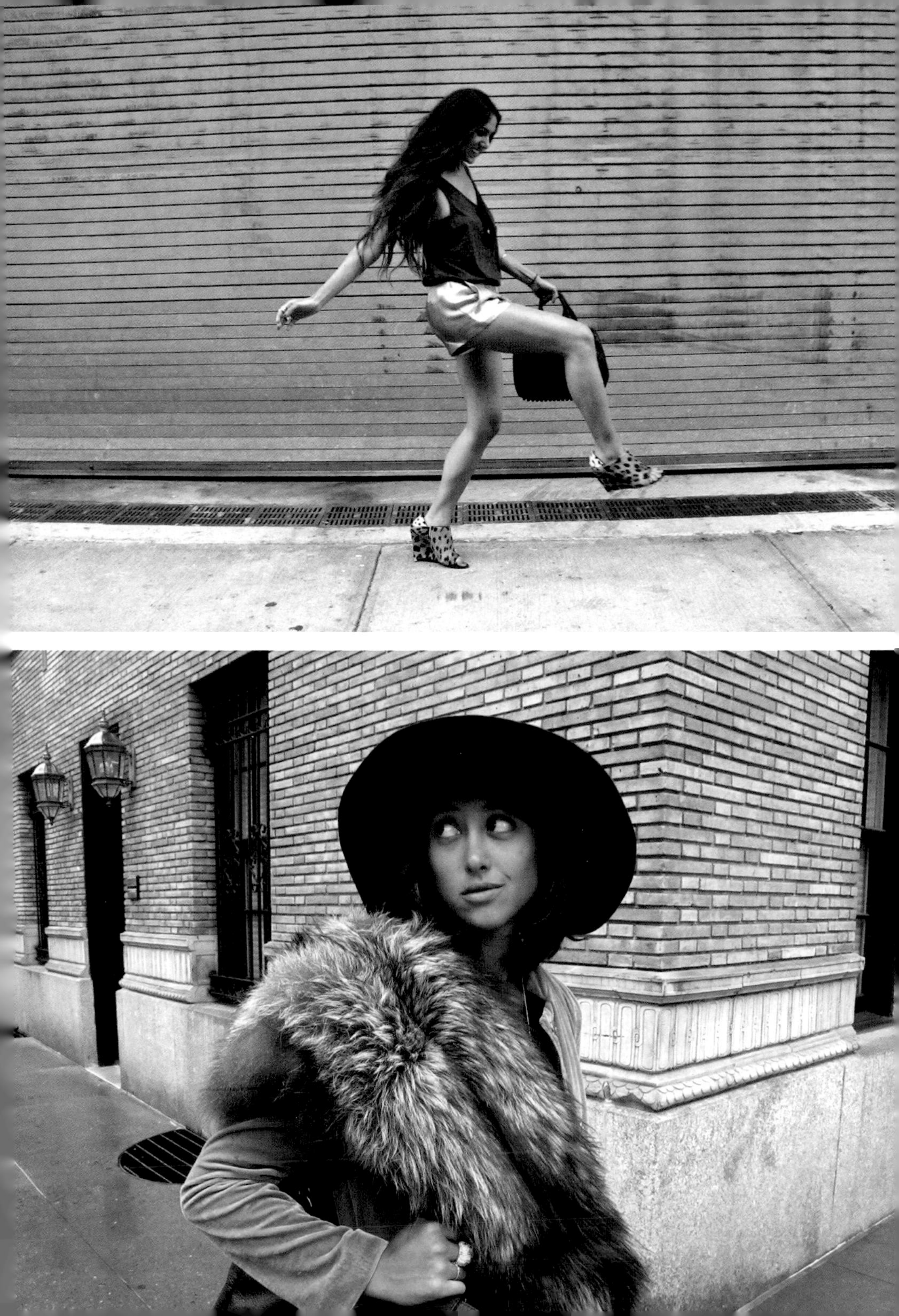

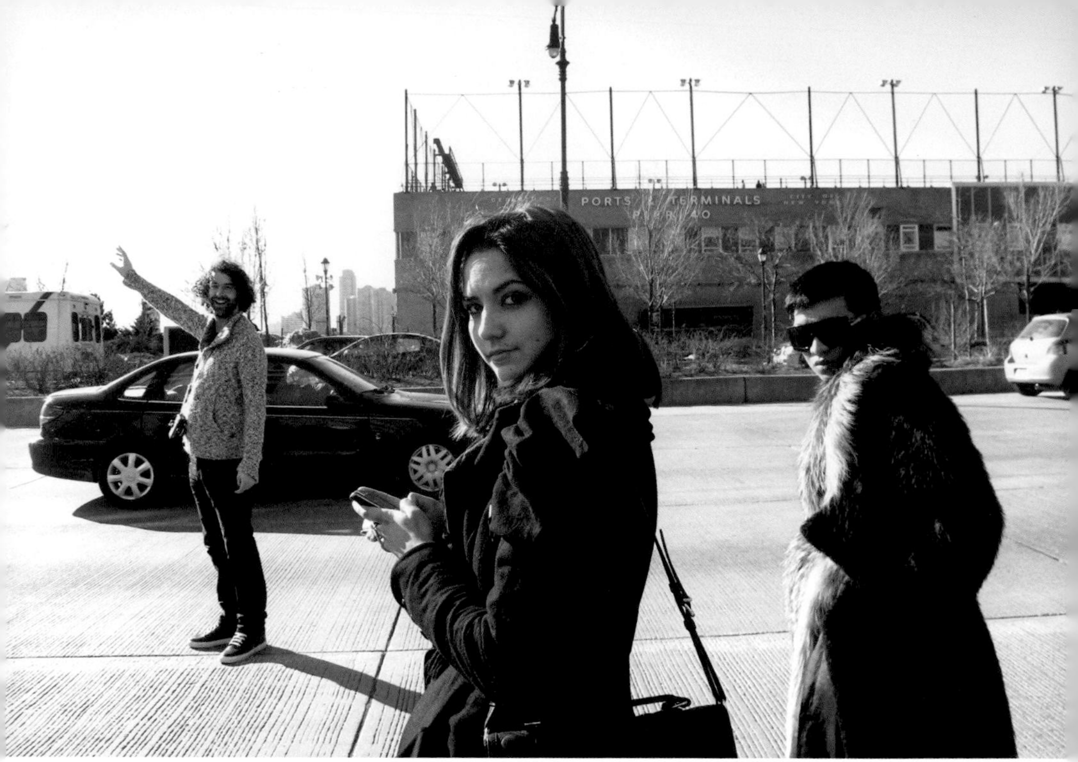

PORTS
TERMINALS

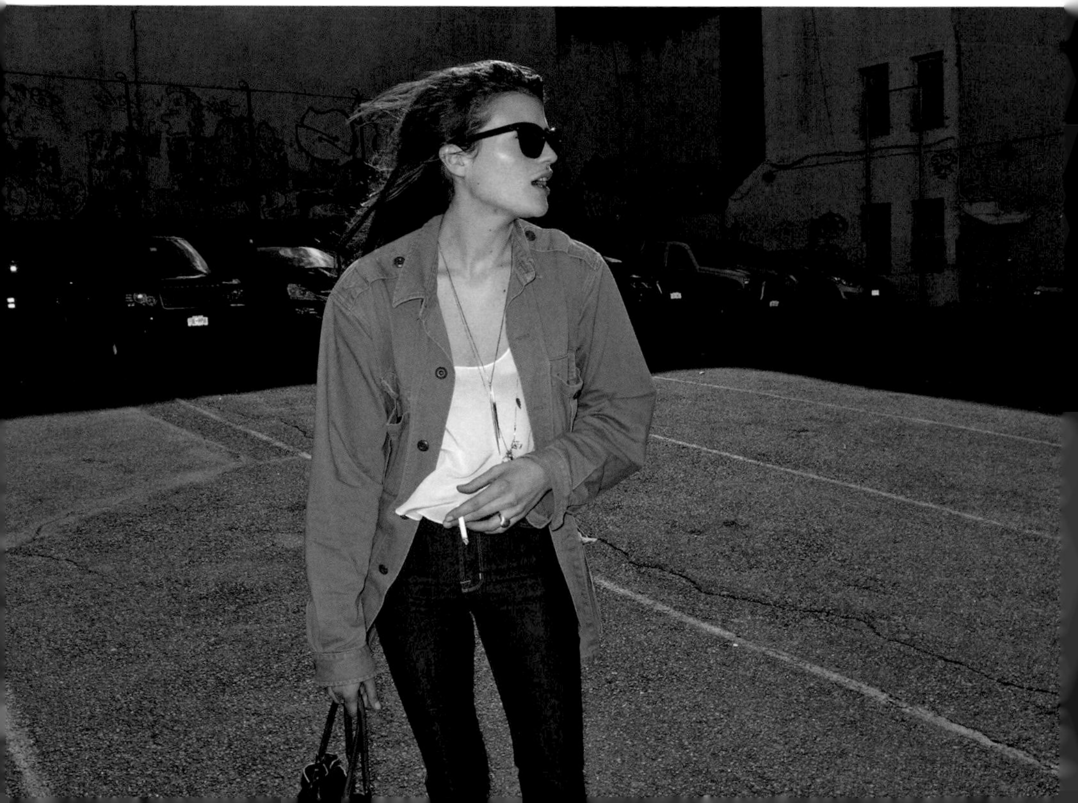

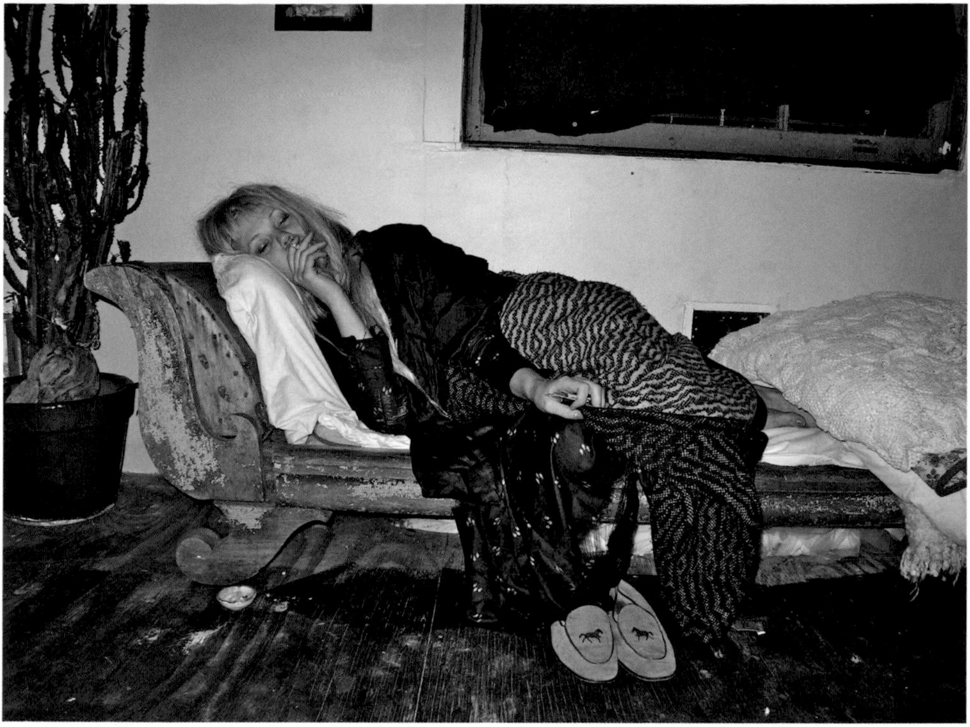

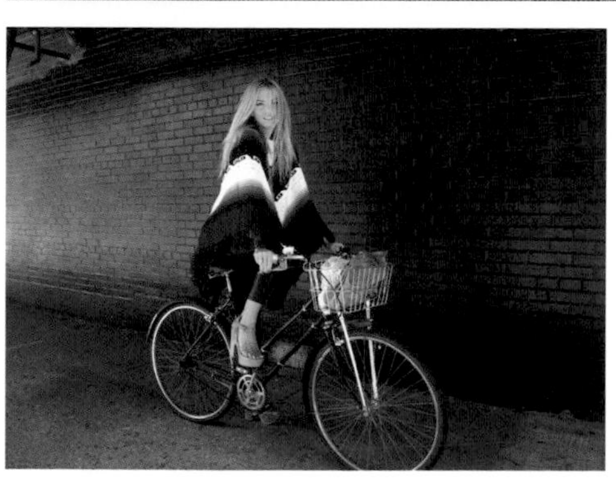

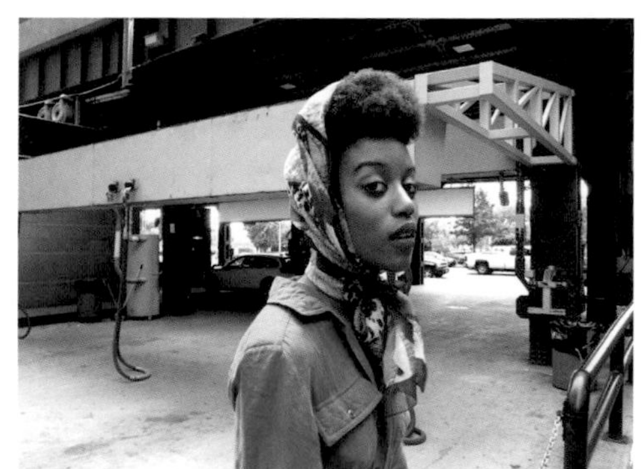

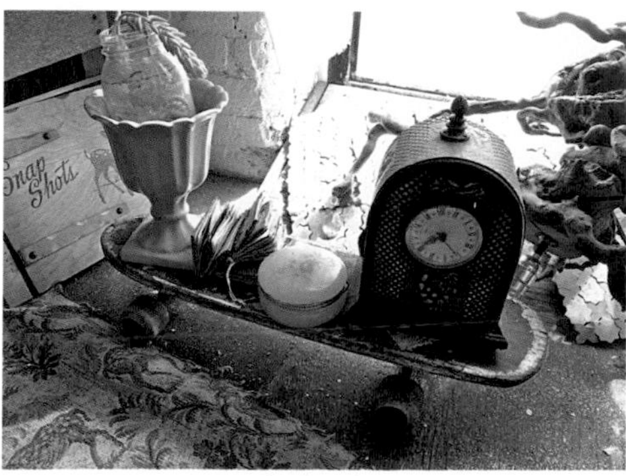
Snap Shots

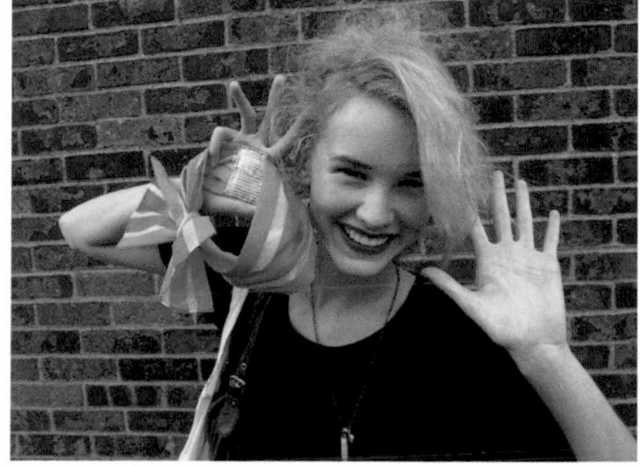

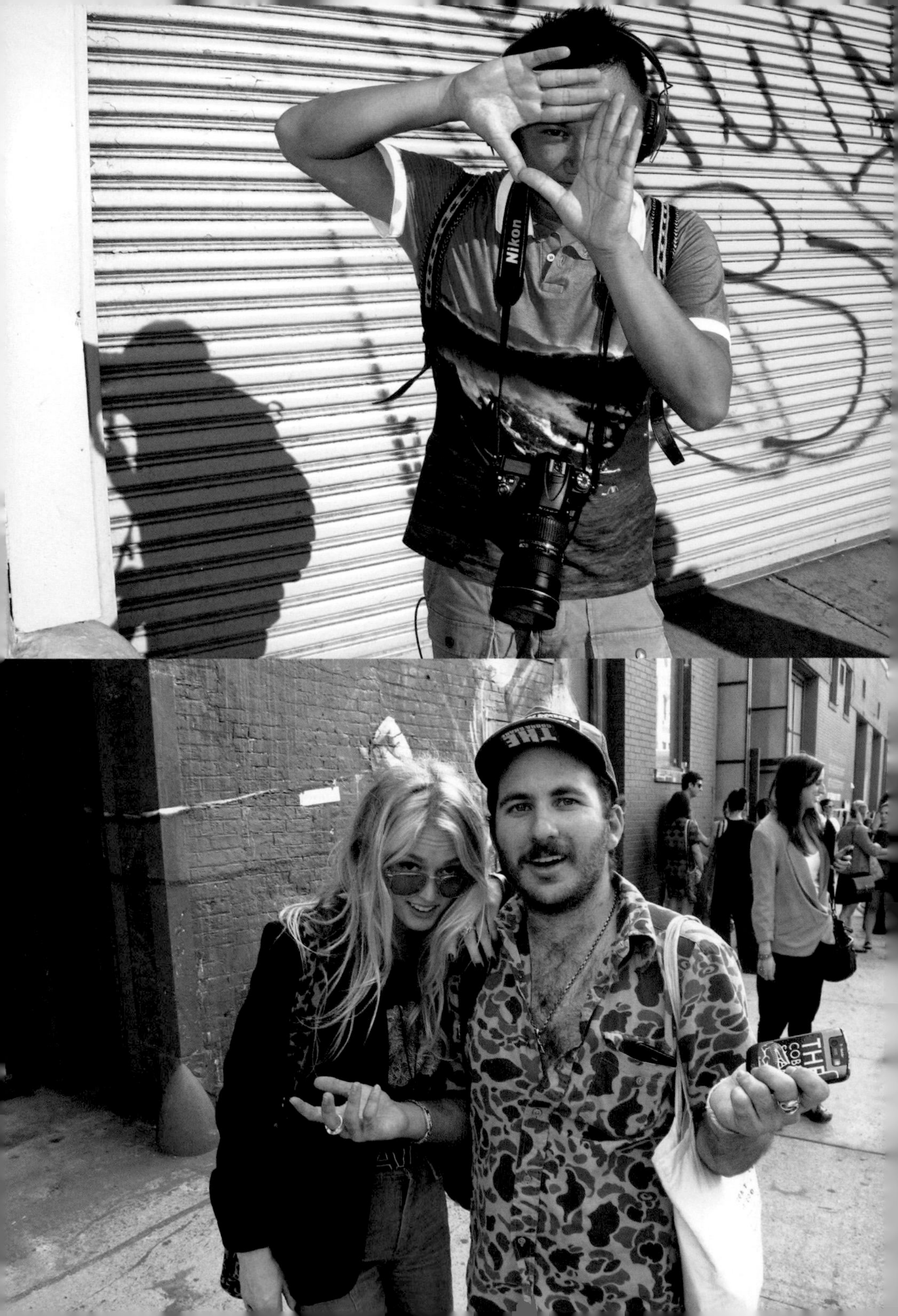
Nikon
THE

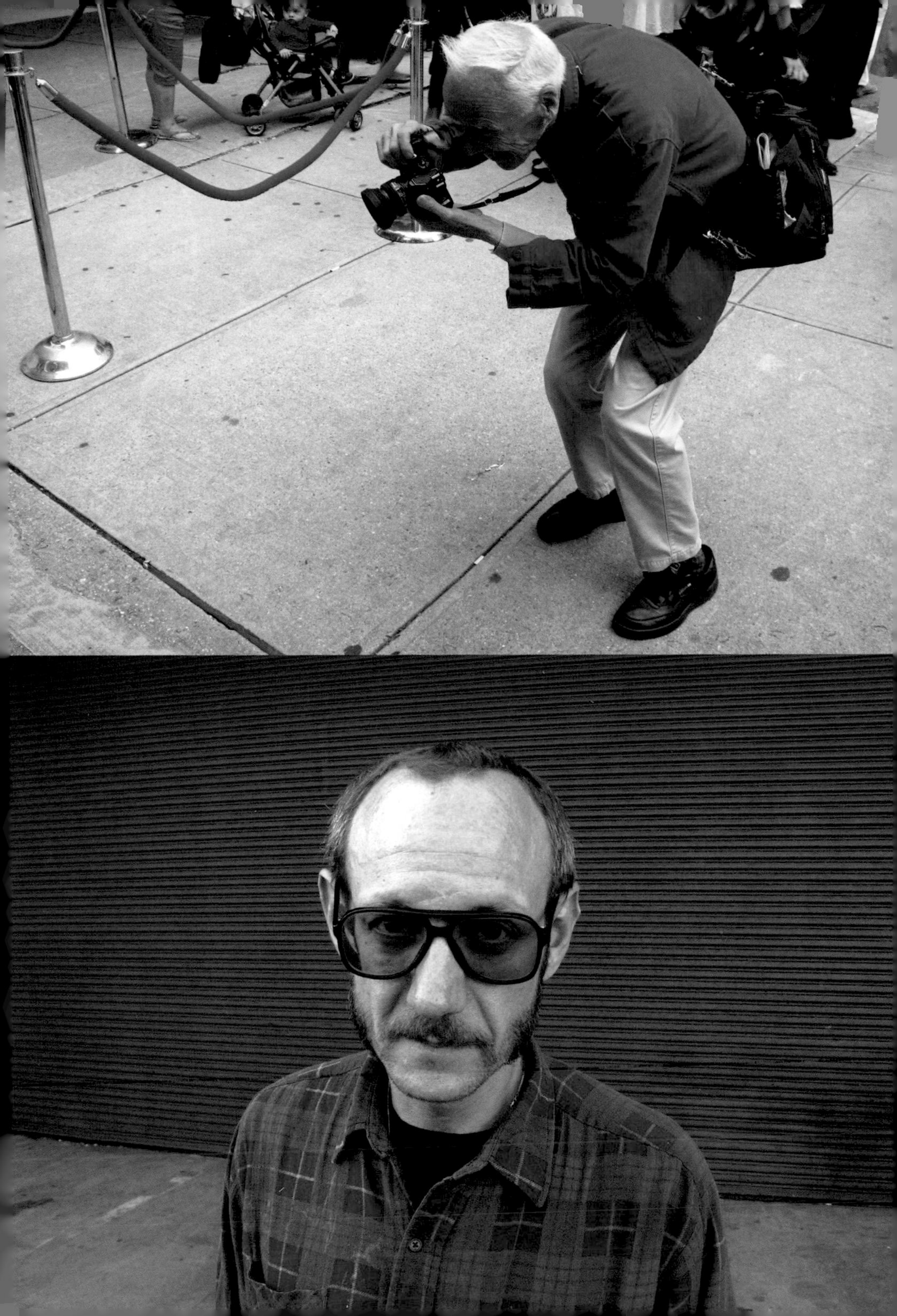

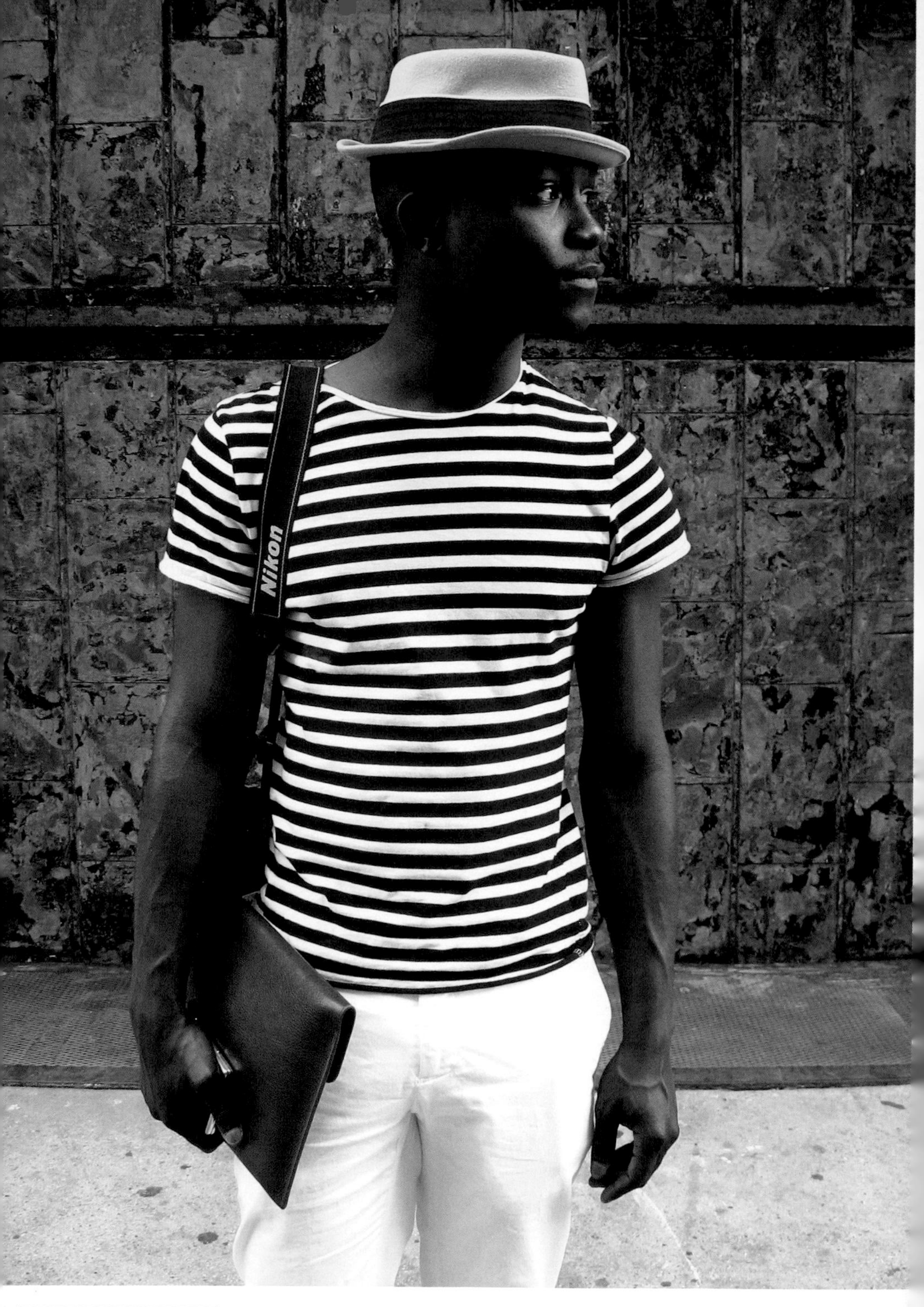
Nikon

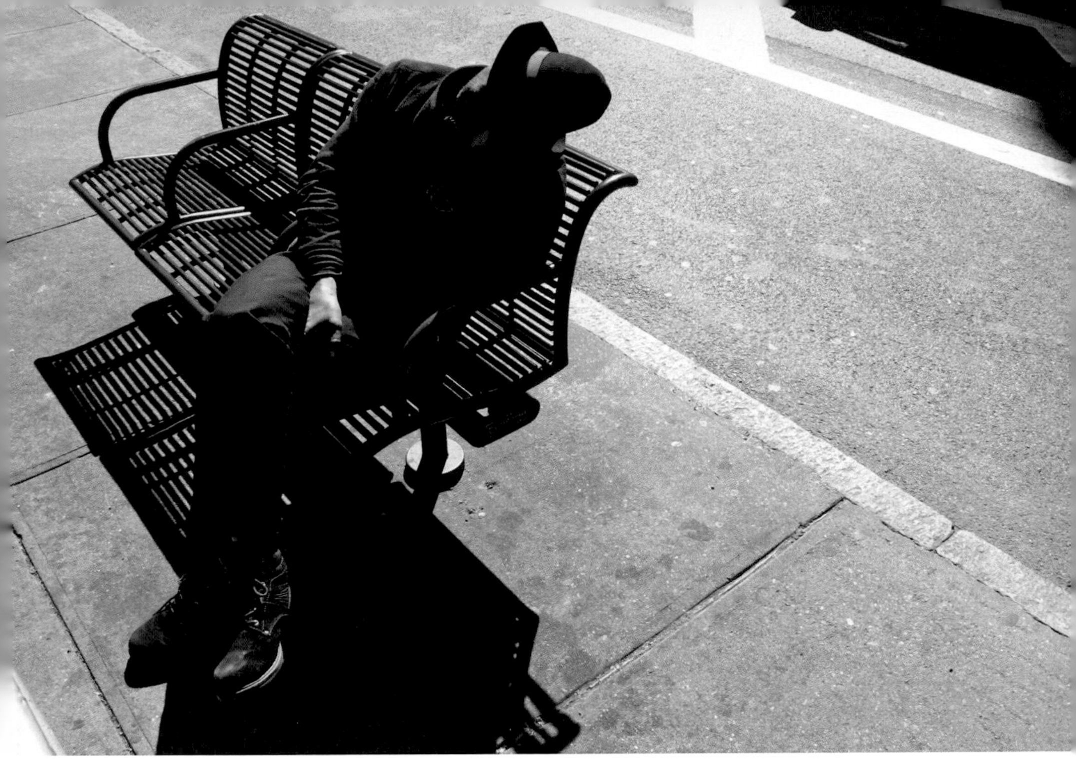

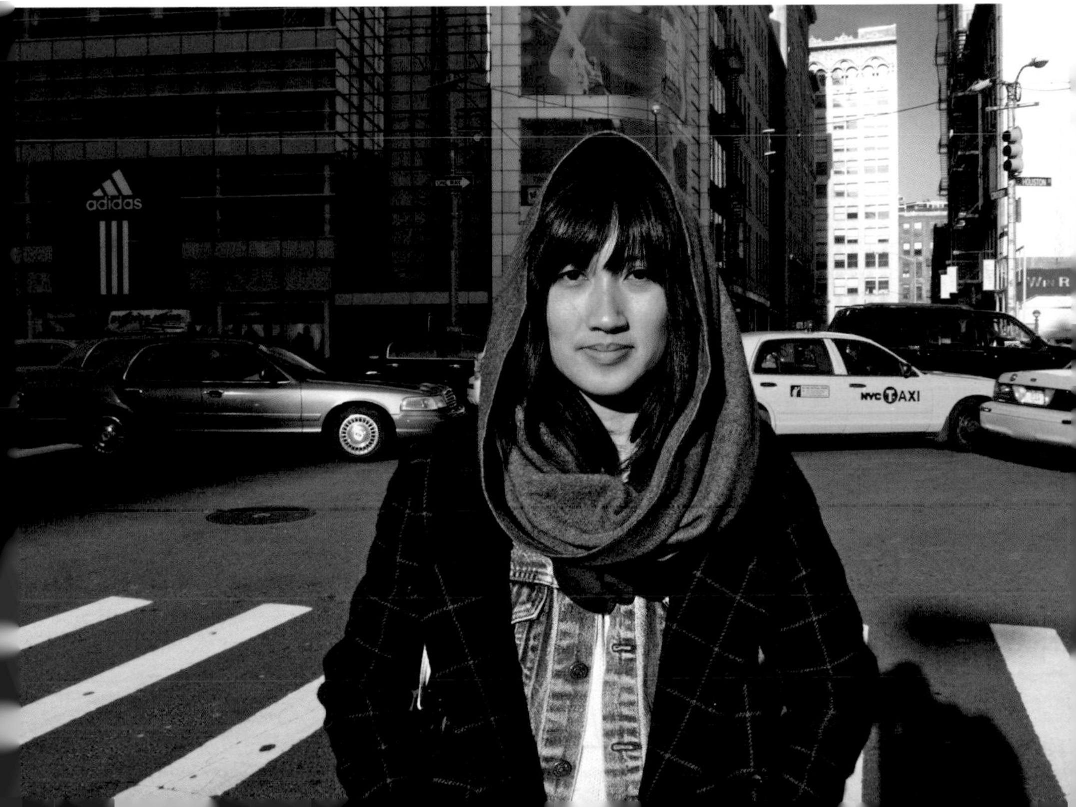

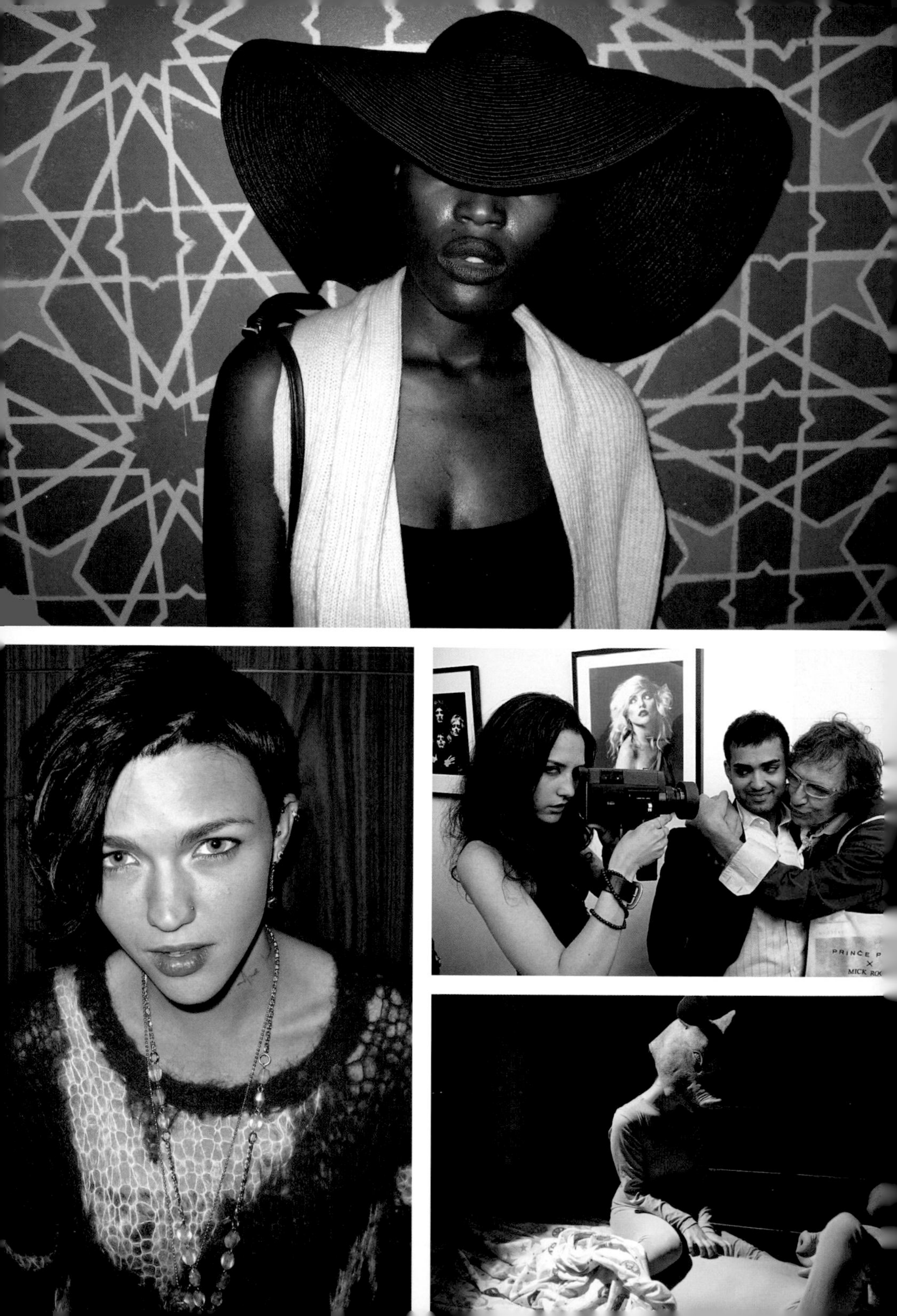
PRINČE
X
MICK

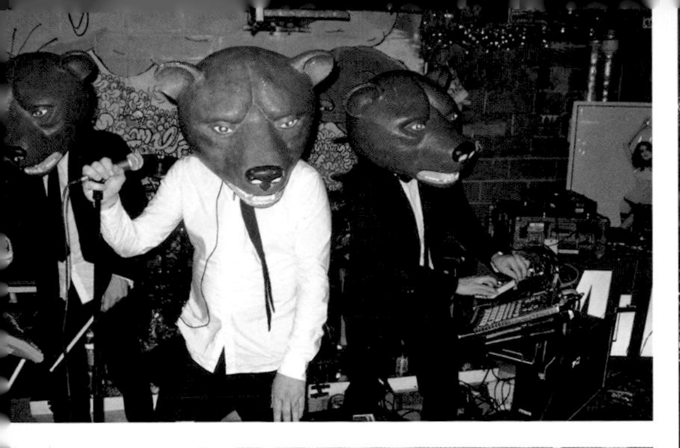

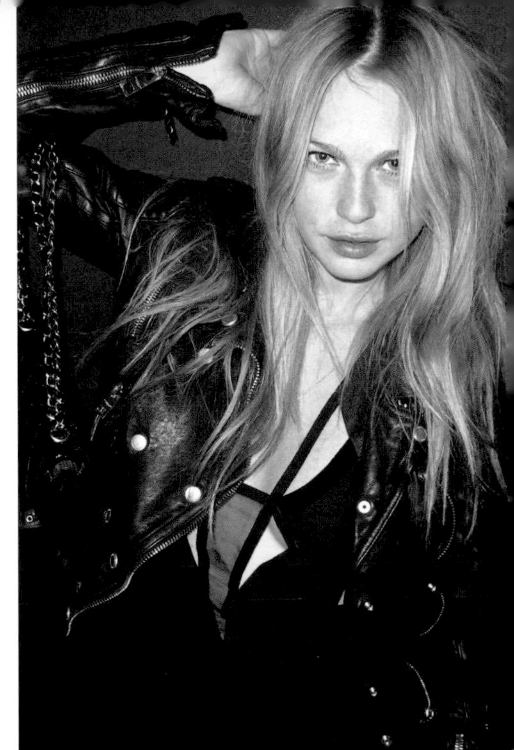

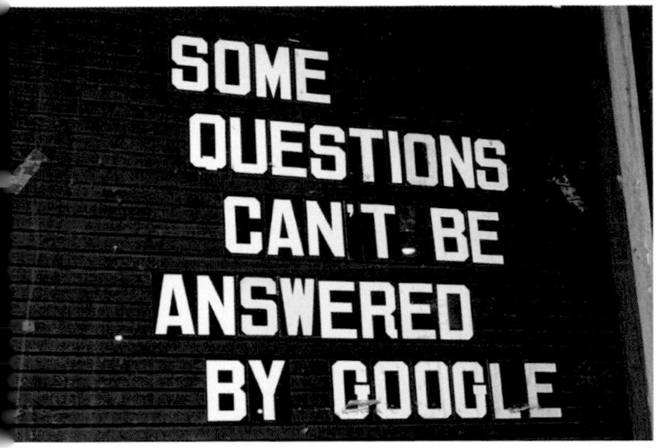

SOME
QUESTIONS
CAN'T BE
ANSWERED
BY GOOGLE

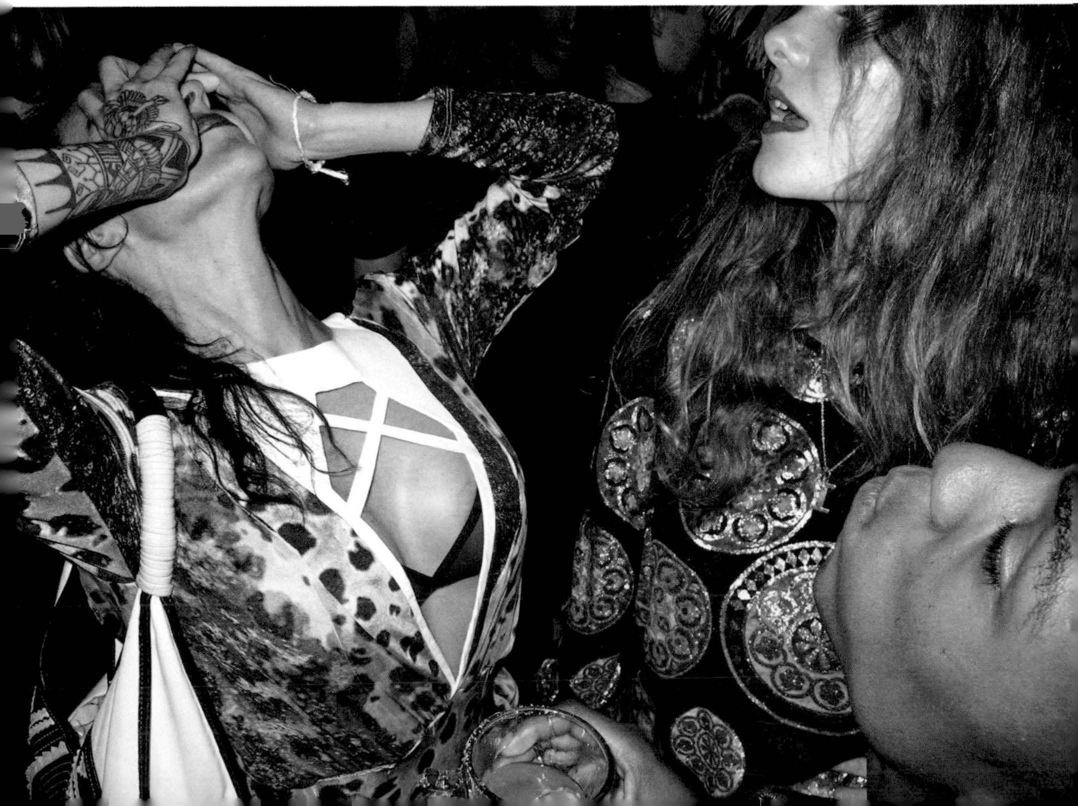

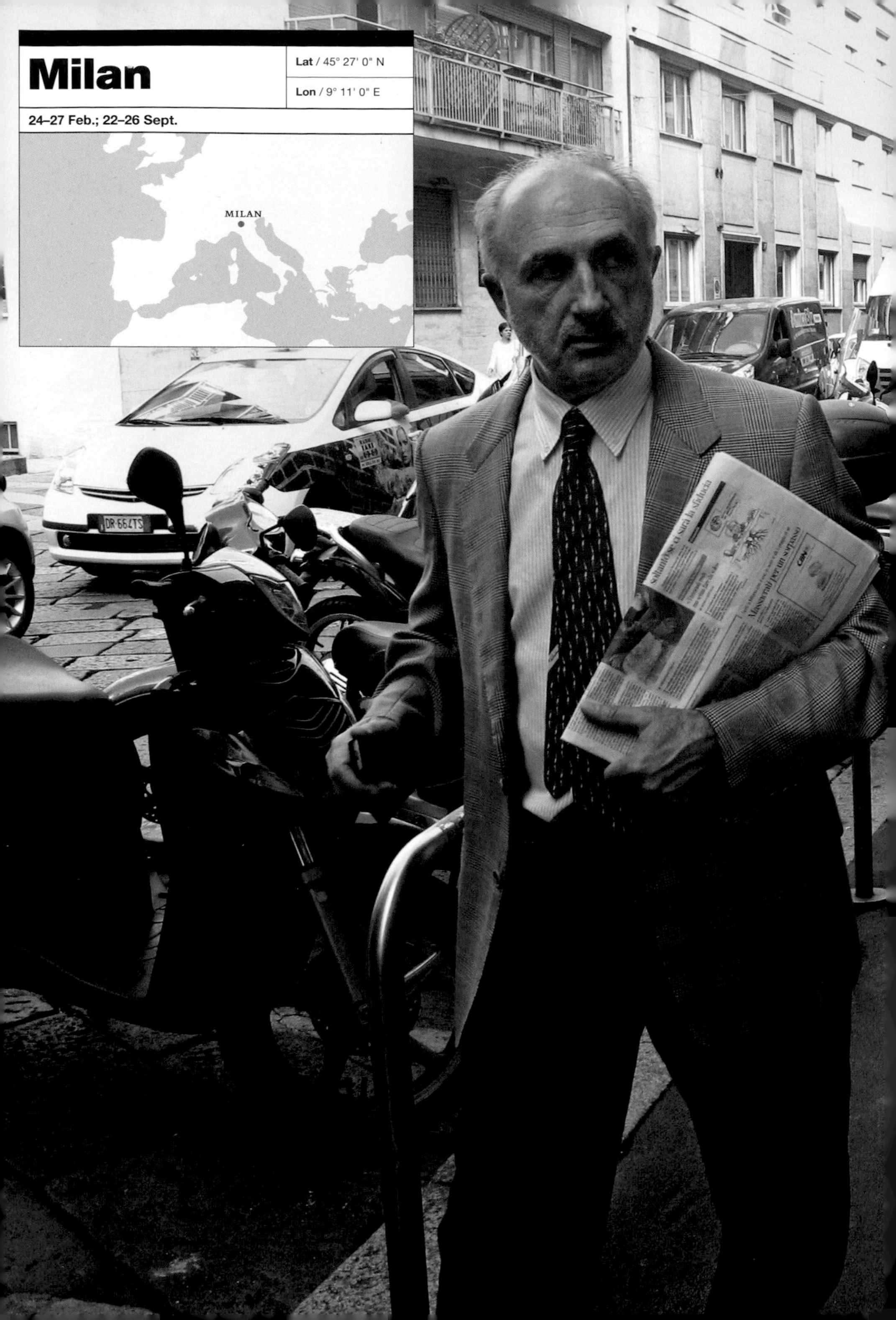

Milan

Lat / 45° 27' 0" N

Lon / 9° 11' 0" E

24–27 Feb.; 22–26 Sept.

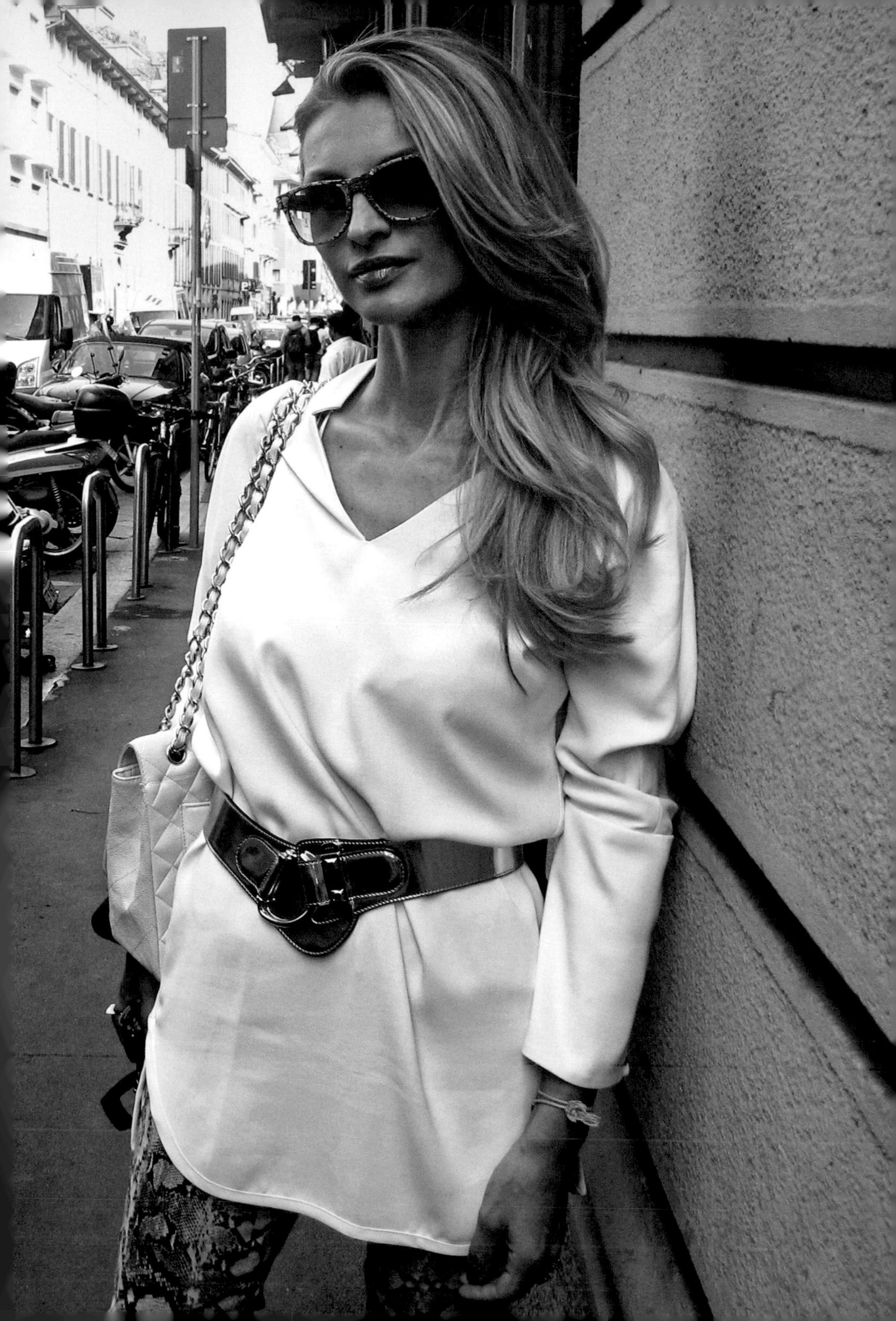

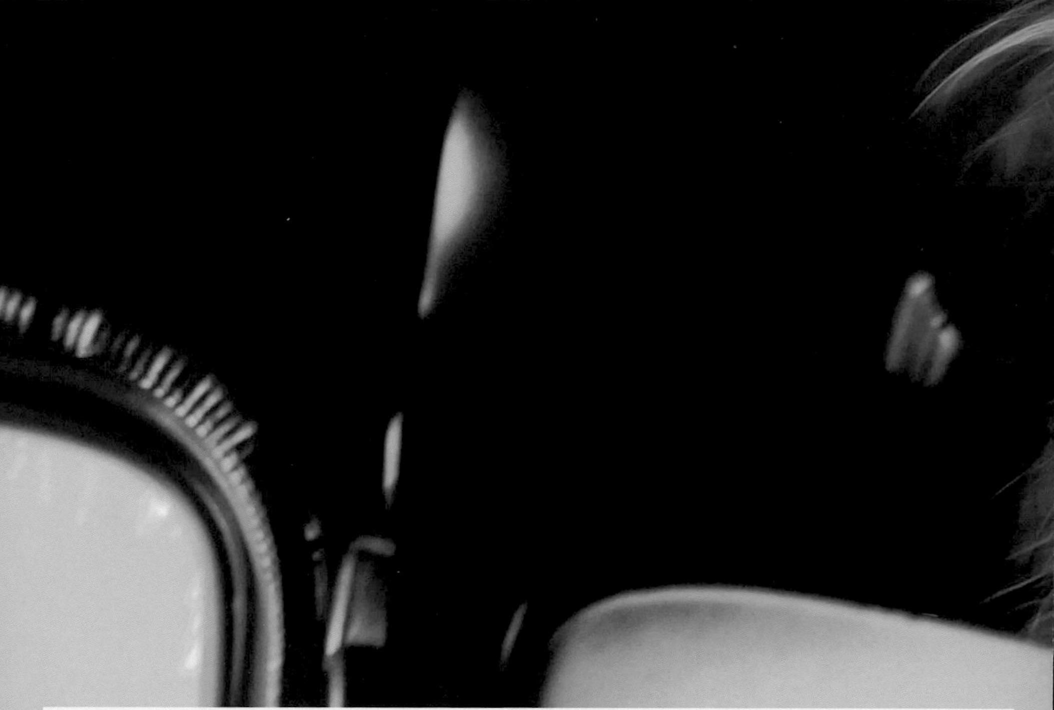

“Milan is a bit of a mystery to me. It’s the capital of Lombardy, historically the home of perfect taste, and from its neoclassical architectural marvels to its streets full of men in tailored suits riding their Vespas, every element of the environment has been harmoniously designed for centuries, with everything in just the right measure. But nowadays Milan seems to be forgetting its classic heritage and instead chasing a soulless kind of ‘brandmania’ more than anywhere else in Europe. It’s as if many Milanese have for some reason recently lost their cultural self-confidence and now can’t live without constant ‘logo confirmation’. You adjust your pair of glasses with their visible Prada logo while having a coffee at Marc by Marc Jacobs Café before going to the Bulgari Hotel for dinner and probably ending up at Just Cavalli Hollywood afterwards. To me all this conspicuous consumption feels like a kind of poverty. On the street you see a few beautifully, classily dressed people, but not much in the way of cutting-edge street style. It’s not a place for public experimentation. There are lots of creative people around, but they seem to operate in a very hidden box.”

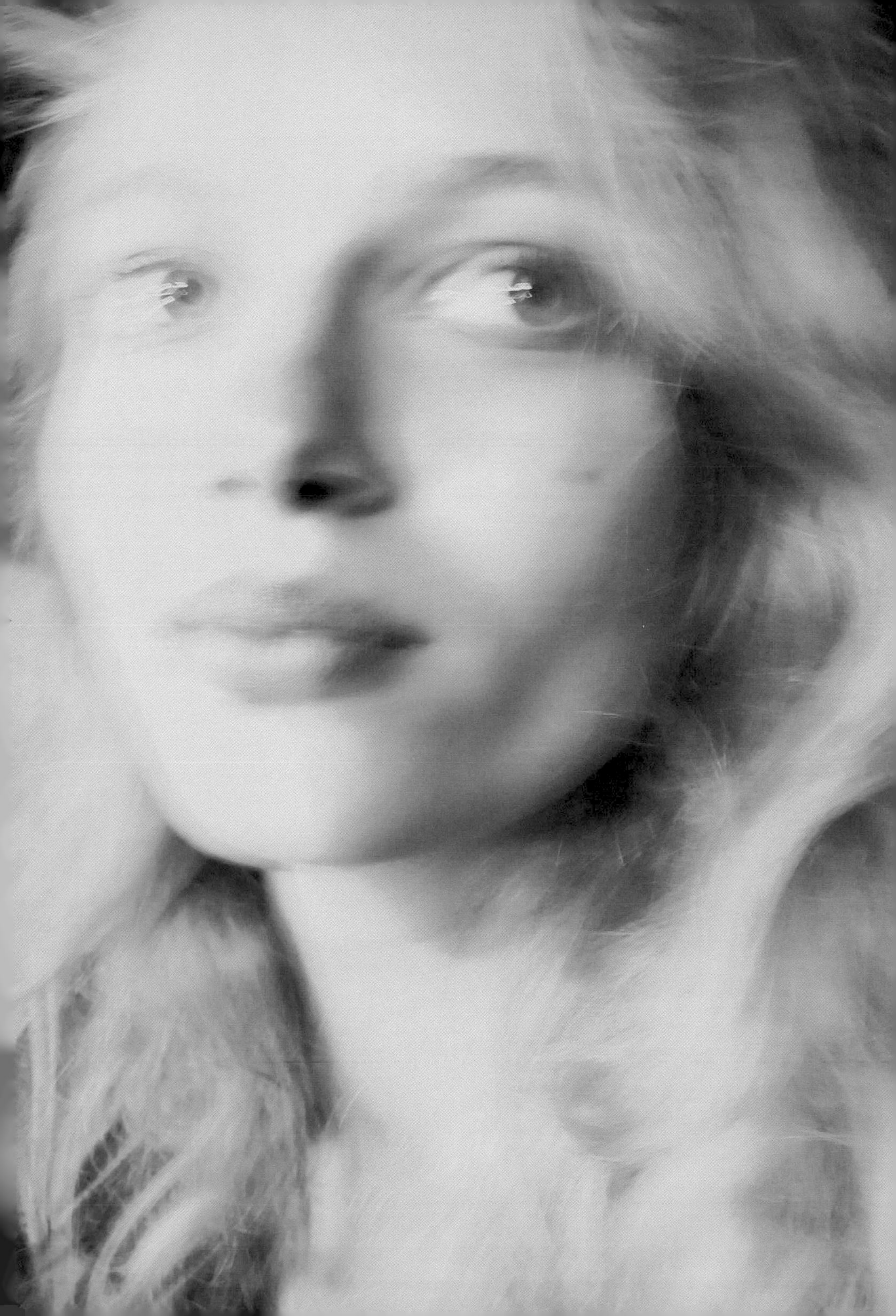

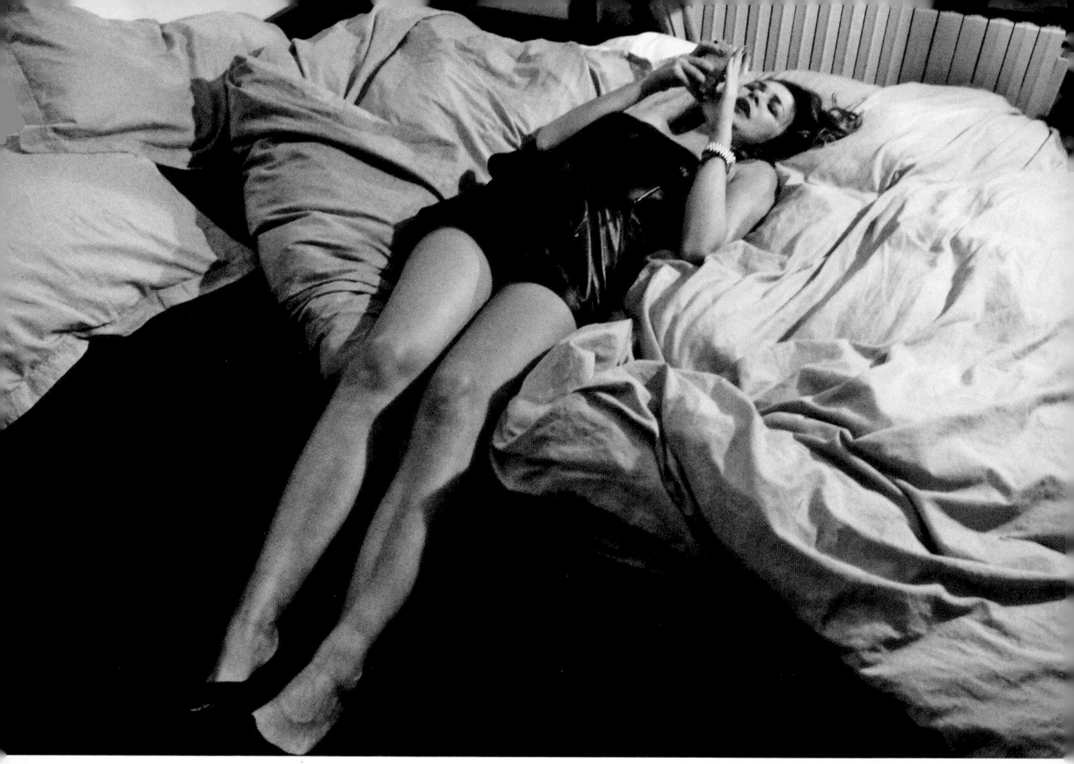

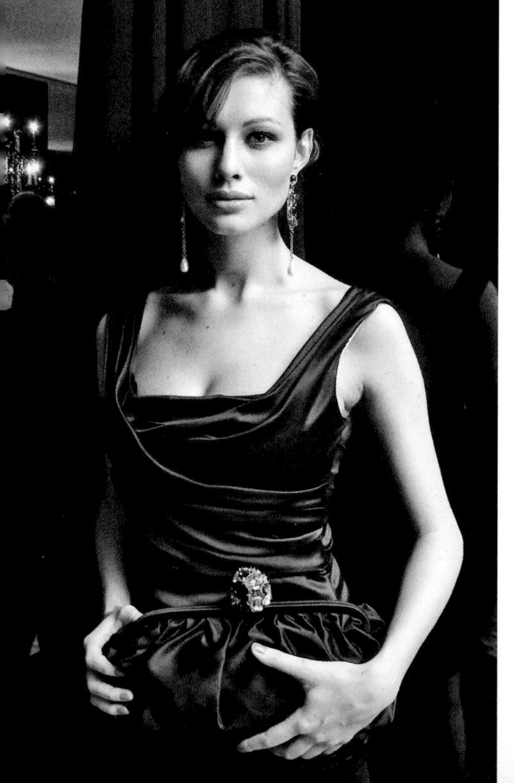

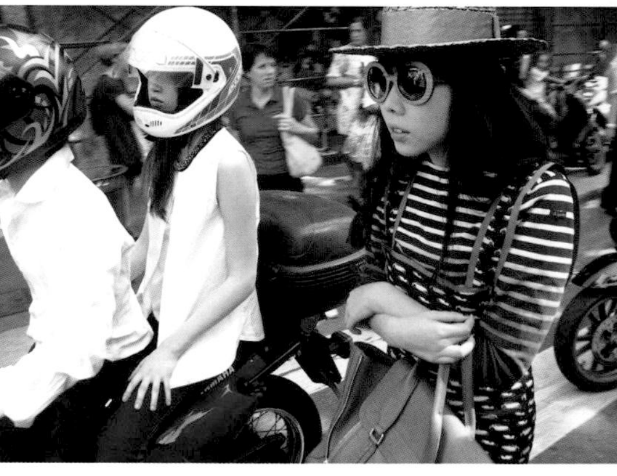

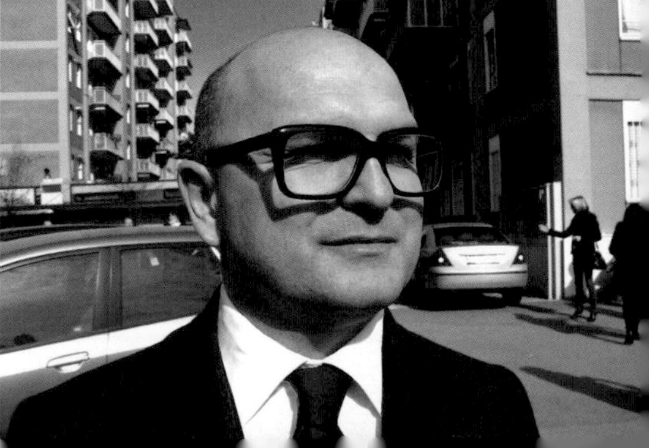

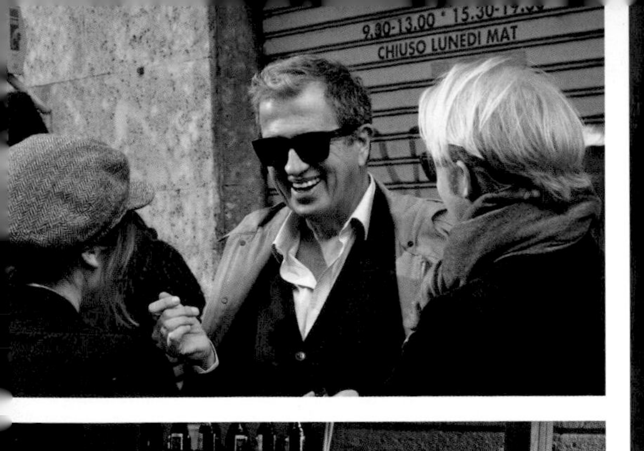
CHIUSO LUNEDI MAT

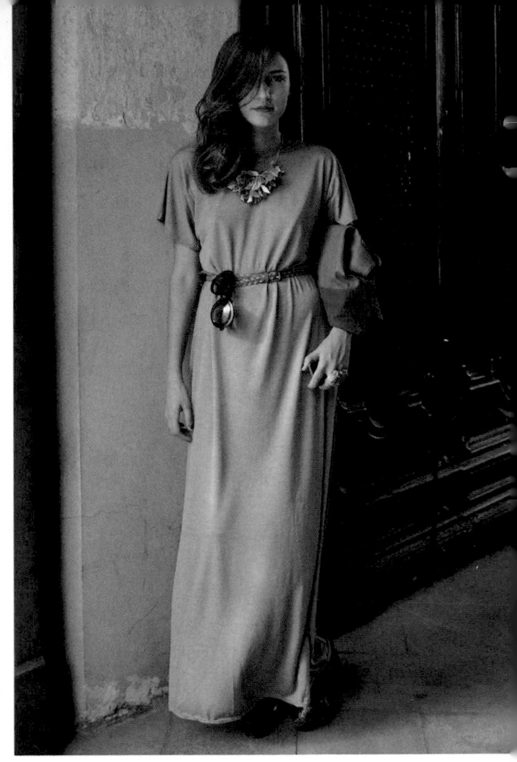

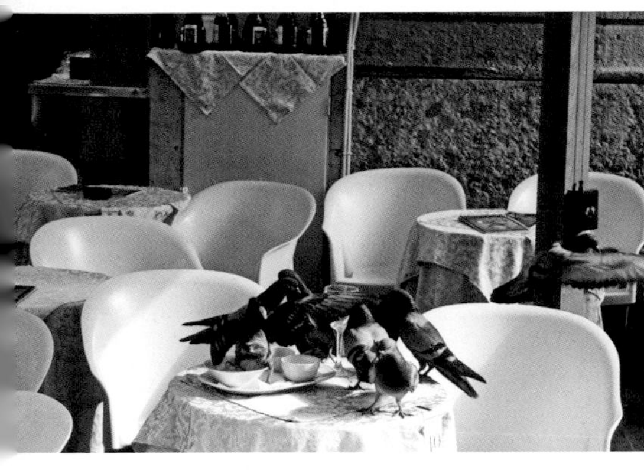

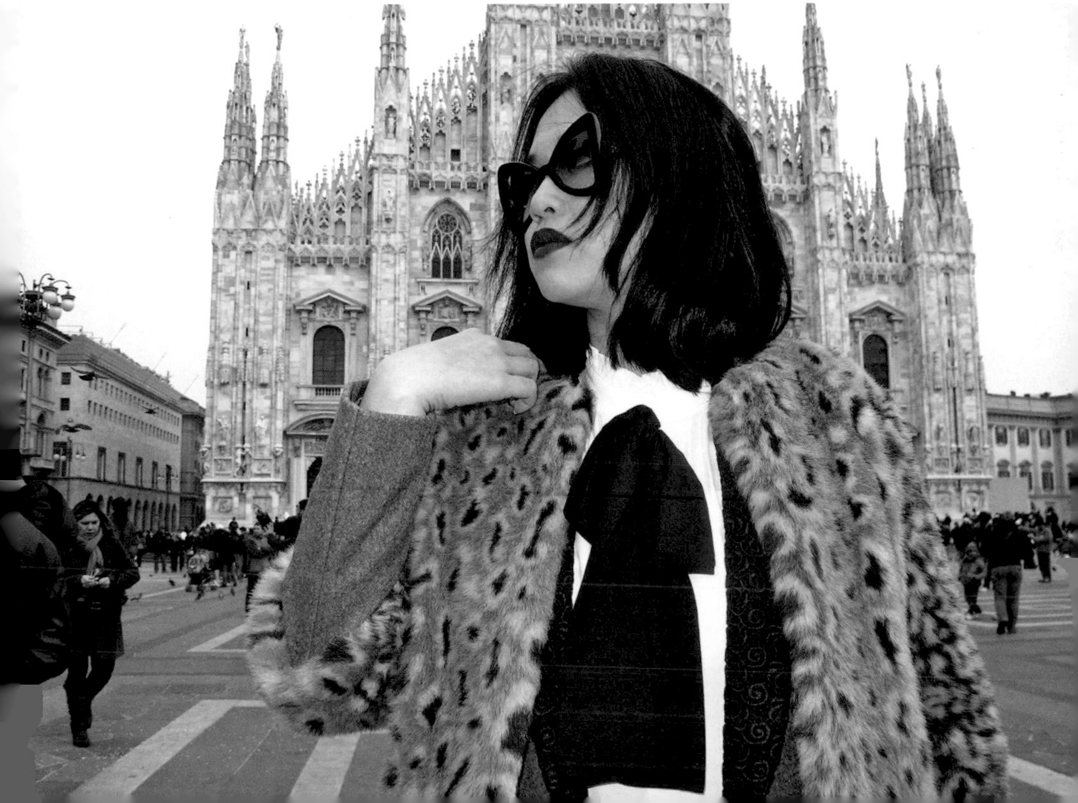

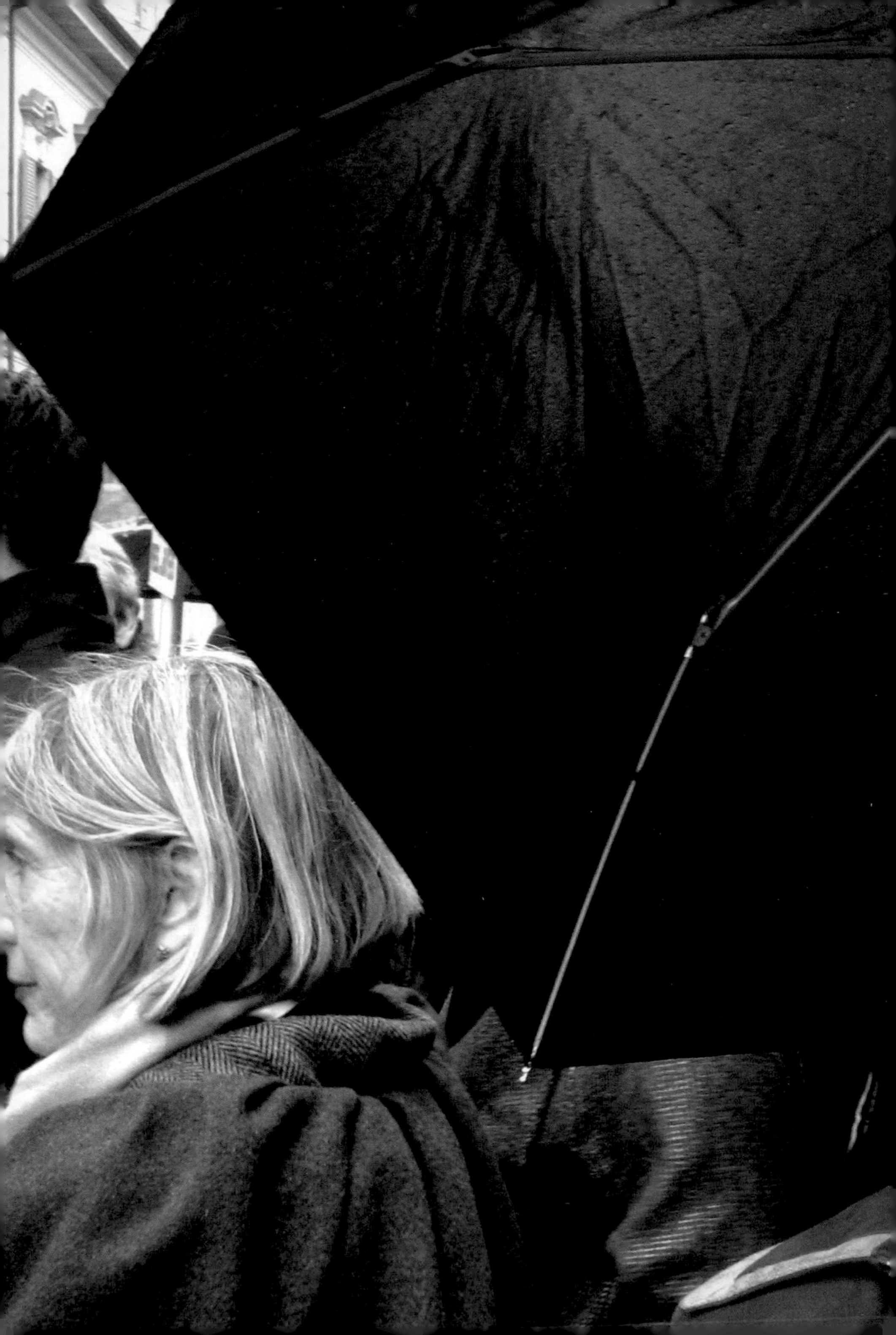

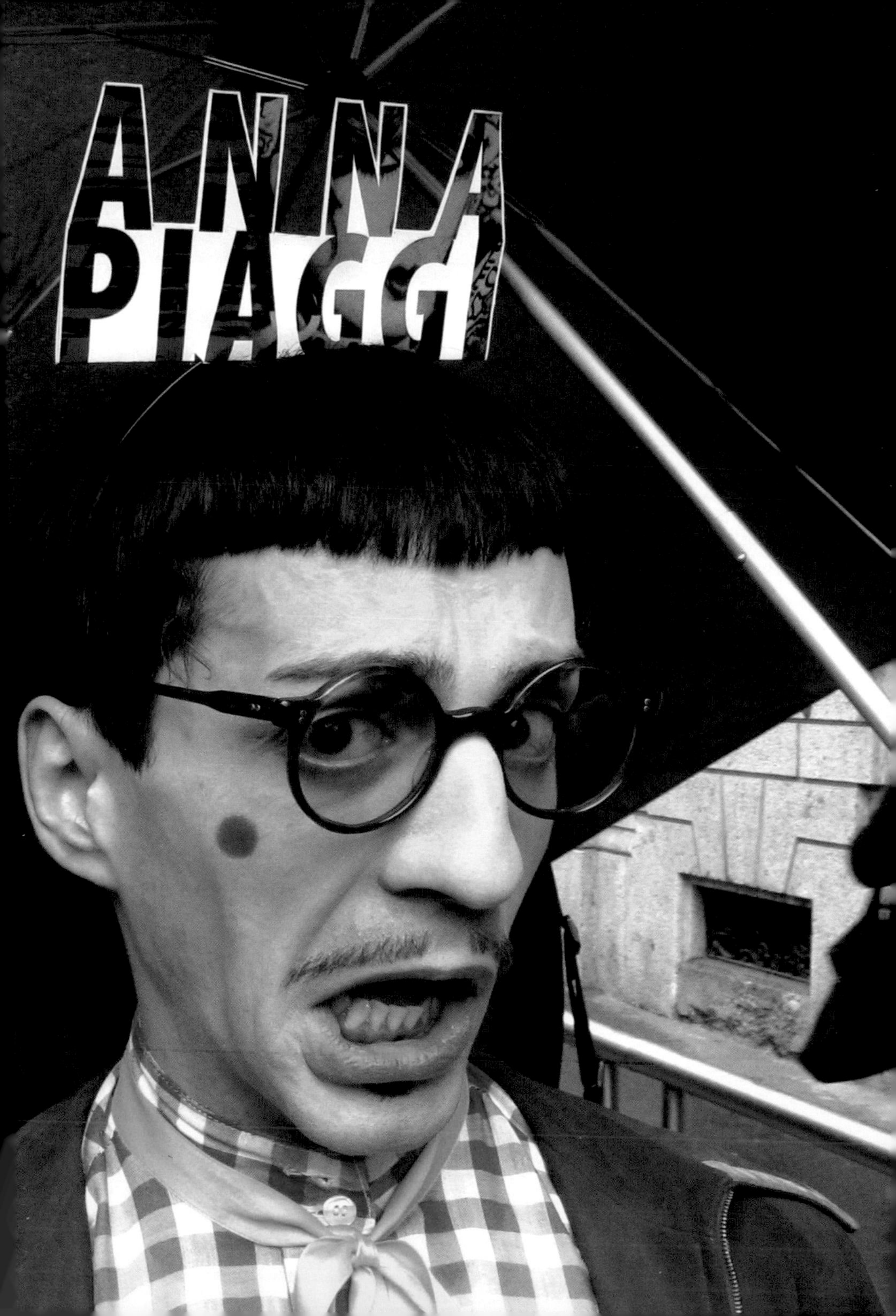
ANNA
PIAGG

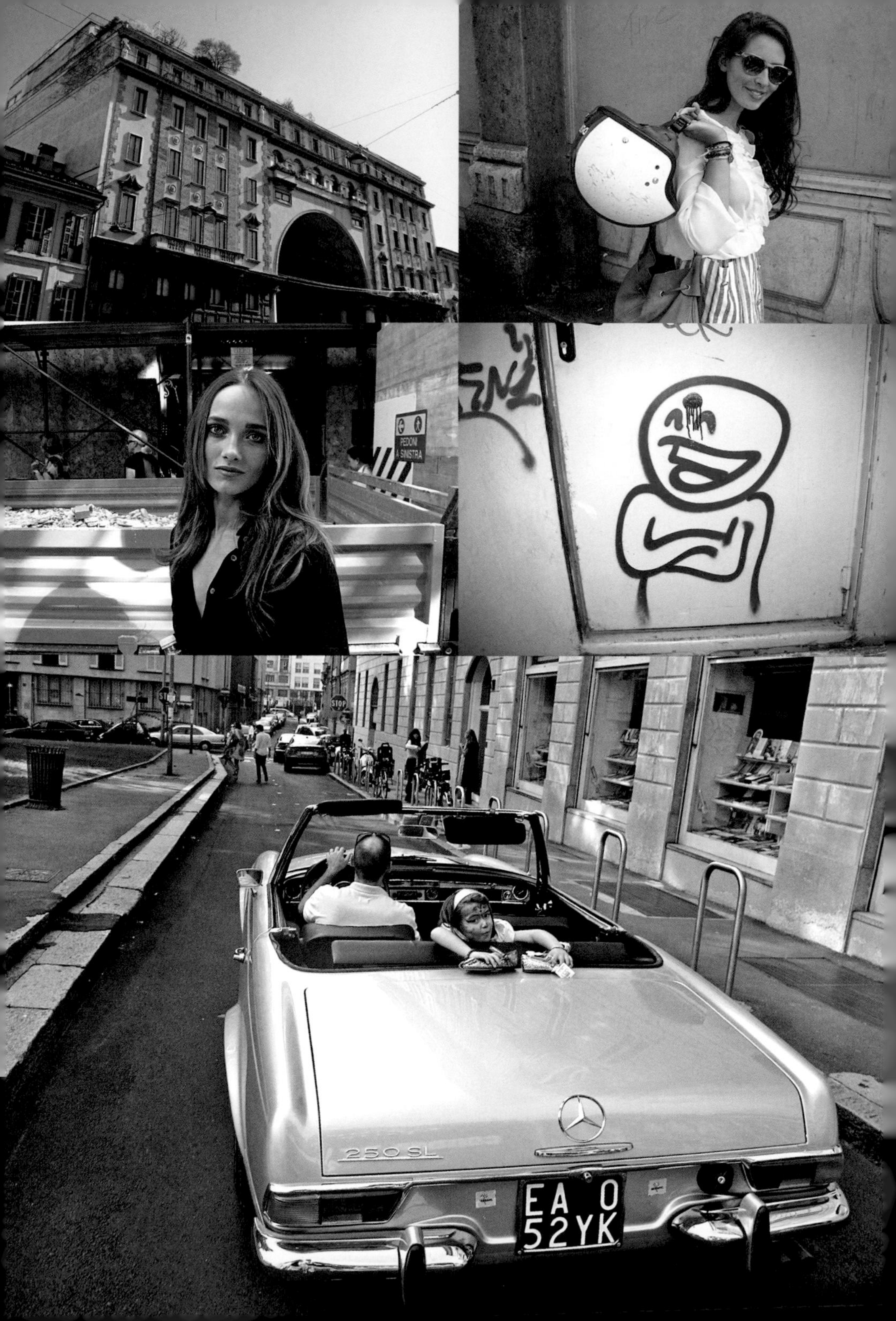
PEDONI
A SINISTRA
250 SL
EA 0
52YK

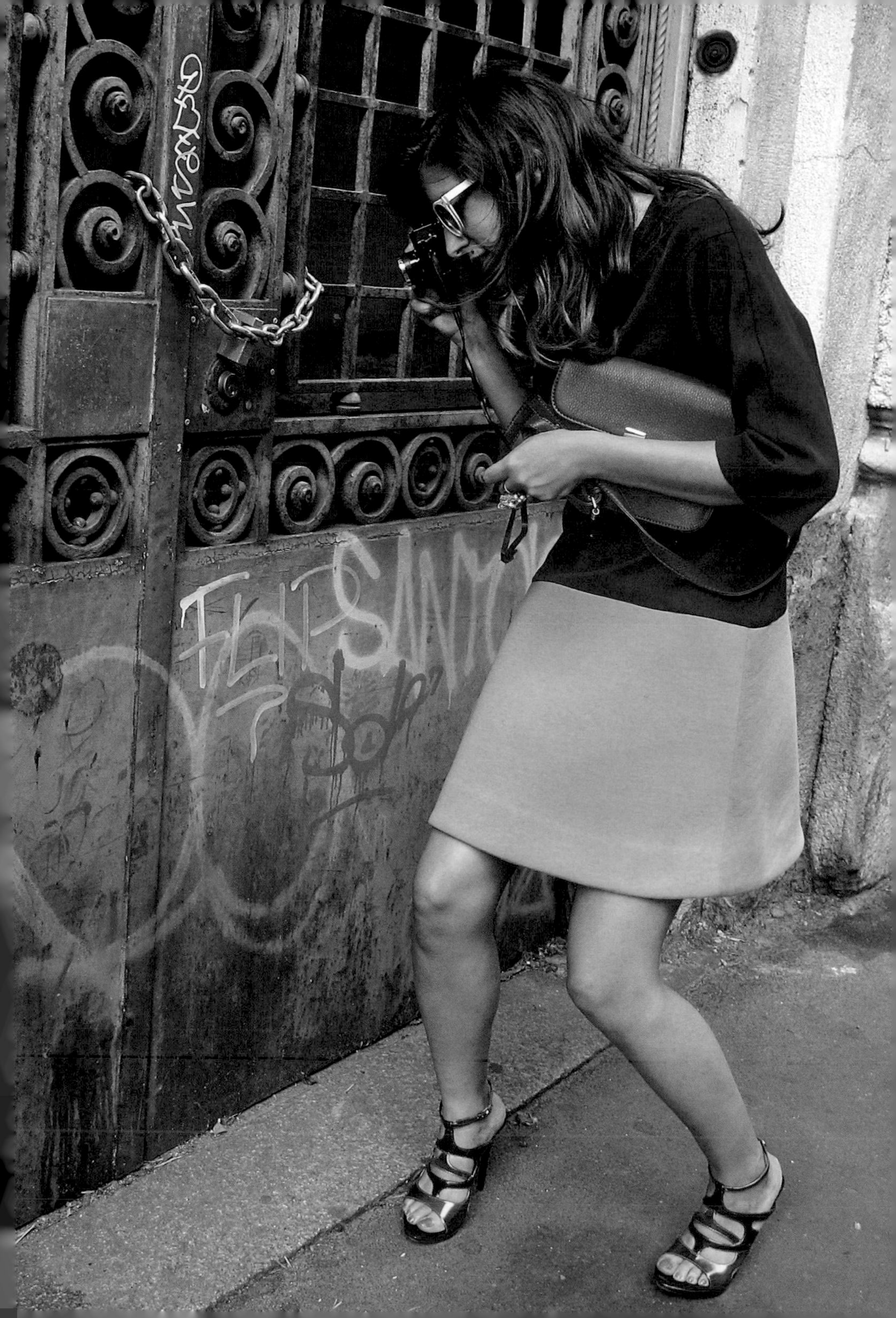

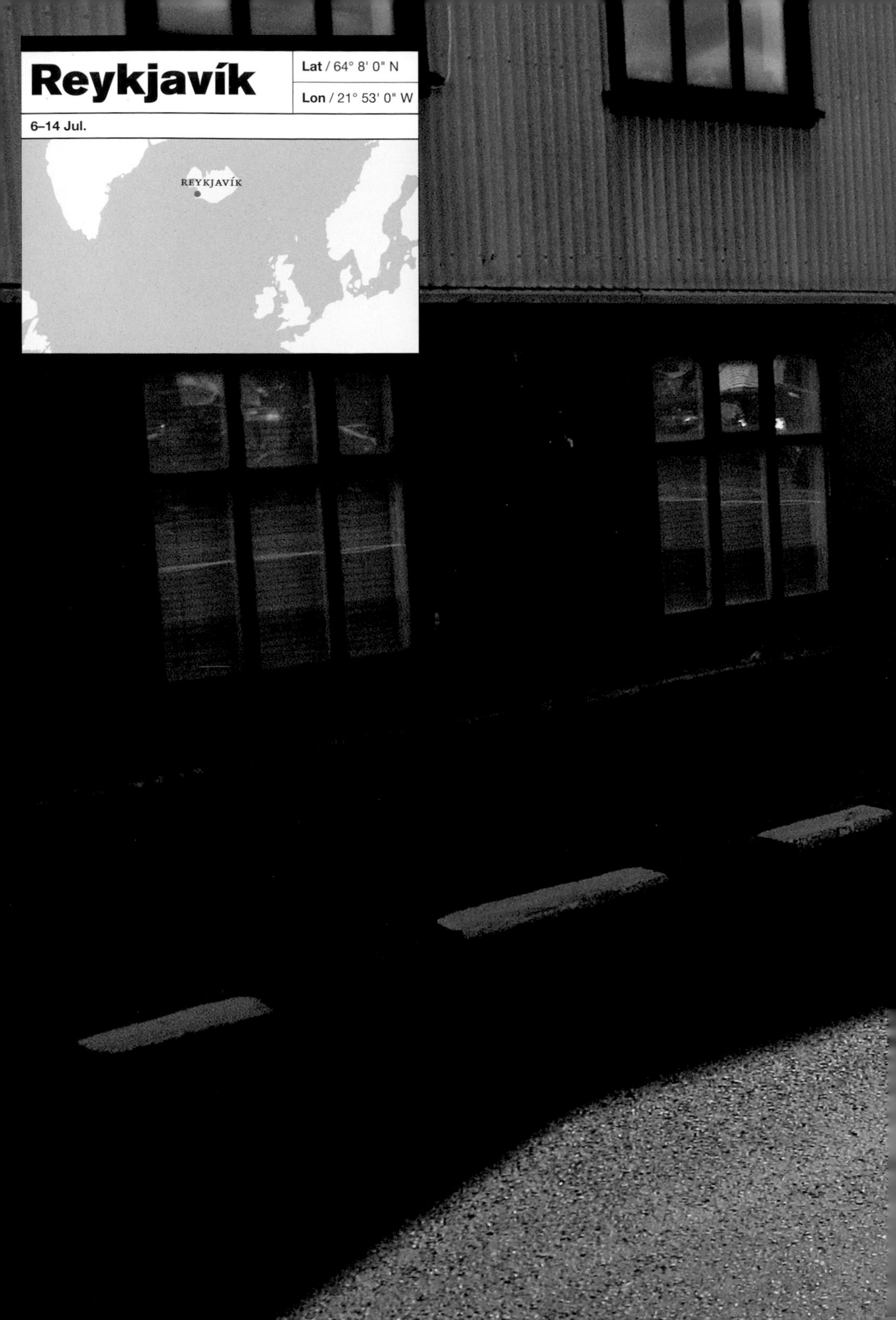
Reykjavík
Lat / 64° 8' 0" N
Lon / 21° 53' 0" W
6–14 Jul.
REYKJAVÍK

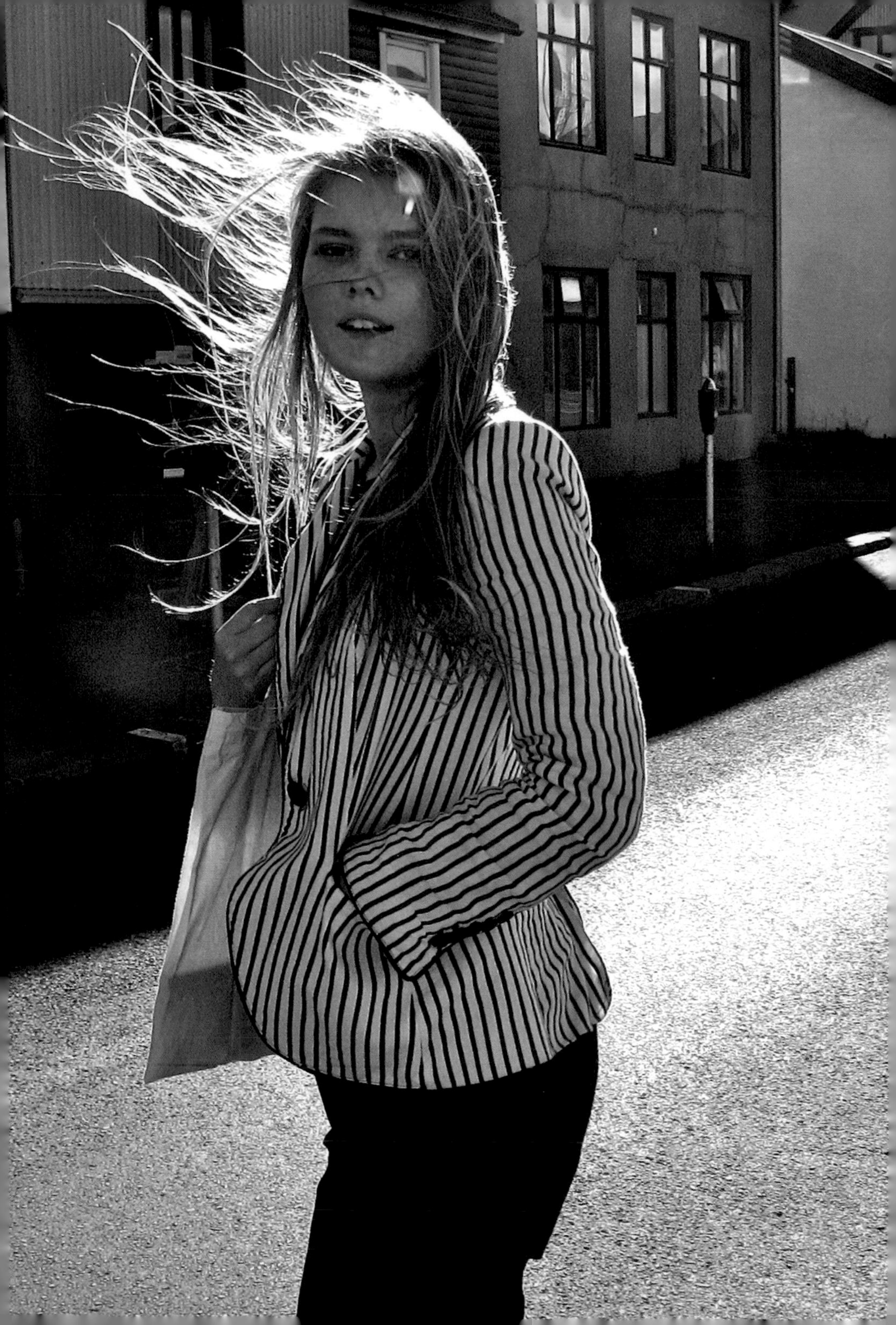

“I need my dose of Reykjavík at least a few times a year. No other city in the world can be both so happening creatively and so connected to nature at the same time. Cities with populations of only 200,000 souls are rarely very relevant when it comes to contemporary culture, but for some reason, this remote and climatically hostile little piece of land located just below the Arctic Circle is home to the highest density of talent per square kilometre I've ever seen. When you walk downtown, it seems like everyone you meet is an artist, a fashion designer or playing in a band. Only a few decades ago, Iceland was one of the poorest countries in Europe, until the modification of a fishing law in the 1980s transformed the volcanic island into one of the wealthiest. Somehow this sudden elevation created a favourable context for the arts. In 1987, the world first heard about Icelandic music when the song 'Birthday' by The Sugarcubes became an indie hit in the UK and the USA. A few years later, Björk, the band's lead singer, started a solo career, securing a spot for Iceland on the map of international coolness, followed by groups such as Sigur Rós and Gus Gus. In the 2000s, Reykjavík began hosting its own music festival called Iceland Airways, showcasing new bands, both Icelandic and international. Airways was one of the first things that made vistors travel to Iceland for something other than its landscapes. Same for me. I went there for the first time in 2000 to do some hiking in the mind-blowing highlands, thinking that Reykjavík was boring. When I came back in 2006 for Airways, I was shocked to find so much positive madness, so many cool bands I'd never heard of before and so many people with a unique 'Face Hunter' style. Airways was followed by myriad festivals of all kinds, from short films to contemporary art. Since 2010, the world's northernmost capital city has even had its own fashion week: Reykjavík Fashion Festival, where designers like Mundi and Ziska present their eccentric work to the international press. It's a great atmosphere. Despite the recent economic upheaval, Icelanders still love to party so much and so hard that when the bars and clubs close, it seems like every house in Reykjavík is hosting an afterparty that lasts forever.”

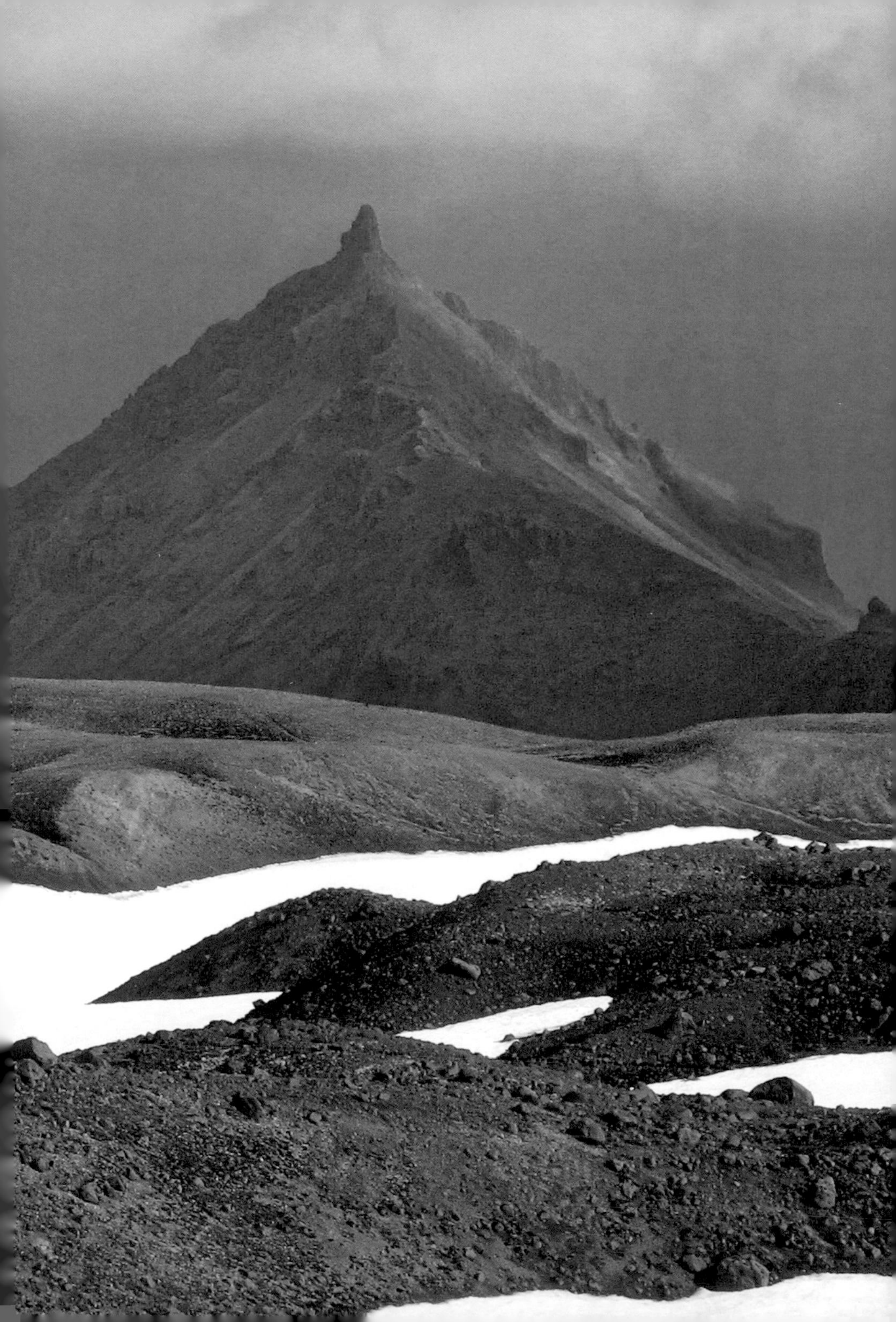

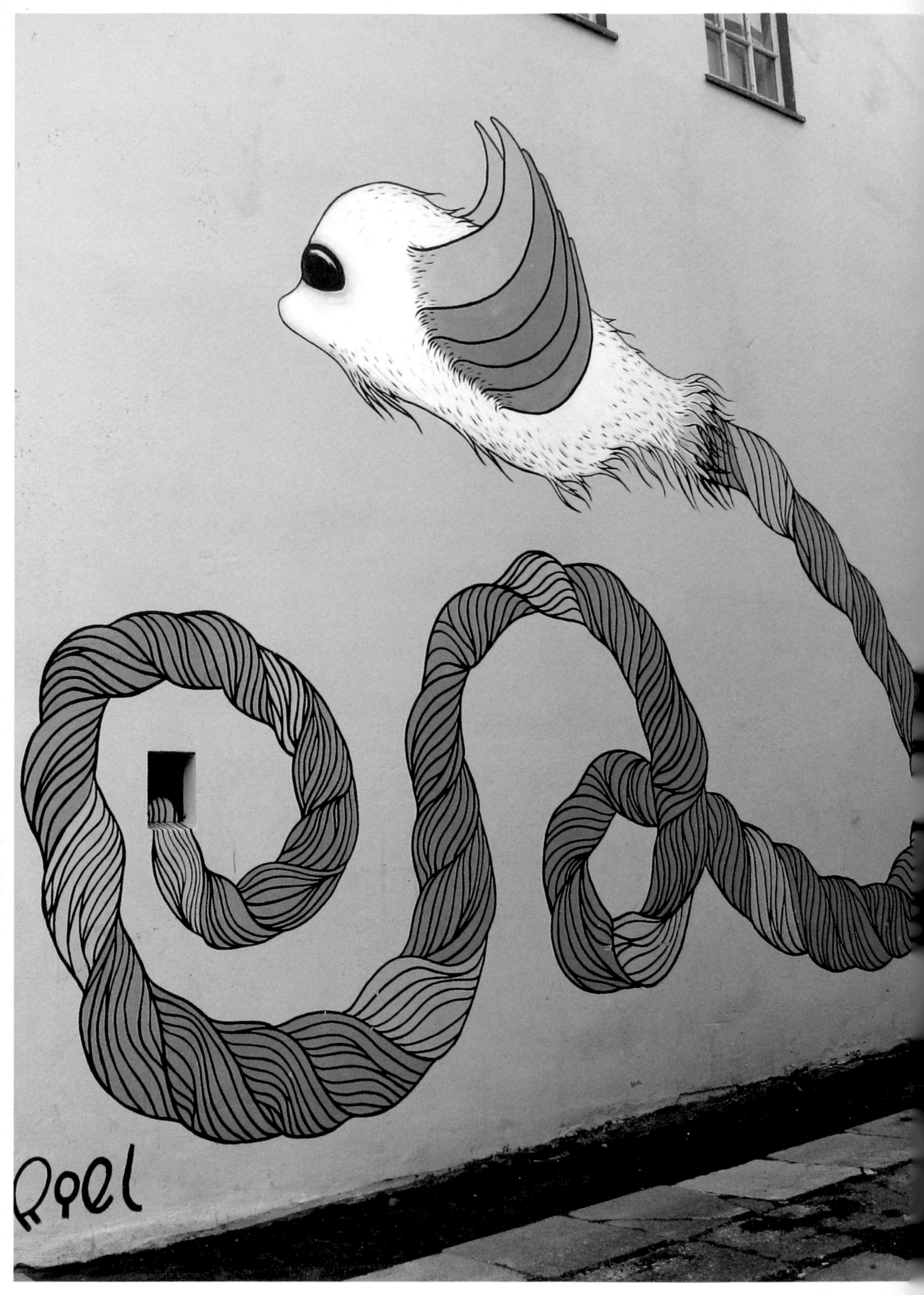
Roel

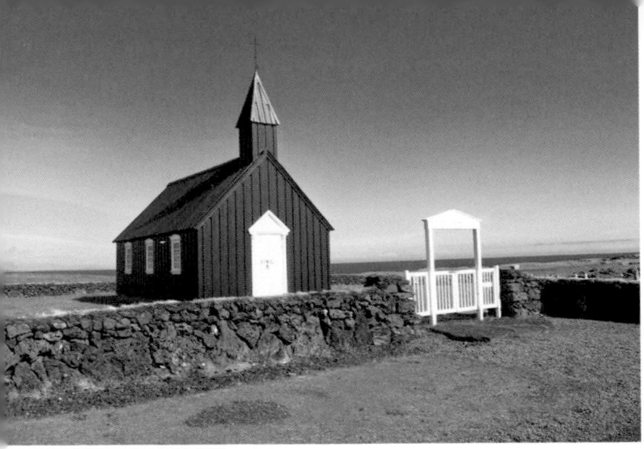

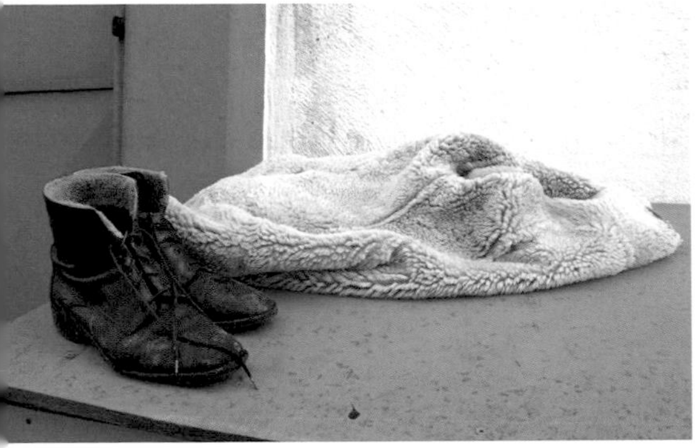

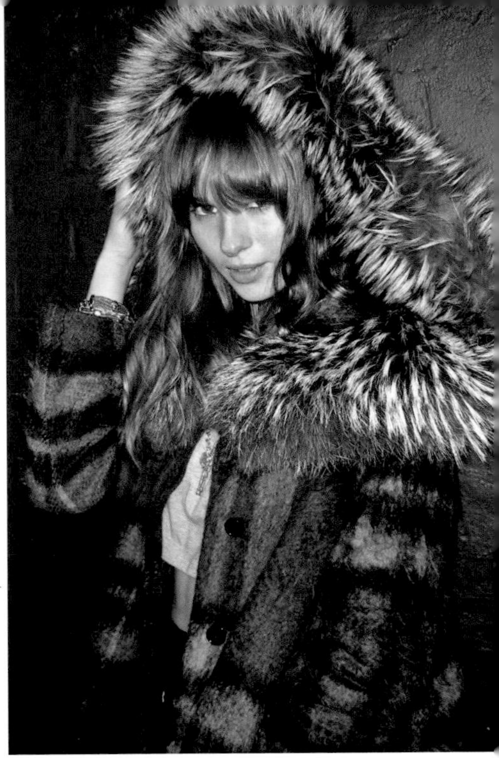

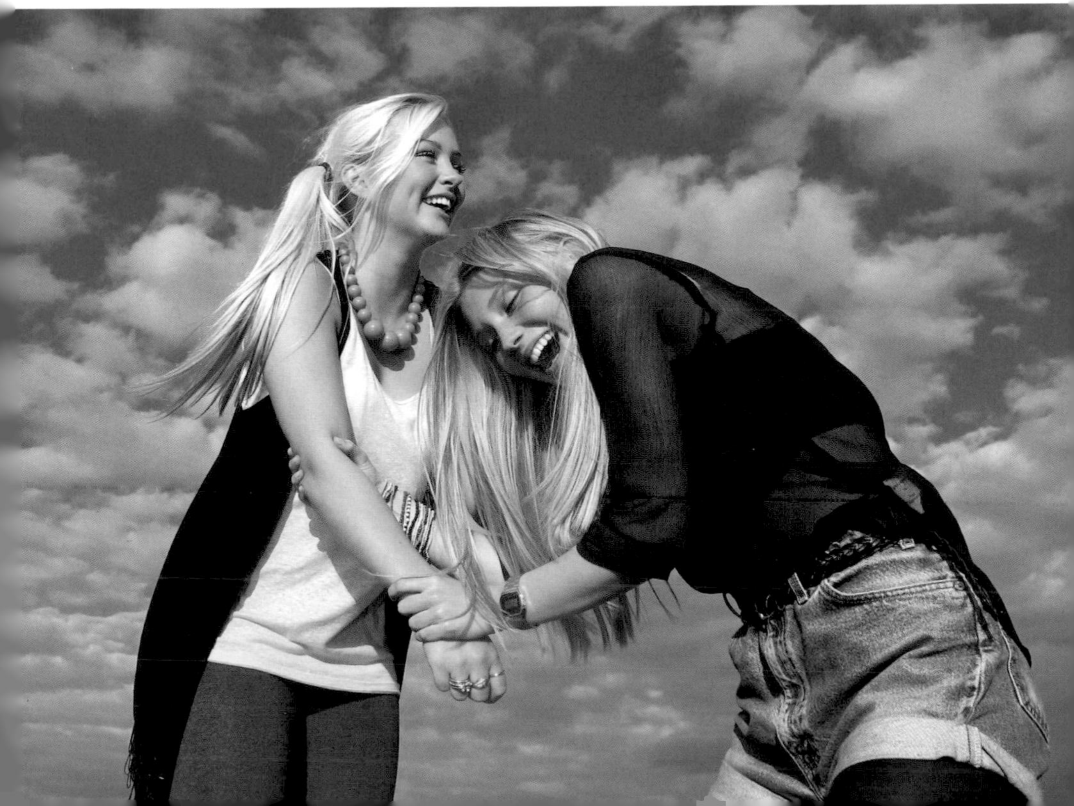

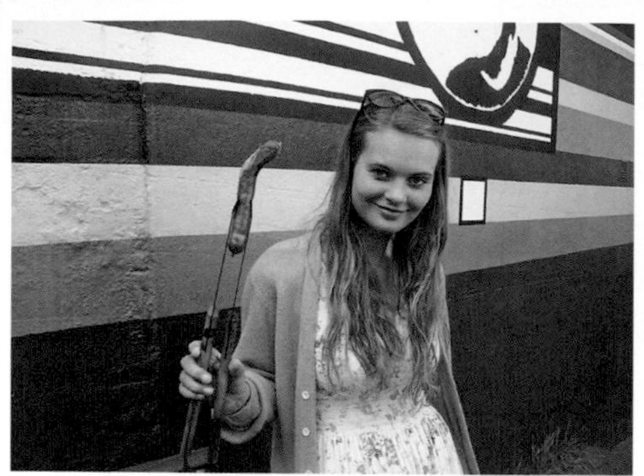

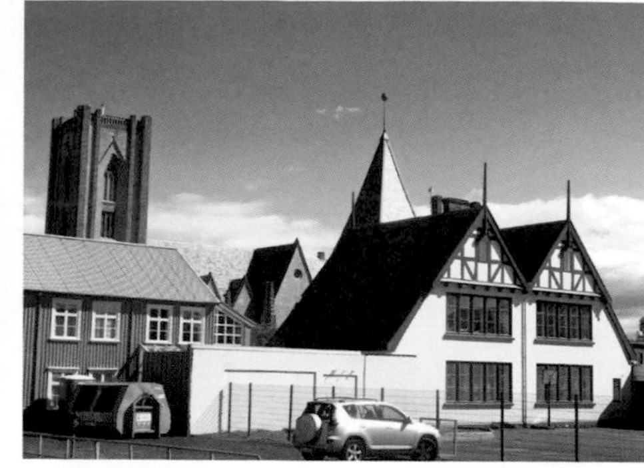

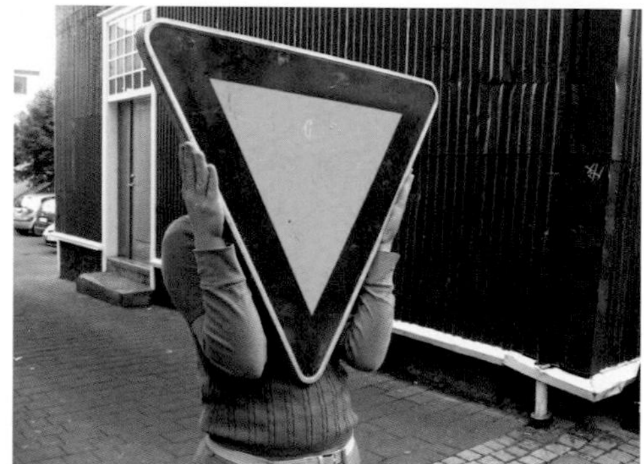

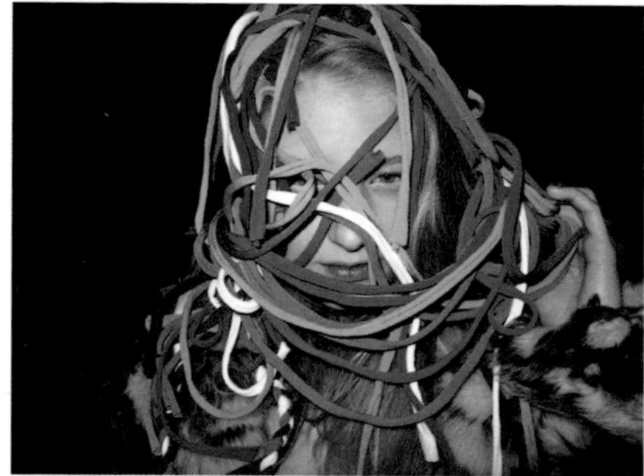

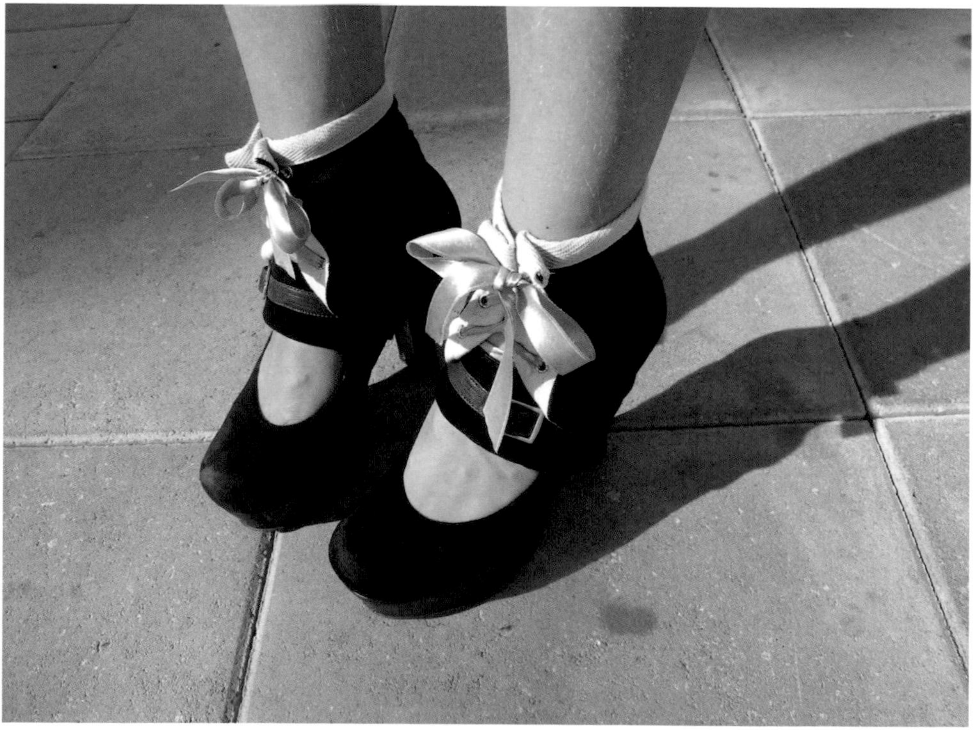

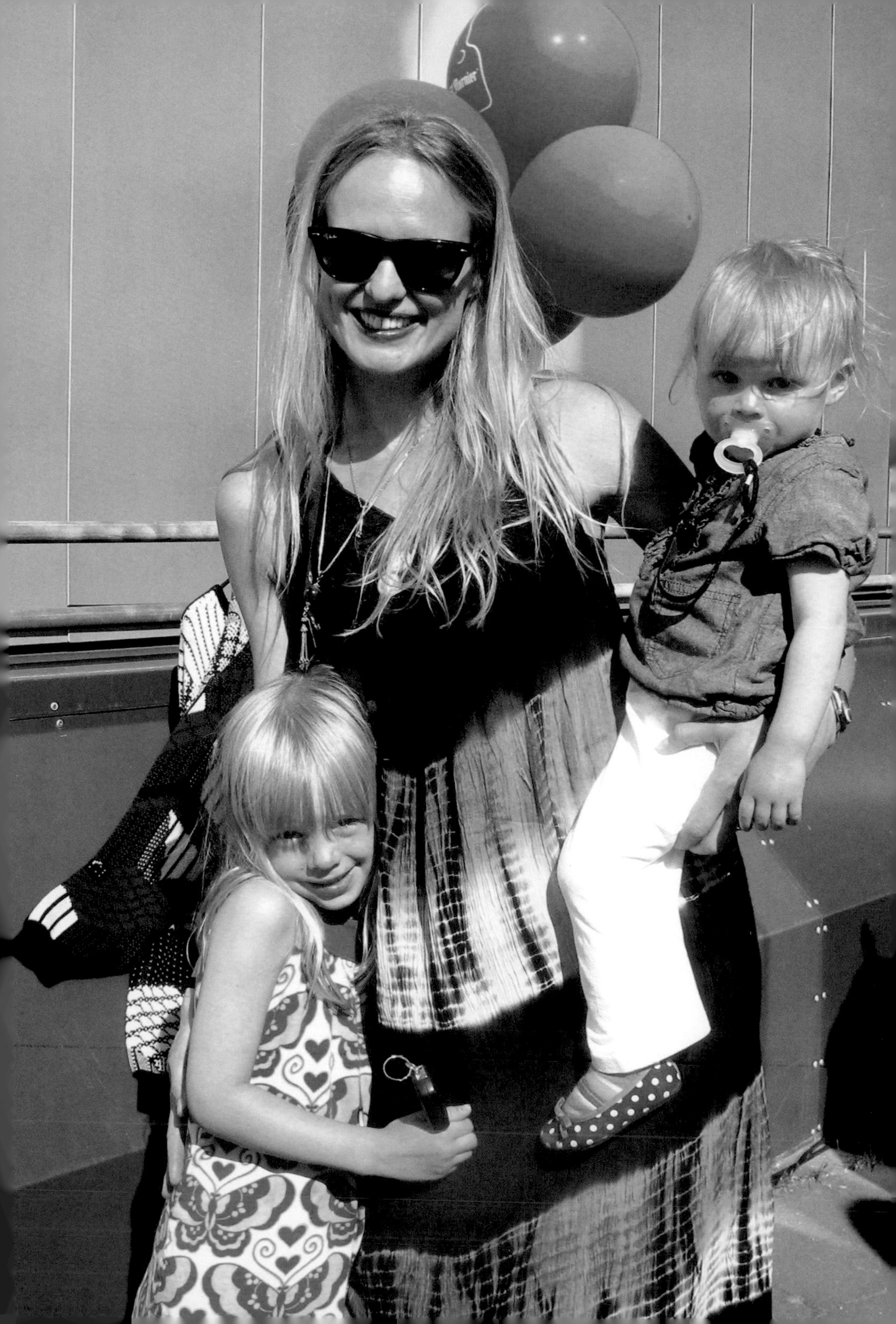

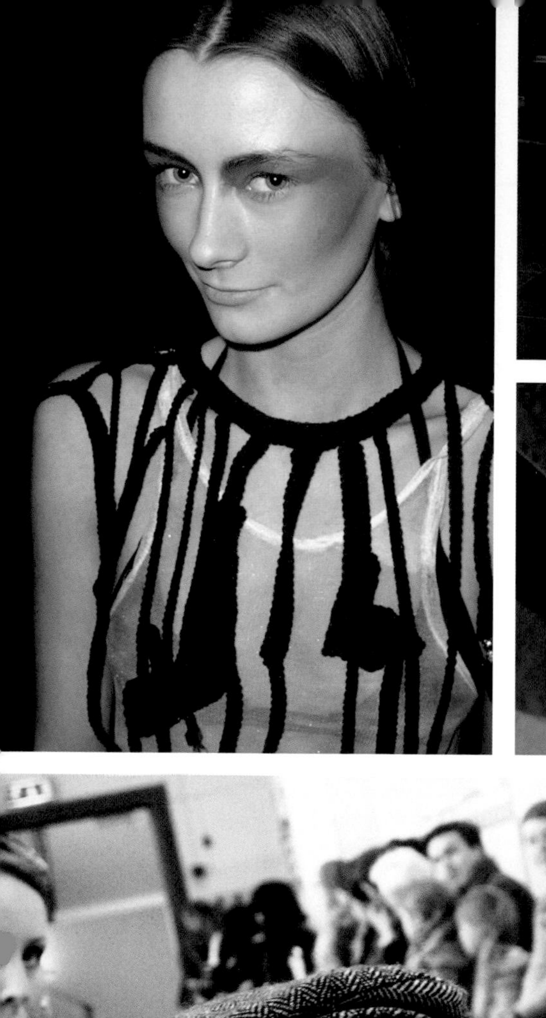

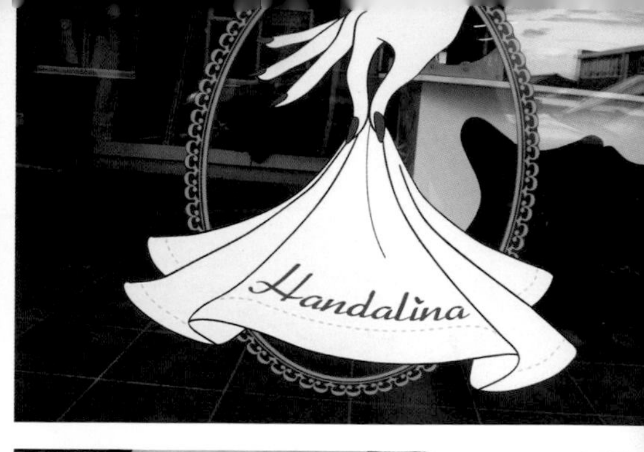
Handalina

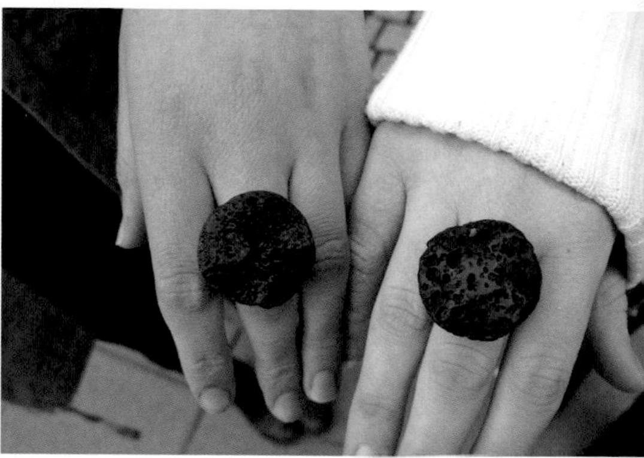

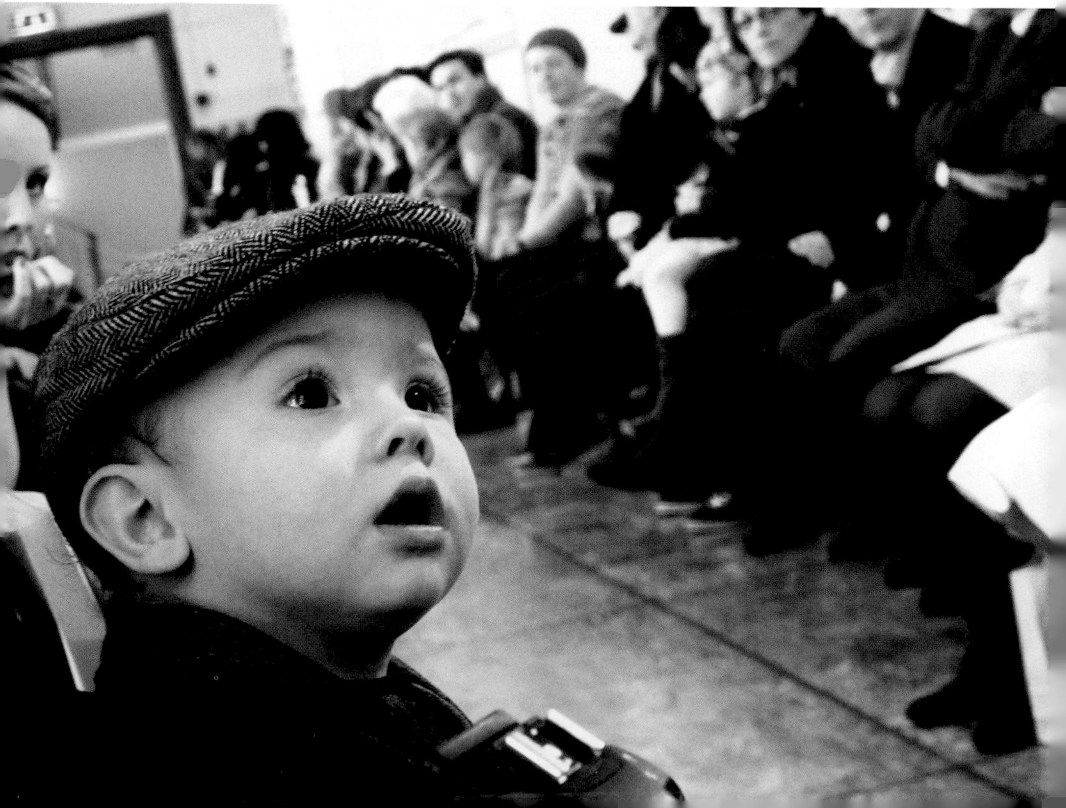

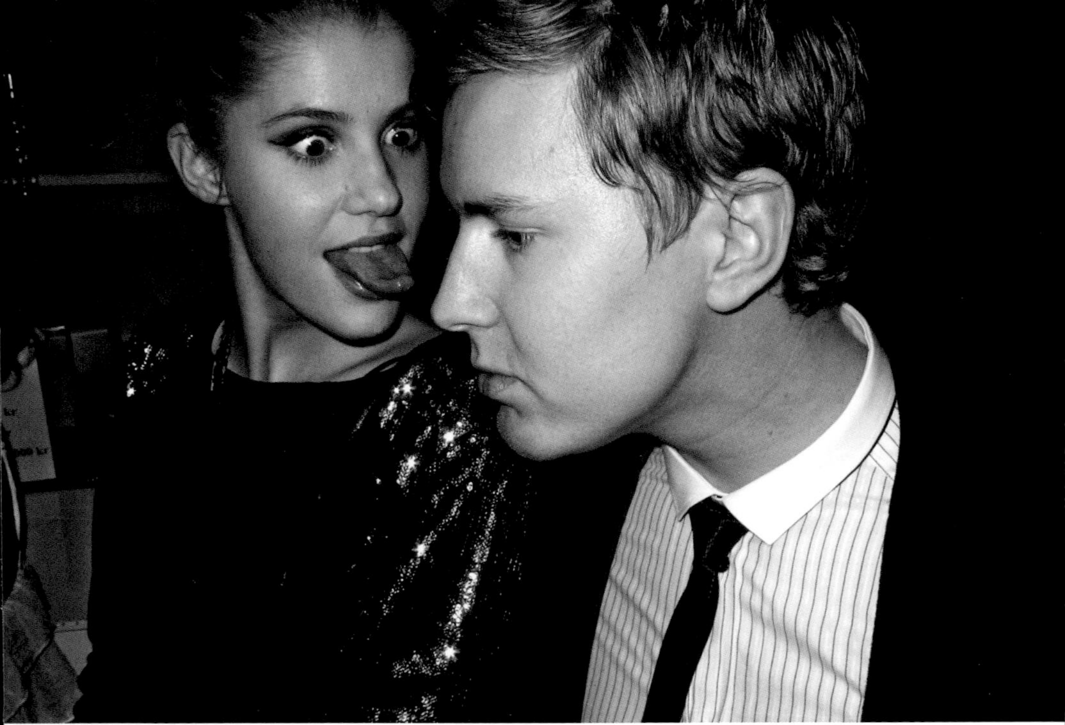

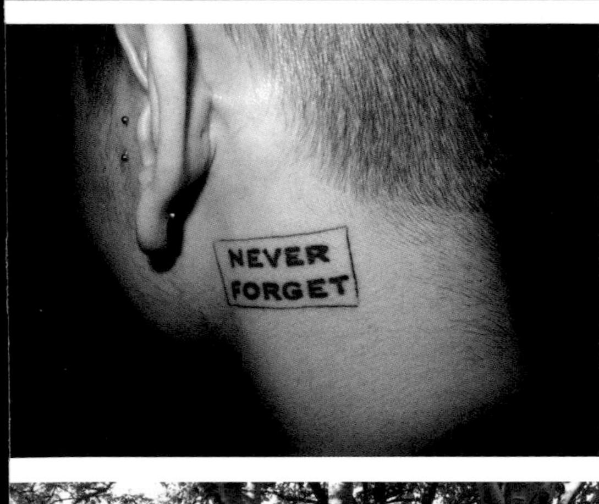
NEVER
FORGET

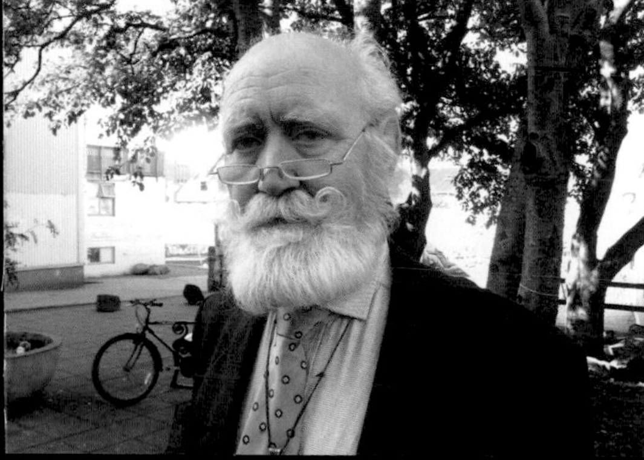

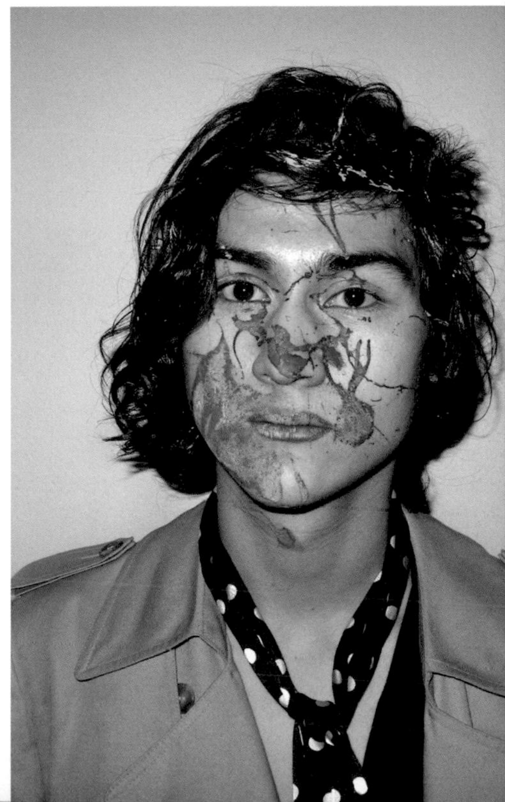

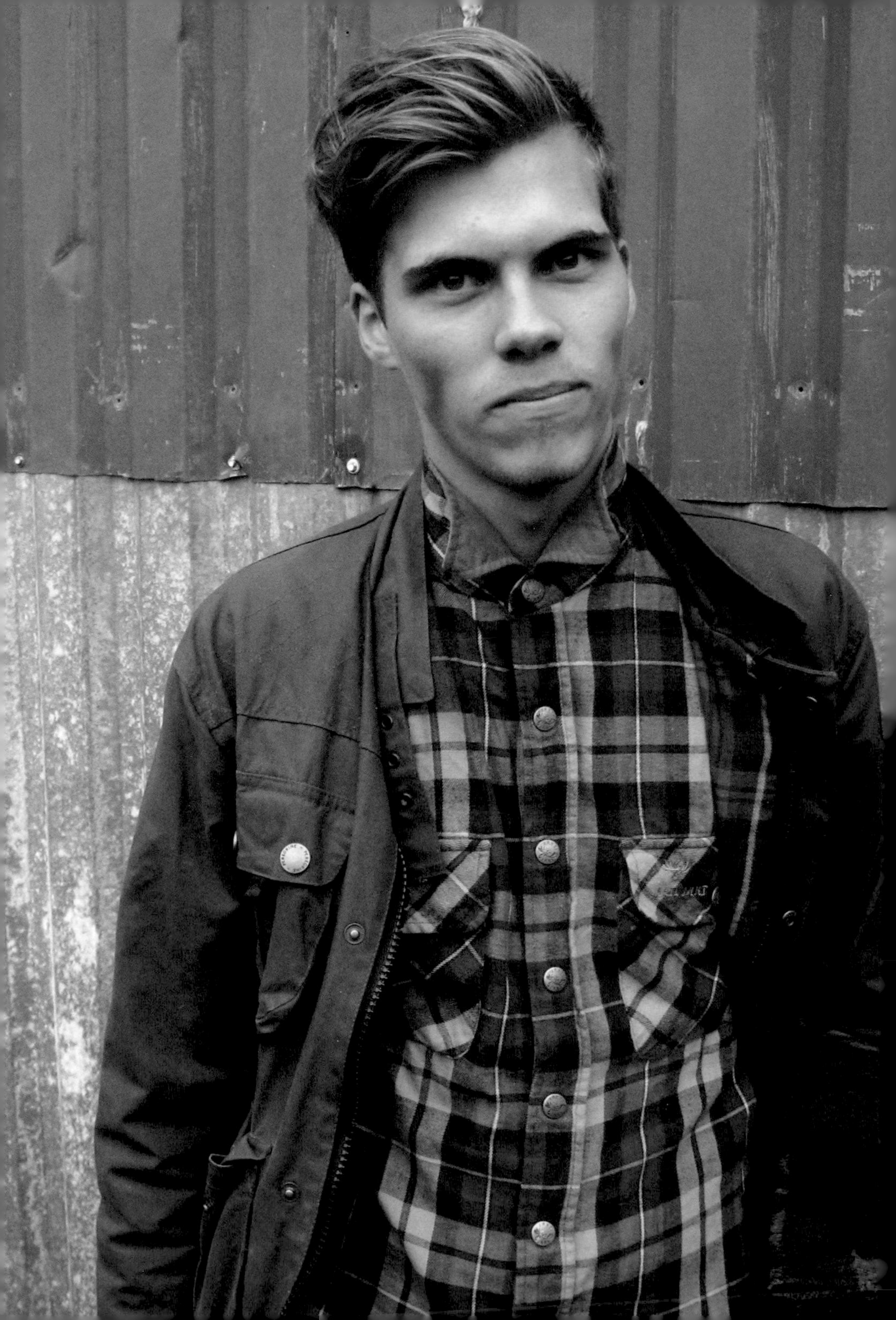

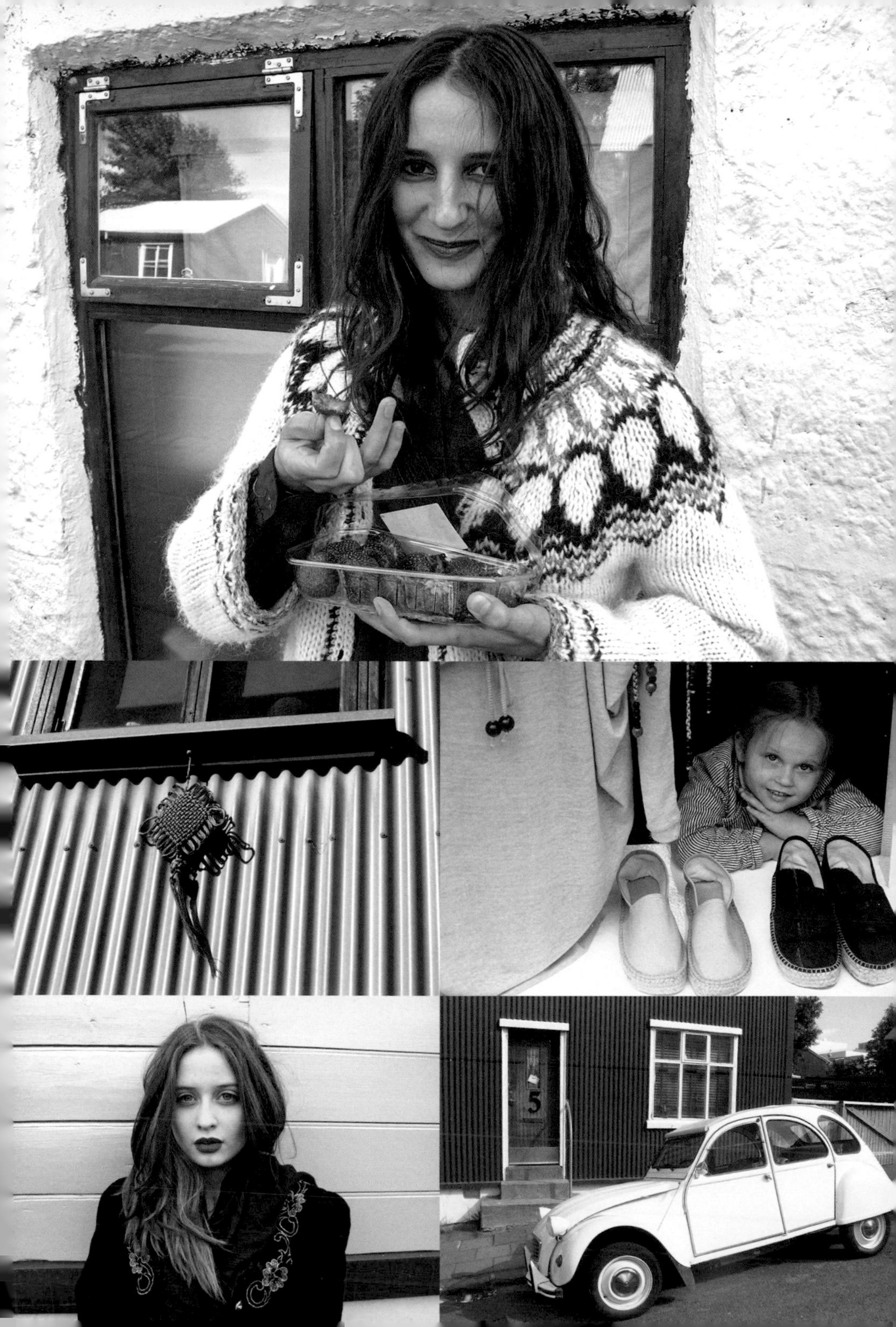
5

São Paulo

Lat / 23° 33' 0" S

Lon / 46° 38' 0" W

28 Jan.–5 Feb.

SÃO PAULO

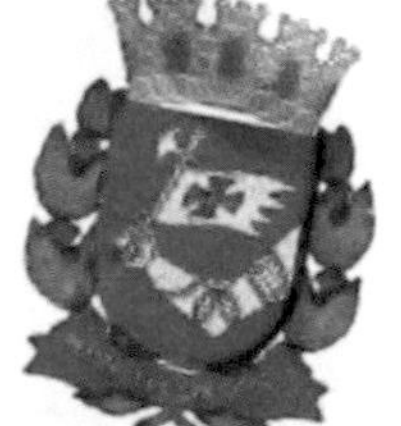

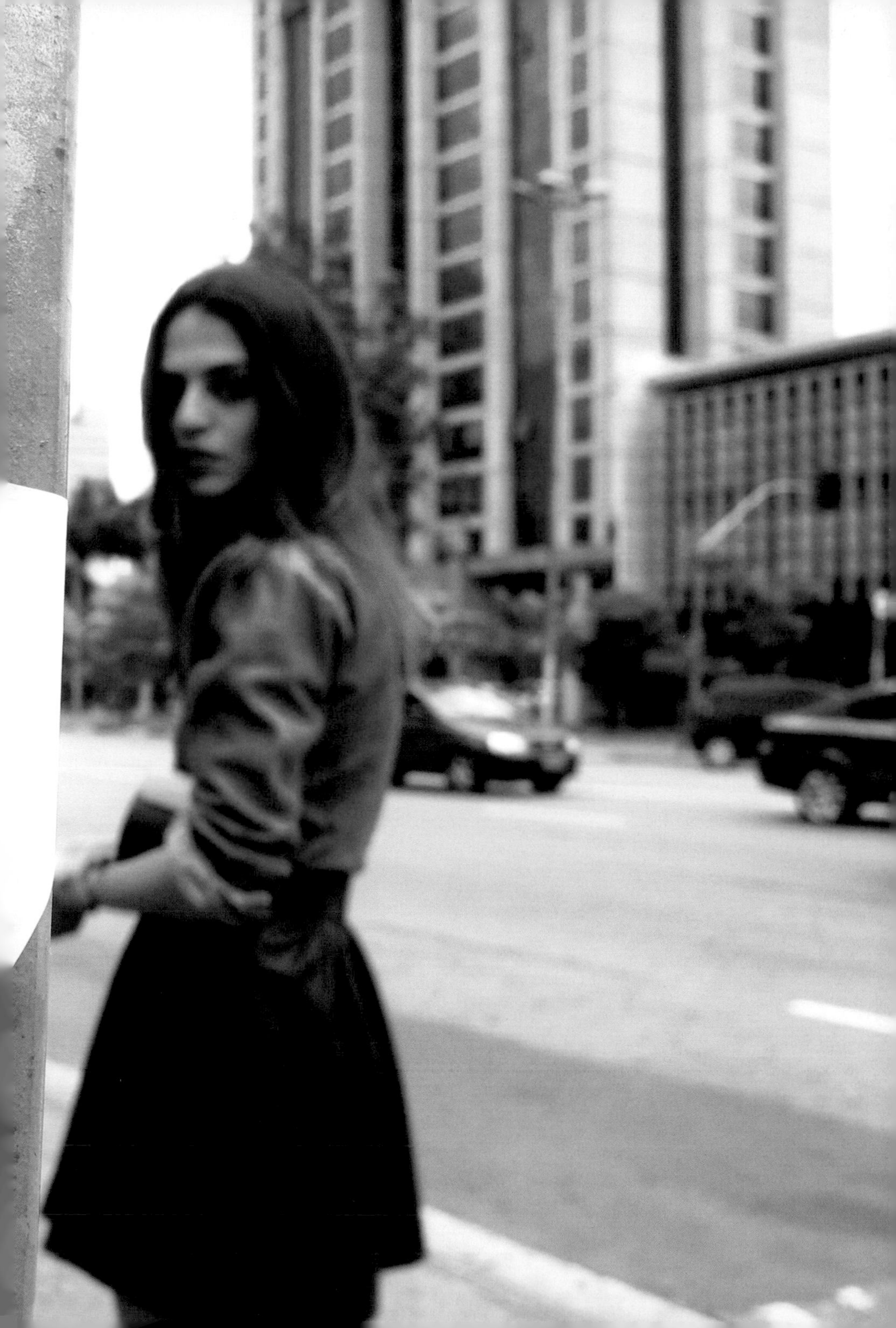

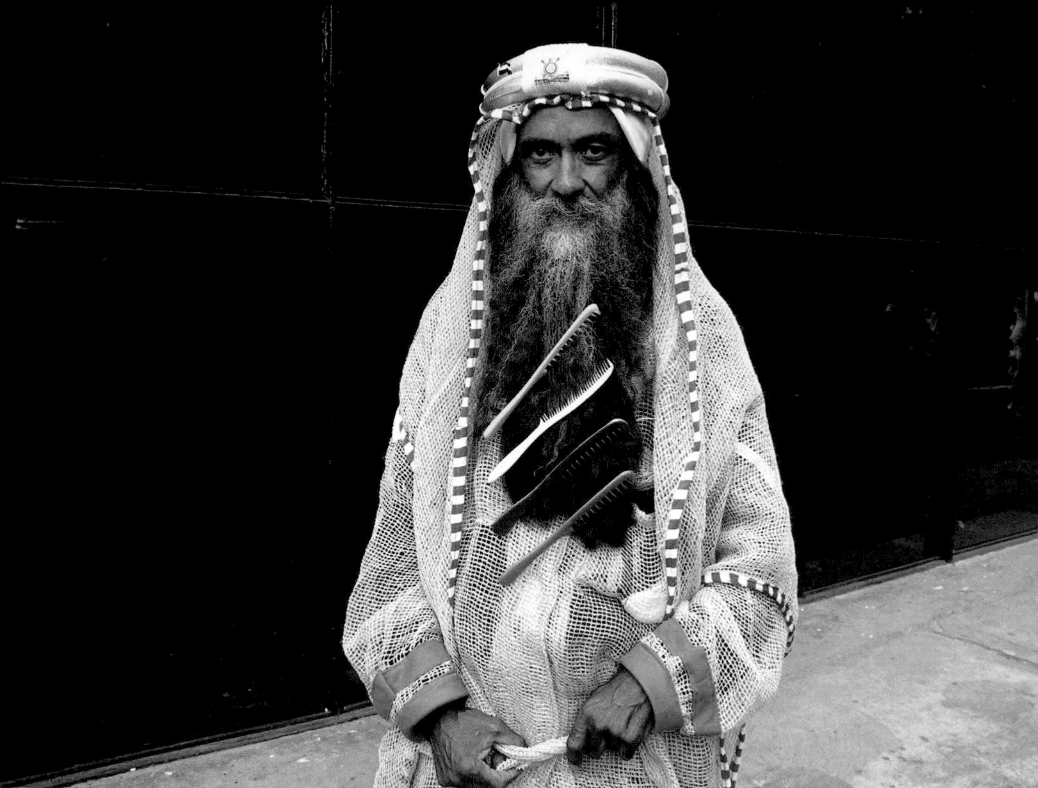

" I love São Paulo's combination of concrete brutalist architecture and sensual tropical vegetation. It's the ultimate urban jungle, wild, powerful and uncontrolled. It's also a world capital of street art, with thousands of hidden spots and stunning cryptic Pixação graffiti, which is only found in São Paulo and Rio de Janeiro, painted by gangs to mark their territories. São Paulo is the city that gives me the most powerful sense of itself, more so than New York or London. Even though it is one of the biggest and most happening urban metropolises in the world, you won't meet many tourists there, because they tend to go straight to the beaches instead. I love being in cities where there are hardly any foreigners – it makes travel more meaningful. Women in São Paulo play with personal style more freely; men tend to be more conservative as there is a big fear among many straight Brazilian men of being seen as gay, which translates into a fear of dressing elegantly. So it's not uncommon to see amazing, creatively dressed women on the arms of men who look like school headmasters. One night I went downtown with my friend Erlend (who doesn't exactly look like a school headmaster) from the band The Whitest Boy Alive (p. 57, lower right) because we wanted to experience walking through what is commonly considered a very dodgy part of town, with a reputation for violence and prostitution. In that part of São Paulo, you mainly see fantastic but very dilapidated 1920s Chicago-style skyscrapers, which have a look of faded grandeur. After a bit of hesitation, our local friends agreed to take us there, but when the police saw our unusual group wandering around they insisted on escorting us, driving their car next to us while we walked. The streets were almost empty, except for the homeless people, drug dealers, prostitutes and street cleaners. It was totally surreal. "

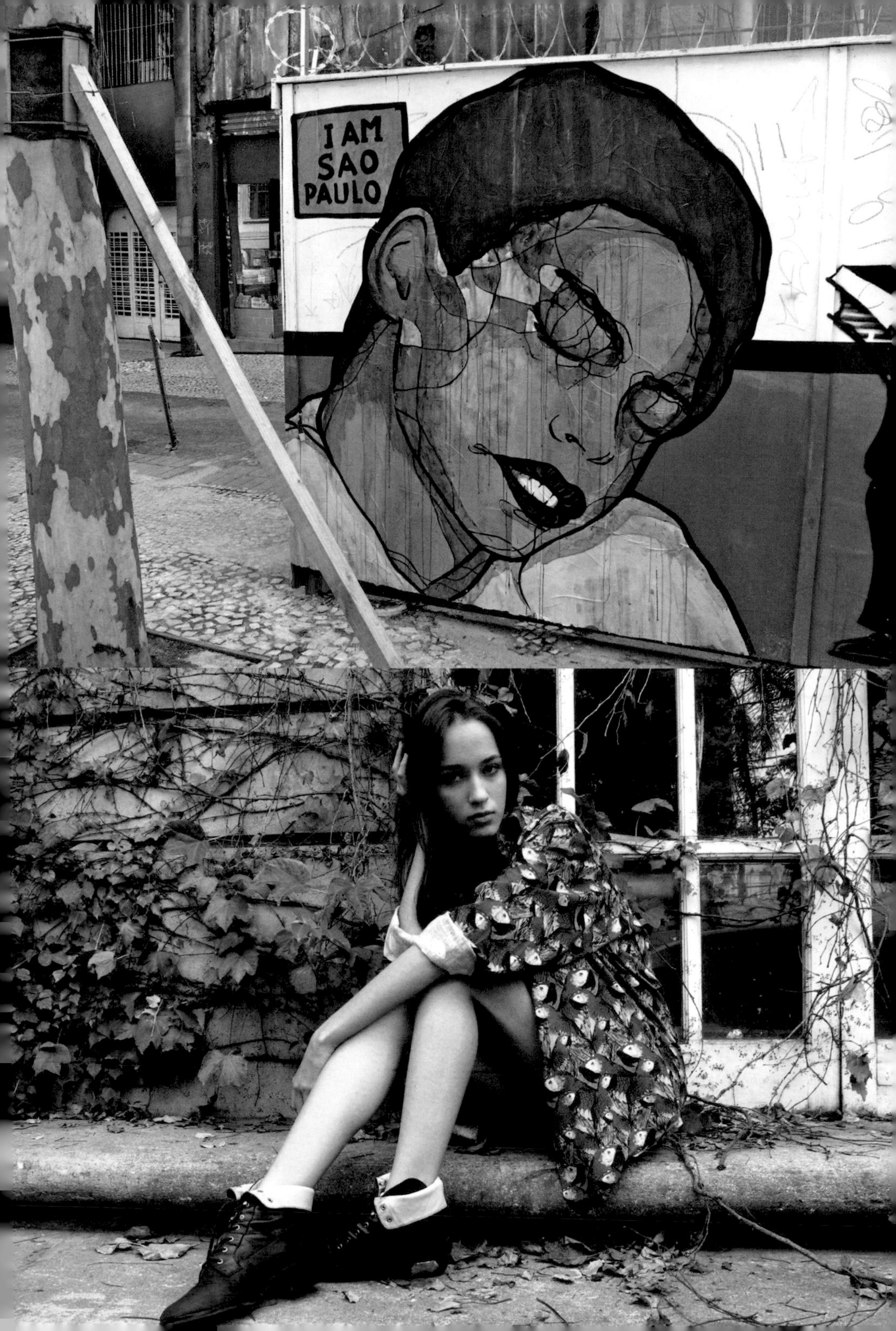
I AM
SAO
PAULO

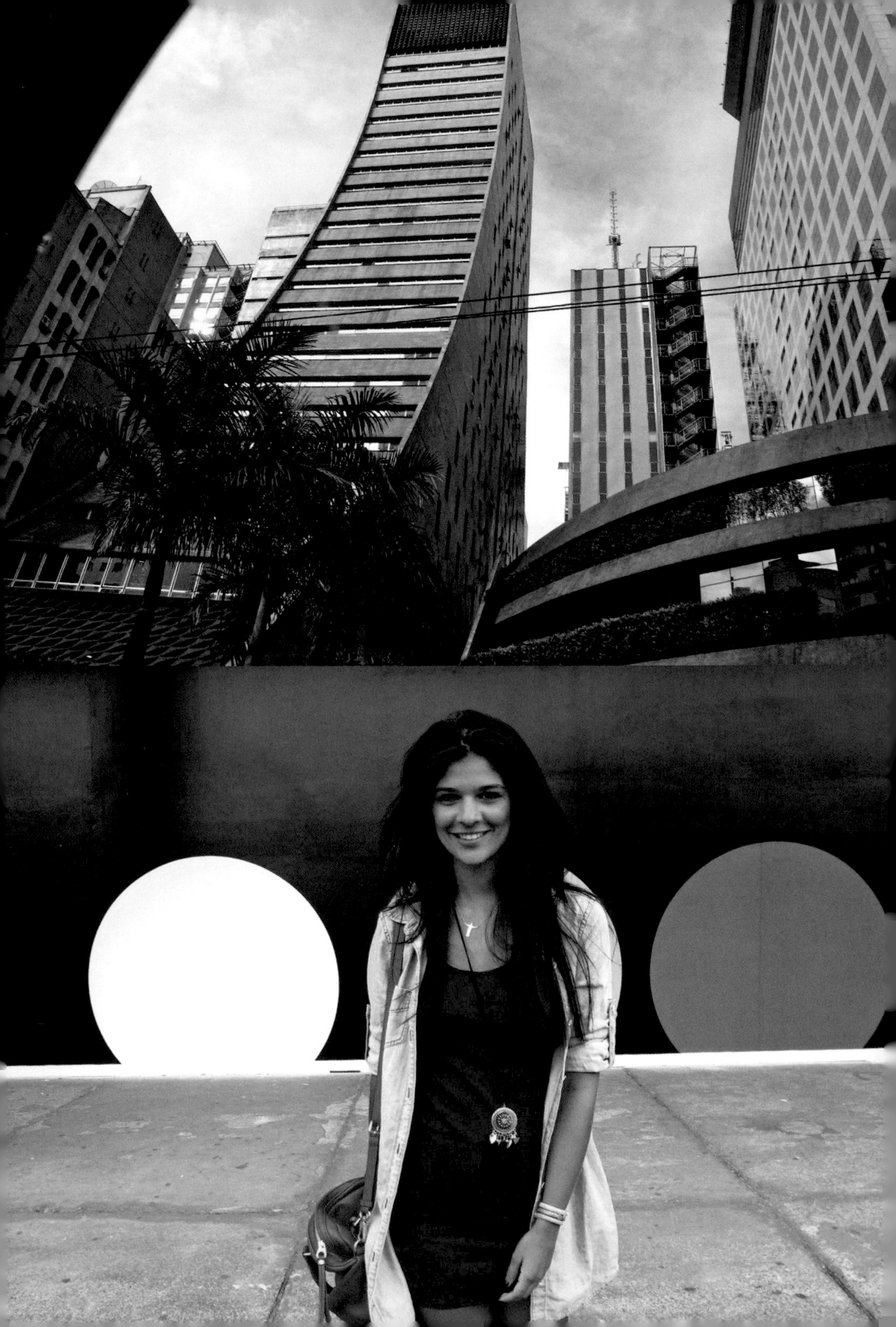

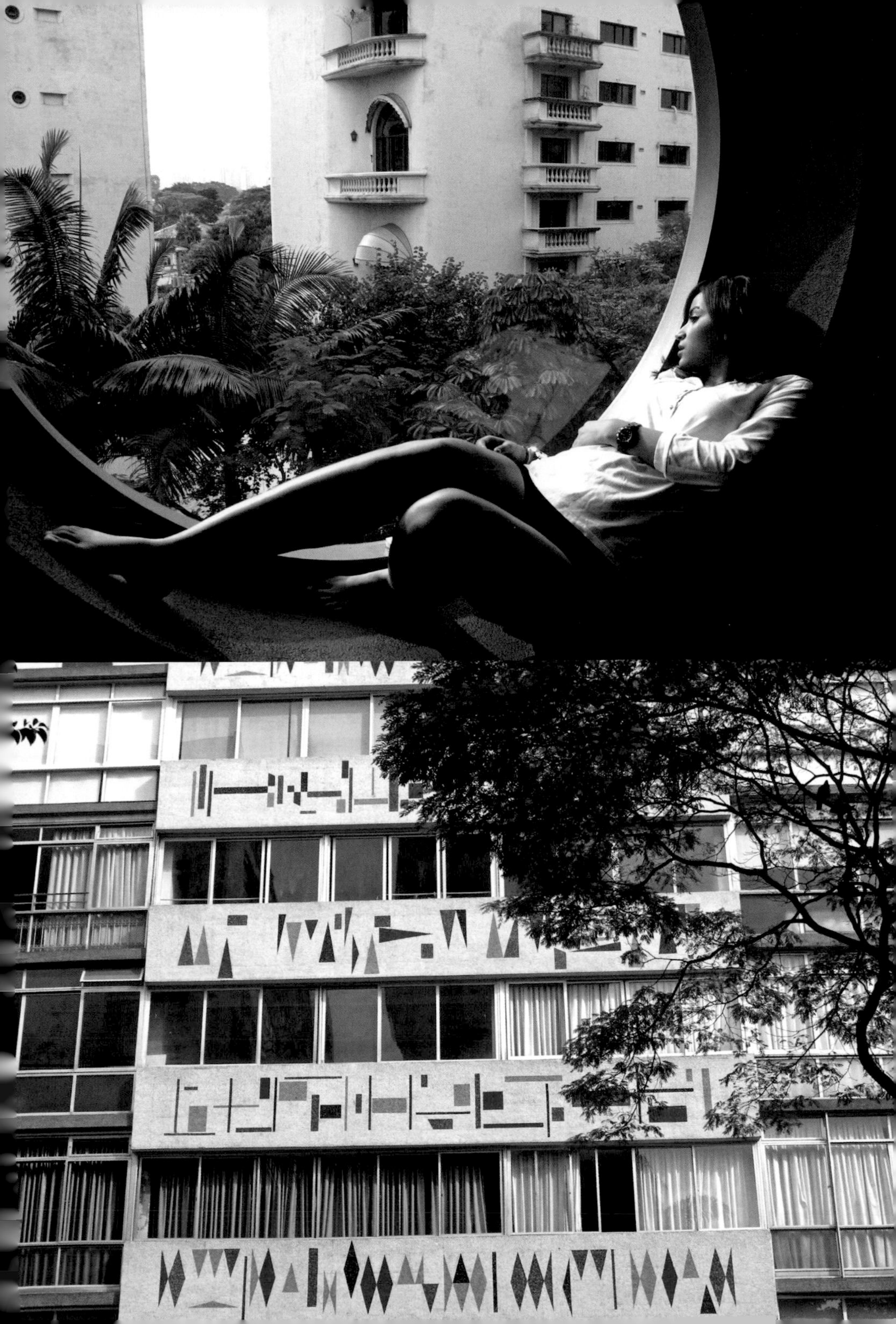

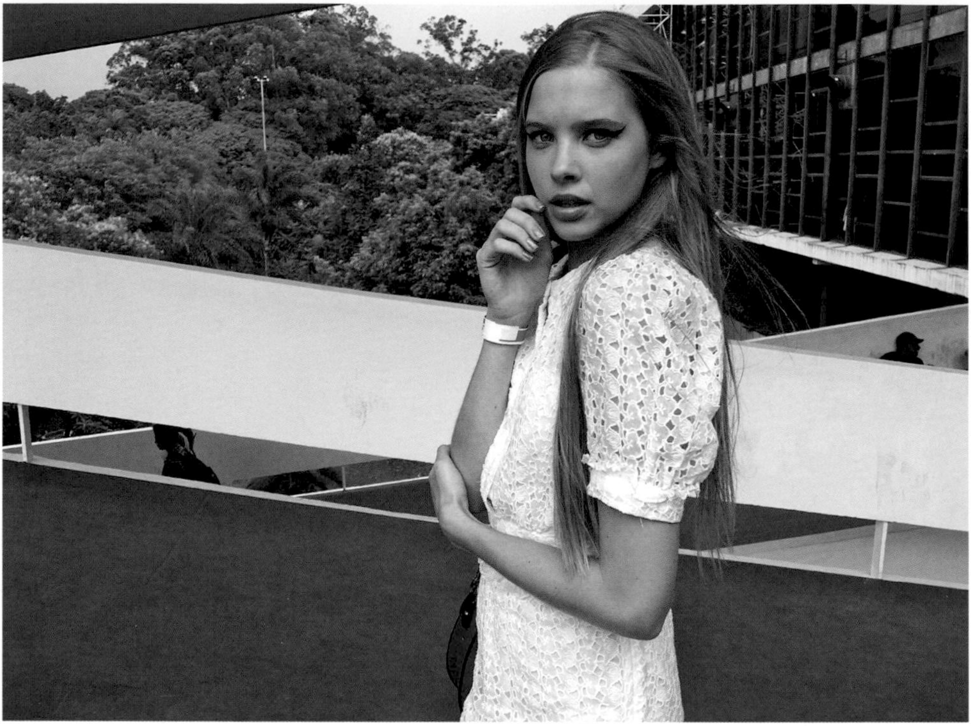

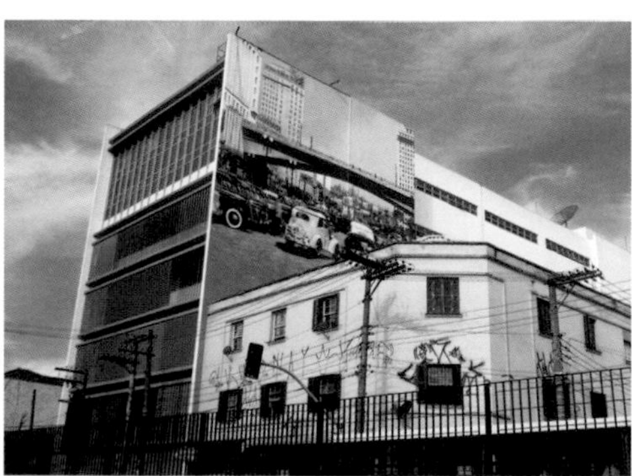

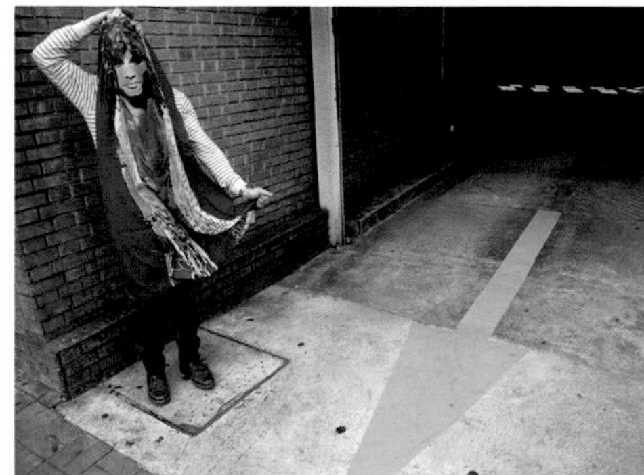

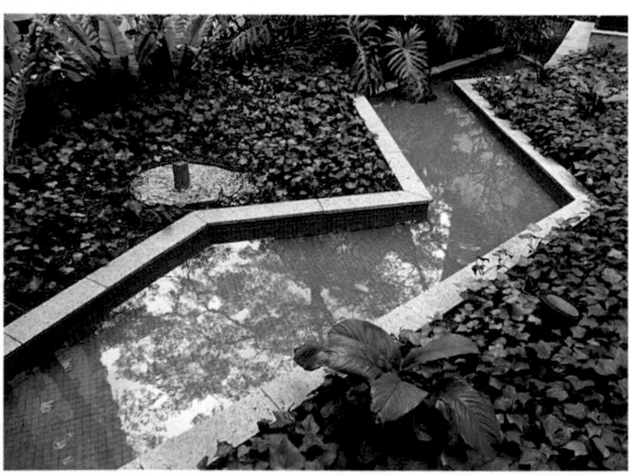

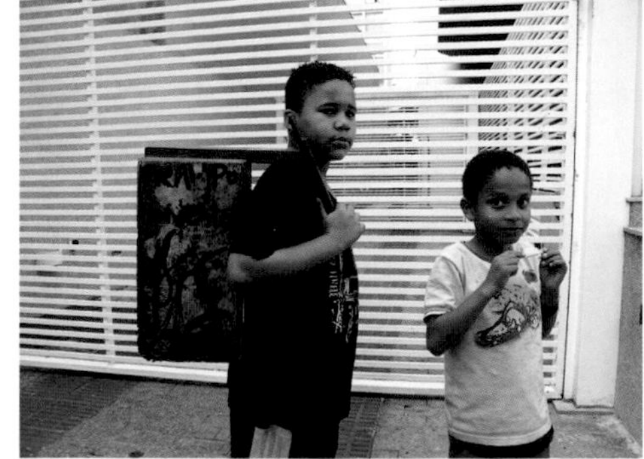

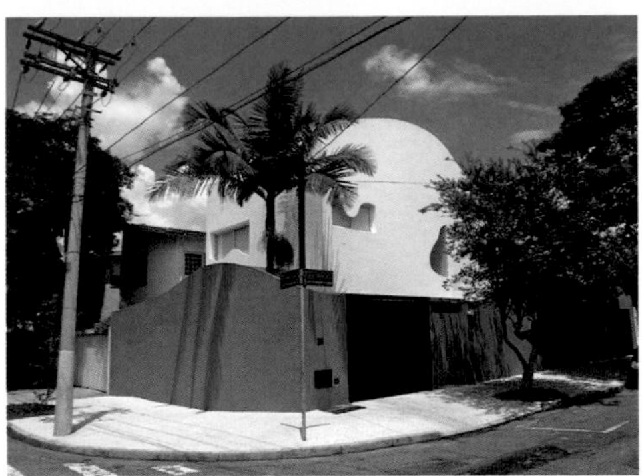

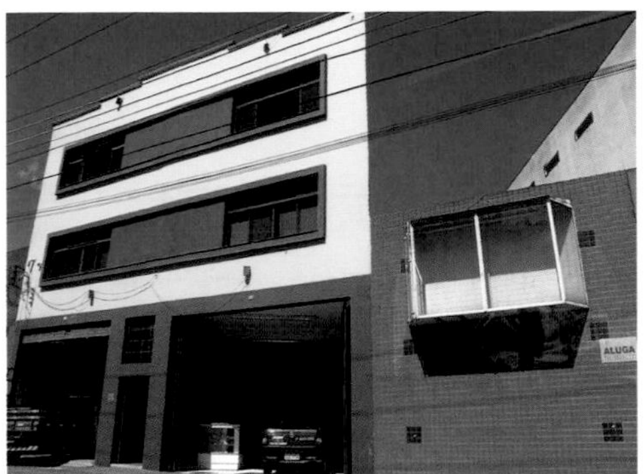
ALUGA

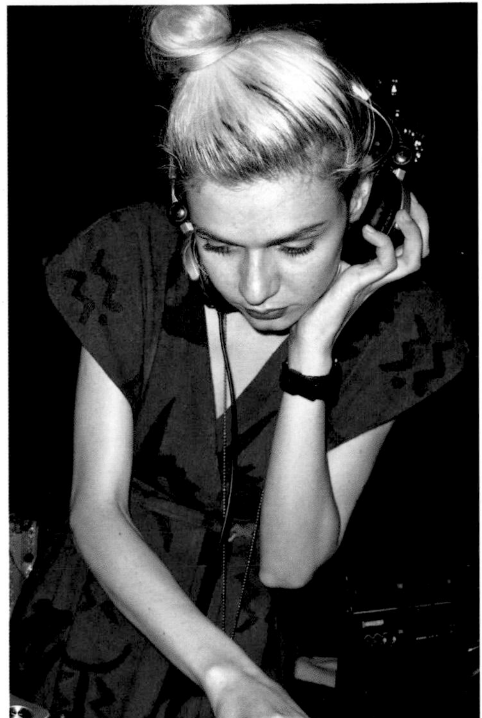

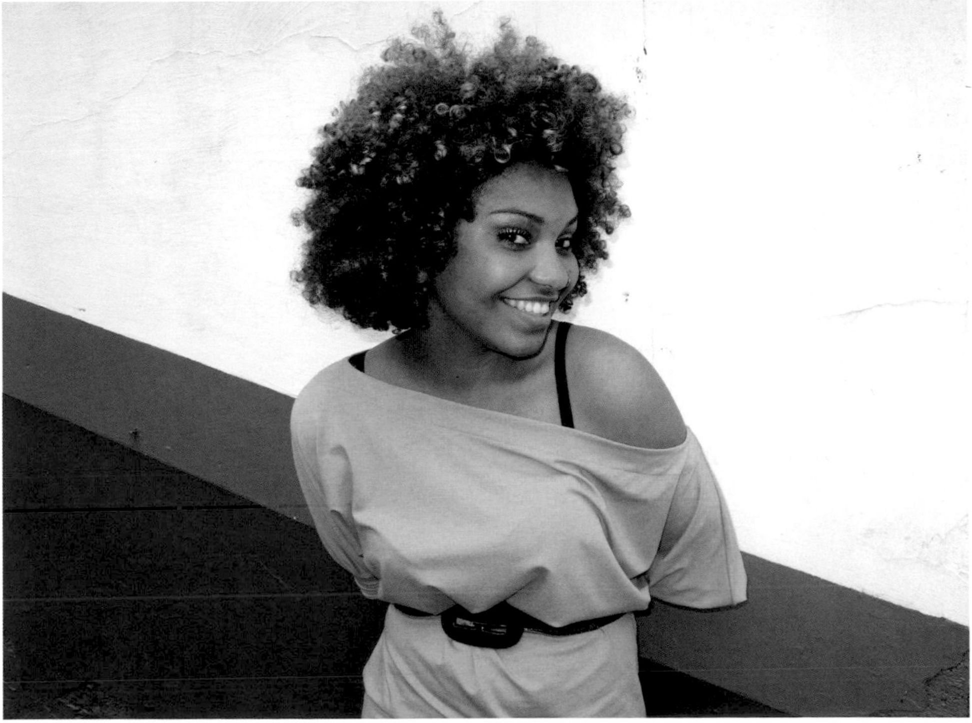

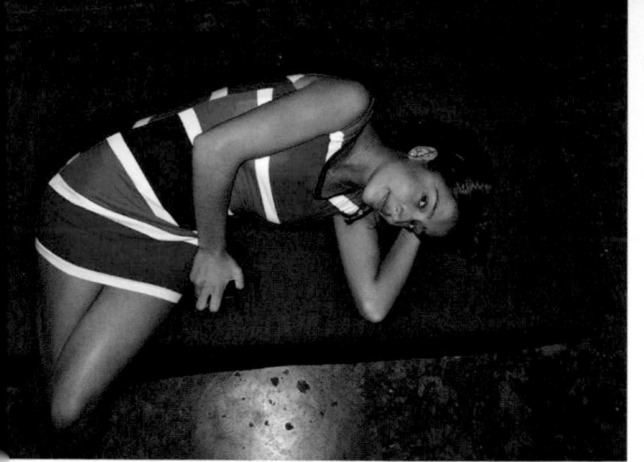

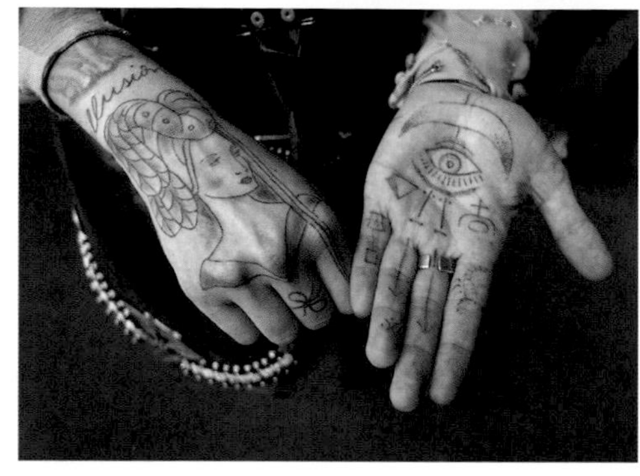

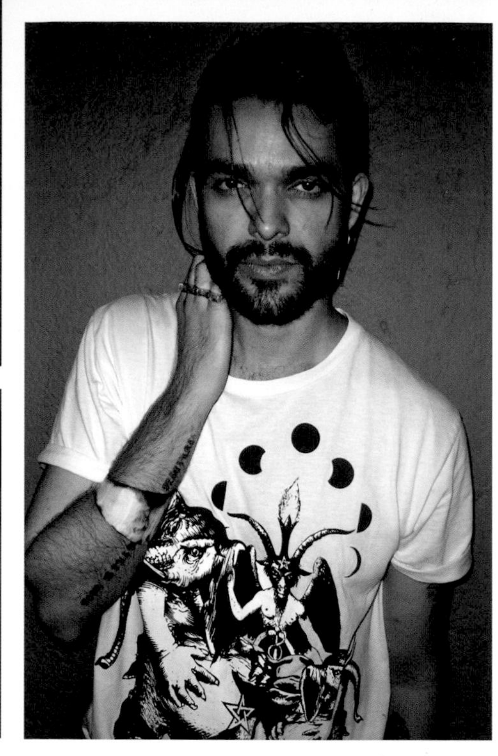

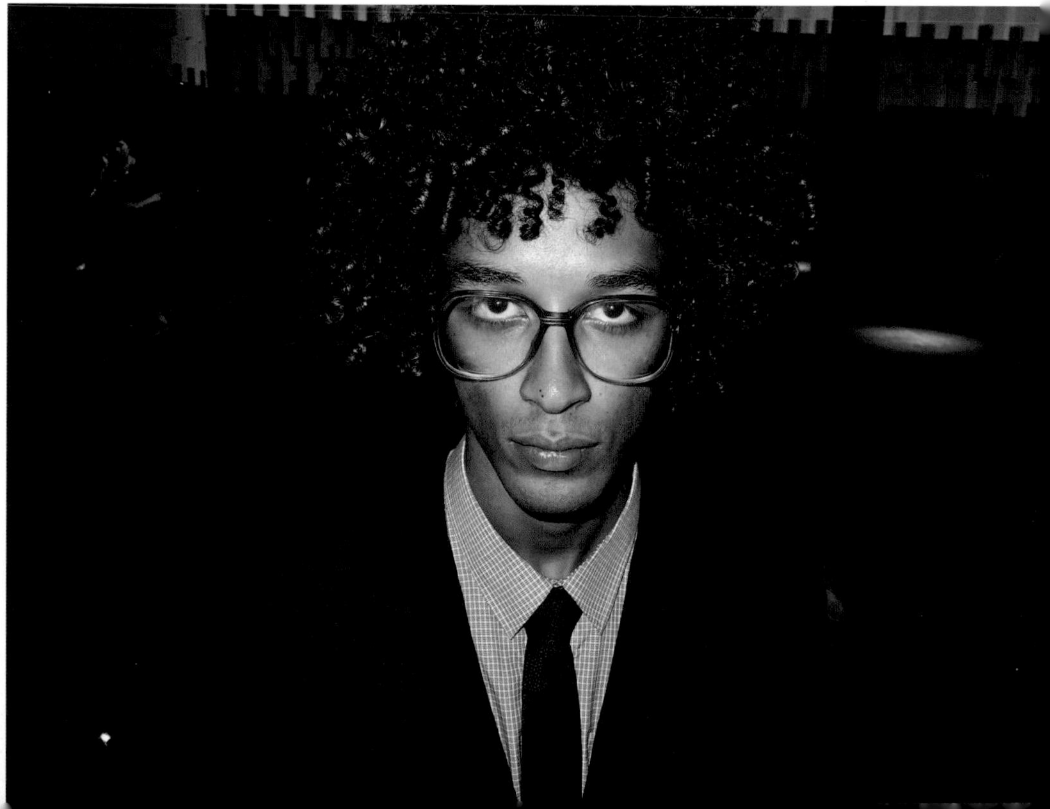

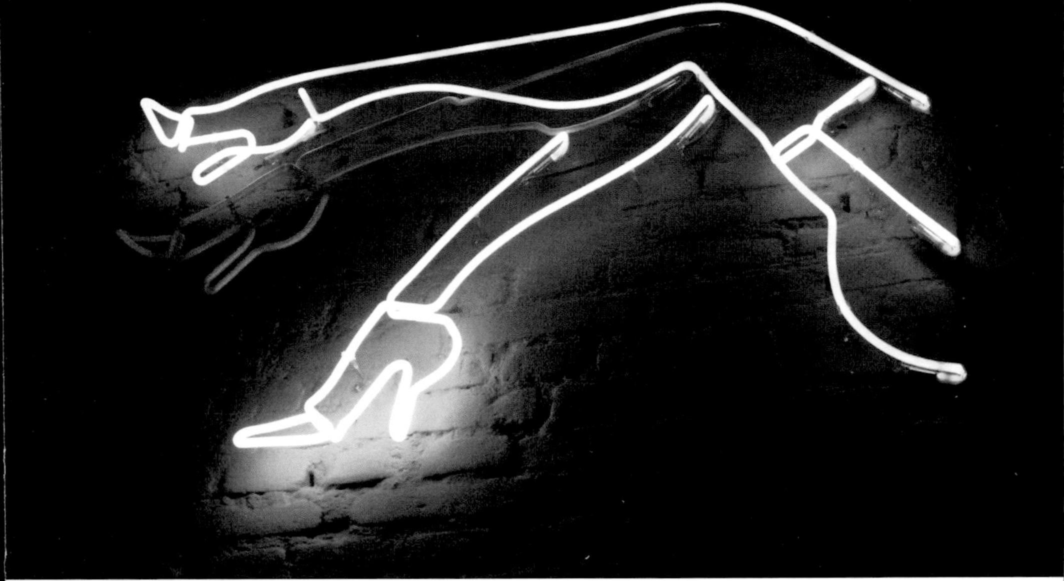

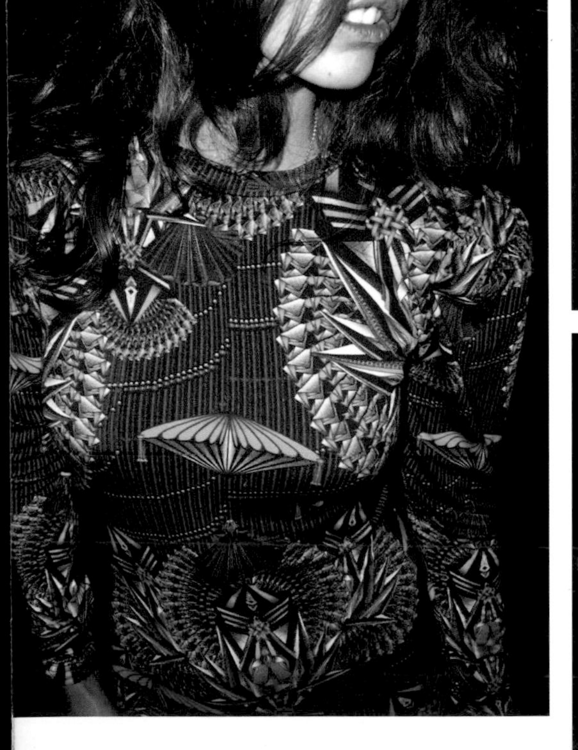

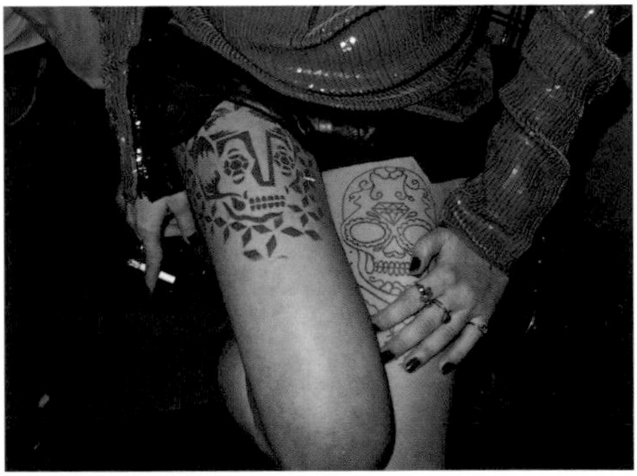

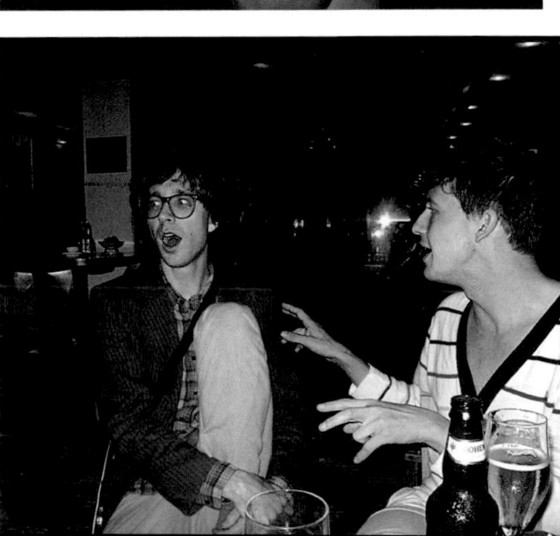

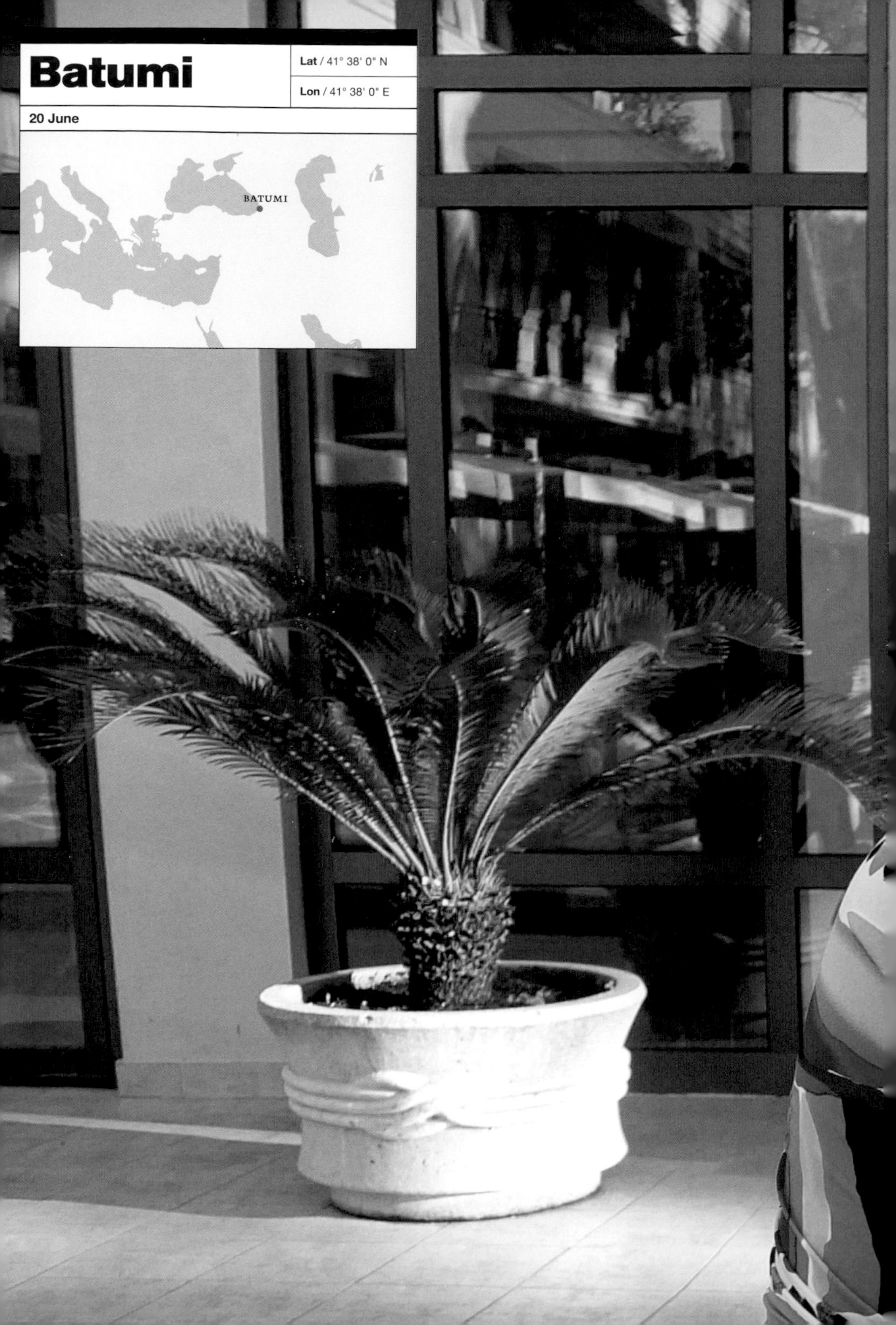
Batumi
Lat / 41° 38' 0" N
Lon / 41° 38' 0" E
20 June
BATUMI

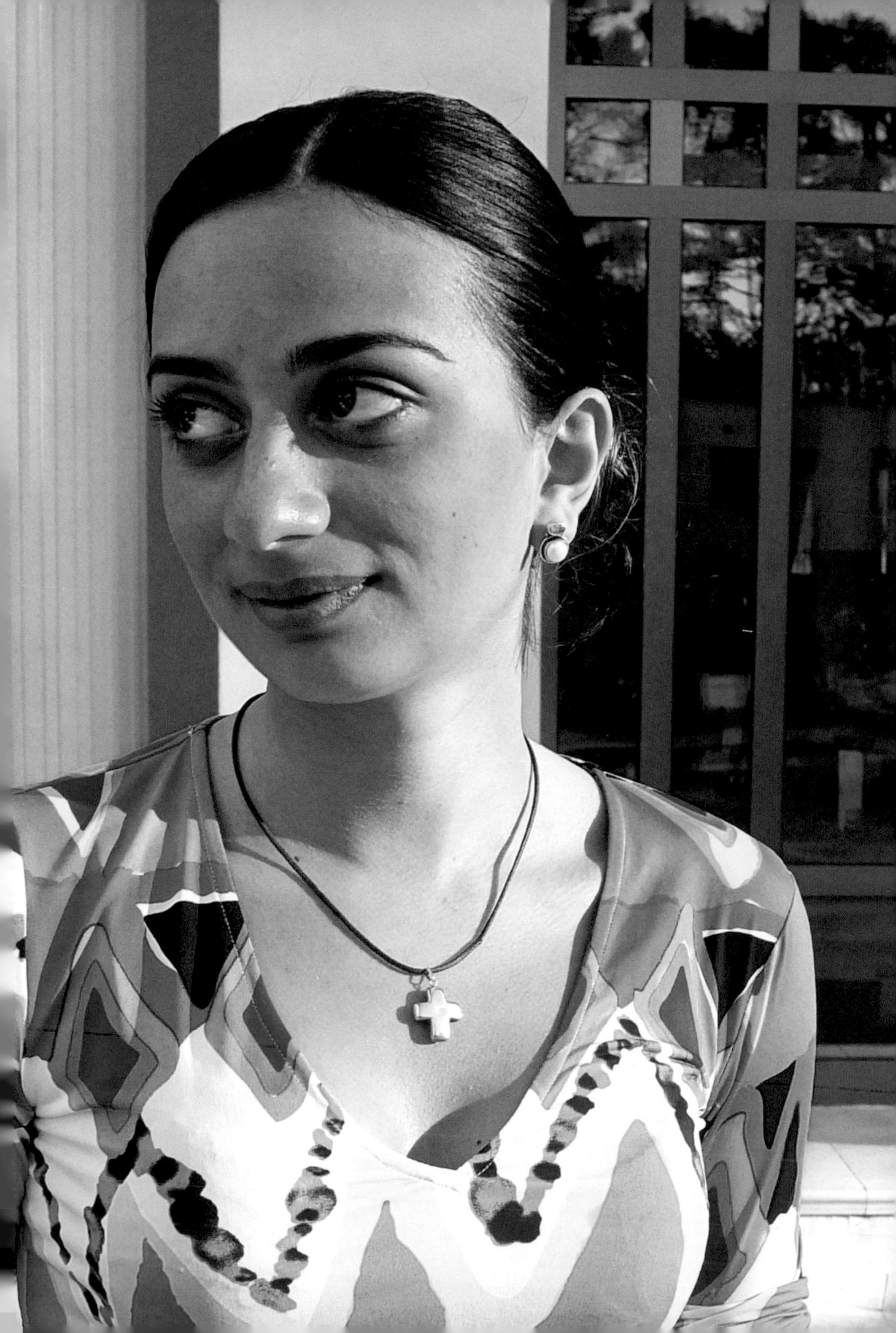

“Nothing can prepare you for Batumi, one of the most beautifully strange places on earth. There are no visual clichés to overcome, as there are when you visit India or China, because so few people have ever heard of this place, let alone photographed it for a travel brochure. Located in a subtropical zone on the Black Sea coast of Georgia (not the one in the USA!), at the intersection of Asia, the Mediterranean, the Middle East and Eastern Europe, it is possibly the most exotic place I have ever been to, with stunning turquoise water, unexpected street art, Dubai-style tourist attractions (just starting up), palm trees and lush, verdant greenery that could be mistaken for Hawaii or Indonesia. Goats and cows still wander in the streets alongside the traffic. The eclecticism of the architecture is insane: pastel-coloured hotels that look like transplants from Miami's South Beach sitting next to a neoclassical-inspired theatre and Soviet-era concrete apartment buildings. It's not only visually that Batumi is different: it's amazing that Georgian language and culture have survived for so many centuries while surrounded by powerful neighbours like Russia and Turkey. To me the Georgian language sounds a bit like Hebrew and looks like Thai or Urdu when it's written out. The food is very rich, lots of smoked cheese and lamb, a bit like Turkish meze where you have lots of small dishes, and there is usually someone in charge of keeping the glasses filled at dinner. Batumi was a popular resort during the Soviet era but is now starting to attract vistors from outside CIS countries. It still has a bit of port-city roughness, however, and there is something slightly melancholic about people's demeanor, which keeps it from feeling like a typical beach resort. I went there for a fashion event called Be Next, a contest for Georgian fashion designers. At the end of the final show everyone went out of the beach and released Chinese lanterns over the sea. It was a magical moment.”

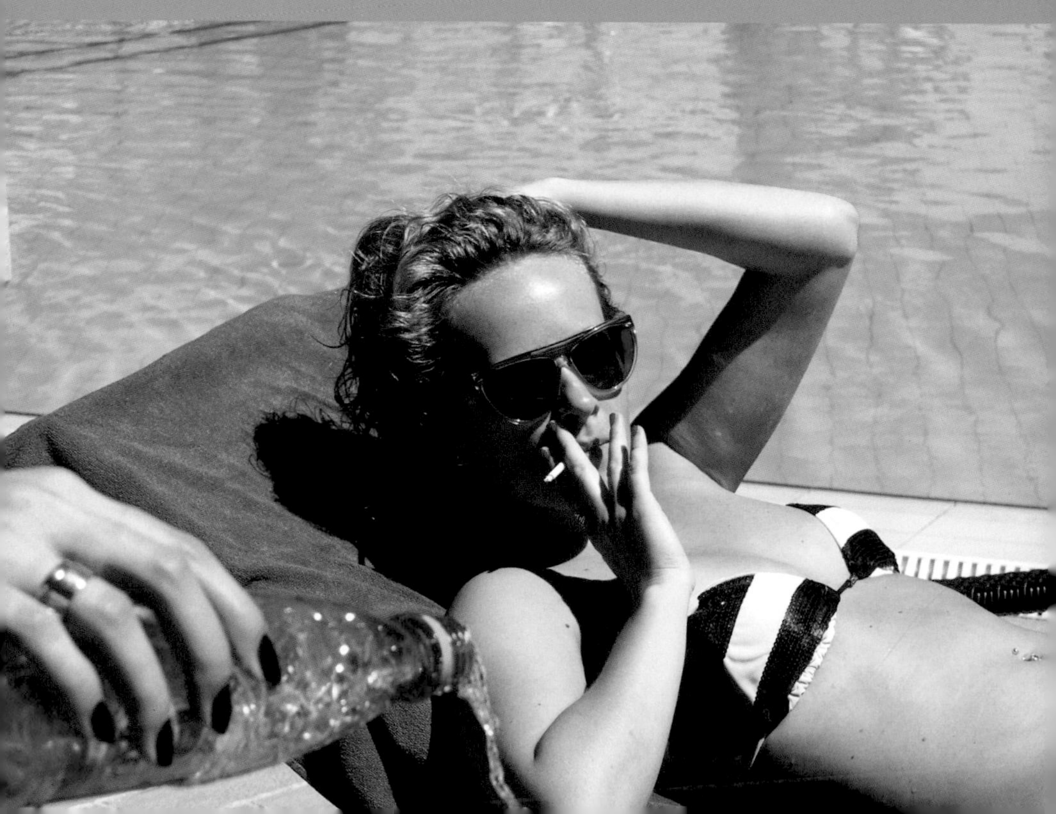

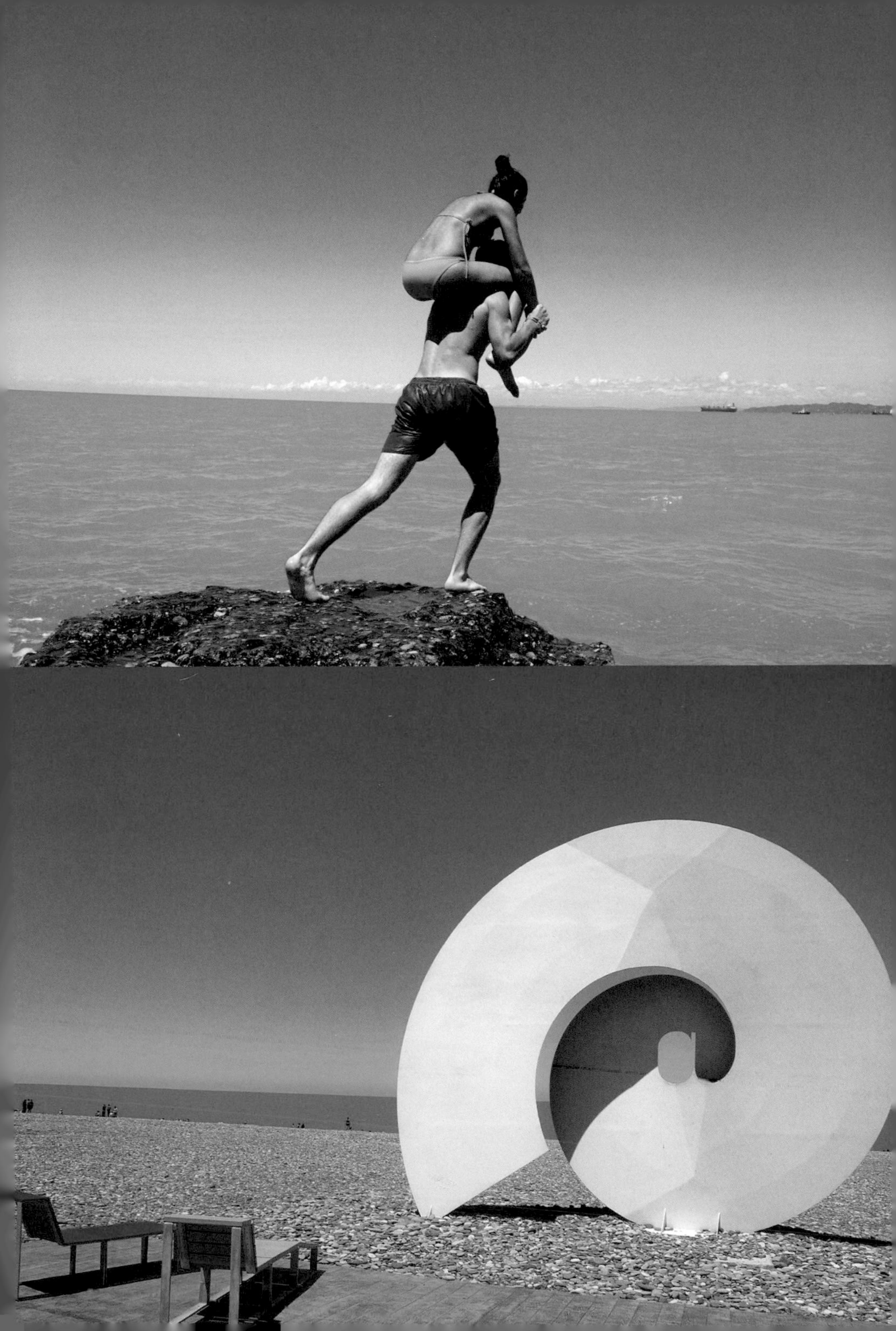

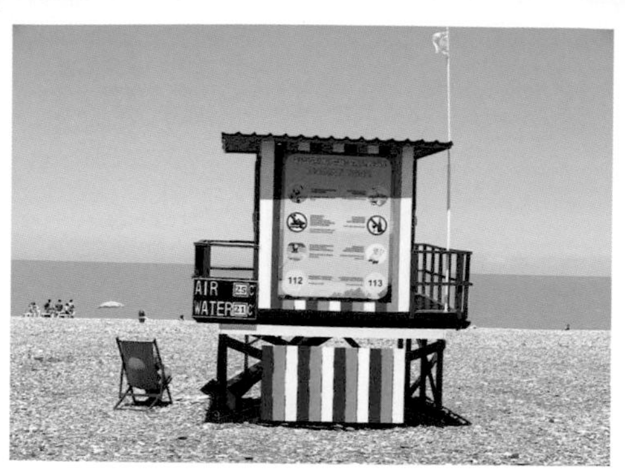
AIR
WATER
112
113

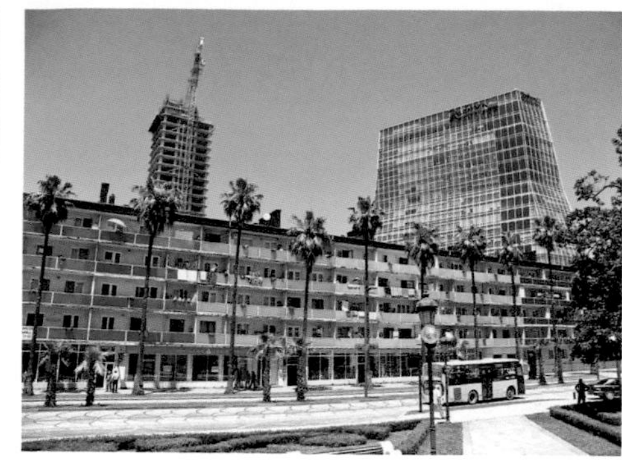

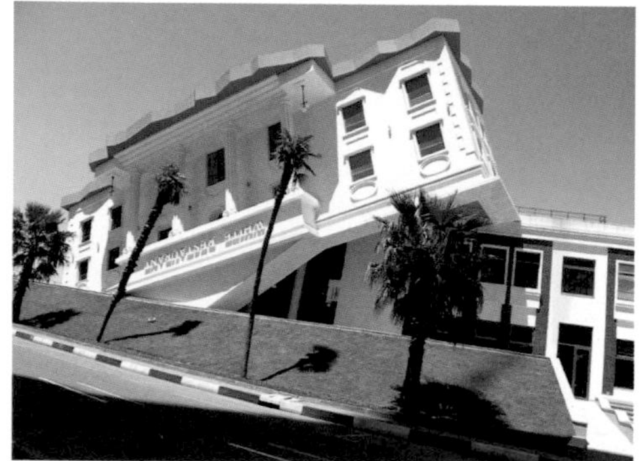

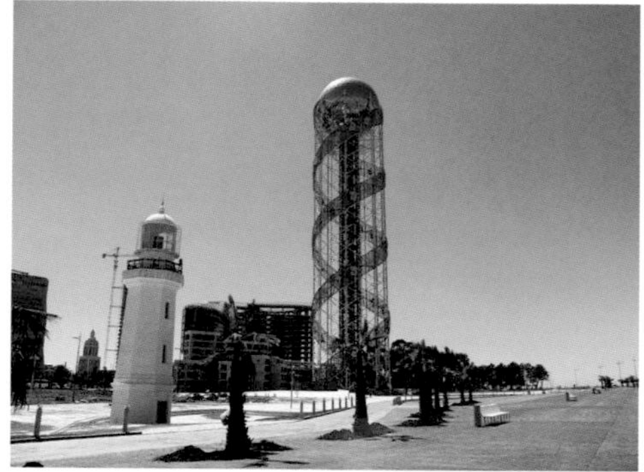

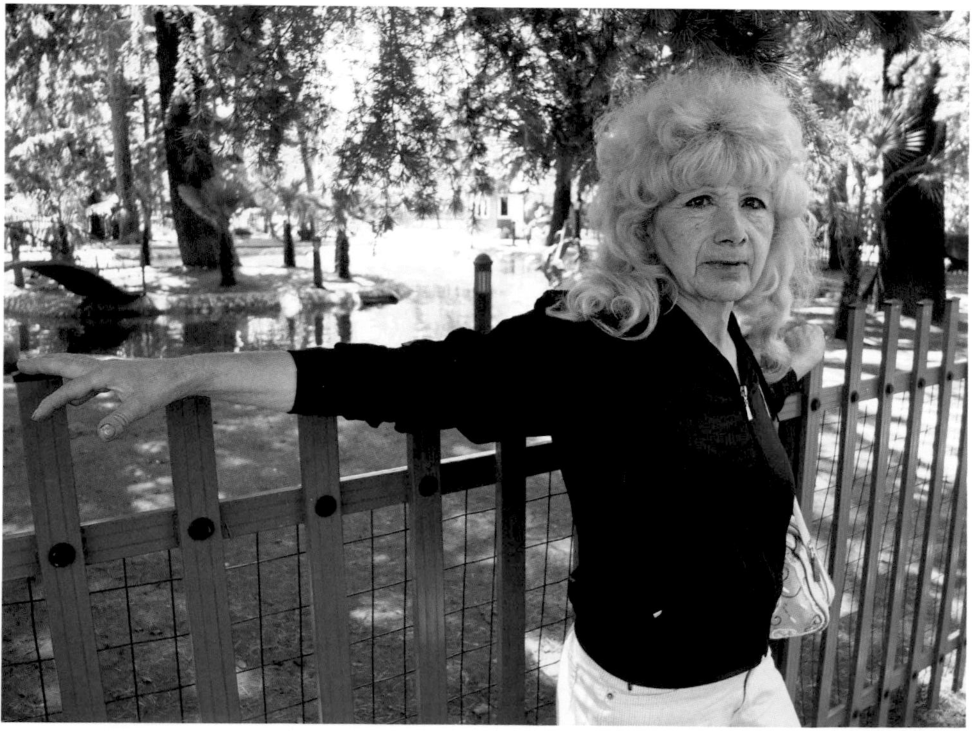

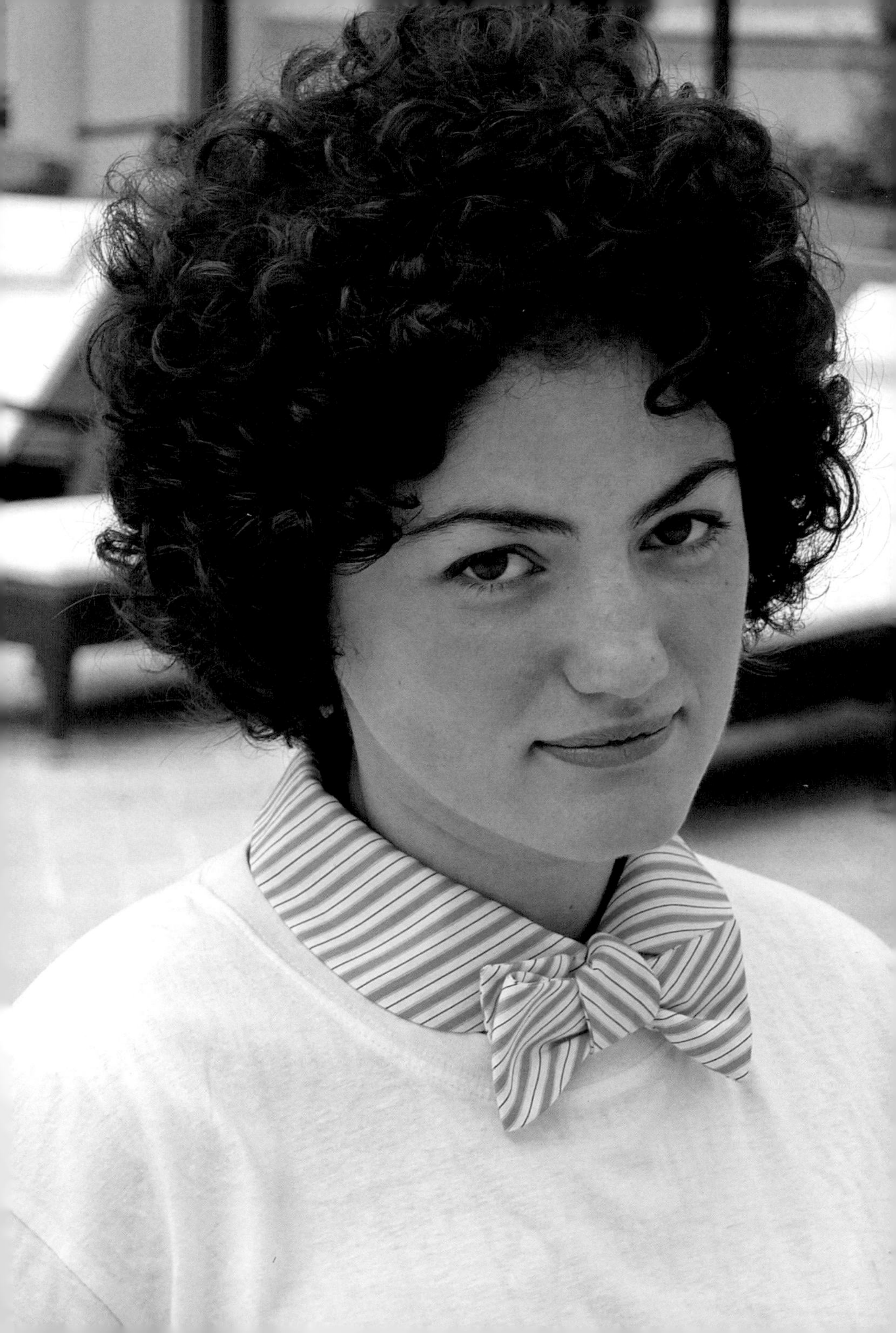

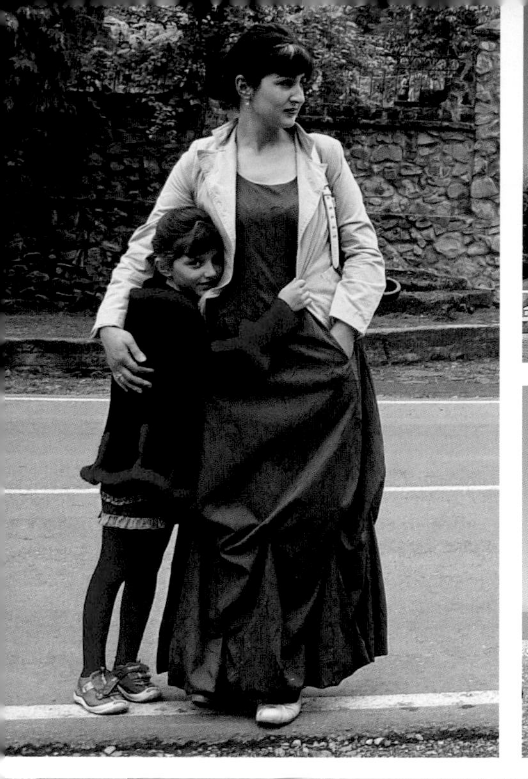

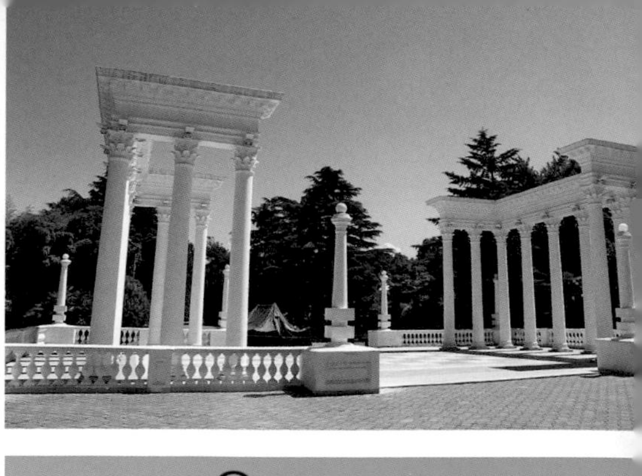

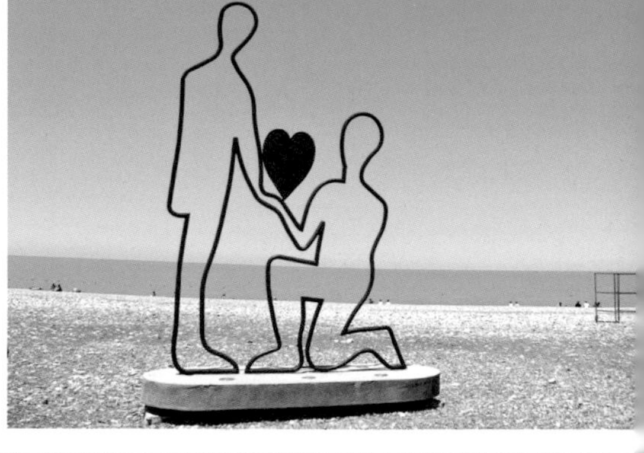

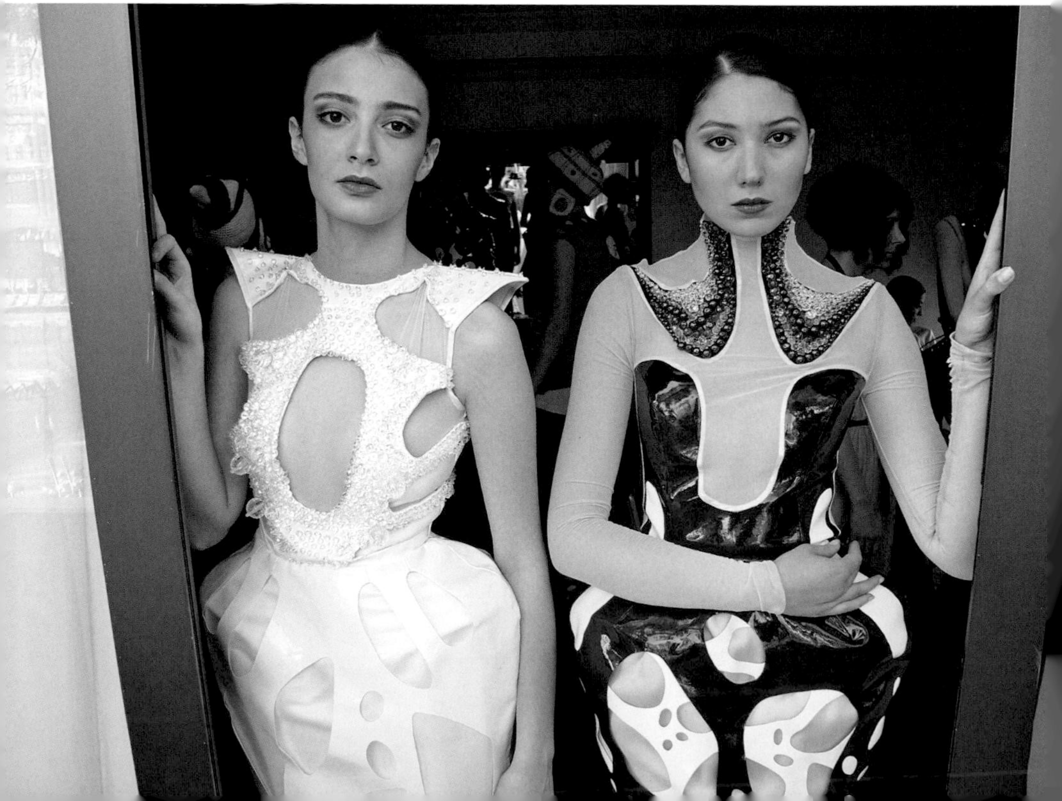

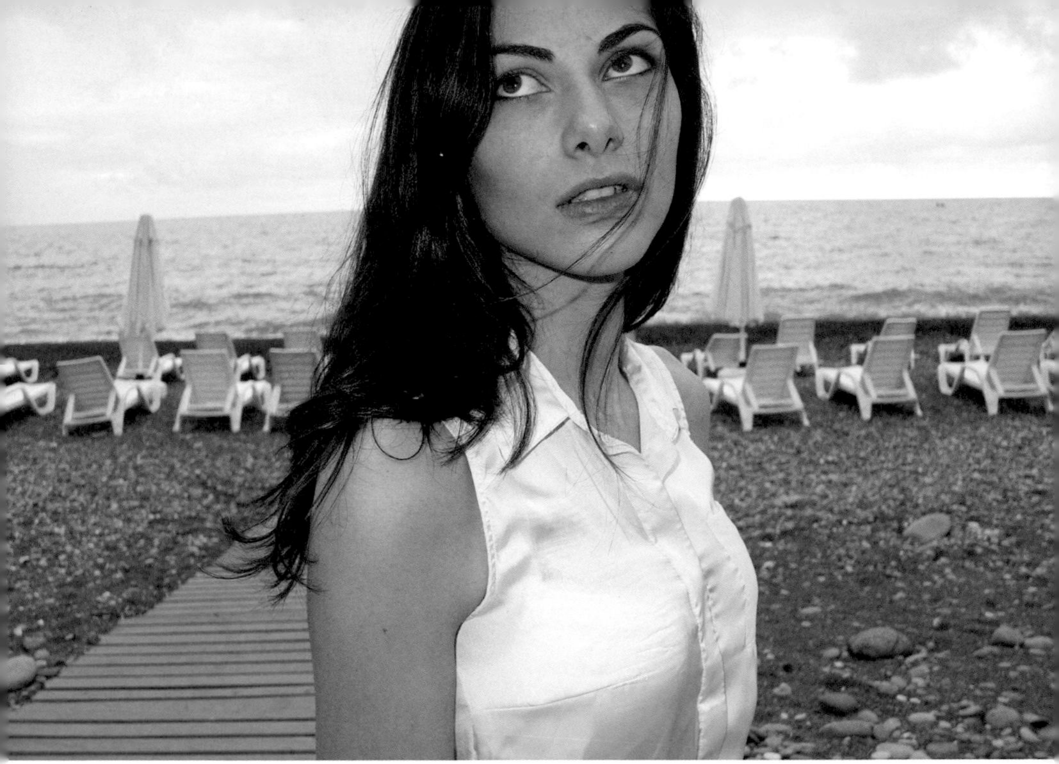

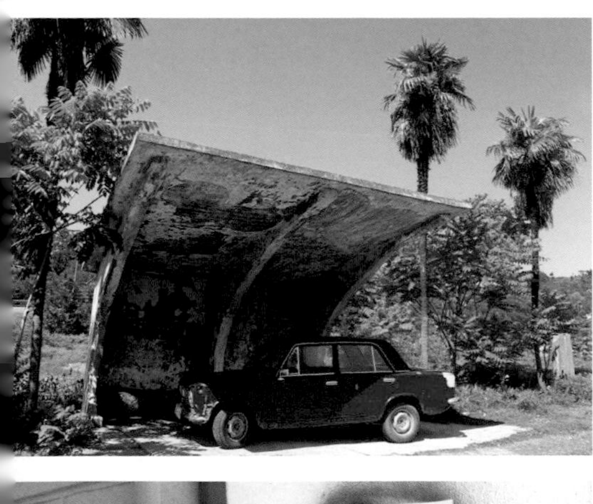

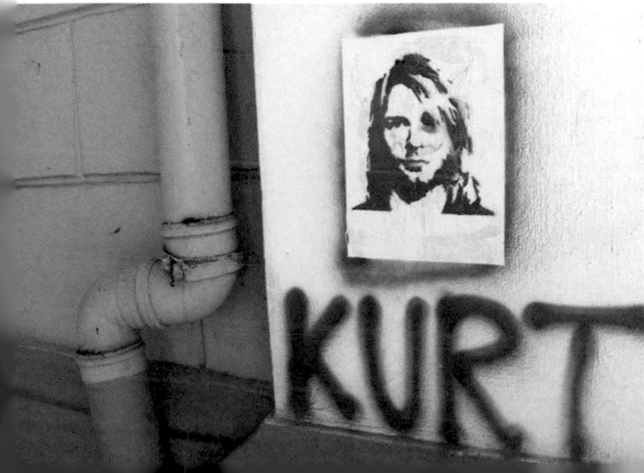
KURT

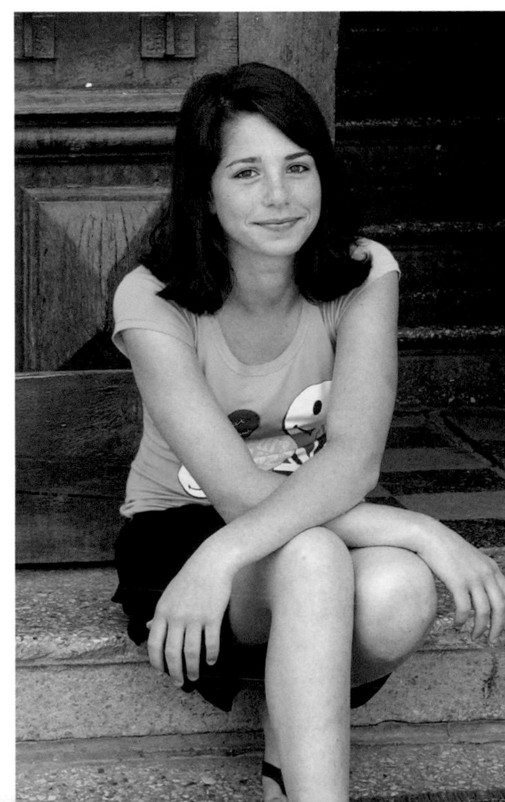

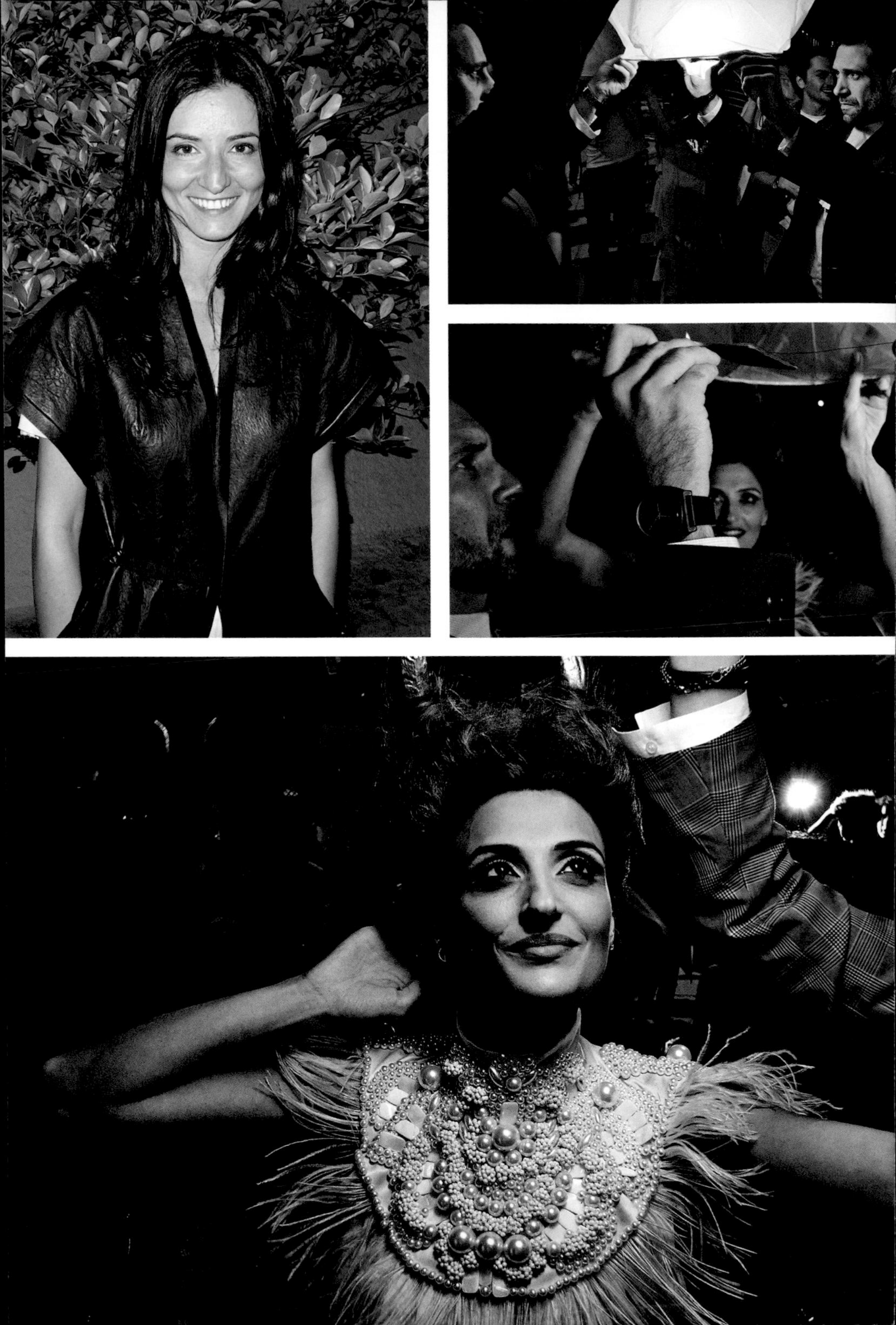

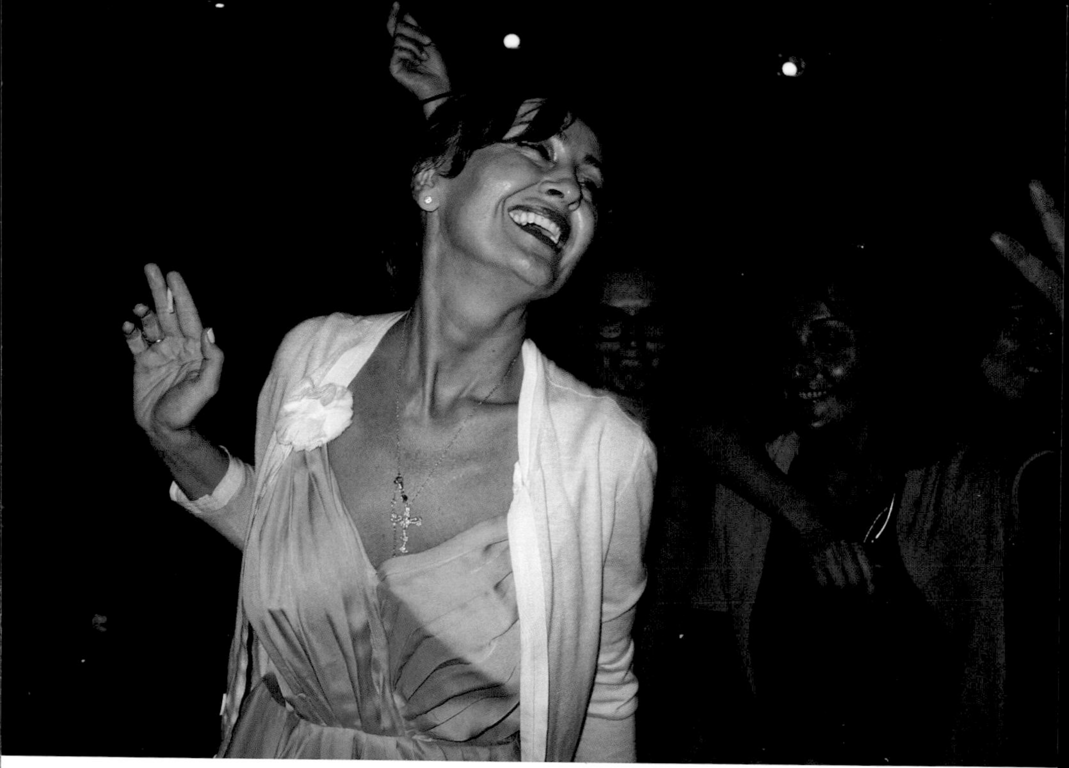

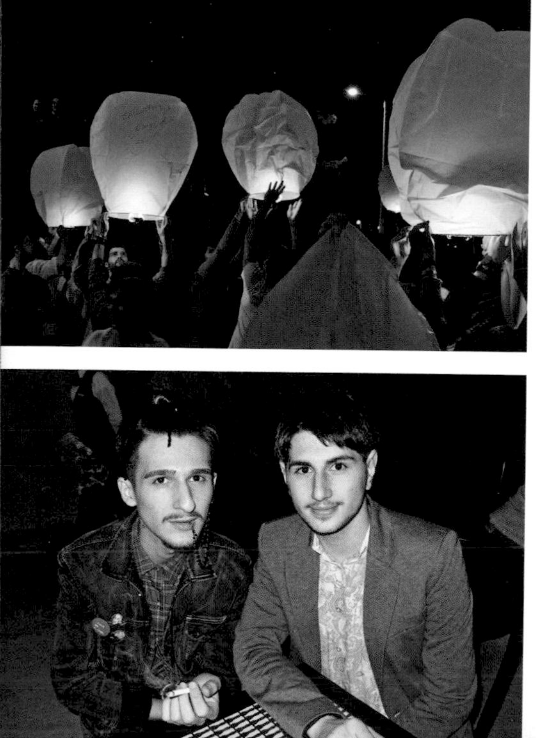

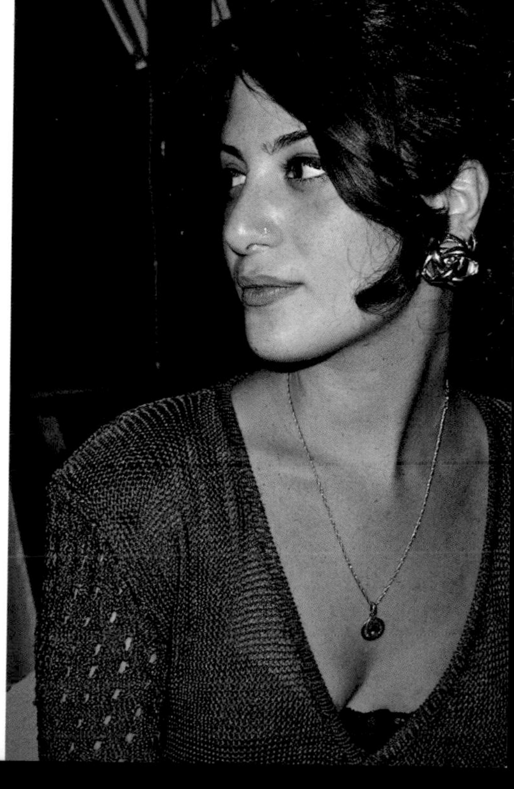

Beirut

Lat / 33° 53' 0" N

Lon / 35° 29' 0" E

28 Jul.–1 Aug.

BEIRUT

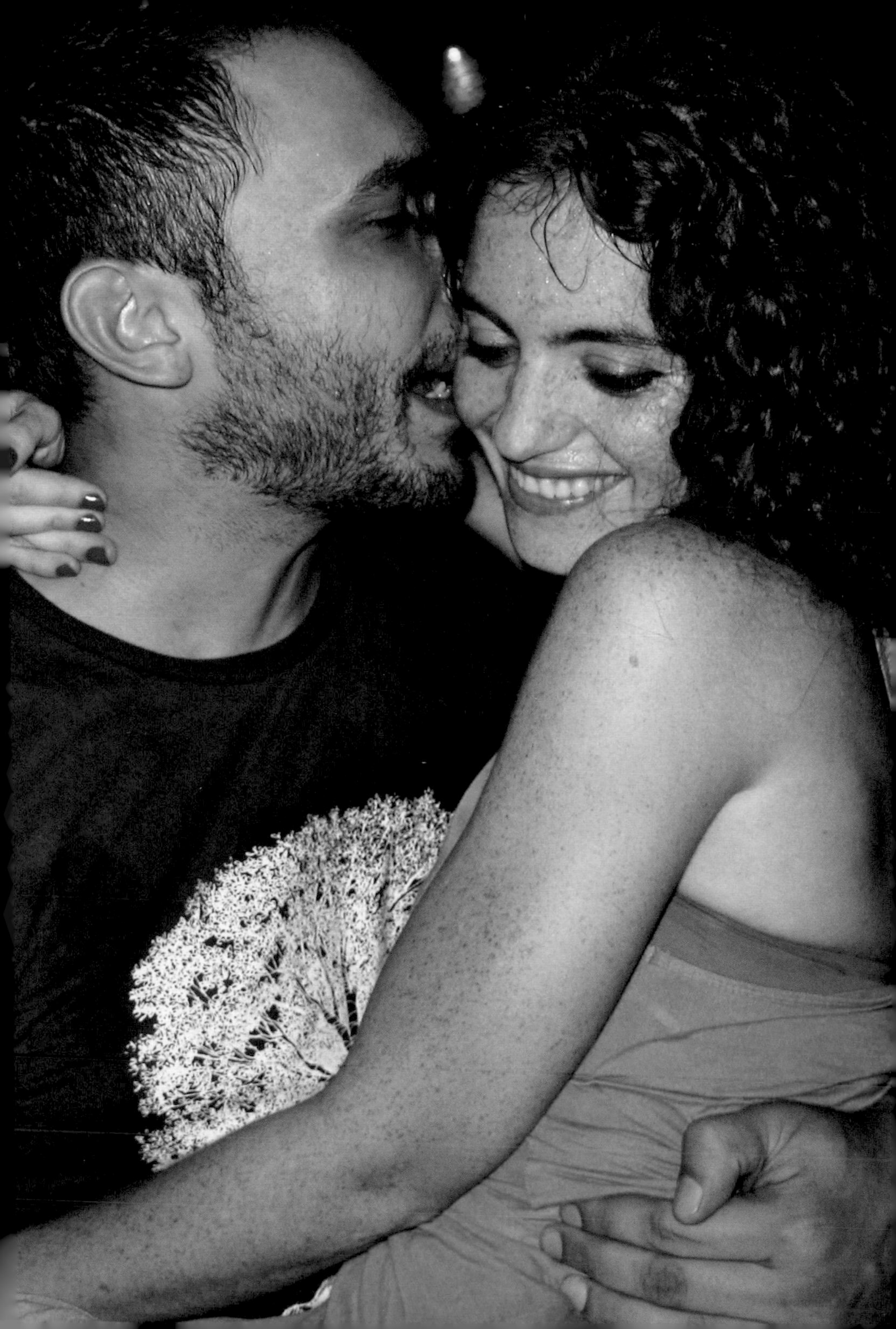

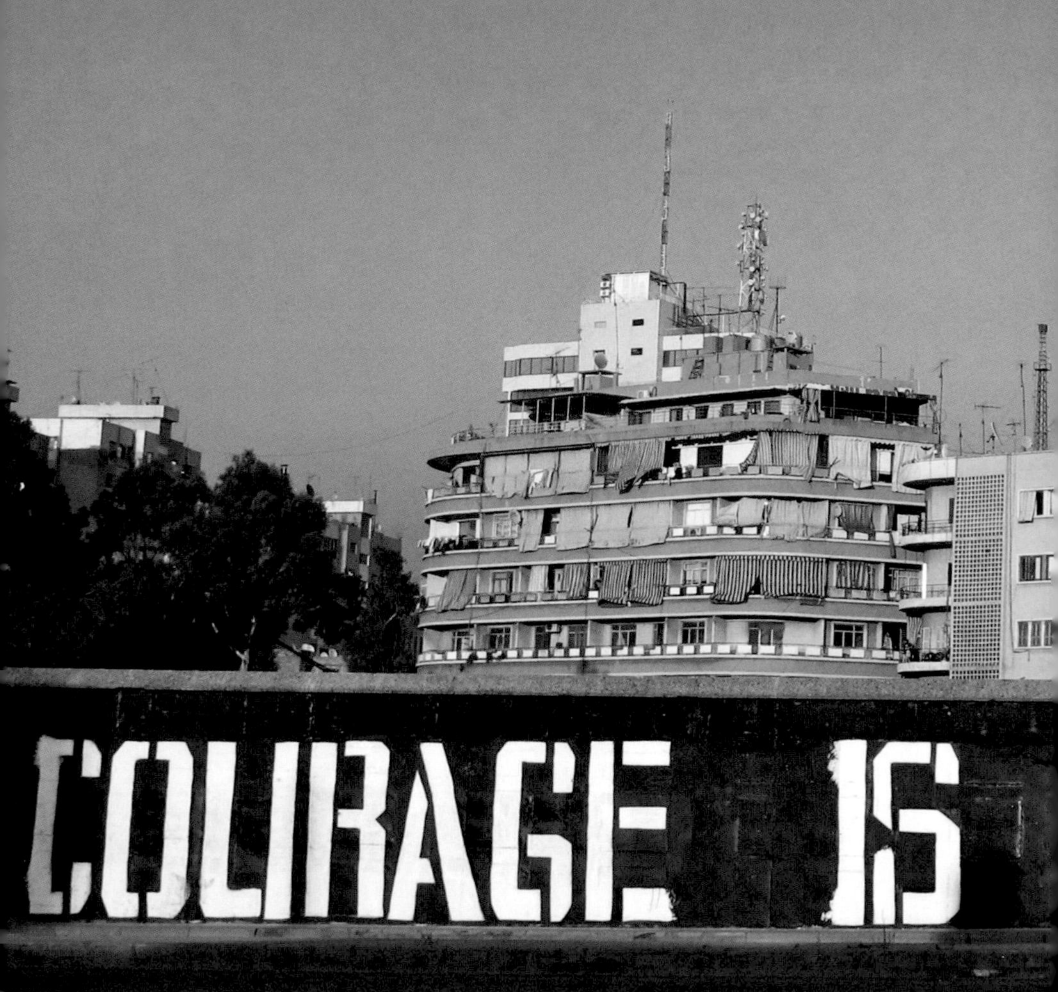

“ Beirut is possibly the most fascinating and open-minded place I've been to in the Middle East. It's a city with multiple personalities that constantly contradicts itself. You can see, smell, taste and do everything – and its opposite extreme – all in the same street. You talk to a sexy and liberated girl about her extremely conservative dad; you see children playing happily in front of a building covered in bullet holes. Walking around the city you feel very safe, but then you pass the house of someone important and see the gates guarded by a tank – not just armed security guys, but a tank! – and you realize what kind of upheaval this city has been through in the past few decades. People in Beirut have an incredible appetite for good food, fun parties and all the pleasures of life, which I think has partly come from experiencing this tough political situation. There is a complex interplay of French, English and Arabic language and culture in the city, as well as a large Armenian community that immigrated after the

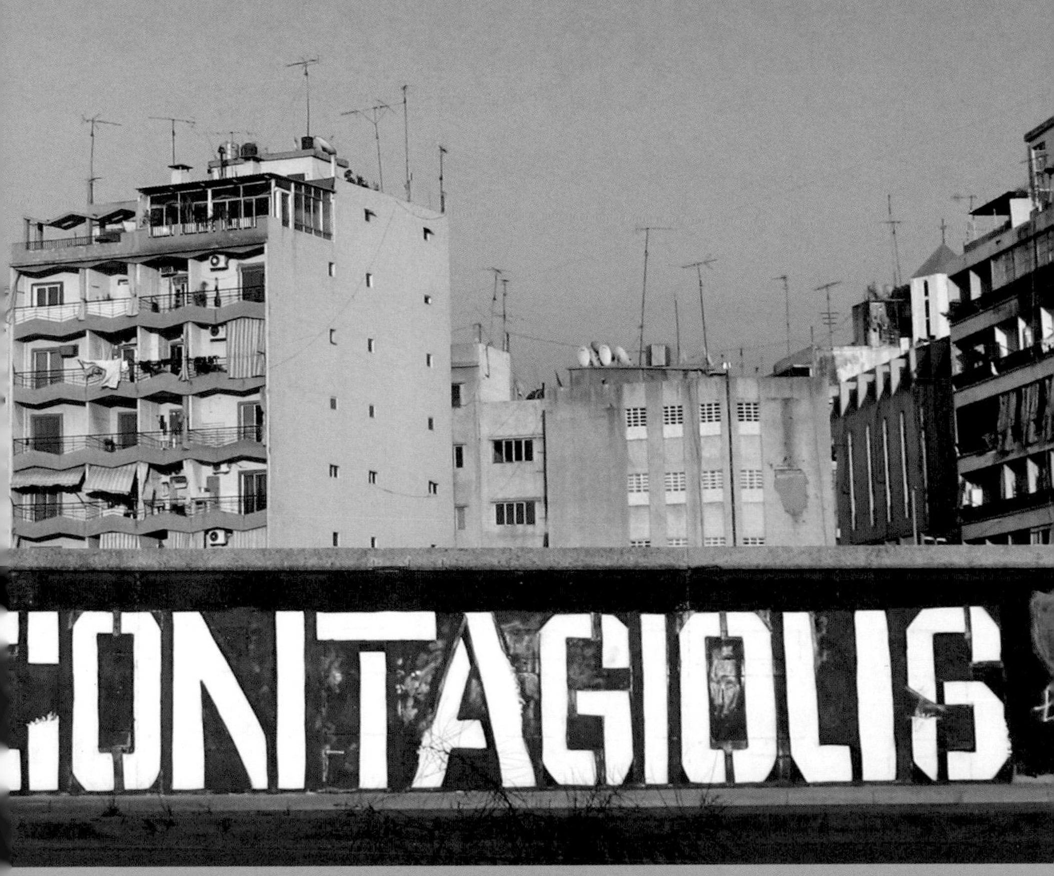

genocide of 1915. The fourth-generation Armenian–Lebanese still preserve their great-grandparents' cultural heritage, and there are lots of amazing Armenian restaurants. There are parts of the city that are very Westernized, where people dress in a style indistinguishable from that of most Europeans; other neighbourhoods are more traditional. Women in Beirut dress in a very feminine way, and only a few cover their hair. I was surprised by how relatively open the gay scene was compared to that of other Middle Eastern cities. I had a fantastic time at a semi-legal foam party held on the rooftop of a former candy factory where a whole spectrum of people – gay, straight and everything in between – had a great time together. I was also impressed with the furniture design scene: lots of up-and-coming designers working in a very minimalist, almost Scandinavian style, with a few oriental twists. Beirut is a city that challenges your expectations on so many different levels. ”

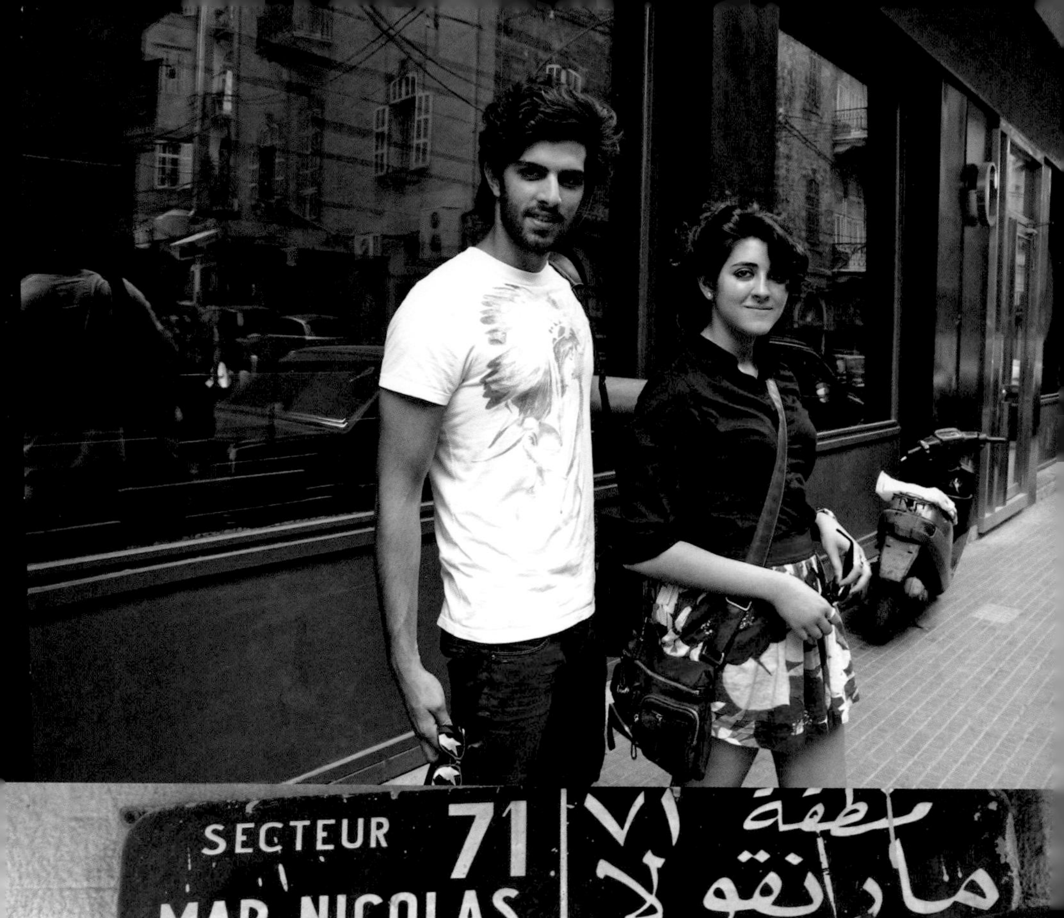

SECTEUR 71 | منطقة ٧١
MAR. NICOLAS | مار نقولا

RUE 52 | شارع ٥٢

شارع بطرس داغر
RUE BOUTROS DAGHER

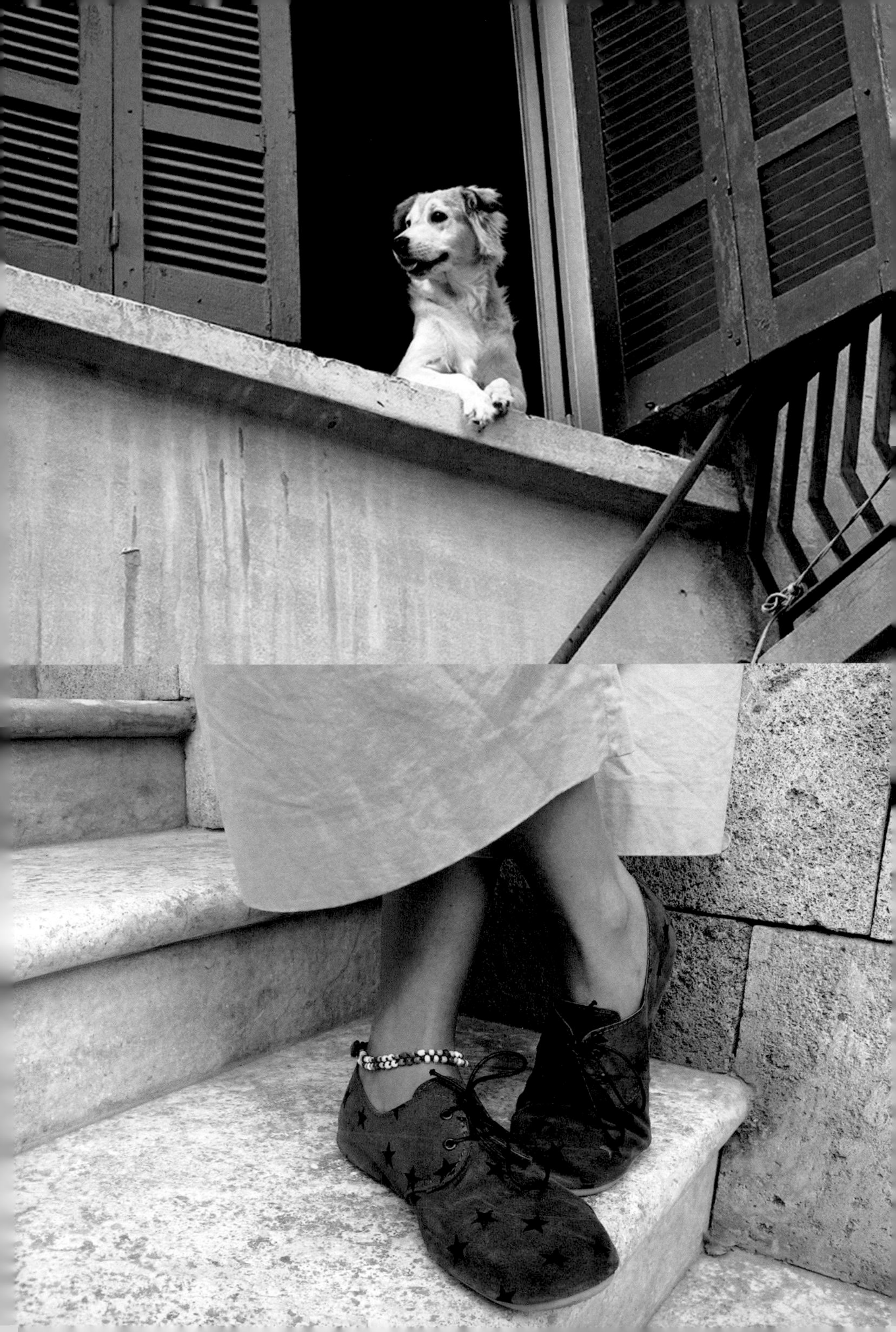

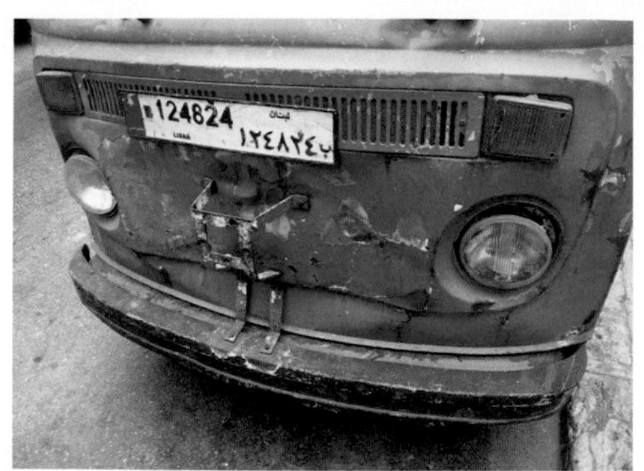
124824

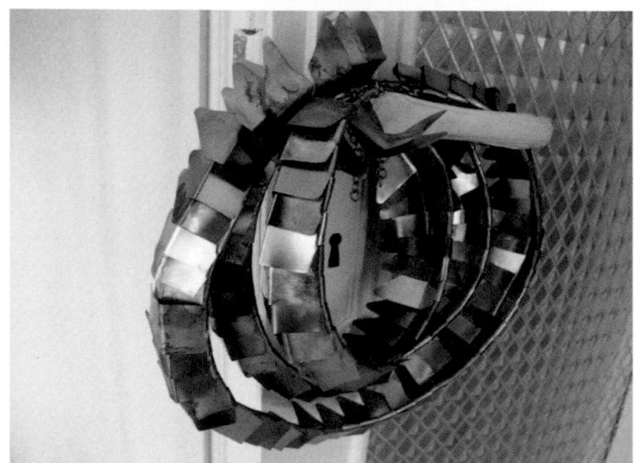

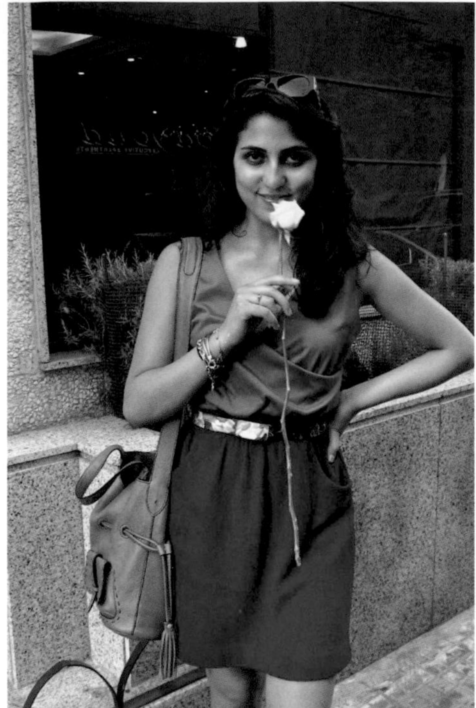

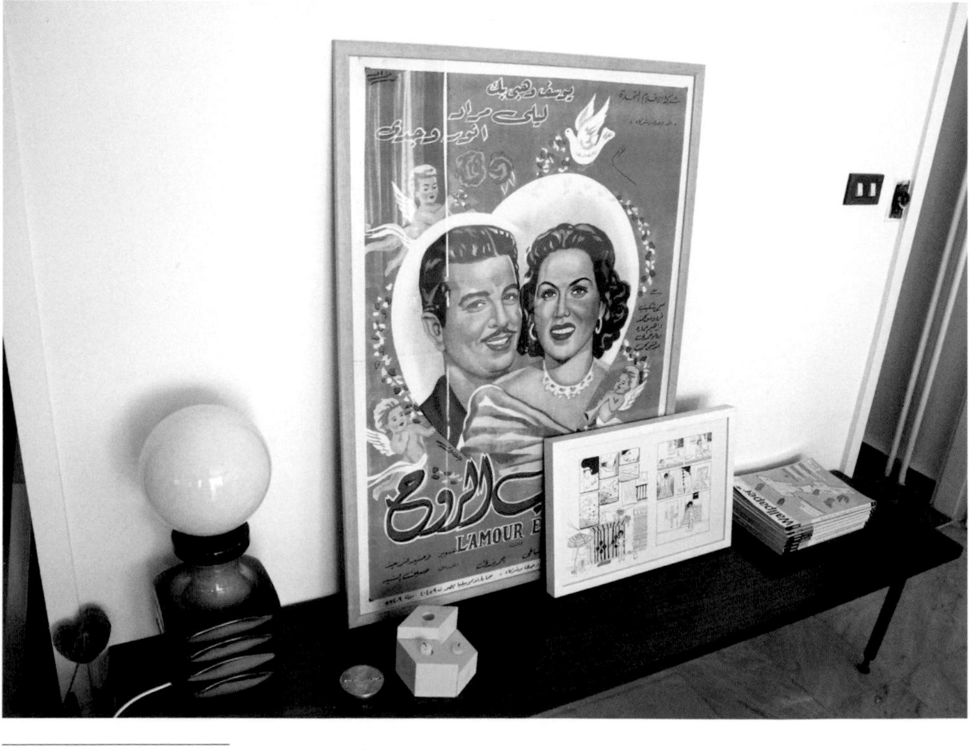

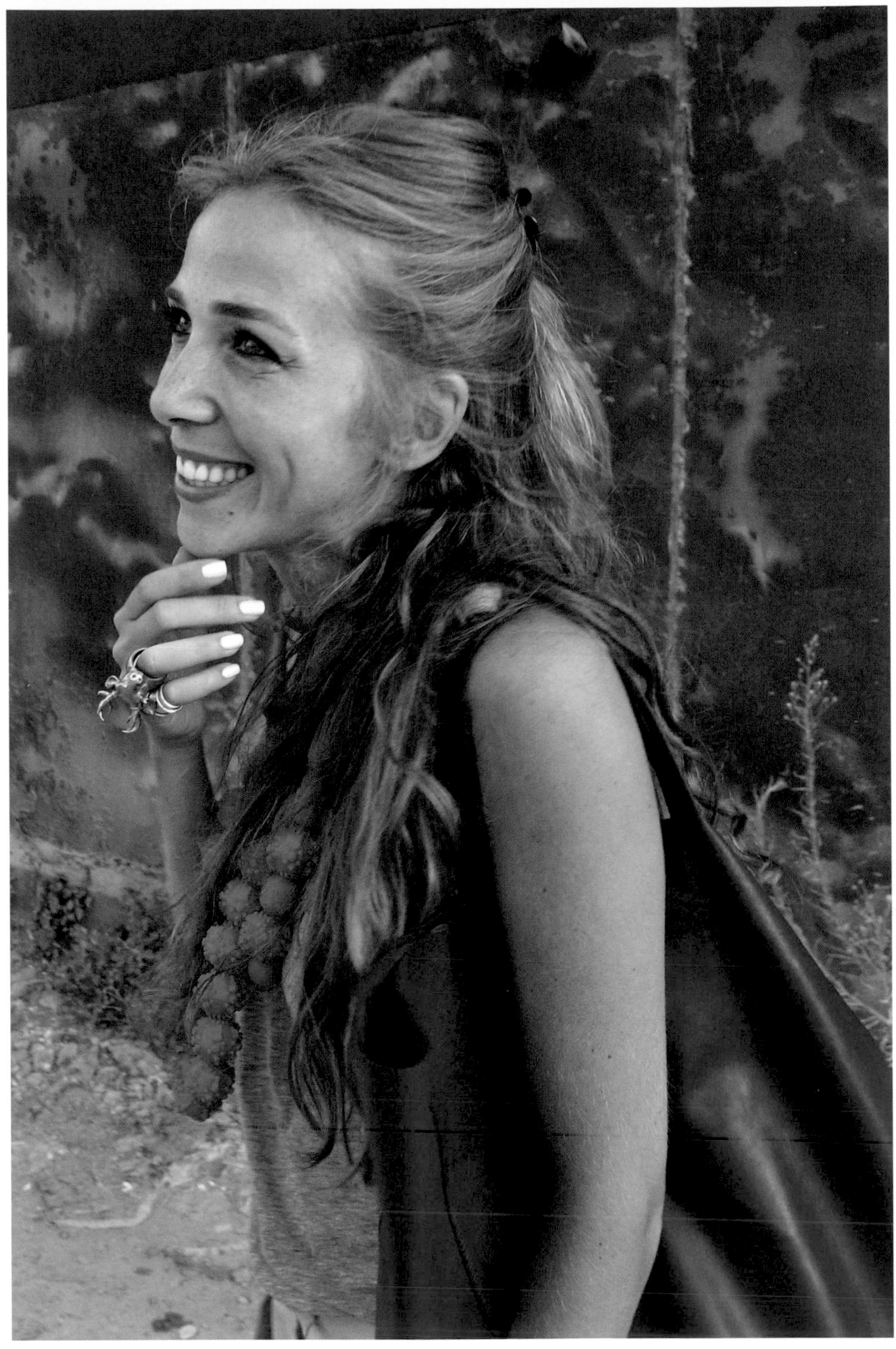

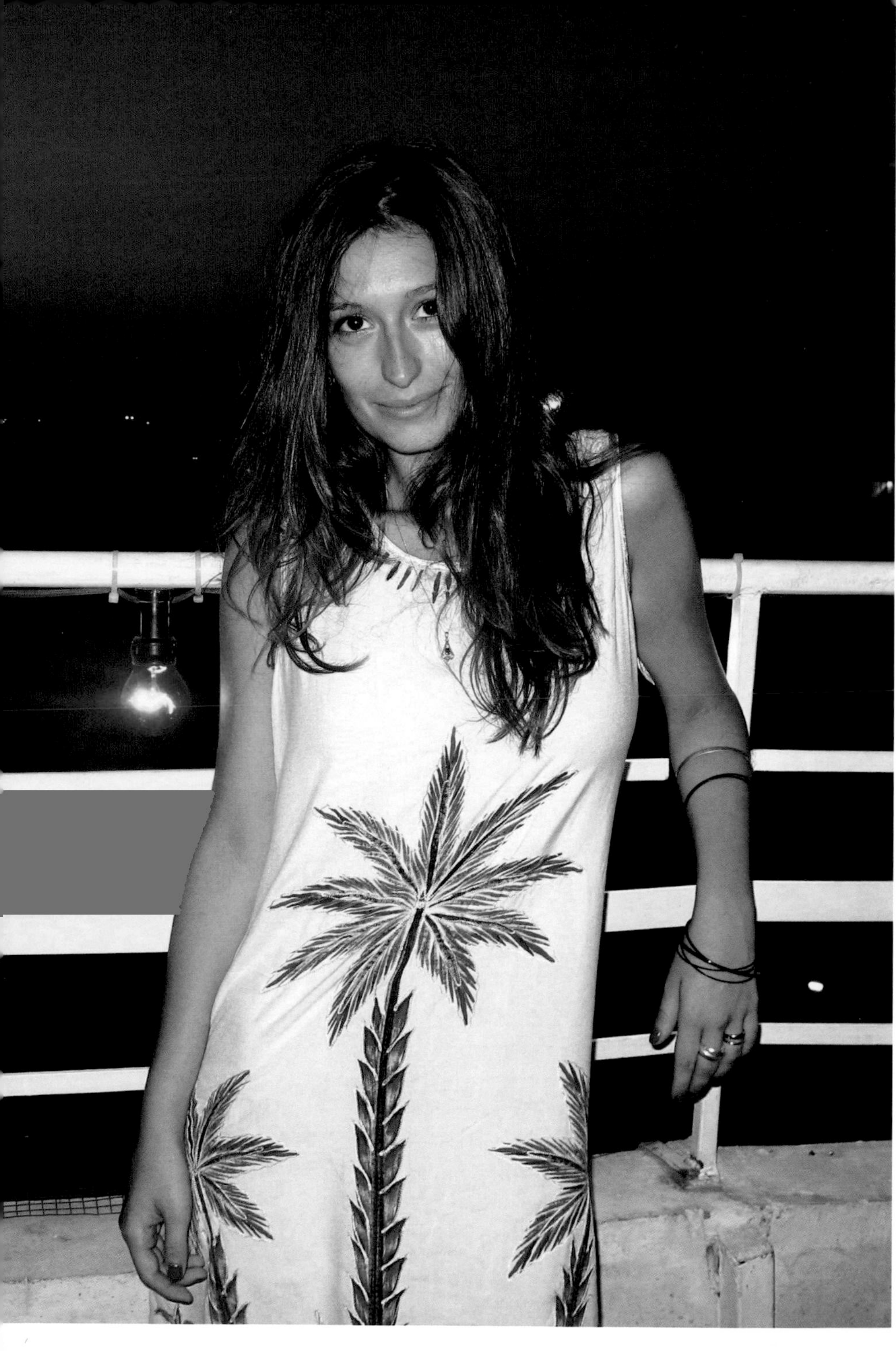

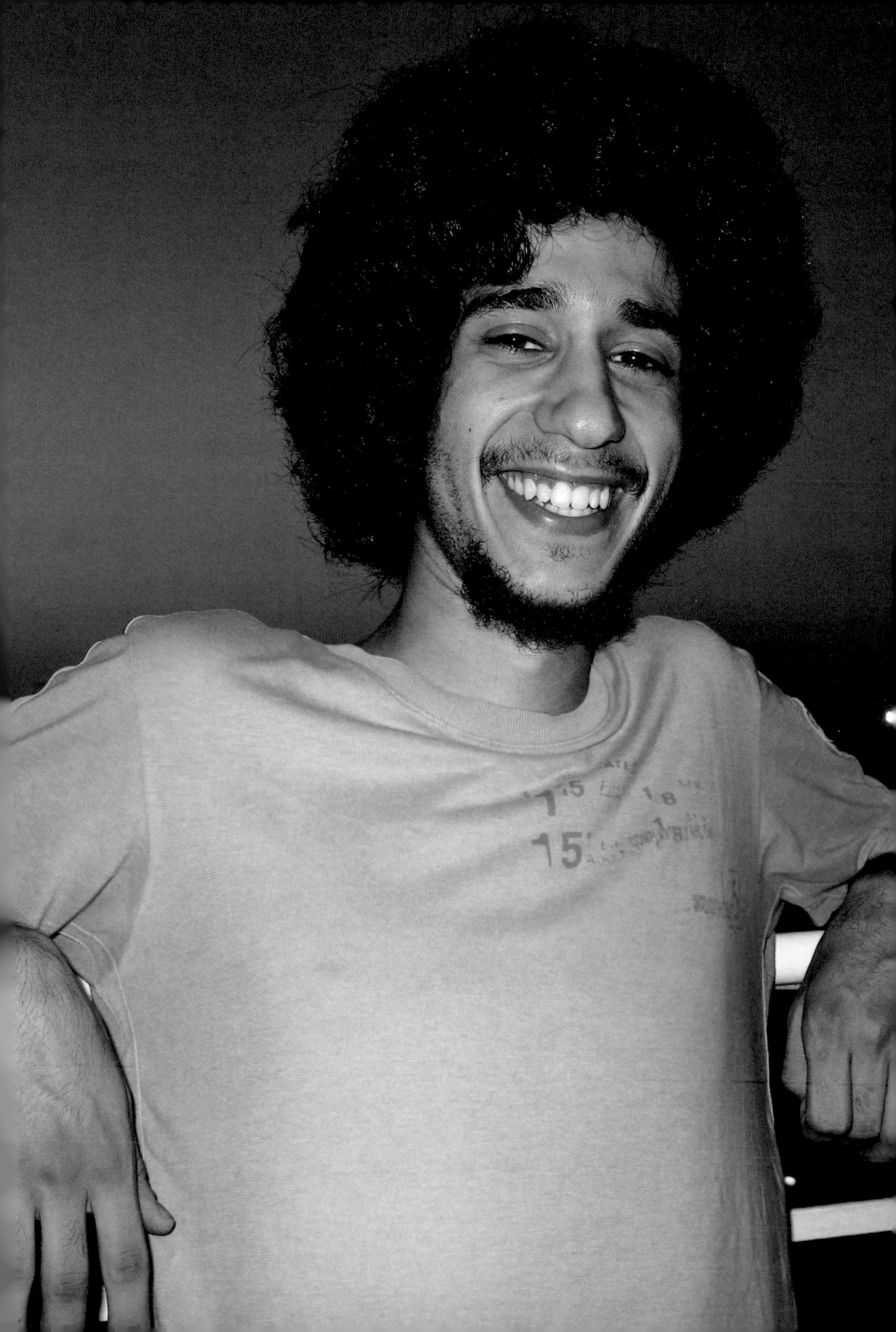

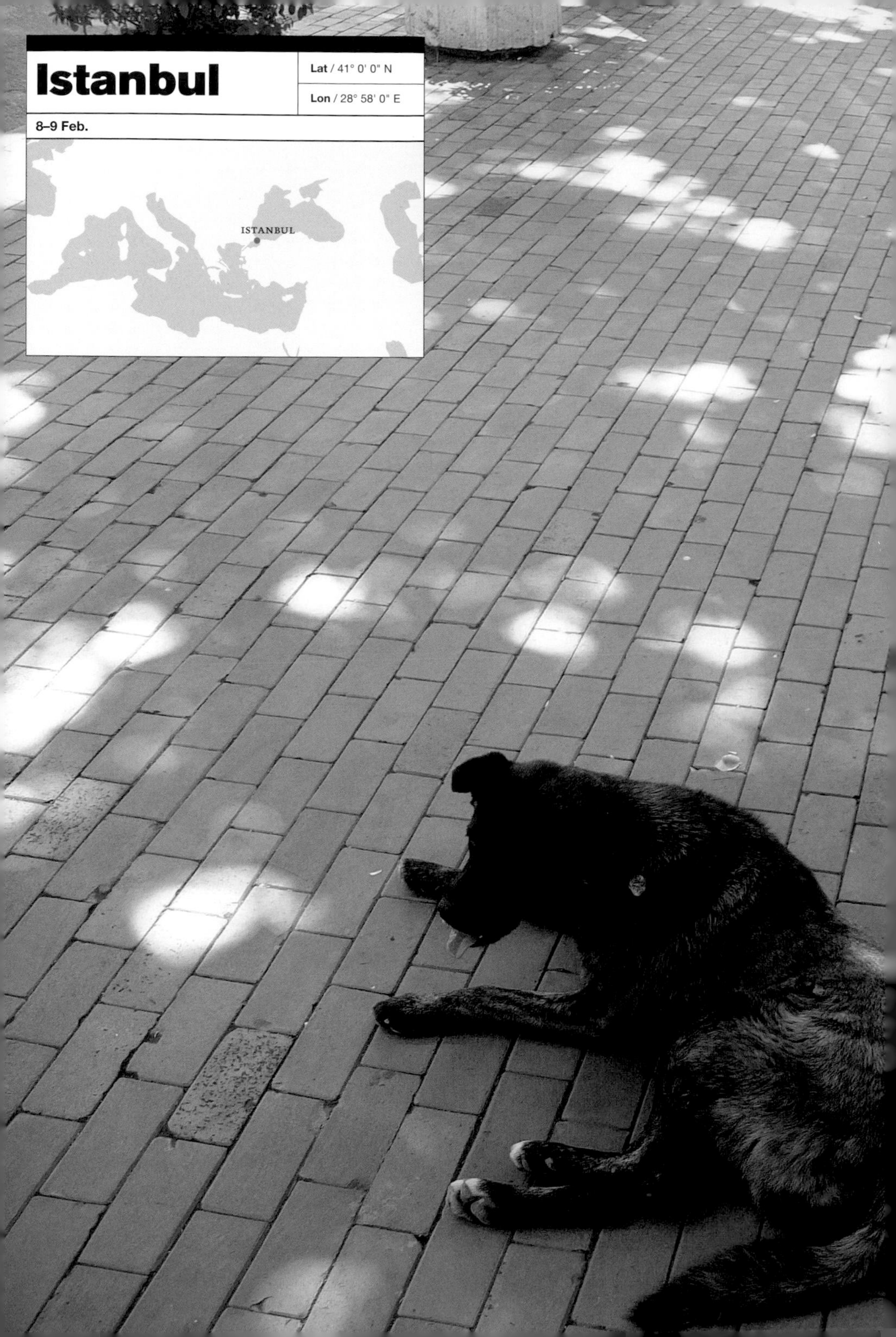
Istanbul
Lat / 41° 0' 0" N
Lon / 28° 58' 0" E
8–9 Feb.
ISTANBUL

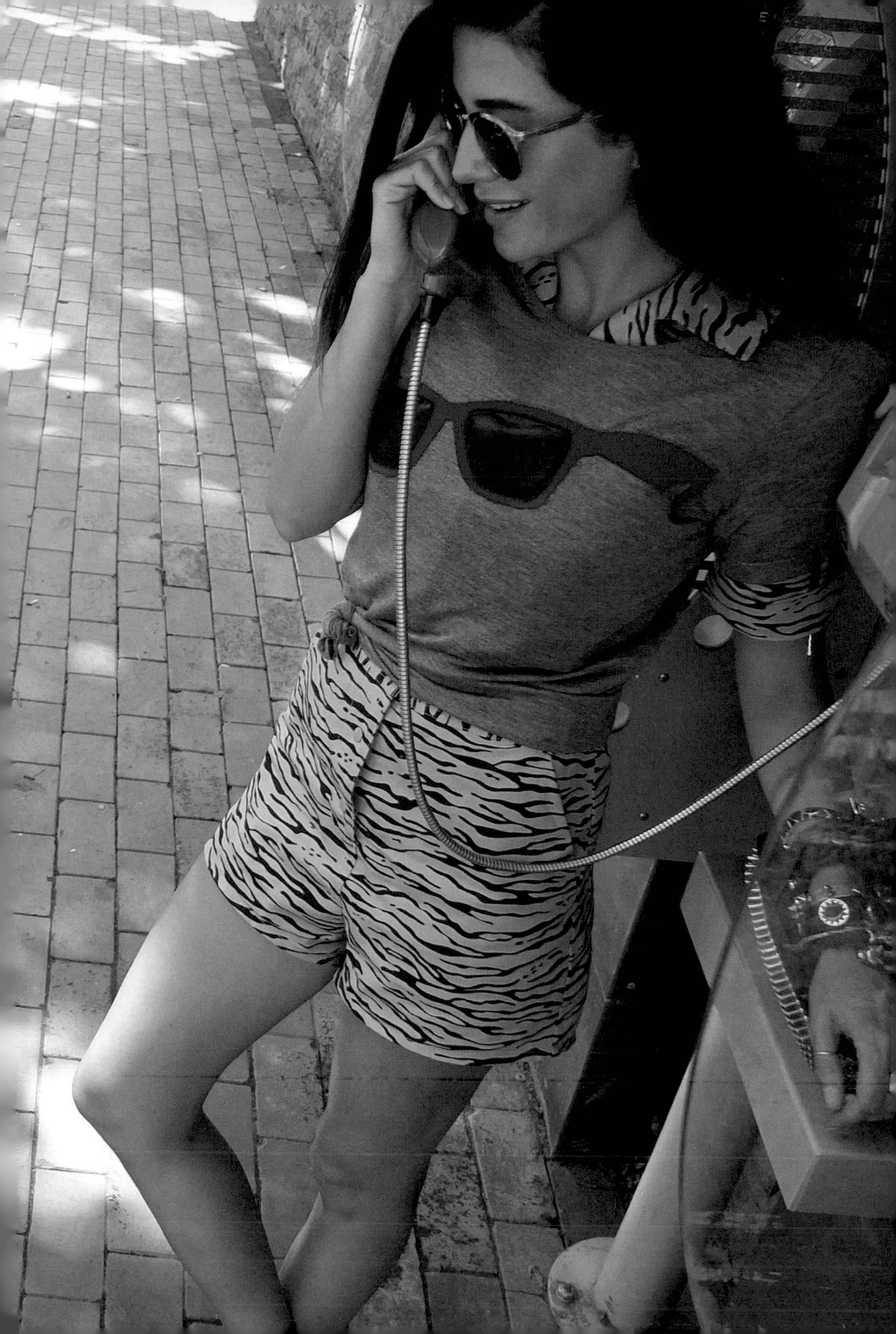

“ The clichéd thing is to say that Istanbul is the crossroads where East meets West. It's partly true – you see a very Westernized lifestyle existing alongside a traditional, oriental culture. I've been there many times and I think it's one of the coolest places in either Europe or Asia. There's a lot of support for new Turkish designers, and pockets of people who care intensely about fashion and are very creative and daring in what they wear. My favourite part of the city is Arnavutköy, which has amazing wooden mansions from the Ottoman period, very charming and elegant – it reminds me a bit of the older parts of Bergen, Norway. Arnavutköy is the one neighbourhood in Istanbul that doesn't yet – at least at the time of writing! – have a Starbucks. A lot of visitors focus on the minarets, the mosques and the bazaar and think Istanbul is a more old-fashioned place than it actually is. I was most recently there working on a street-photoshoot project with a local designer, Aslı Filinta, for Turkish *Vogue*. It showed me a completely different side of the city that tourists never see – the It girls, the booming fashion scene – it's very Face Hunter Friendly.

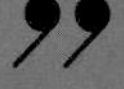

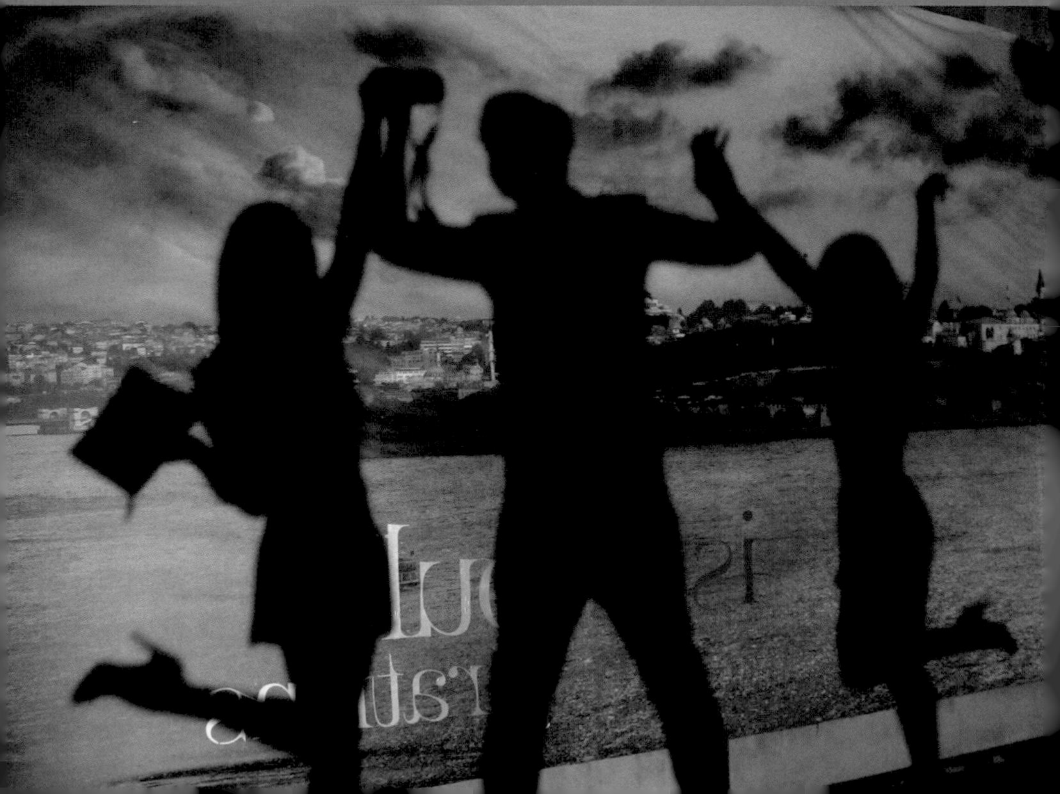

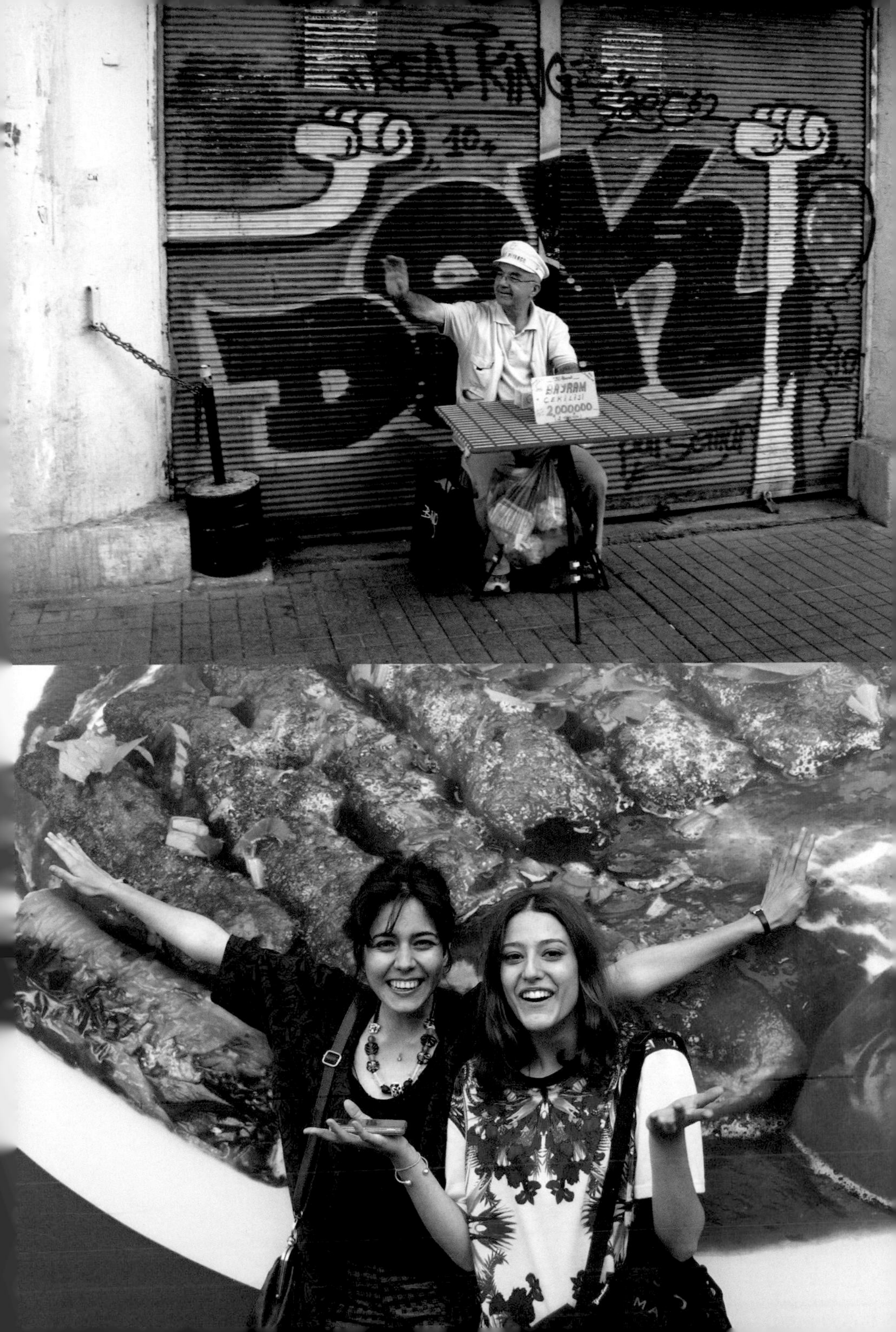
BAYRAM
ÇEKİLİŞİ
2,000,000

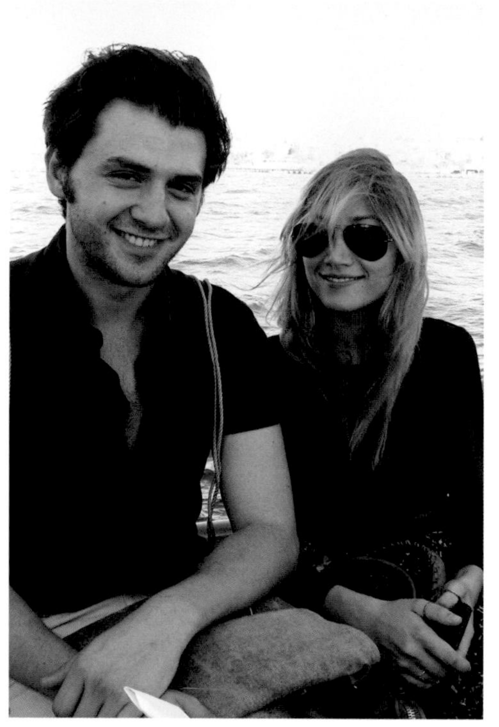

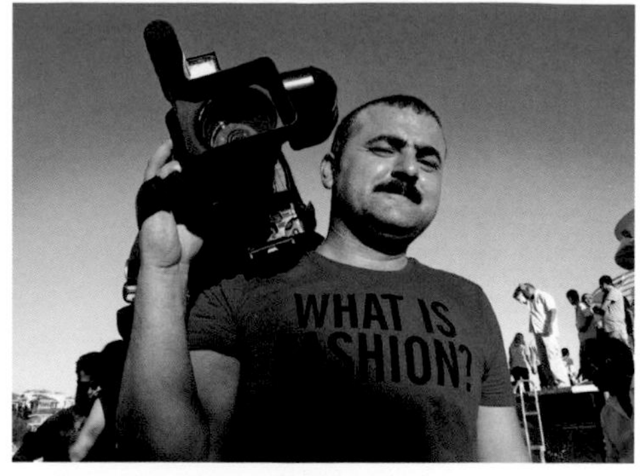
WHAT IS
SHION?

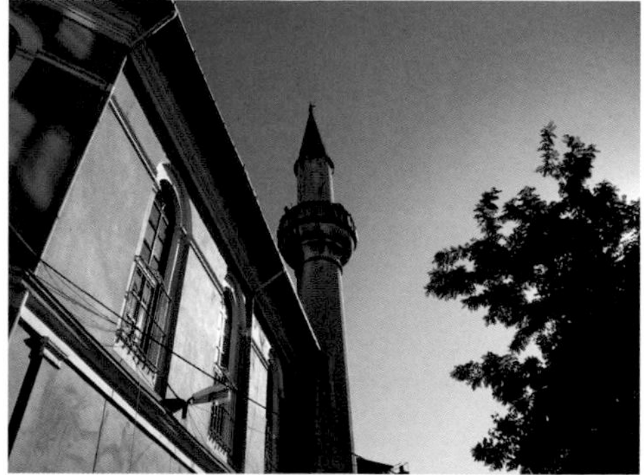

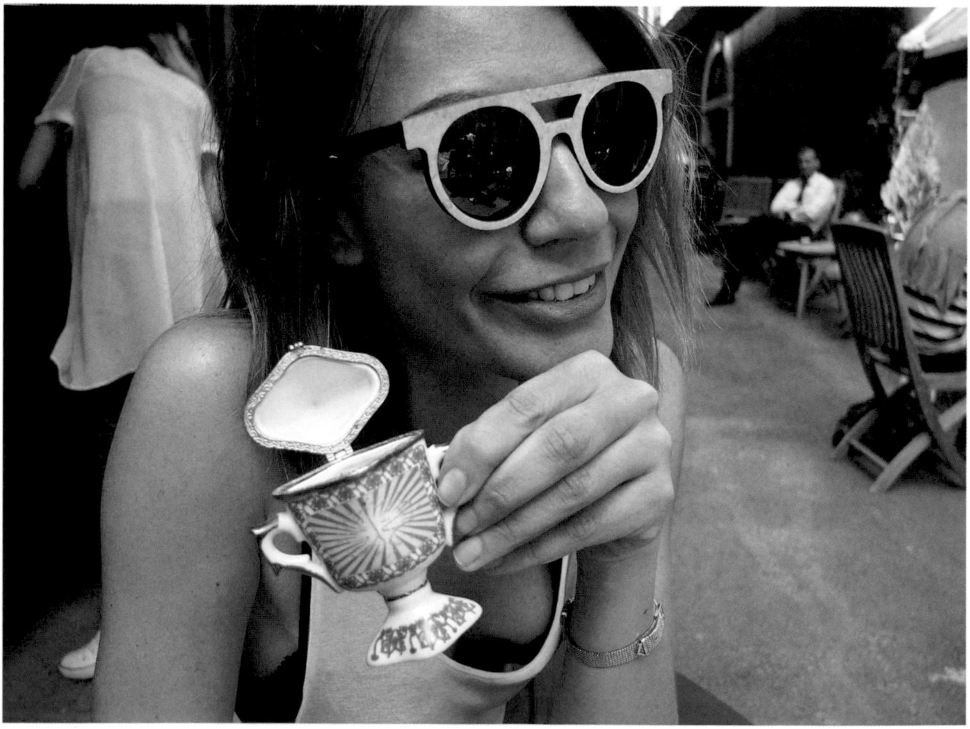

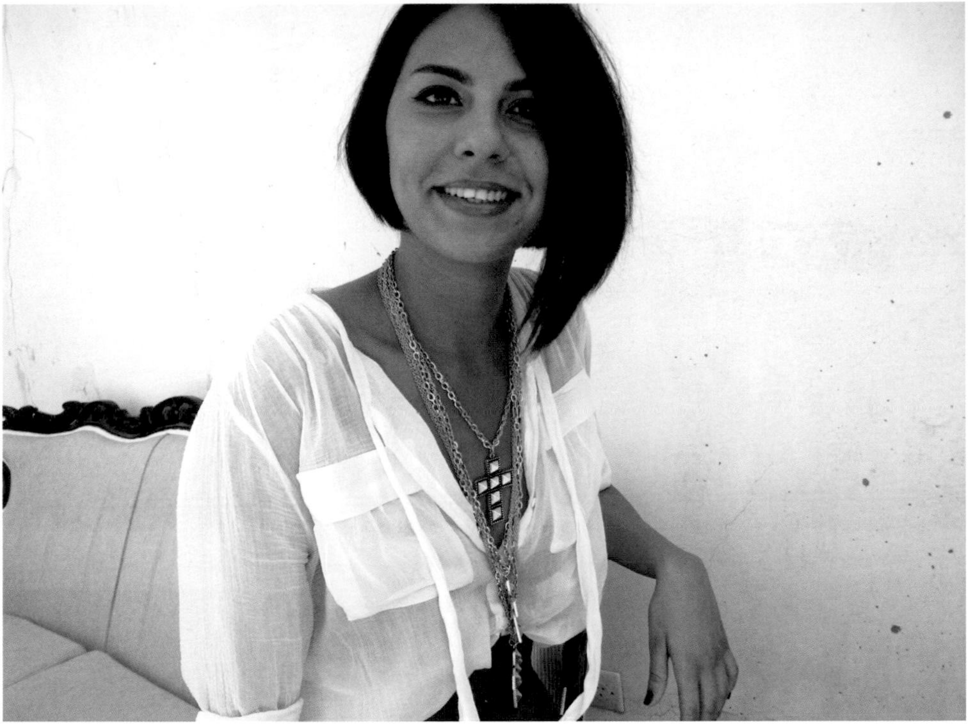

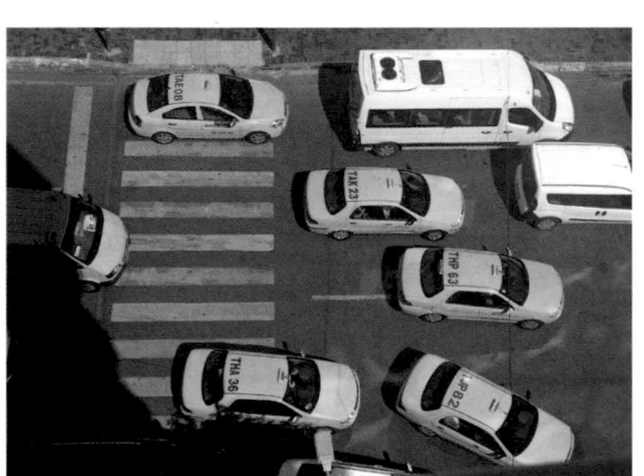
TAK 23
TMP 63
THA 36

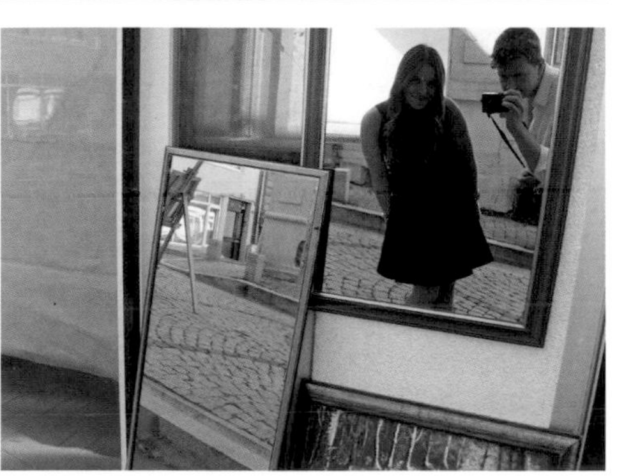

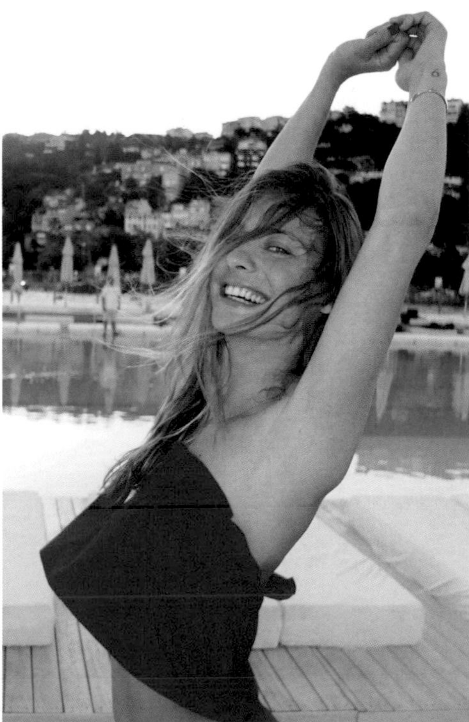

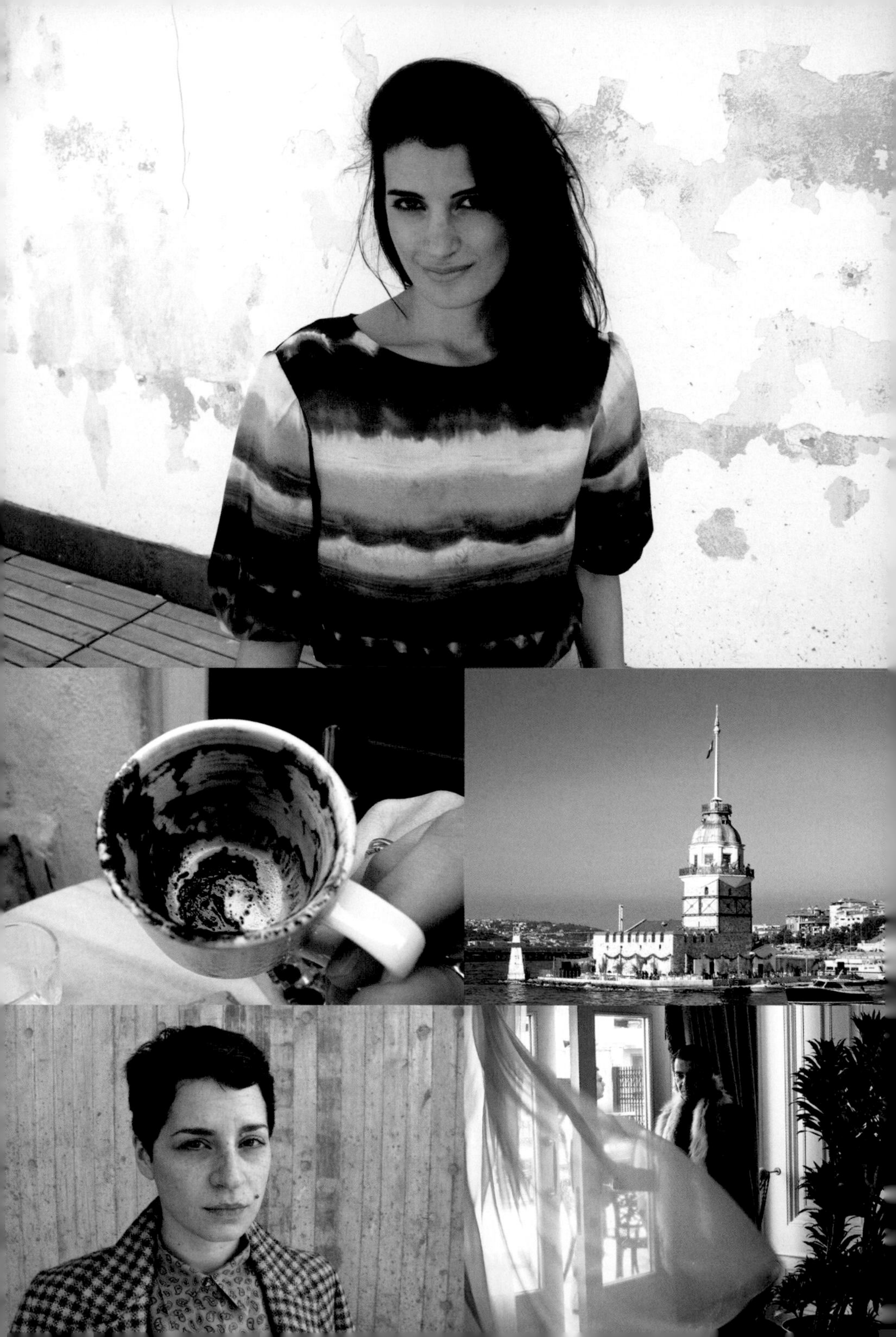

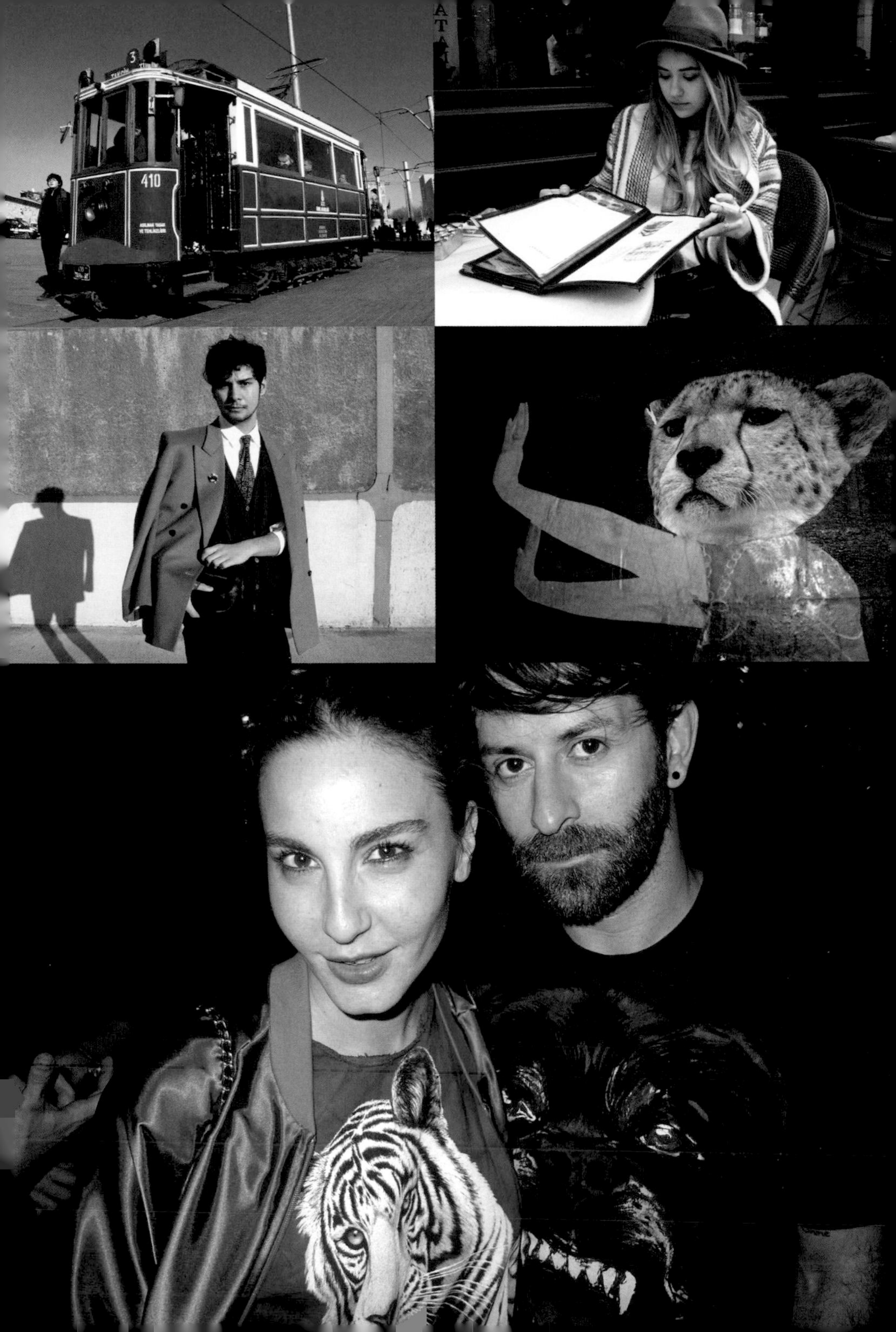

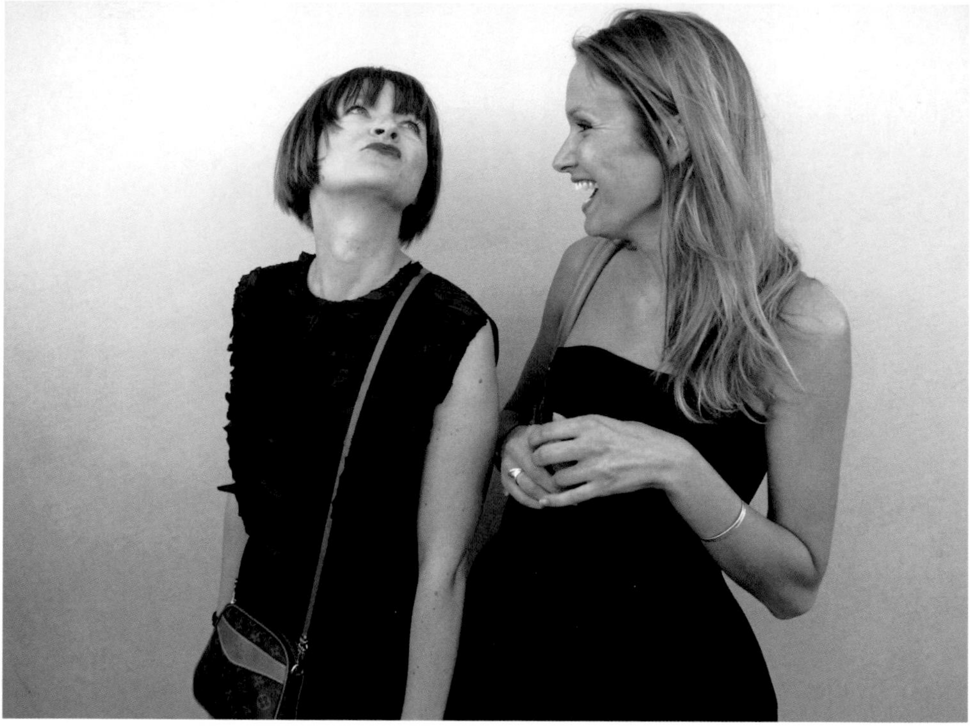

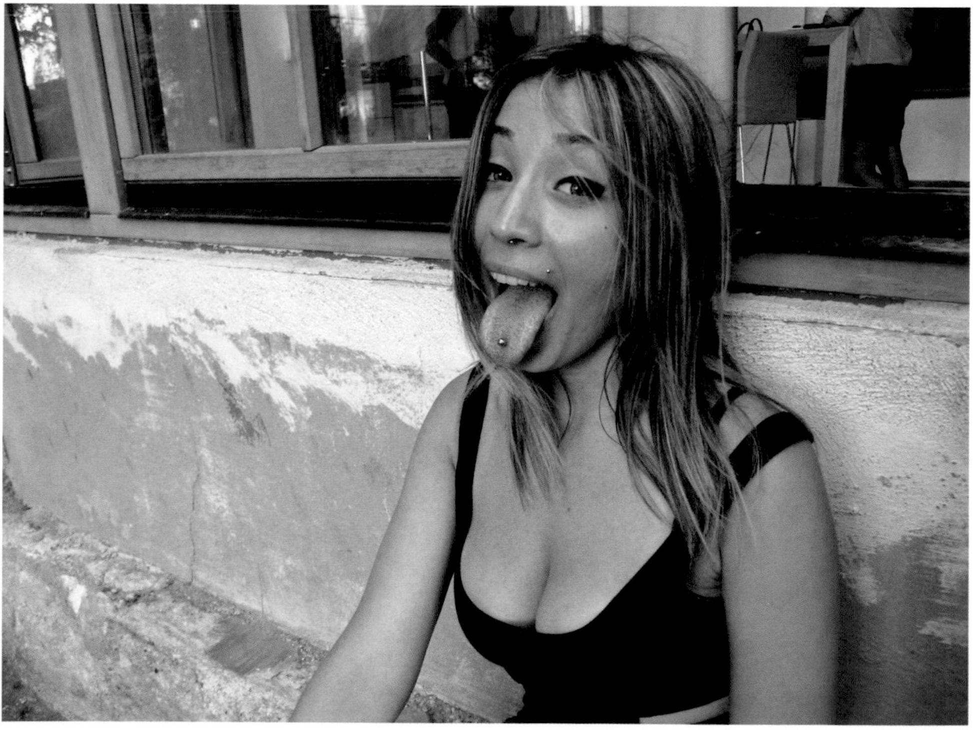

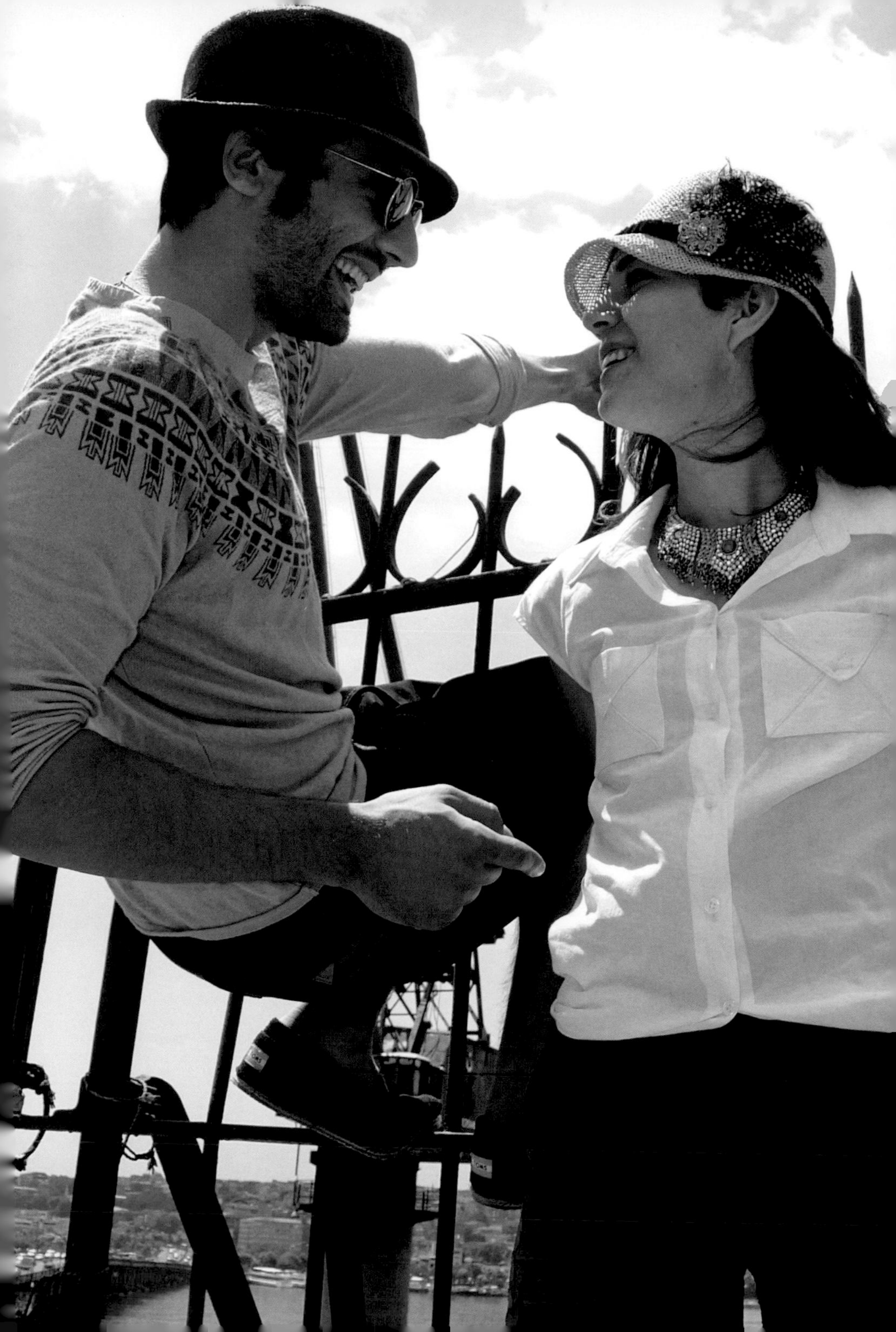

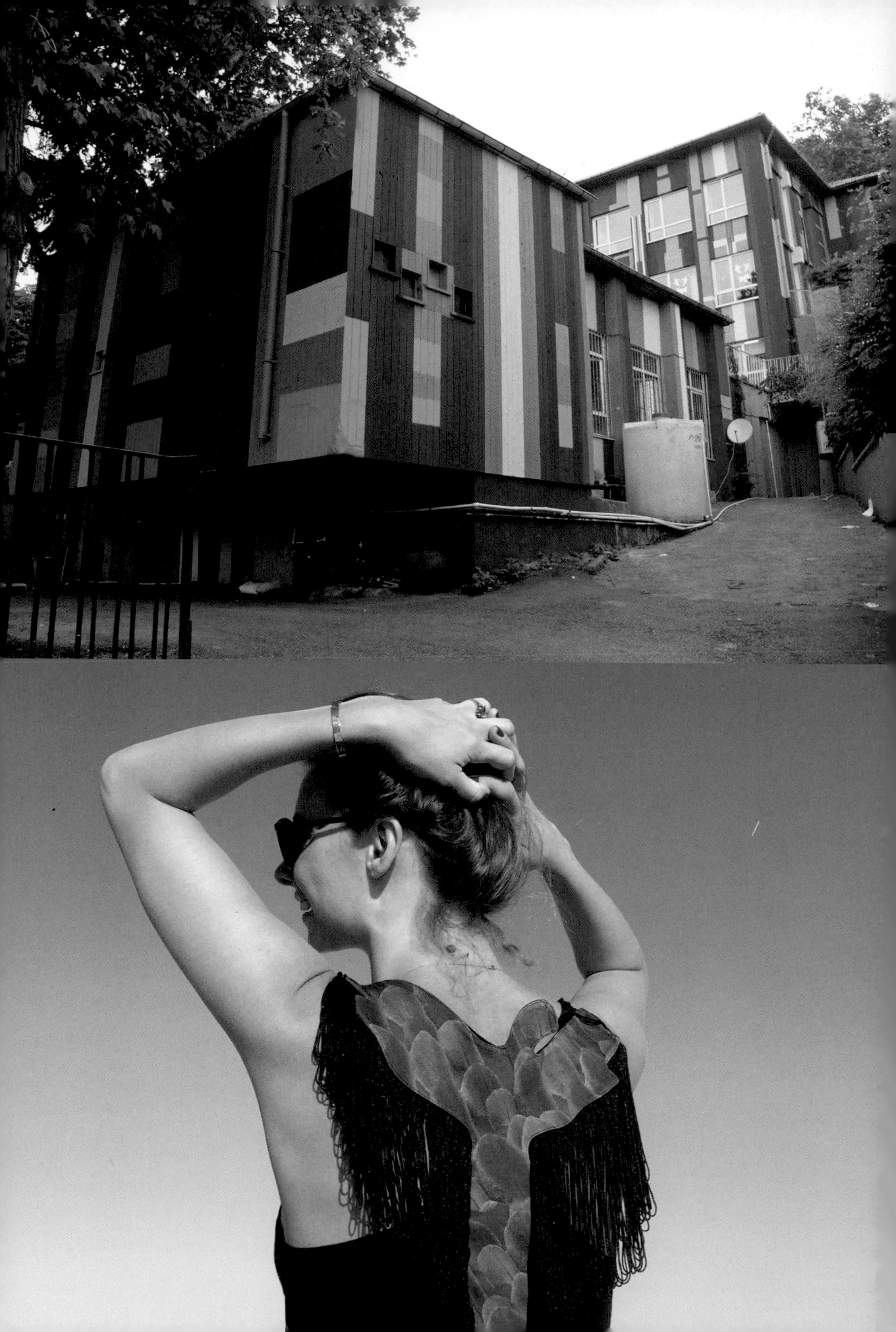

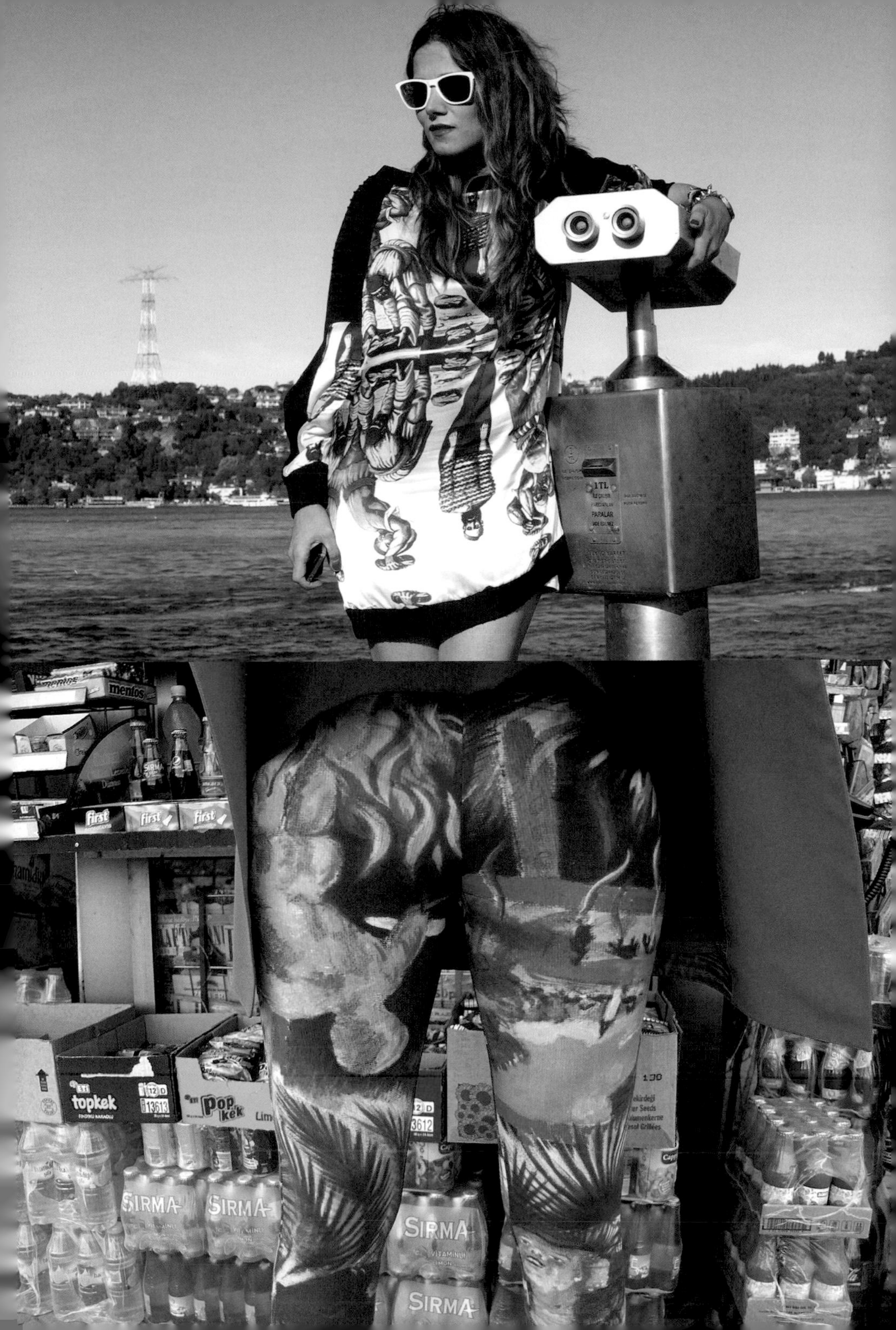

1TL
PARALAR
mentos
first
first
first
topkek
13613
Pop kek
3612
SIRMA
SIRMA
SIRMA
SIRMA

Seoul

Lat / 37° 33' 0" N

Lon / 126° 58' 0" E

20–24 Apr.; 5–7 Dec.

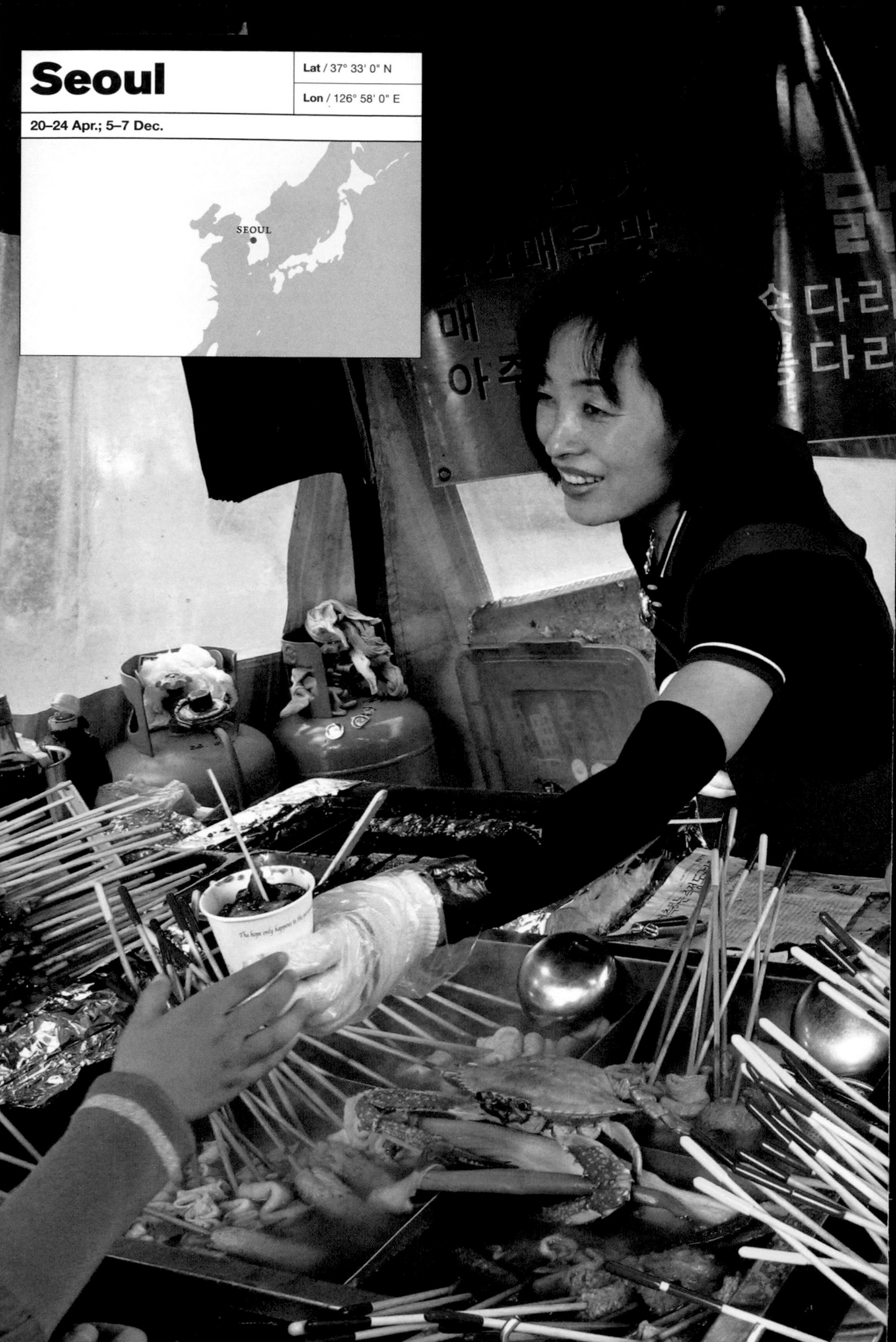

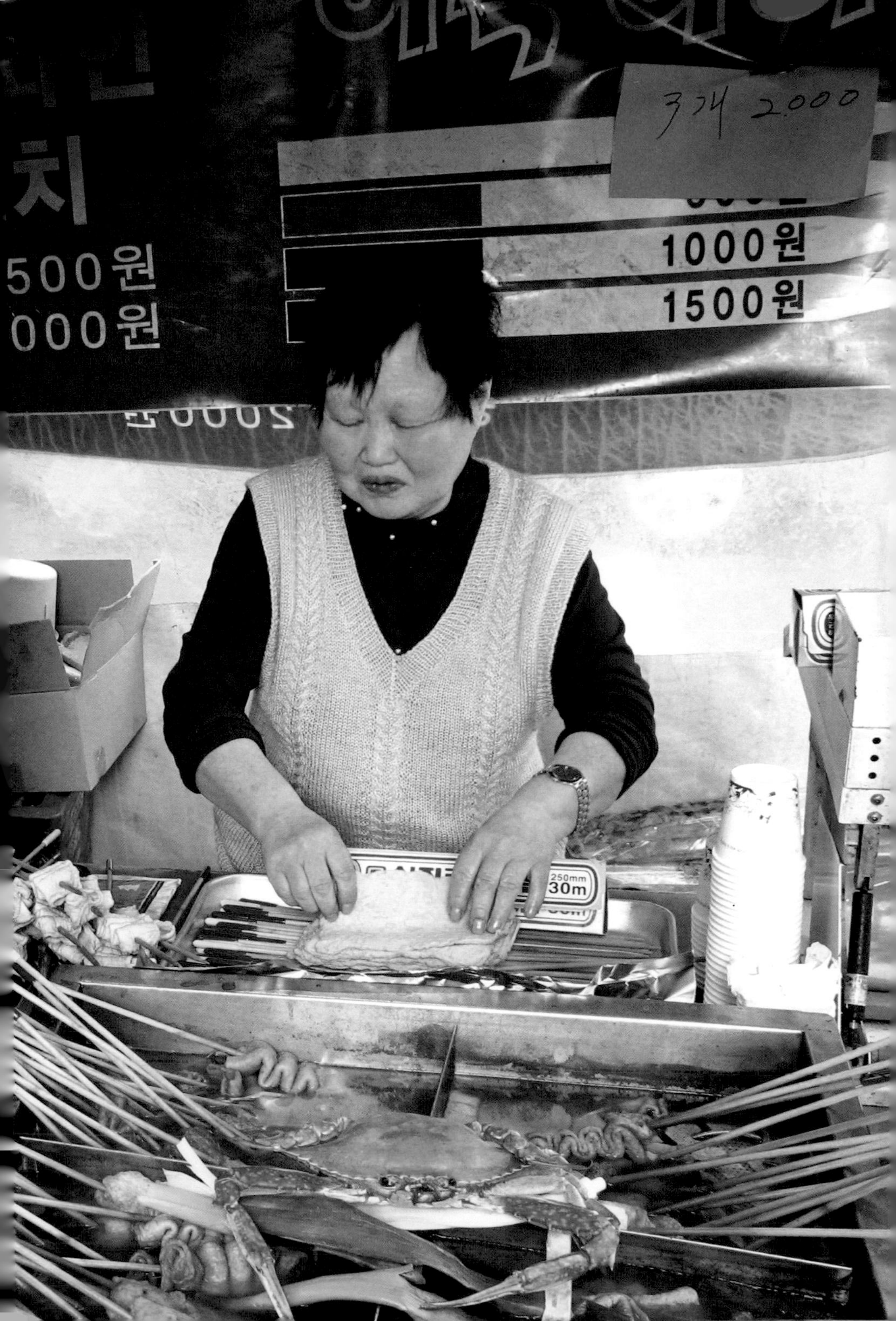
3개 2000
1000원
1500원

“It’s difficult not to describe Seoul in comparison to Tokyo, the quintessential super-advanced, hi-tech and innovative city in the Far East. To me Seoul feels more mysterious and undiscovered than Tokyo, more romantic and melancholic, full of areas with houses closely packed together and small cosy cafés with arty details. Tokyo’s style is colourful and cute; Seoul’s is more serious and grown-up, more grey – but in a good way. It’s one of the cities where you see the most well-dressed straight men in the world. It’s the opposite of Brazil: Korean men love looking smart and sharp, very hi-tech preppie. (Korea was one of the first viable markets for men’s grooming products.) Women in Seoul dress very elegantly, more classically than the men, with lots of black. (Somehow I managed to find enough women wearing colours to please the book’s designer for this section!) The ‘couple look’, which is popular throughout Asia, is especially big in Seoul: on the weekends couples will dress in matching outfits, especially matching American-style sweatshirts with obnoxious brand logos. The food is amazing, though if you don’t like spicy food, don’t even go to Korea: you’ll suffer. I did a photoshoot for *Nylon* Korea and they threw a great party on the rooftop of their company offices with lots of fantastic little details, including Face Hunter-themed cupcakes. You see the same attention to detail in people’s outfits. The first time I visited Seoul I was taken to a Korean ‘booking club’. The concept is that the guys book a table on their own for the evening and then the waiters introduce them to a series of different women in quick succession. It looks creepy but actually isn’t, though it is a bit like speed-dating meets the floor of the New York Stock Exchange. I was the only Western guy there and I didn’t know how the process worked. It felt like I’d been thrown headfirst into Korean culture and it was sink or swim!”

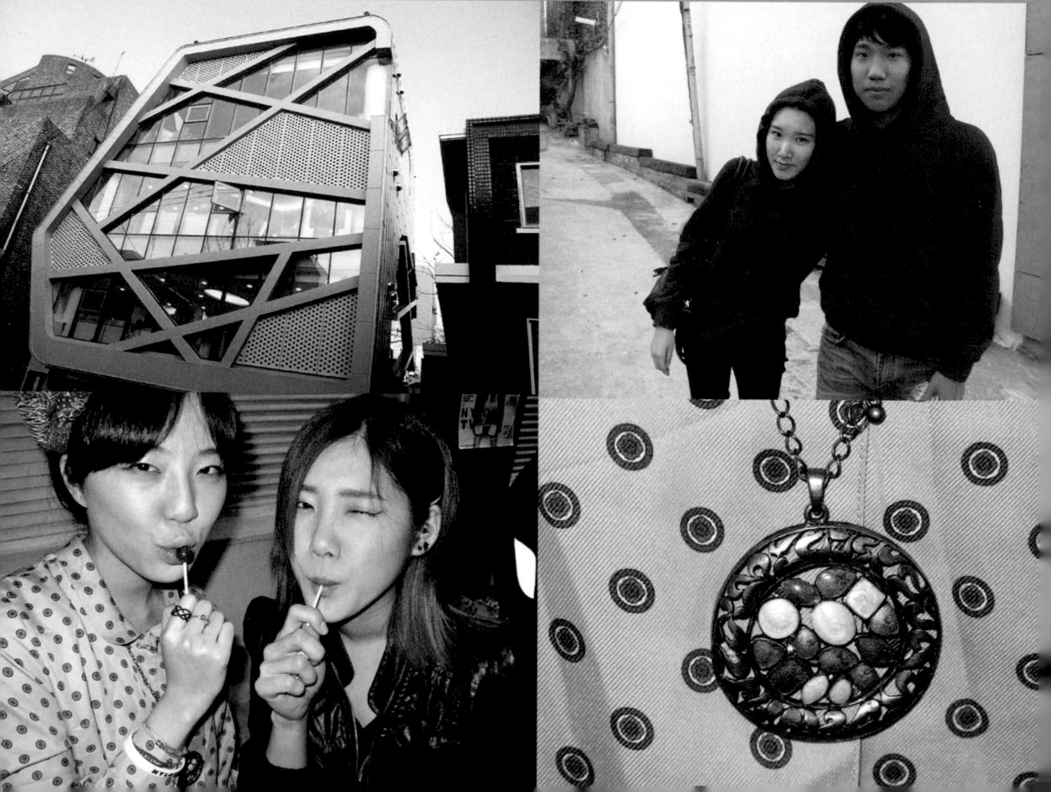

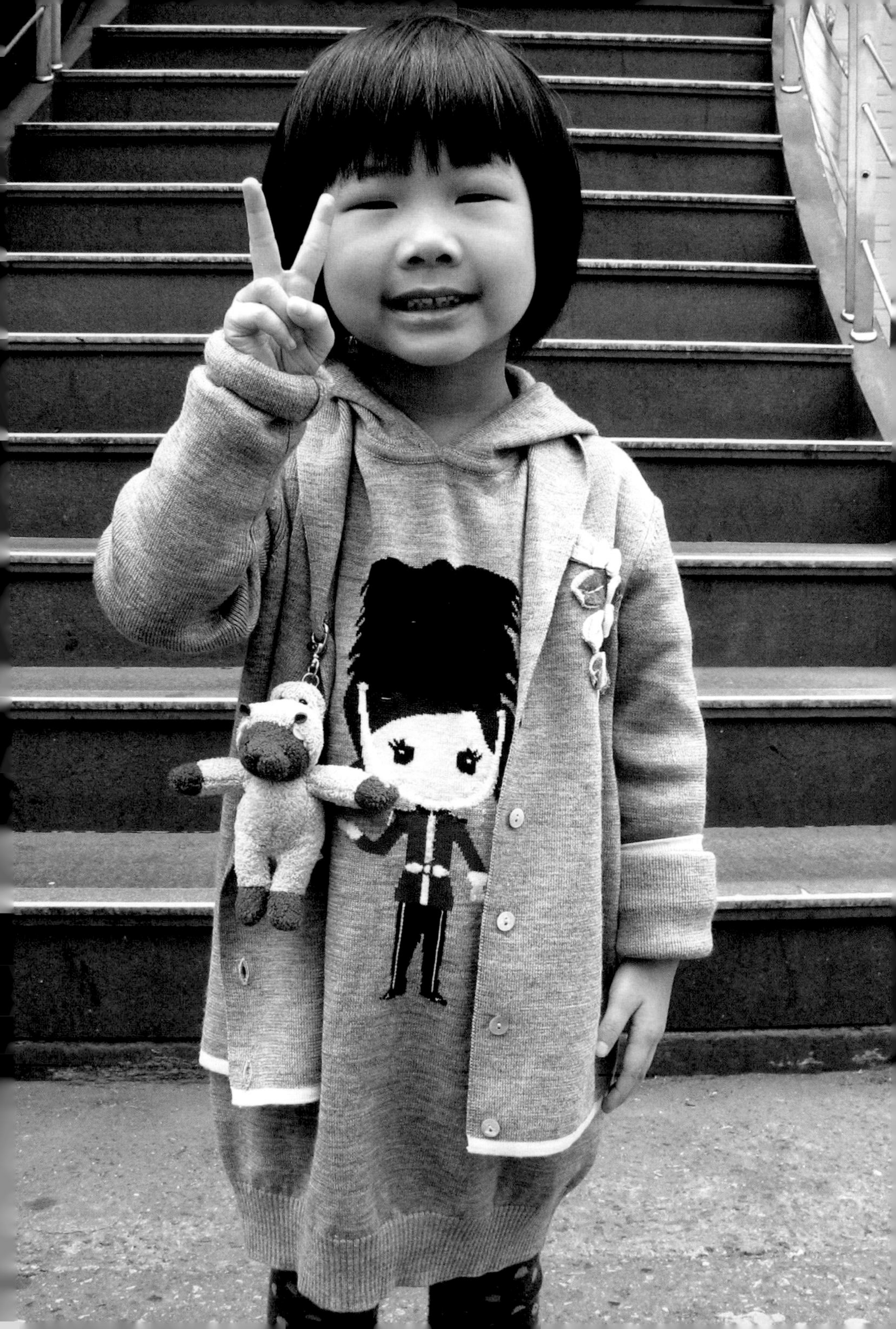

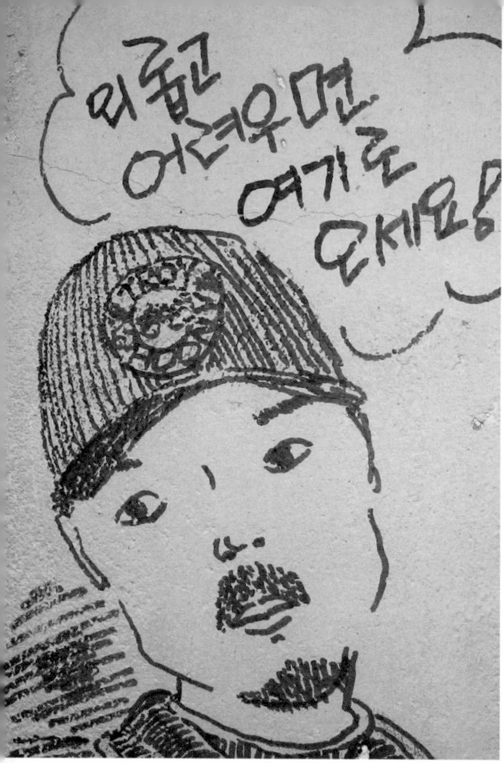

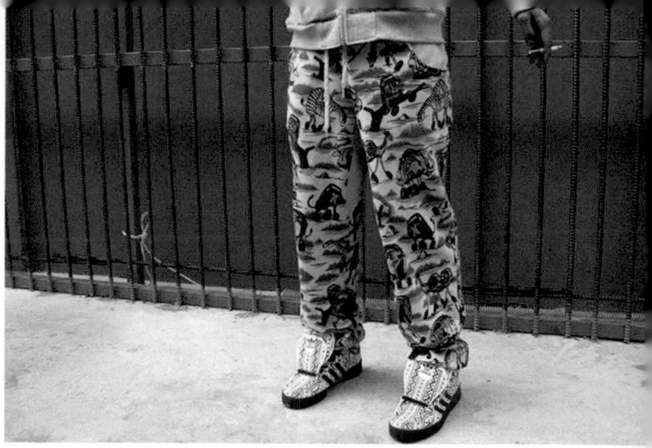

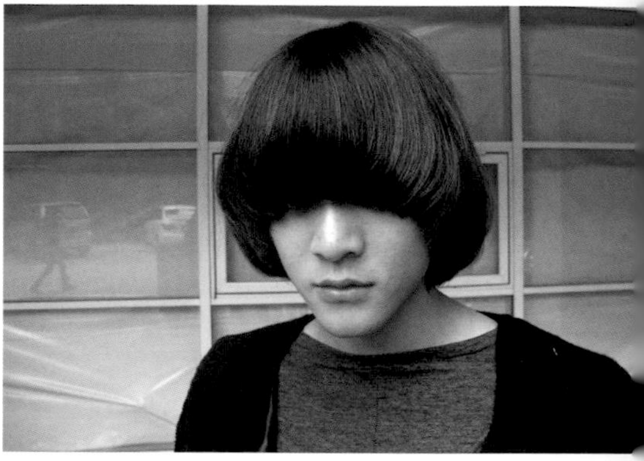

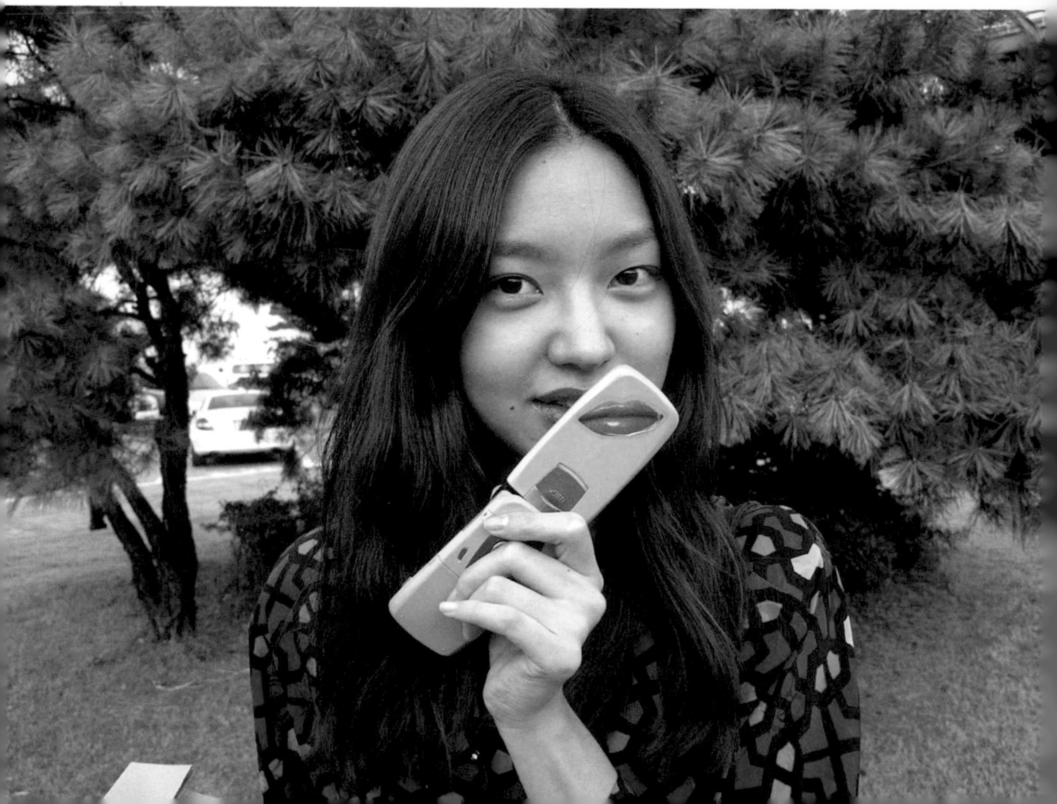

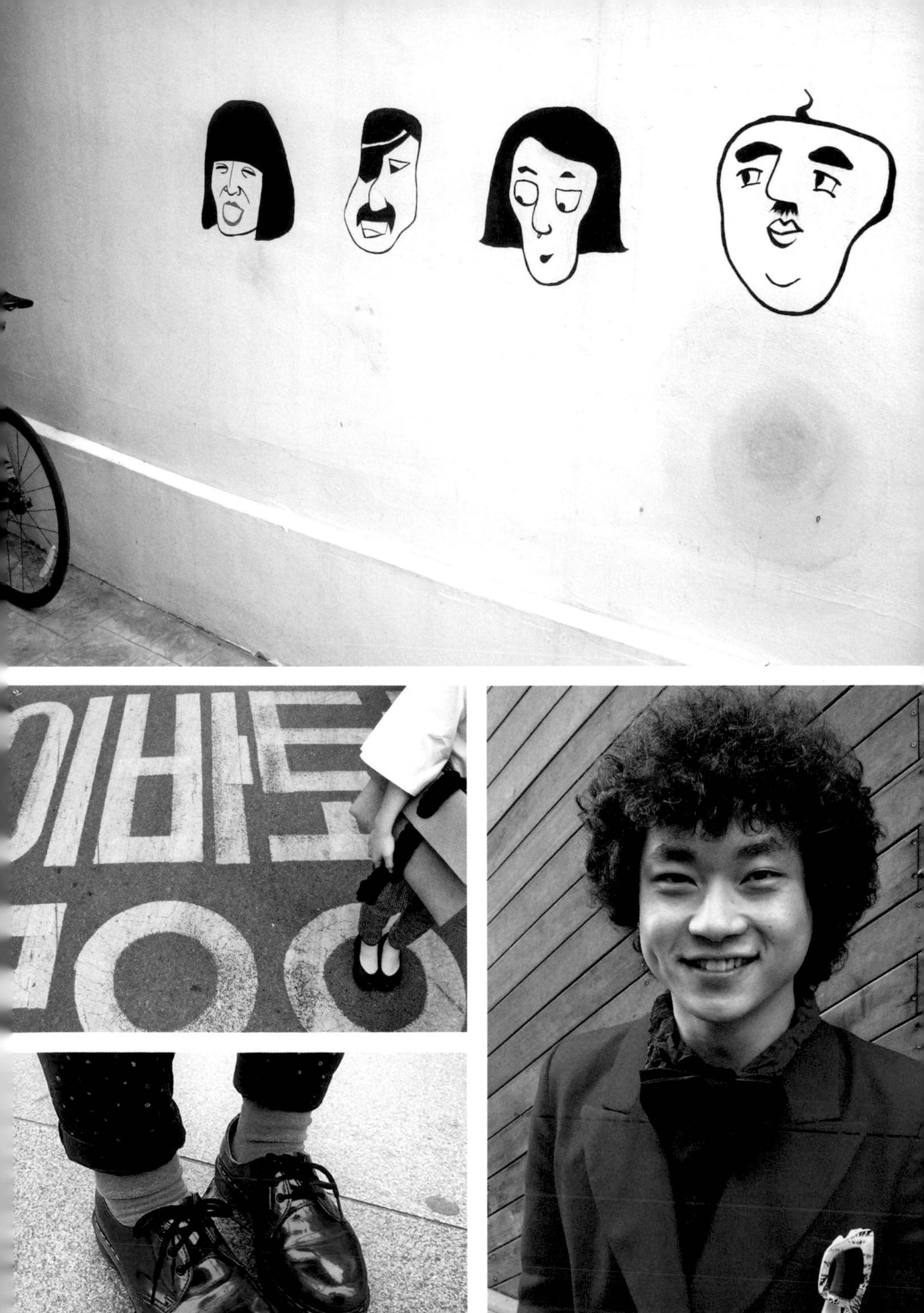

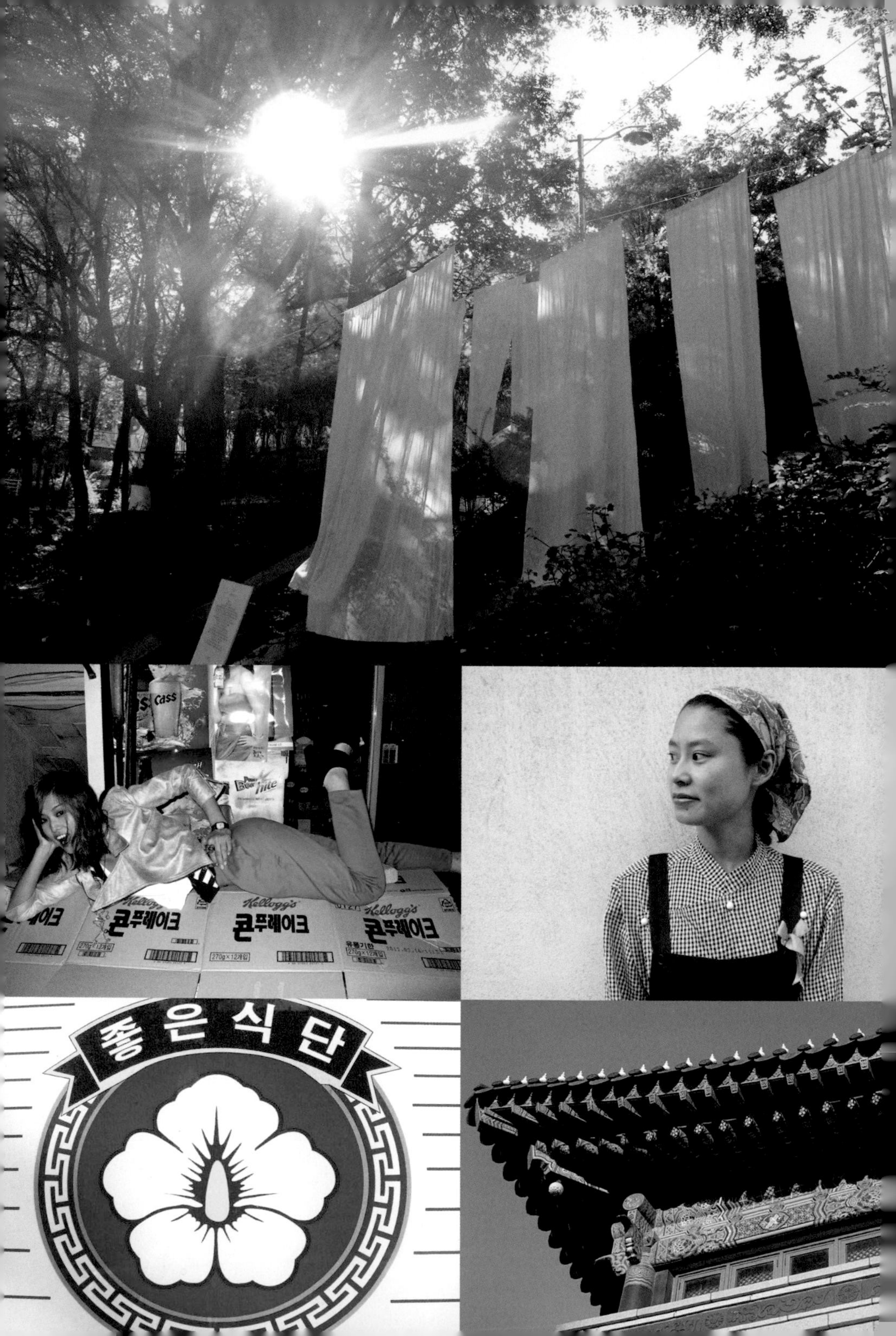
Cass
Kellogg's
콘푸레이크
270g×12개입
유통기한
좋은식단

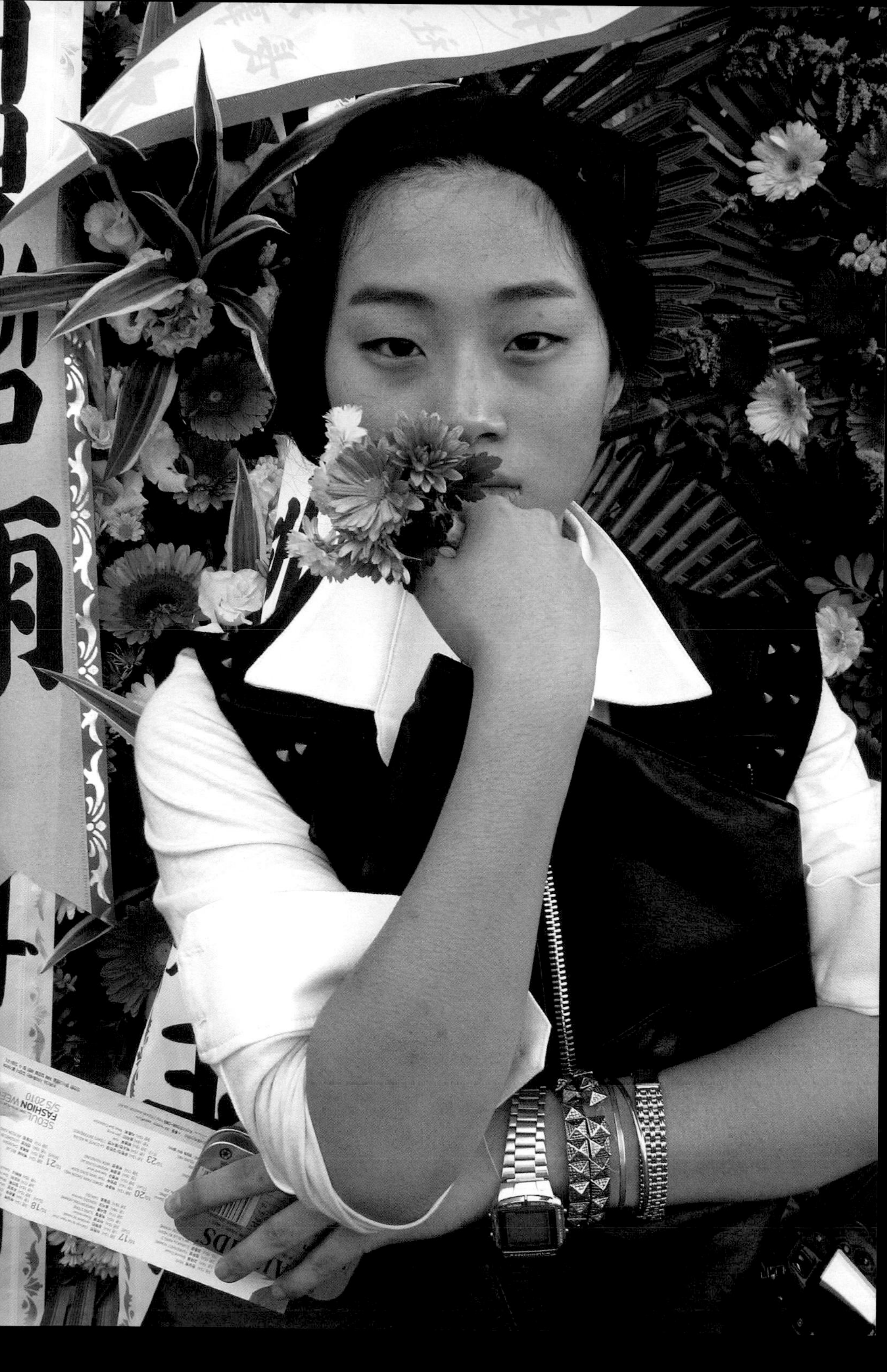
SEOUL
FASHION WEE
S/S 2010

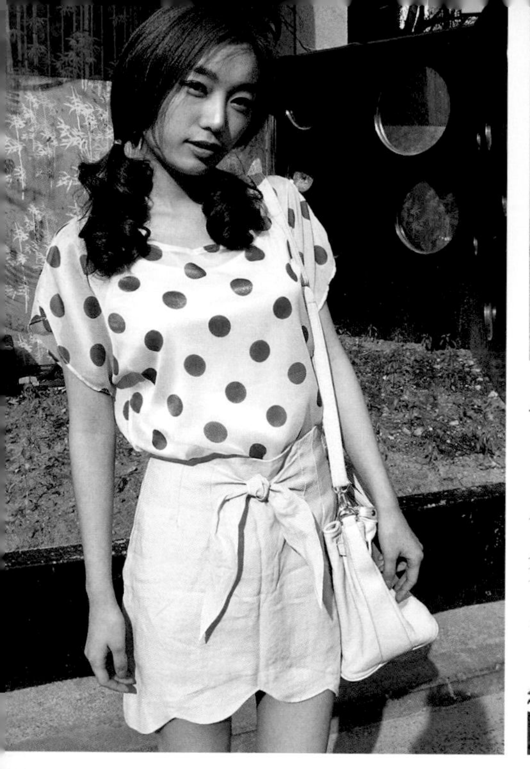

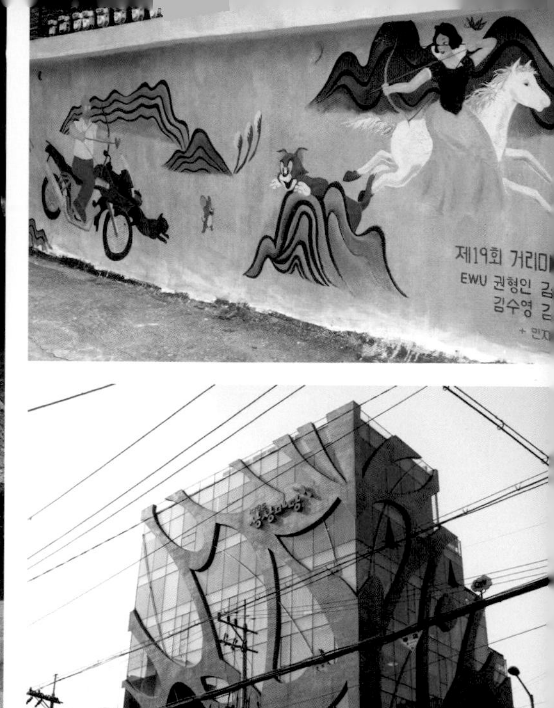
제19회 거리미
EWU 권형인
김수영

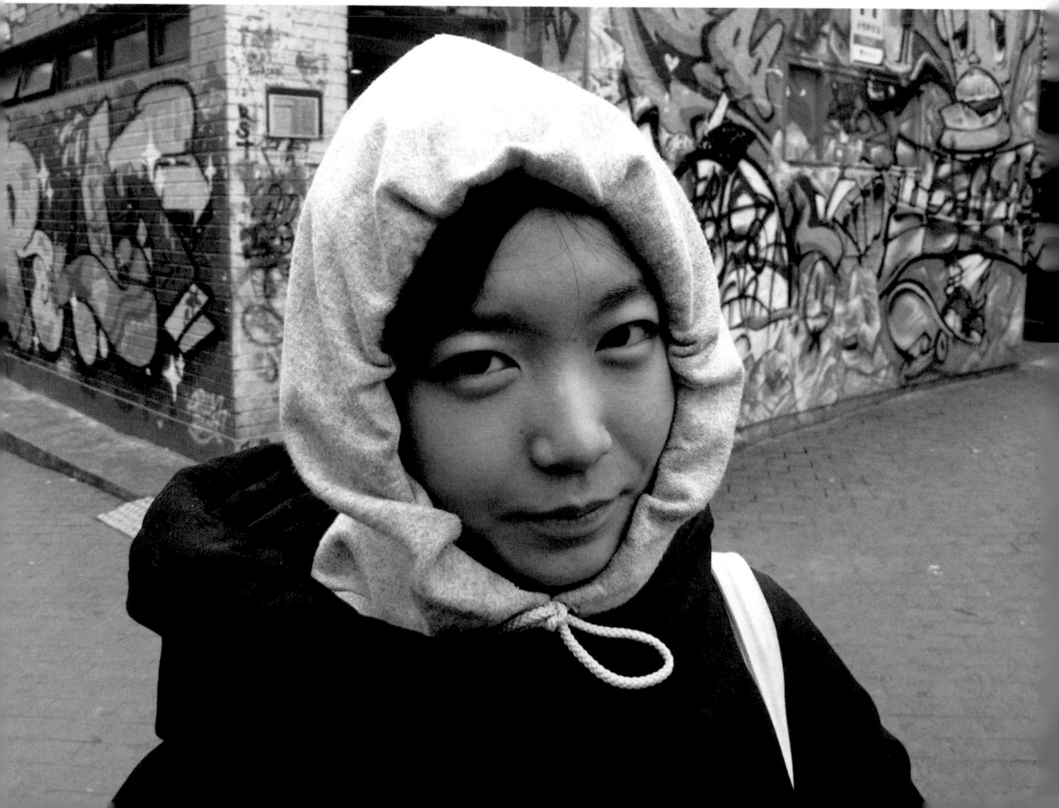

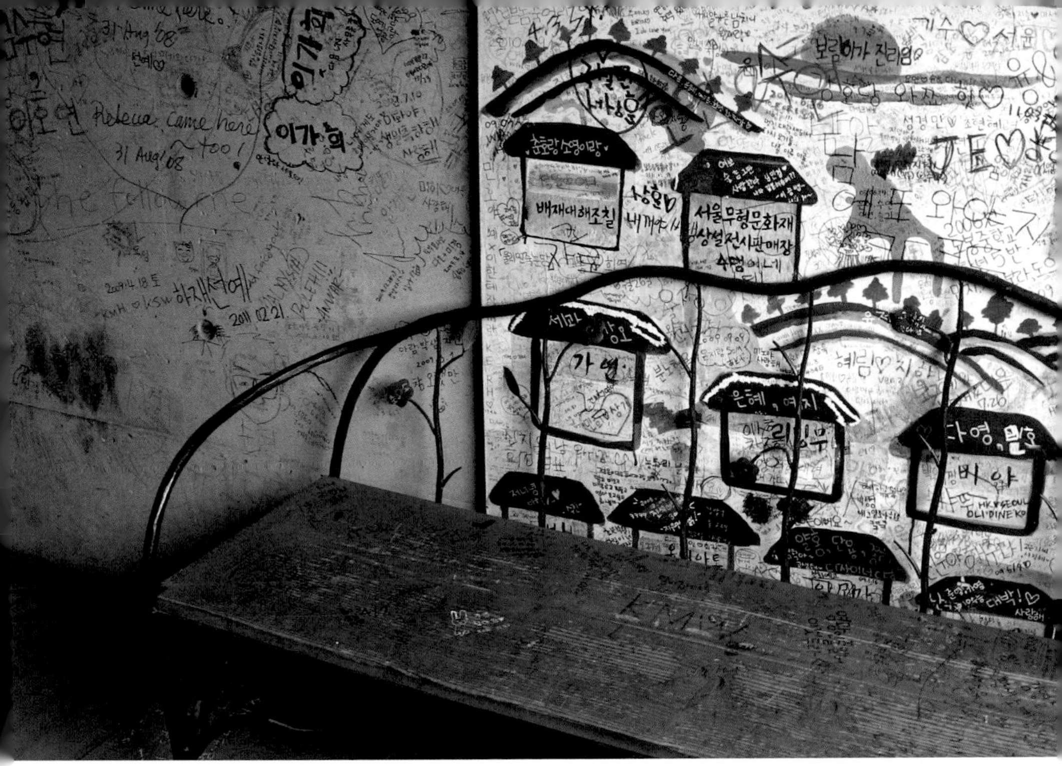

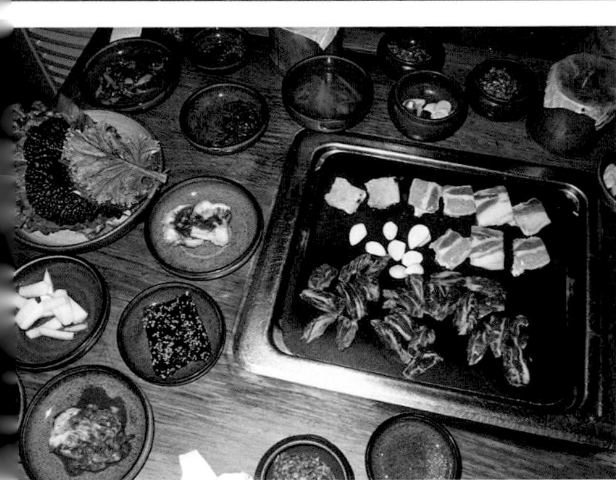

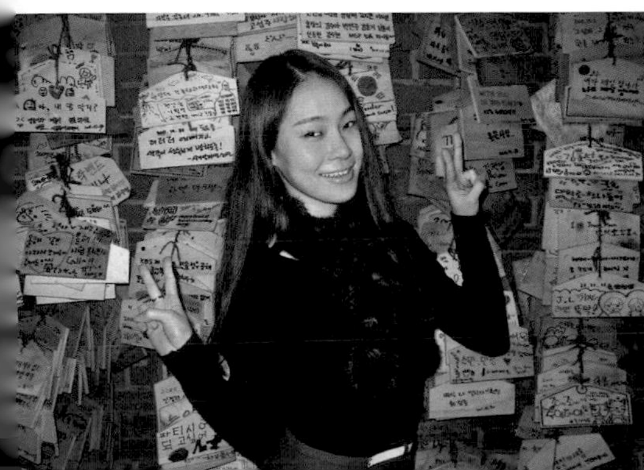

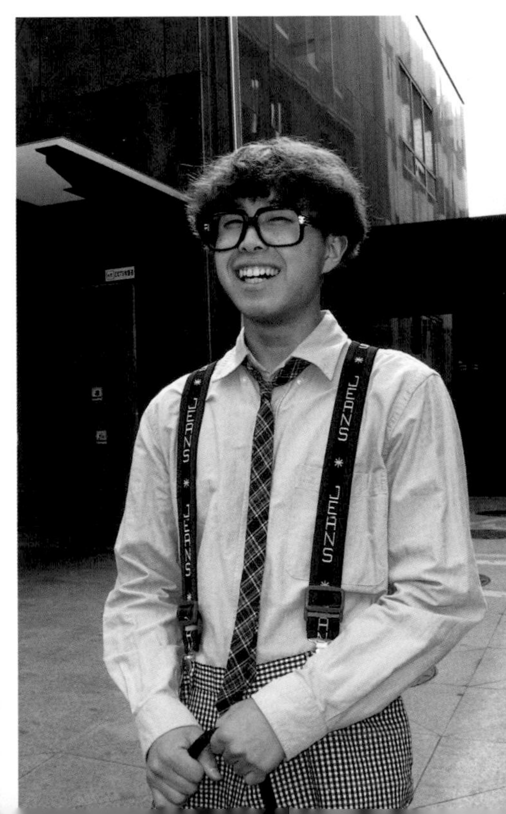
JEANS
JEANS
JEANS

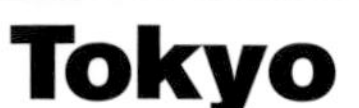

Tokyo

Lat / 35° 41' 0" N

Lon / 139° 11' 0" E

25–27 Apr.; 12 Dec.

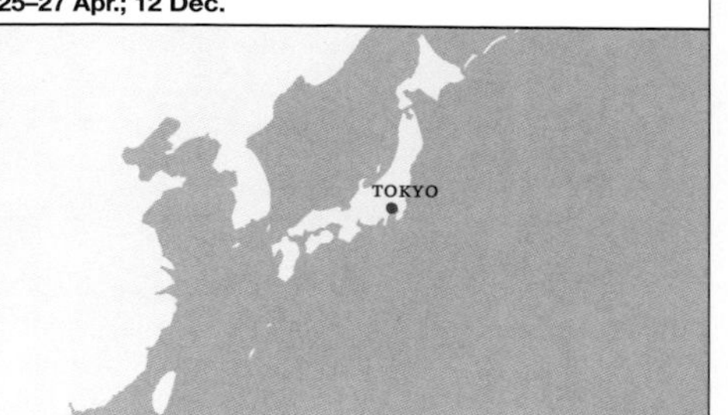

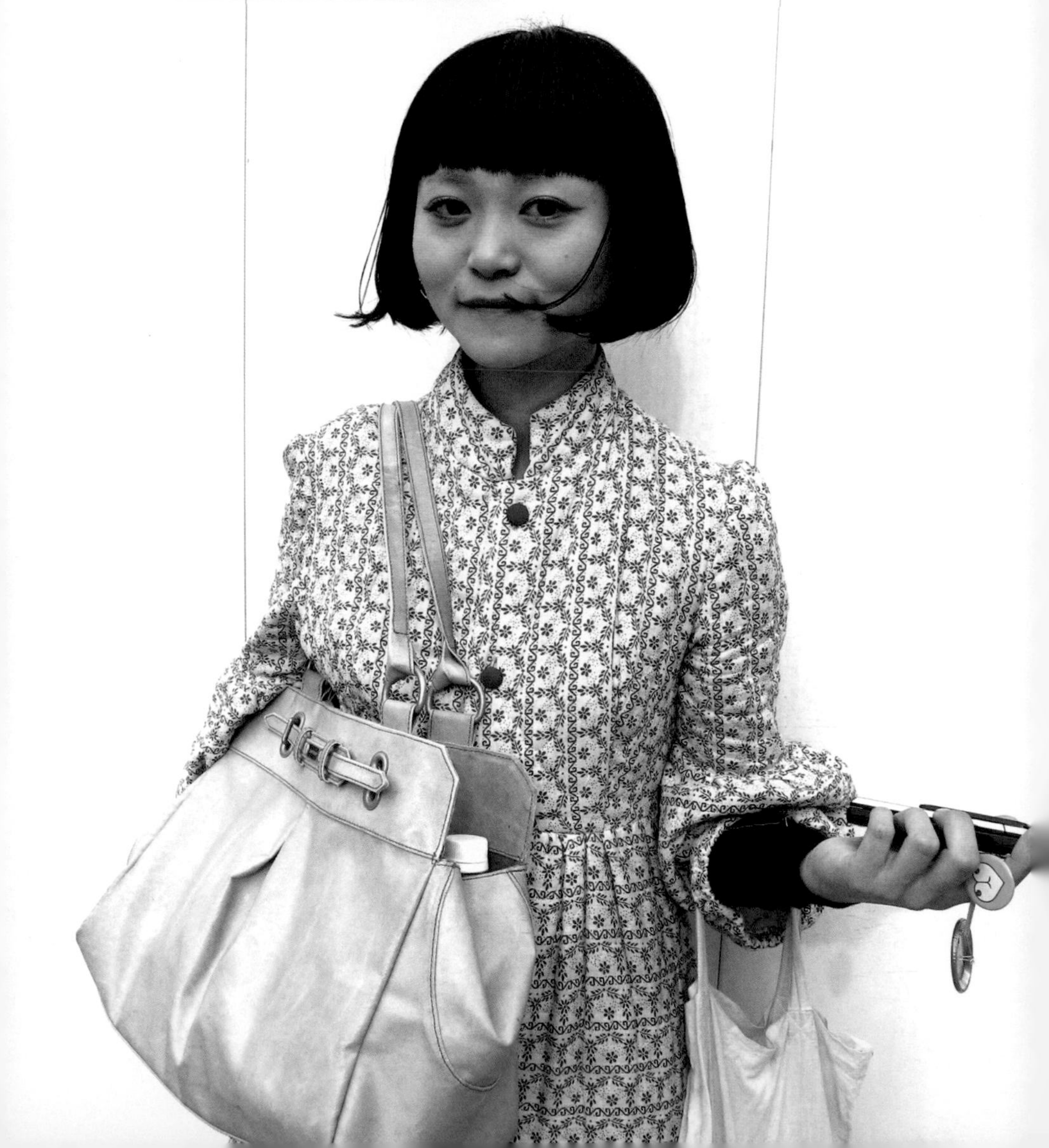

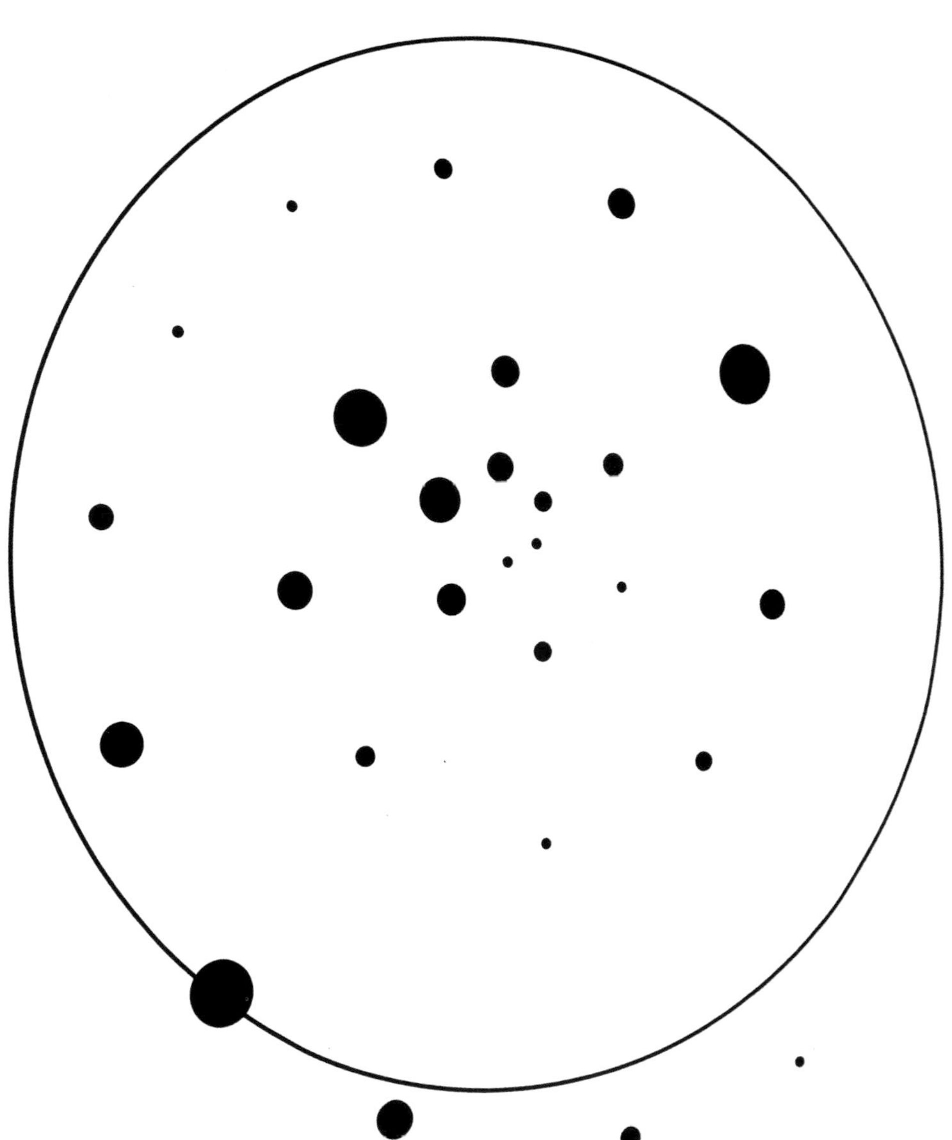

“In Tokyo it seems like everything is designed to be playful. On one hand it is a very serious and structured society, where everyone, especially workers, operates according to strict rules. But on the other hand it can be very fun aesthetically – even serious company logos look like children's manga illustrations. Every component of daily life and public space is very modern, innovative and carefully designed. Western aesthetics look very plain and old-fashioned in comparison. Tokyo is of course one of the major style capitals of the world, along with London, Paris and New York, but it's much more experimental – it's the most truly postmodern fashion scene in the world. You see all the elements of popular and traditional culture deconstructed and used in unexpected combinations in Tokyo. It's mainly down to the young people who rebel against the rigidly formatted society. But it's still hard to adequately explain the scale and visual excitement of the place: the degree of sophistication and creativity is just mind-blowing. But playful as it is, Tokyo can also be a very lonely place, as there's a culture of keeping your distance and your reserve. As a Westerner it can be especially difficult to make connections with local people.”

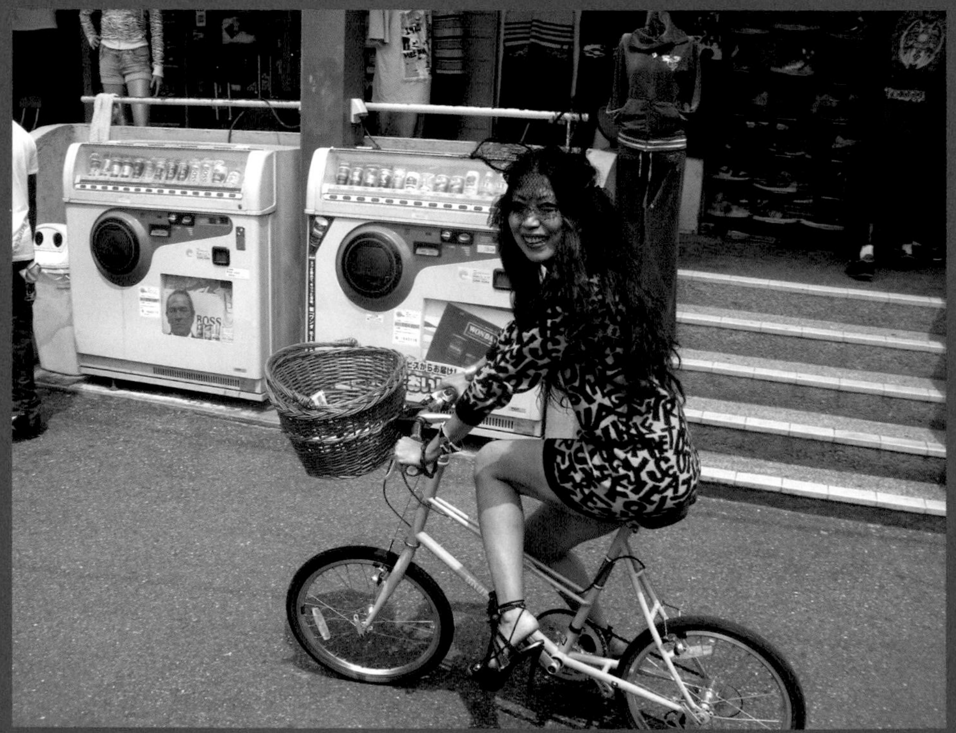

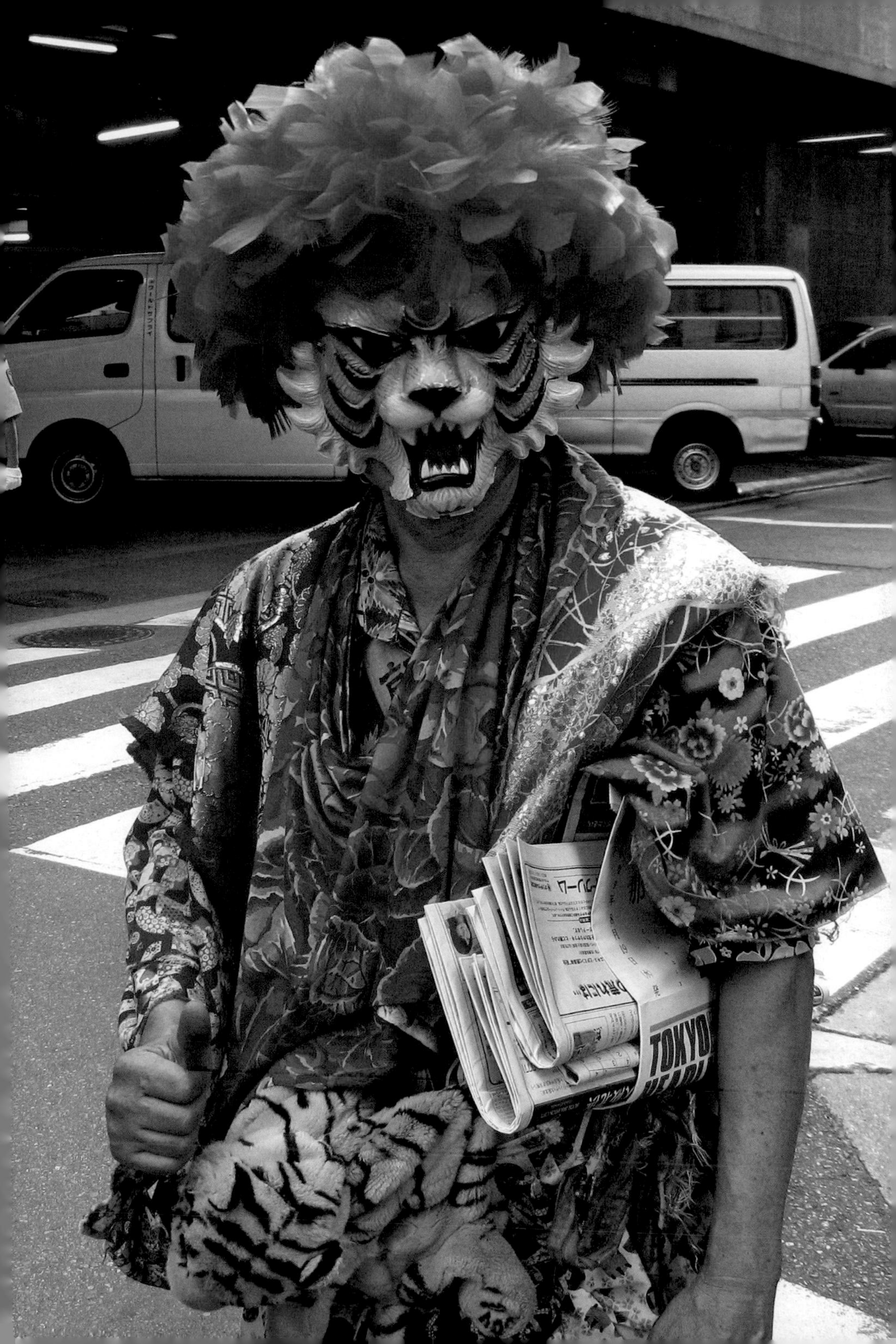
TOKYO

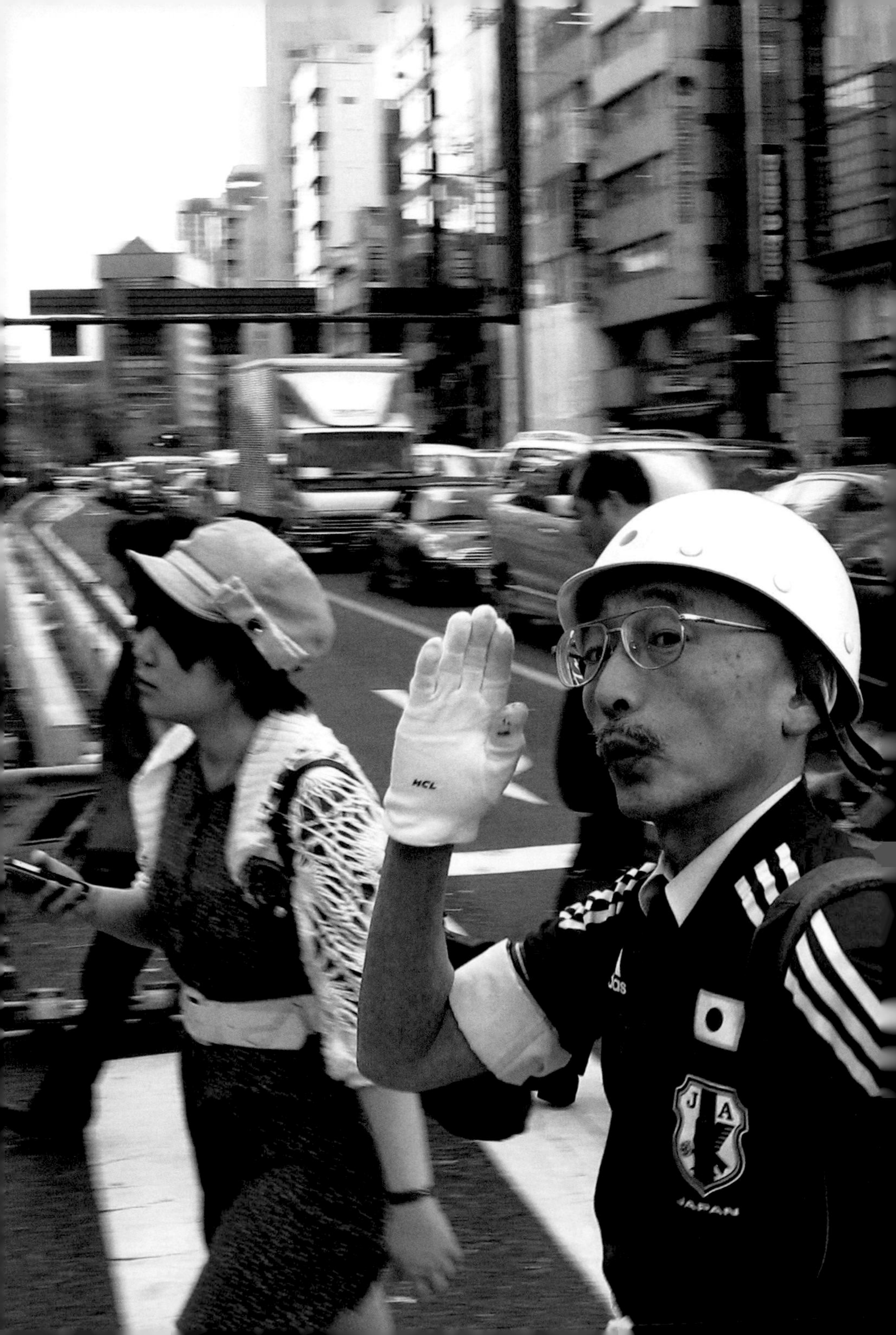
HCL
JA
JAPAN

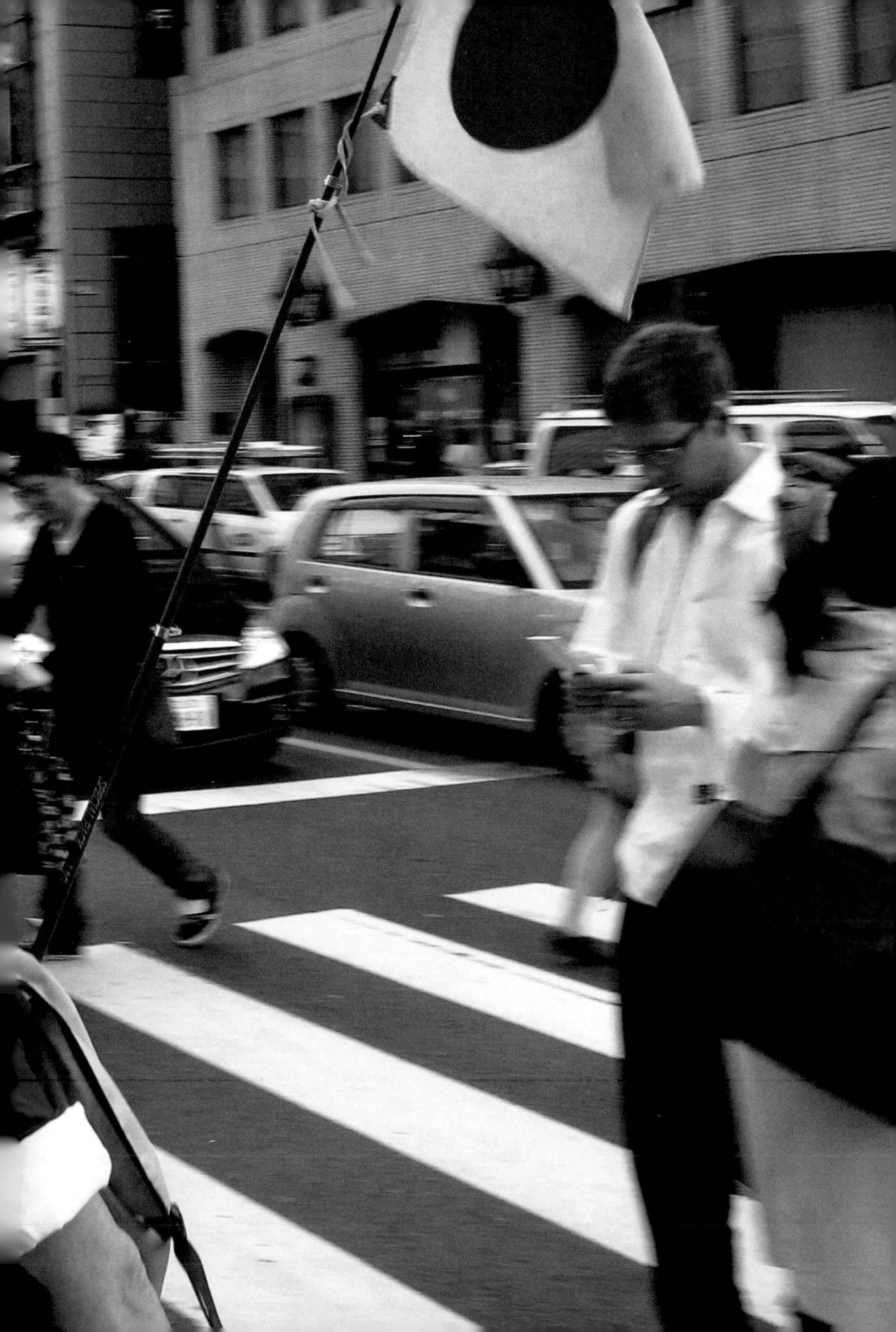

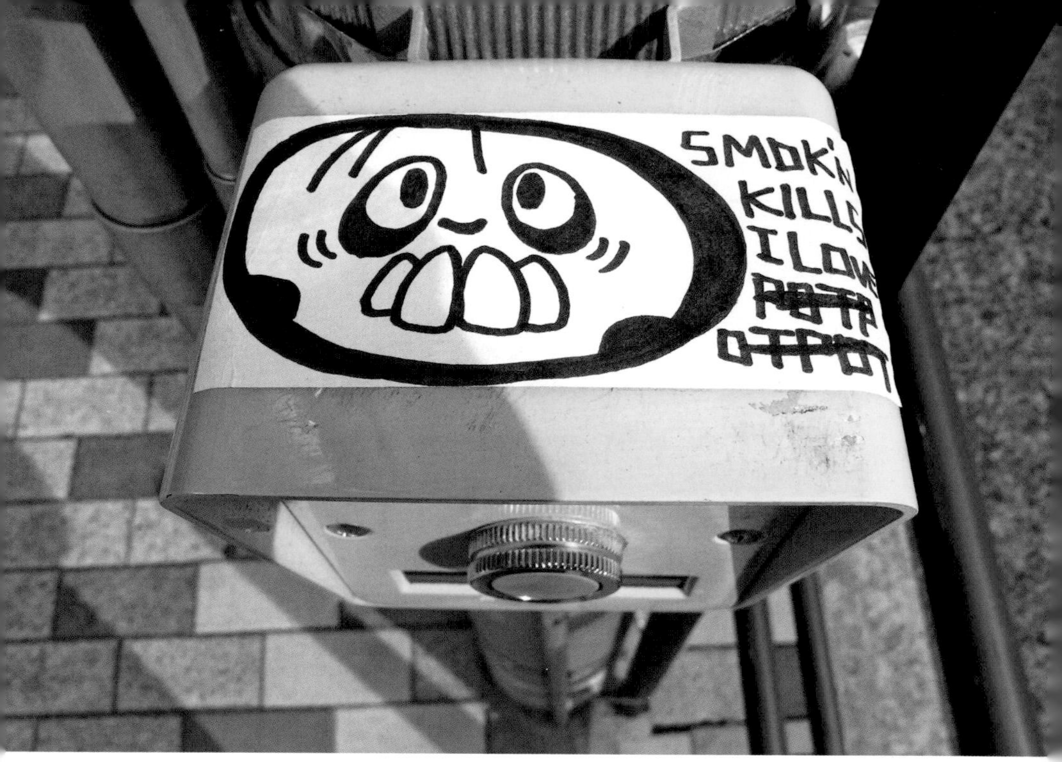

SMOK'N
KILLS
I LOVE

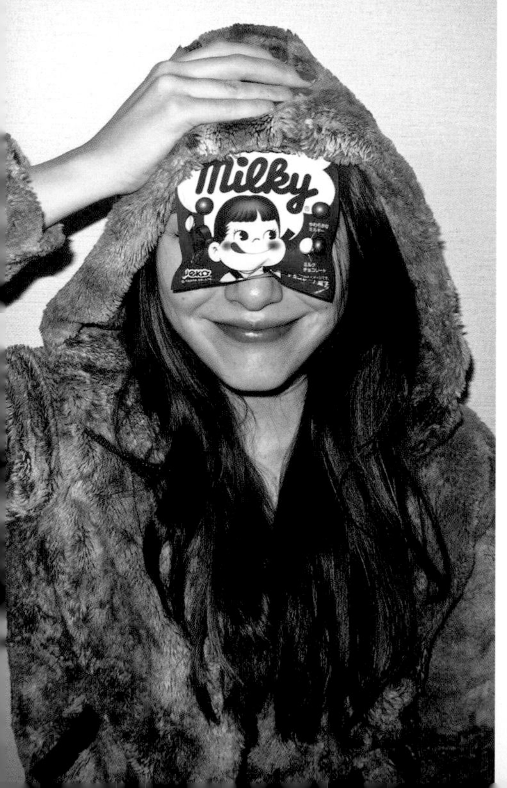
Milky

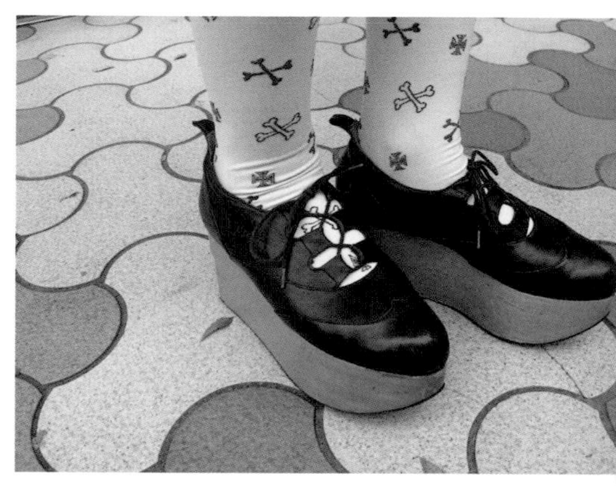

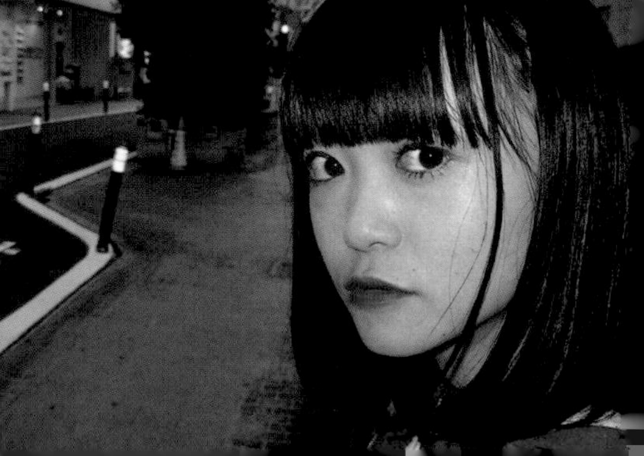

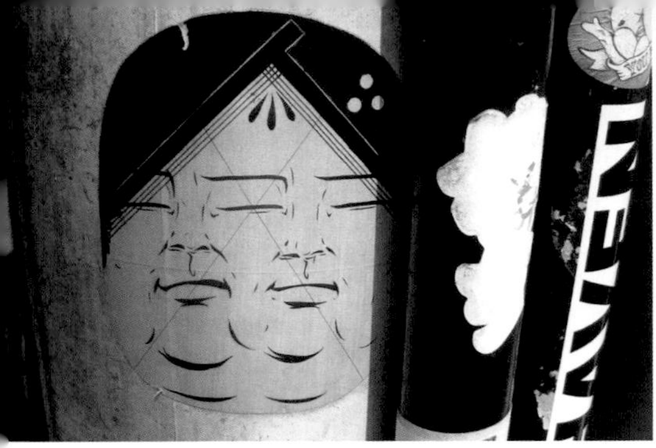

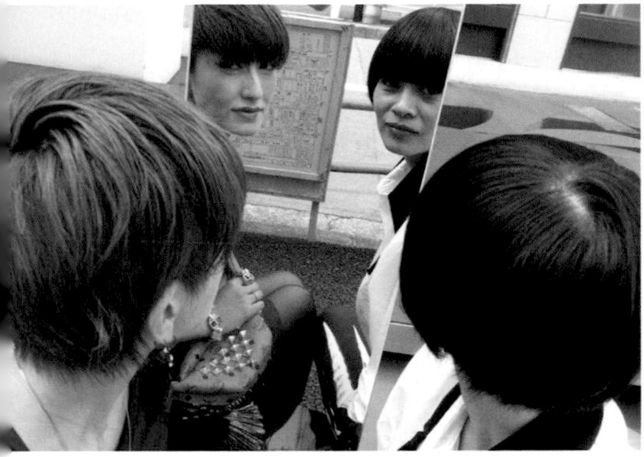

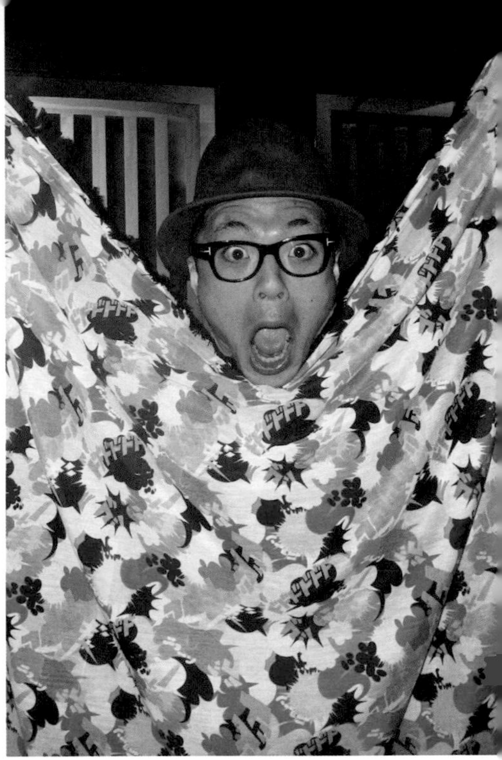

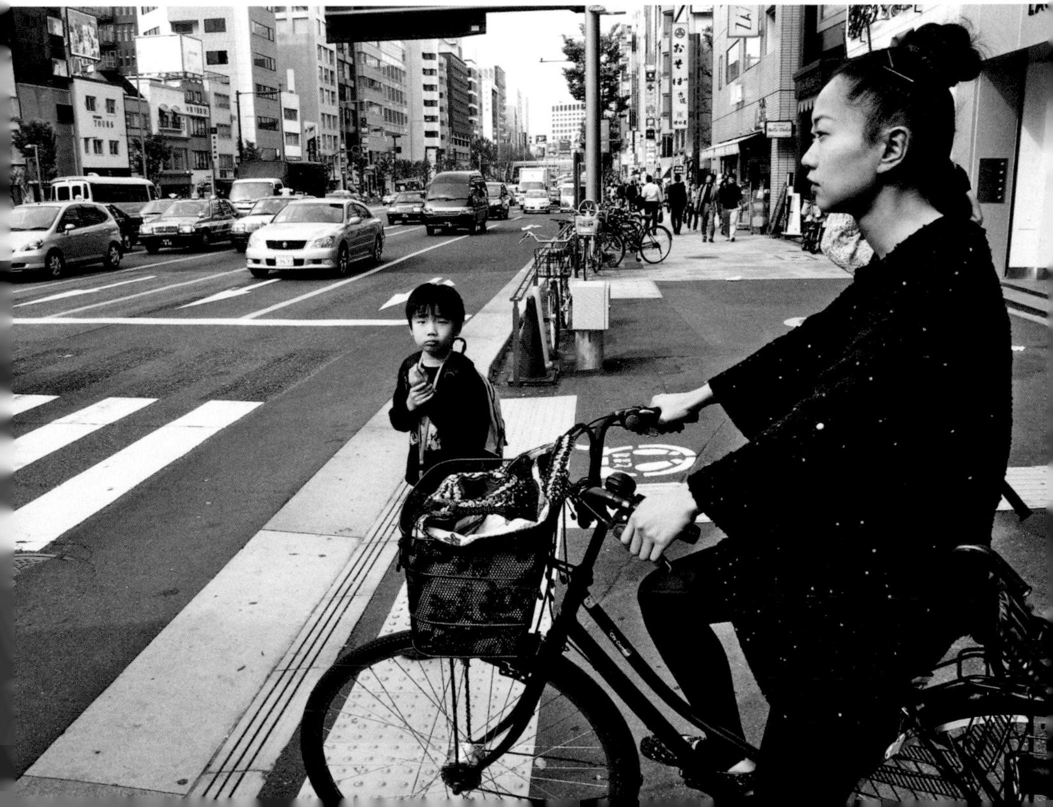

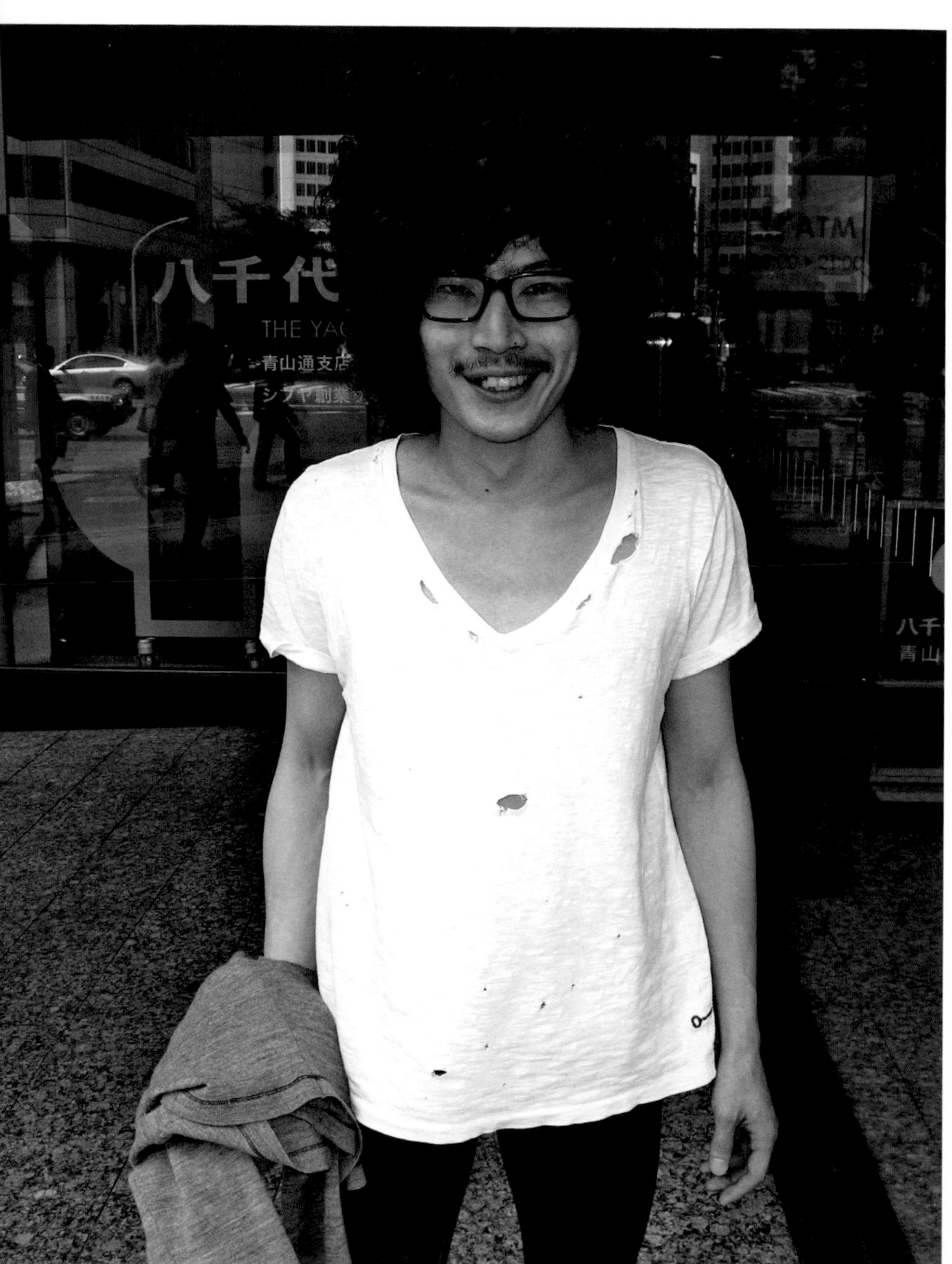
八千代
青山通支店
ATM

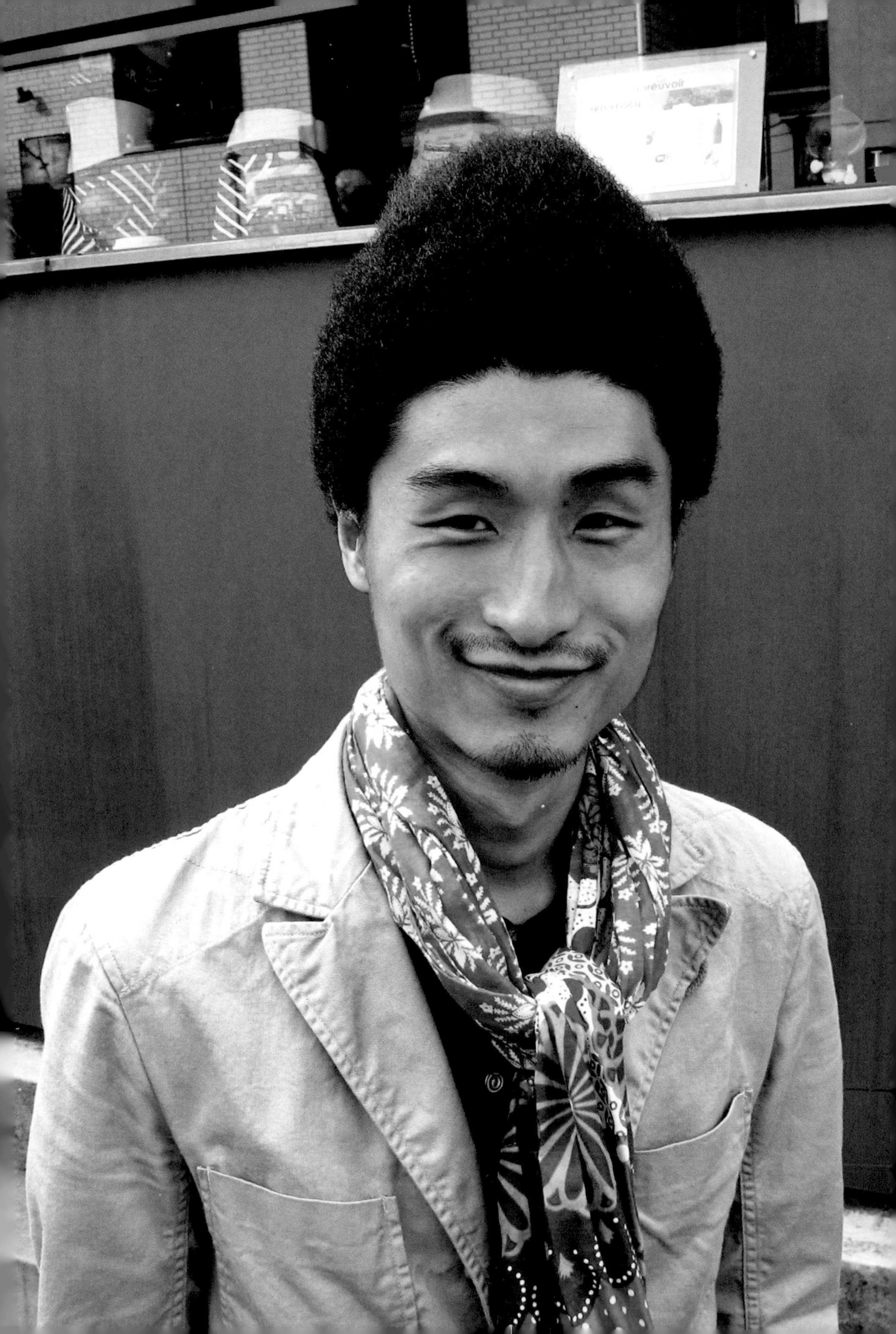

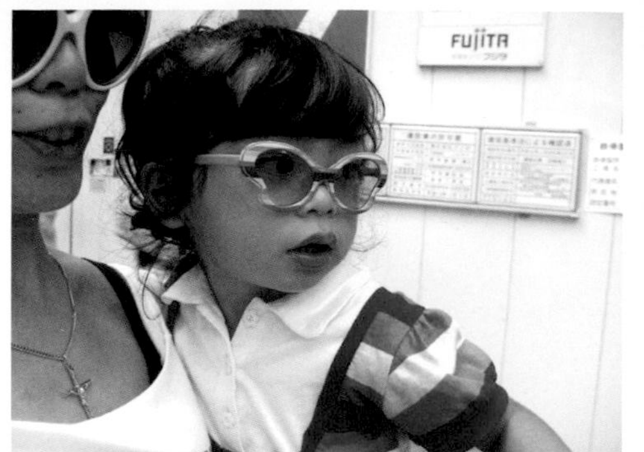
FUJITA

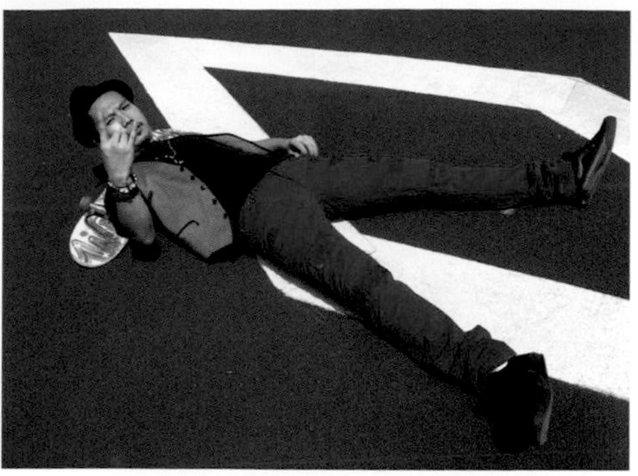

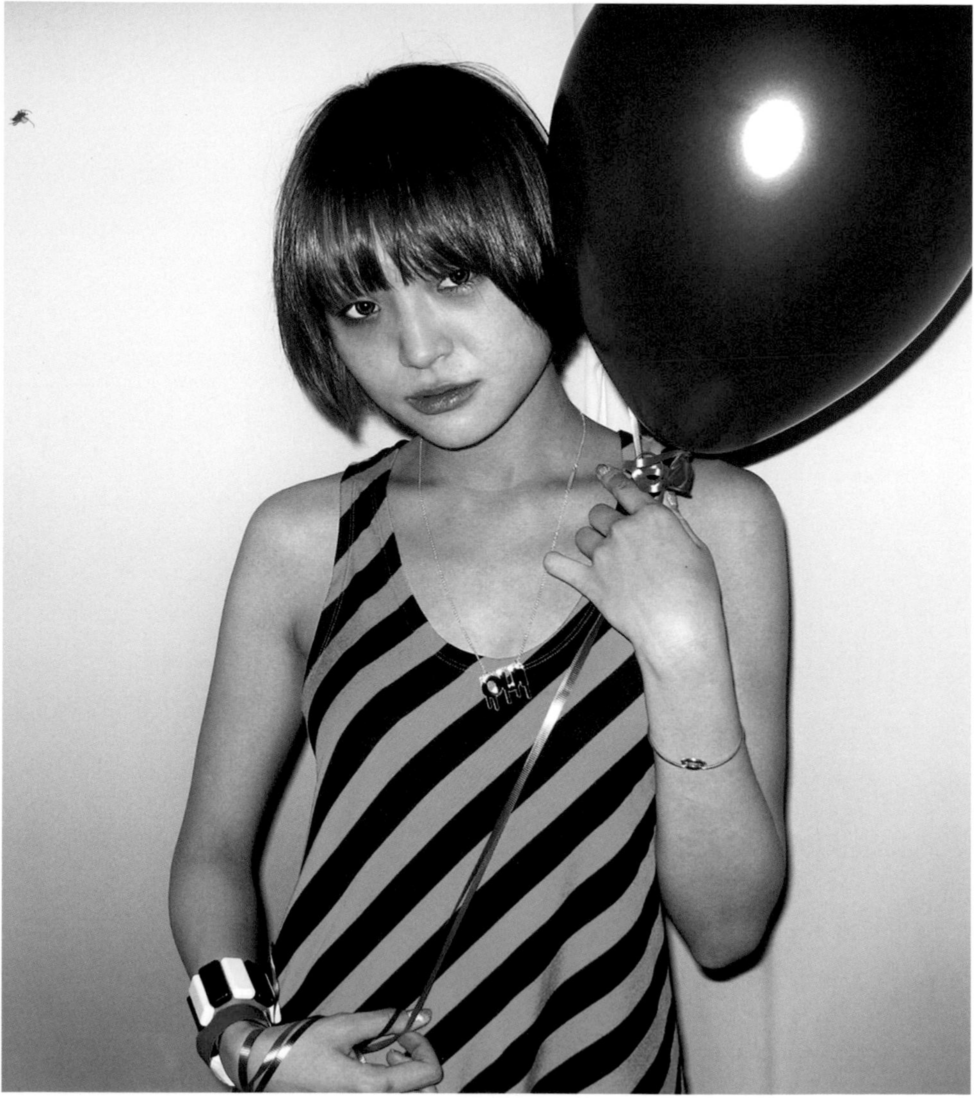

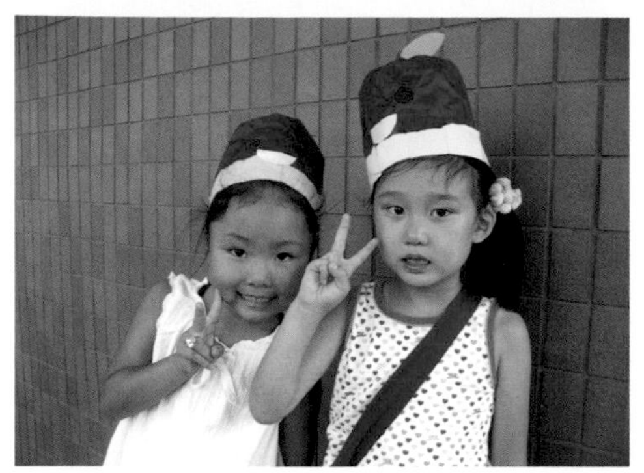

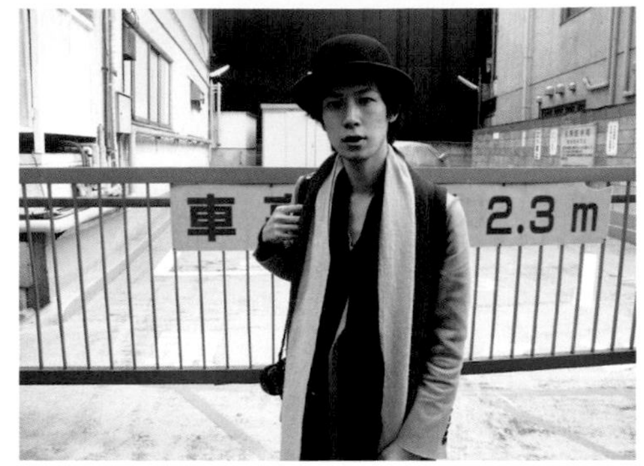
2.3 m

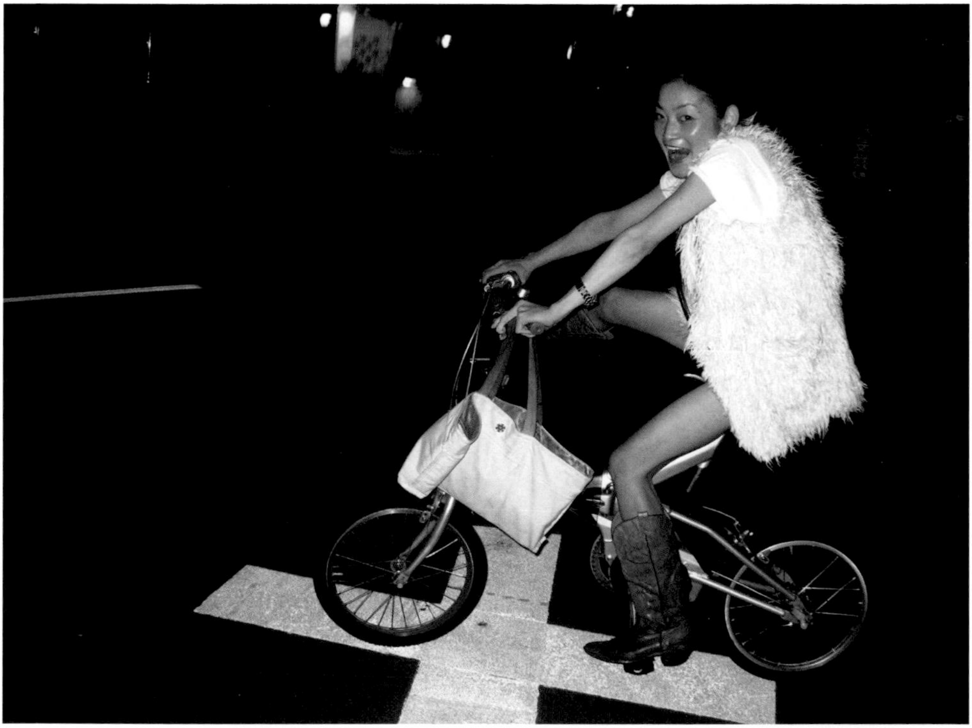

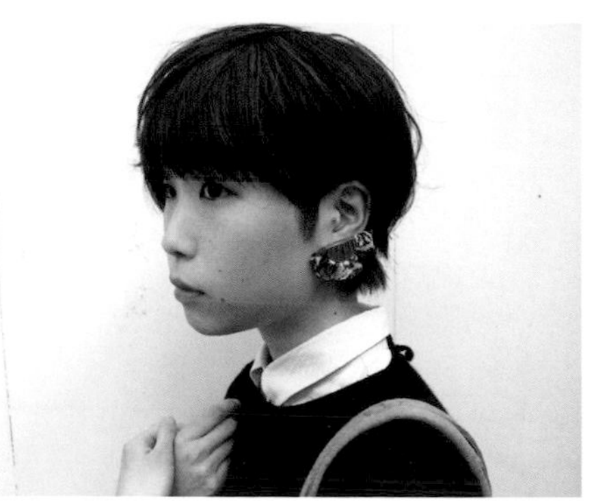

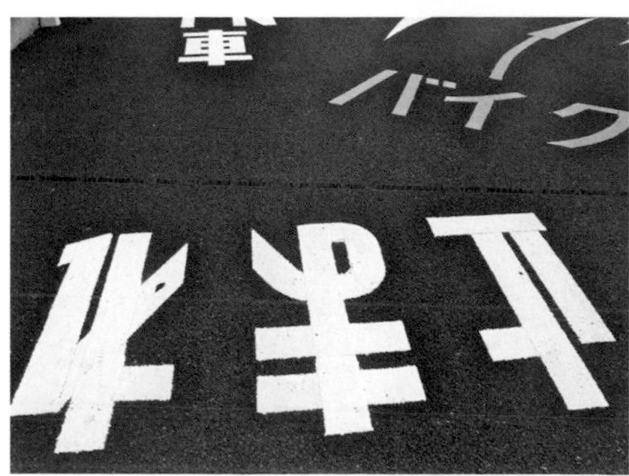

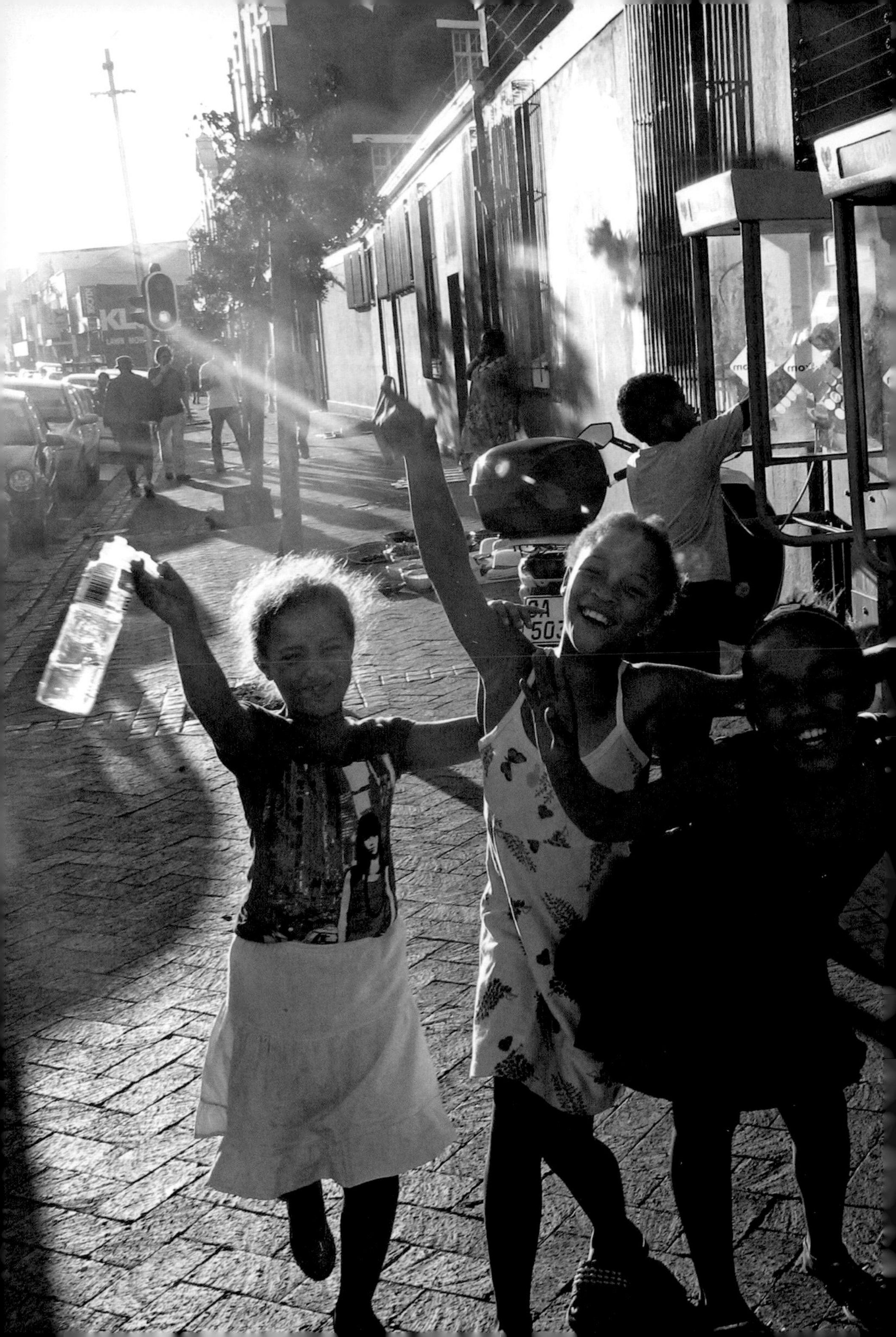

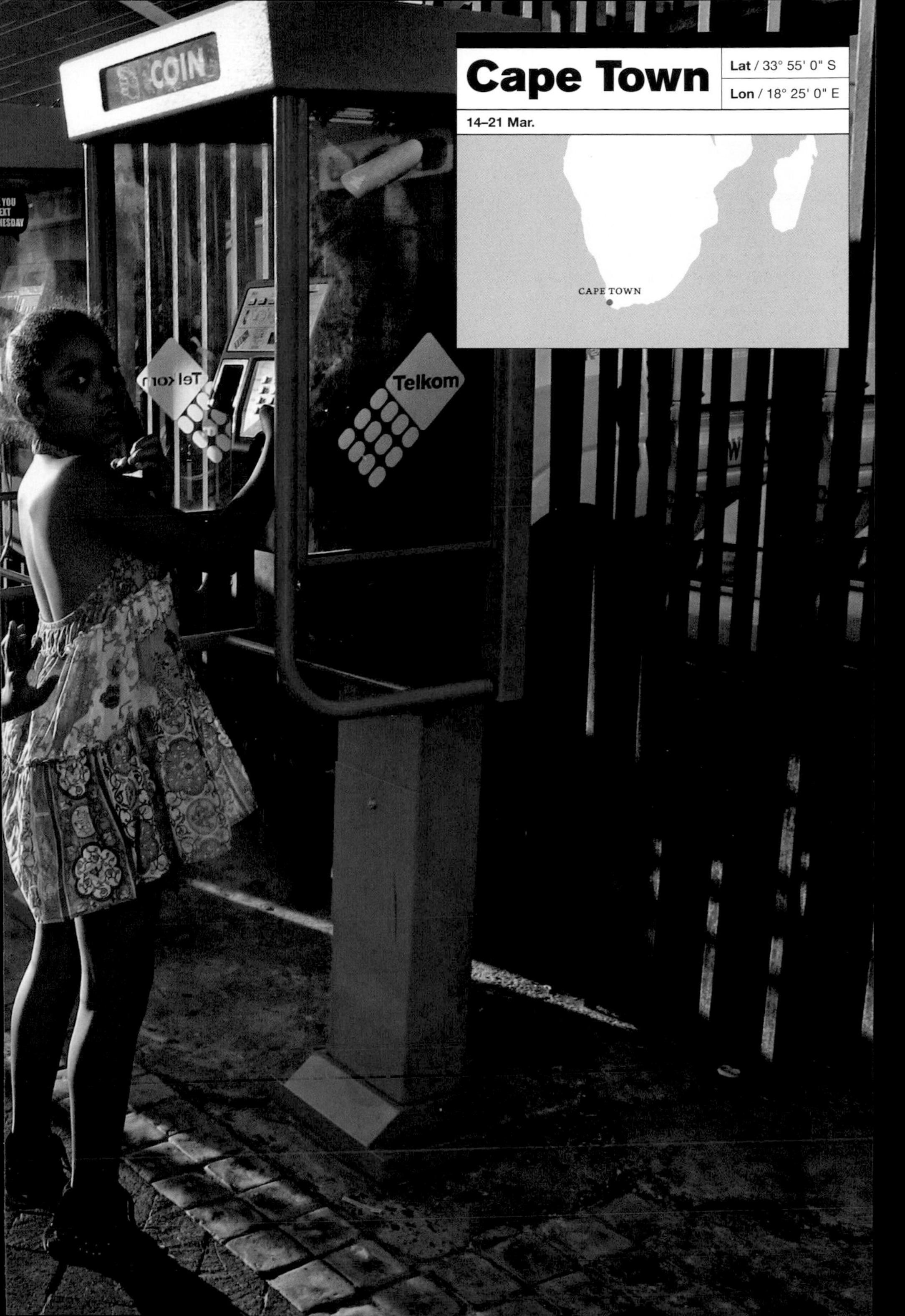

Cape Town

Lat / 33° 55' 0" S

Lon / 18° 25' 0" E

14–21 Mar.

“Cape Town has the most beautiful scenery of any city in the world. It’s surrounded by seven mountains and the ocean, and in some parts of the city it’s easy to forget you’re in a city at all. If you’re looking for fashion inspiration, the younger people in the black communities have a great style all their own, combining traditional African elements, such as printed fabrics and jewelry, with modern European and American fashions. When I visited I went to Mzoli’s in the Gugulethu township (overleaf). It’s a giant street party held by a local butcher shop. Every Sunday wealthy and middle-class people from the city and poor and working-class people from the townships meet to enjoy cold beer and fantastic barbecue. We queued for four hours to buy our meat (by the kilo!) from the barbecue team in a hot, smoky room that looked like Dante’s Inferno, before moving to the dance floor, where you eat with your hands (no cutlery allowed!) while dancing to African electronica. One of my all-time top experiences in Africa.”

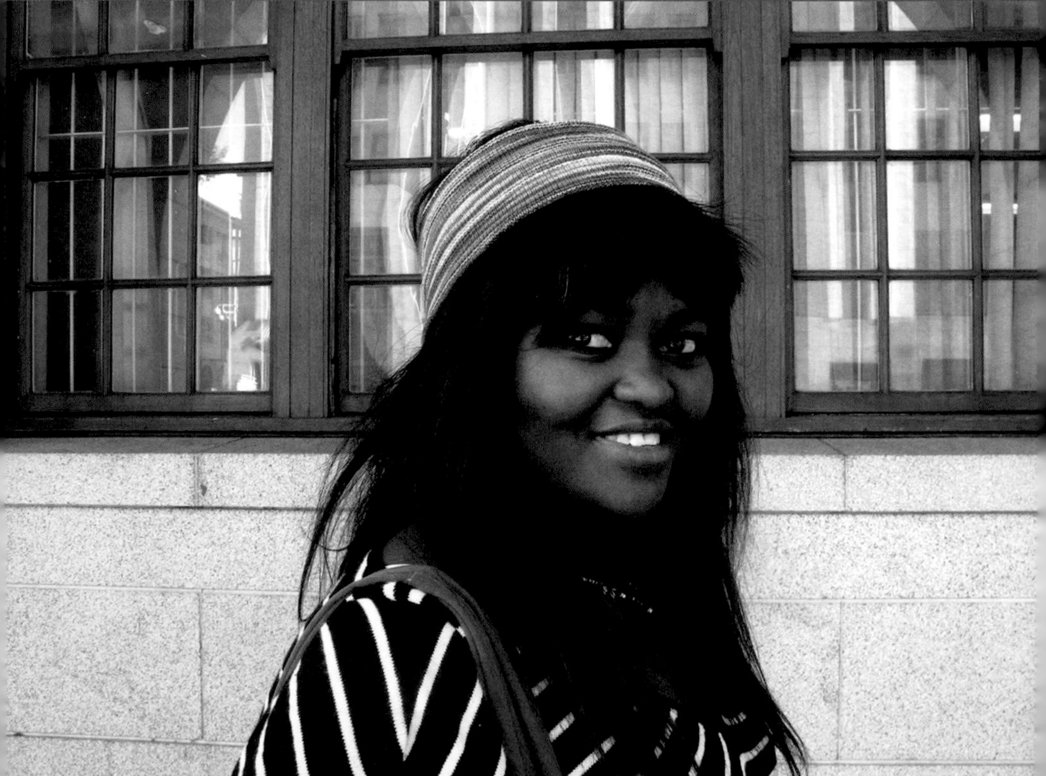

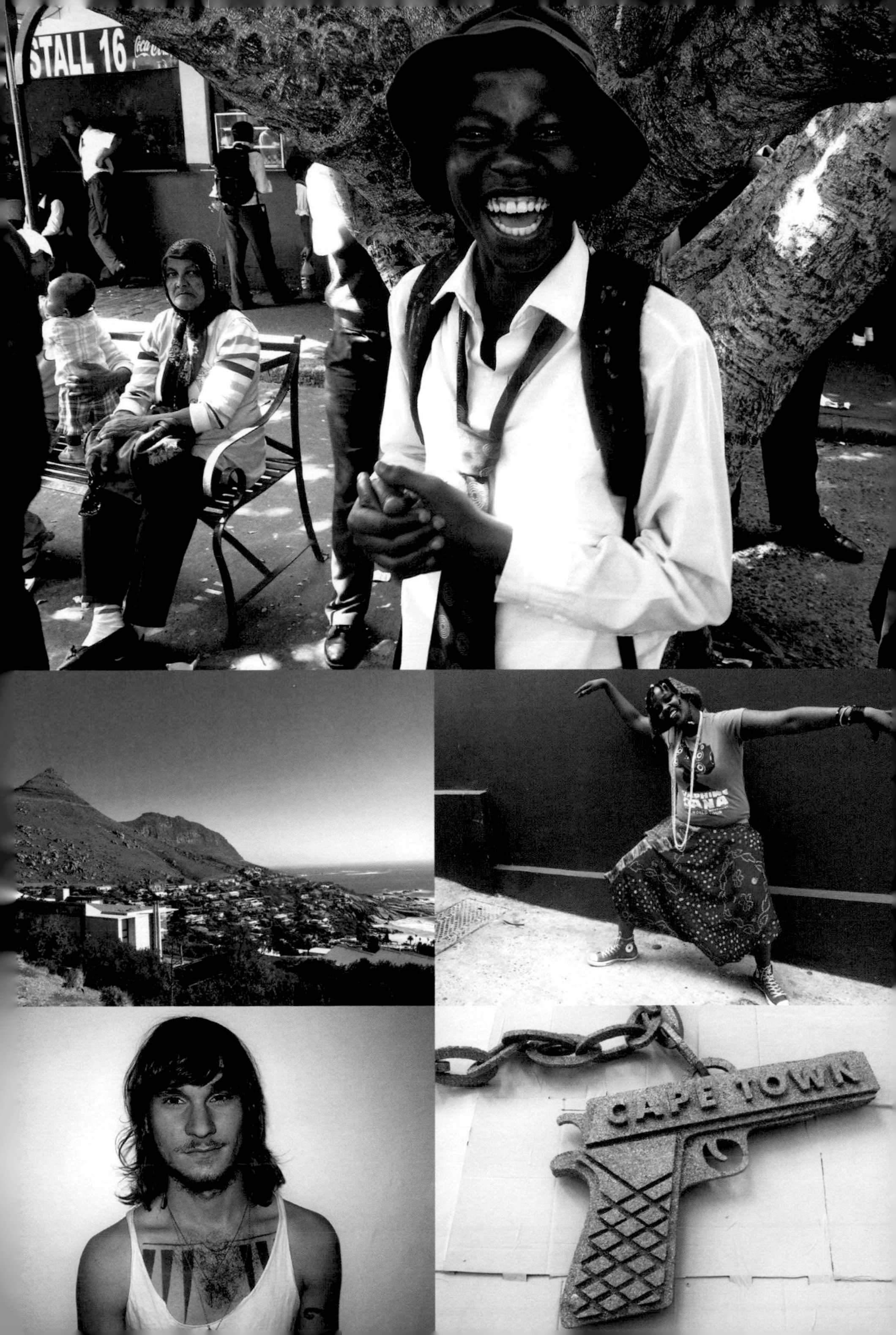
STALL 16
CAPE TOWN

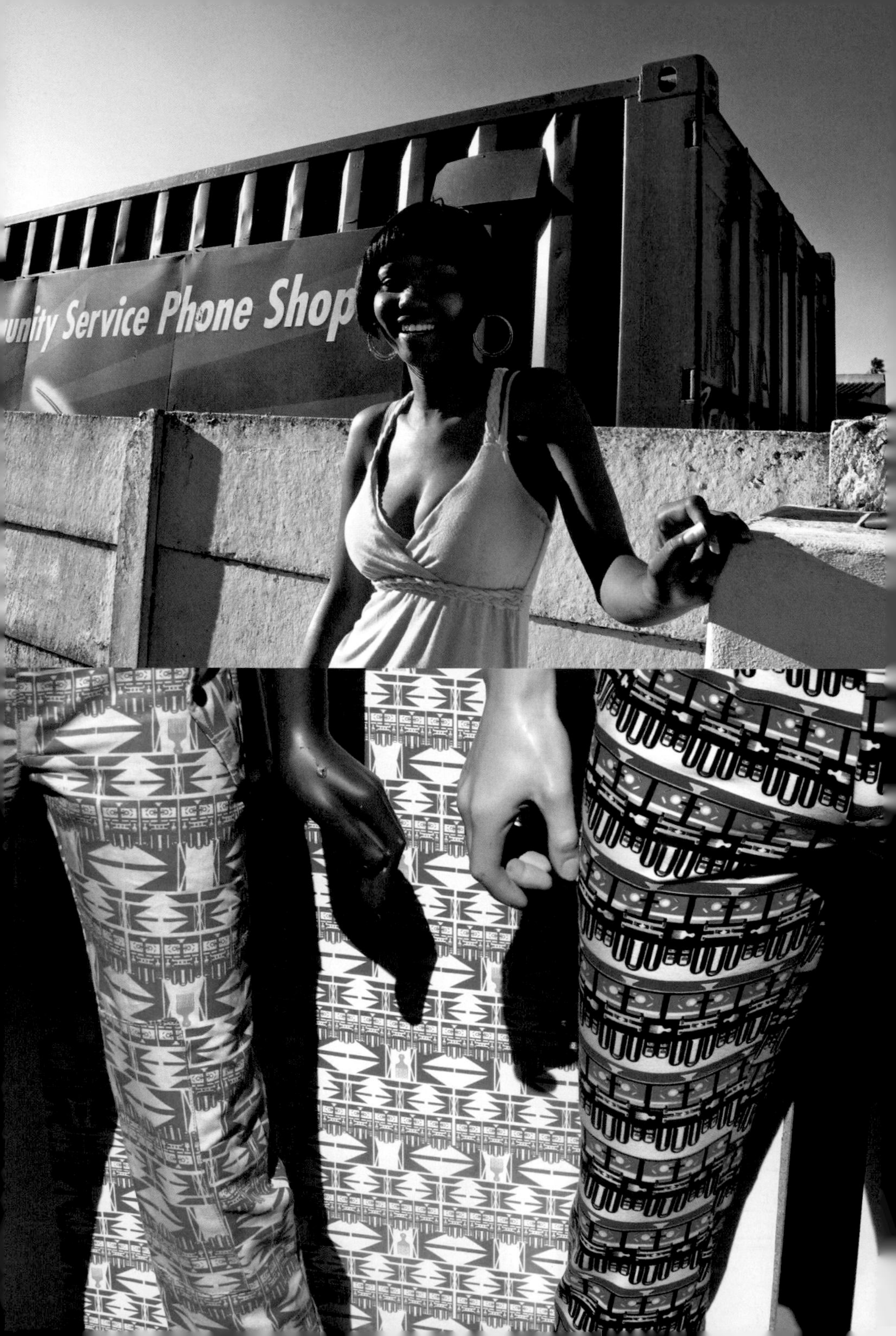
unity Service Phone Shop

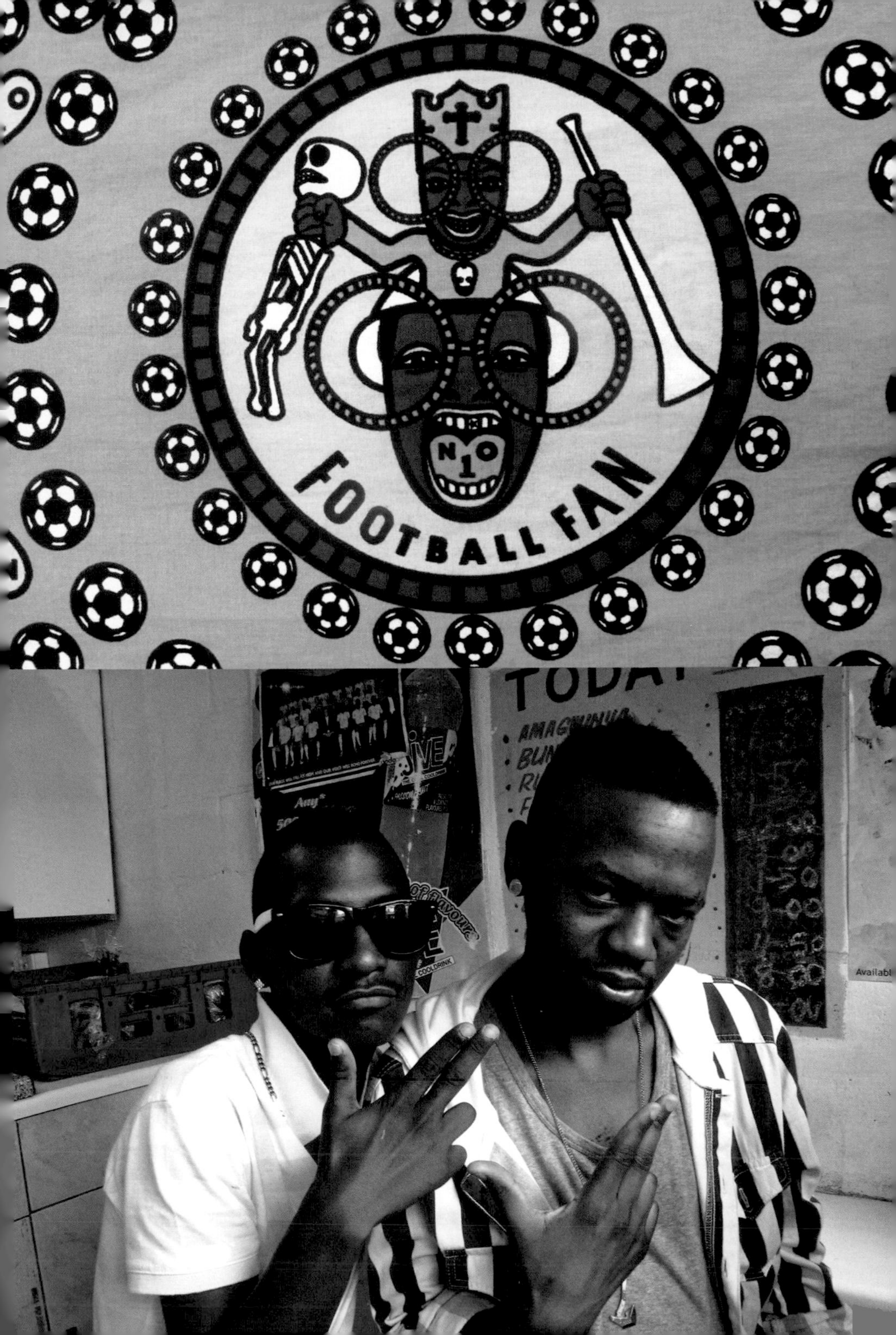
FOOTBALL FAN

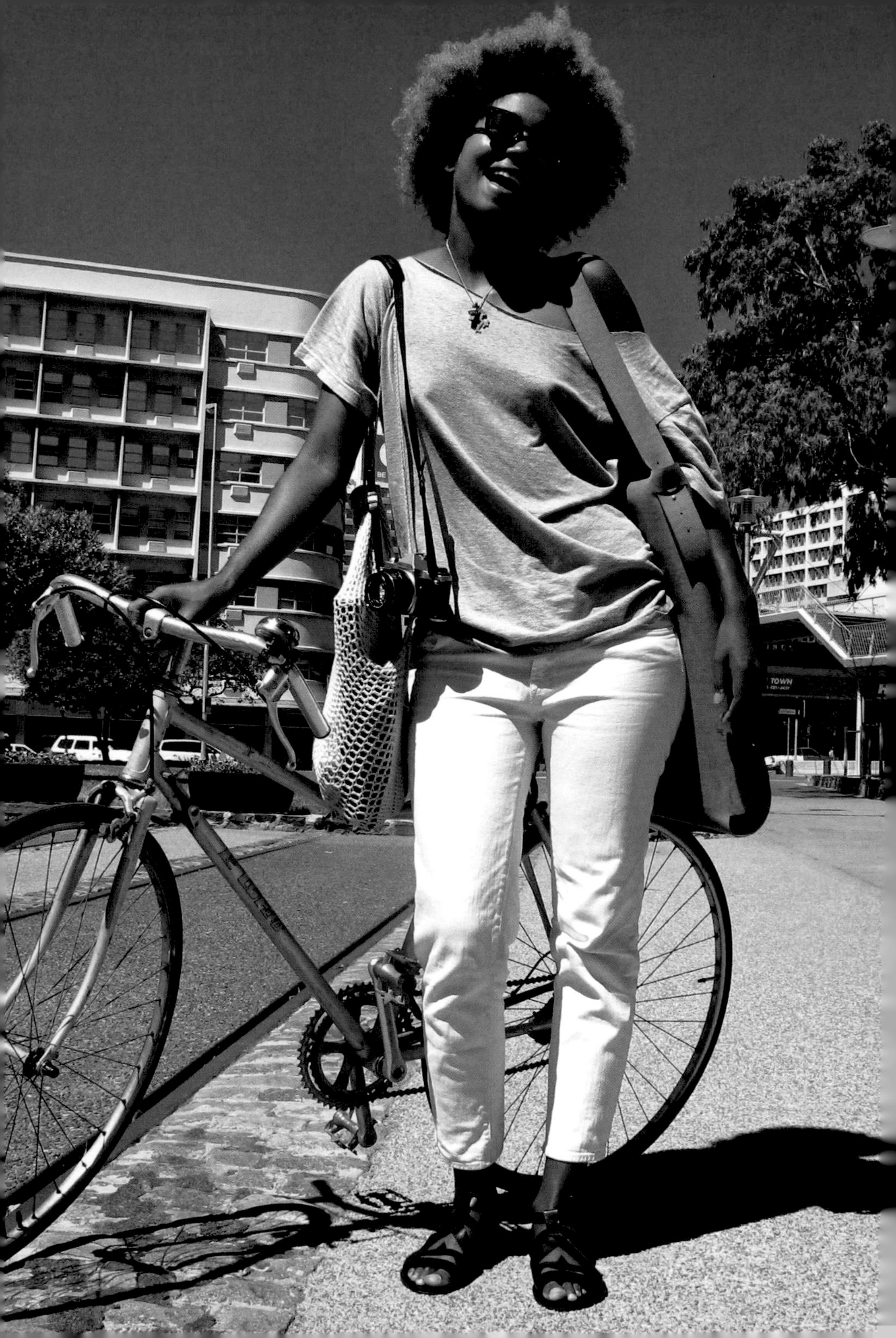
TOWN

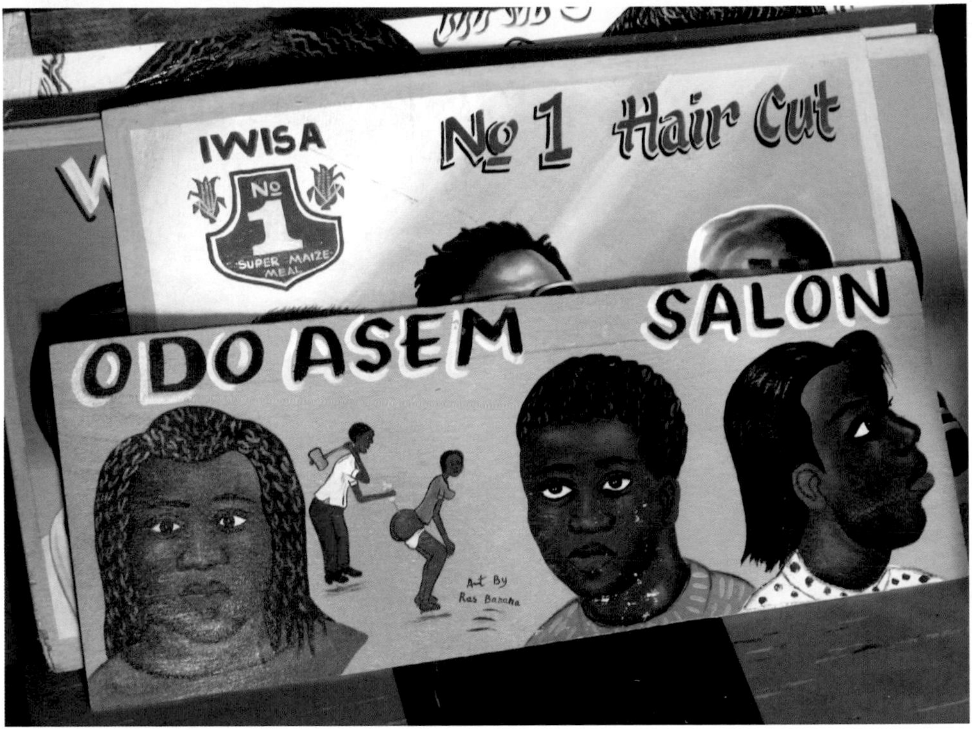
IWISA
No 1
SUPER MAIZE MEAL
No 1 Hair Cut
ODO ASEM SALON
Art By
Ras Banana

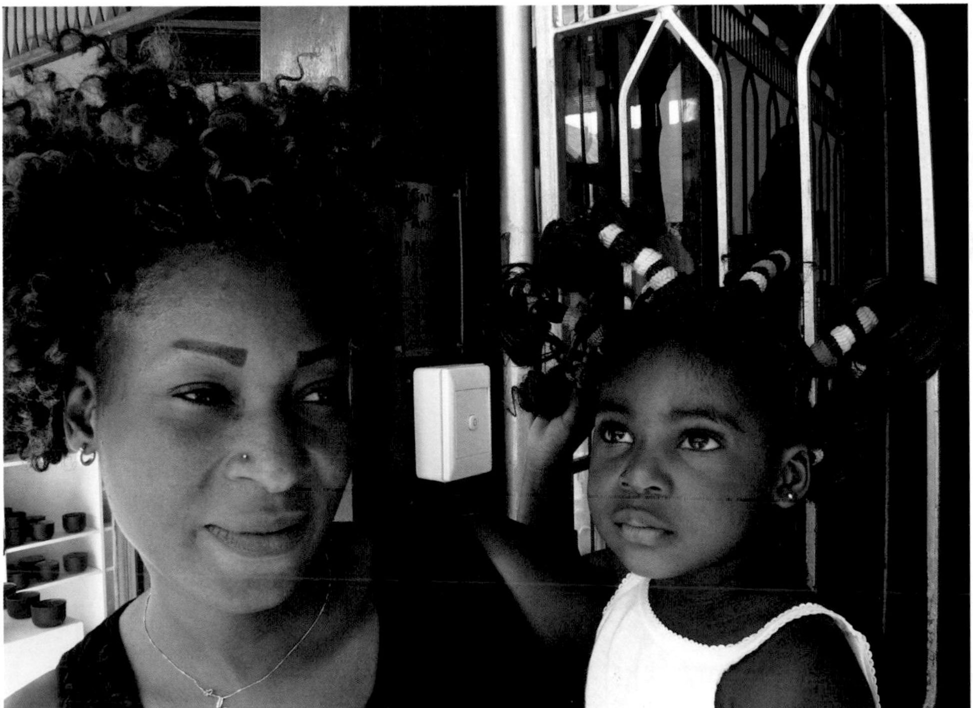

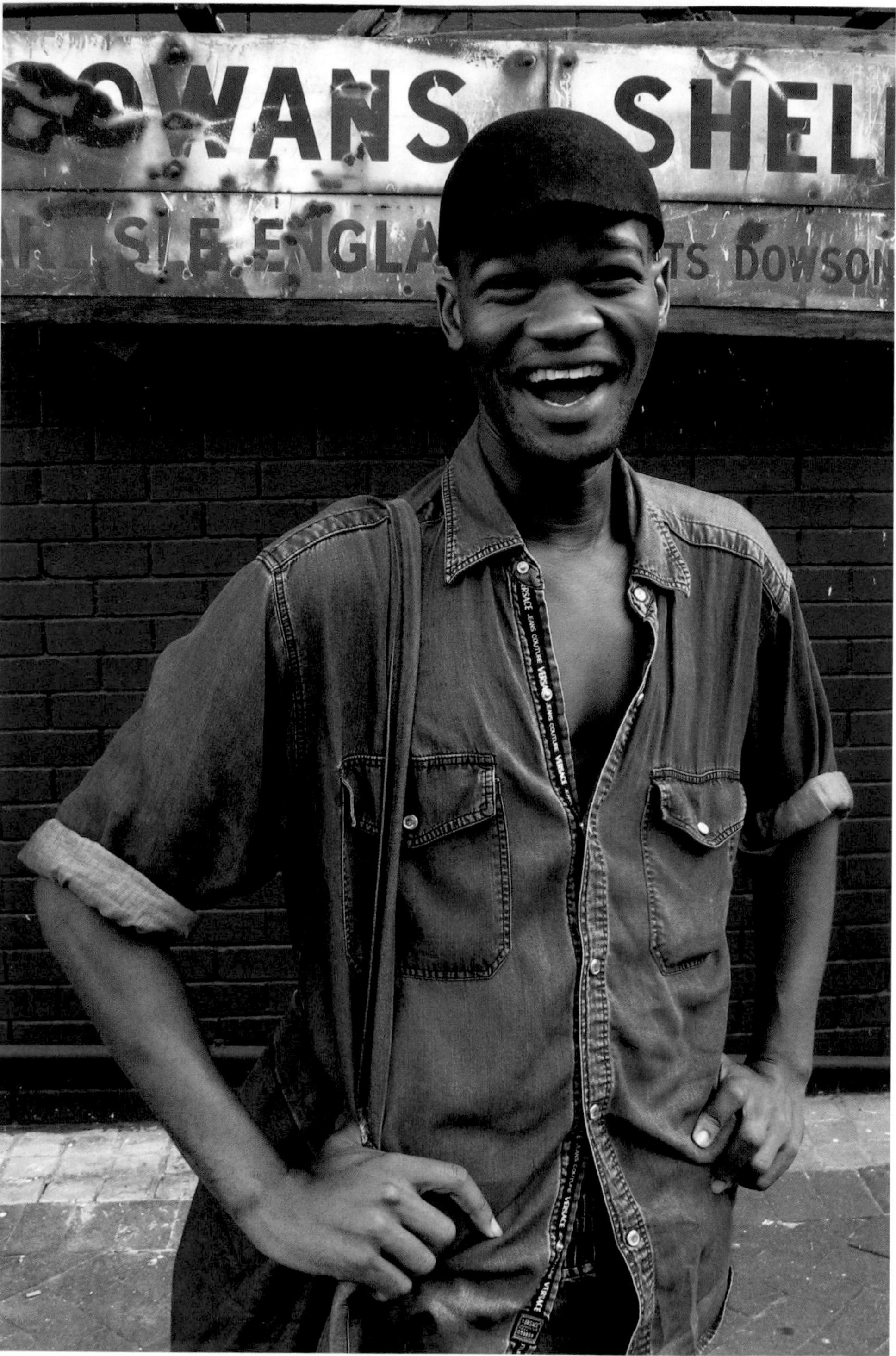
DOWSON
VERSACE JEANS COUTURE

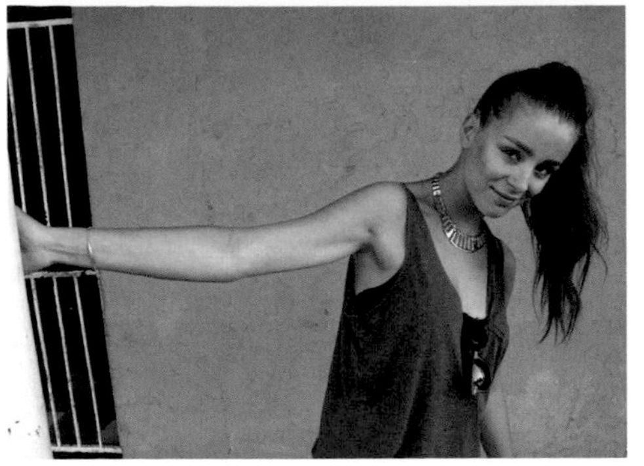

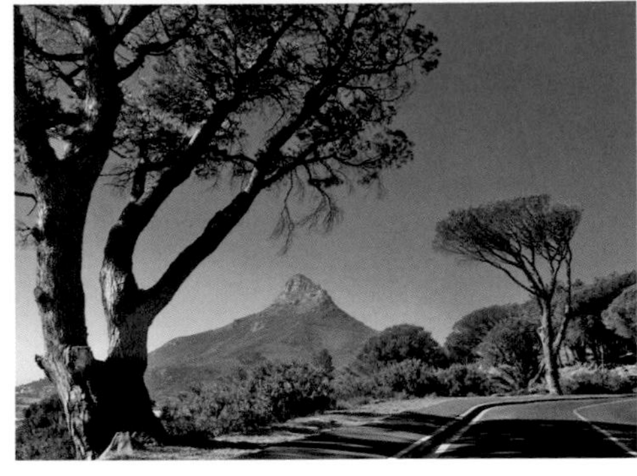

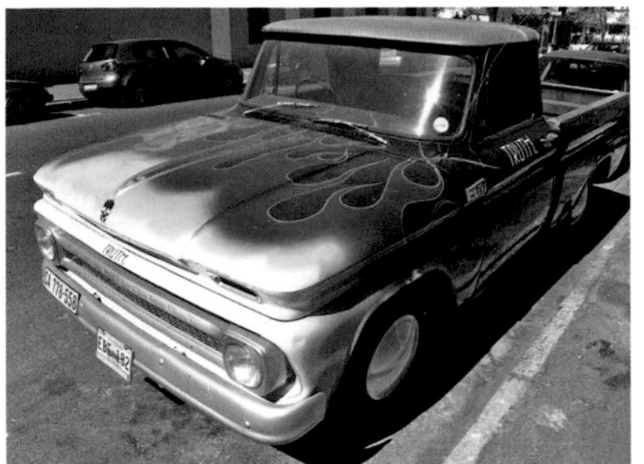

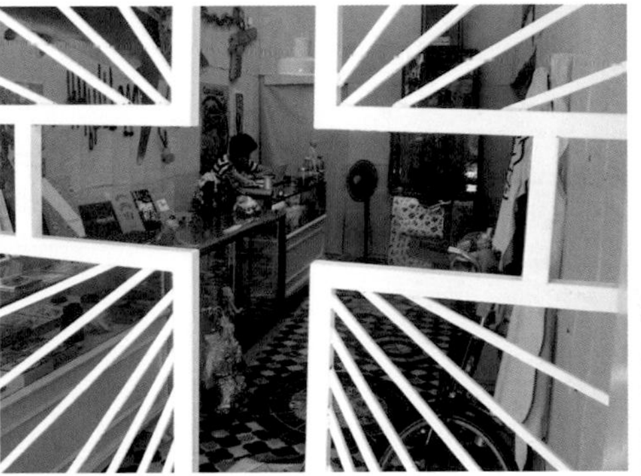

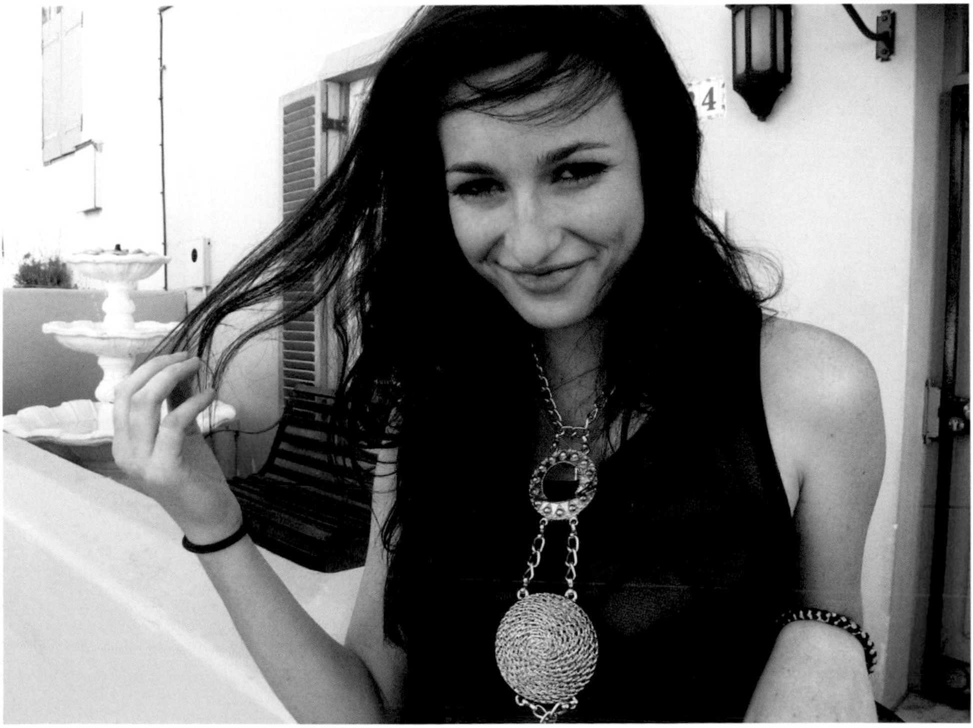

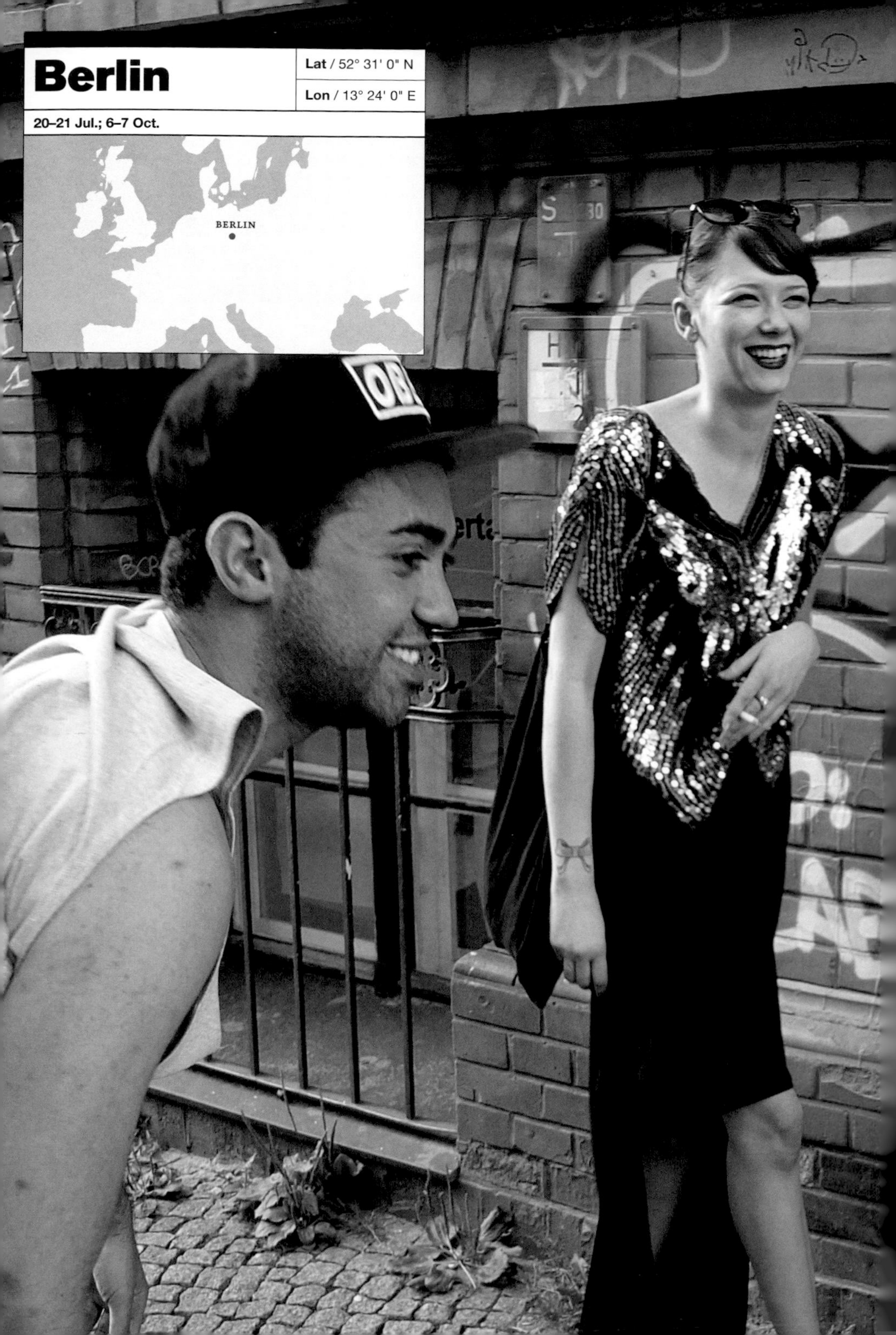

Berlin
Lat / 52° 31' 0" N
Lon / 13° 24' 0" E
20–21 Jul.; 6–7 Oct.
BERLIN

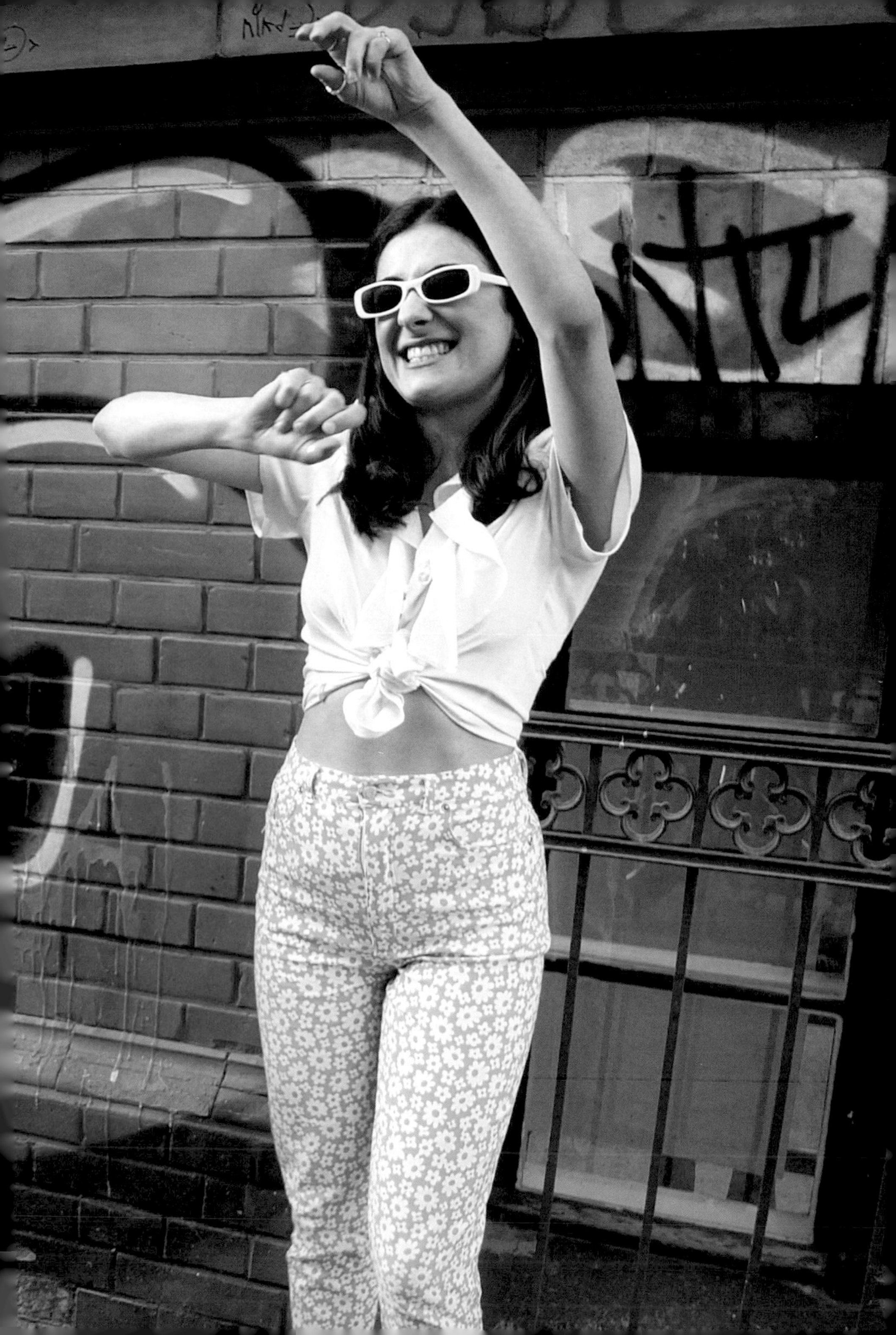

“Berlin is like a big, arty playground. After having been a hyper-tense friction-point for international superpowers during the Second World War and the Cold War, the city finally deserved some fun. Berlin has since become one of the most liberated places in Europe. It seems like there are no limitations of any kind. It’s one of the few places in the world – including New York – where you can really party 24/7. Without the typical quaint, charming old town that you see in almost every other European city, Berlin’s centre feels very exotic to me. It’s an improbable architectural patchwork of 19th-century neoclassicism, 1920s modernism, 1960s Socialist architecture and an unusual amount of unoccupied space. Berlin is also the best place to get my favourite cocktail: the Moscow Mule, which is made out of vodka, ginger beer, lime juice and cucumber. Briefly famous in 1940s Hollywood, for some reason the Moscow Mule has recently made a comeback in Berlin – Europe’s city that never sleeps.”

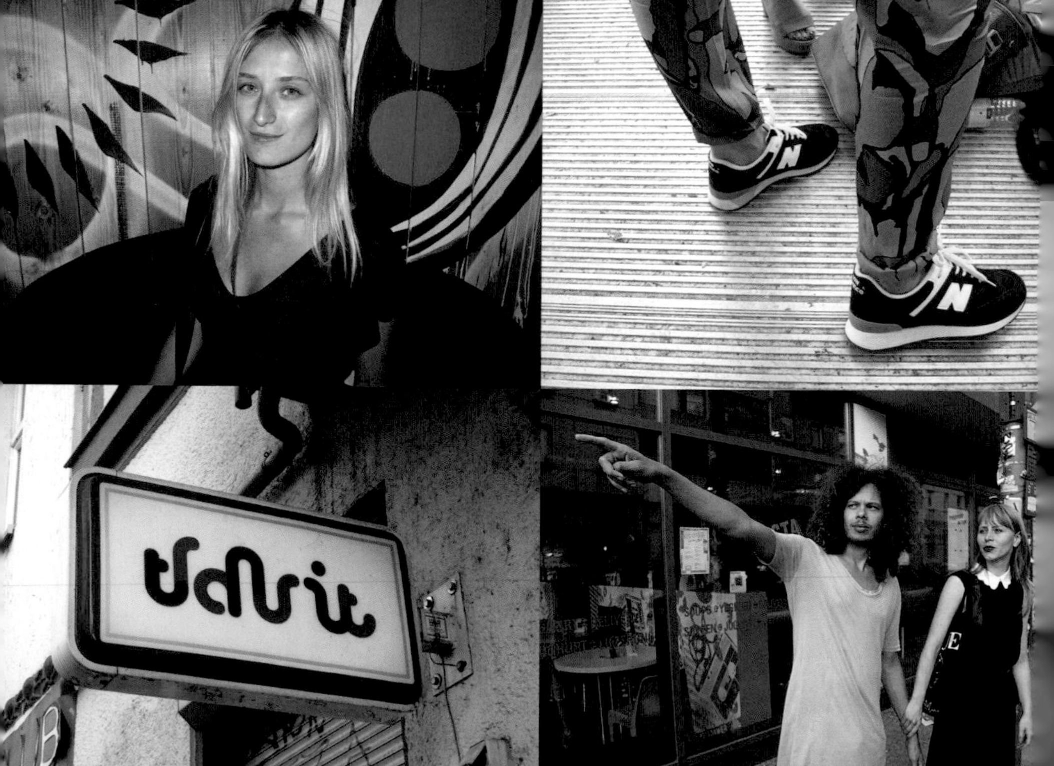

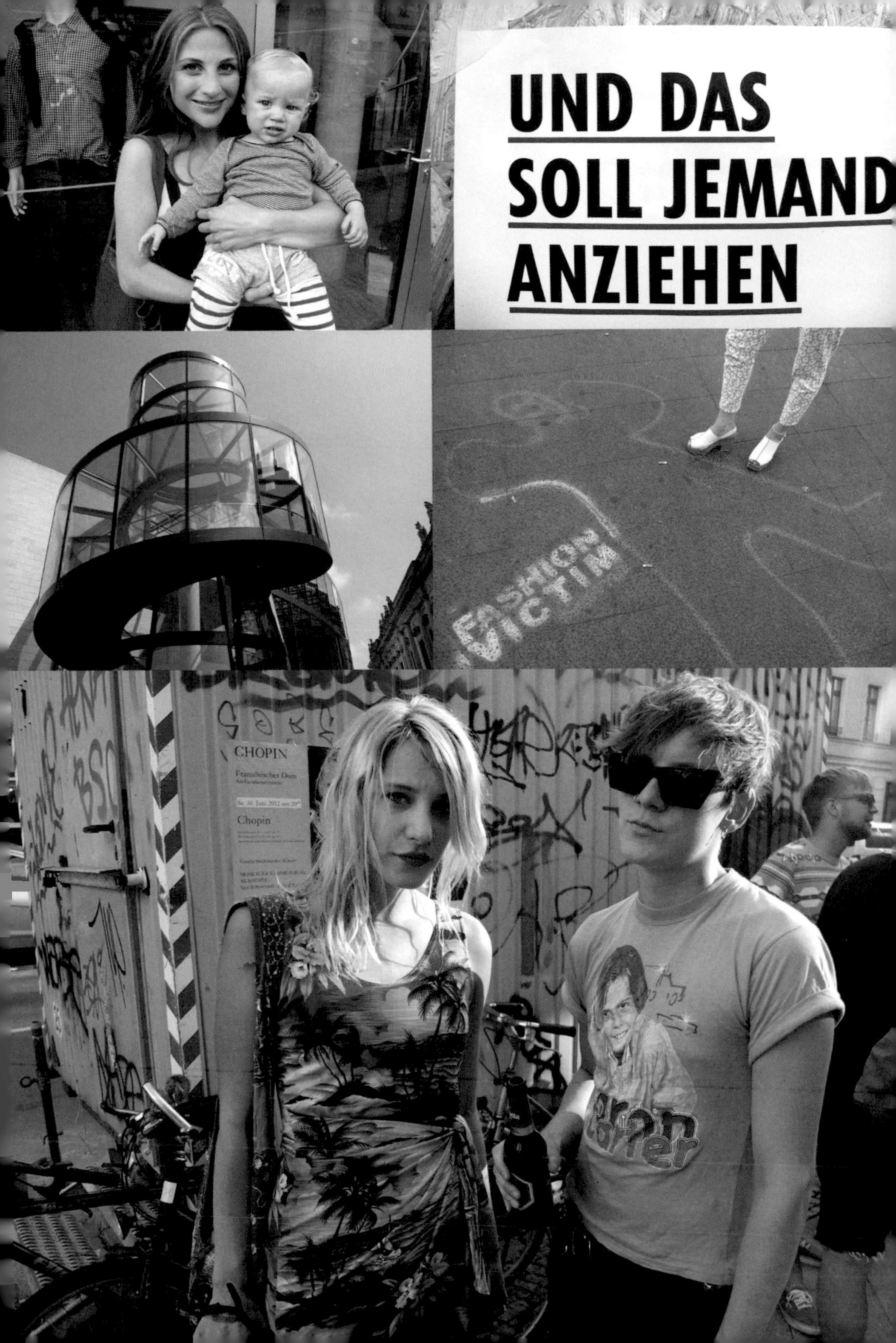
UND DAS
SOLL JEMAND
ANZIEHEN
FASHION VICTIM
CHOPIN
Französischer Dom
Chopin

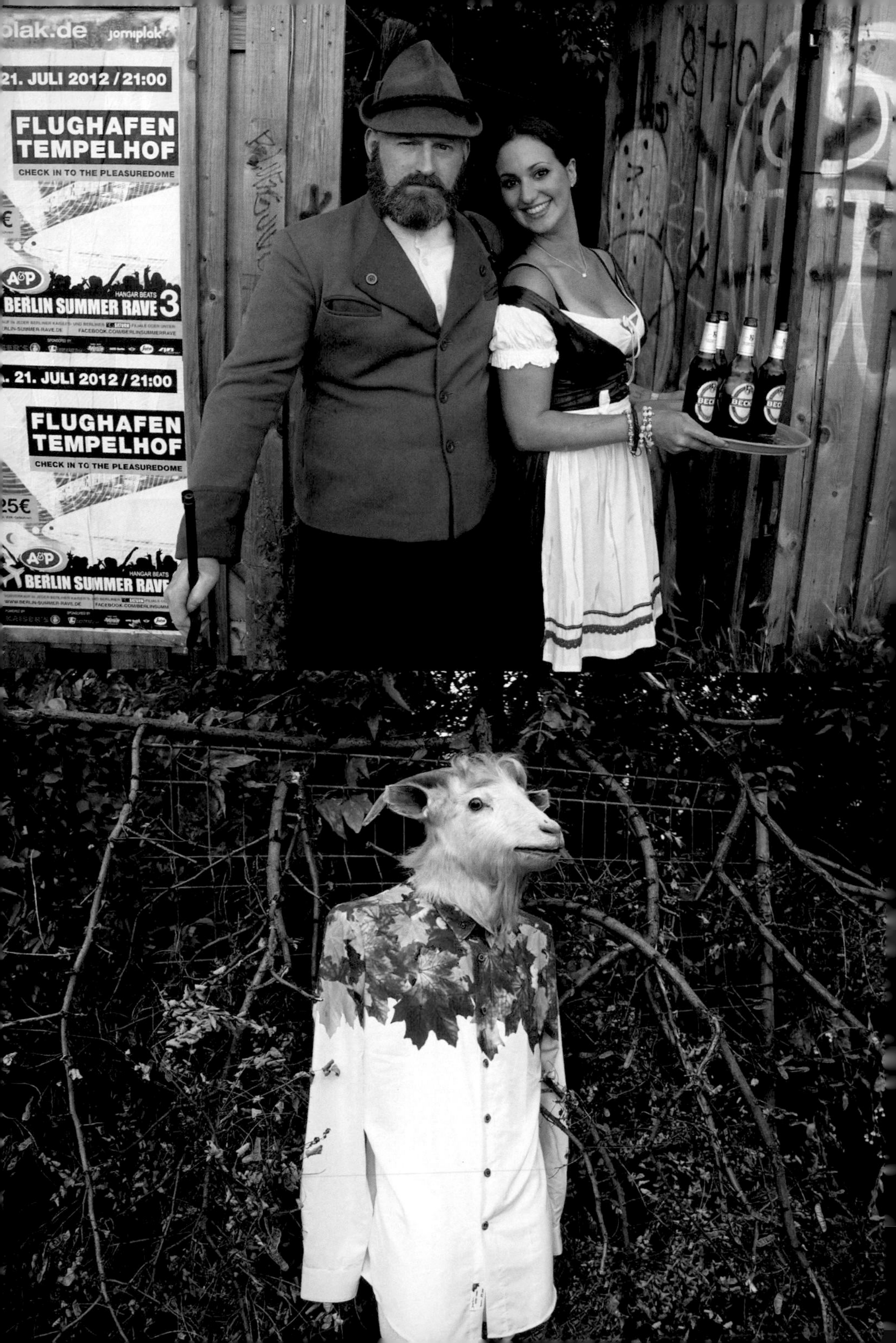

jomiplak
21. JULI 2012 / 21:00
FLUGHAFEN
TEMPELHOF
CHECK IN TO THE PLEASUREDOME
A&P
HANGAR BEATS
BERLIN SUMMER RAVE 3
FACEBOOK.COM/BERLINSUMMERRAVE
21. JULI 2012 / 21:00
FLUGHAFEN
TEMPELHOF
CHECK IN TO THE PLEASUREDOME
25€
A&P
HANGAR BEATS
BERLIN SUMMER RAVE

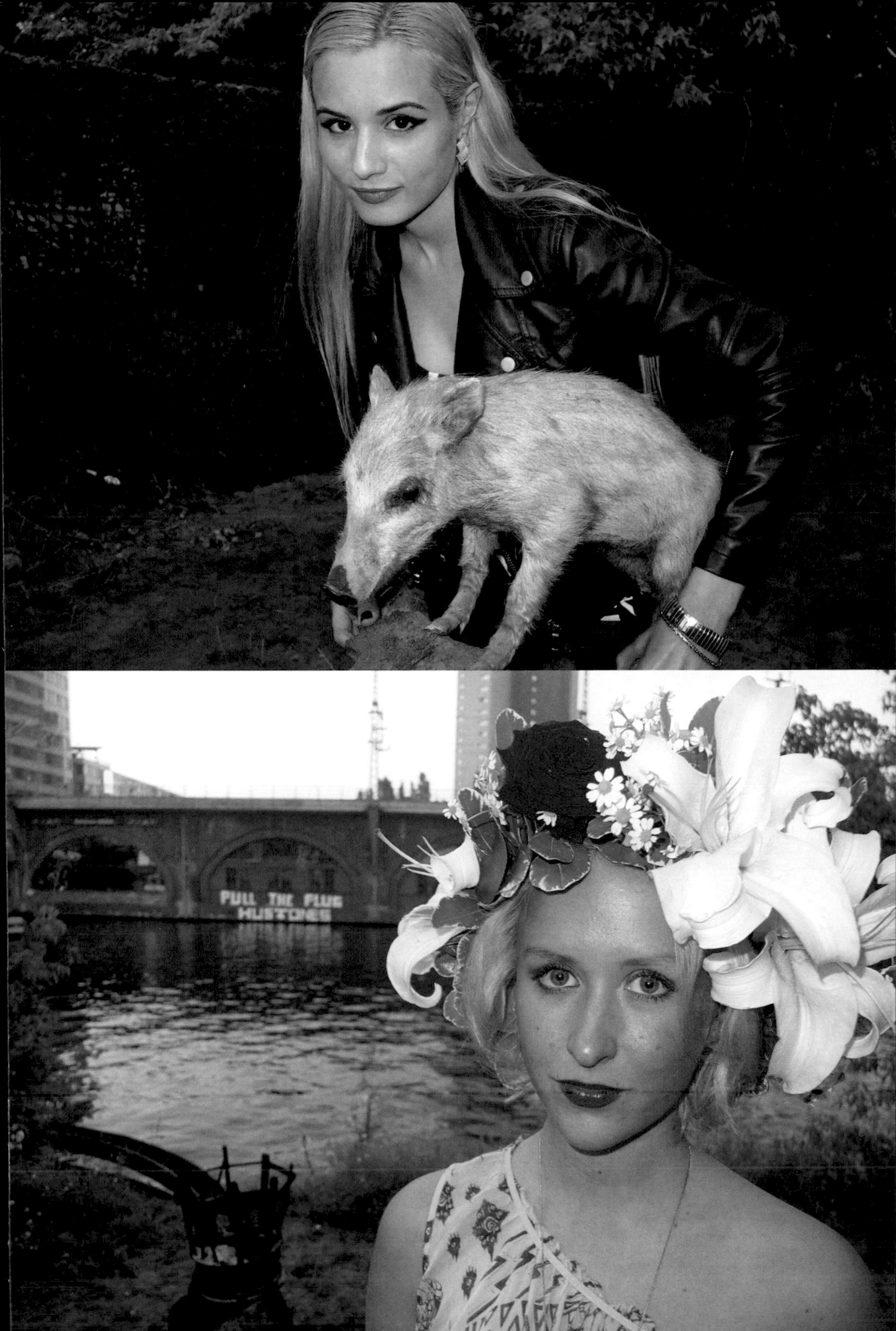
PULL THE PLUG

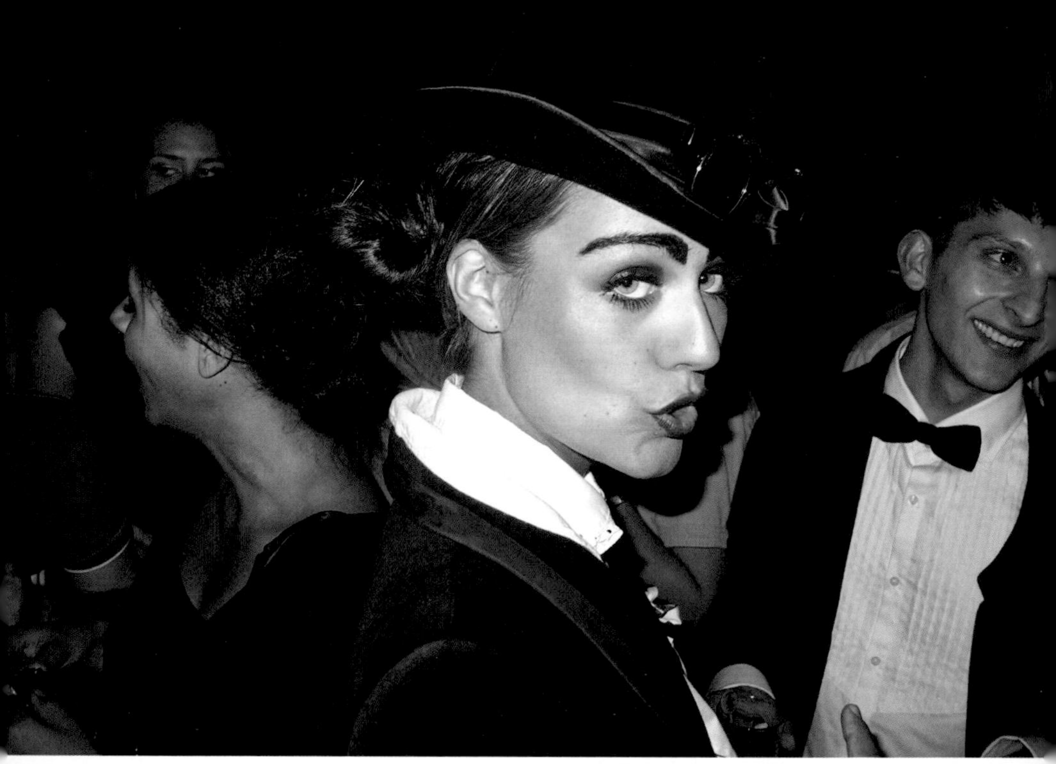

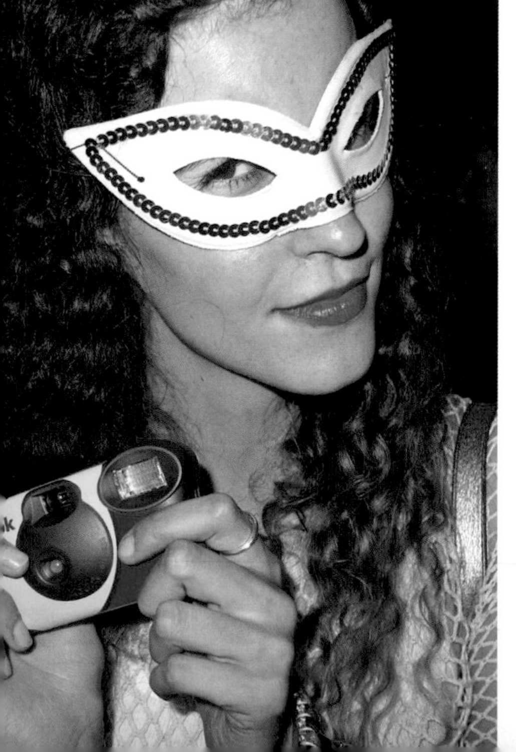

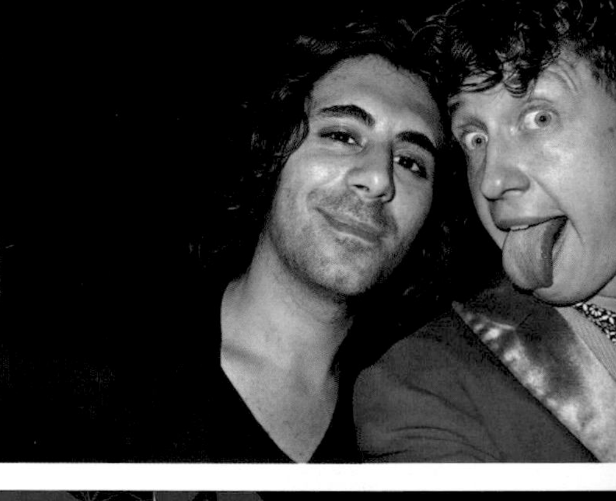

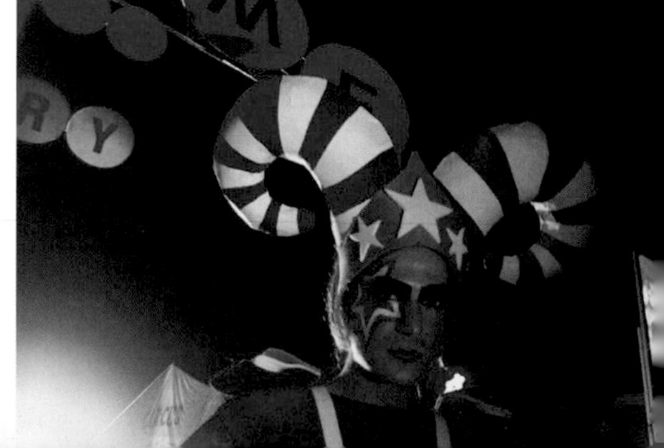

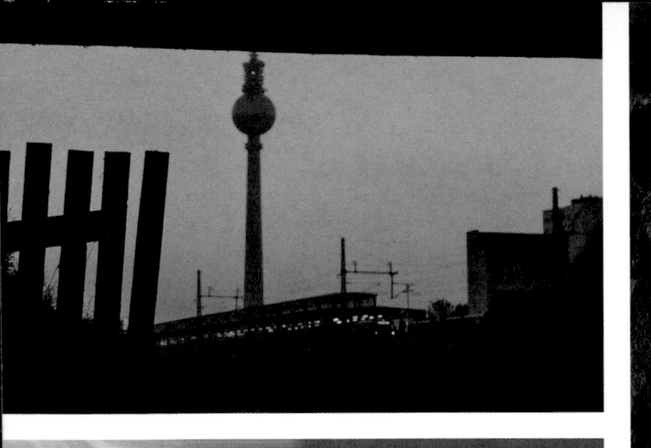

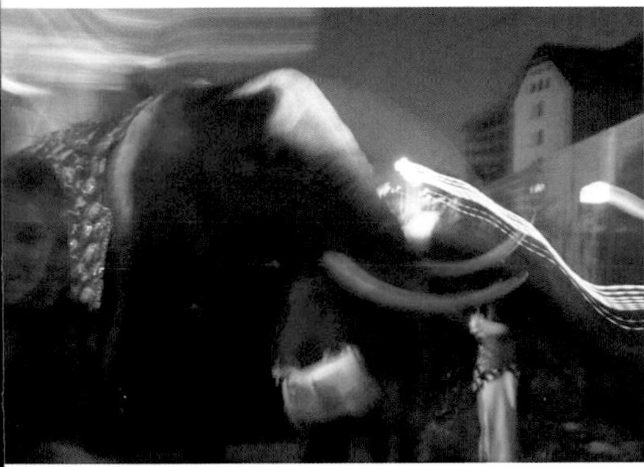

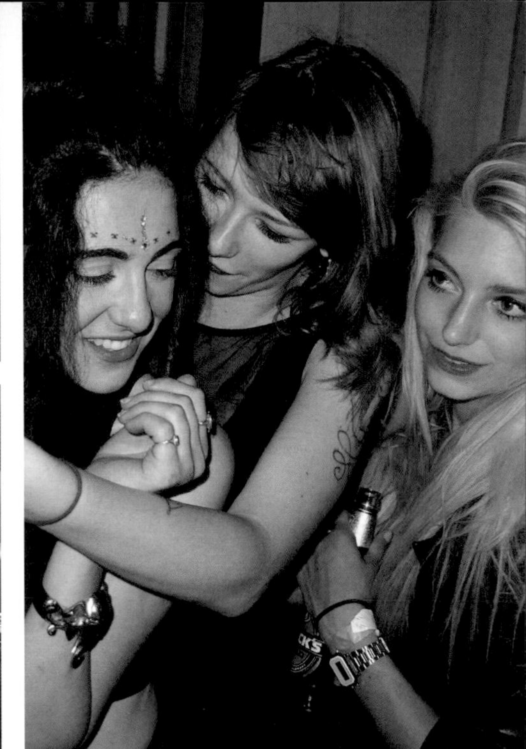

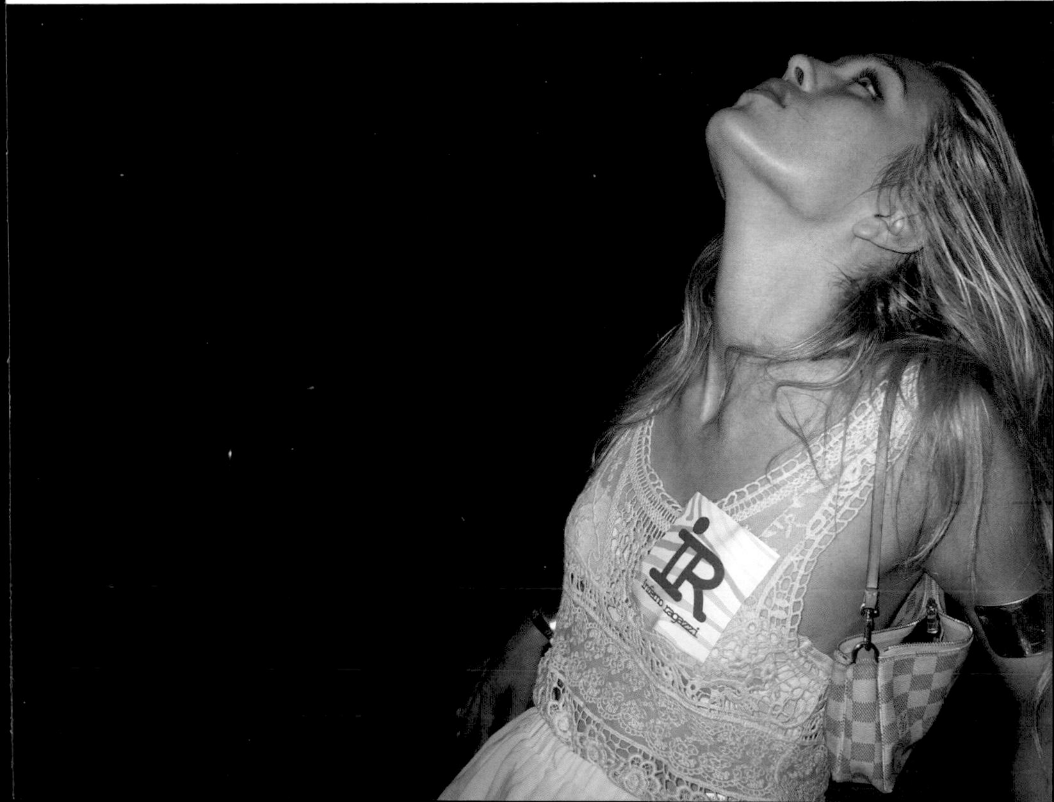

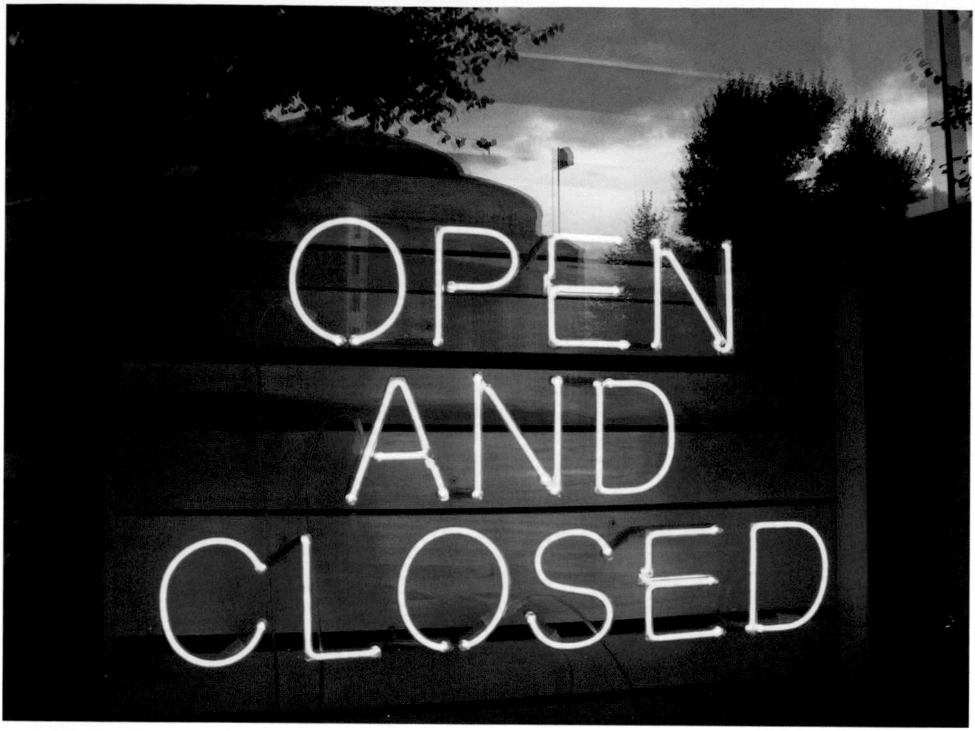
OPEN
AND
CLOSED

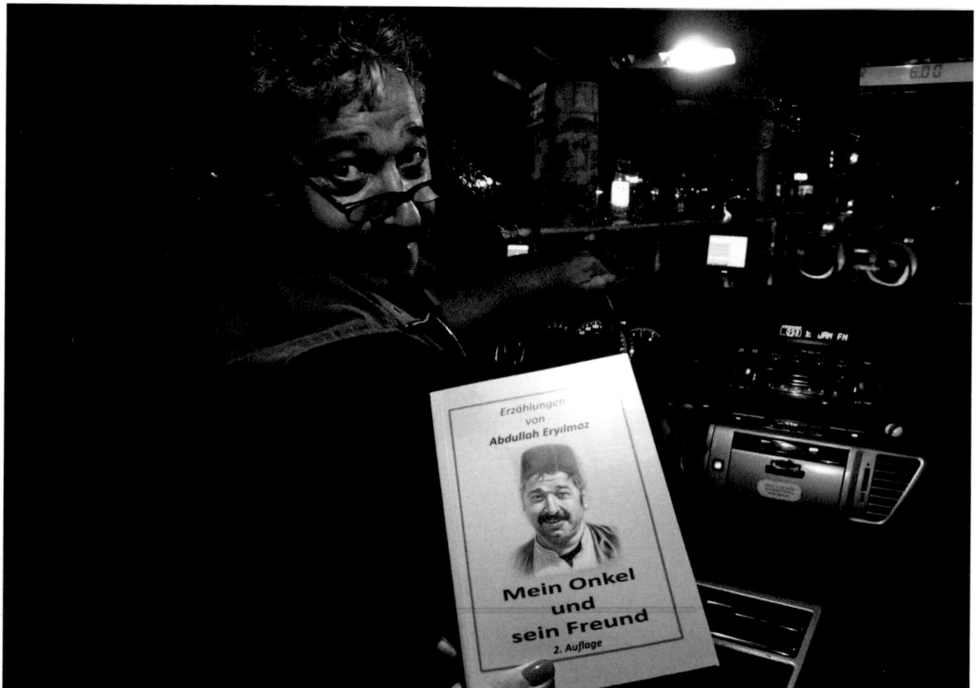
Erzählungen
von
Abdullah Eryılmaz
Mein Onkel
und
sein Freund
2. Auflage

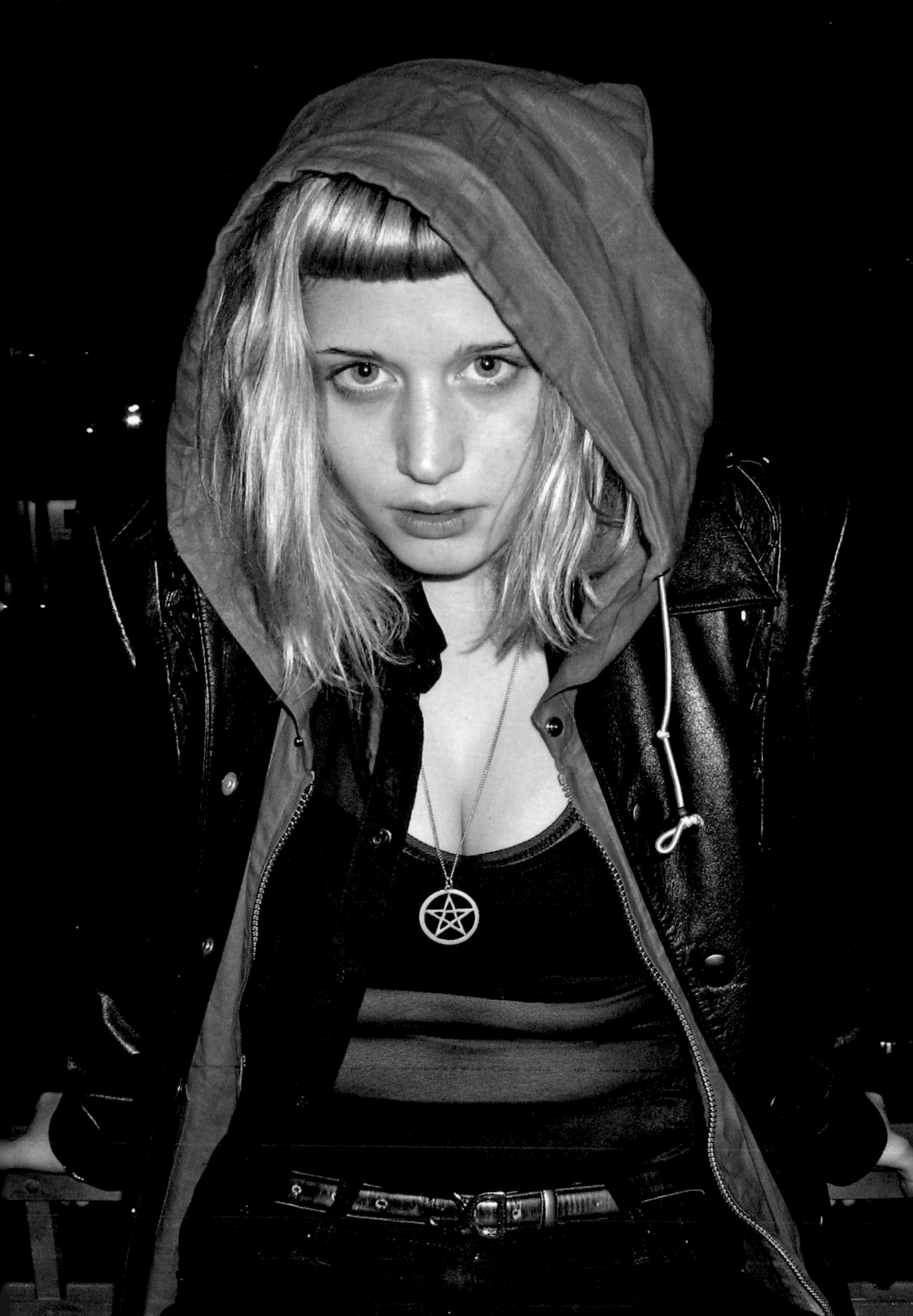

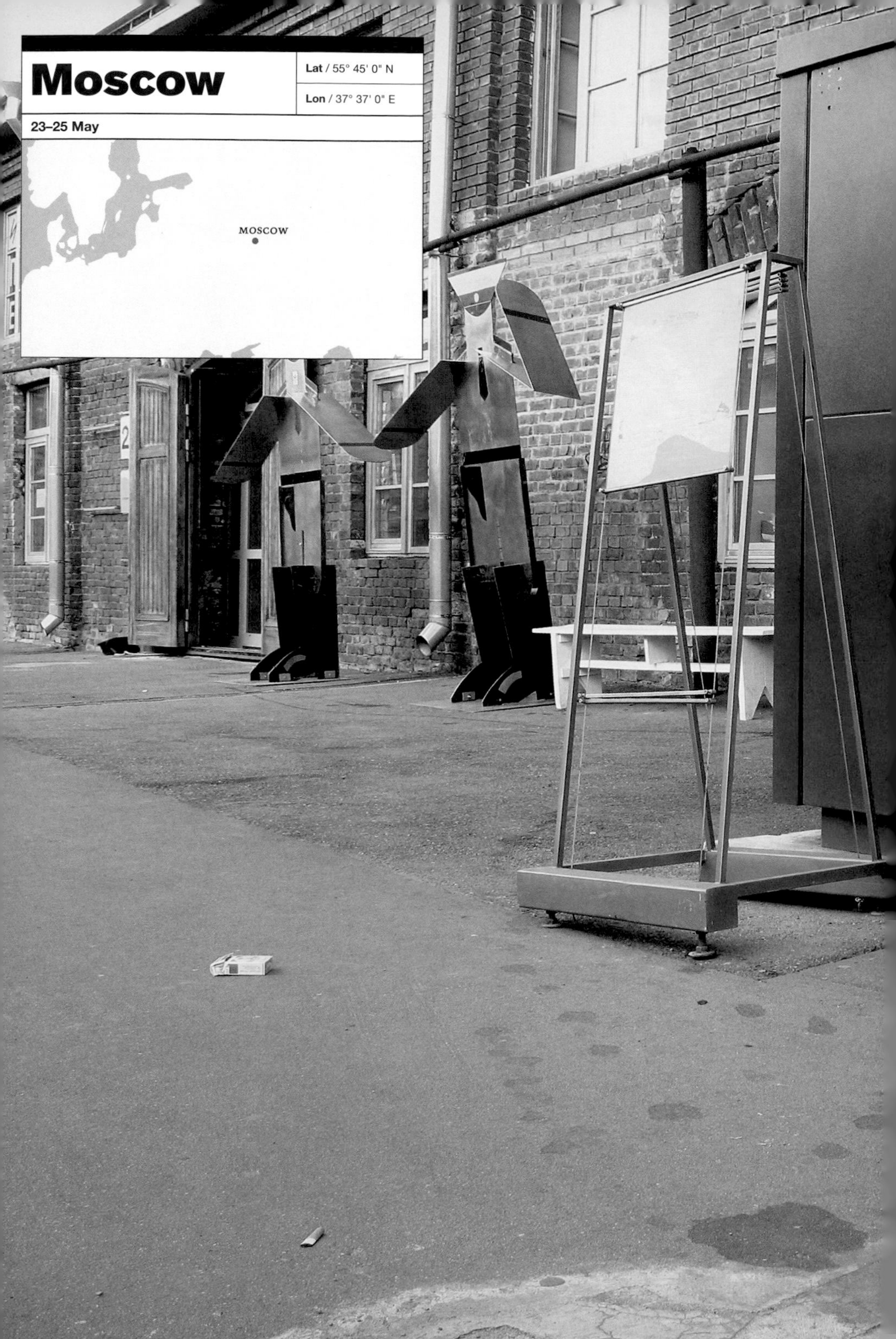
Moscow
Lat / 55° 45' 0" N
Lon / 37° 37' 0" E
23–25 May
MOSCOW

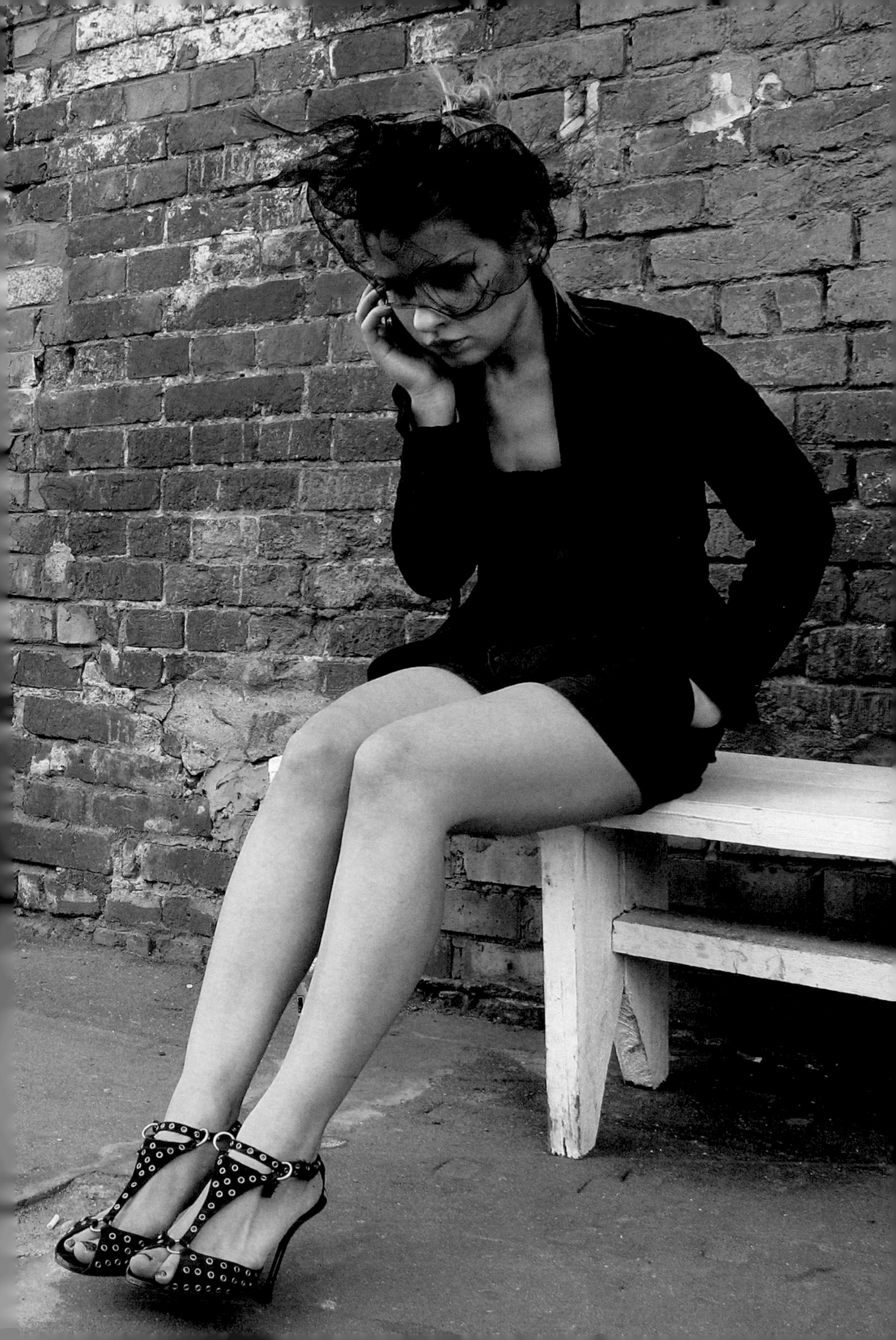

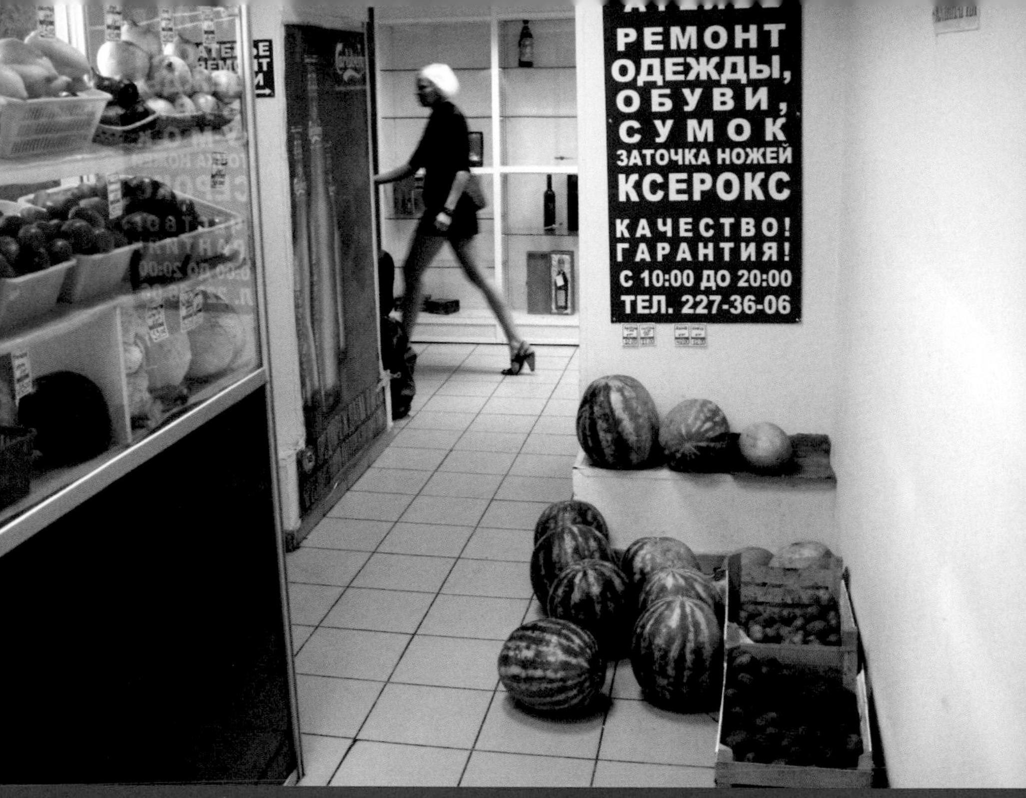

“I had heard so many scary stories about Moscow that I'm ashamed to say I was pretty nervous about visiting for the first time. So it was a pleasant surprise to find a certain normality there – and incredibly warm hospitality – but a certain madness as well. On my first night in Moscow, we went to an underground beach party in the basement of a shut-down restaurant. It was dark and rainy outside, but inside they'd trucked in tonnes of sand, inflatable pools and fresh fruit. The energy and atmosphere was amazing and people were getting pretty wild – in Moscow there is definitely the mentality that you party like there's no tomorrow. The city has an incredible night-time culture: lots of nightclubs and 24-hour restaurants. Fashion shops usually stay open until midnight and grocery superstores are open 24/7. It's perfect for me because I'm someone who likes to go to bed late and go to a restaurant if I'm hungry at 3 AM. Moscow is a city of extremes: some of the worst traffic in the world, despite the gigantic ten-lane avenues; a combination of stunningly beautiful and stunningly horrible architecture; frigid Arctic winters and sweltering hot summers and more billionaires per capita than any other city I know of. People think of Russian style as ostentatious and glamorous, but the people I met in Moscow were cool and edgy in a more subtle and refined way.”

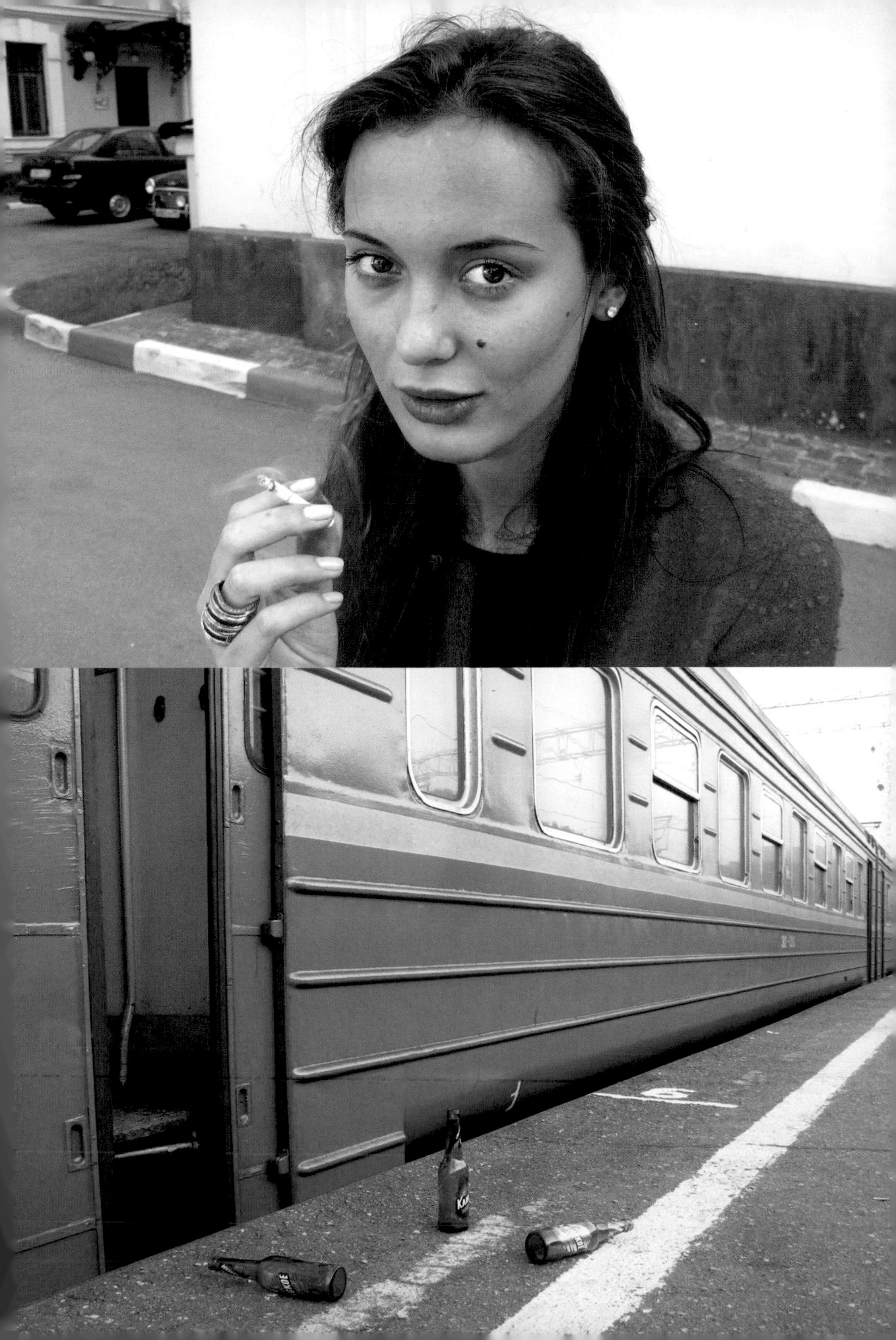

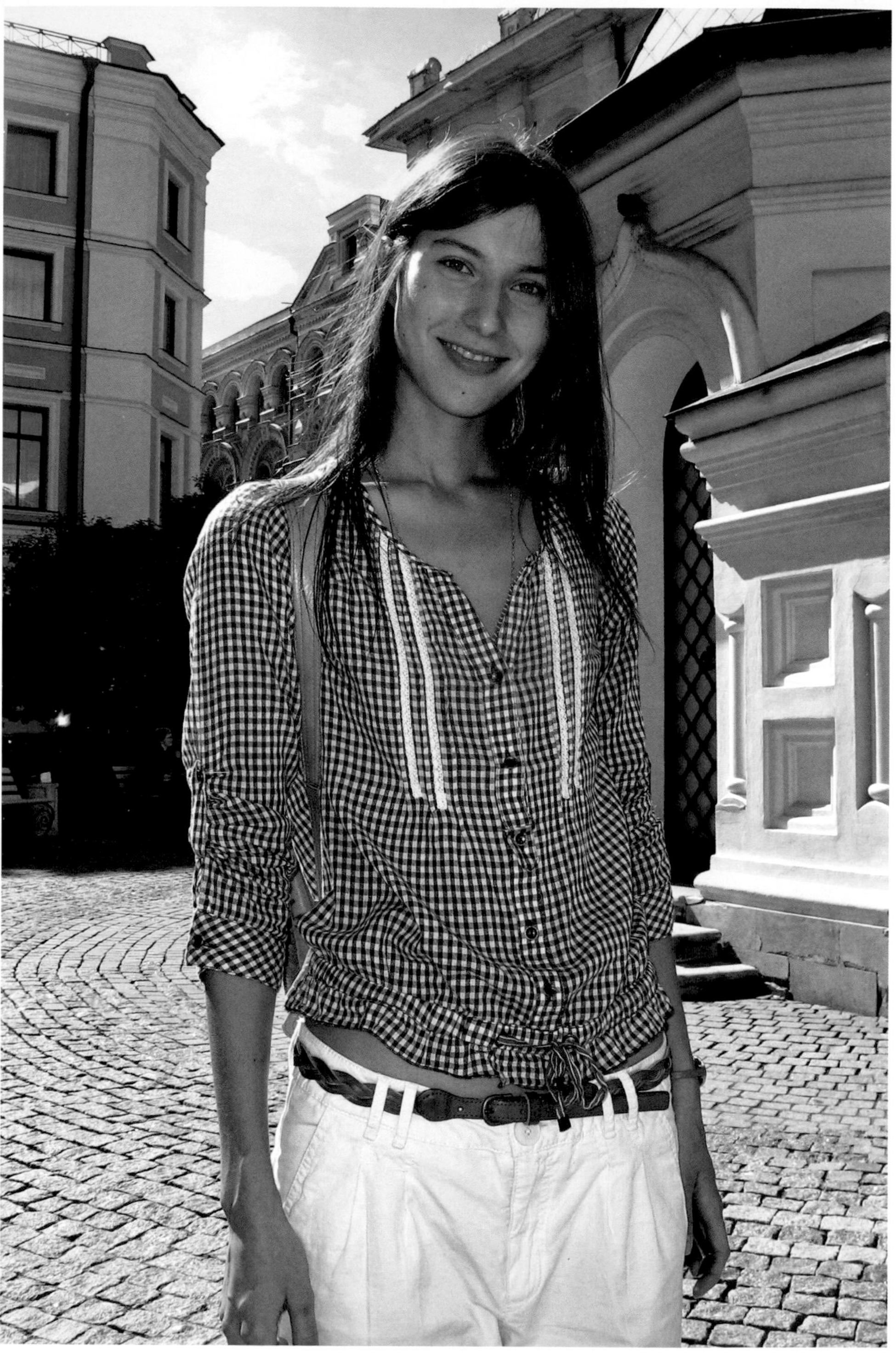

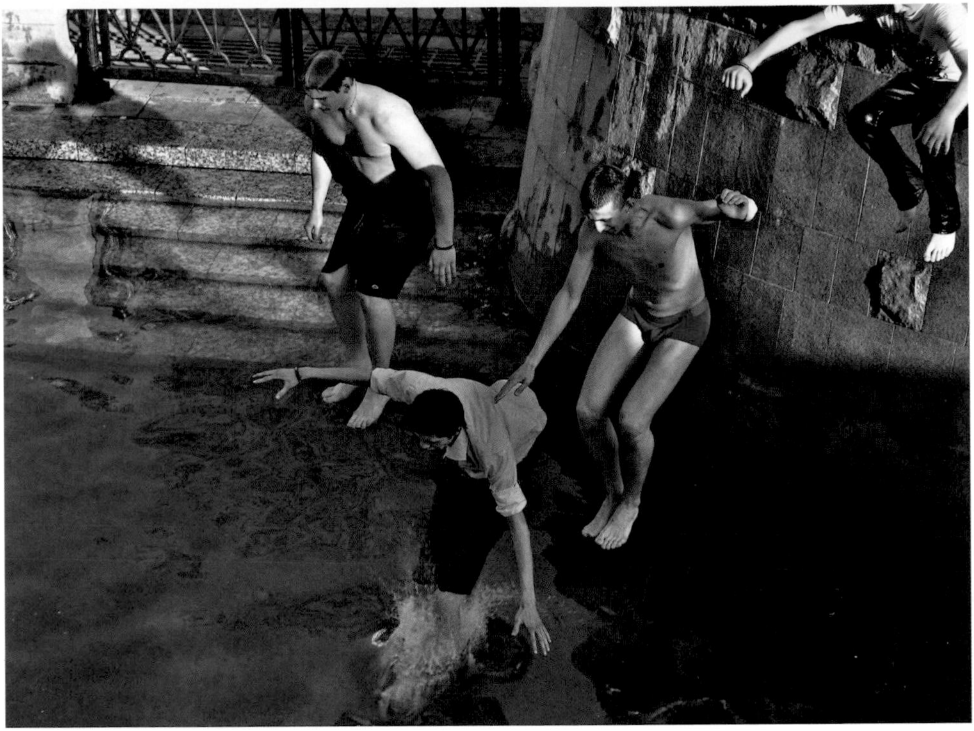

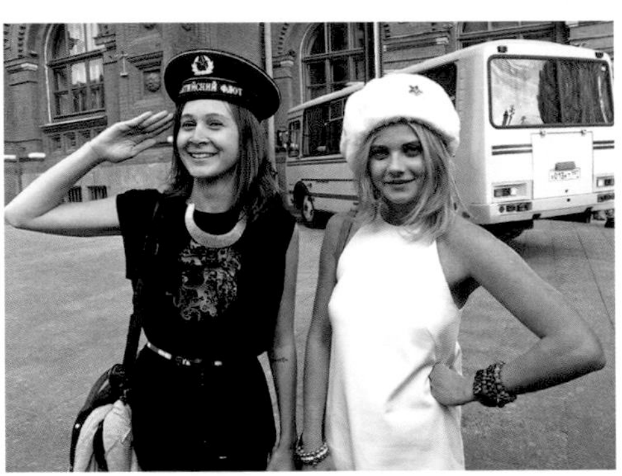

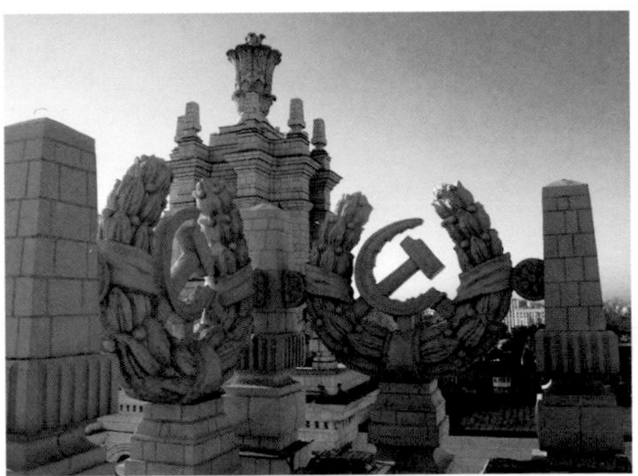

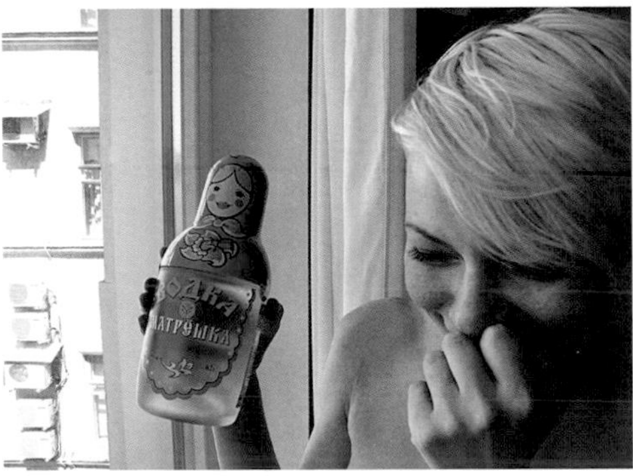

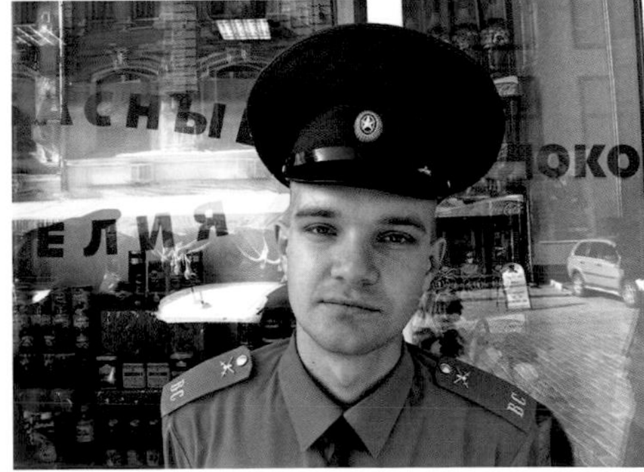

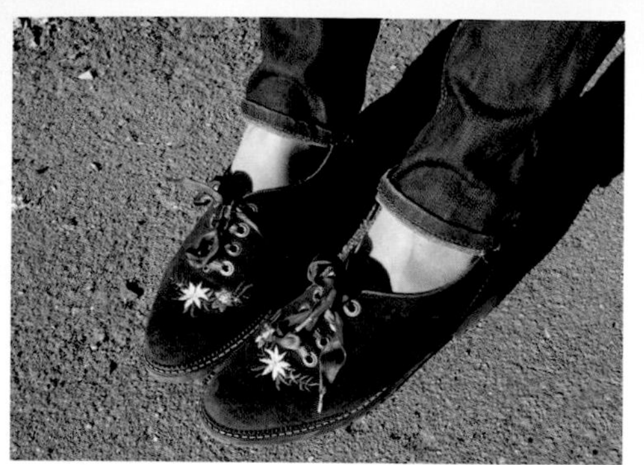

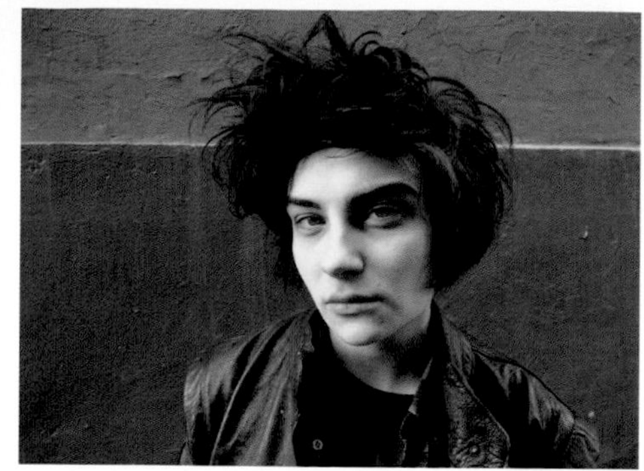

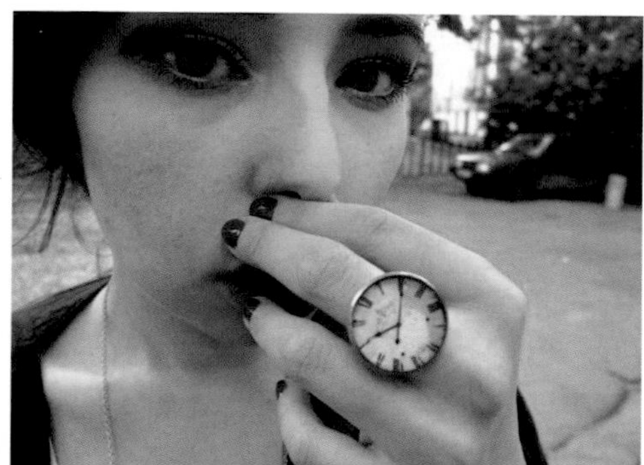

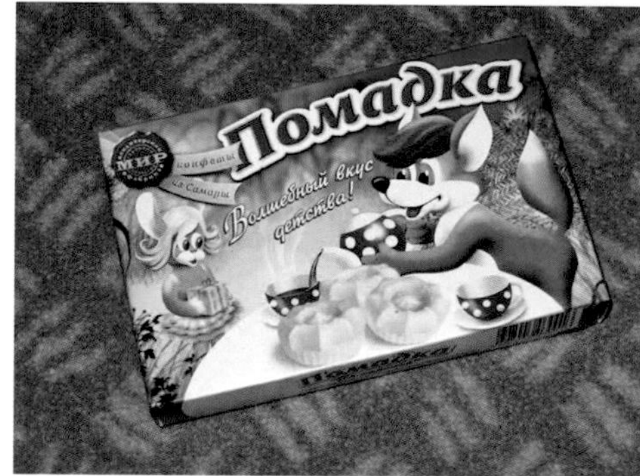
Помадка
конфеты
из Самары
Волшебный вкус детства!
Помадка

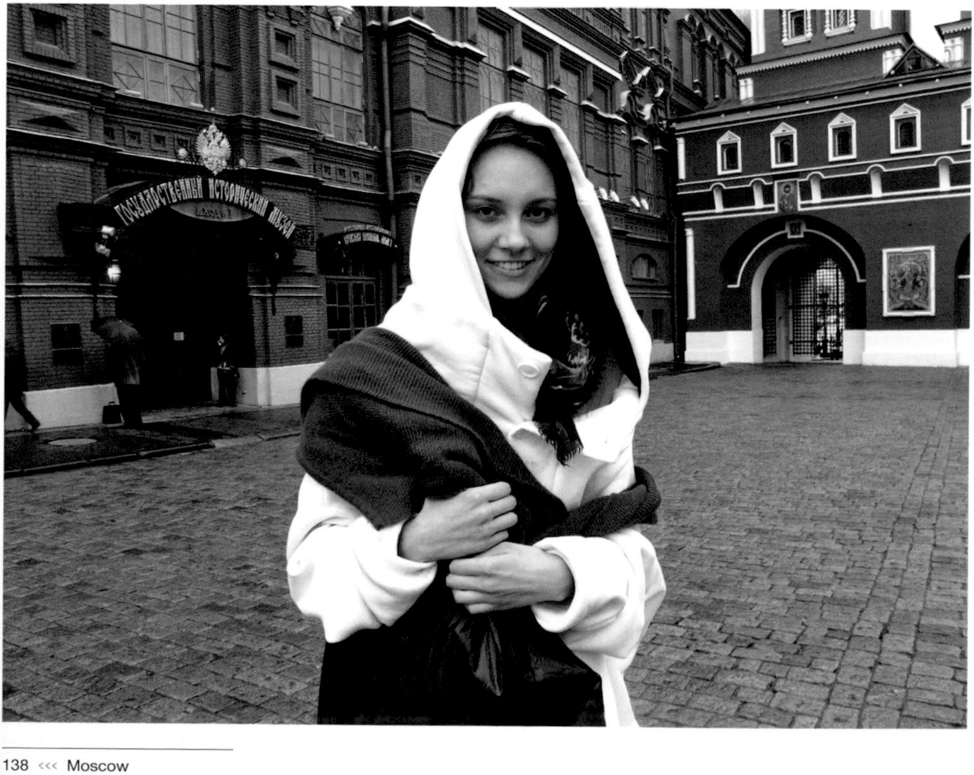

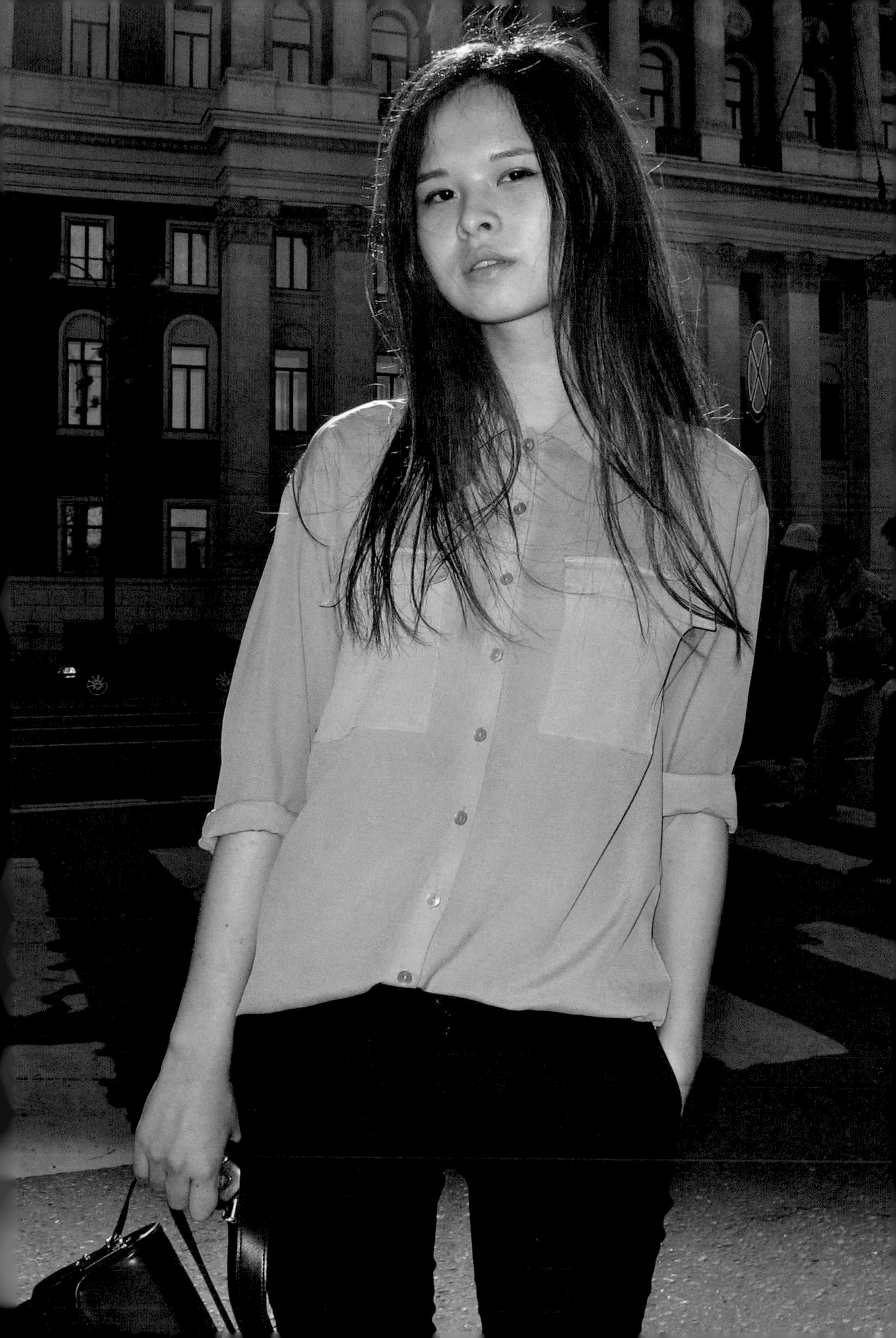

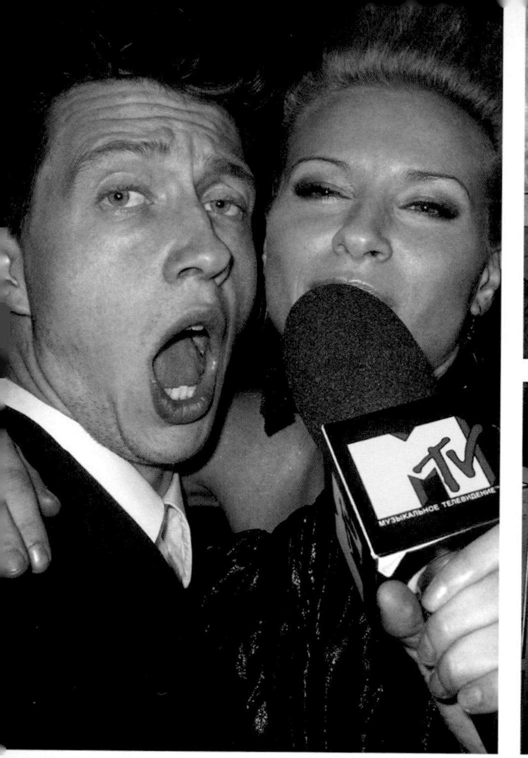
MTV
МУЗЫКАЛЬНОЕ ТЕЛЕВИДЕНИЕ

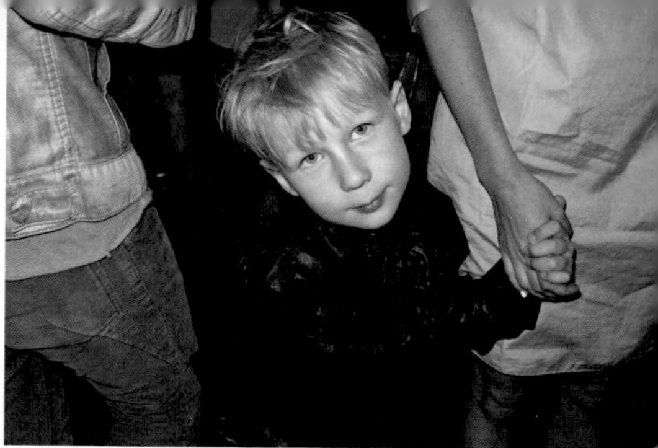

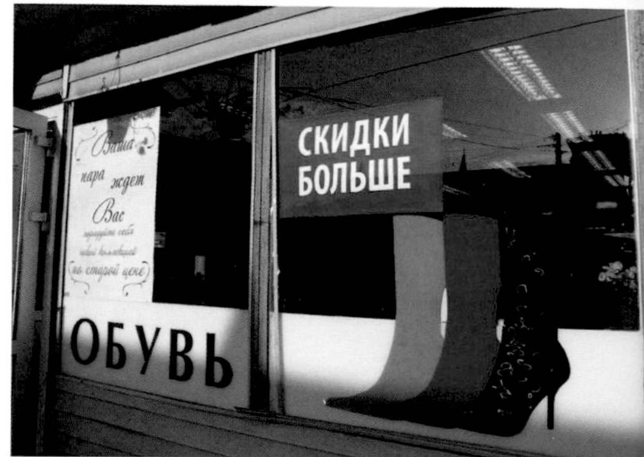
Ваша
пара ждет
Вас
по старой цене
СКИДКИ
БОЛЬШЕ
ОБУВЬ

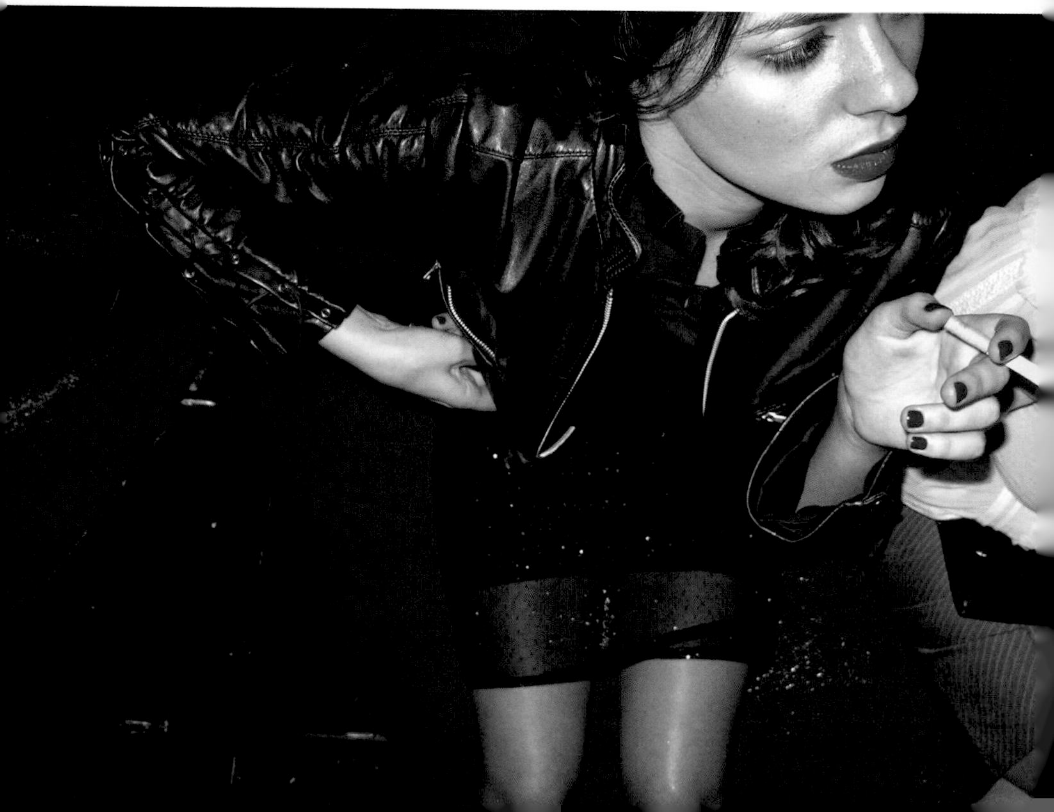

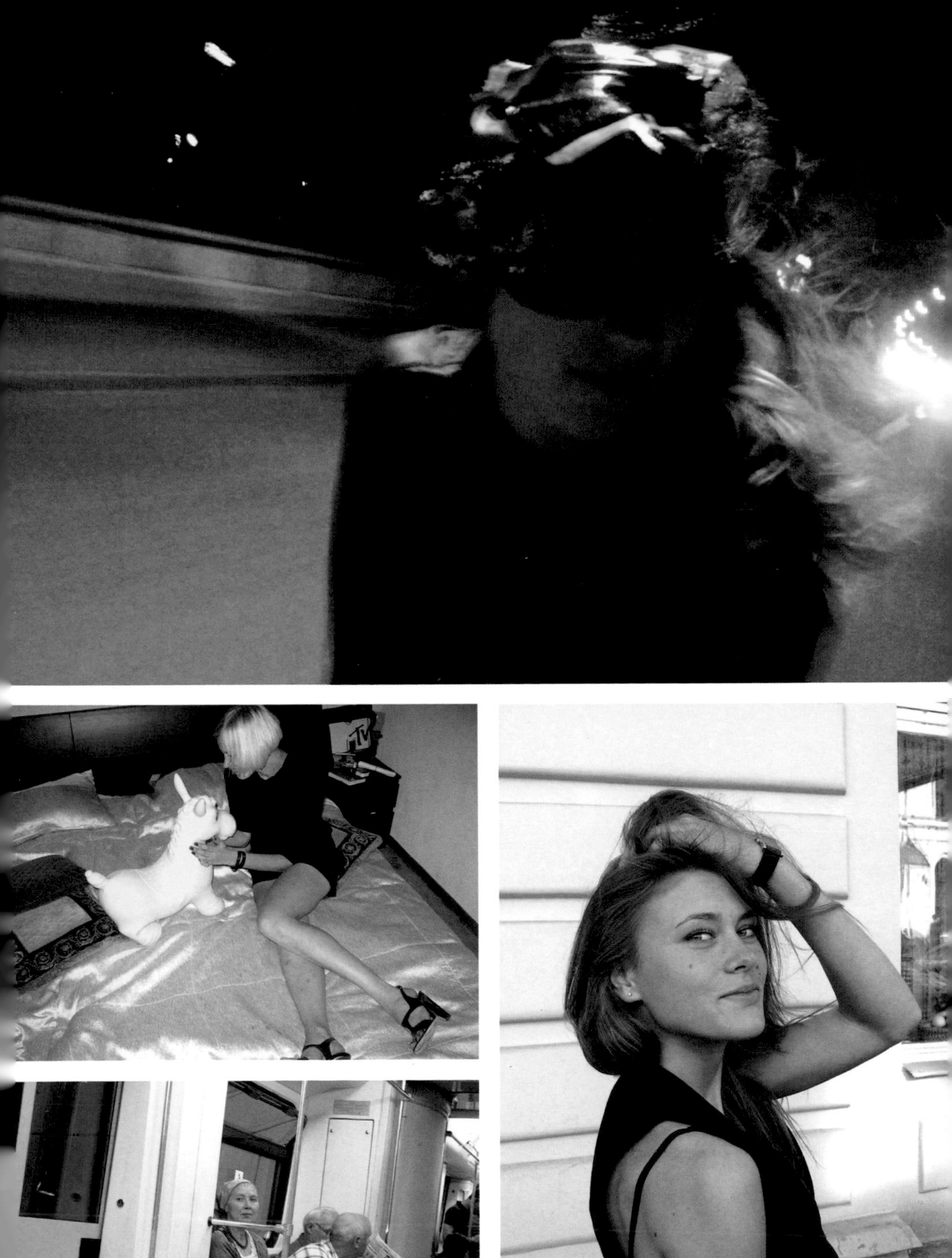

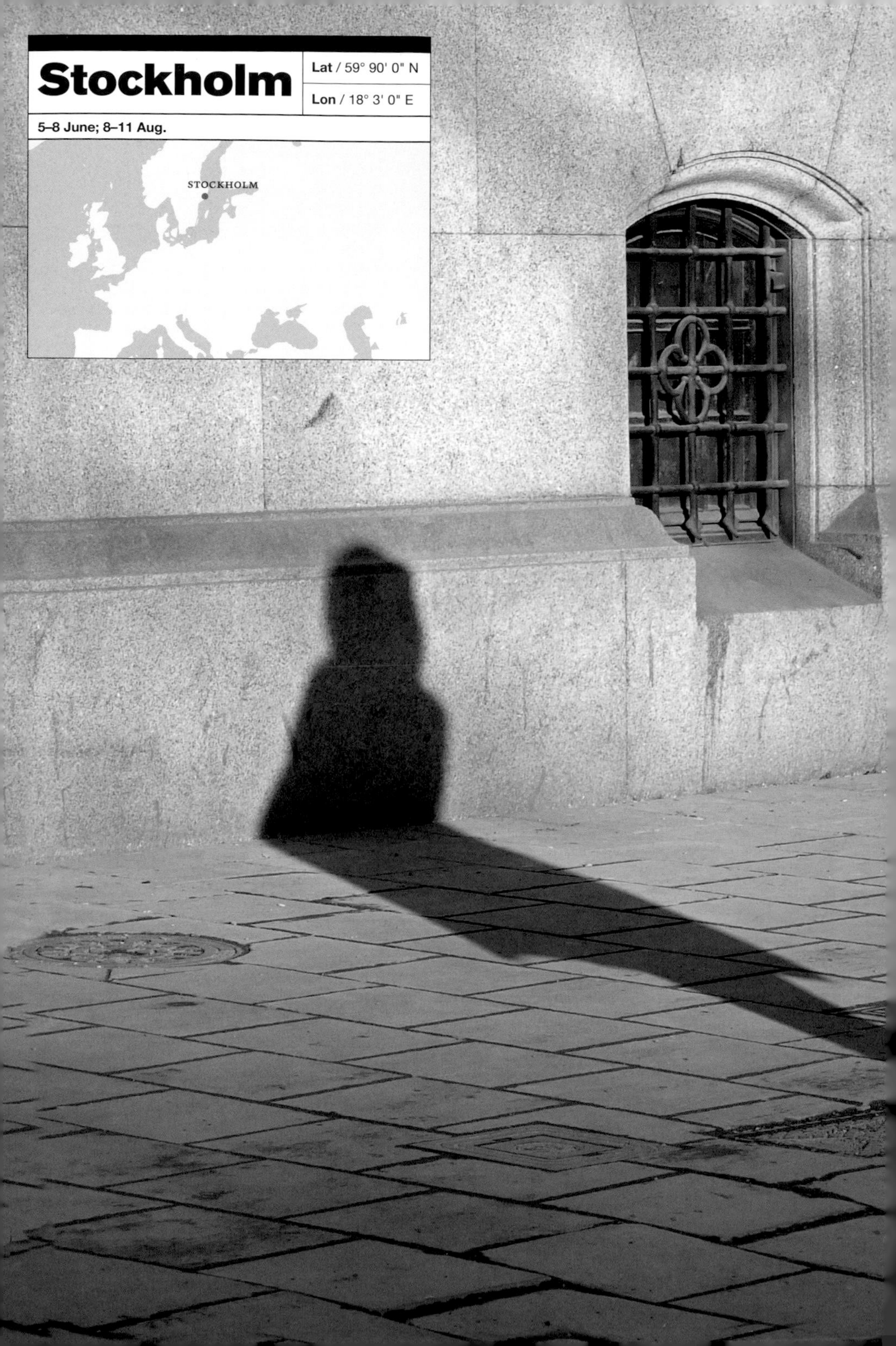
Stockholm
Lat / 59° 90' 0" N
Lon / 18° 3' 0" E
5–8 June; 8–11 Aug.
STOCKHOLM

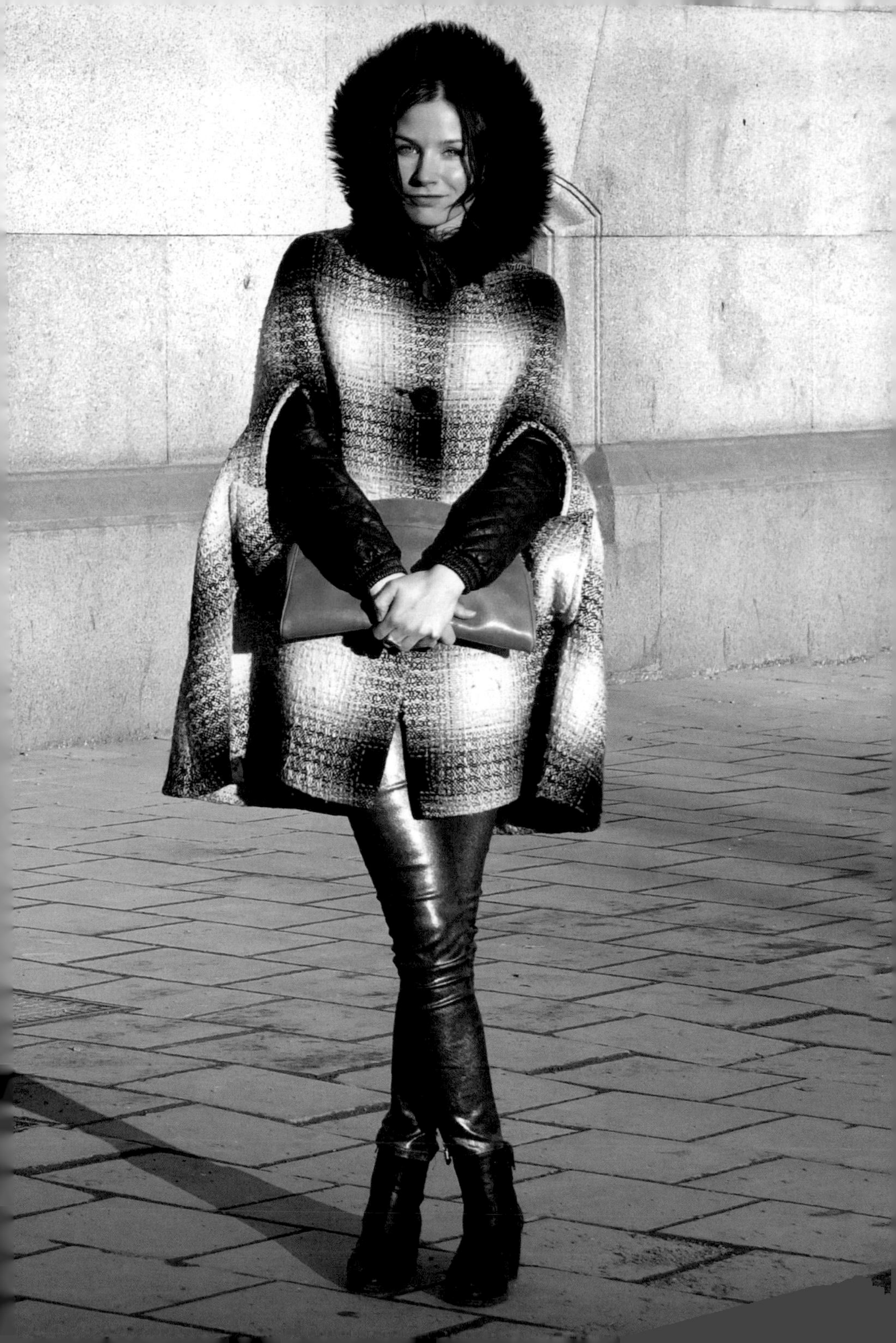

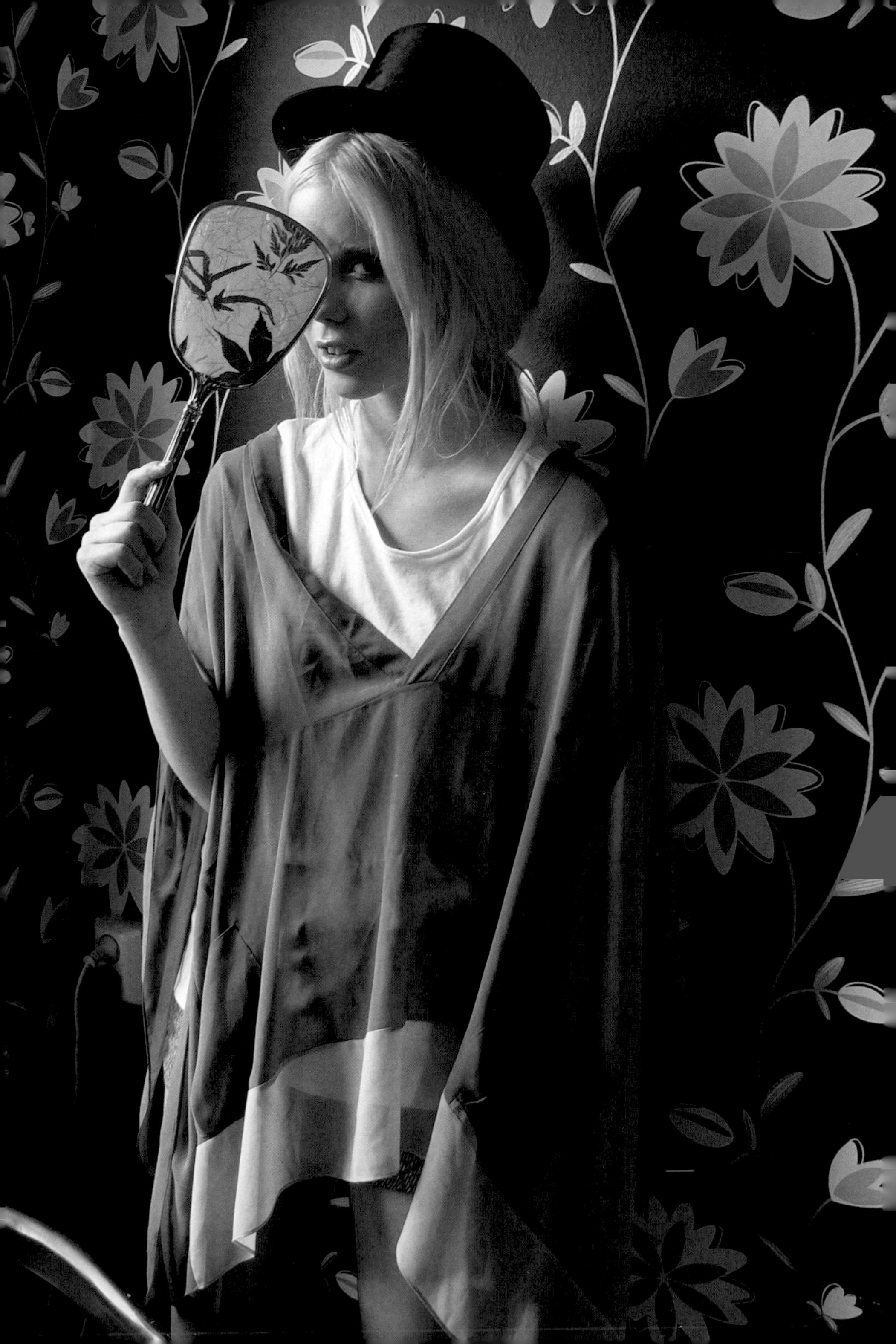

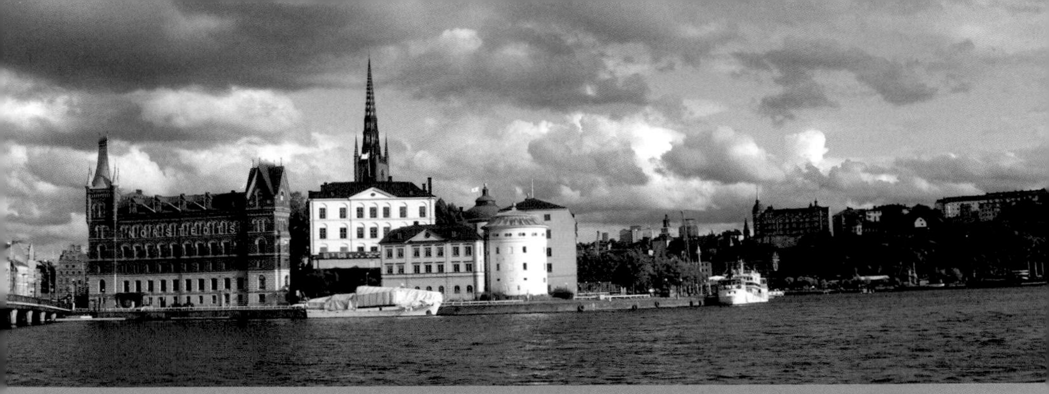

“It’s almost as if Swedes are born with the gene for coolness. Everything in Stockholm, from men’s hairstyles to urban street furniture, is so perfectly and harmoniously designed. Sometimes it looks like the sci-fi movie *Gattaca*. But the ironic part is that Swedish society – and Scandinavian society in general – values humility. This tendency is sometimes called the Law of Jante, which includes ten moral rules, among them: ‘Don’t think you are anything special.’ At the same time Sweden is also one of the places where fashion blogging started. Long before most of you ever heard the word ‘blog’, Stockholm was already home to the first professional fashion bloggers, whose pioneering sites helped to popularize the Swedish look around the world. Swedish brands such as Acne and Cheap Monday probably would not have had the same level of success without the Swedish blogging boom. At the same time, the emphasis is not on brands, but on personal style. Swedes are masters at looking edgy with just a well-cut pair of jeans and a perfectly styled T-shirt. It’s the way each person wears the outfit, styling it for him or herself – rolling up the cuffs and sleeves, for example. The look is a sensible mix of simplicity and quirkiness.”

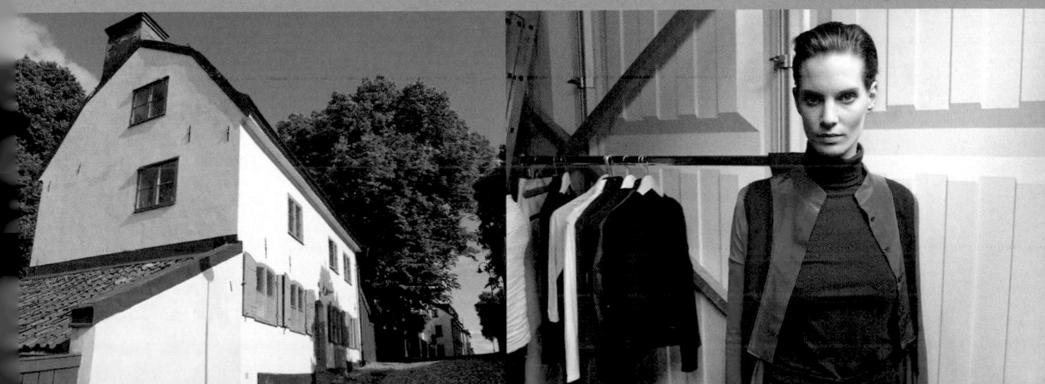

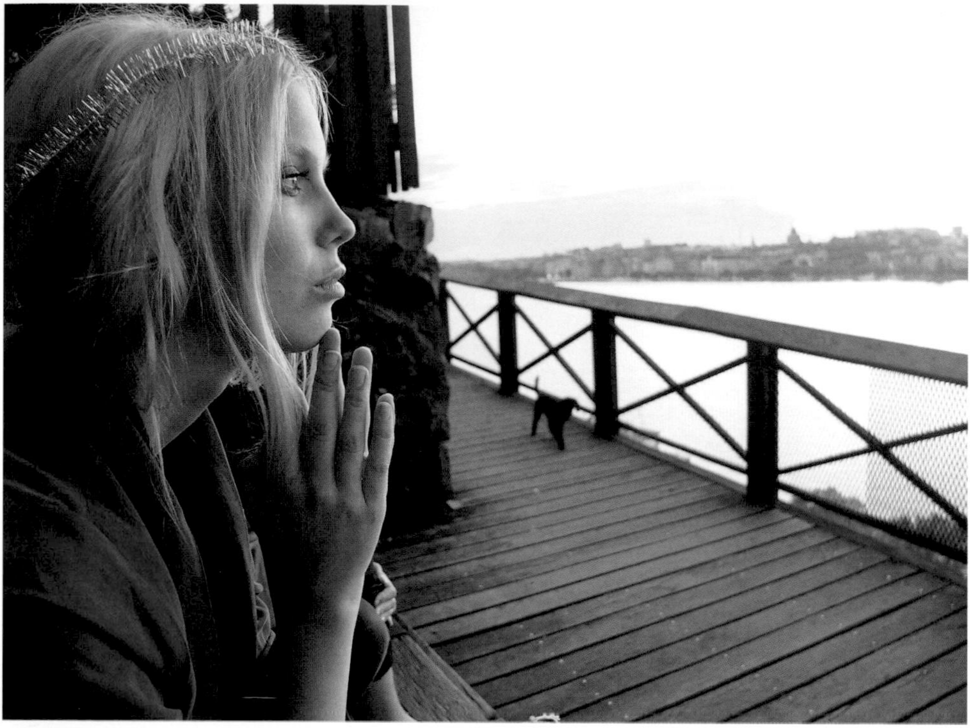

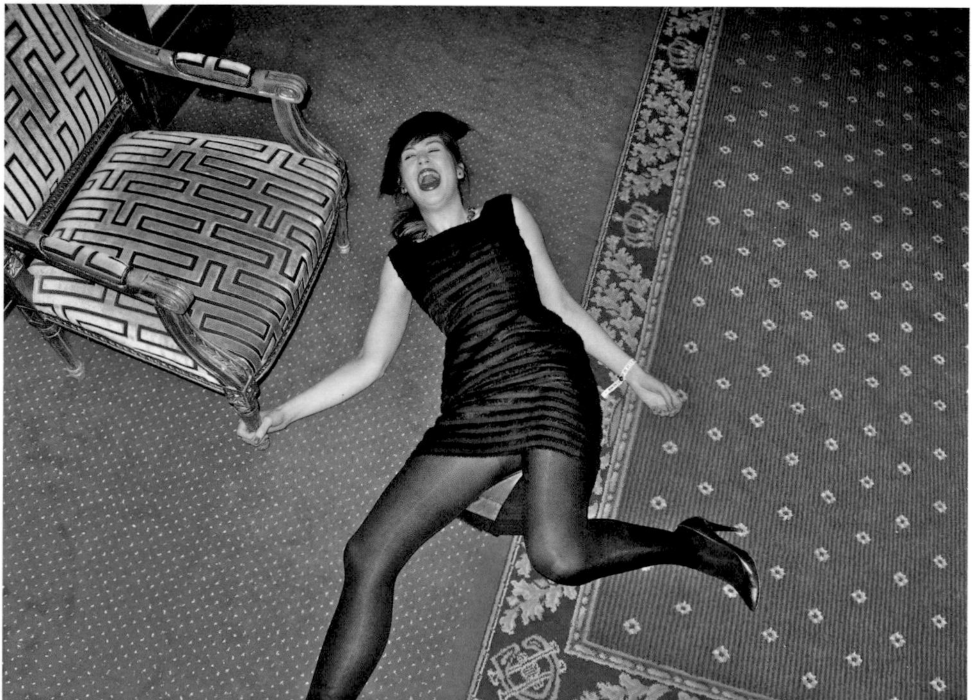

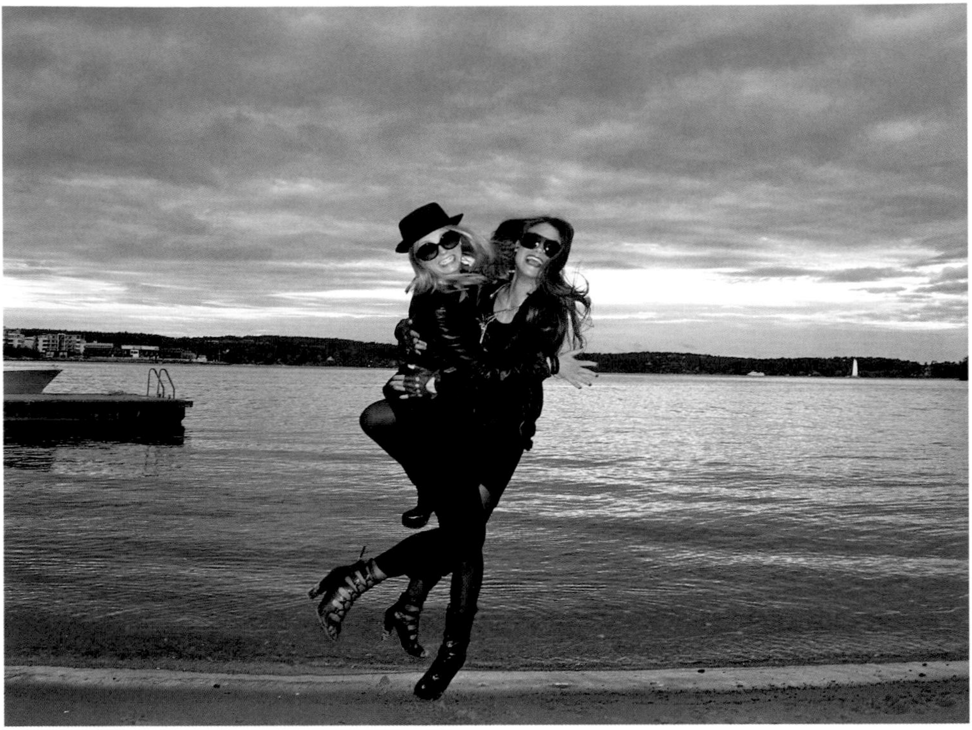

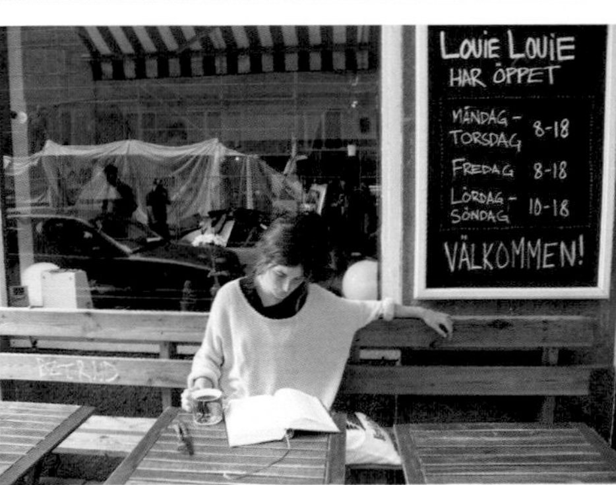
LOUIE LOUIE
HAR ÖPPET
MÅNDAG - TORSDAG 8-18
FREDAG 8-18
LÖRDAG - SÖNDAG 10-18
VÄLKOMMEN!

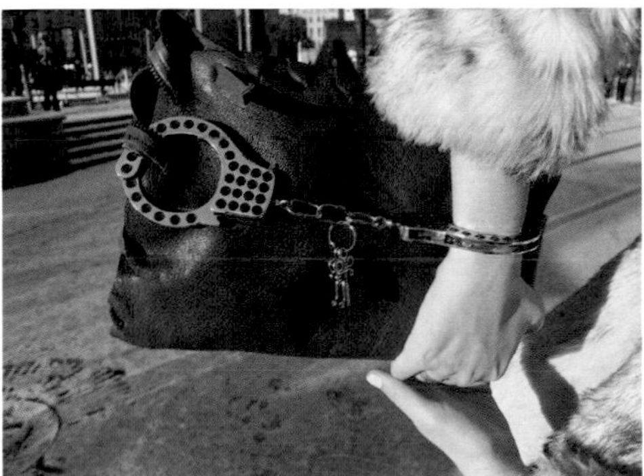

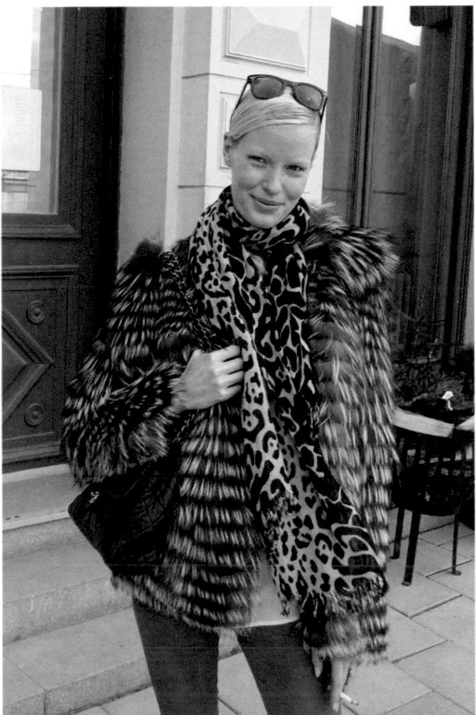

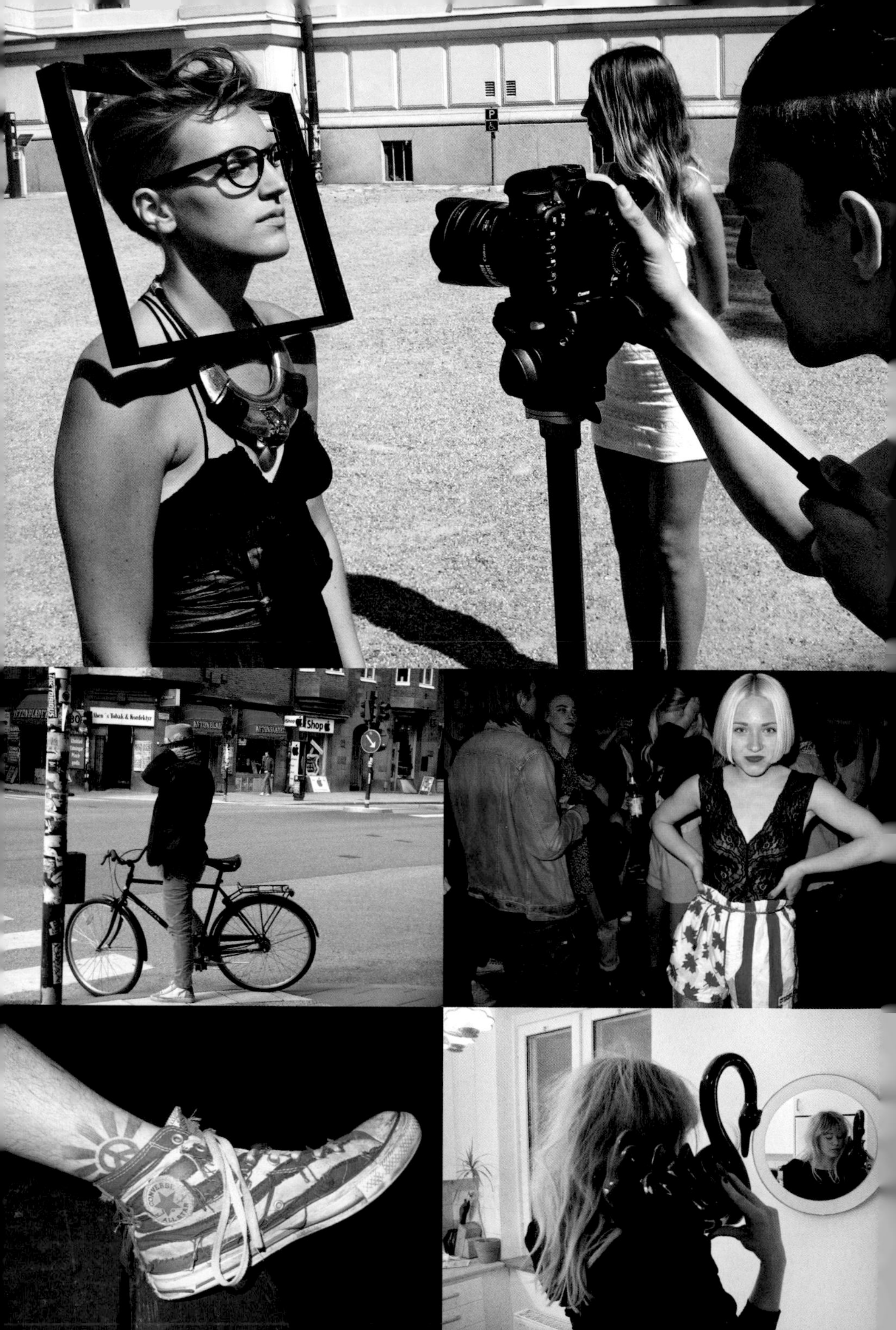
Tobak & Konfektyr
Shop

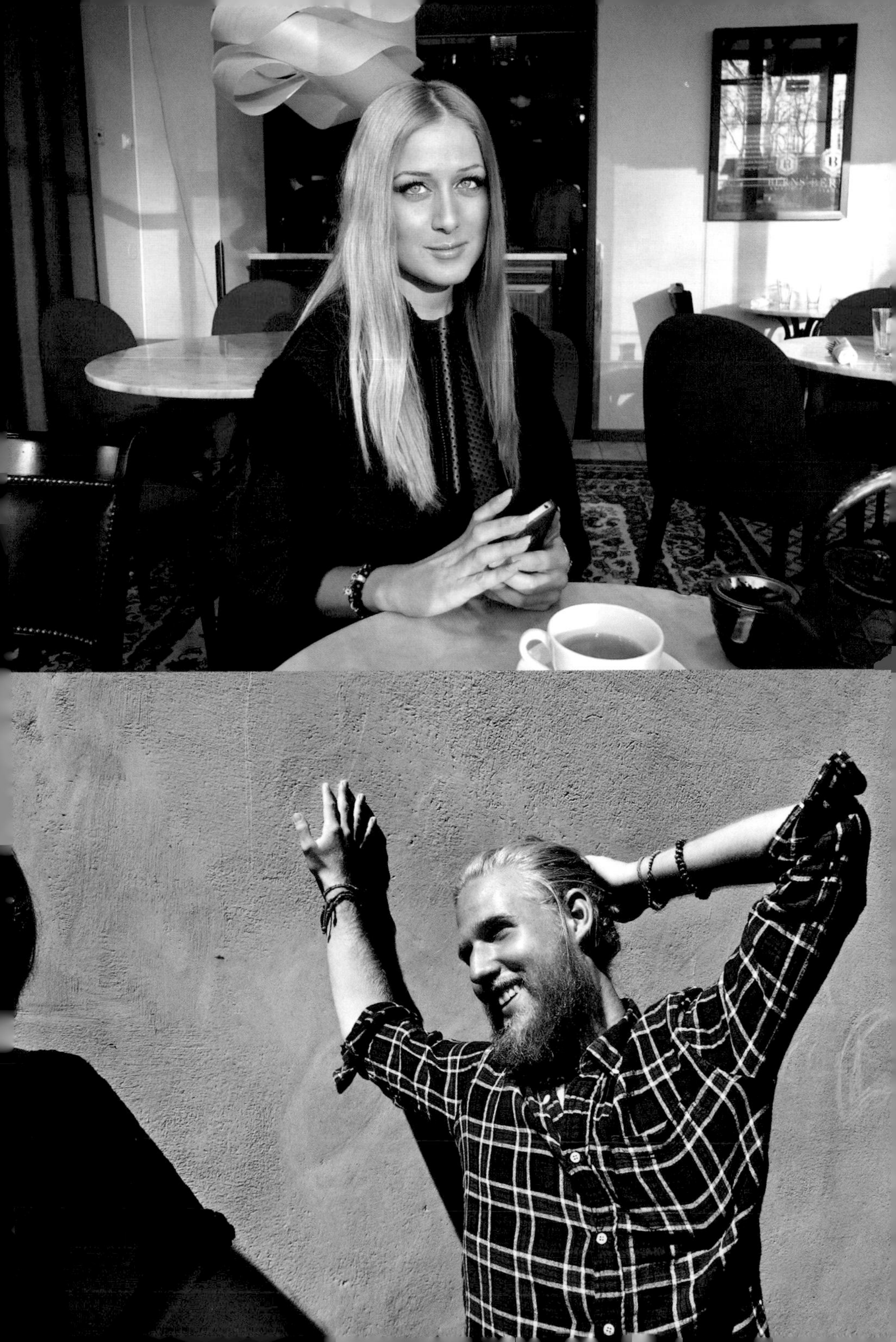

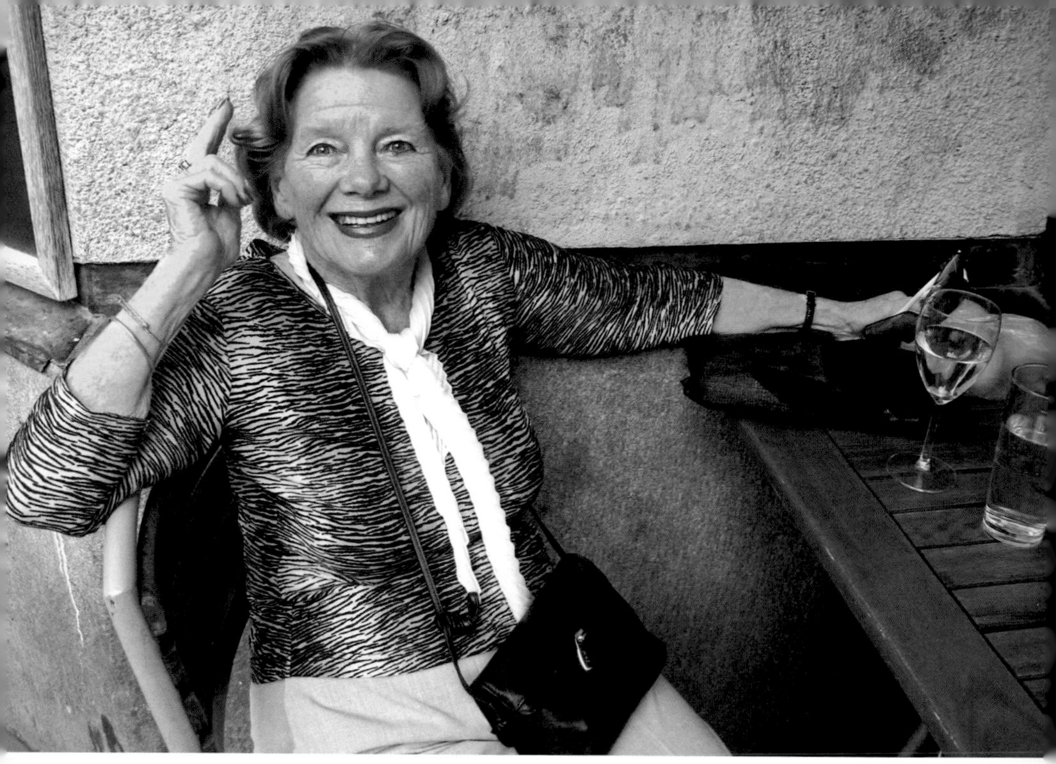

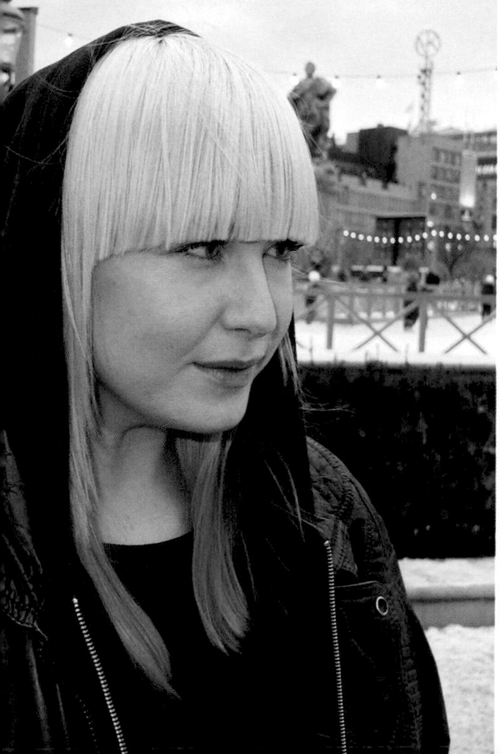

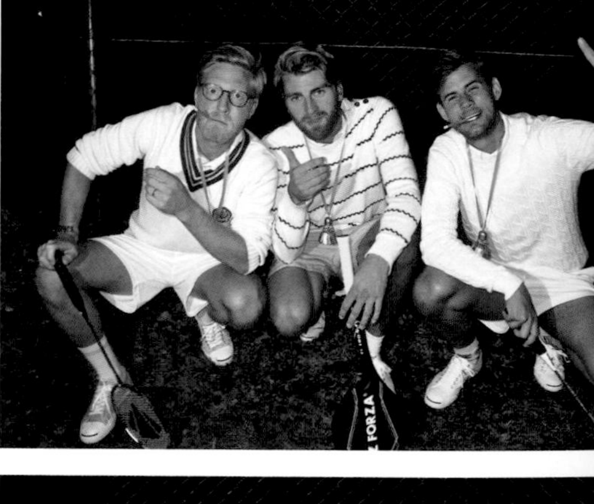

FORZA

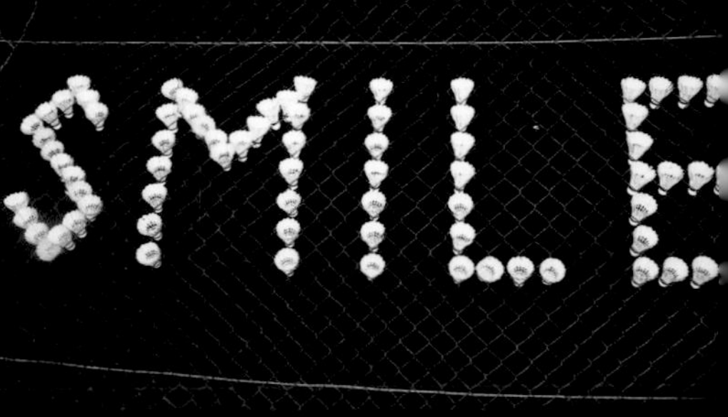

SMILE

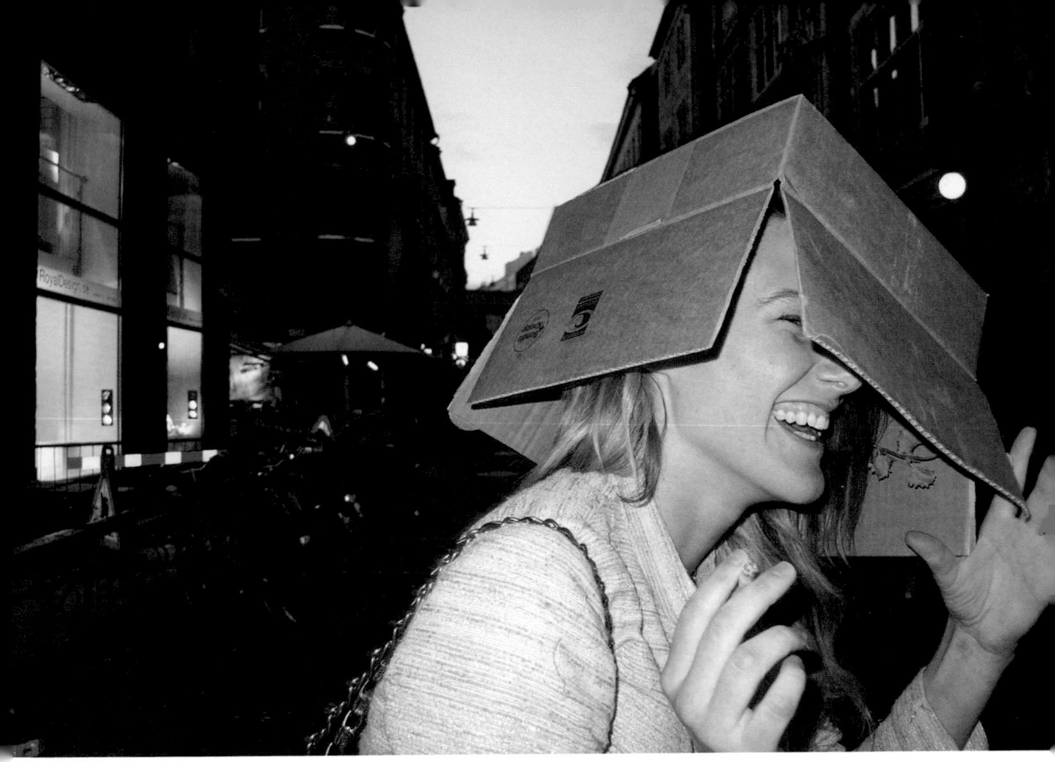

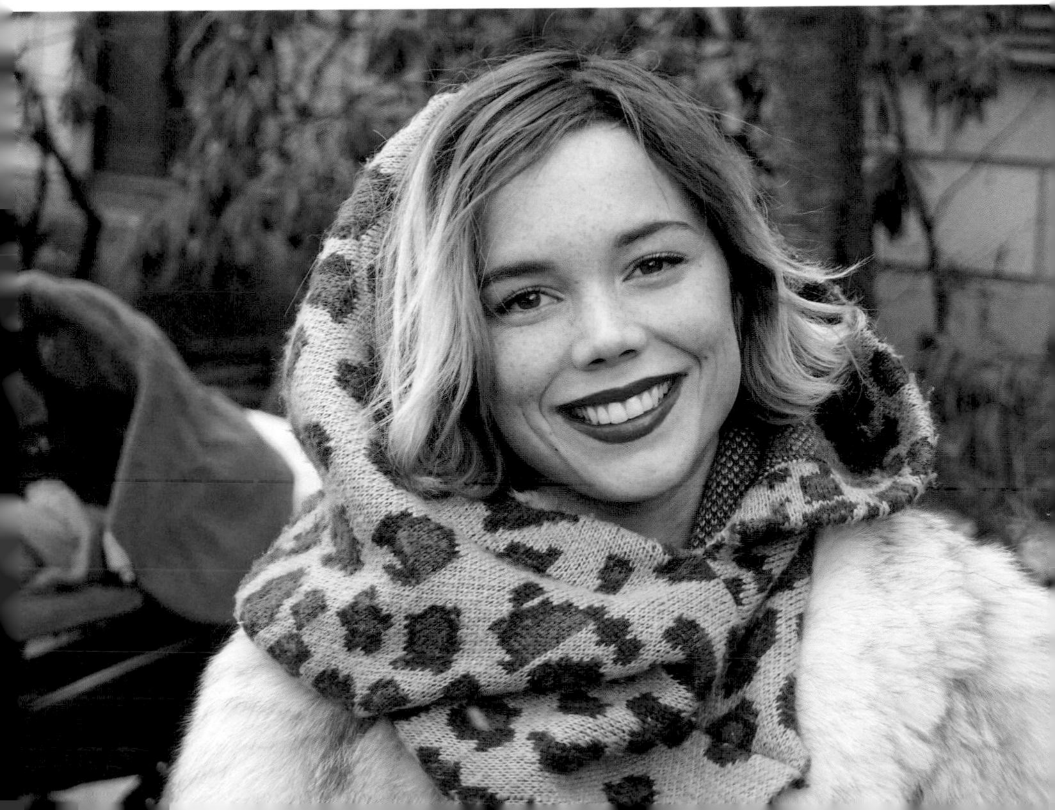

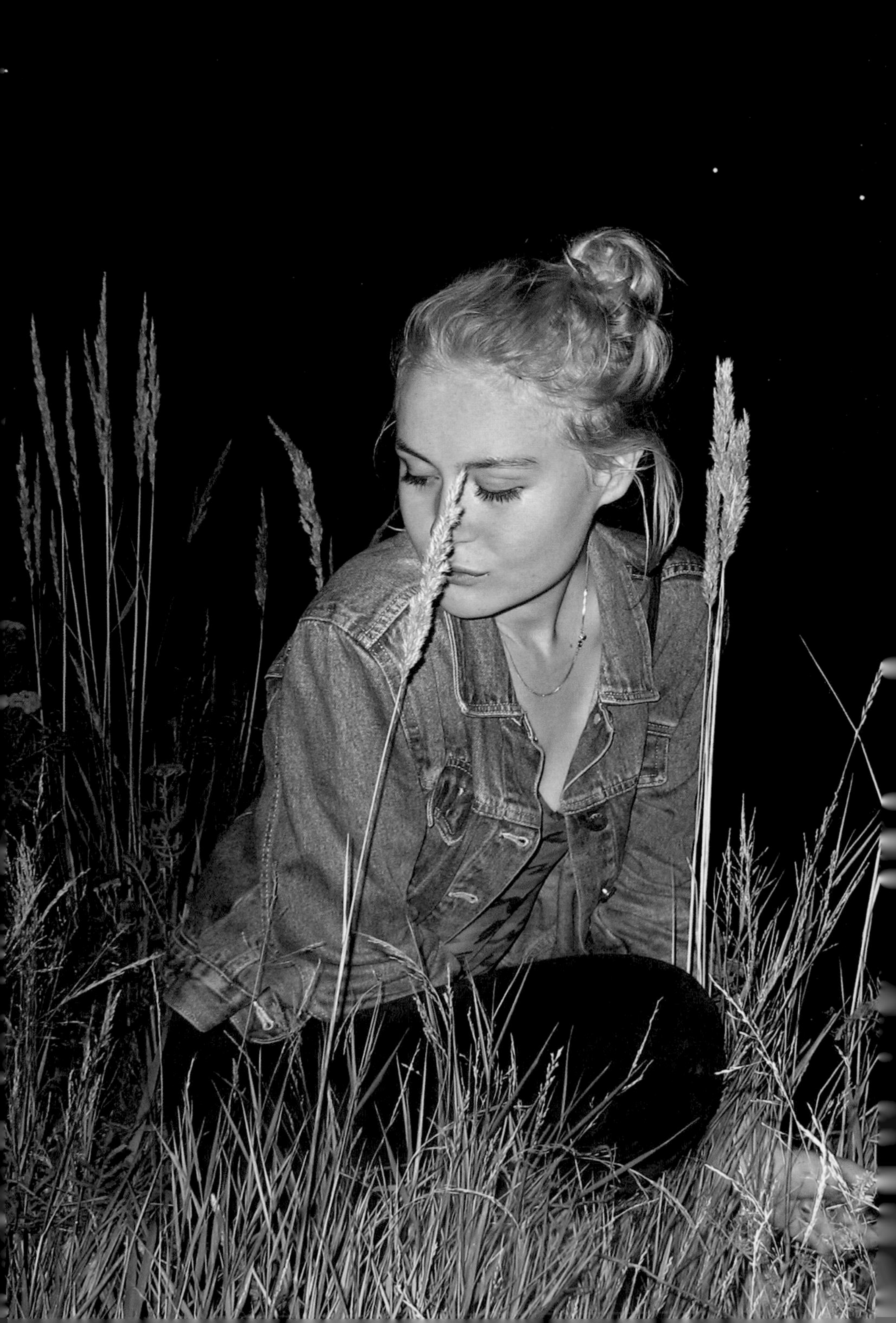

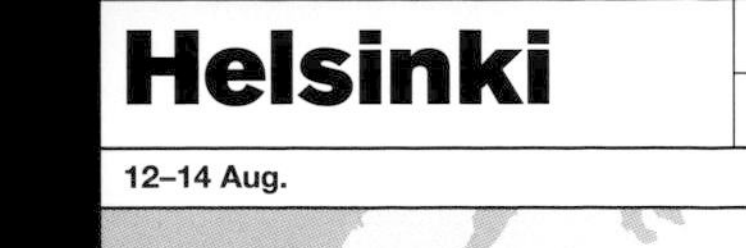

12–14 Aug.

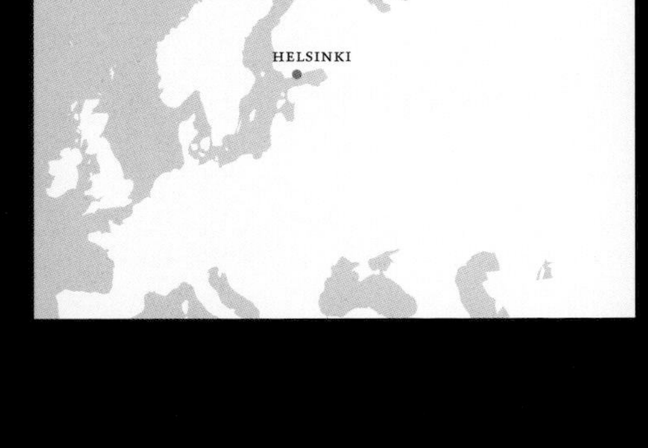

“Helsinki is geeky. In a good way. Finland is a very hi-tech society, with a unique design aesthetic, a kind of quirky minimalism that is different from the style of the rest of Scandinavia. Finland was once very isolated, linguistically as well as geographically, and this has made it fiercely independent. It's hard to talk about the mainstream fashion culture in Helsinki, because there really isn't one – just lots of quirky subcultures existing side by side: Japanese Lolita fashion, Emo kids, 80s heavy metal. Finns love nature as much as they love technology – swimming in lakes, relaxing naked in the sauna, hiking in the woods or walking in the city. Even the iconic Finnish tech firm Nokia started its life as a manufacturer of outdoor footwear. I go to Helsinki whenever I can because I love the city's unique spirit, interesting aesthetics and intelligent lifestyle. A lot of thought and effort goes into making the city as livable as possible. It's inspiring – and geeky. It's a shame that out of all the major Scandinavian cities Helsinki is the one that people seem to know the least about (though I'd secretly prefer it stays that way).

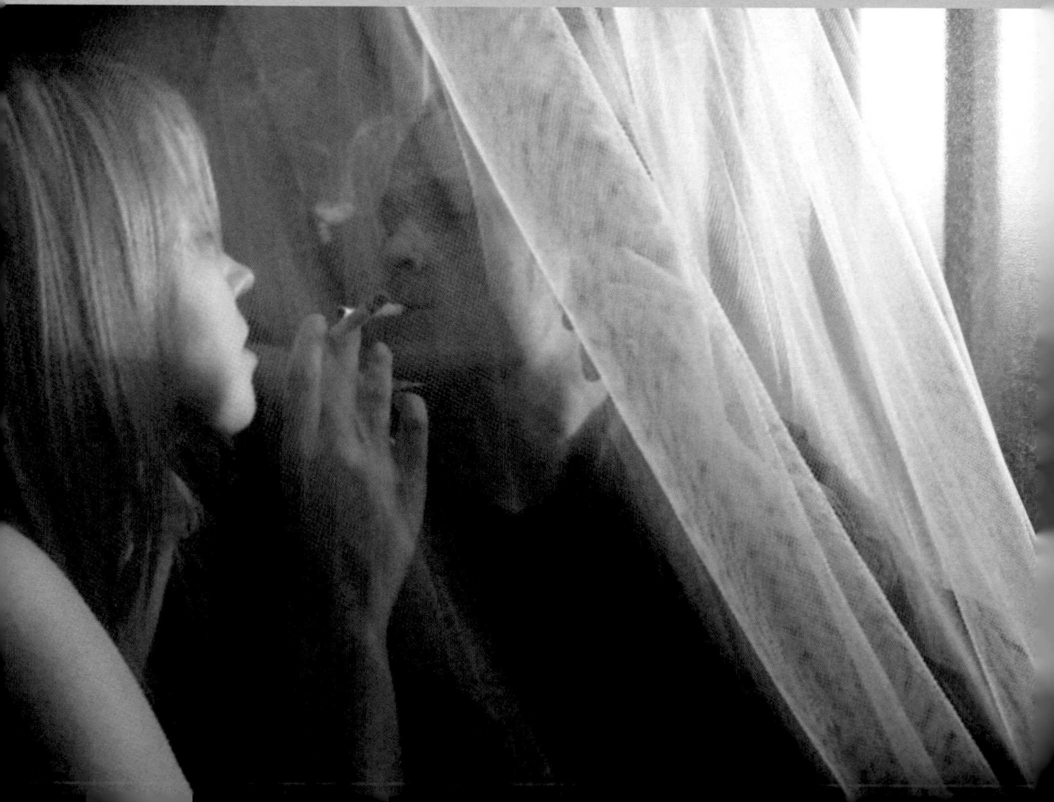

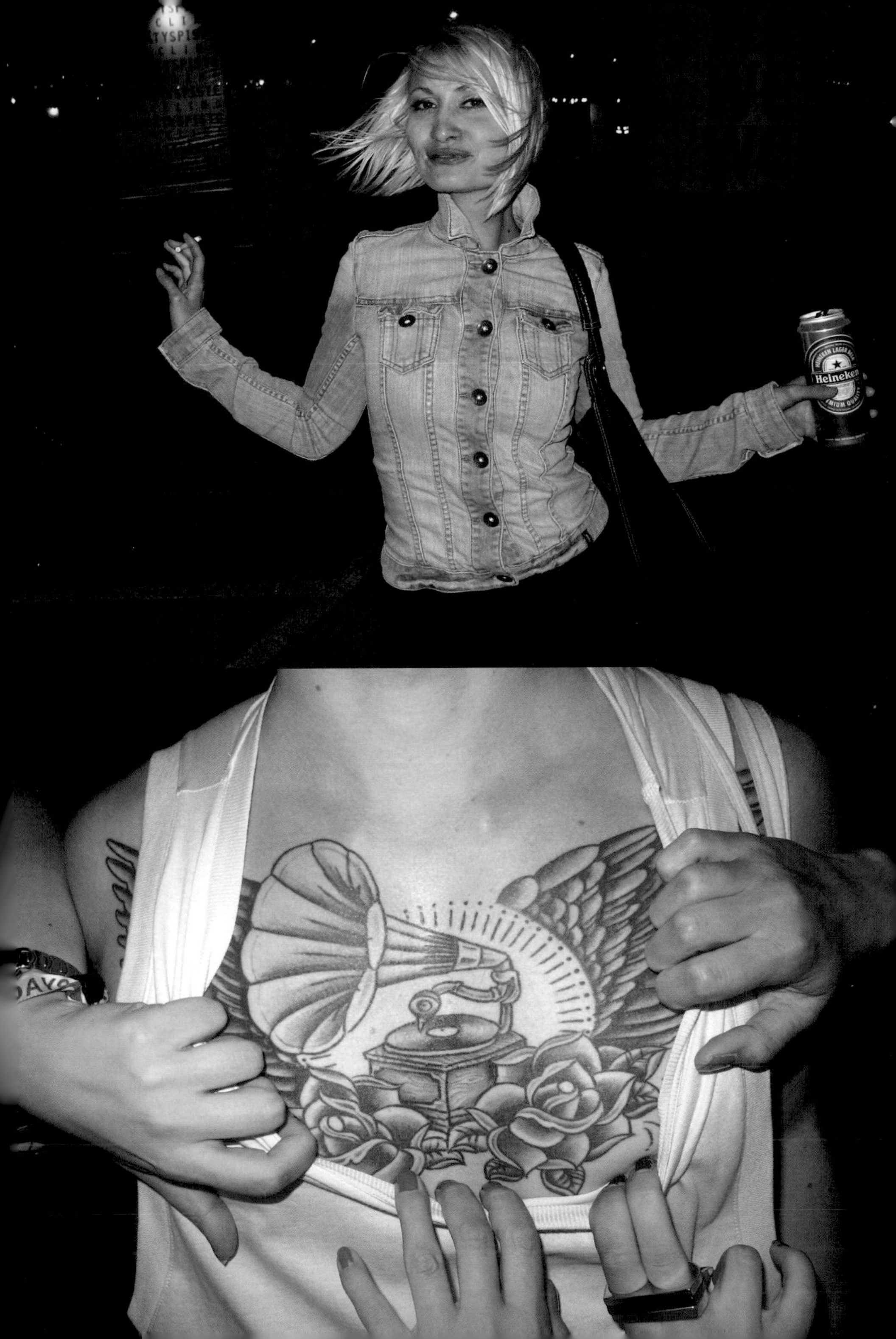
Heineken

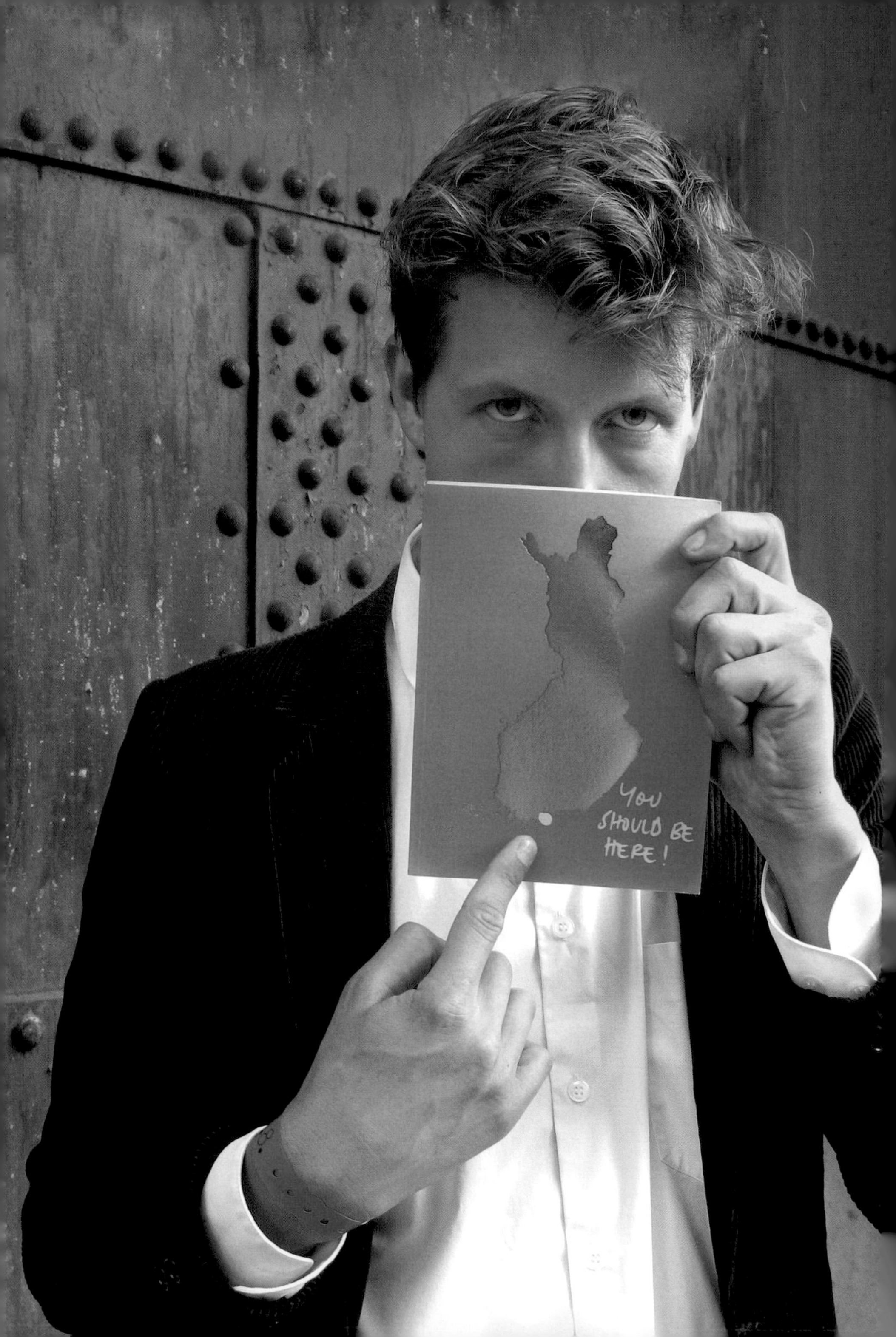
YOU
SHOULD BE
HERE!

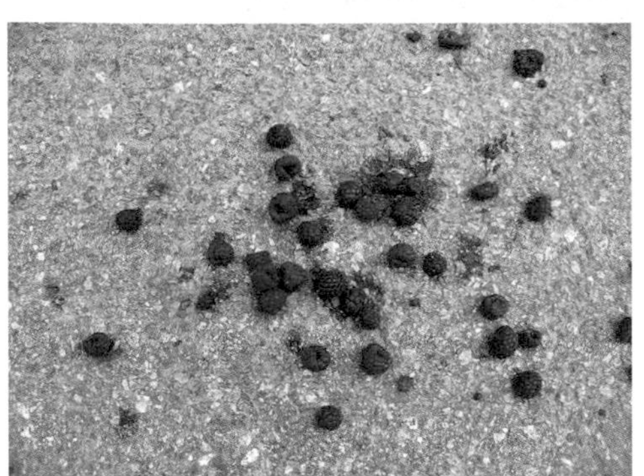

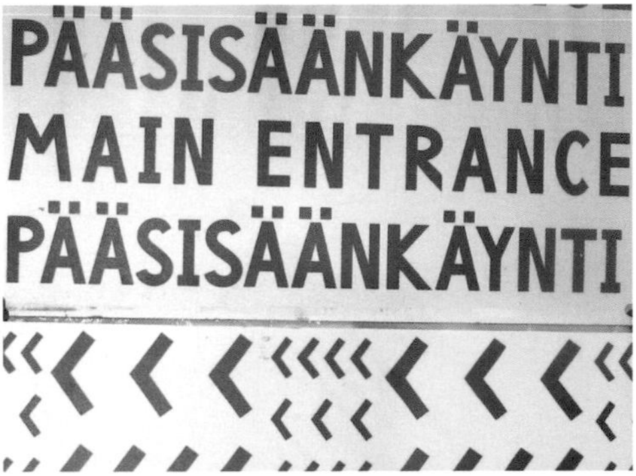

PÄÄSISÄÄNKÄYNTI
MAIN ENTRANCE
PÄÄSISÄÄNKÄYNTI

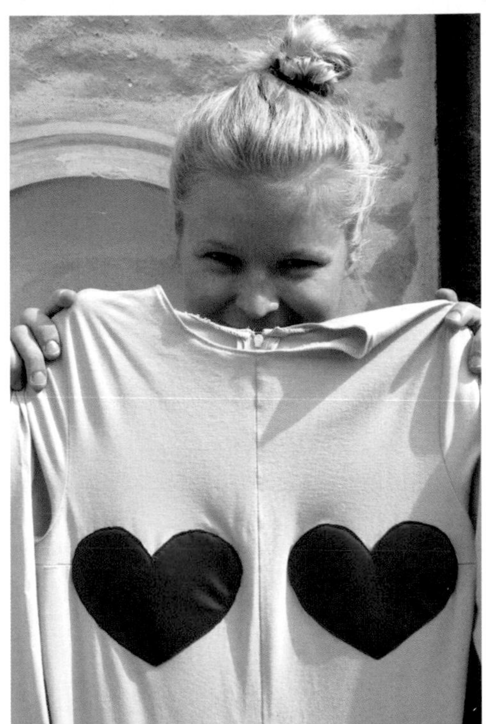

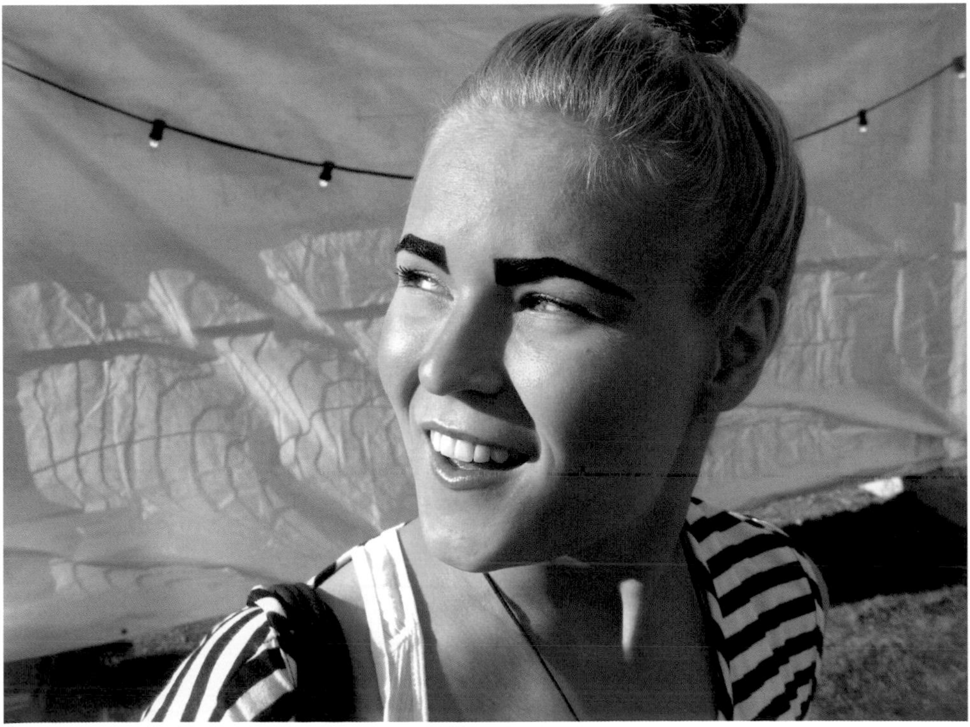

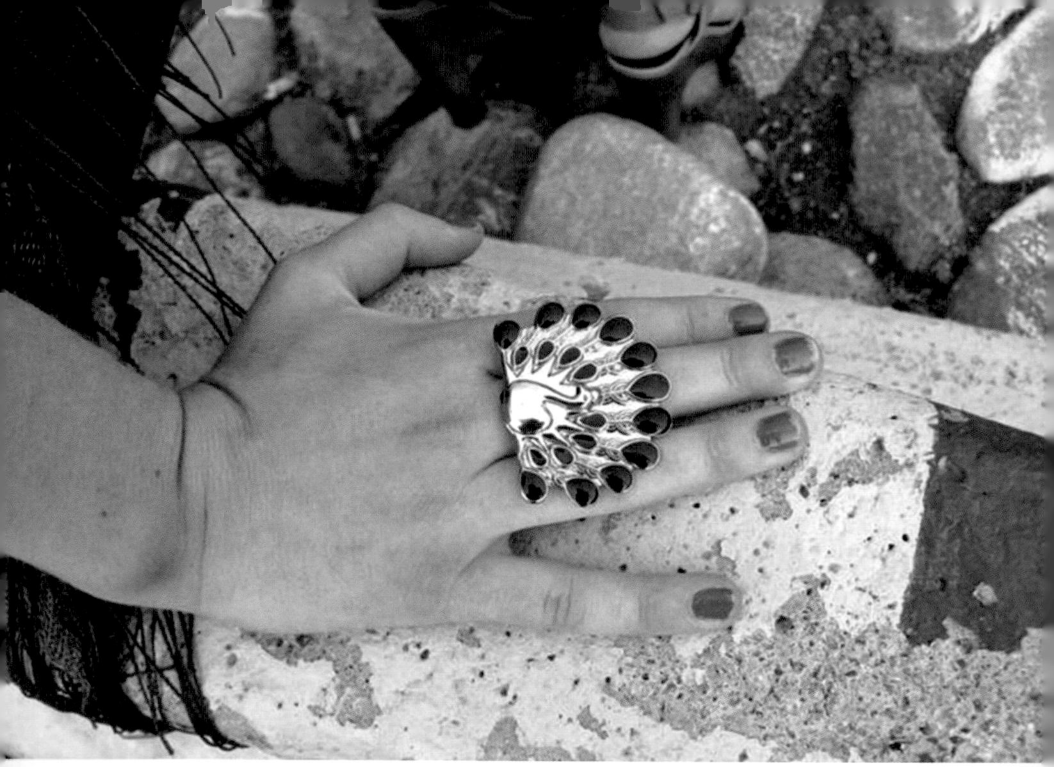

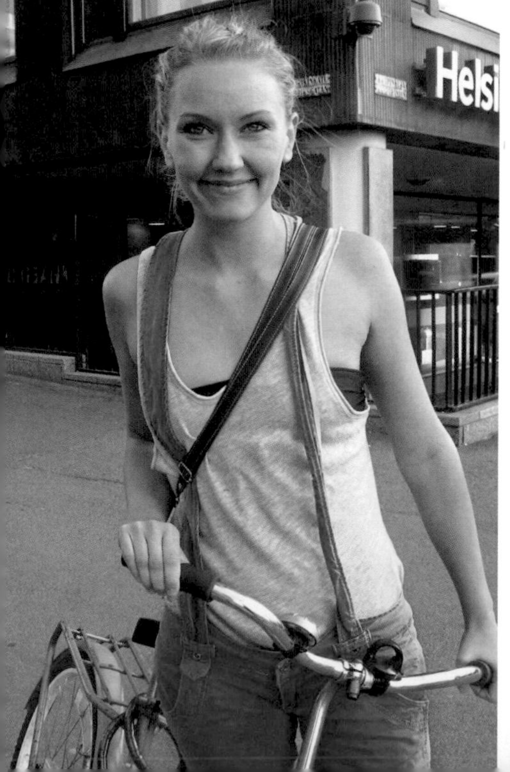
Helsi

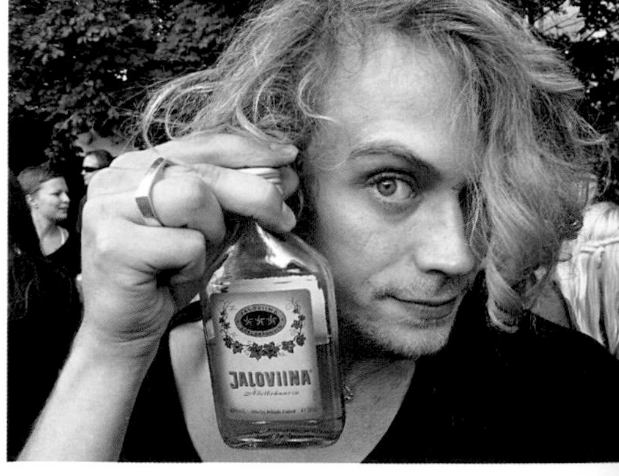
JALOVIINA

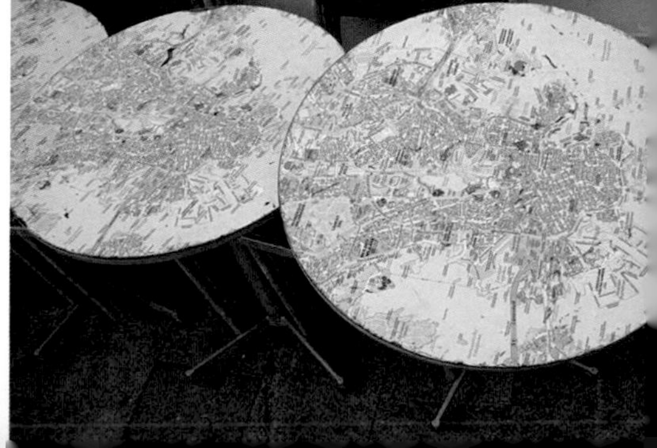

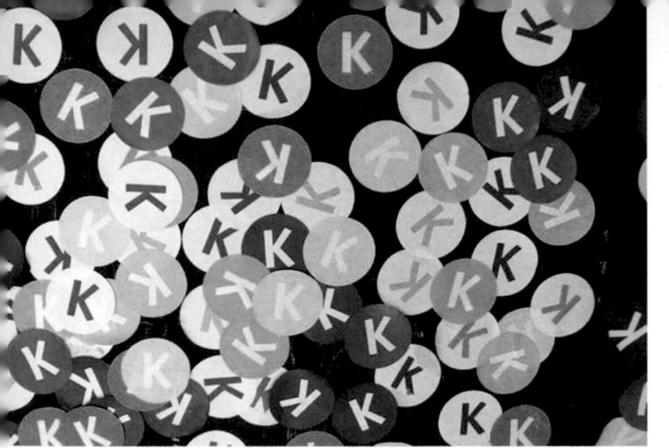

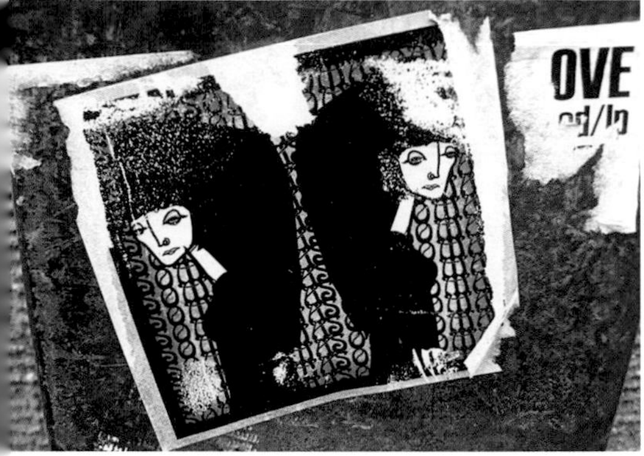
OVE

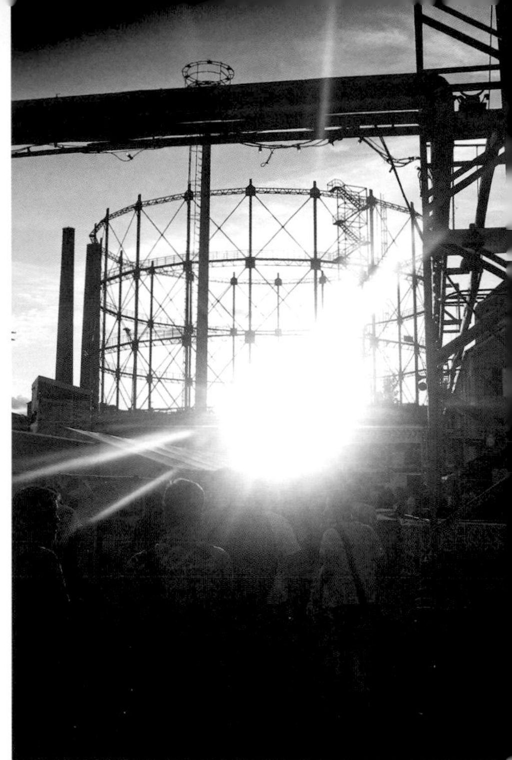

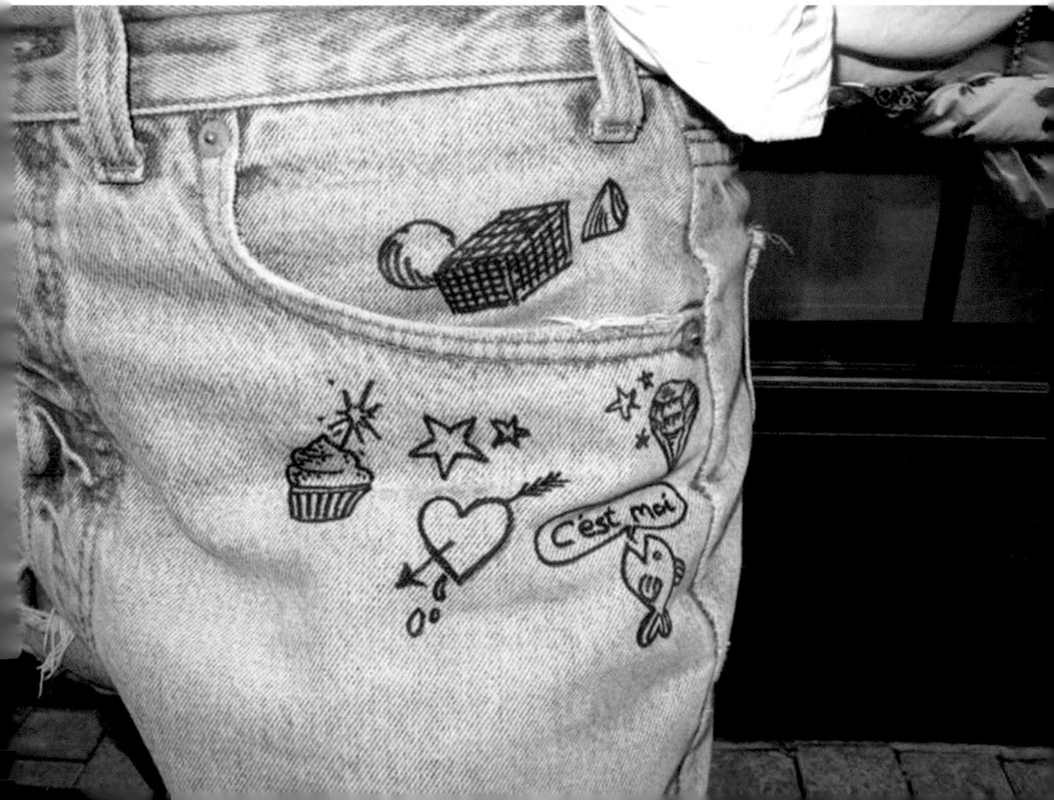

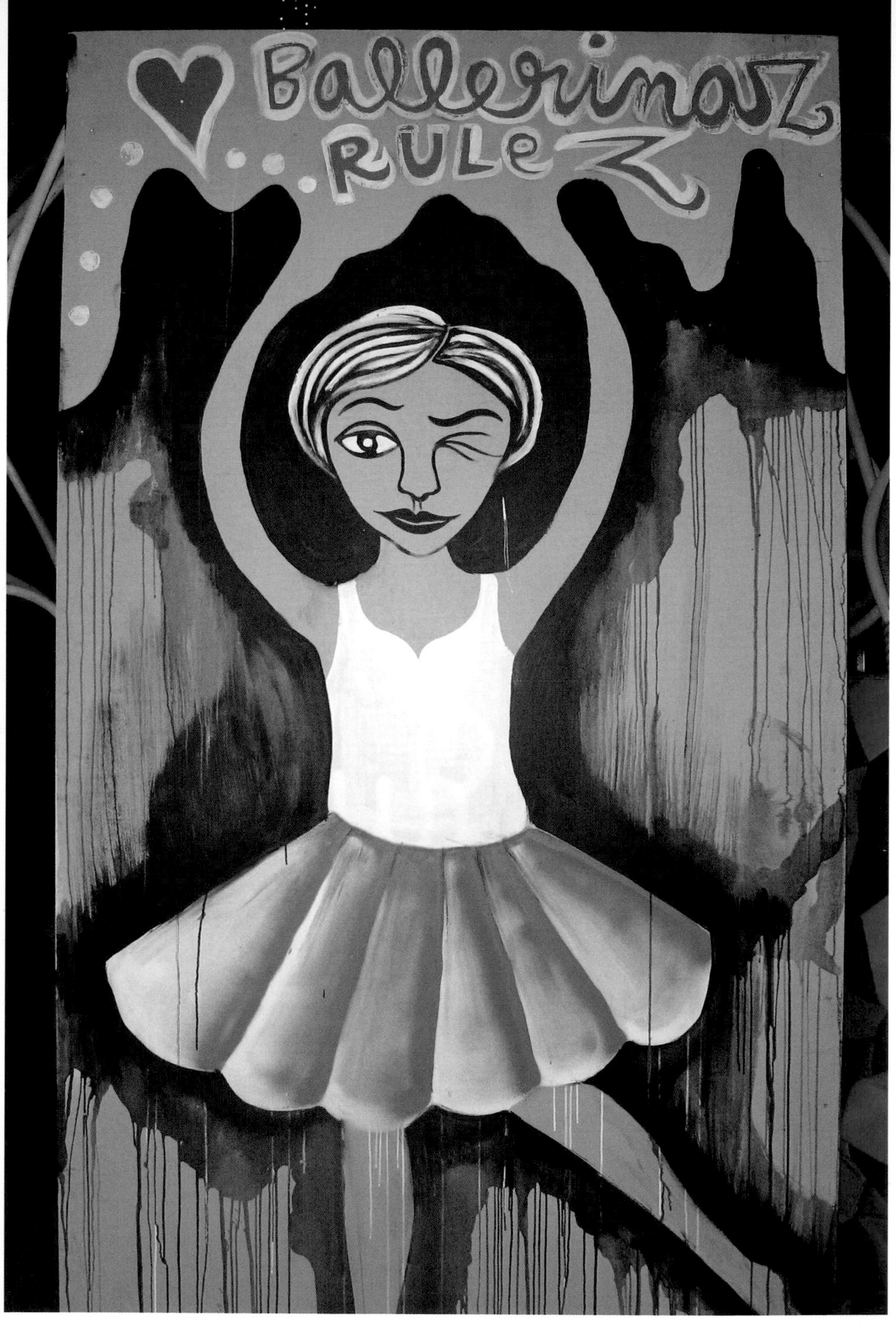
Ballerinaz
RULeZ

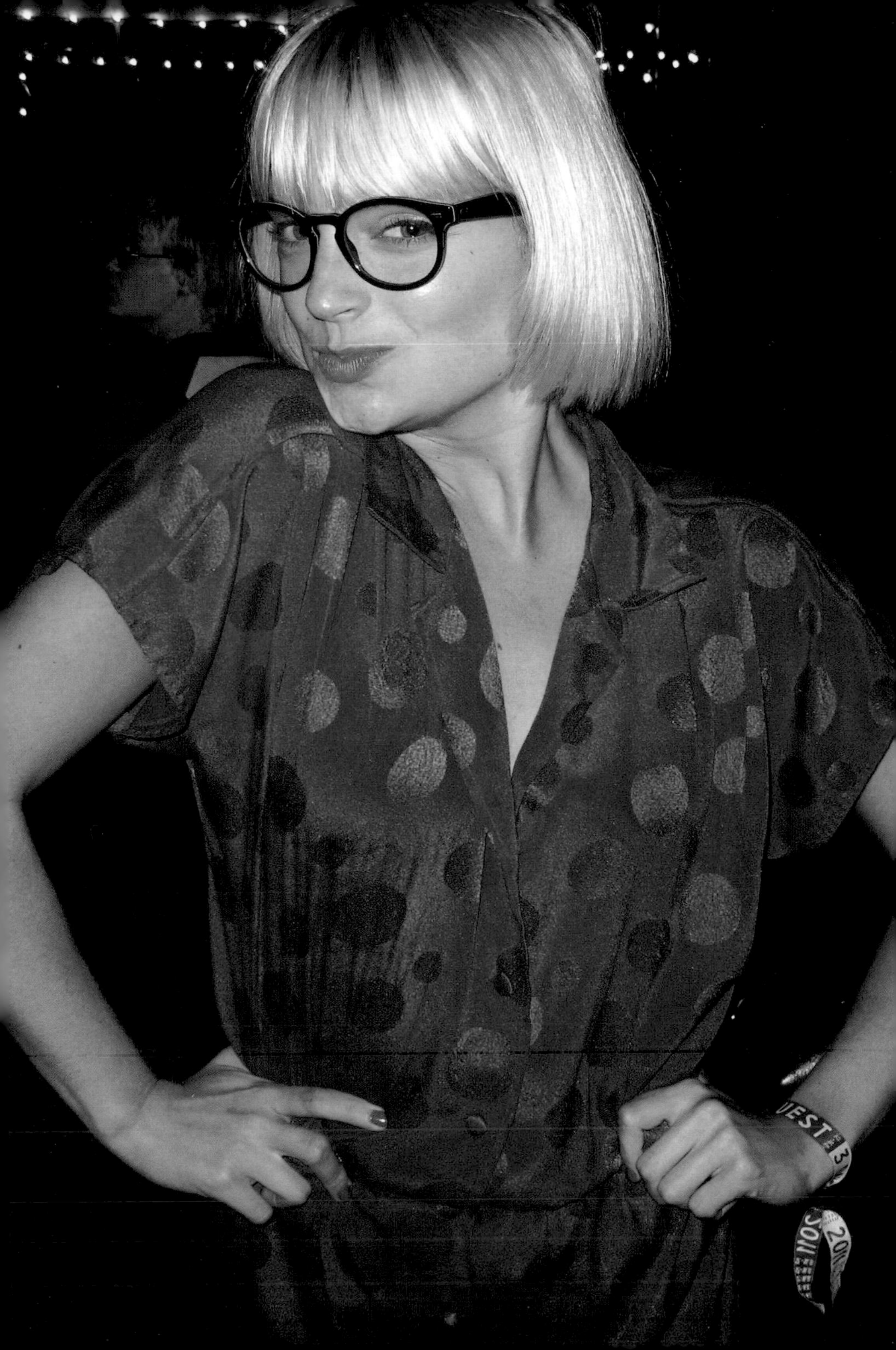

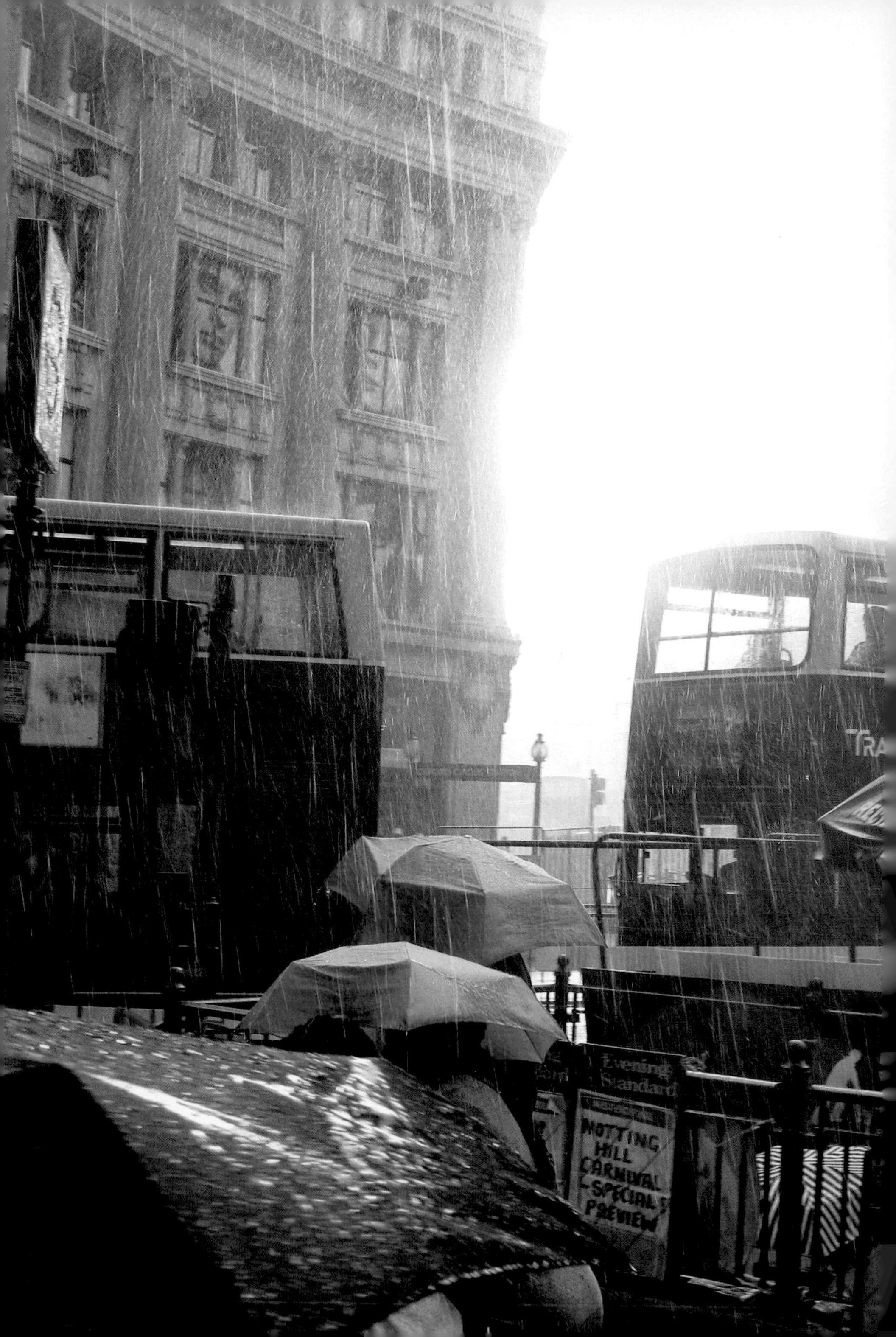

Evening Standard
NOTTING HILL CARNIVAL SPECIAL PREVIEW

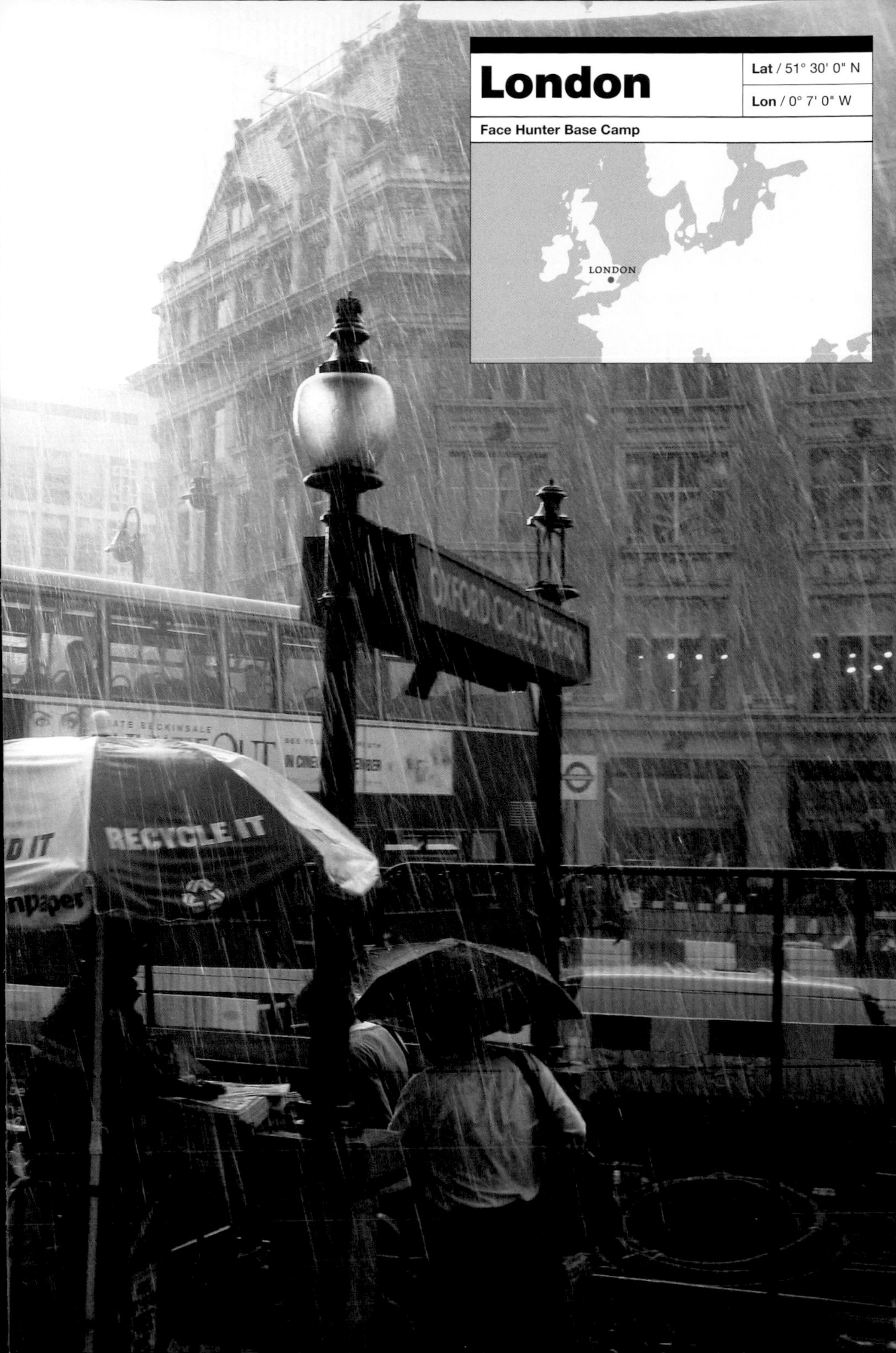

London

Lat / 51° 30' 0" N

Lon / 0° 7' 0" W

Face Hunter Base Camp

“London? I suppose it’s the closest thing I have to a home at the moment. I spend only 10% of my time here, but every time I come back I realize how fantabulous it is. London is the city by which all other cities are measured, but you can’t really measure London itself. It’s a true world hub, at the crossroads of the Americas, Europe, Africa and Asia. Over 300 languages are spoken daily in London, the most of any city in the world. London has always been an incubator for artists, writers, fashion designers and other creatives, and it’s one of the few places where kids truly invent new music and new ways of dressing every season. I live here because A) it’s convenient, and B) because it is the world capital of face-hunting. Here, in no particular order, are my favourite places in London: the Flower Market on Columbia Road in Hackney, which on Sundays is the only place where I have seen young people buying flowers; the Last Tuesday Society gallery store, which has the most incredible collection of bizarre objects including taxidermy and obscure artworks; and La Vie en Rose on Broadway Market (don’t bother trying to find it – it’s since closed. Too bad for me!). And, of course, Heathrow Terminal 5.”

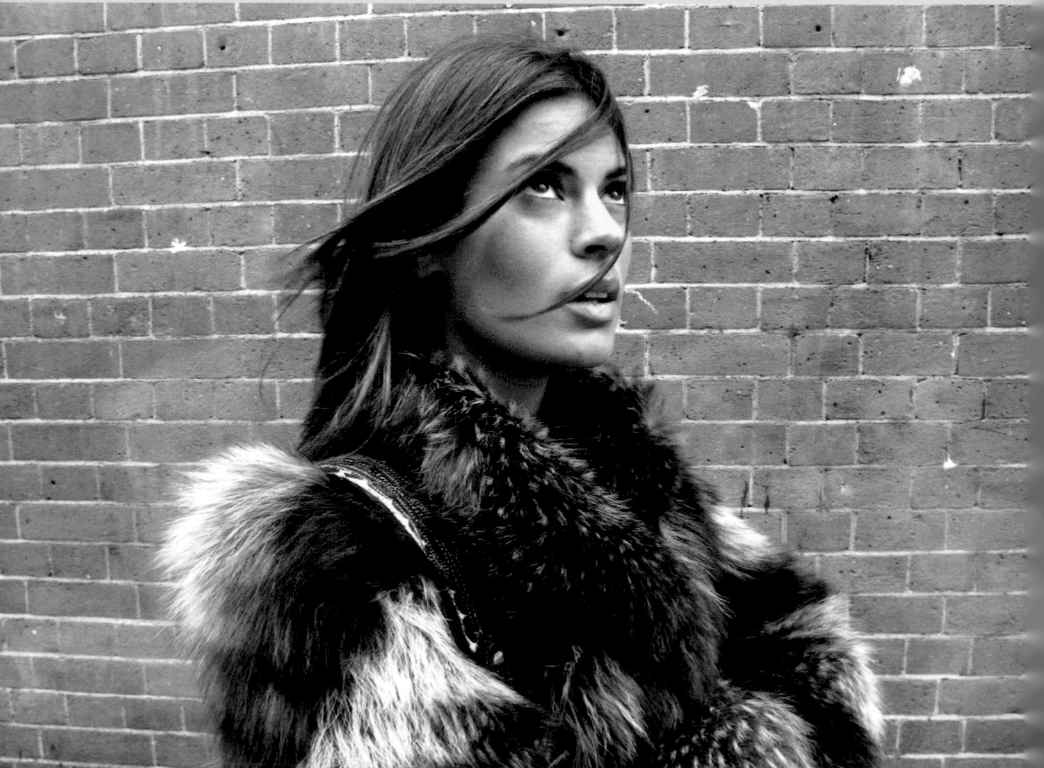

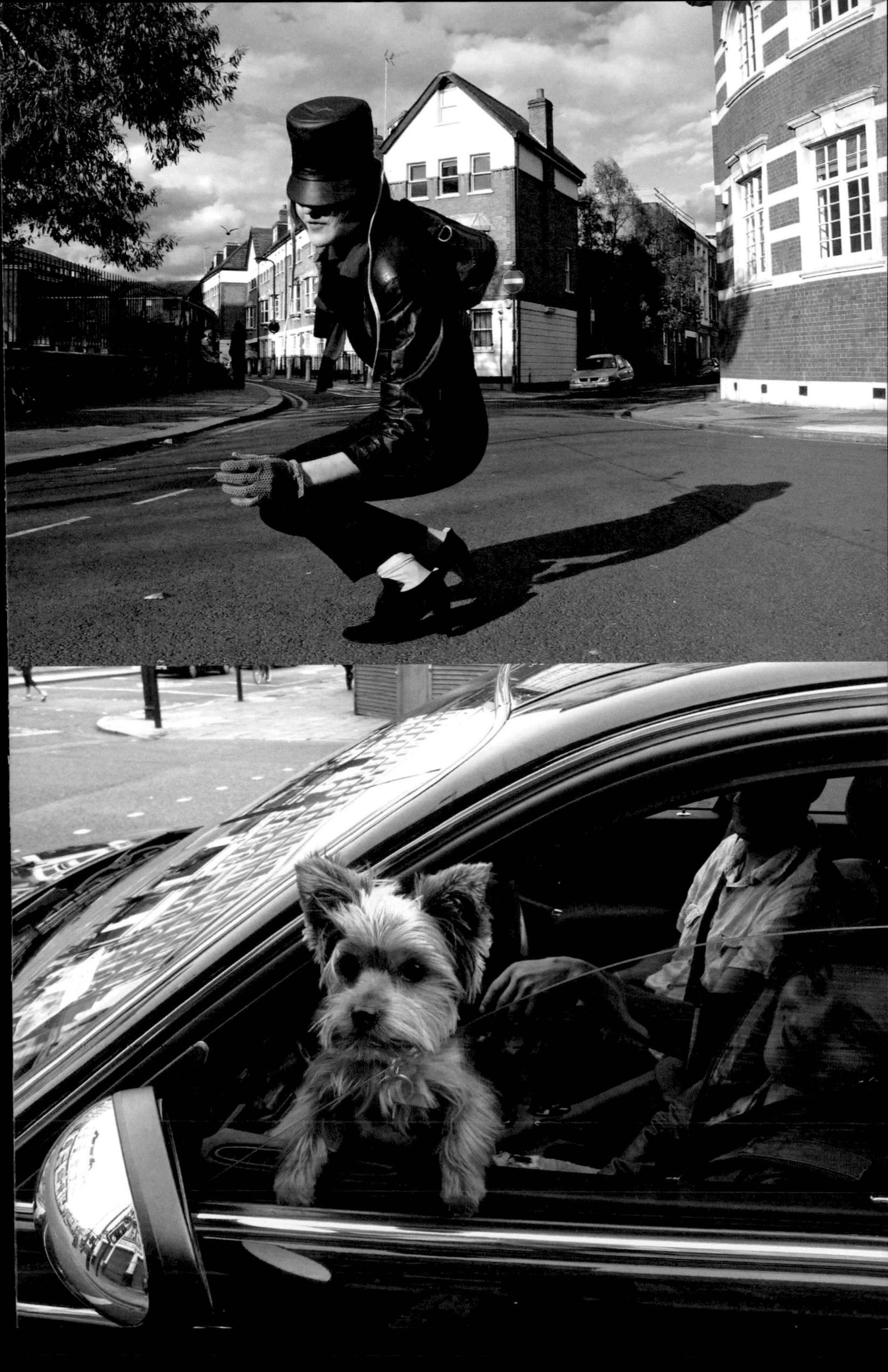

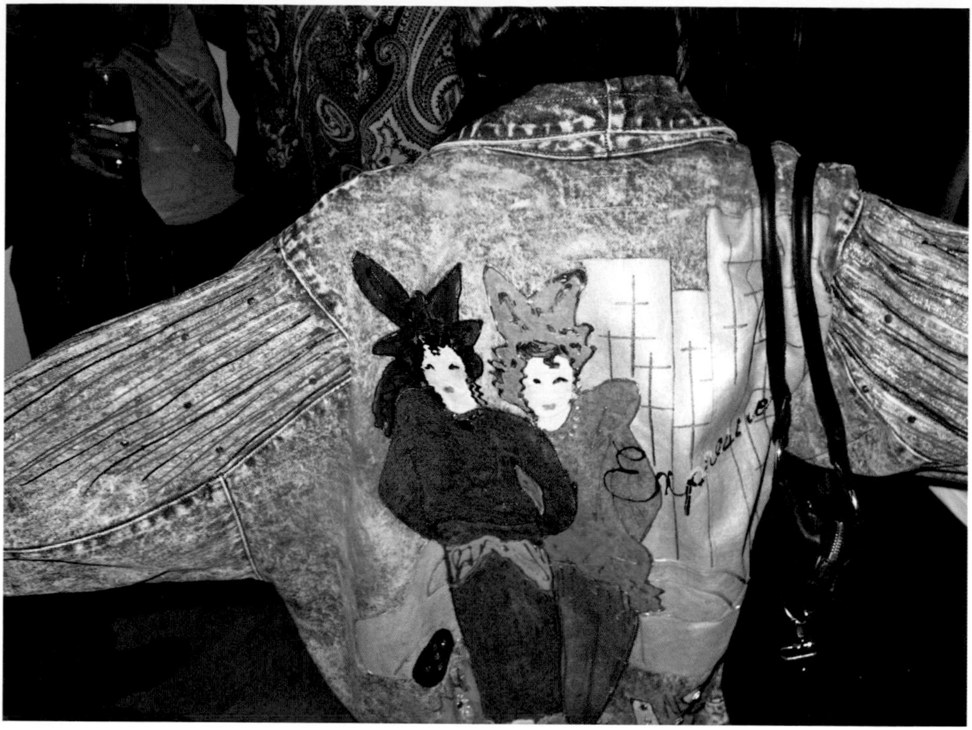

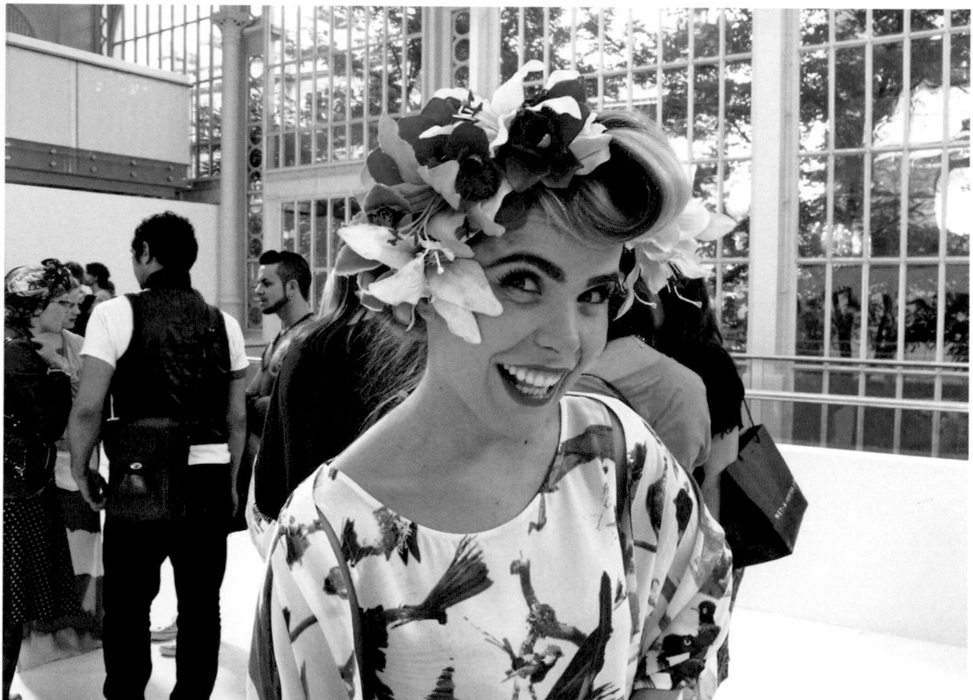

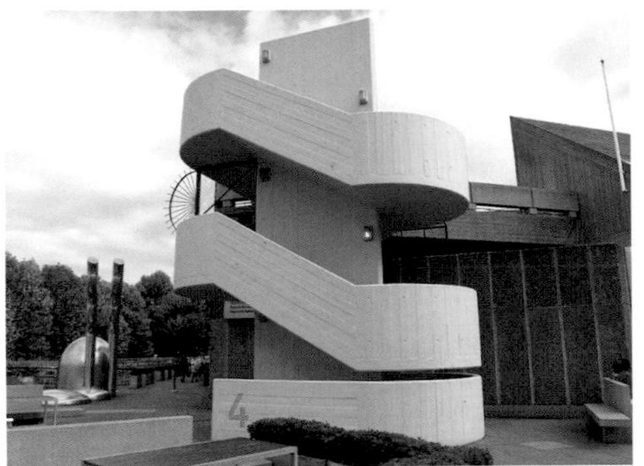

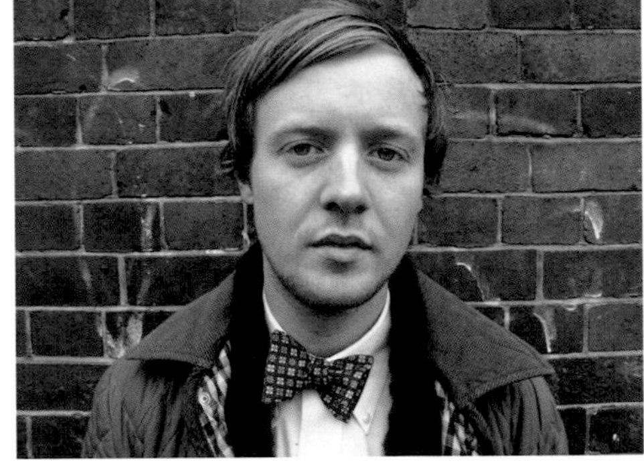

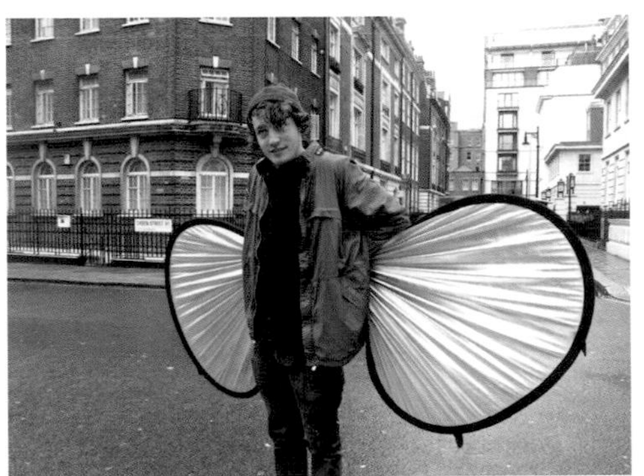

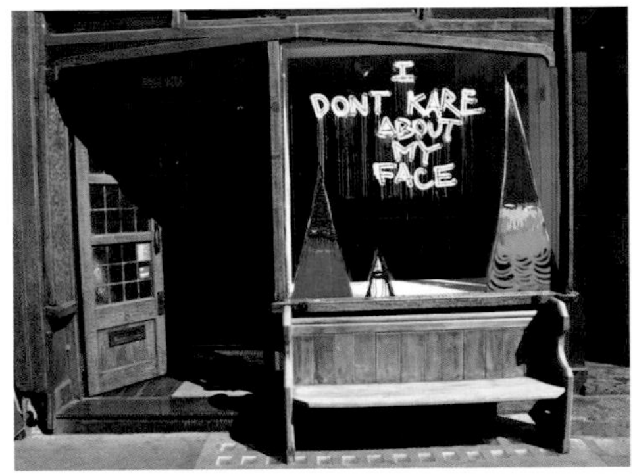
I
DONT KARE
ABOUT
MY
FACE

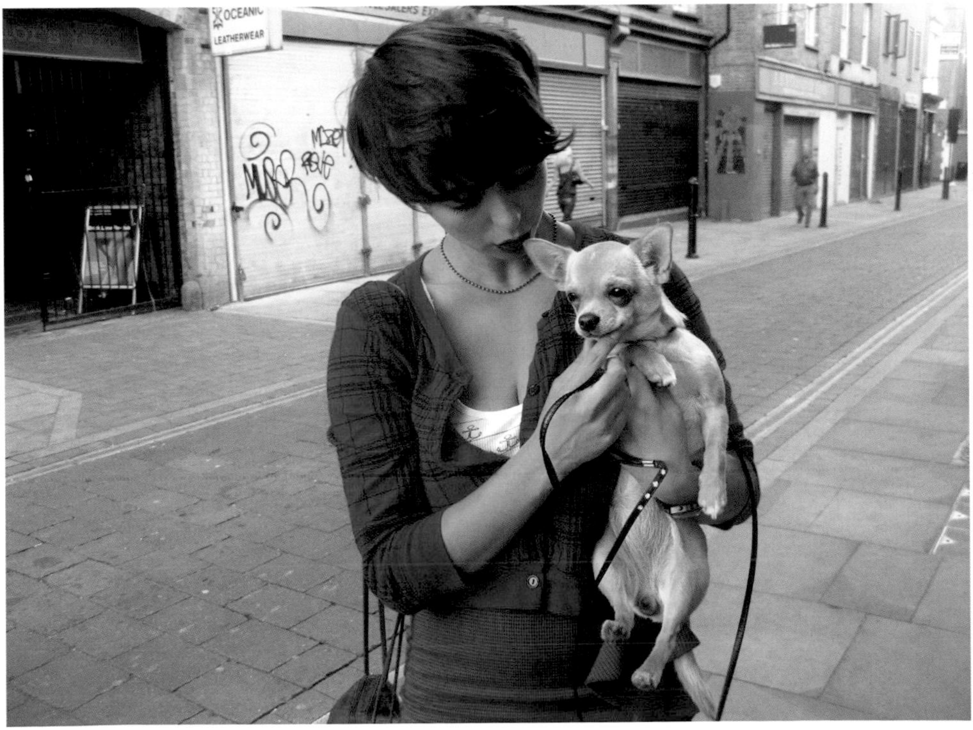

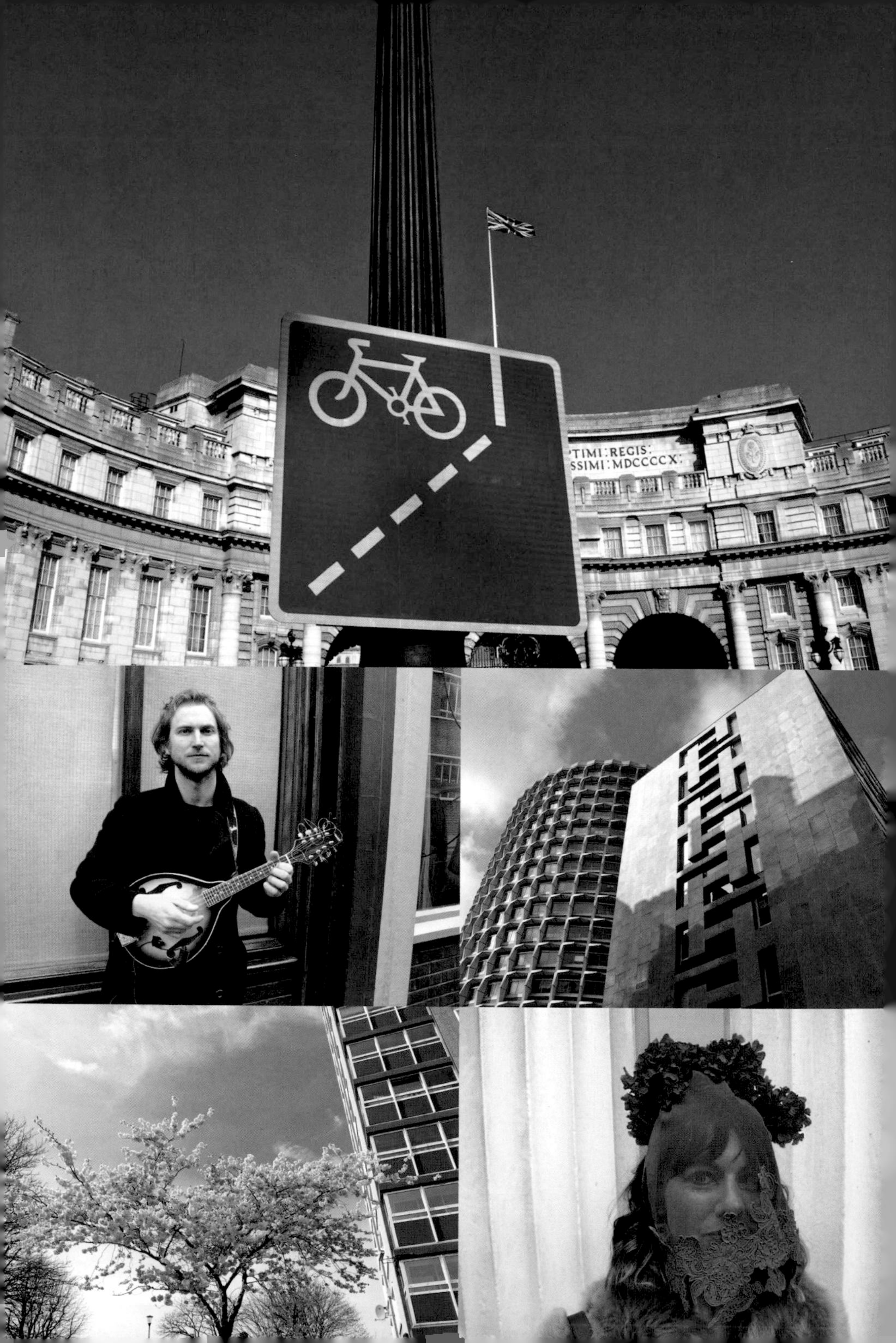
TIMI:REGIS:
SSIMI:MDCCCCX:

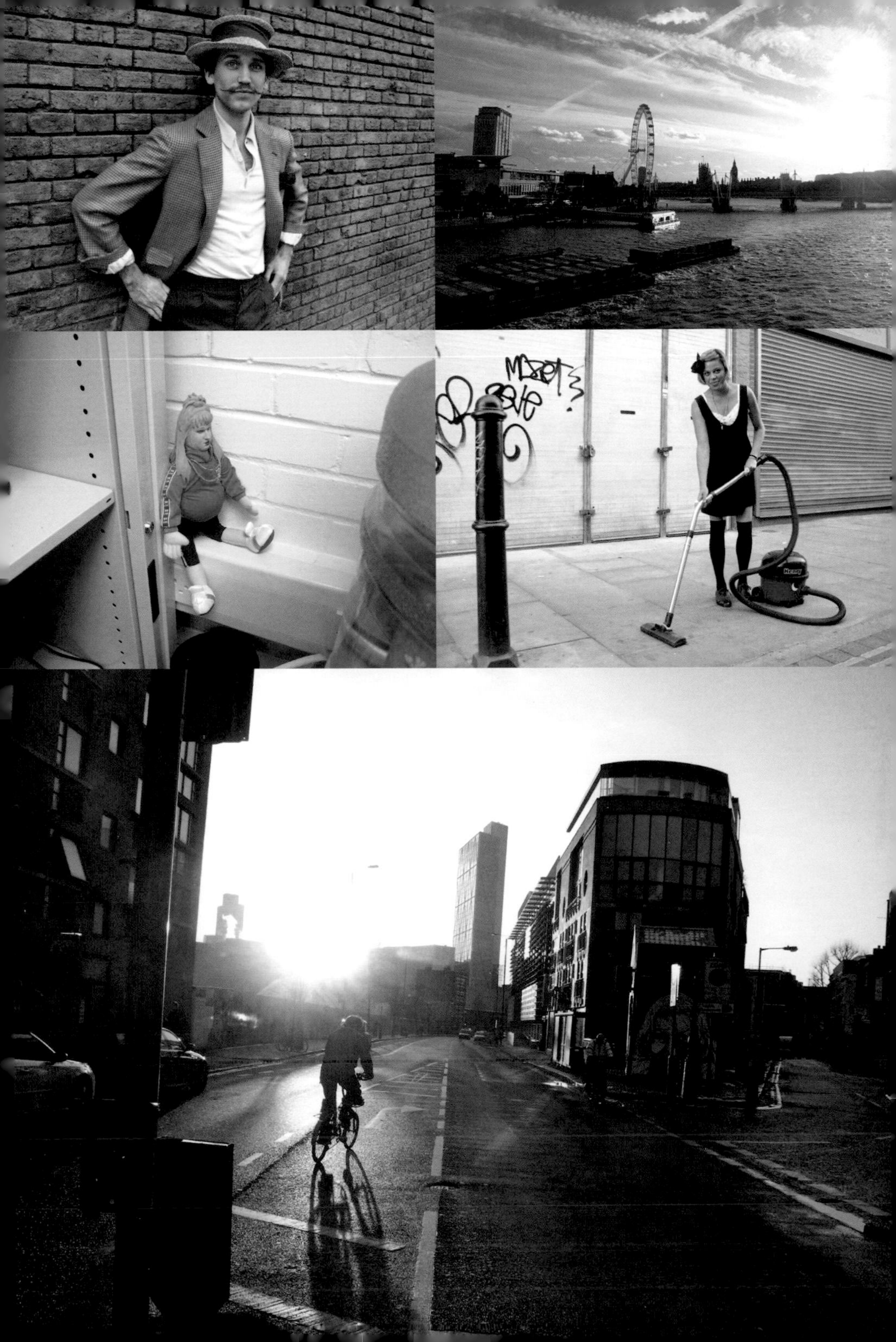

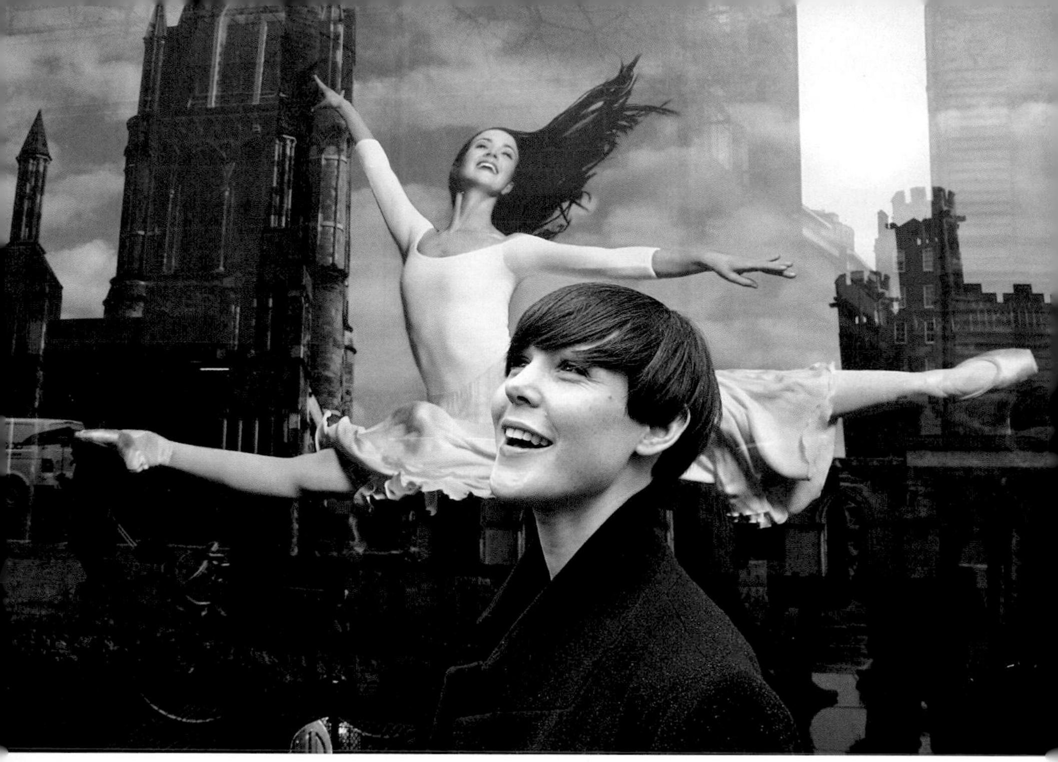

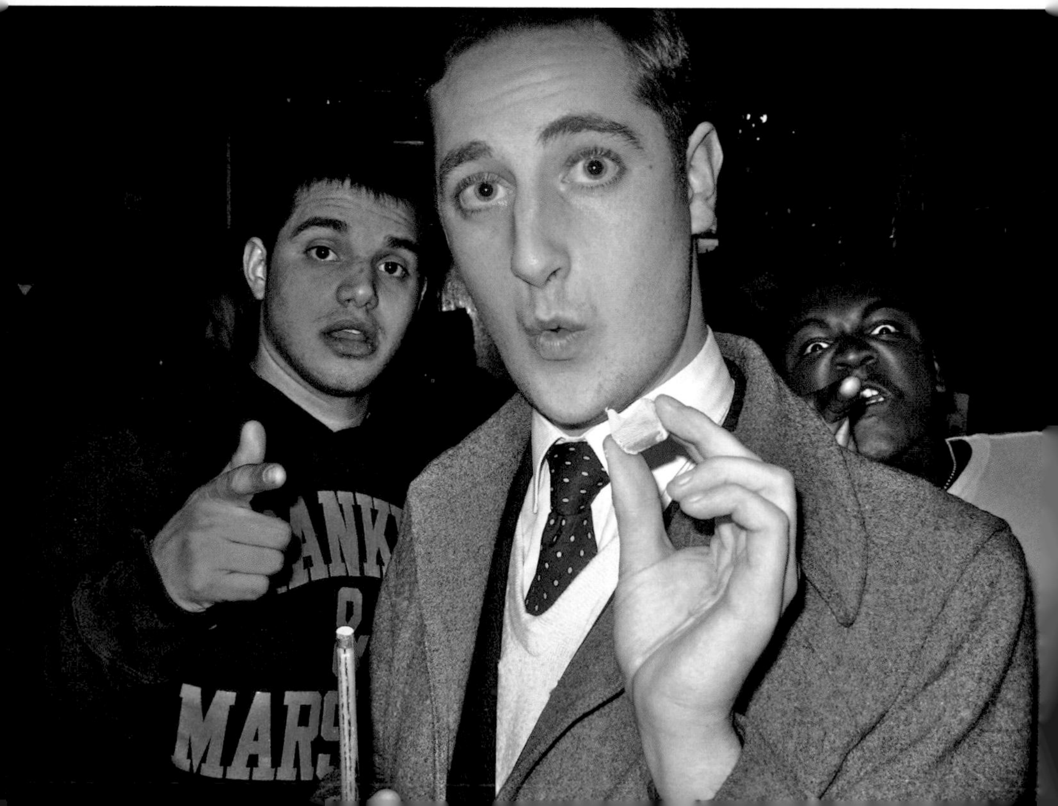

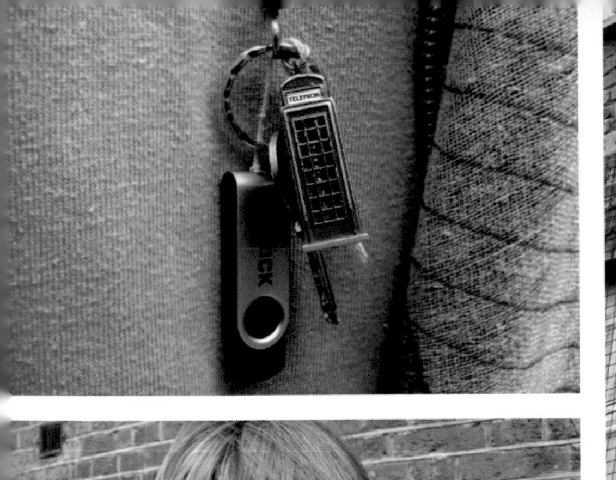

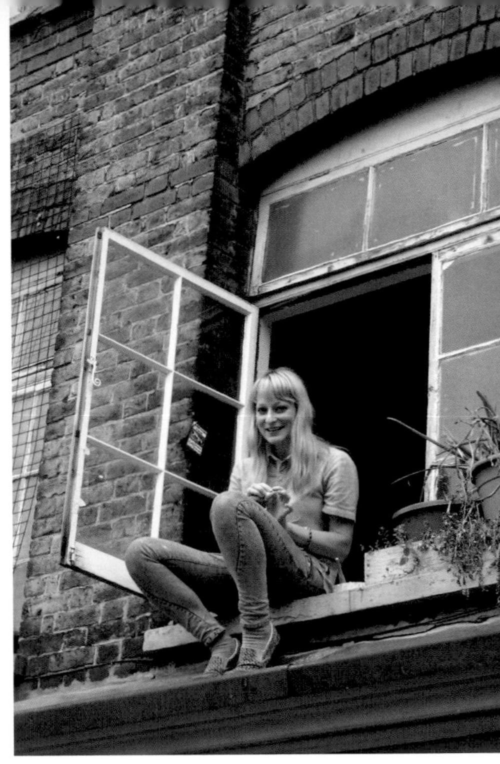

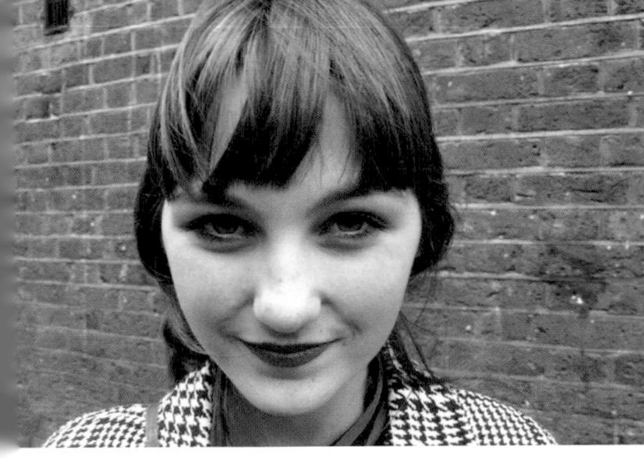

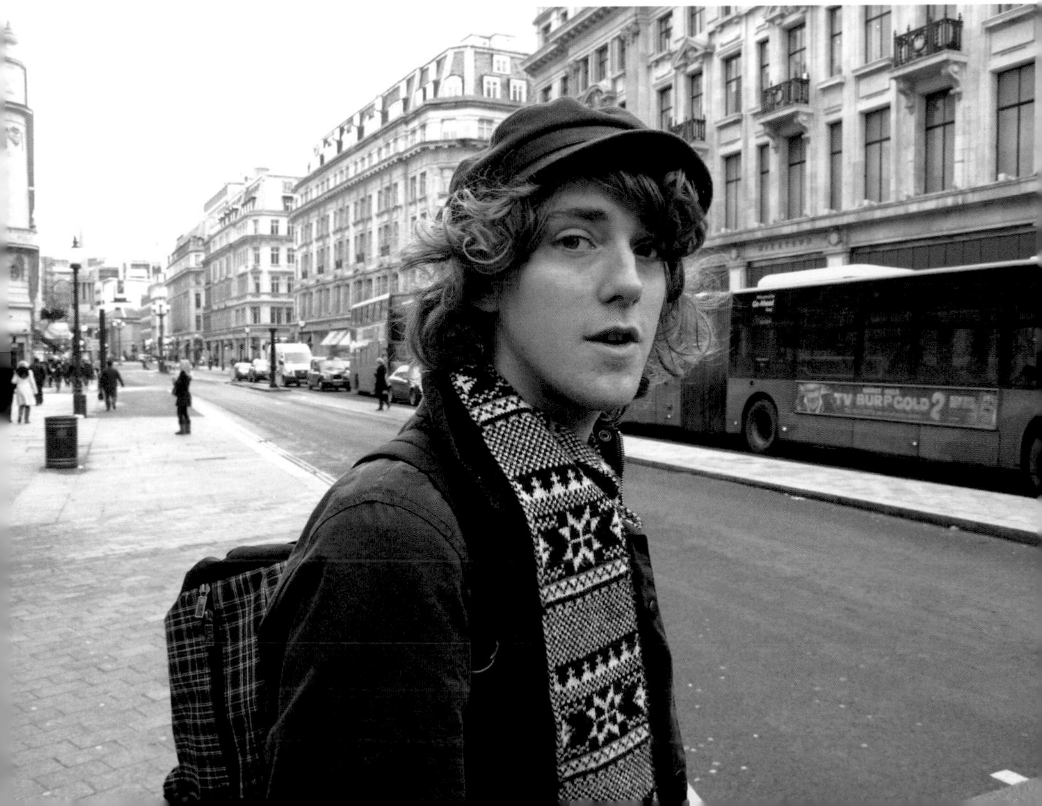

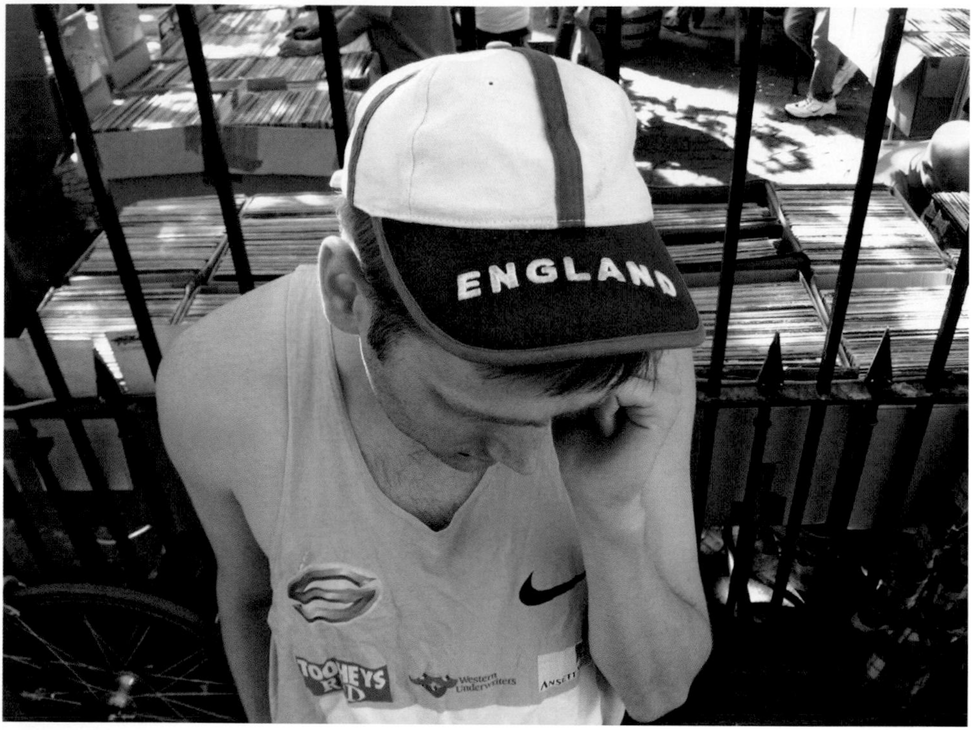

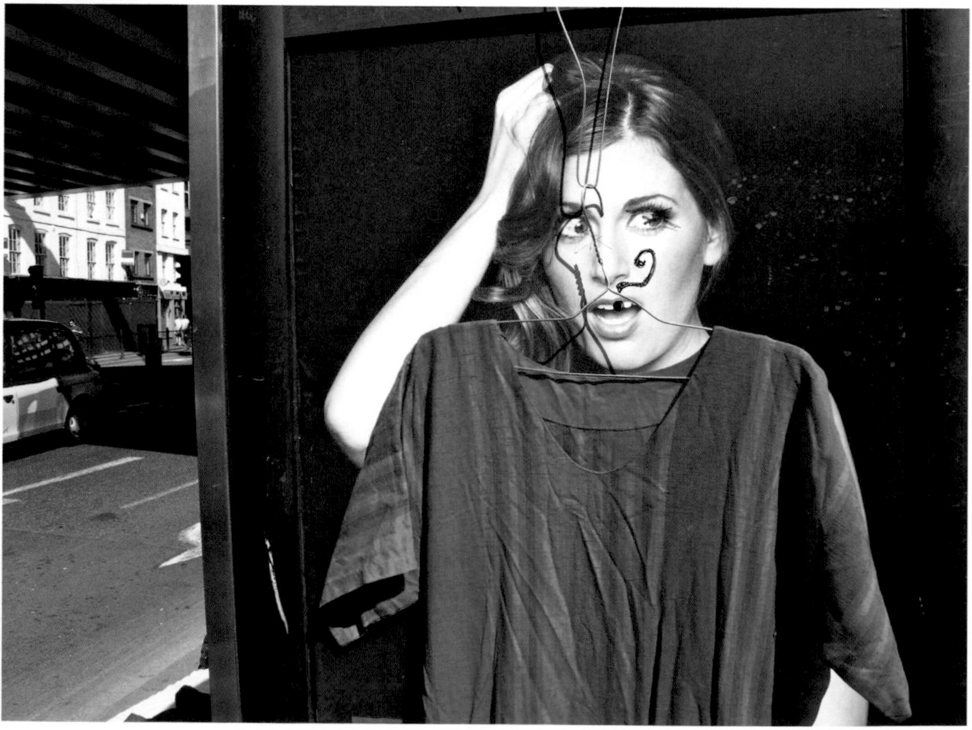

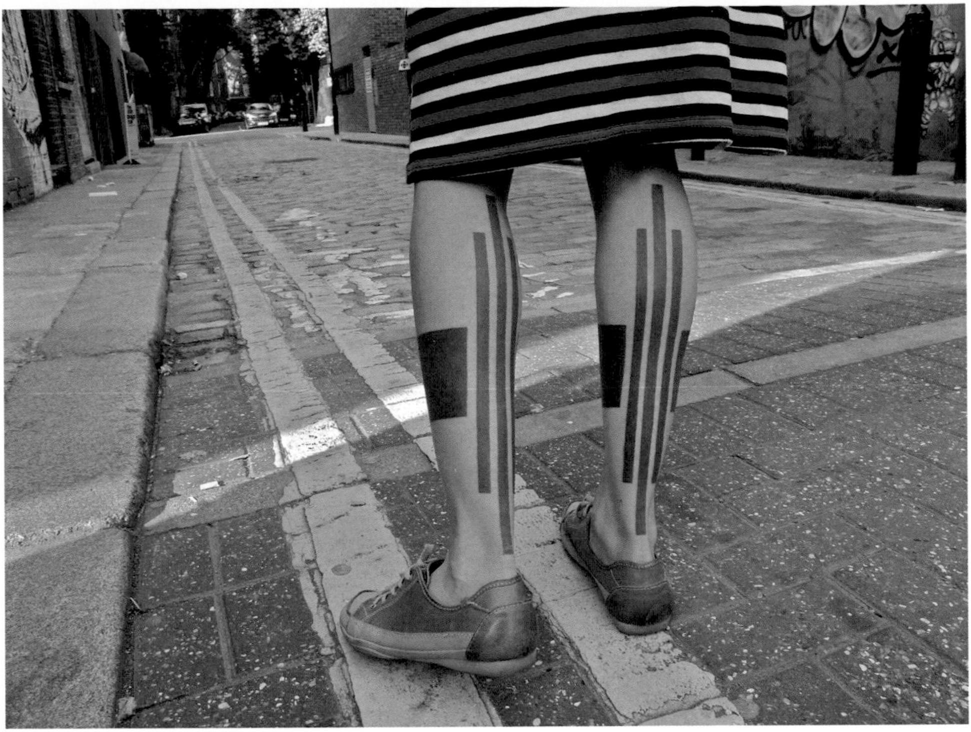

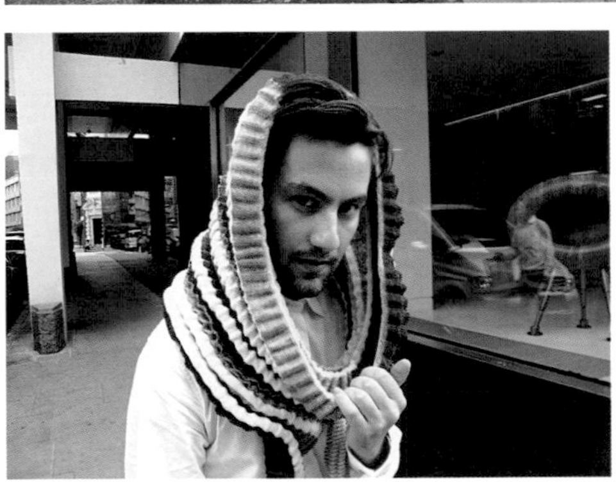

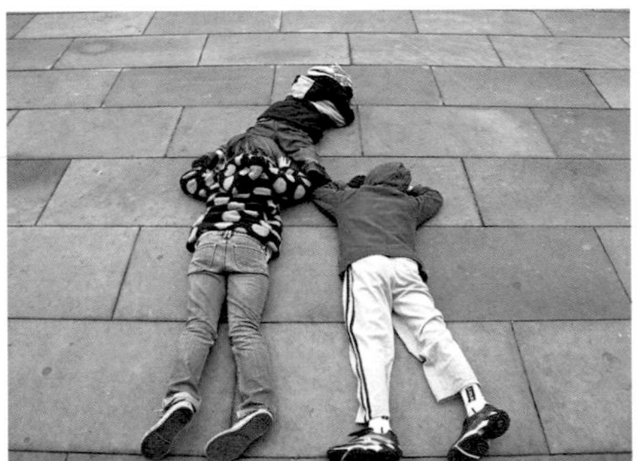

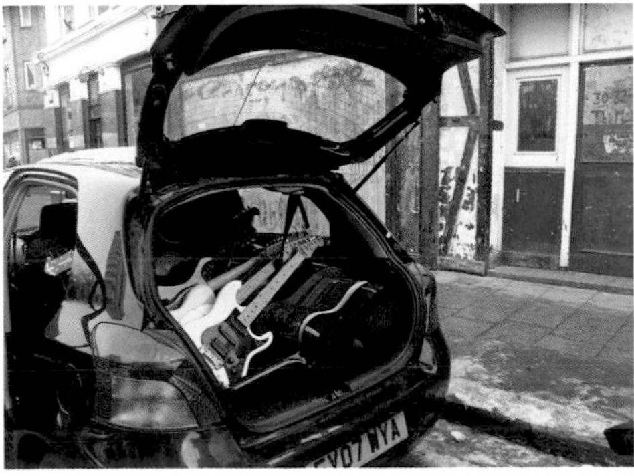

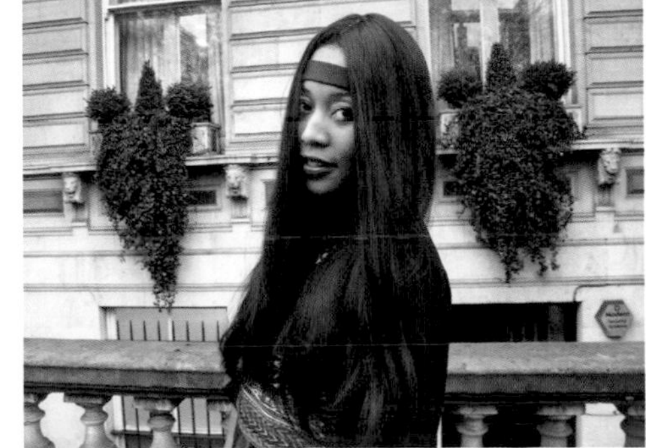

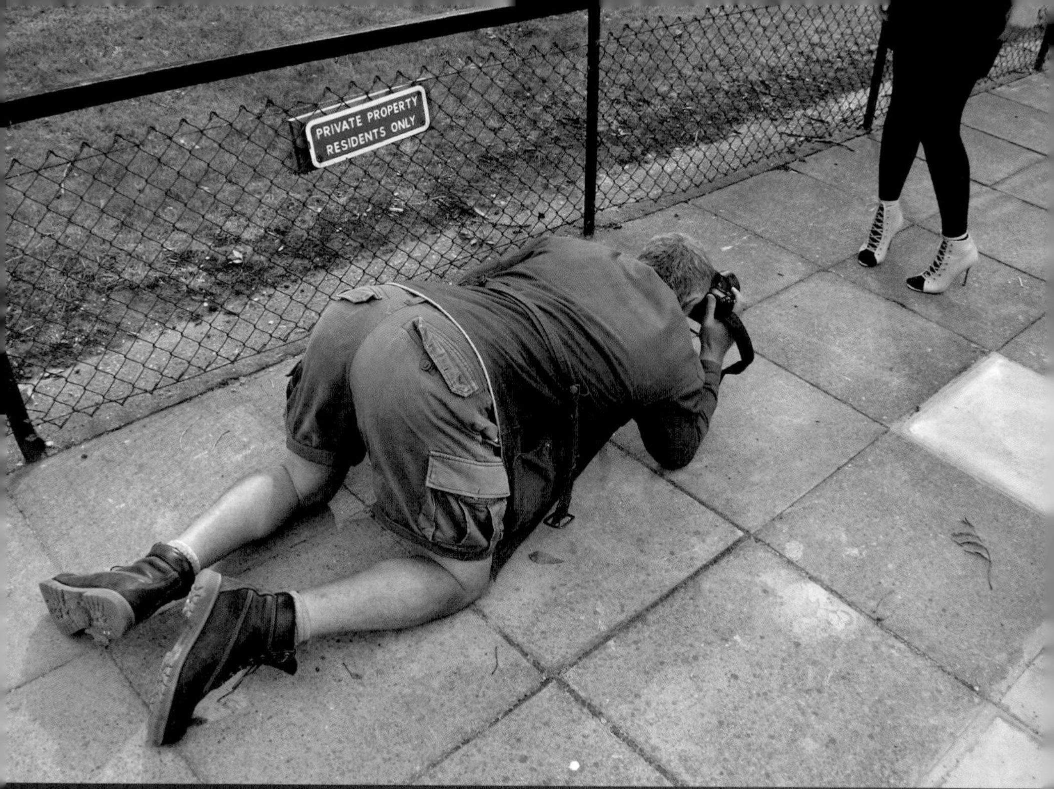

PRIVATE PROPERTY
RESIDENTS ONLY

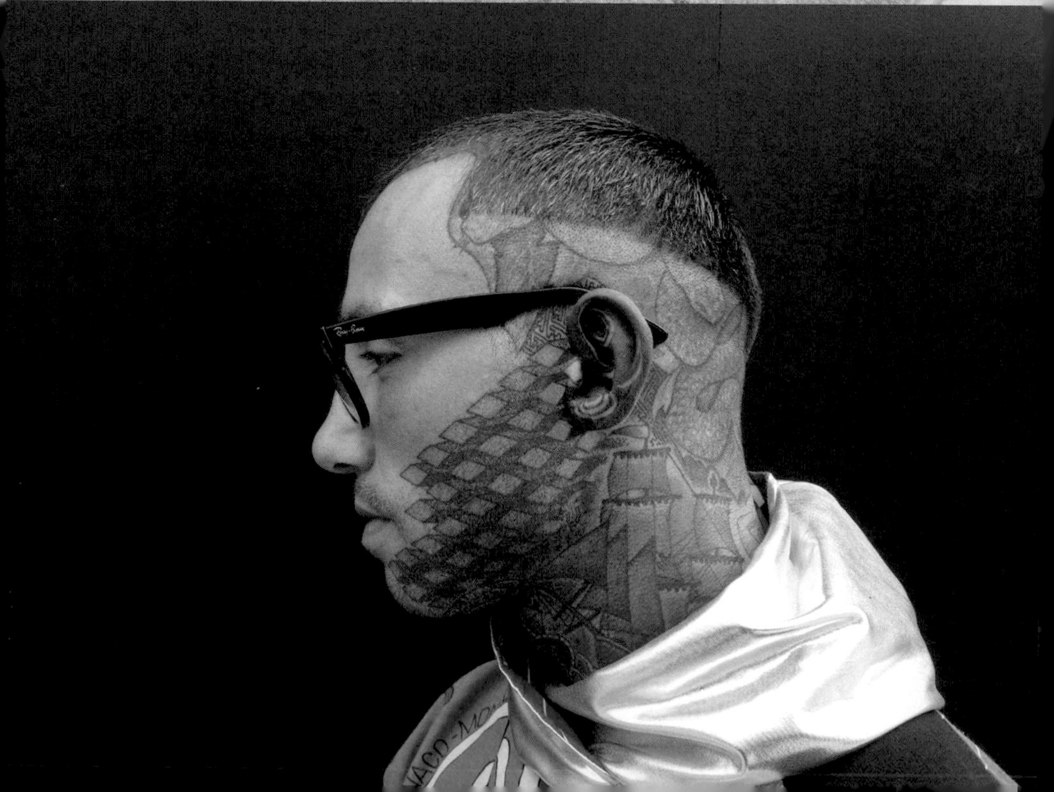

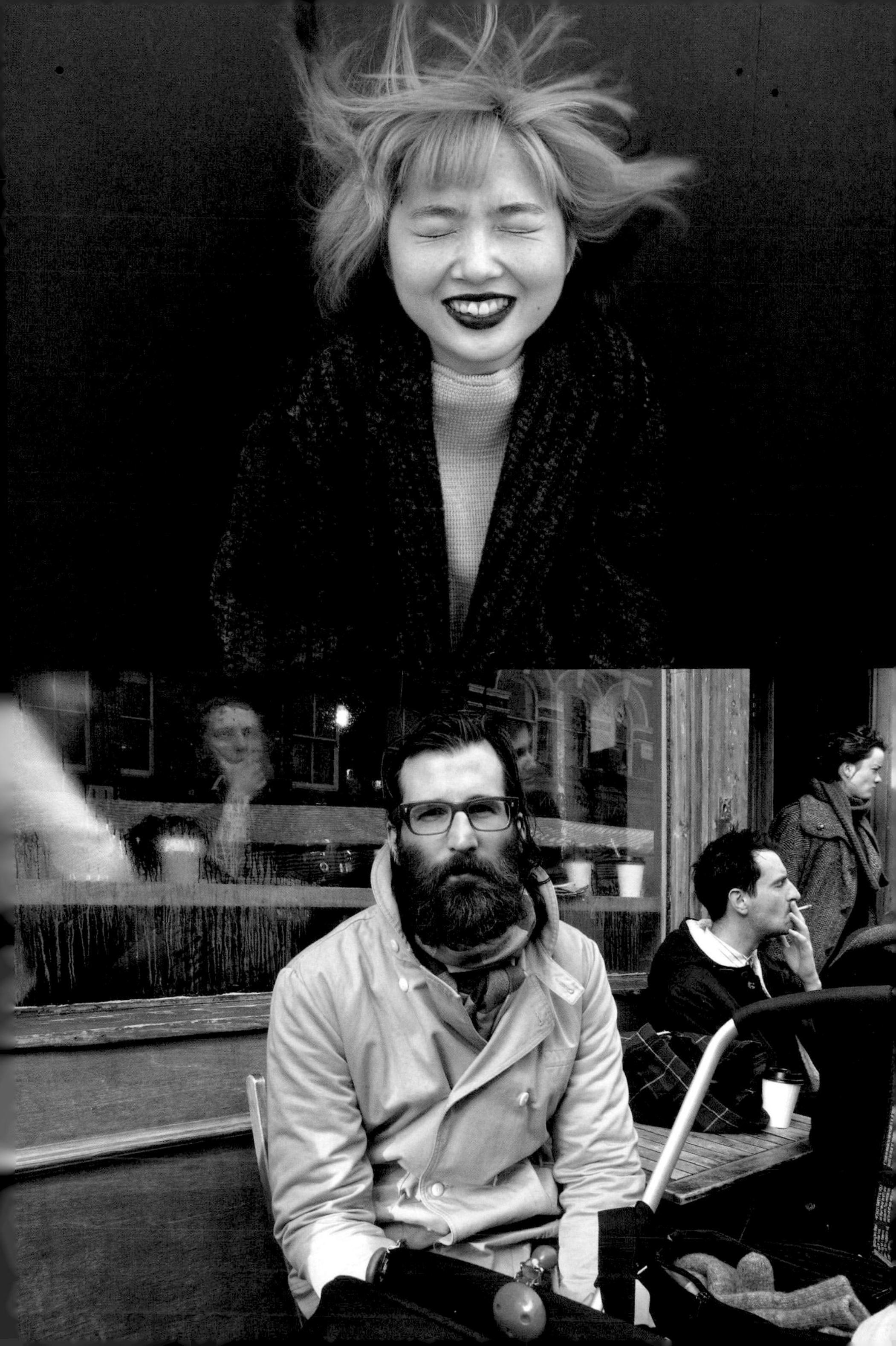

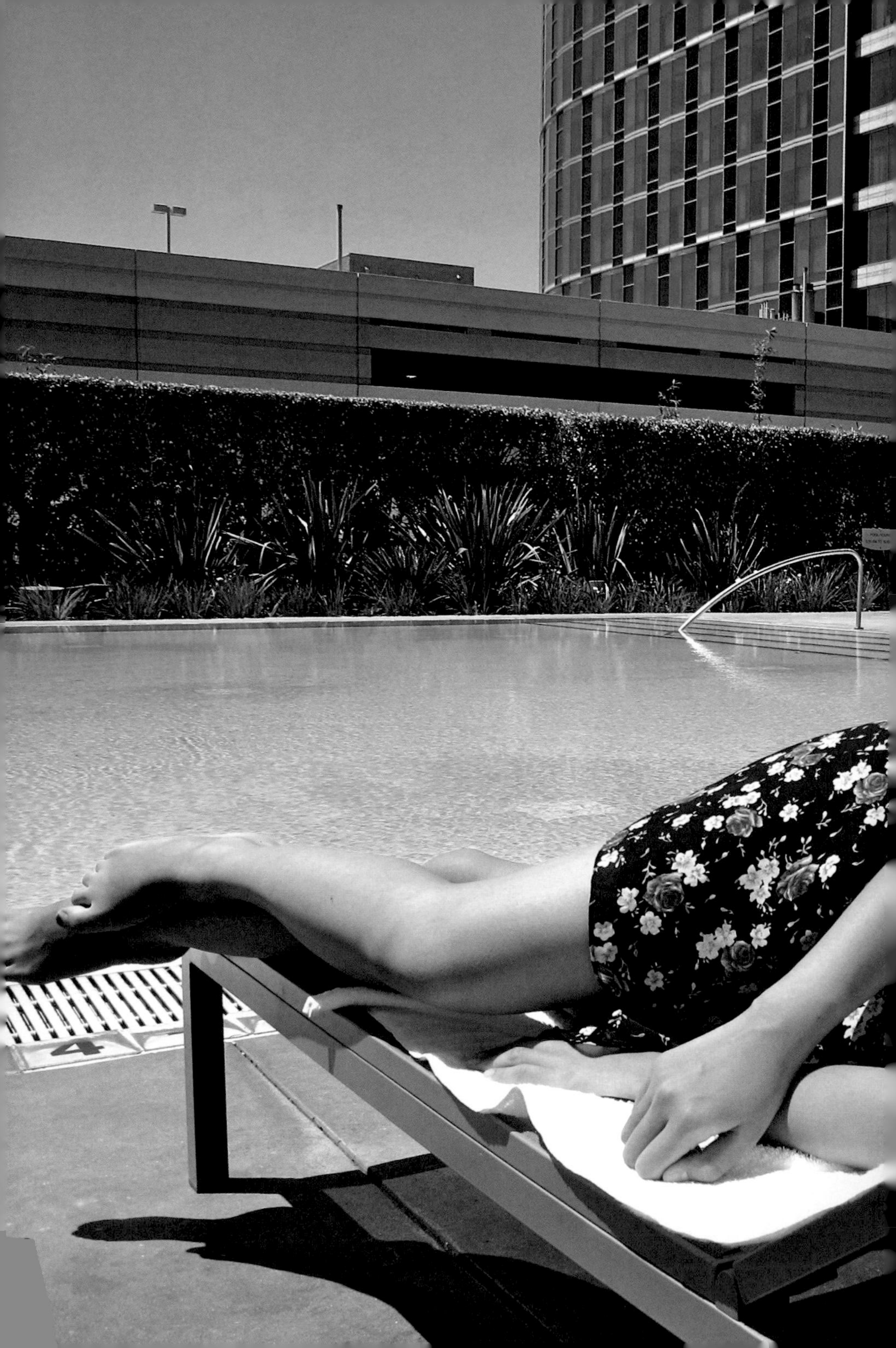

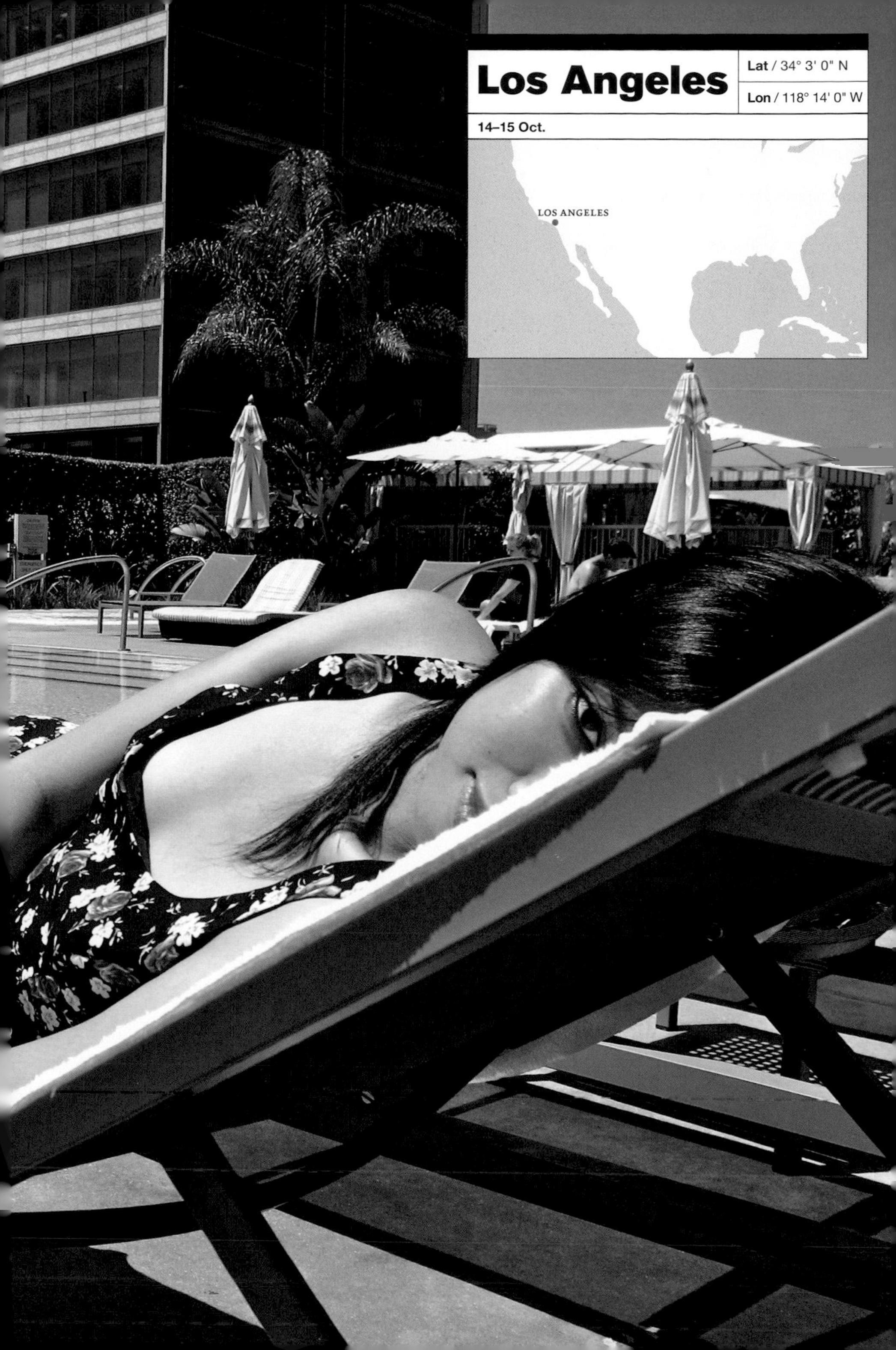
Los Angeles
Lat / 34° 3' 0" N
Lon / 118° 14' 0" W
14–15 Oct.
LOS ANGELES

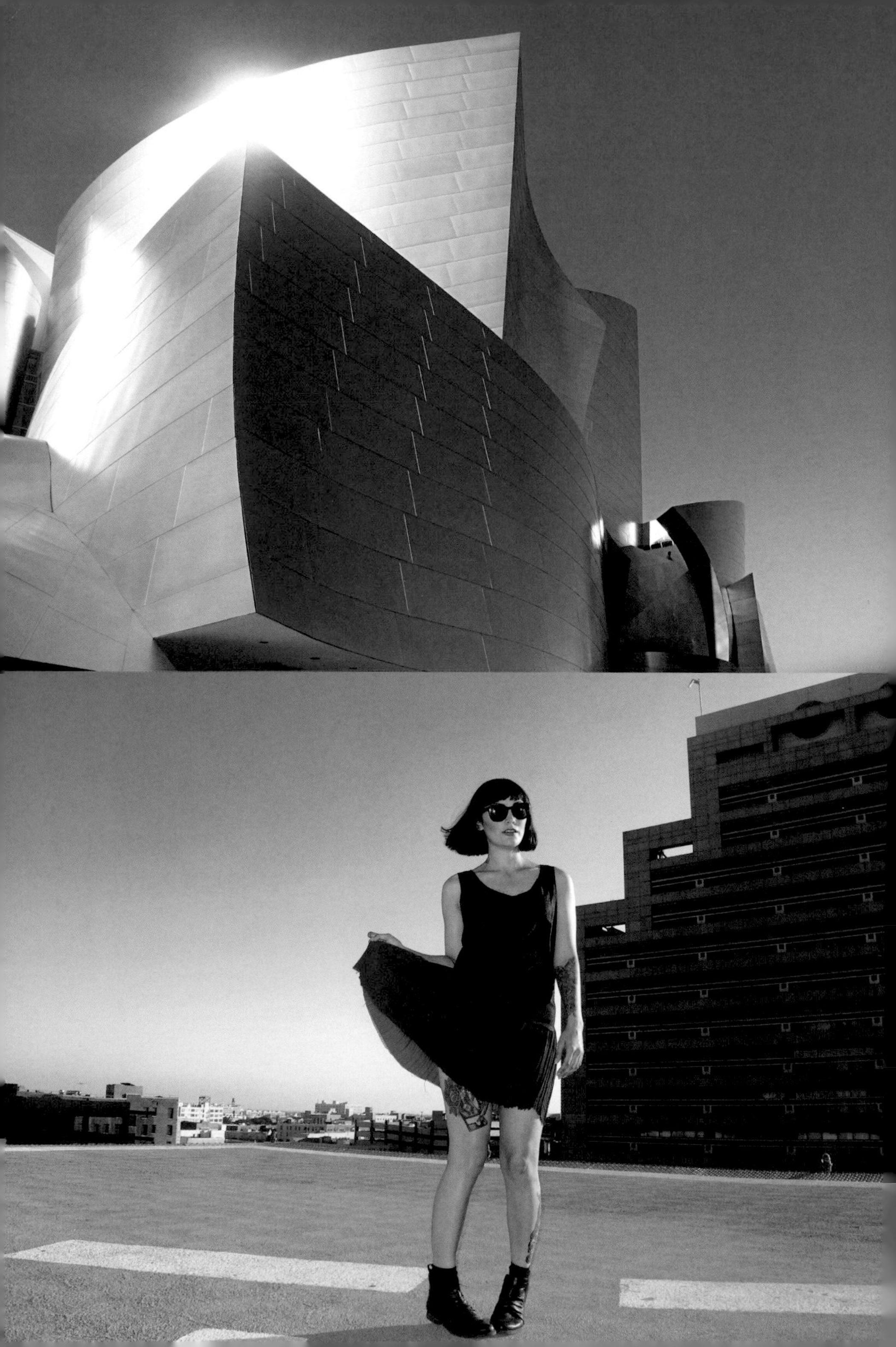

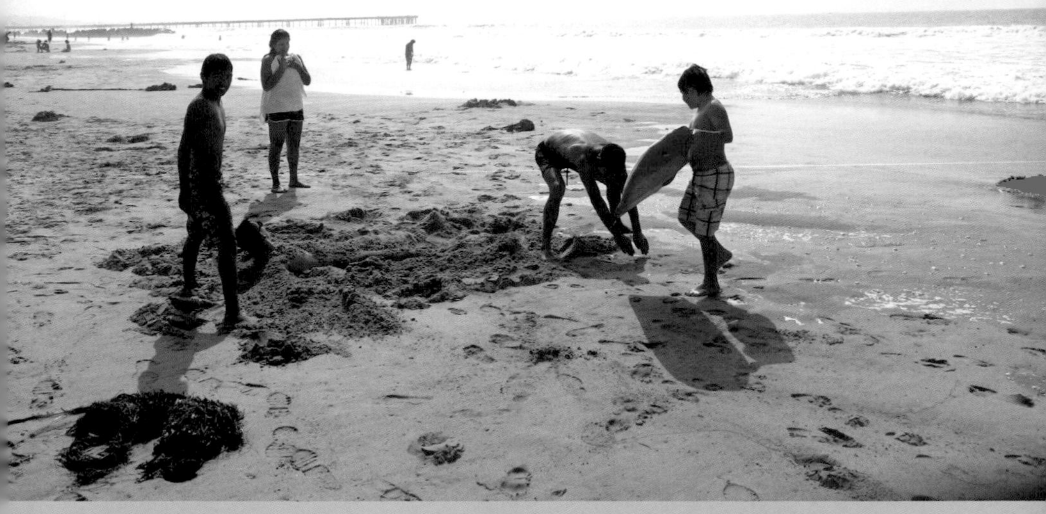

“Los Angeles is a gigantic private city. As big as it is, you don’t actually get to meet very many people in a day. The only crowded places are the highways. As a European I find it very fascinating to be in a metropolis with no centre, where every neighbourhood is essentially a separate city. There’s a laid-back coolness in the air. People will dress up to go to events in the evening, but during the day they don’t bother, since they don’t spend much time in public spaces as they drive from work to the shops and then to the drive-in coffee kiosks. This is a city where people even routinely drive to the gym! (To compensate there is an obsession with maintaining a healthy lifestyle that’s almost a fashion accessory itself.) I’ve never experienced such a sense of freedom, of limitless possibilities, as I did in L.A. – something about having enough physical and mental space to do and be whatever you want.”

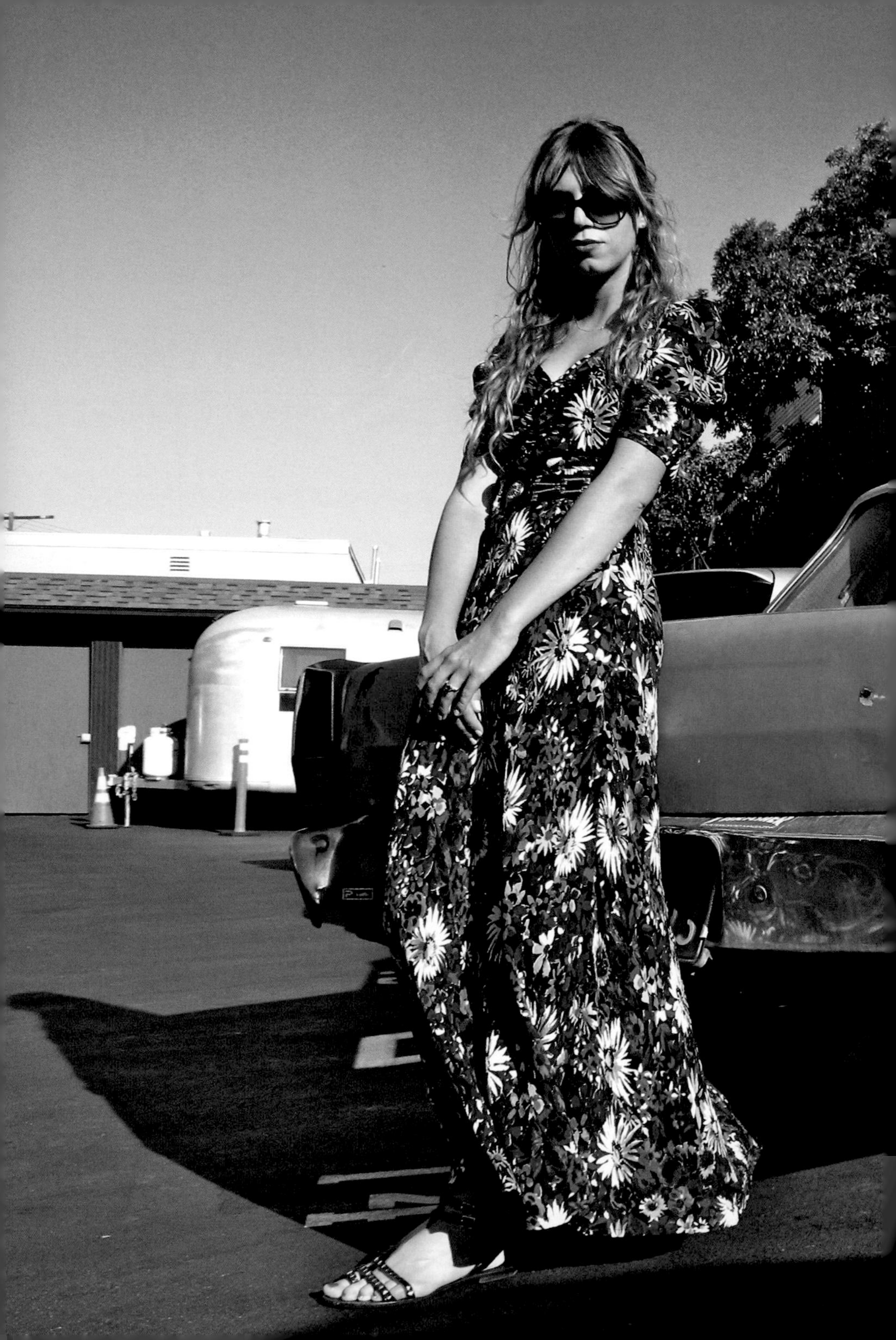

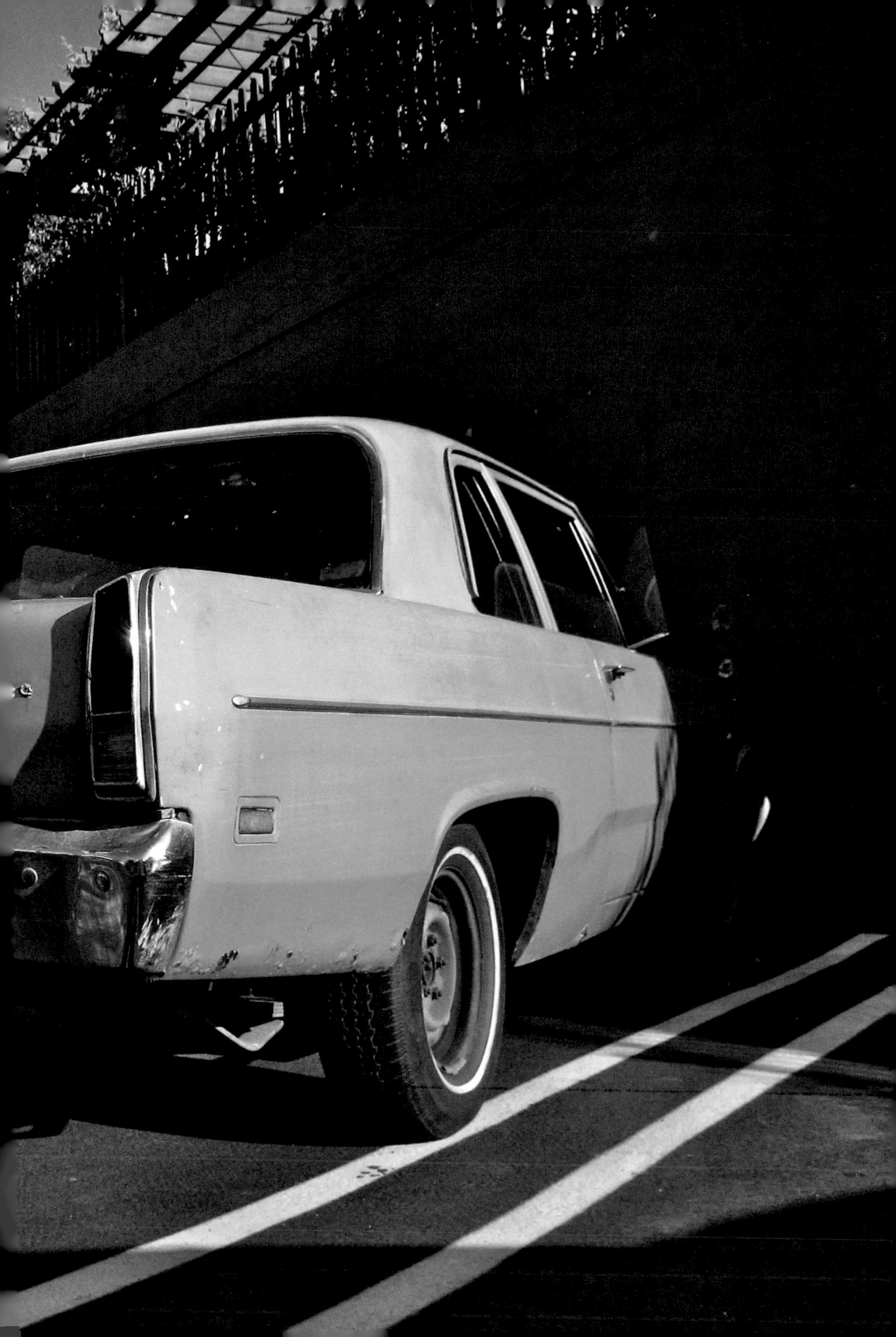

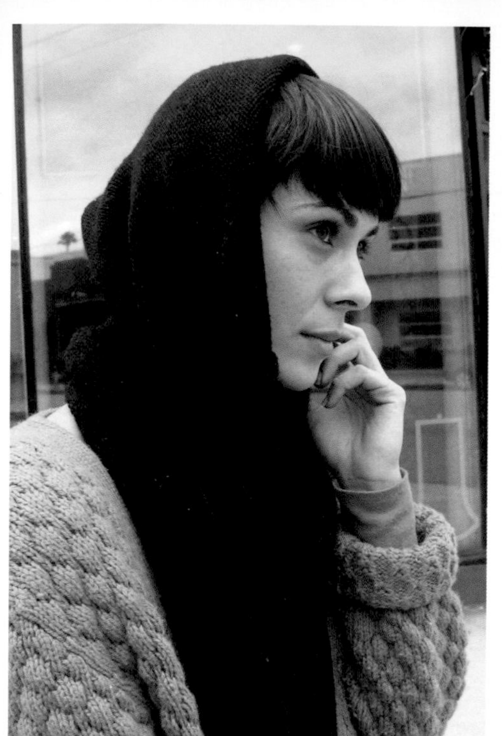

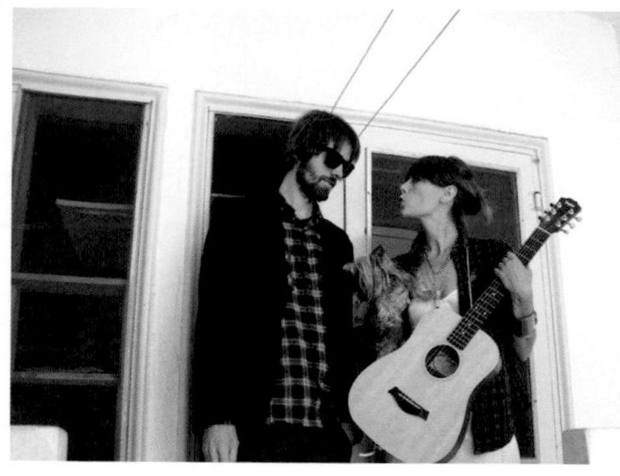

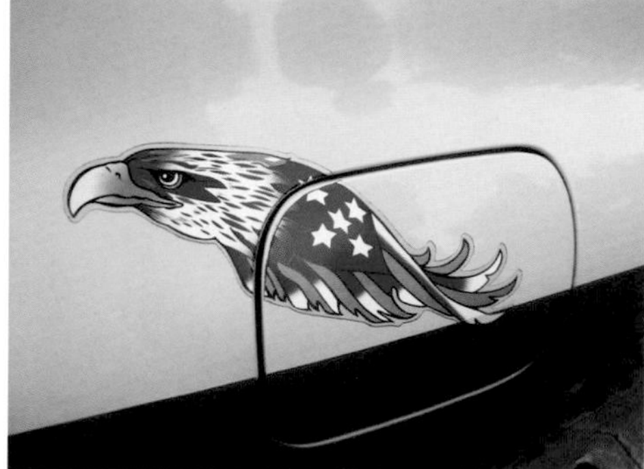

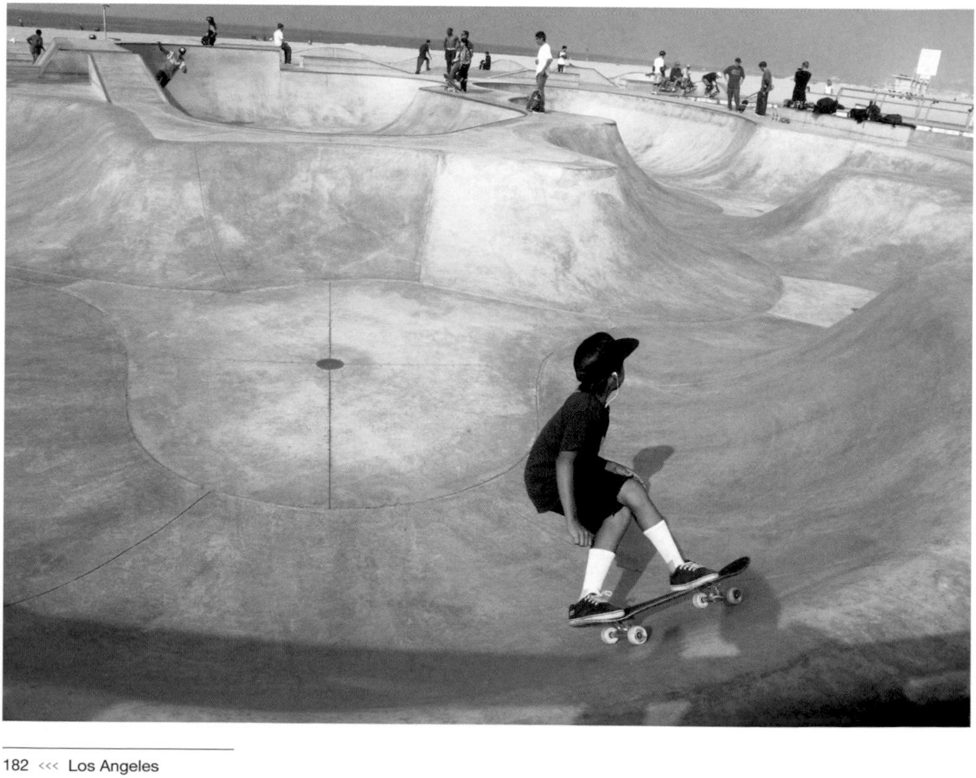

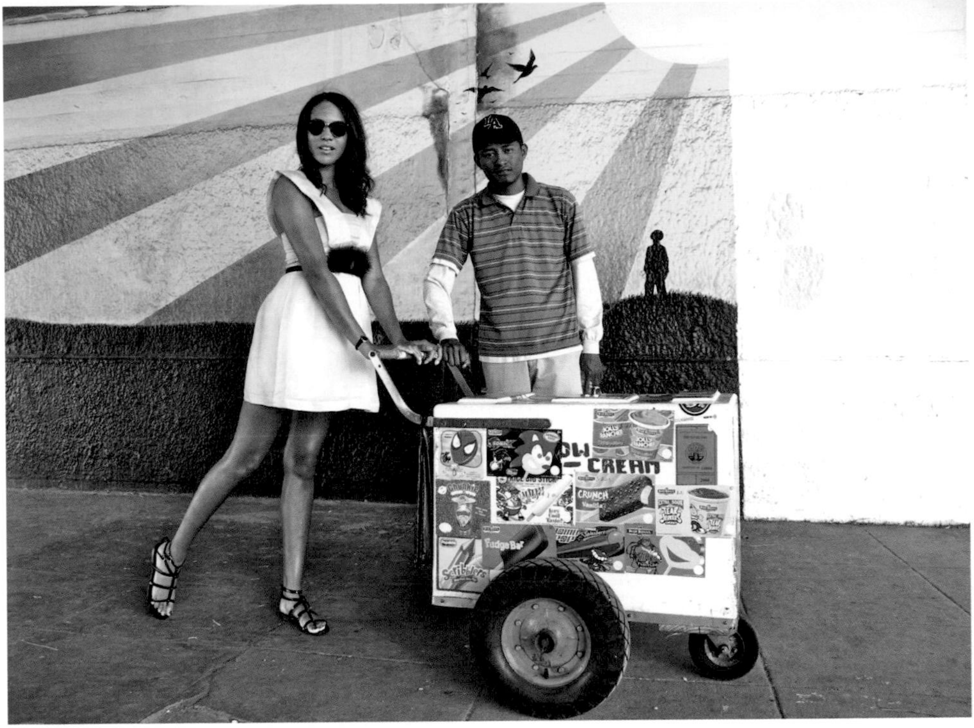

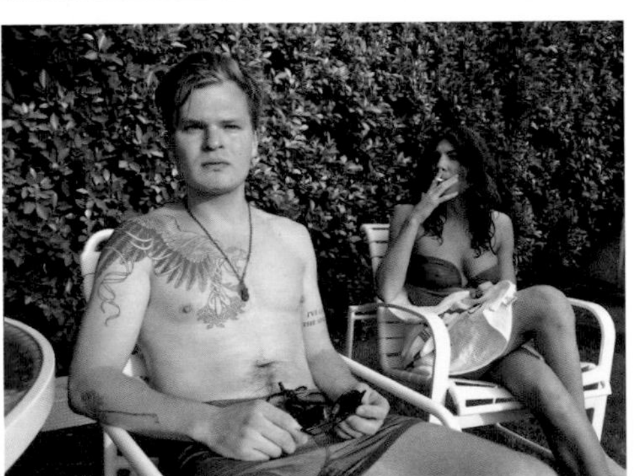

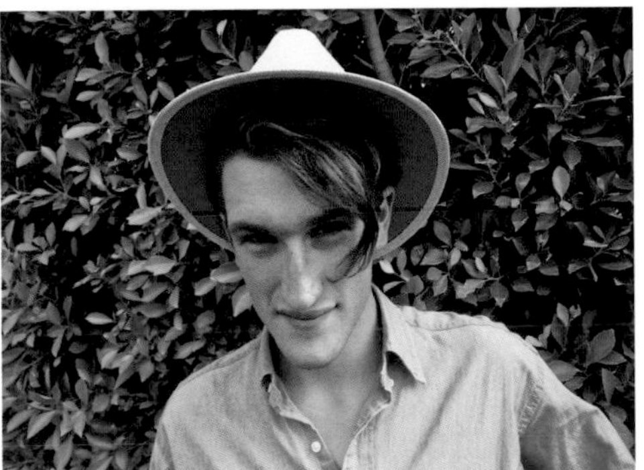

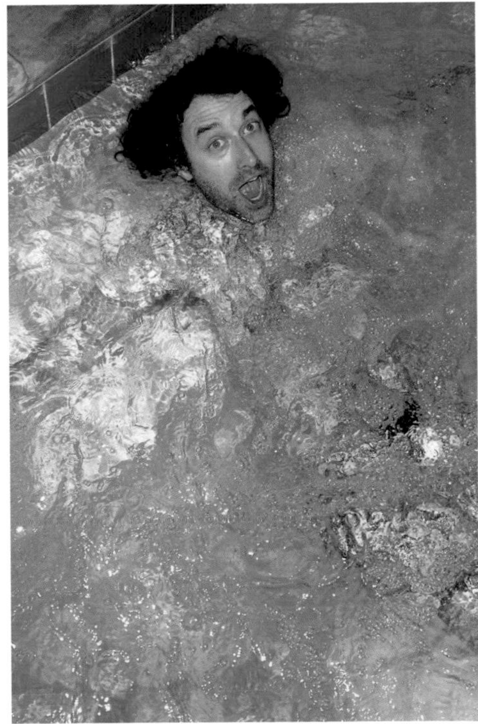

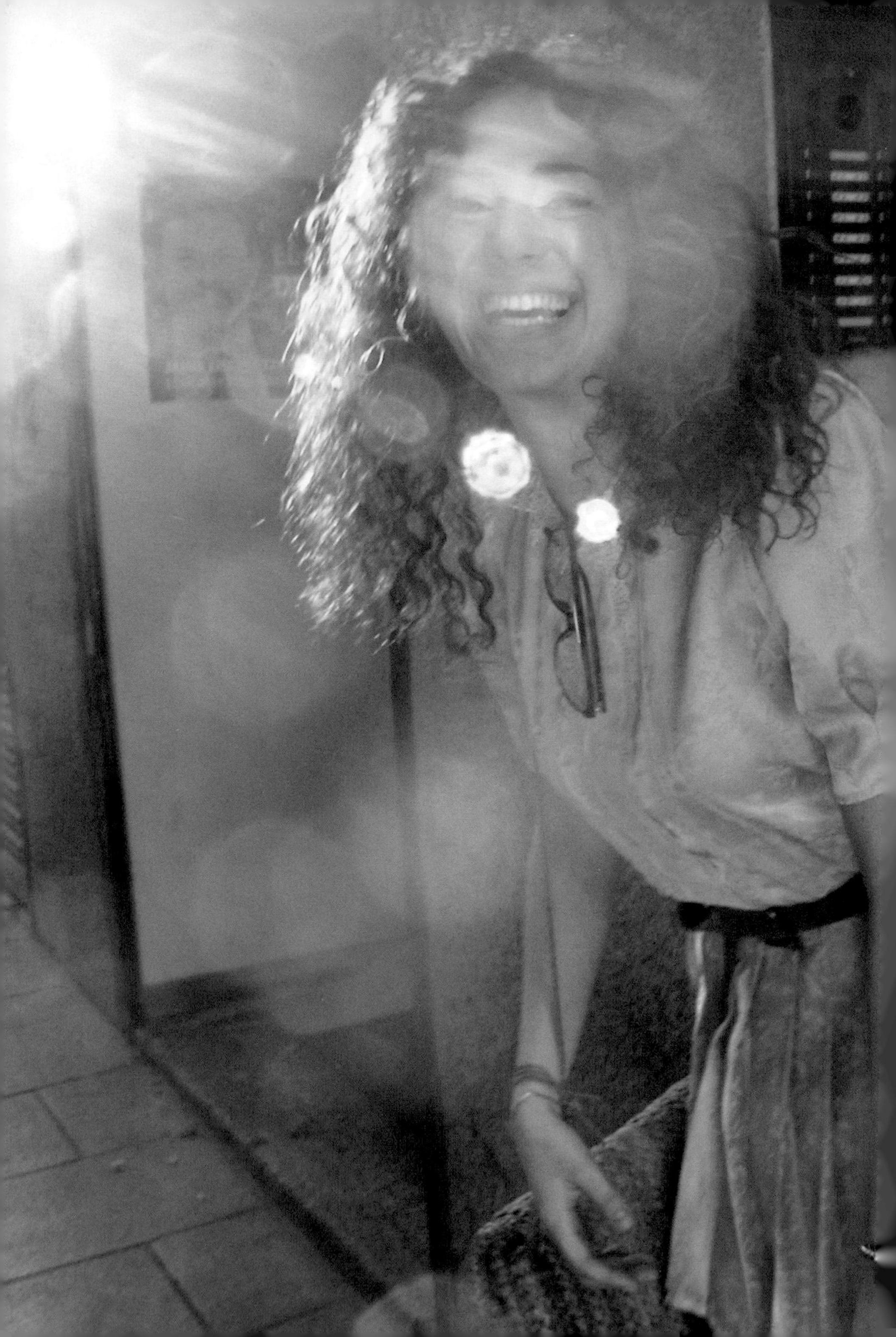

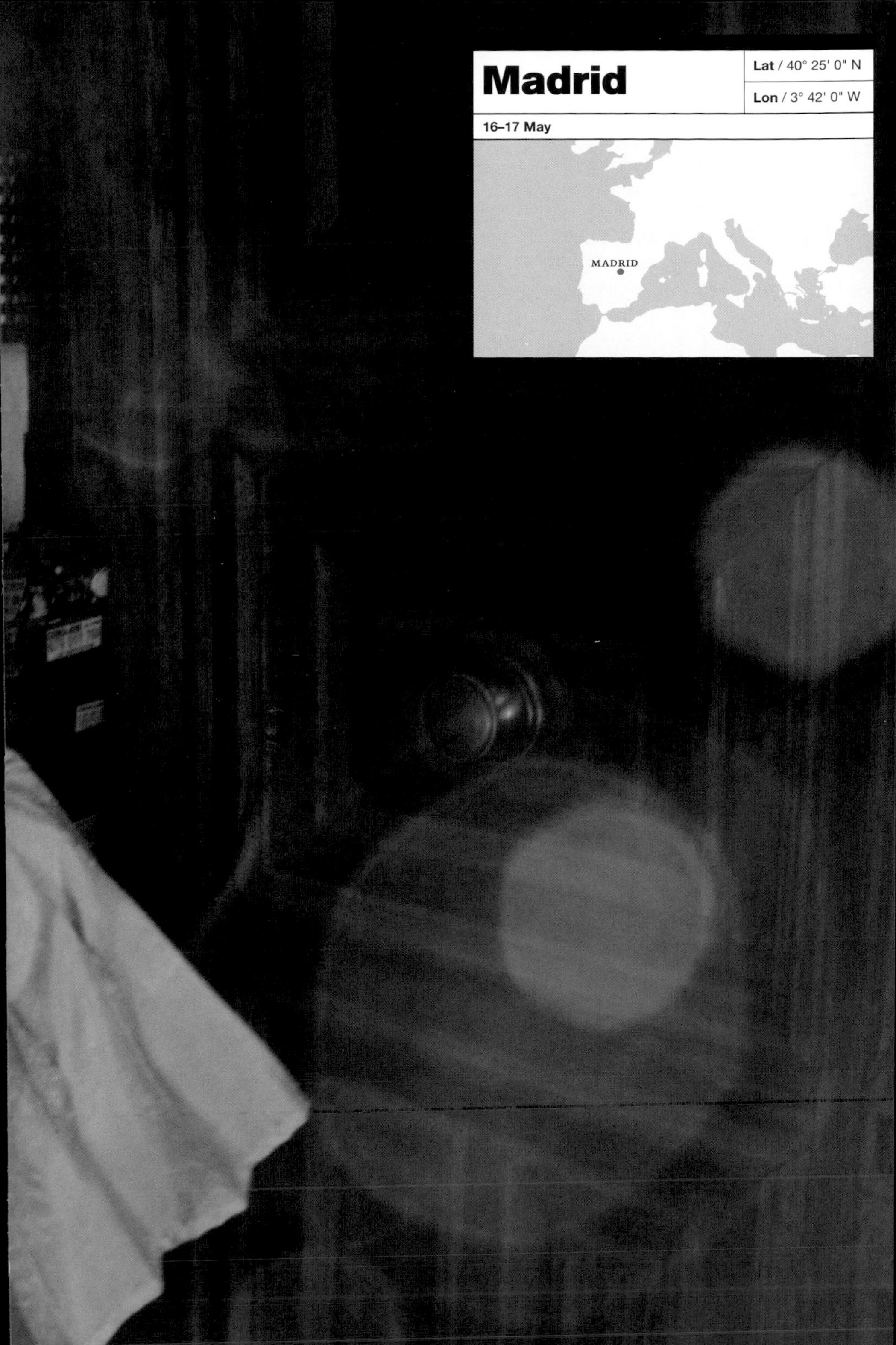
Madrid
Lat / 40° 25' 0" N
Lon / 3° 42' 0" W
16–17 May
MADRID

“People in Madrid say it's 'the new Barcelona'. Within Spain, Madrid is fast becoming the new hotspot for fashion and culture, but many foreigners haven't yet discovered its coolness. Spanish people are some of the most intense party people I have ever met, and Madrid is where I've seen many of the craziest parties of my life (details withheld!). My favourite part of the city (that I remember, at least) is Malasaña, which is cosy and pretty and the perfect place to get an ice cream or breakfast around noon on a sunny terrace after an all-night house party.”

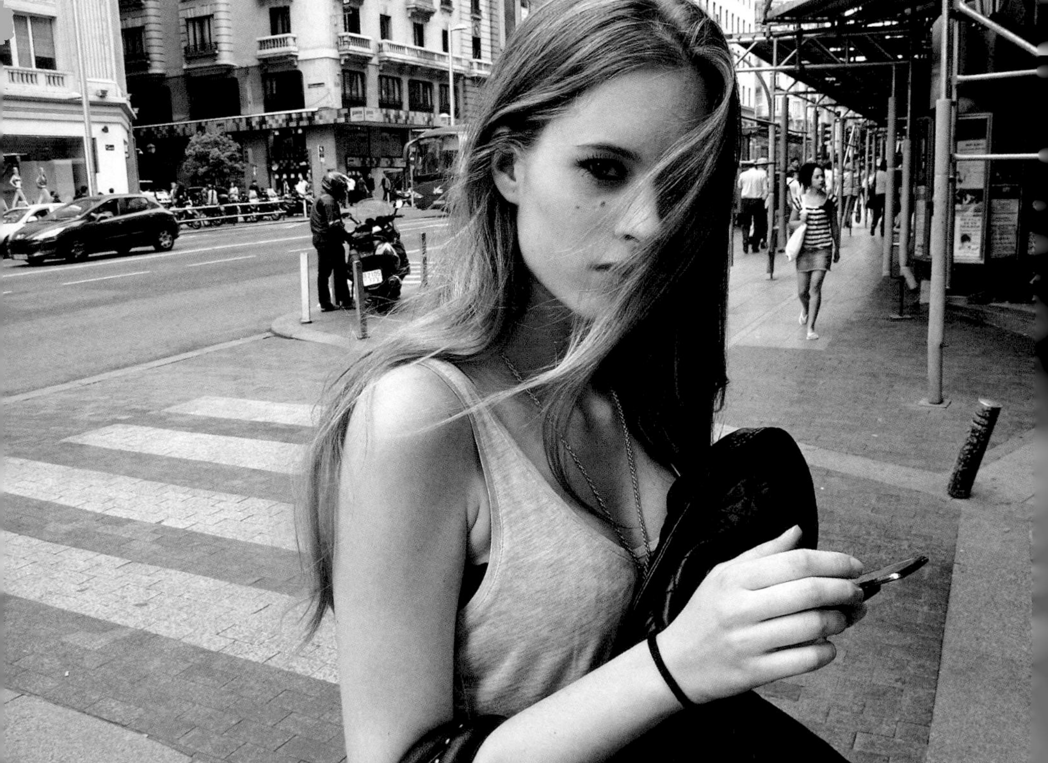

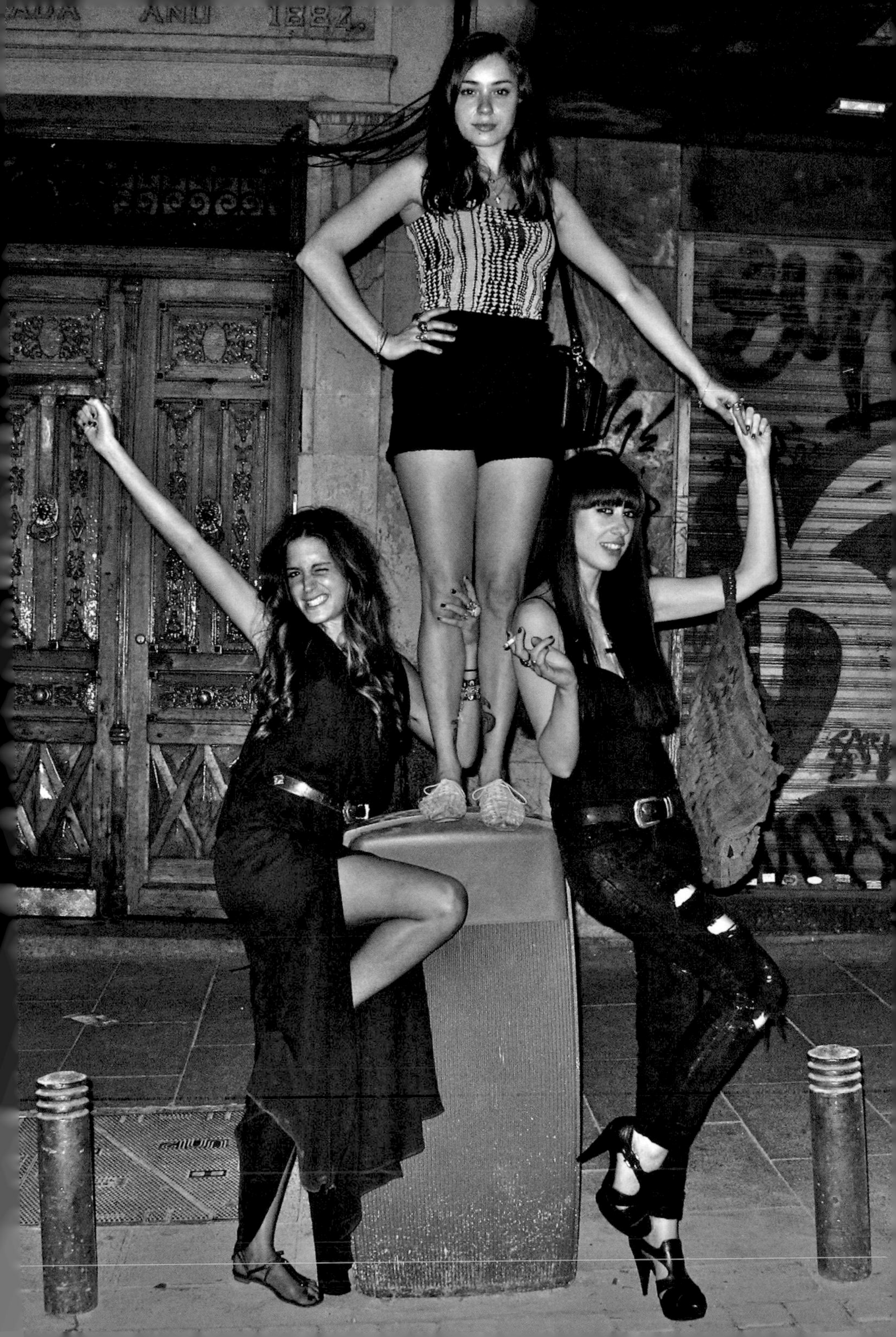

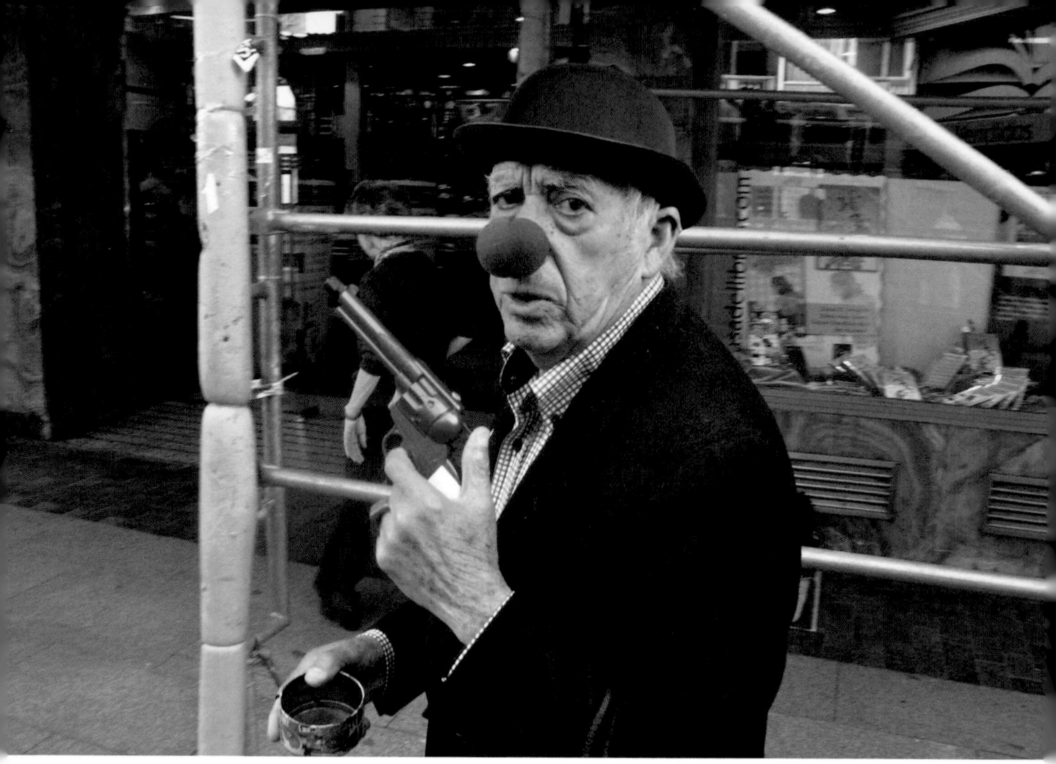

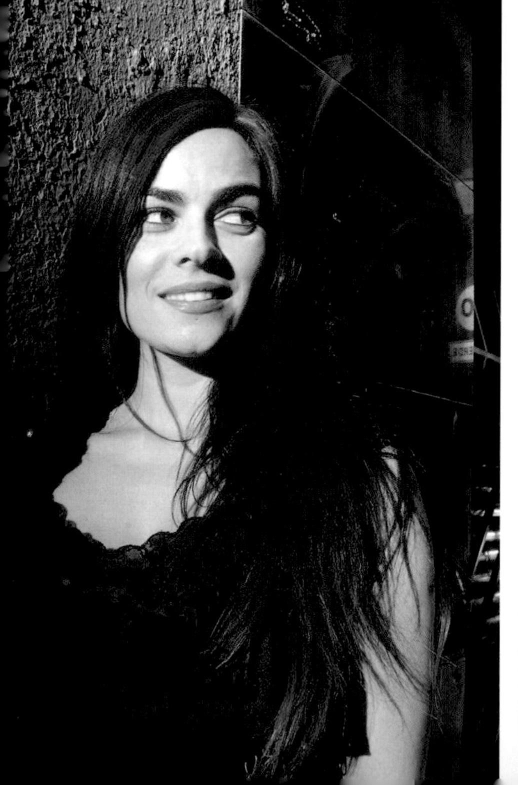

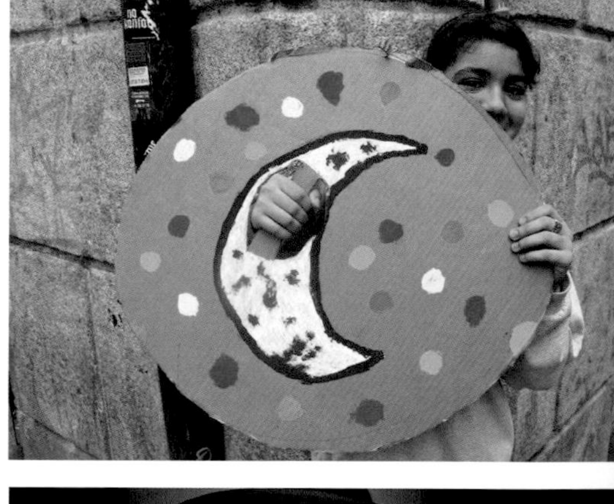

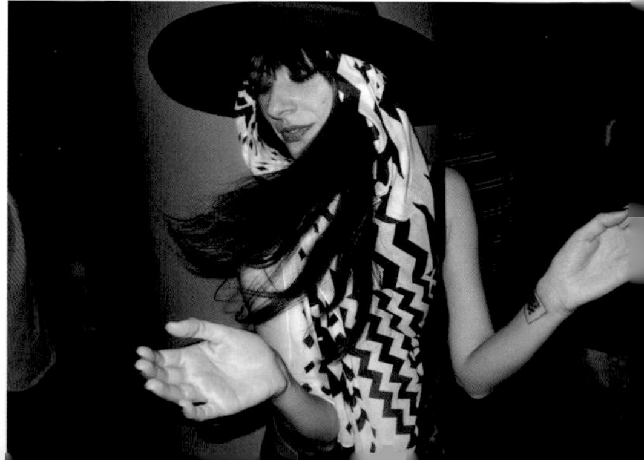

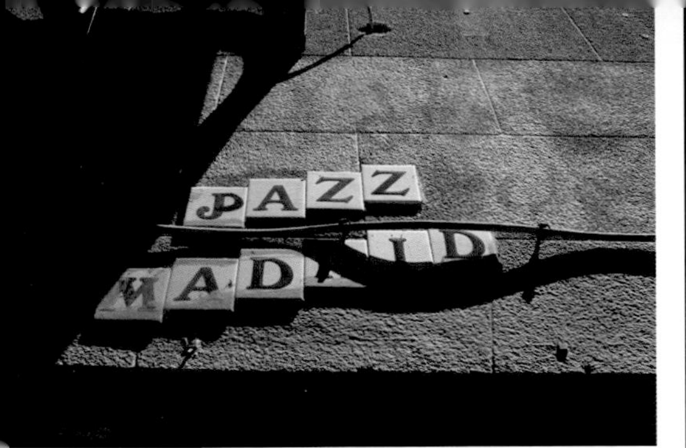
JAZZ

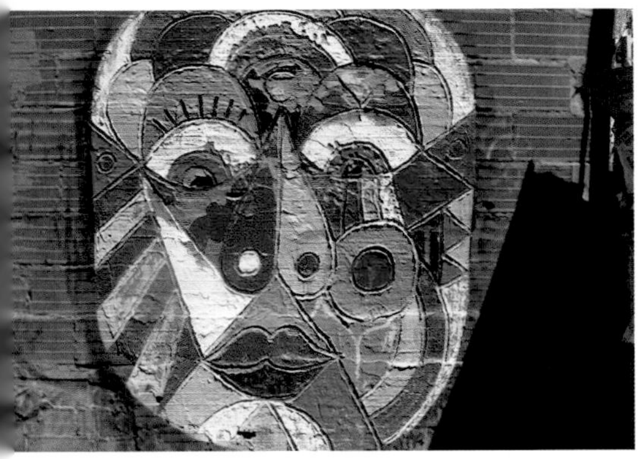

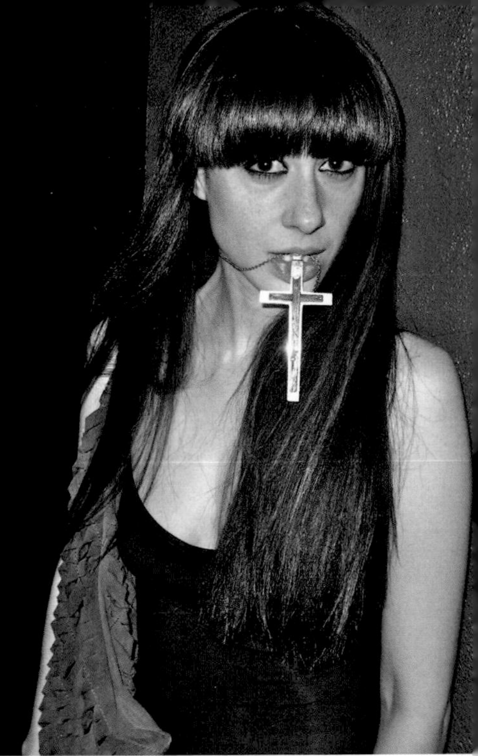

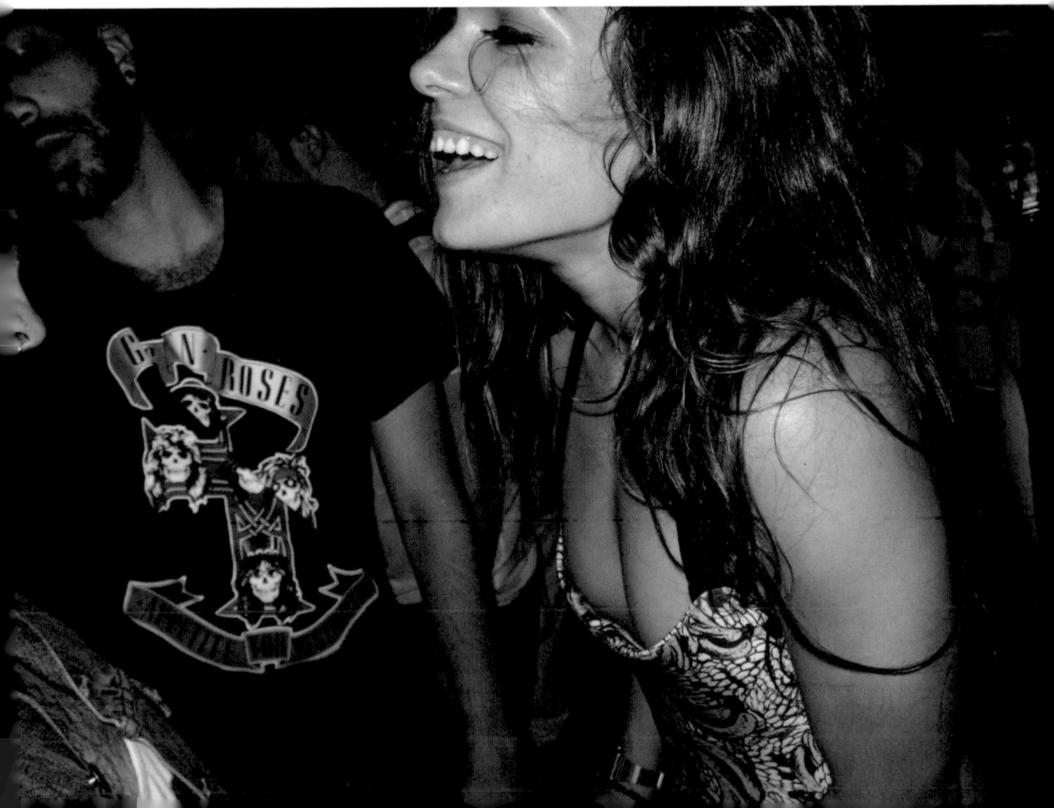

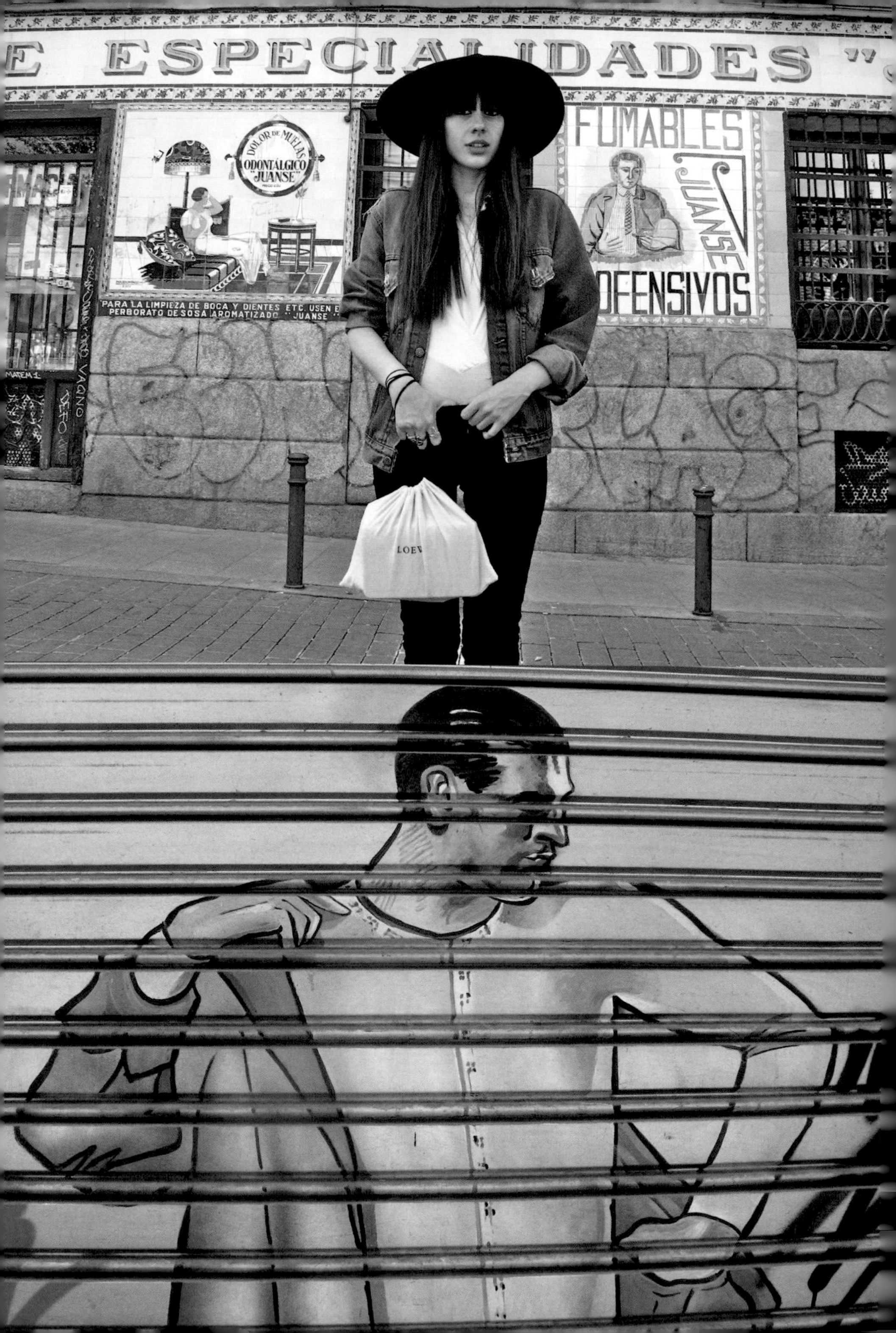
E ESPECIALIDADES "
DOLOR DE MUELAS
ODONTÁLGICO
"JUANSE"
PARA LA LIMPIEZA DE BOCA Y DIENTES ETC. USEN E
PERBORATO DE SOSA AROMATIZADO "JUANSE"
FUMABLES
JUANSE
OFENSIVOS
LOEW

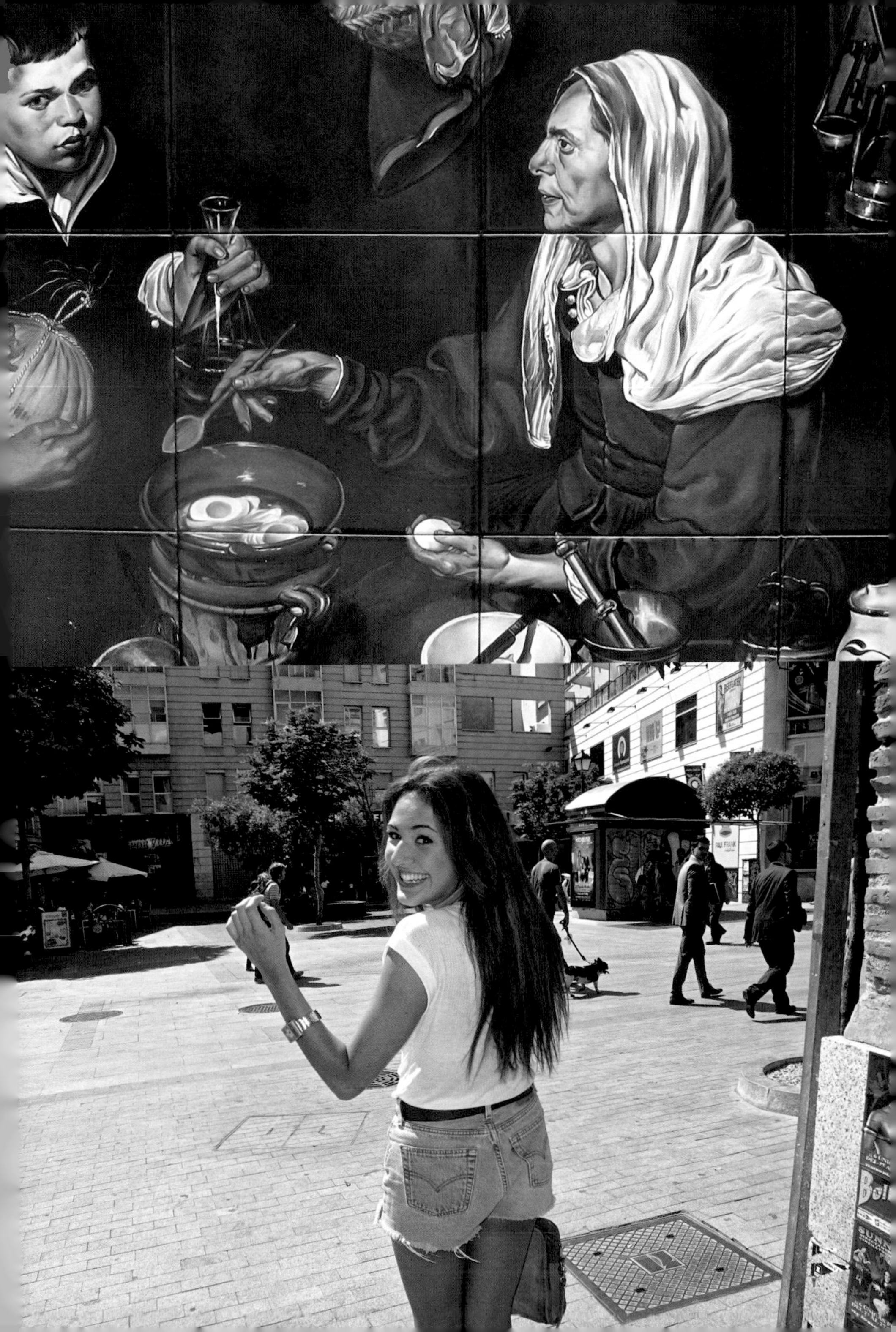

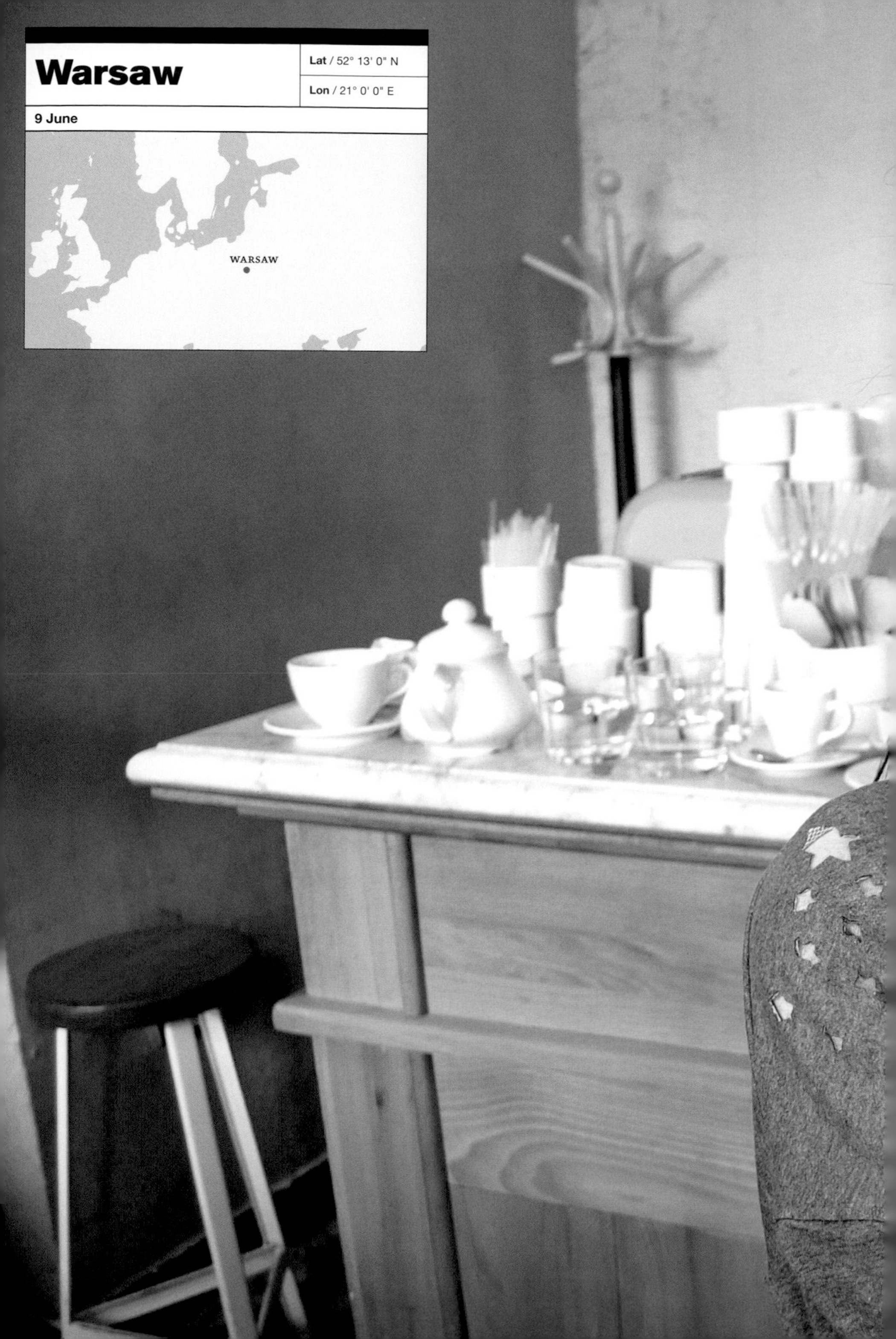
Warsaw
Lat / 52° 13' 0" N
Lon / 21° 0' 0" E
9 June
WARSAW

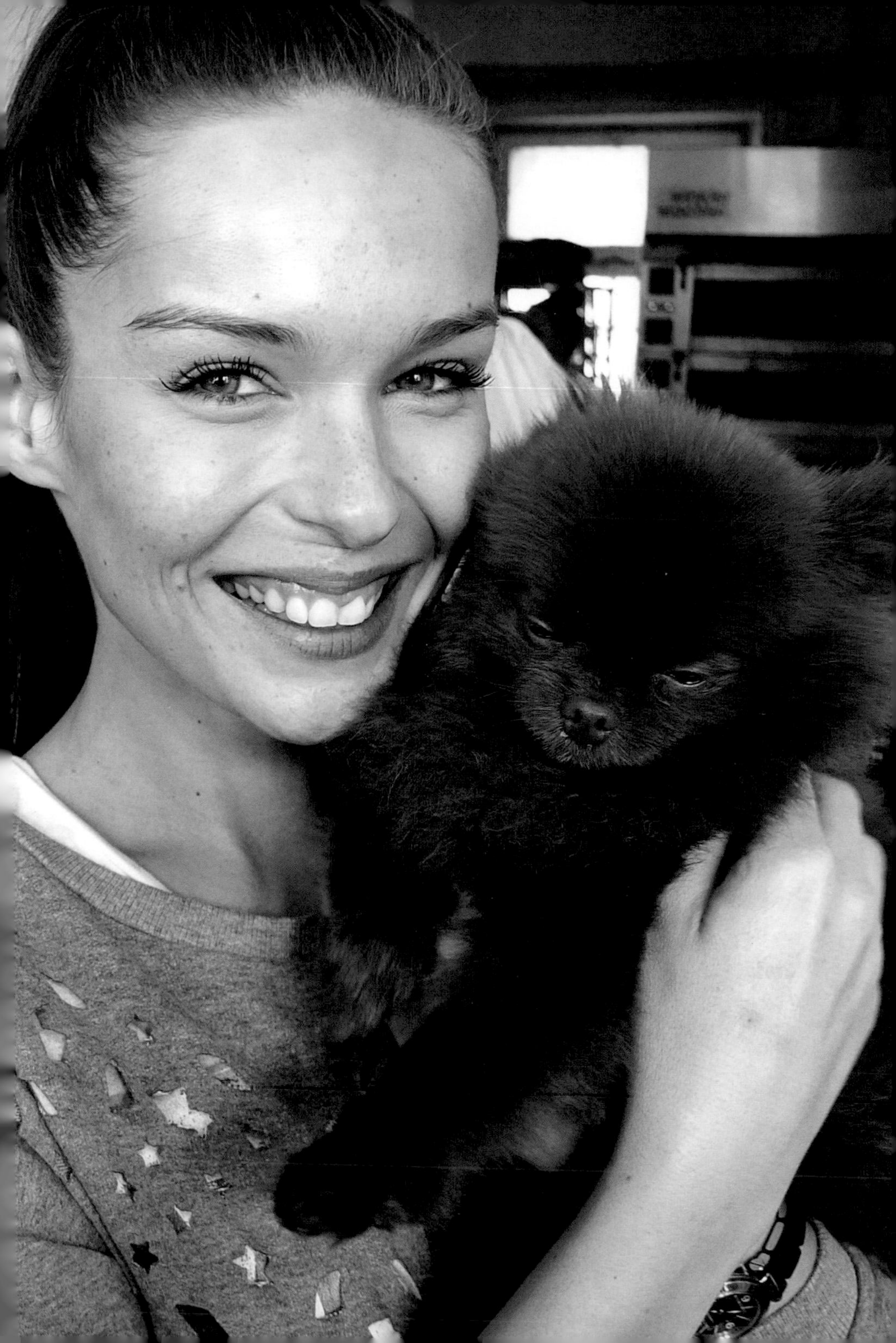

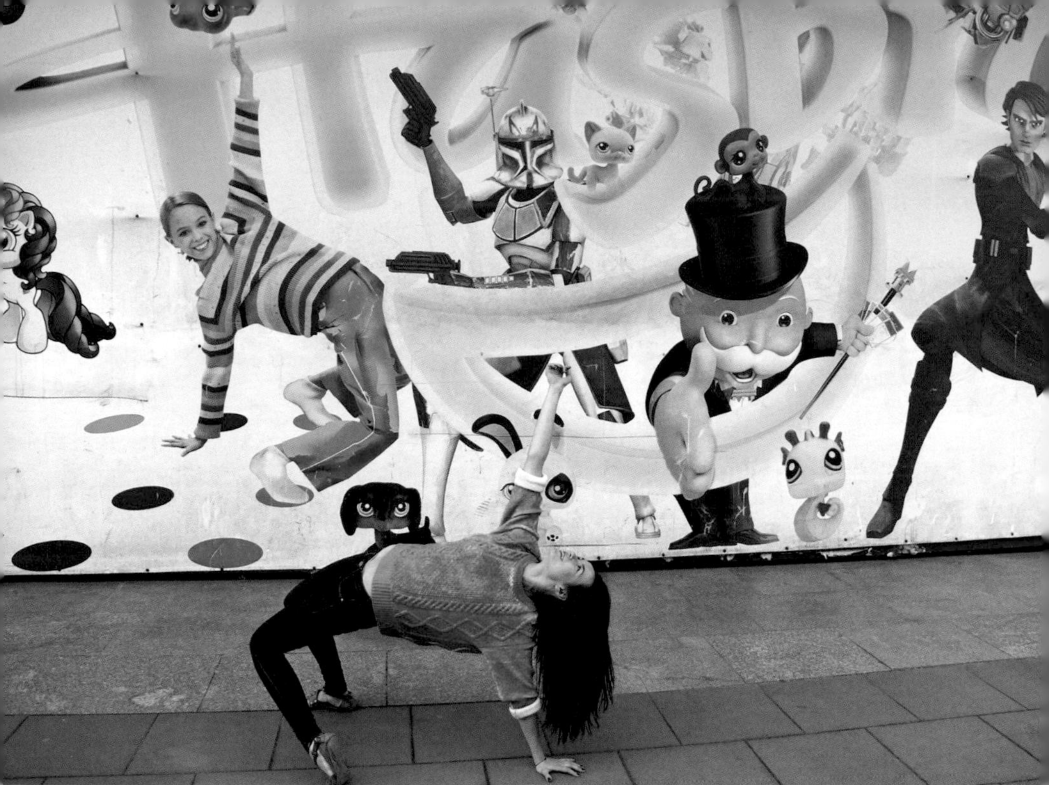

“Warsaw is one of my new favourite cities in Europe. When I first visited five years ago, its Soviet heritage was still slightly palpable, and the city felt like it was trying to catch up with the rest of the world. Now a new generation of people in their early twenties, too young to remember the Communist era at all, is taking over the helm and the result is a city that feels completely fresh and hopeful and is starting to lead the way for the rest of Europe. One of the things I really love about Warsaw summers is the open-air bars, especially PKP Powisle, a Communist-era former train station, and Plac Zabaw, where you'll find several thousand people milling around a huge grassy enclosure outdoors during the long summer nights. There is plenty of *wódka*, but there are rarely any fights – everyone is peacefully having a crazy time.”

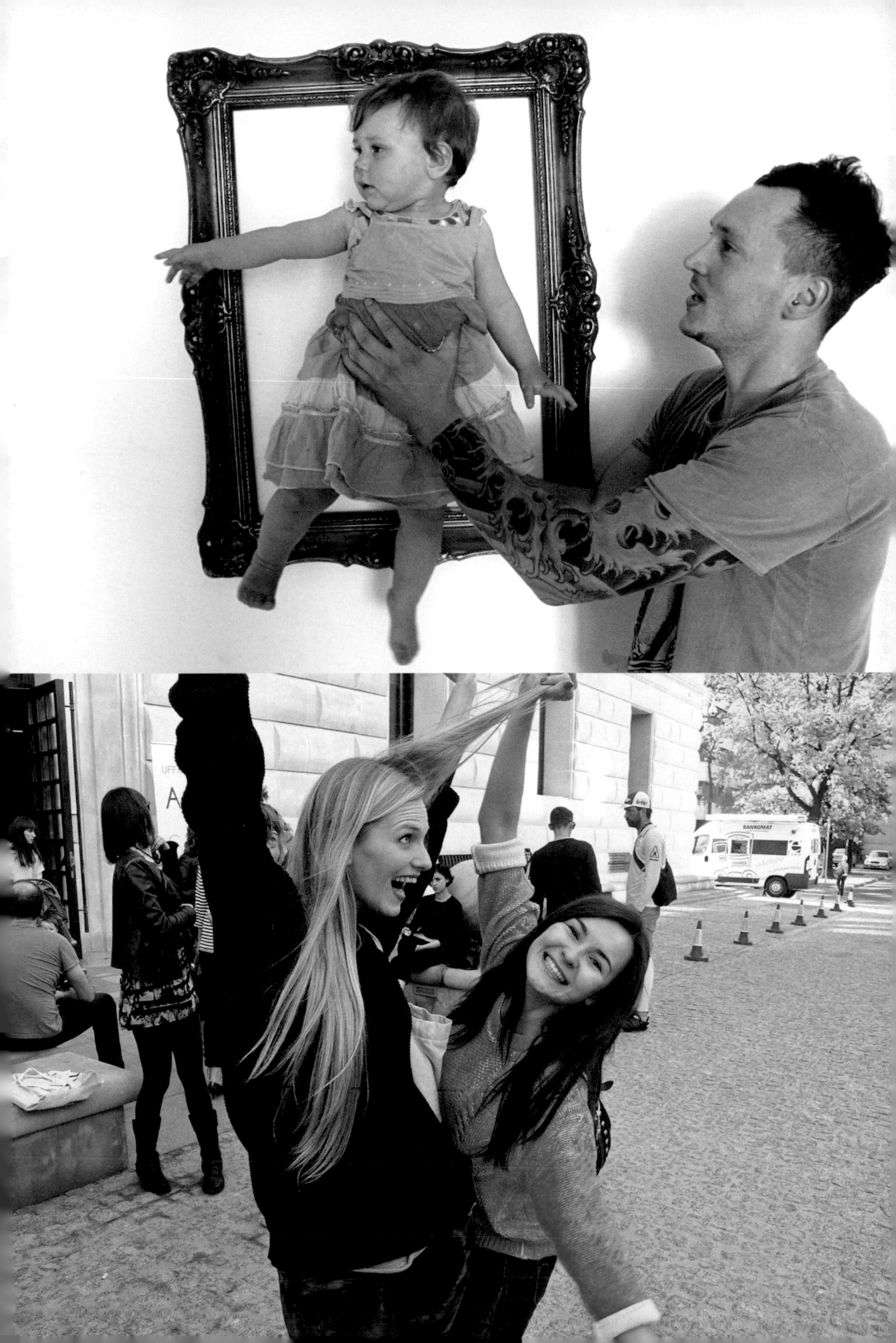
BANKOMAT

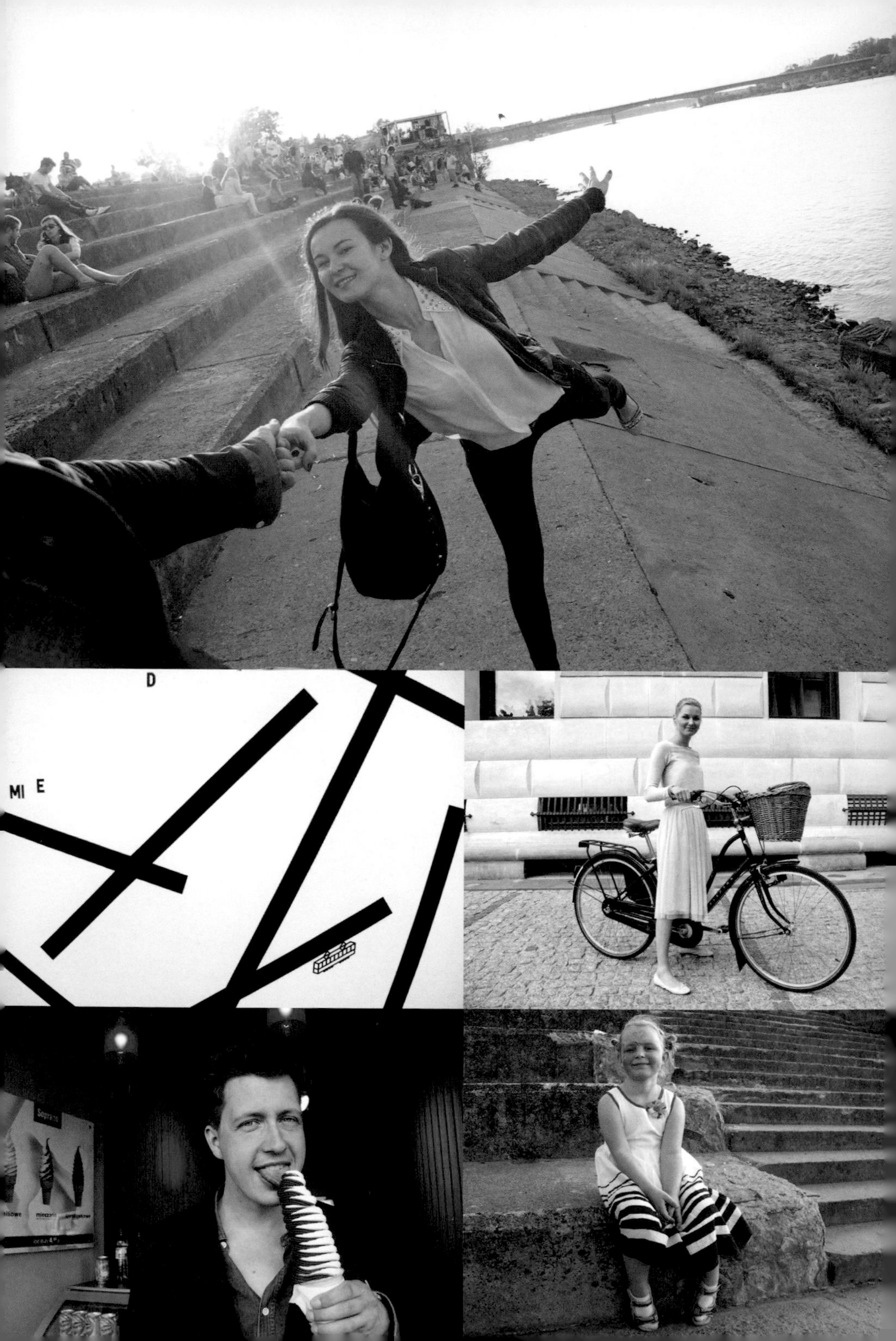
D
MI E

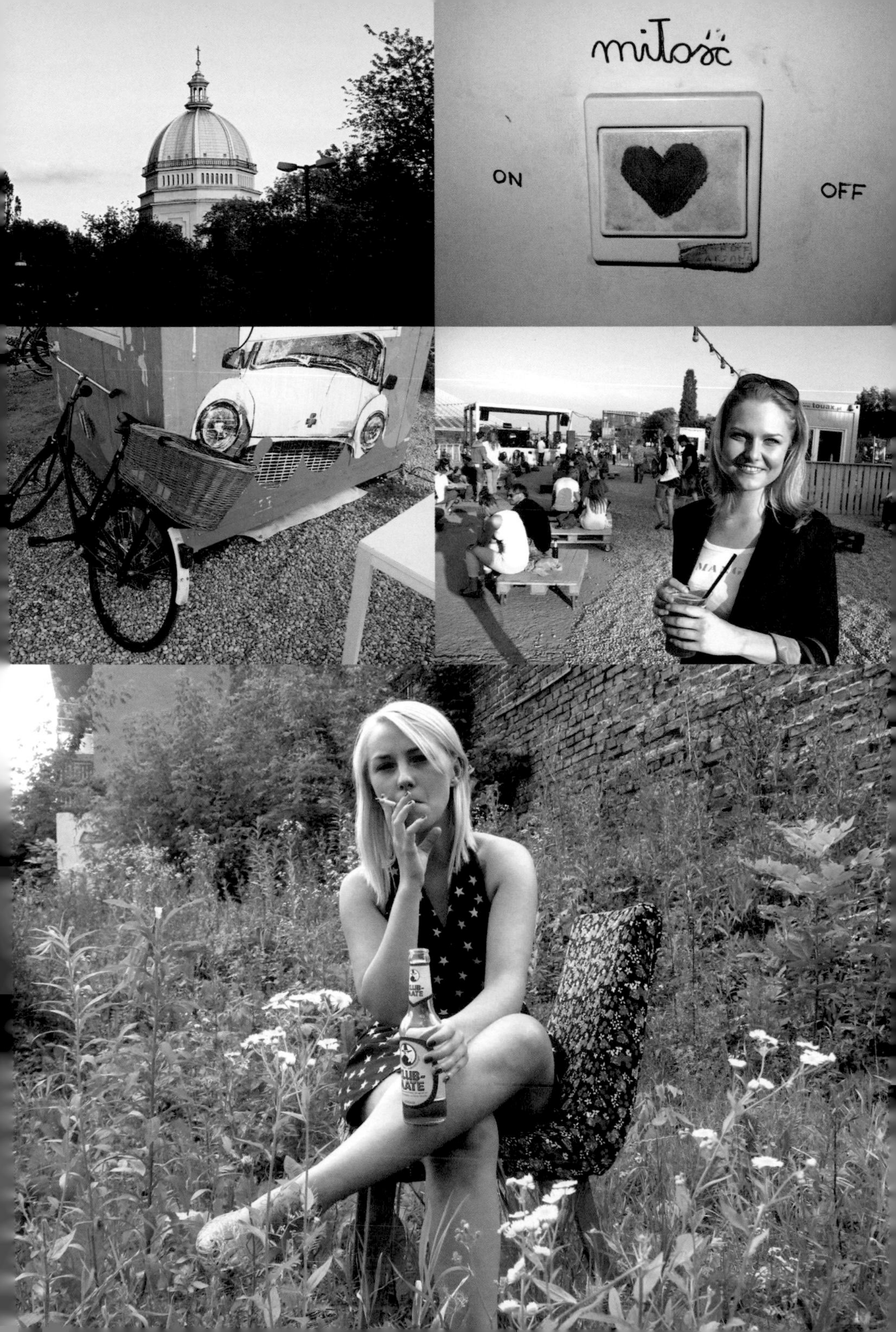
miłość
ON
OFF

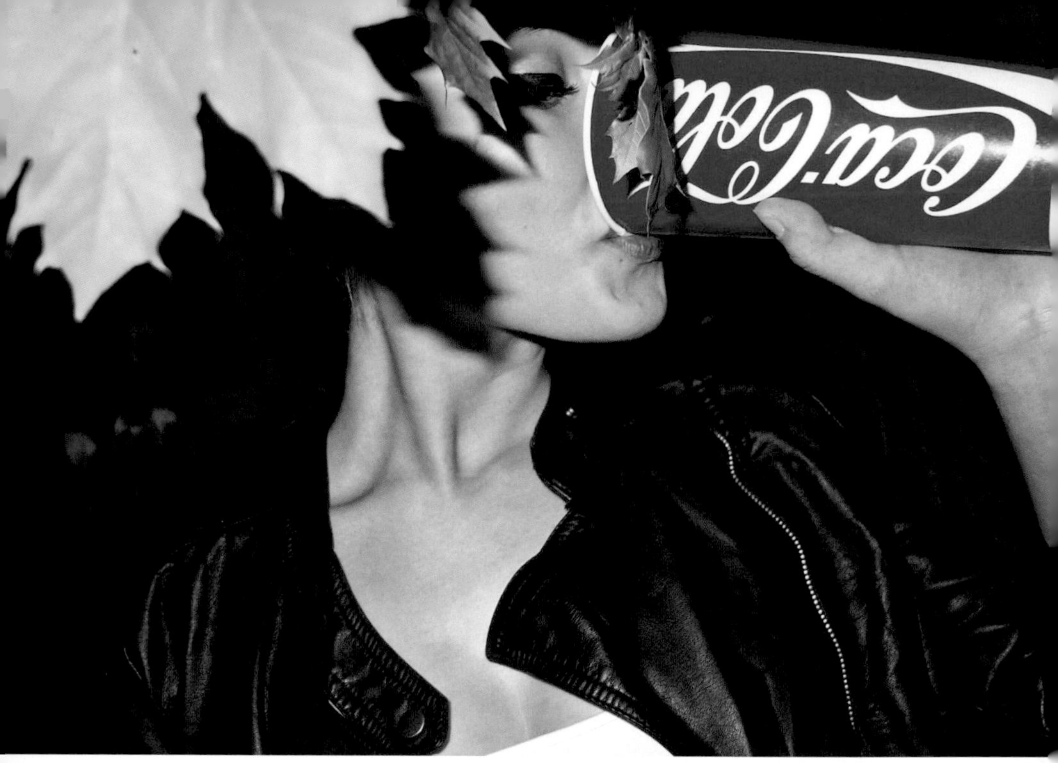

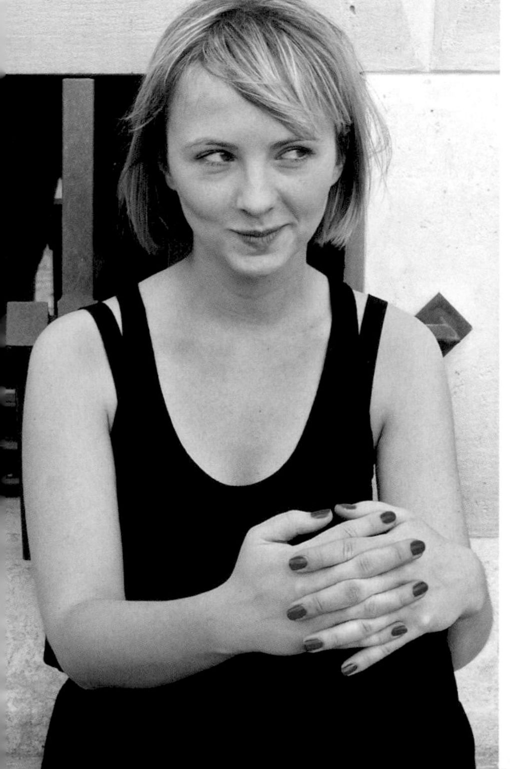

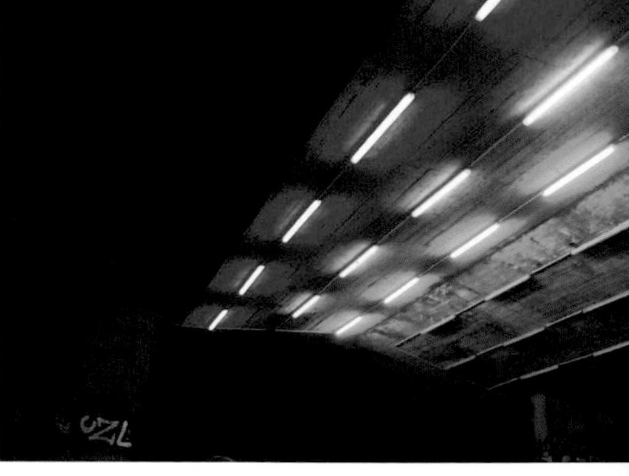

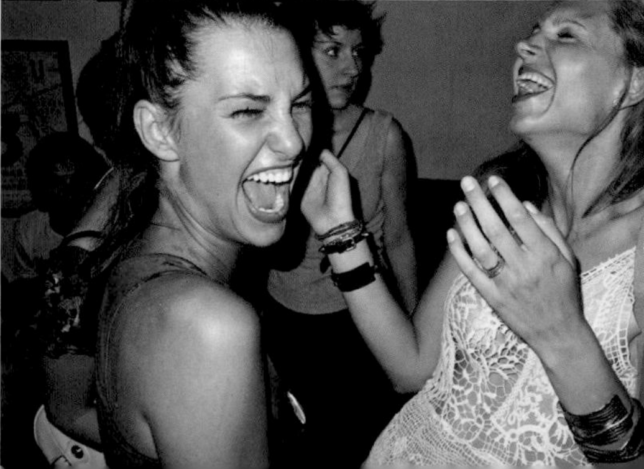

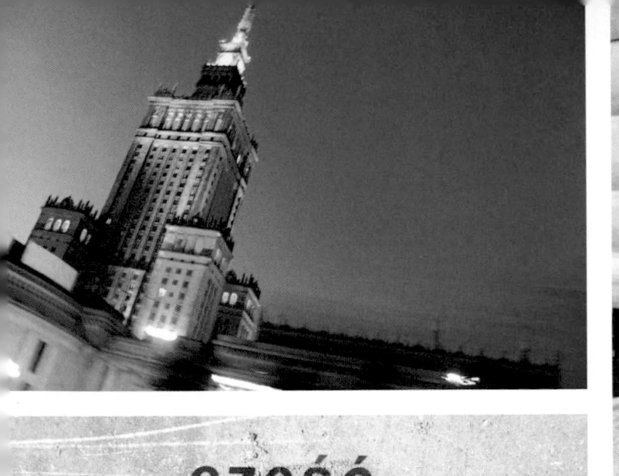

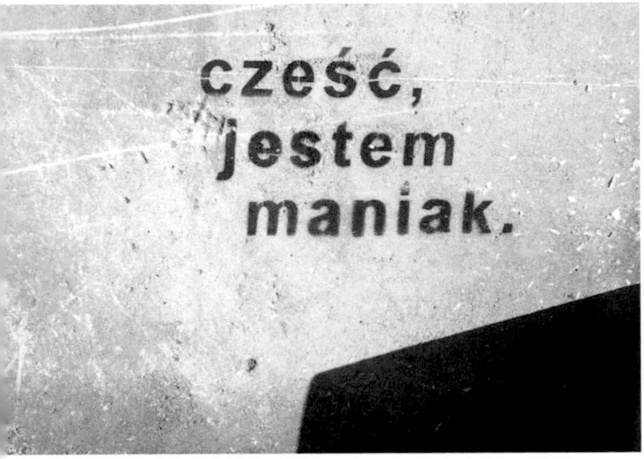

cześć,
jestem
maniak.

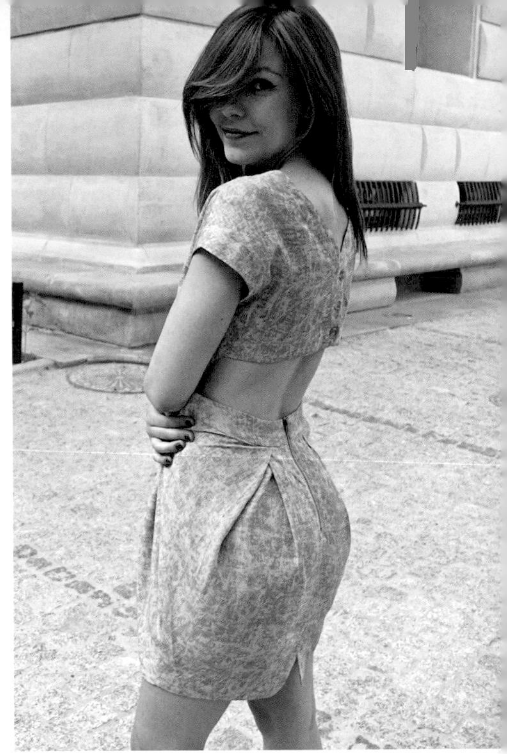

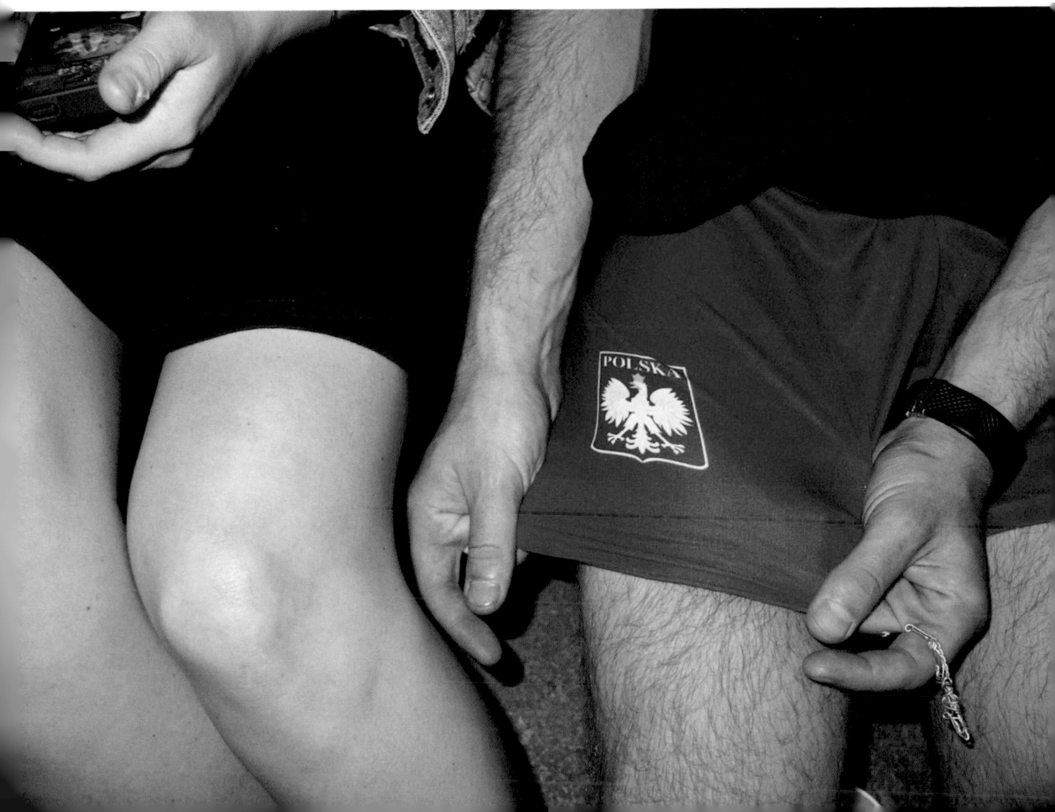

POLSKA

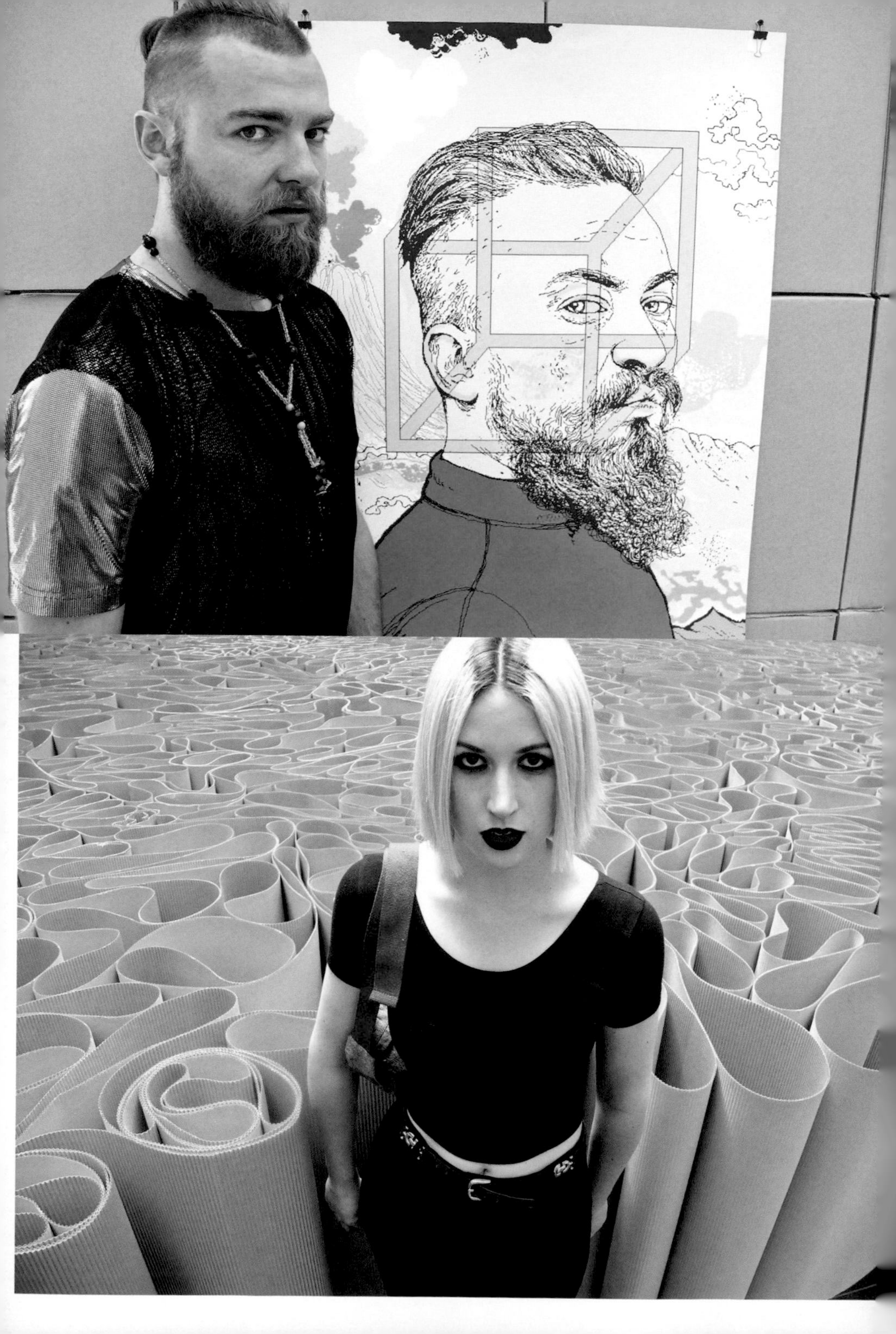

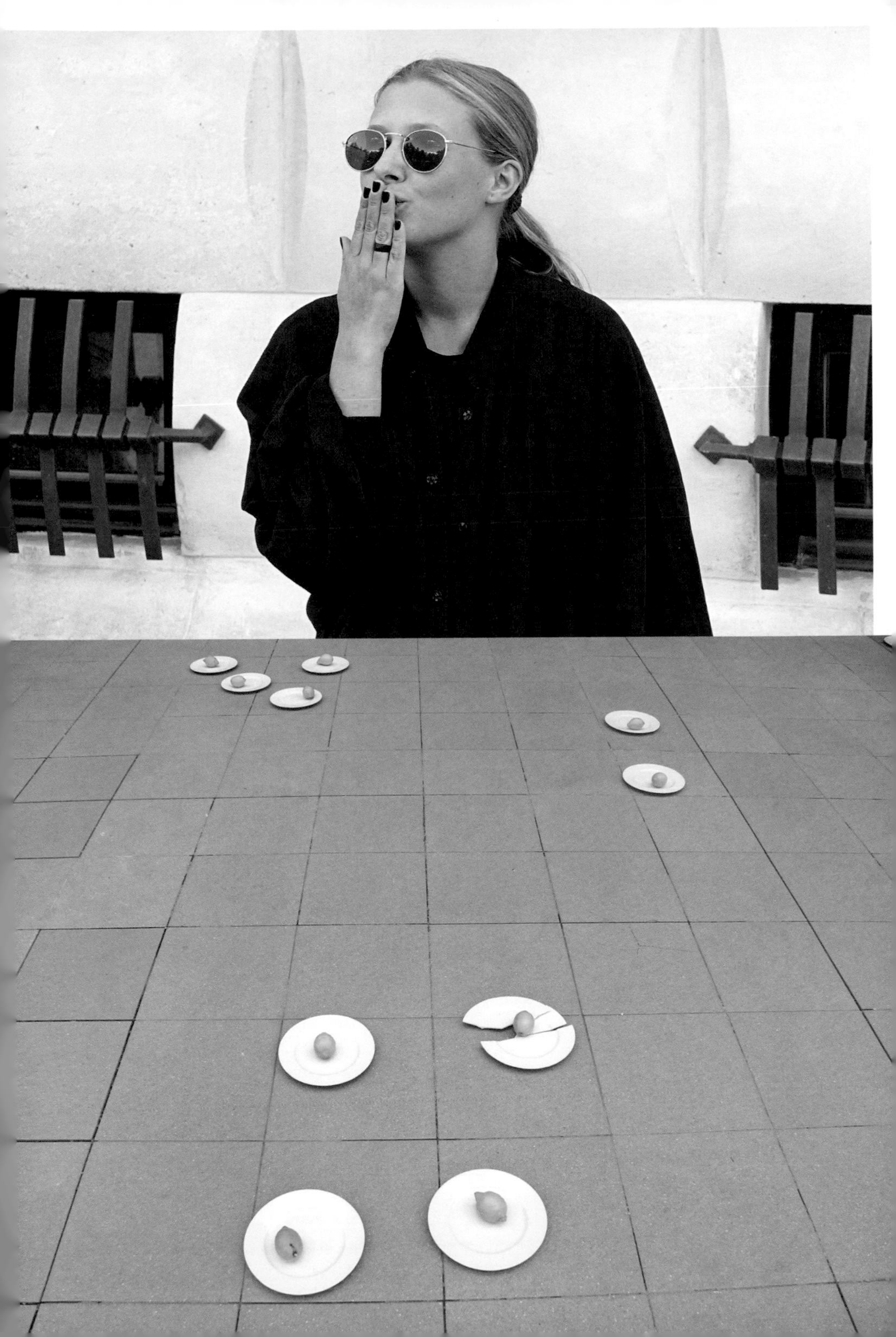

St Petersburg

Lat / 59° 56' 0" N

Lon / 30° 18' 0" E

26–29 May

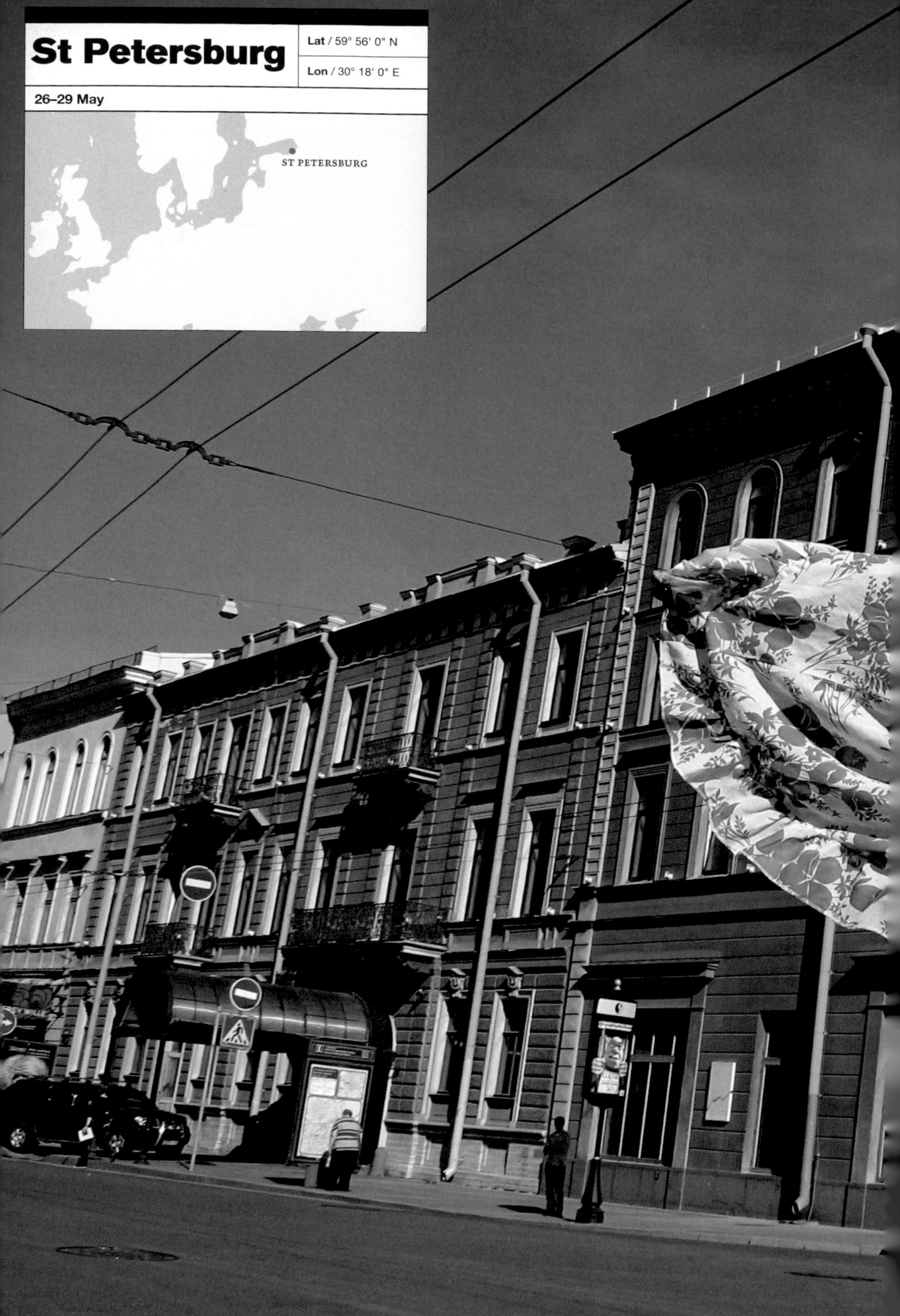

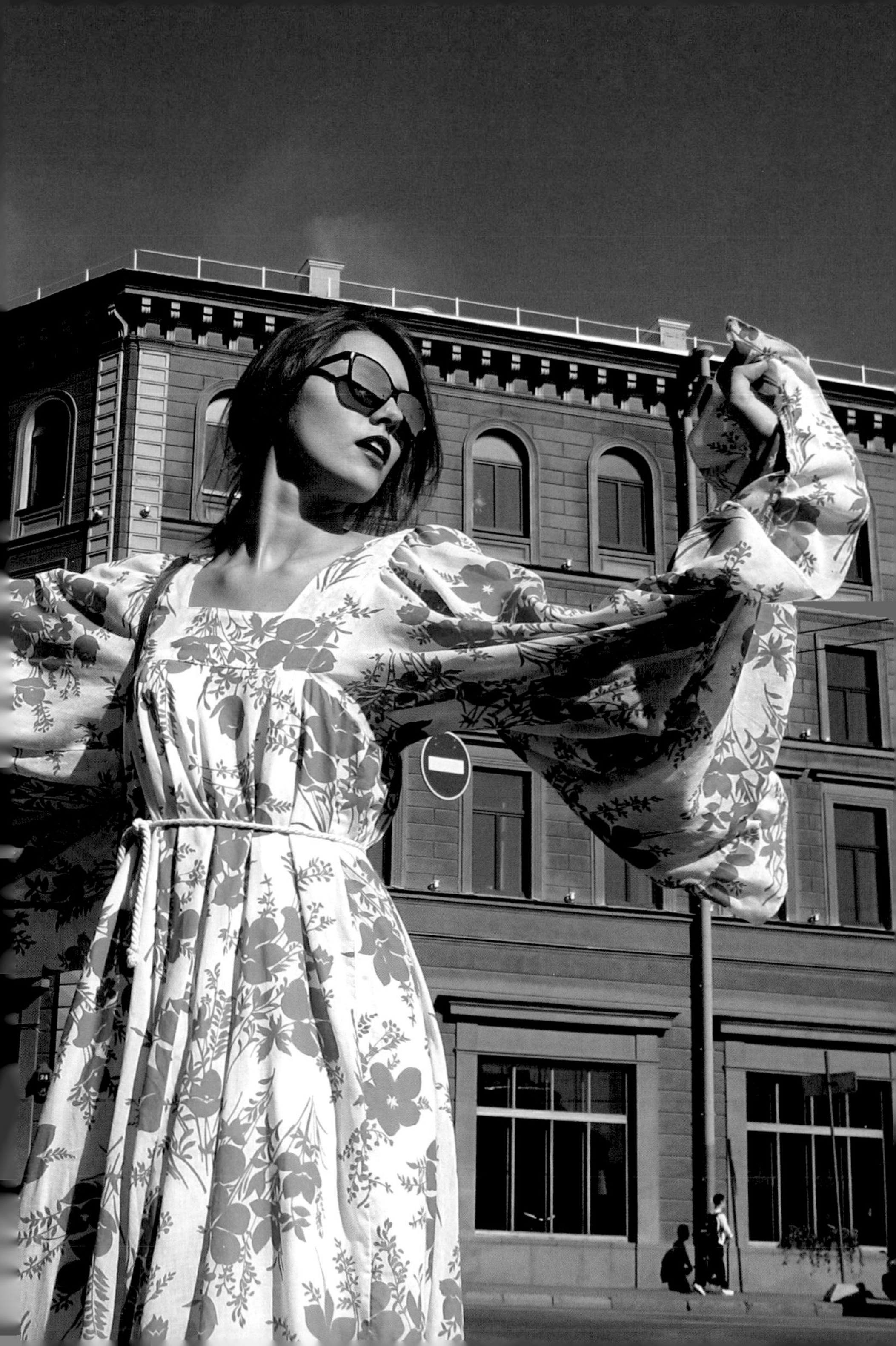

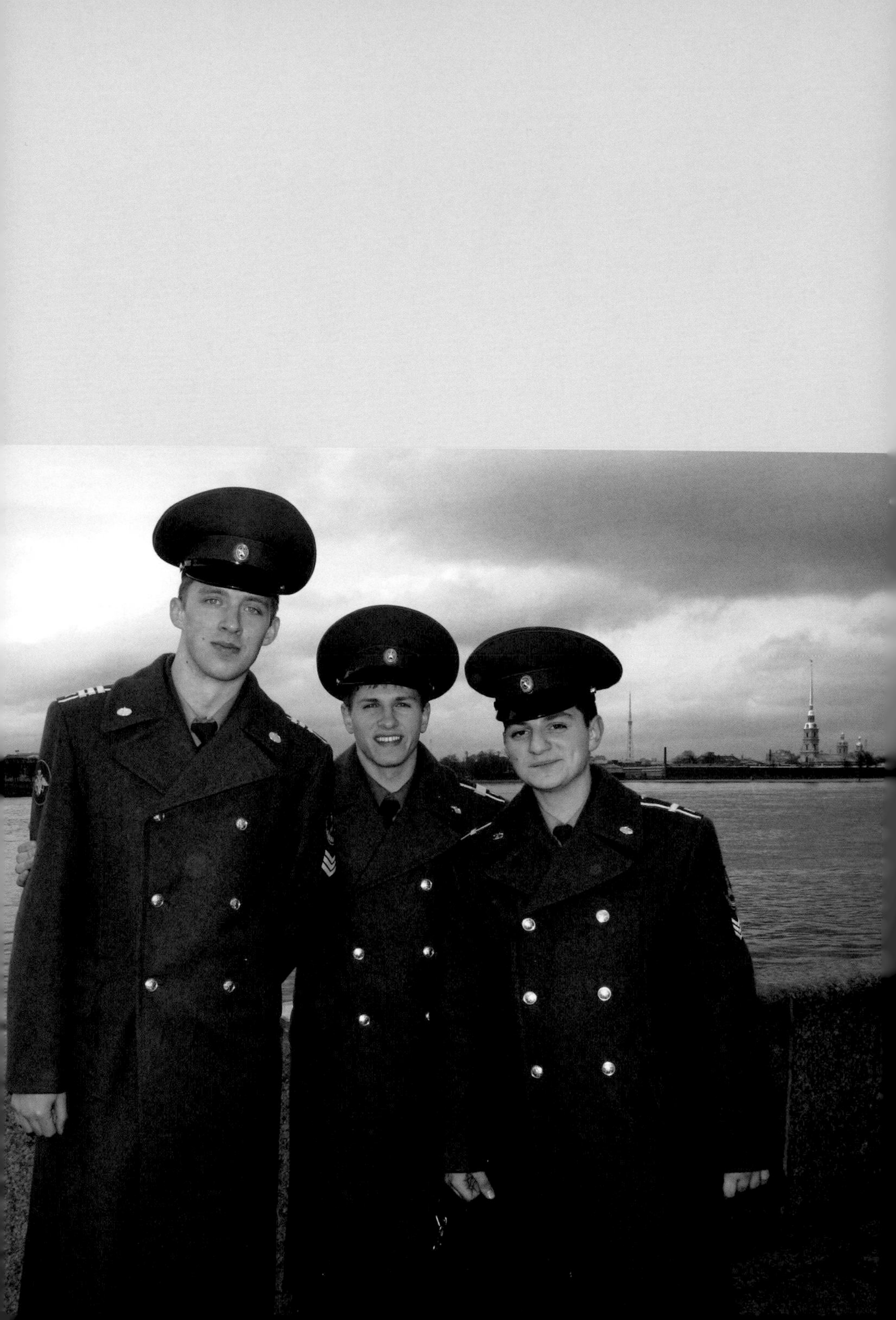

“ Any visit to St Petersburg will always involve the many bridges that criss-cross its rivers and canals. During the summer there's a fine art in calculating the opening times of the various drawbridges to make sure you can get from A to B. One night my friends and I were on our way from one party to another in a randomly hired 'cab' (basically a guy in an unmarked car who will take you anywhere you want to go for 200 roubles). On our way we hit a bridge that was open (p. 211), so the driver positioned the car in line and took a nap for 30 min while we went to watch the bridge open and close. When we finally got to the second party, it turned out to be a 'beach party'(p. 210) held on the banks of the Neva river. It had a magical, Mediterranean feel, with people dancing on the sand and swimming in the pool in the river – until the sun came up and revealed the Soviet-era buildings on the opposite bank.

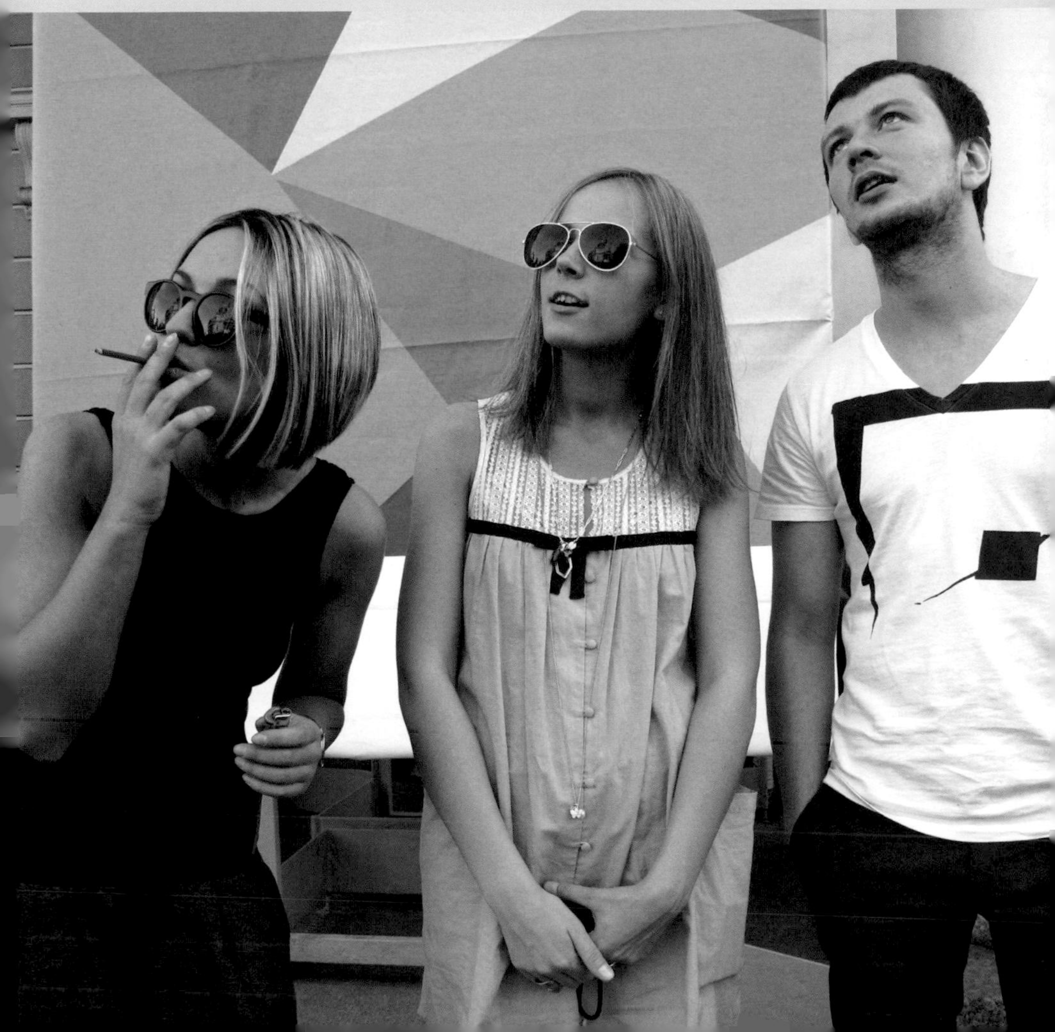

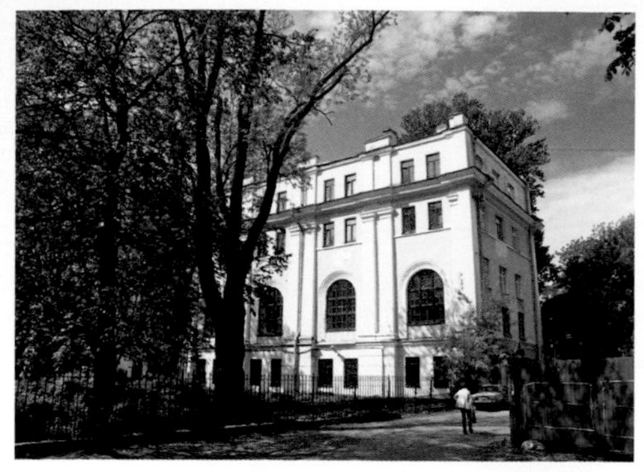

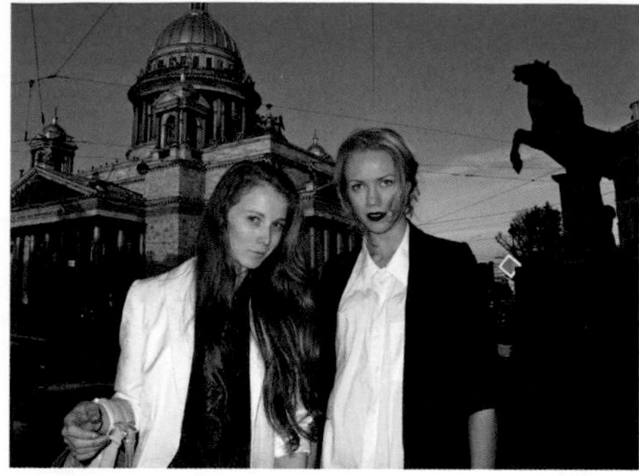

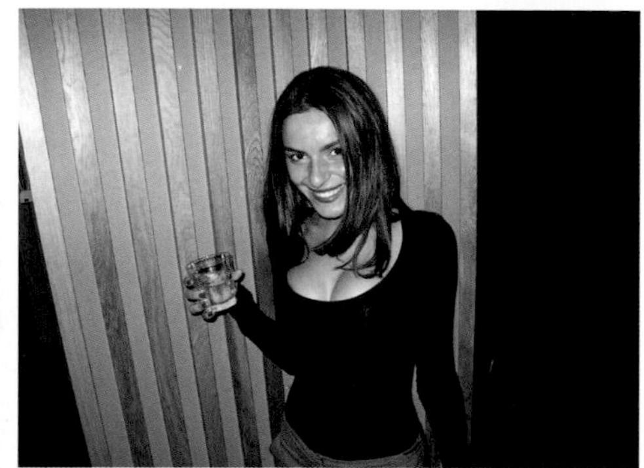

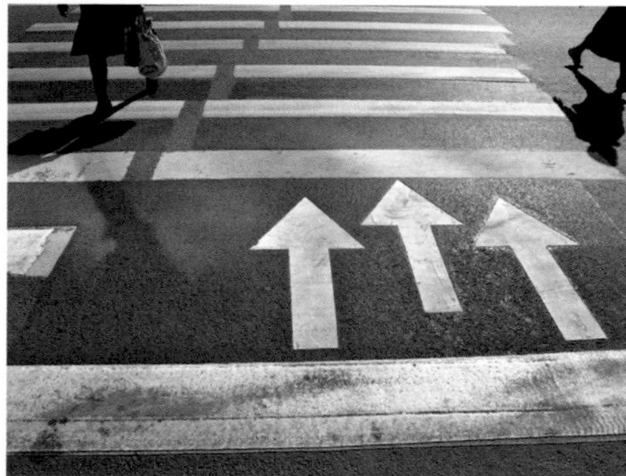

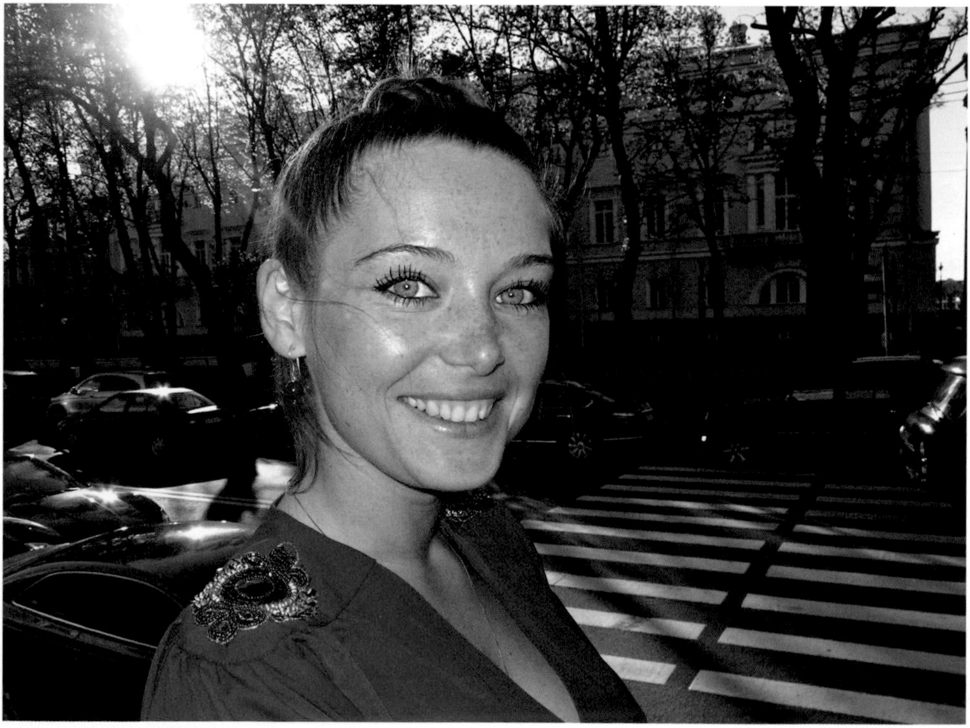

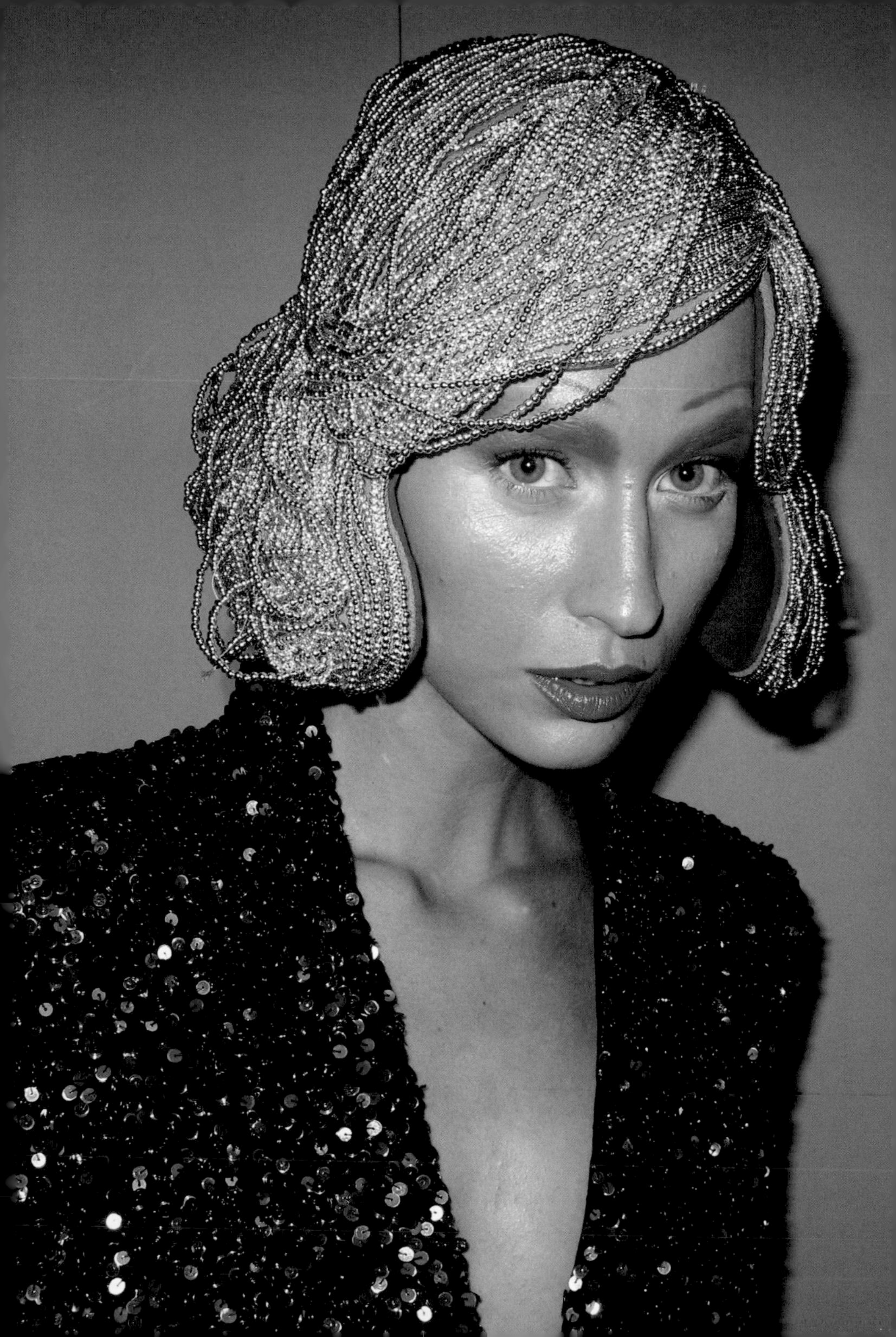

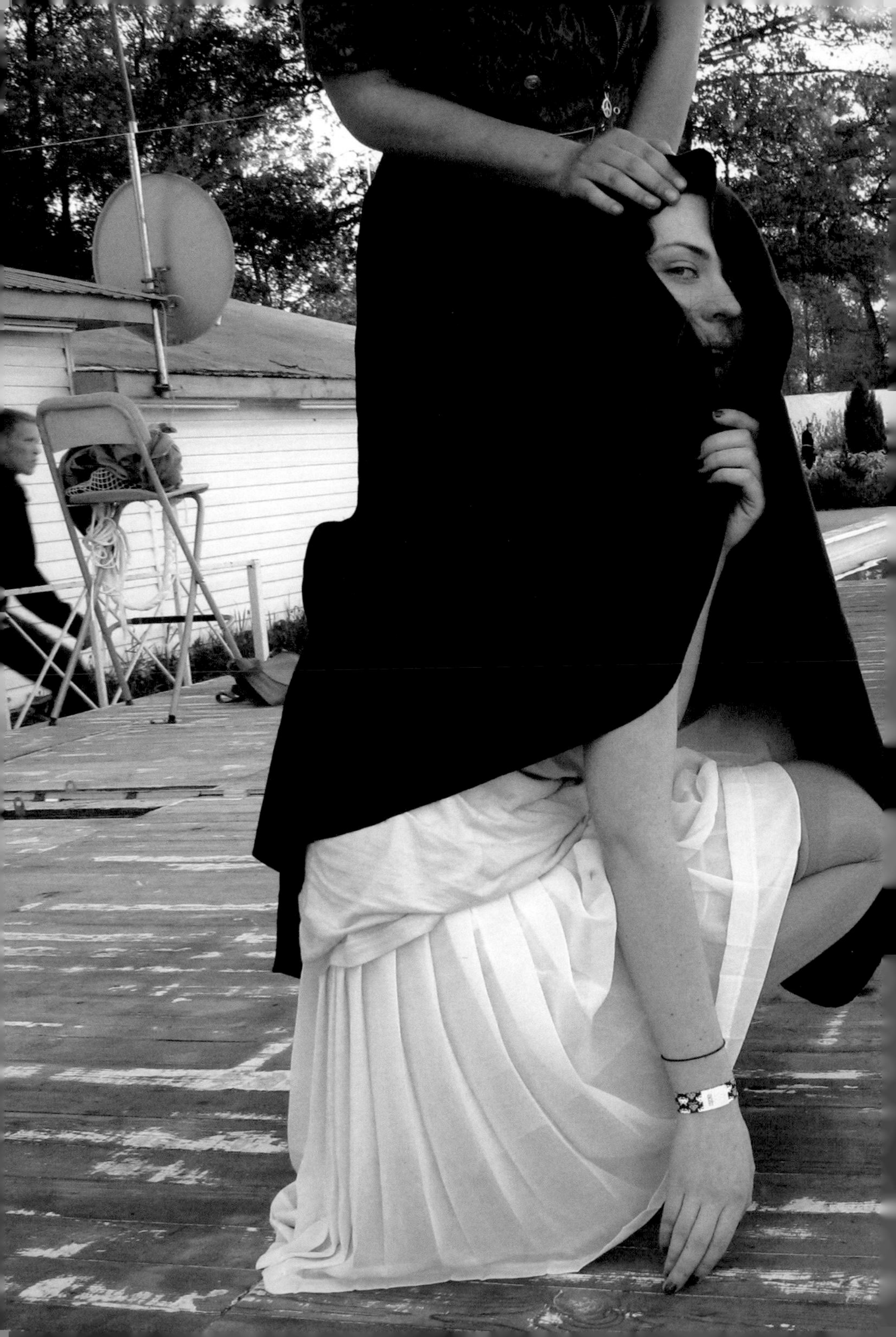

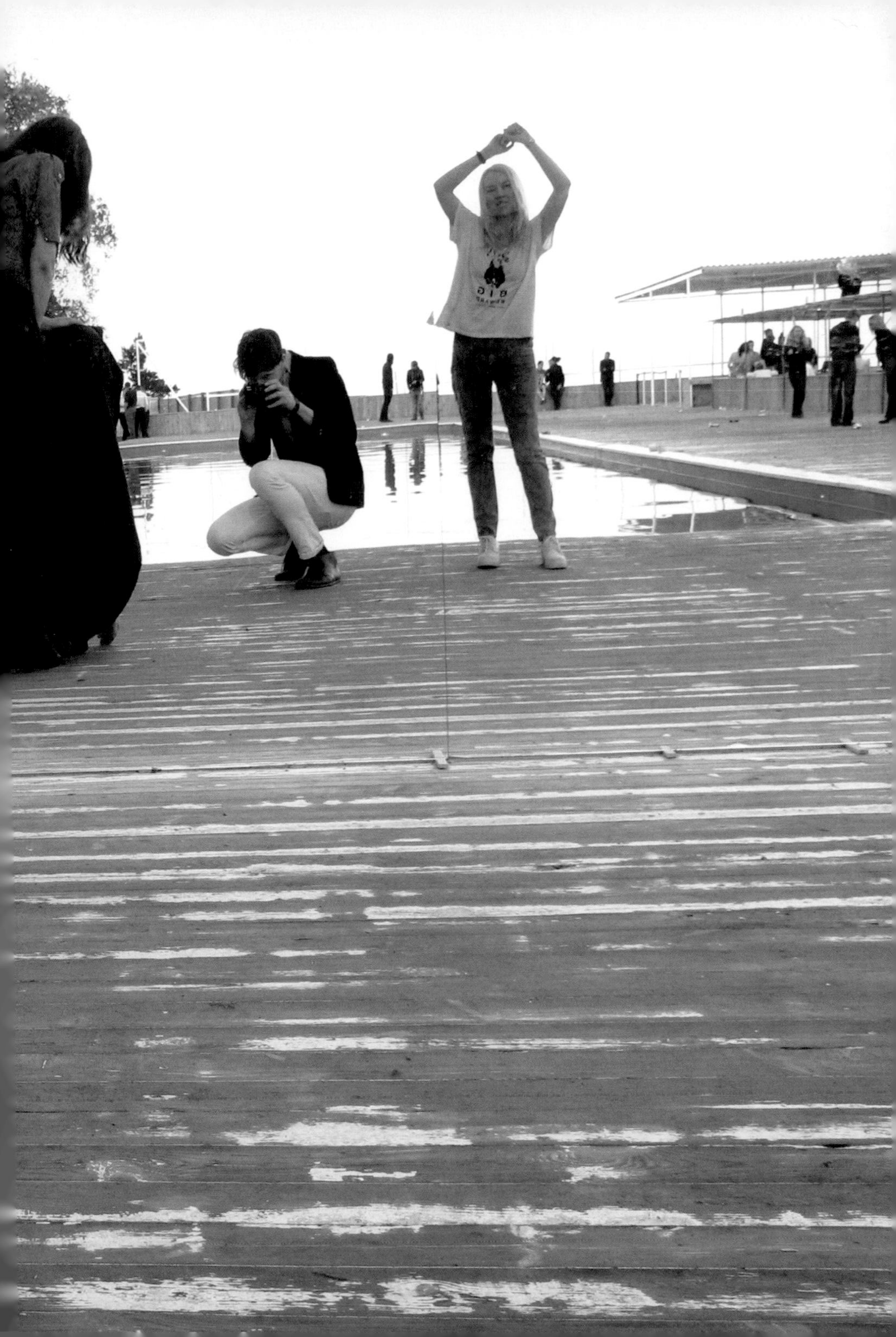

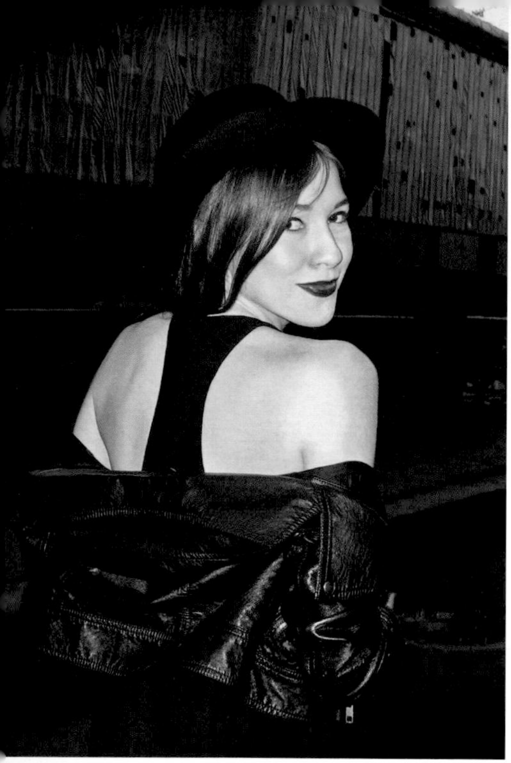

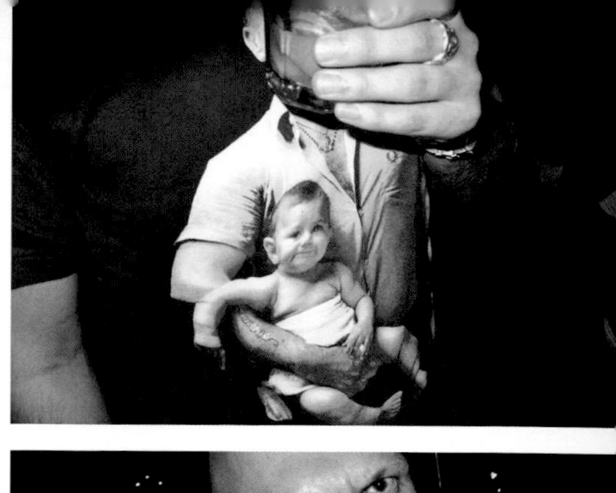

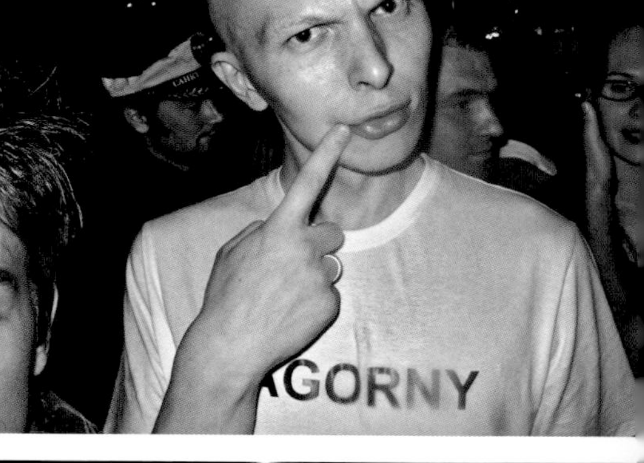
AGORNY

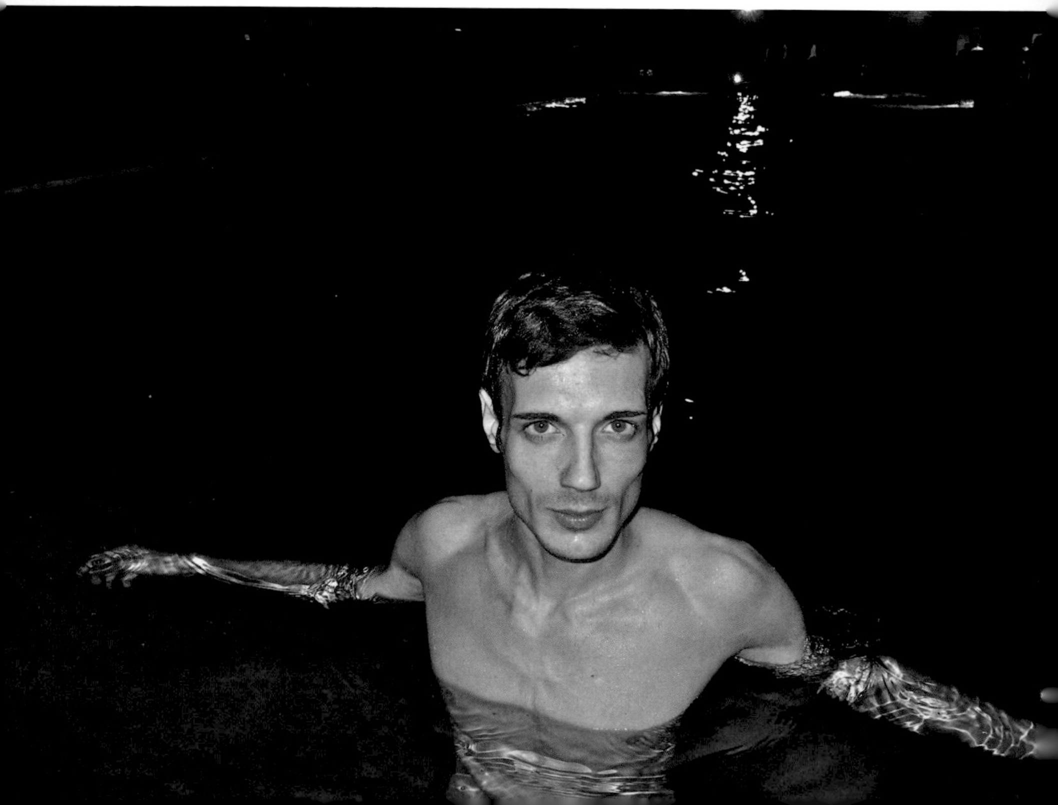

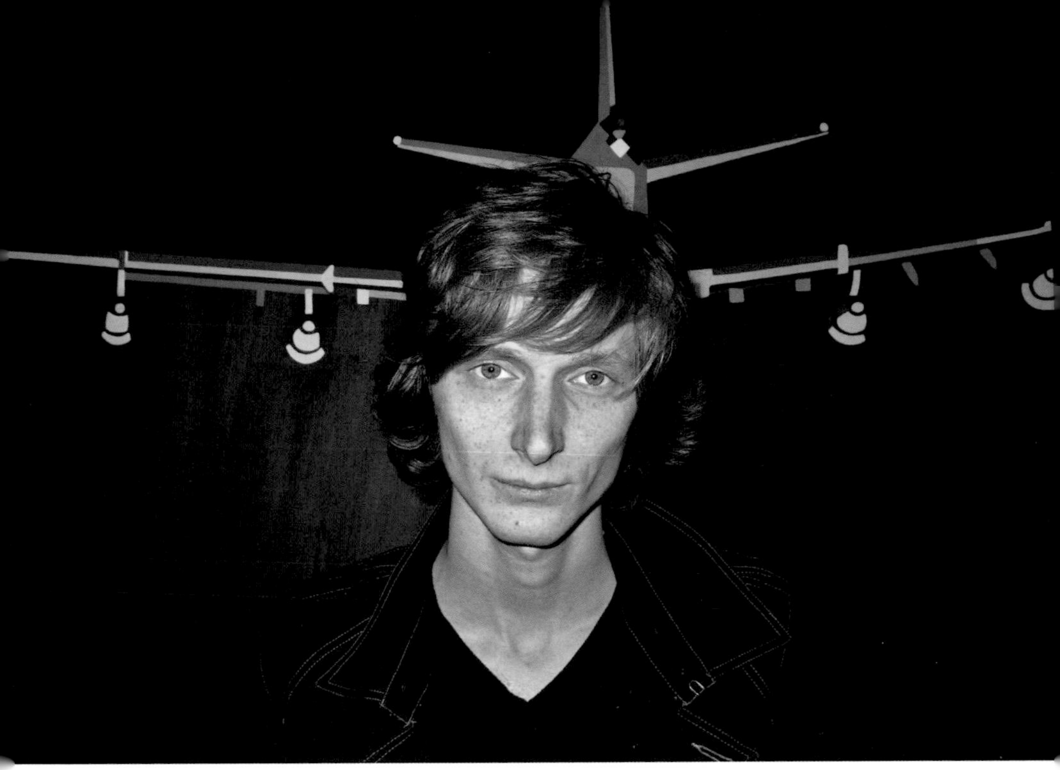

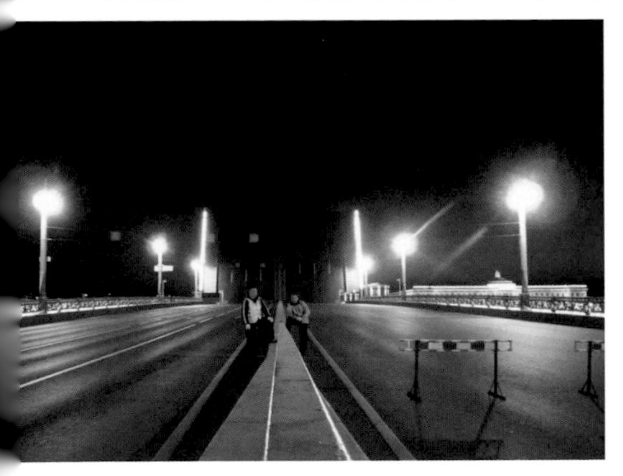

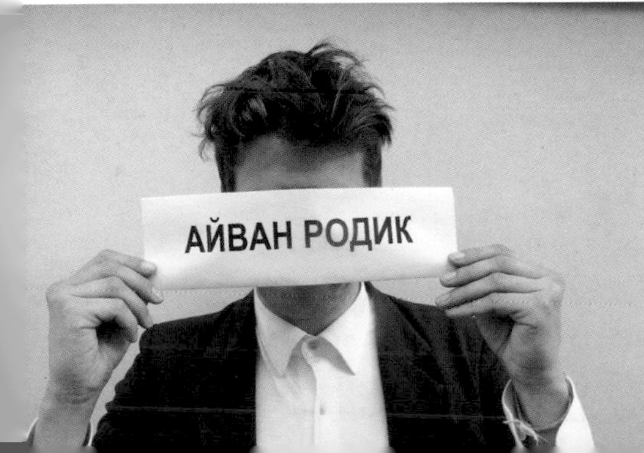
АЙВАН РОДИК

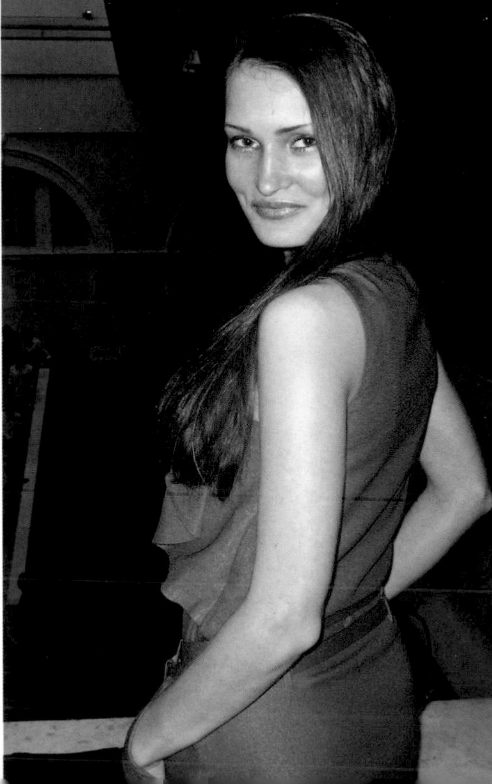

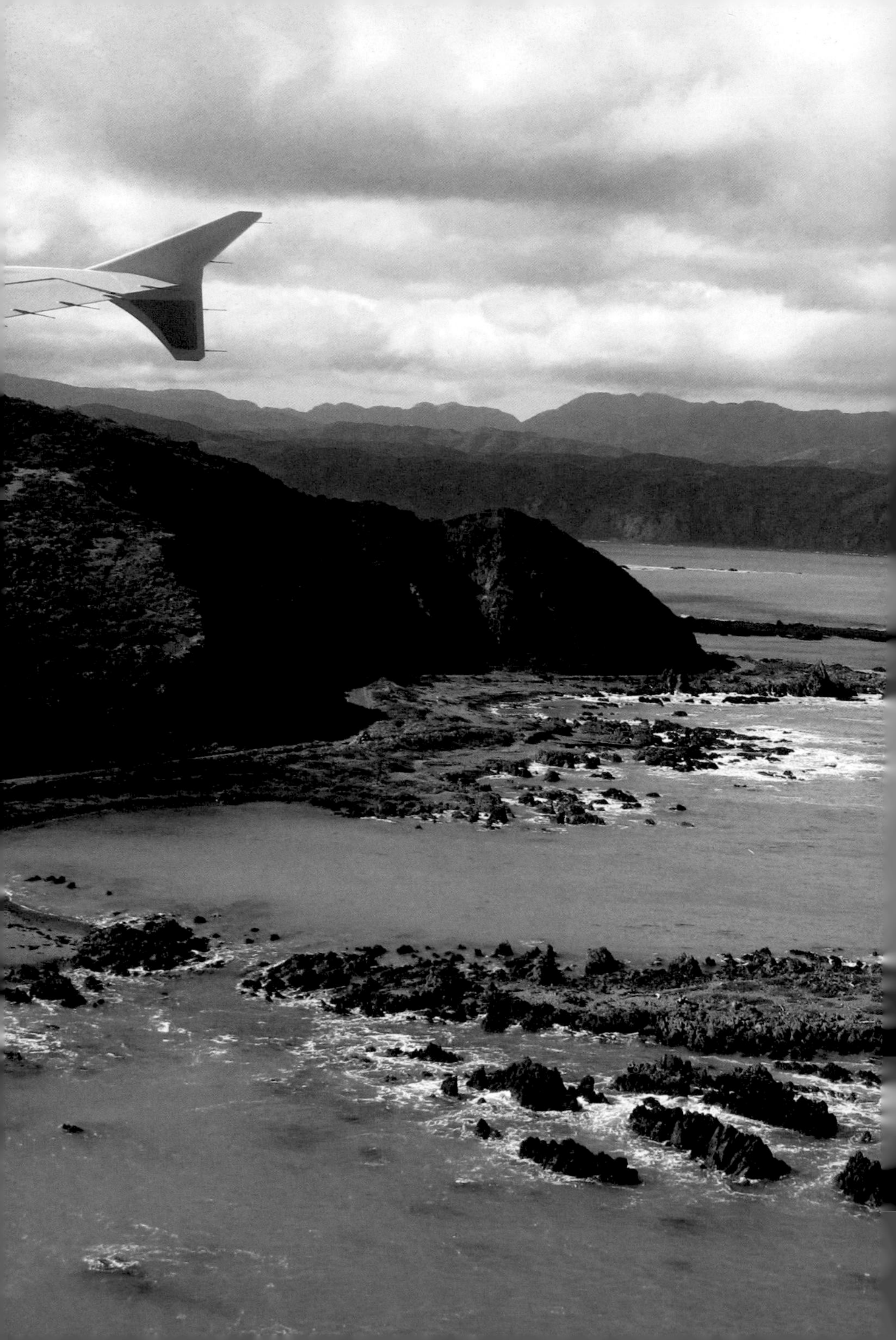

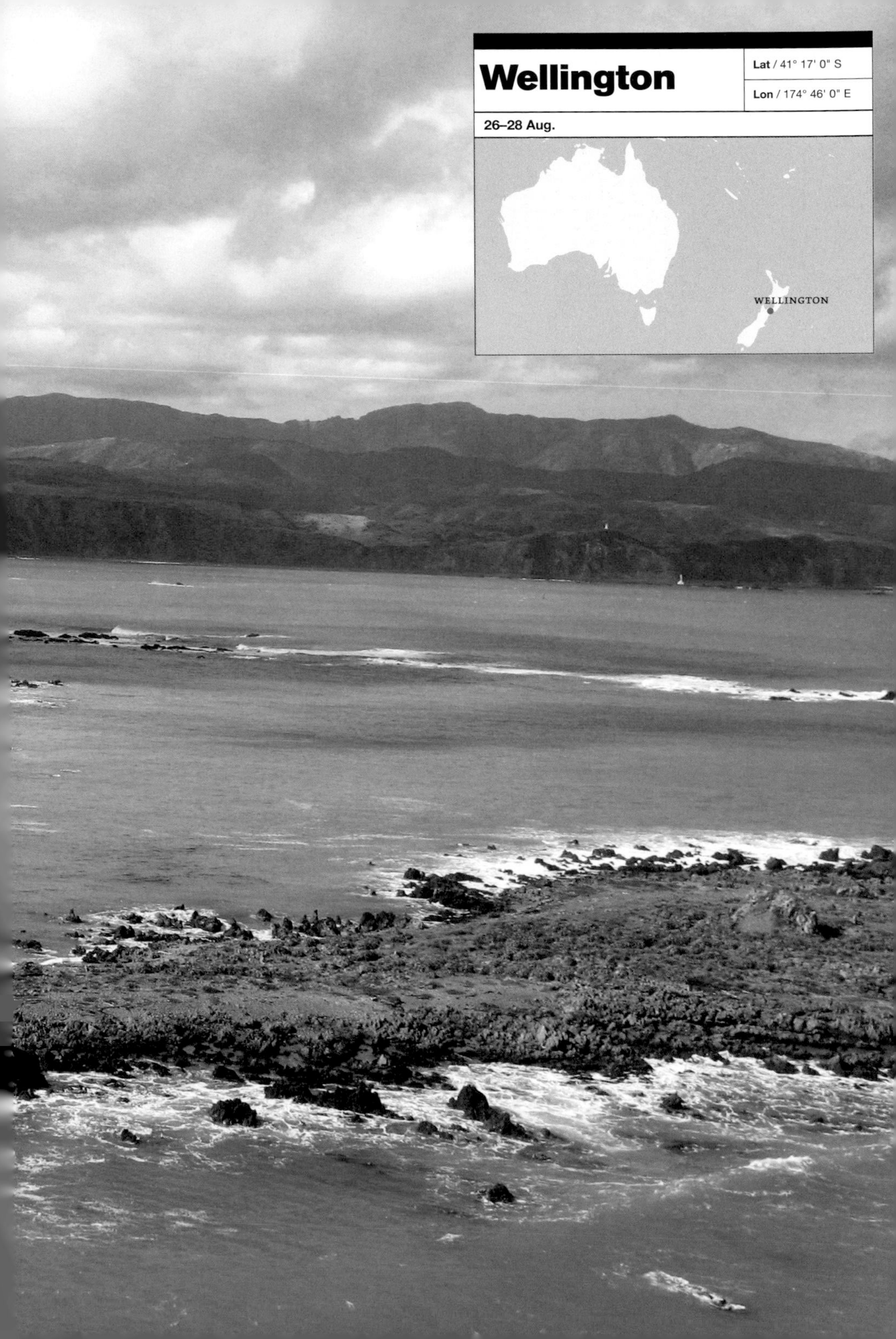
Wellington
Lat / 41° 17' 0" S
Lon / 174° 46' 0" E
26–28 Aug.
WELLINGTON

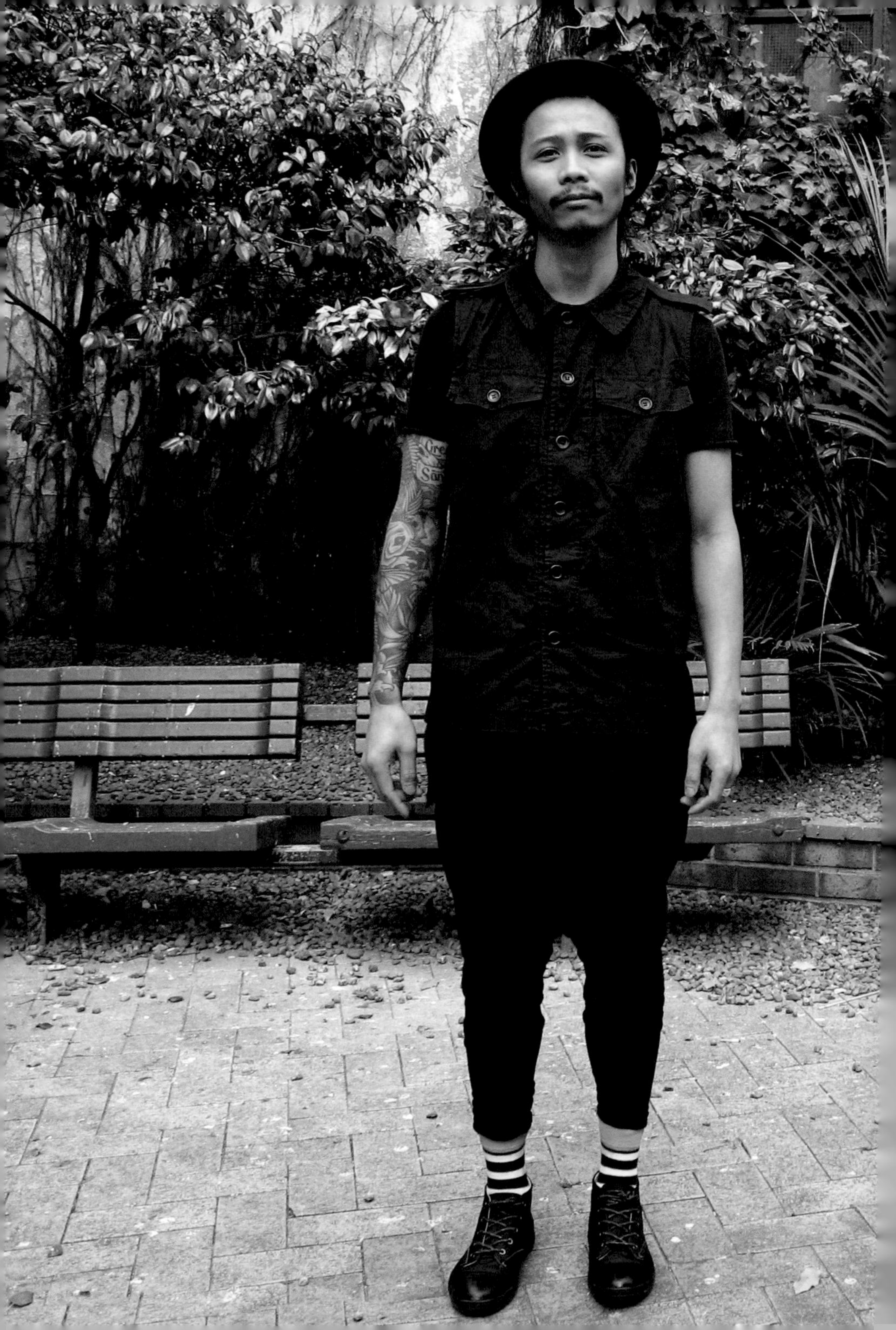

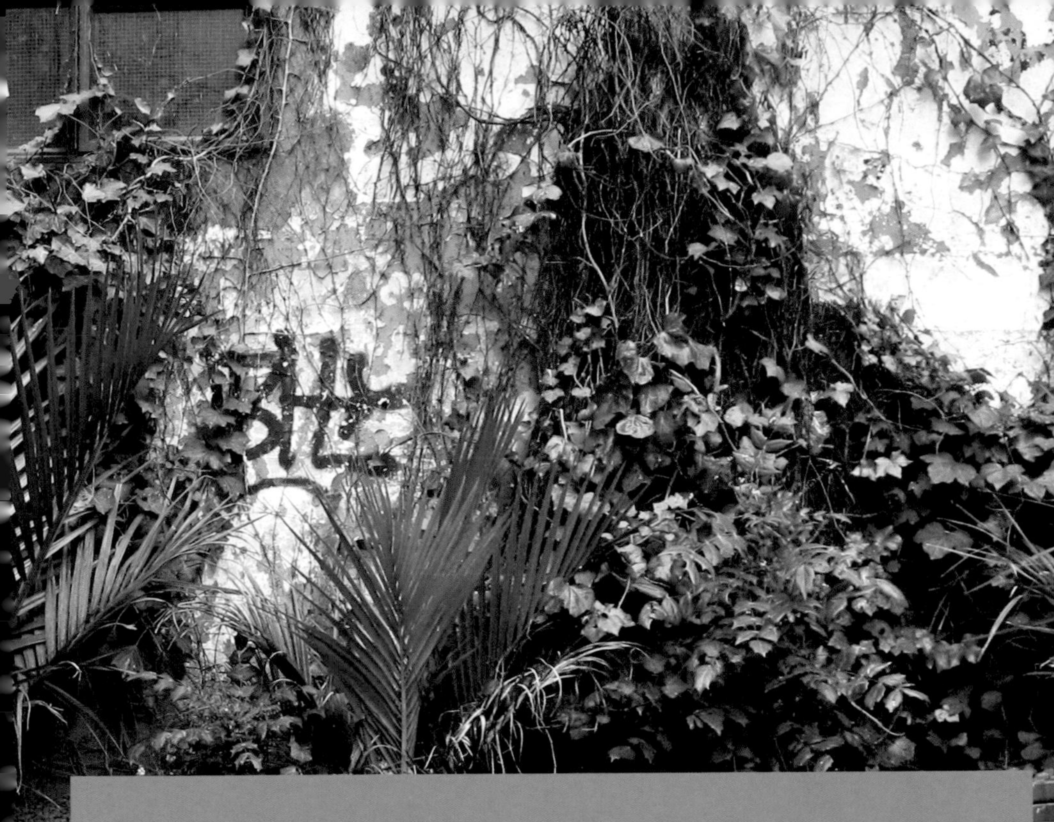

> “To meet the nicest people on earth, you need to fly 24 hours from London. Wellington has the most beautiful approach to an airport I have ever seen: you fly over turquoise water and see jagged rocks emerging from the surf, and then the coastline and the rugged landscape dotted with wooden houses. As a European I expected New Zealand to be similar to Australia, but in fact New Zealand has a very distinct identity. For some reason – maybe because the weather is less reliable and New Zealanders spend less time tanning than do Australians – it seems to me that they have a more complex approach to style and identity. They are also some of the friendliest people I have ever met. When New Zealanders ask ‘How are you?’ you feel they actually care about the answer. There’s a certain camaraderie and low-key approach, an honesty that’s unusual in the Western world. It’s very appealing. Wellington has a beautiful harbour walk and cool local bands. Whereas Auckland is more mainstream, Wellington is a small, cute indie city that is a lot of fun.”

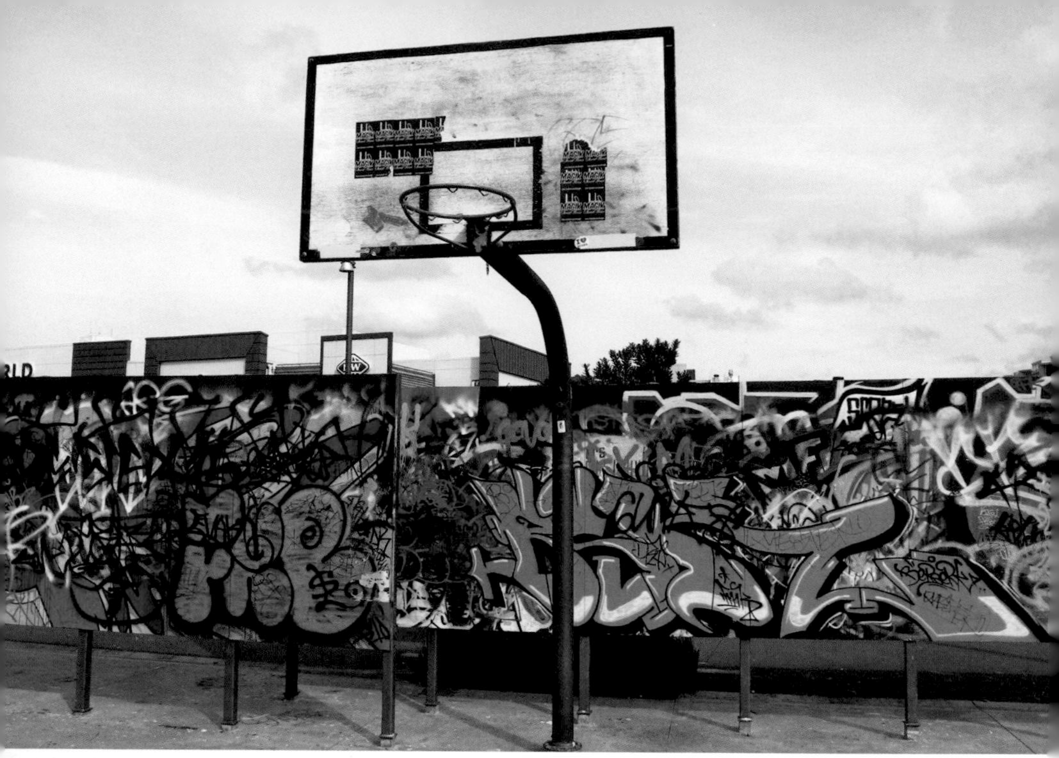

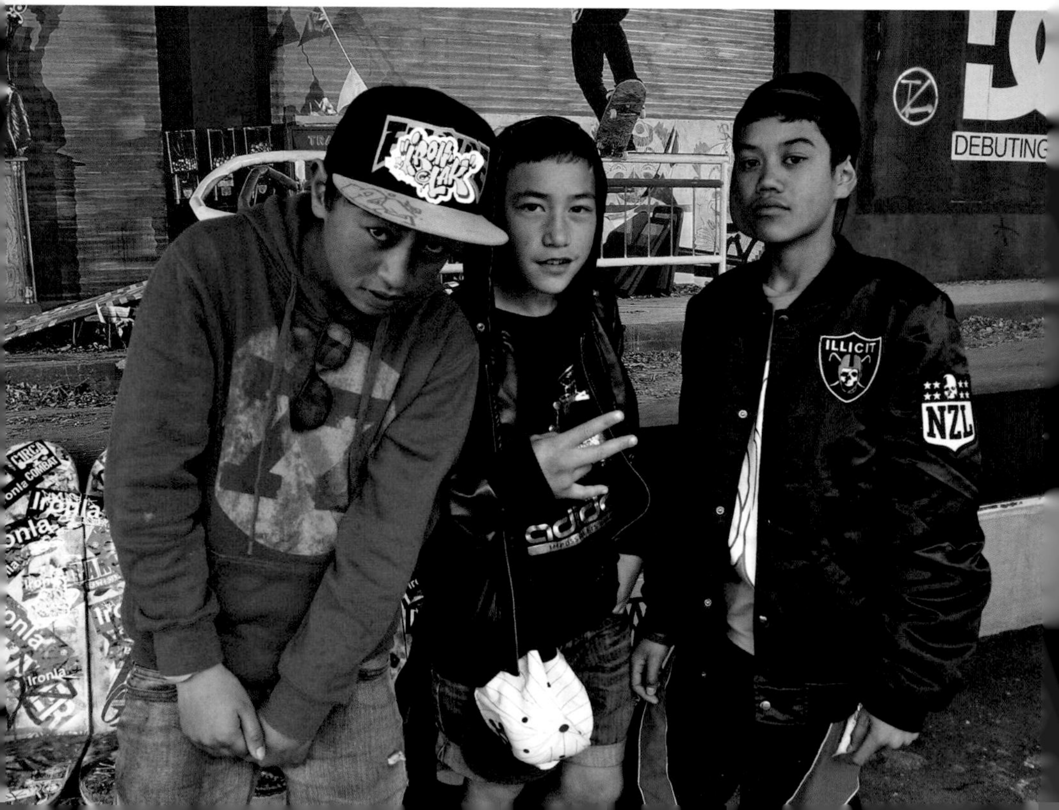

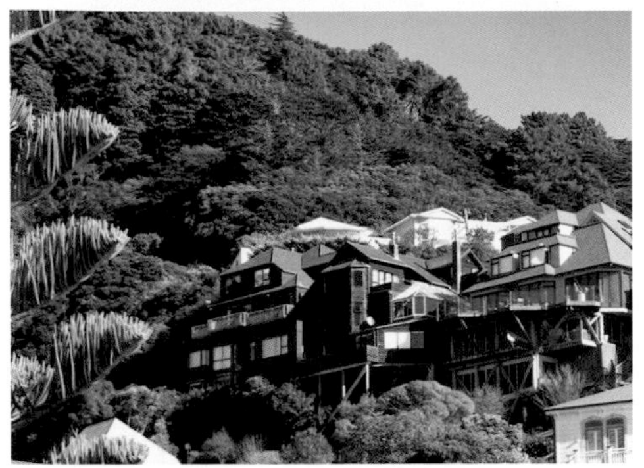

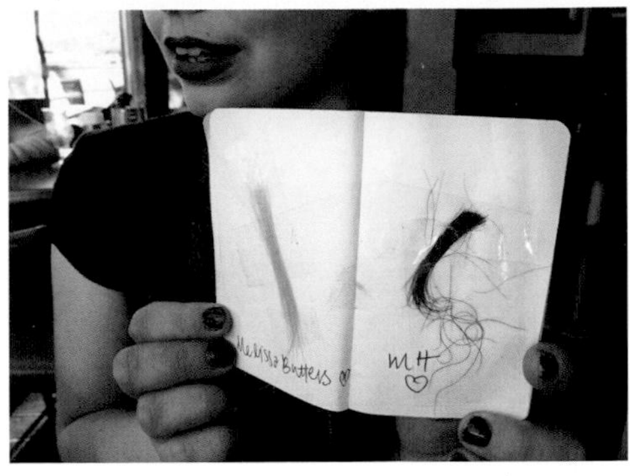

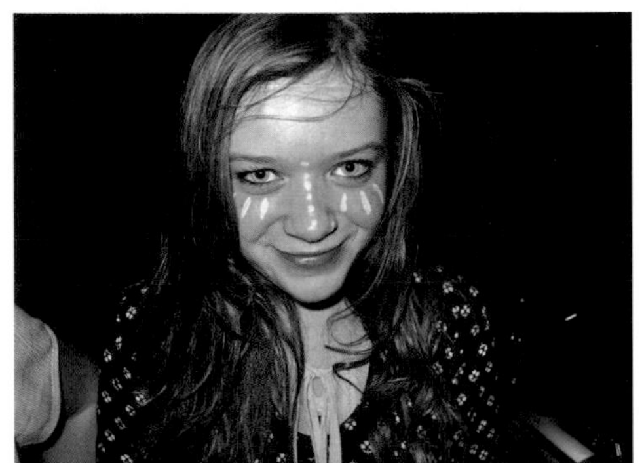

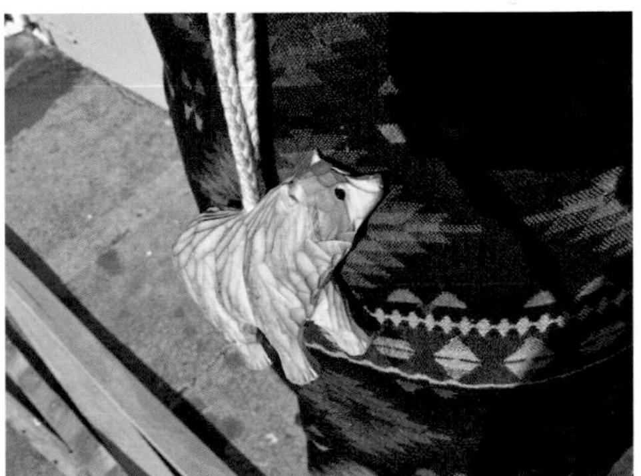

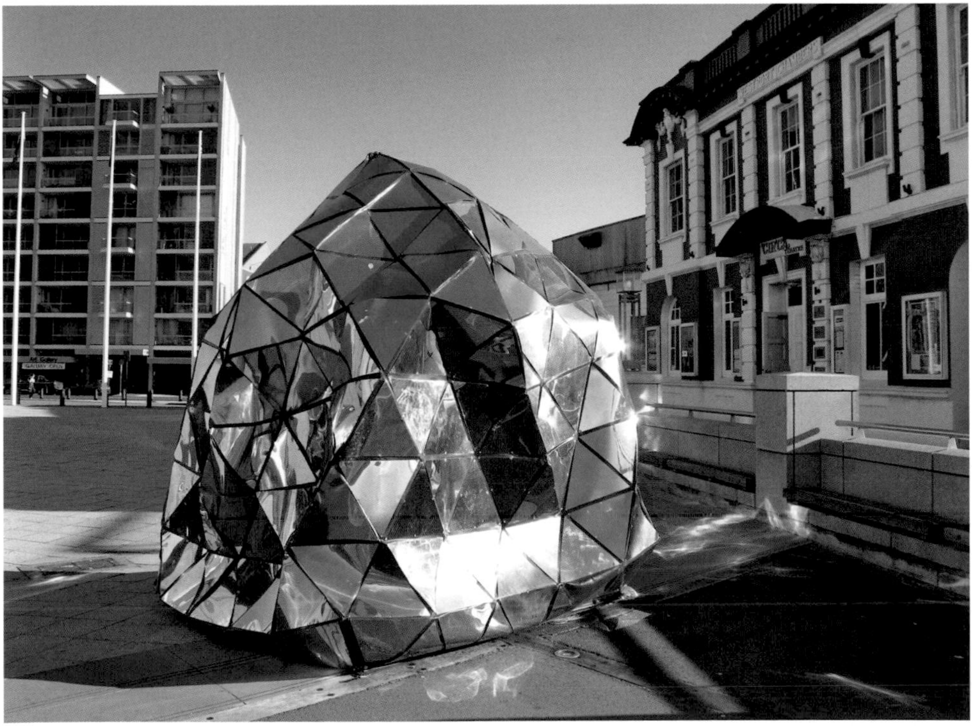

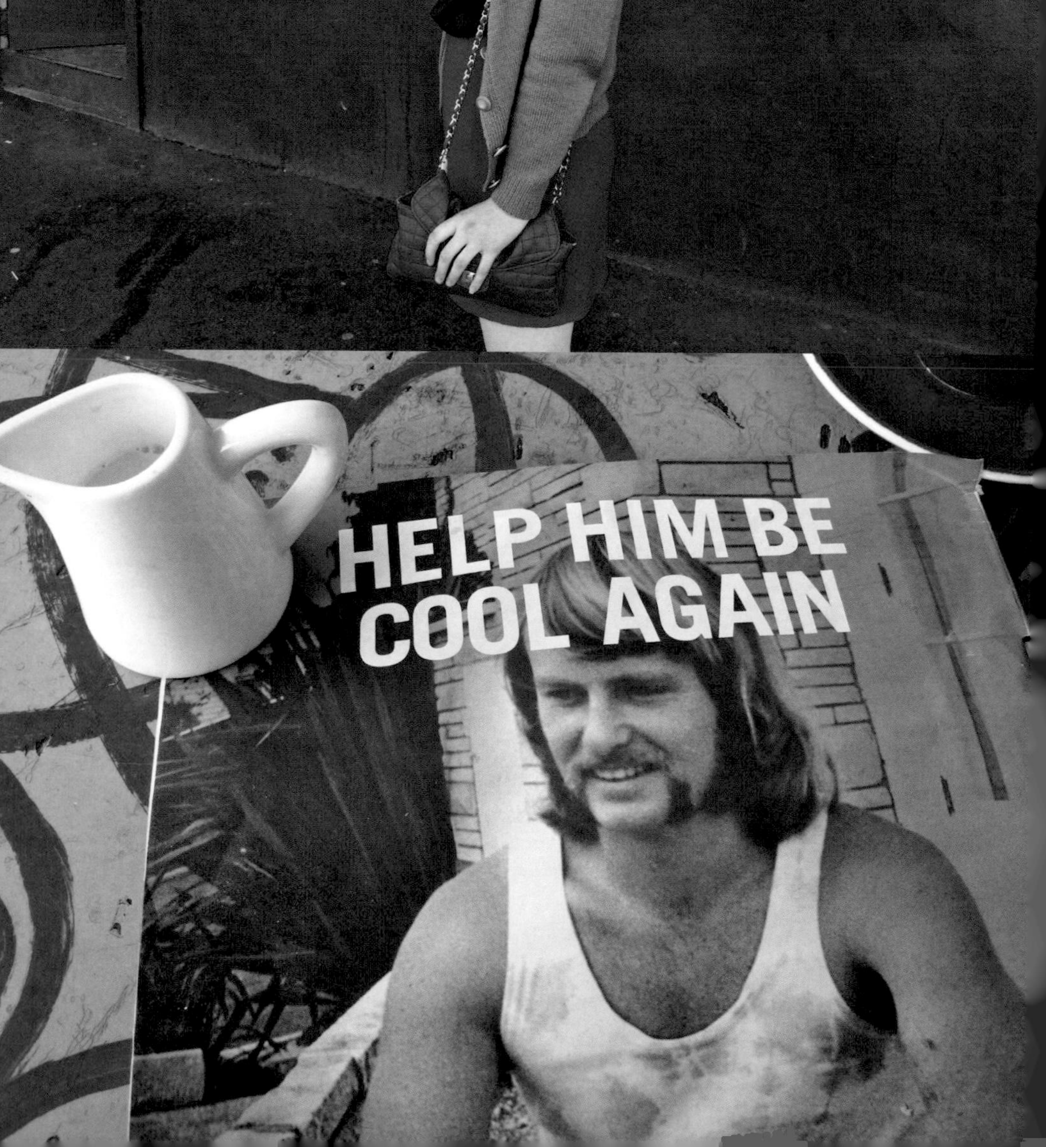
HELP HIM BE
COOL AGAIN

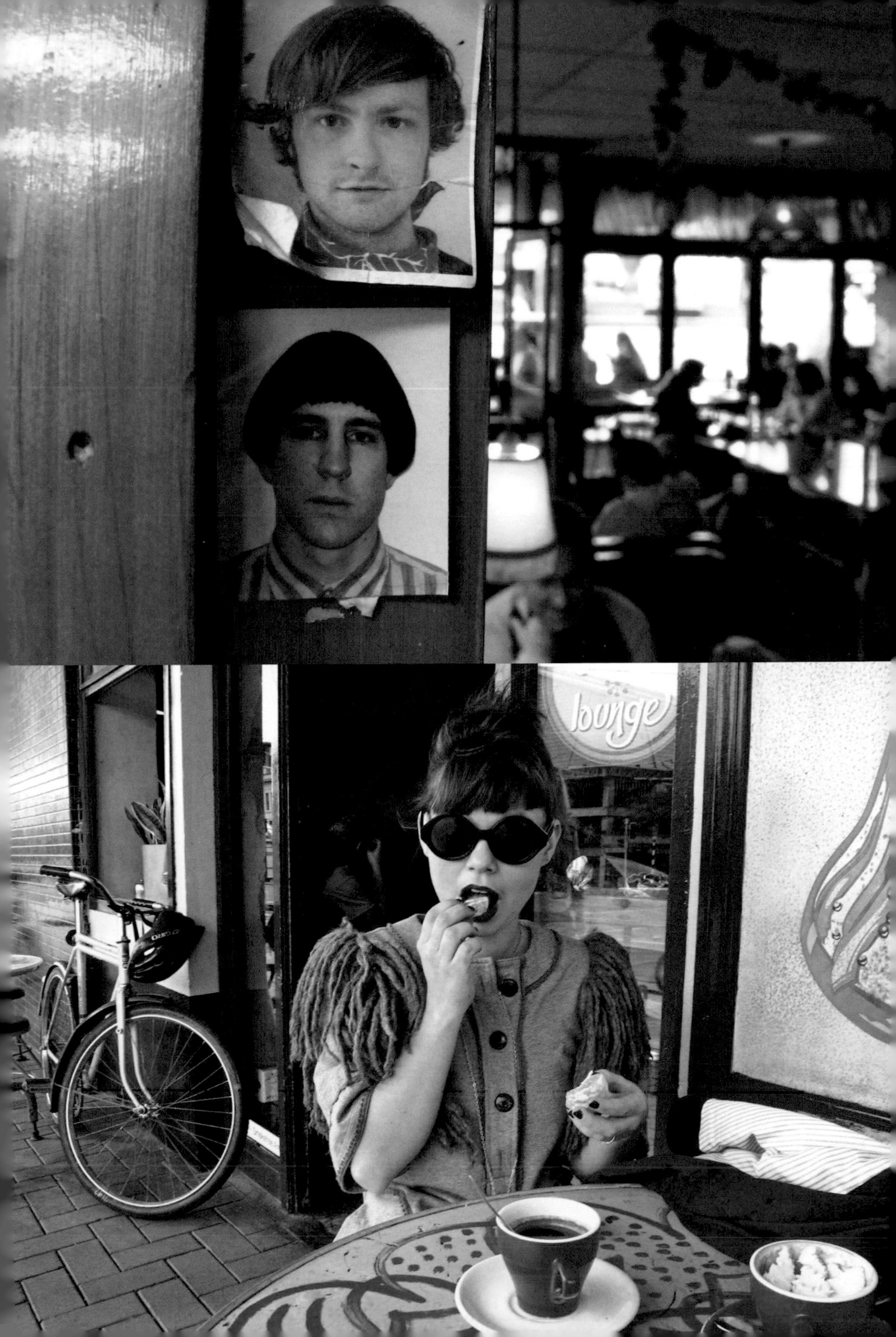
lounge

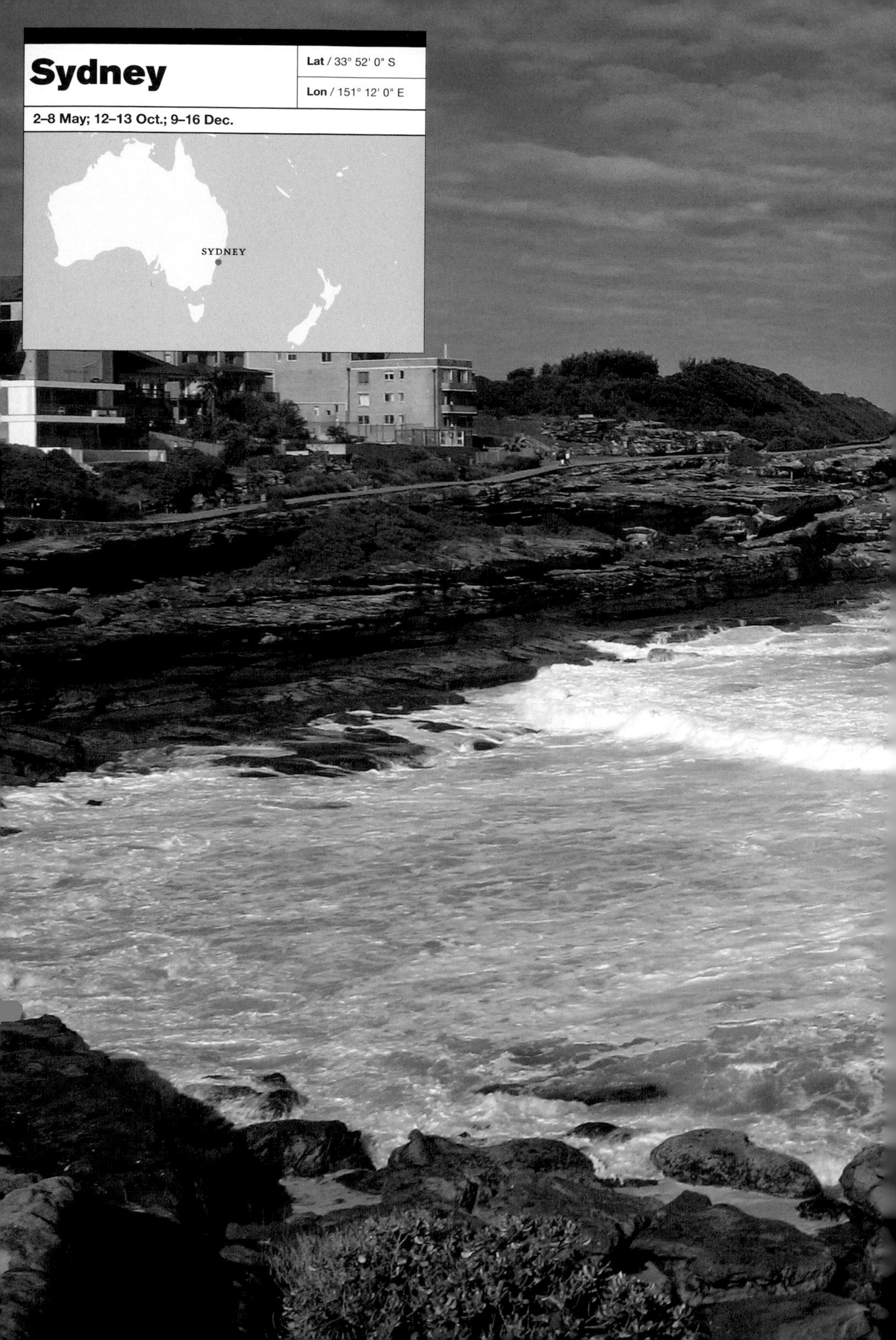

Sydney
Lat / 33° 52' 0" S
Lon / 151° 12' 0" E
2–8 May; 12–13 Oct.; 9–16 Dec.
SYDNEY

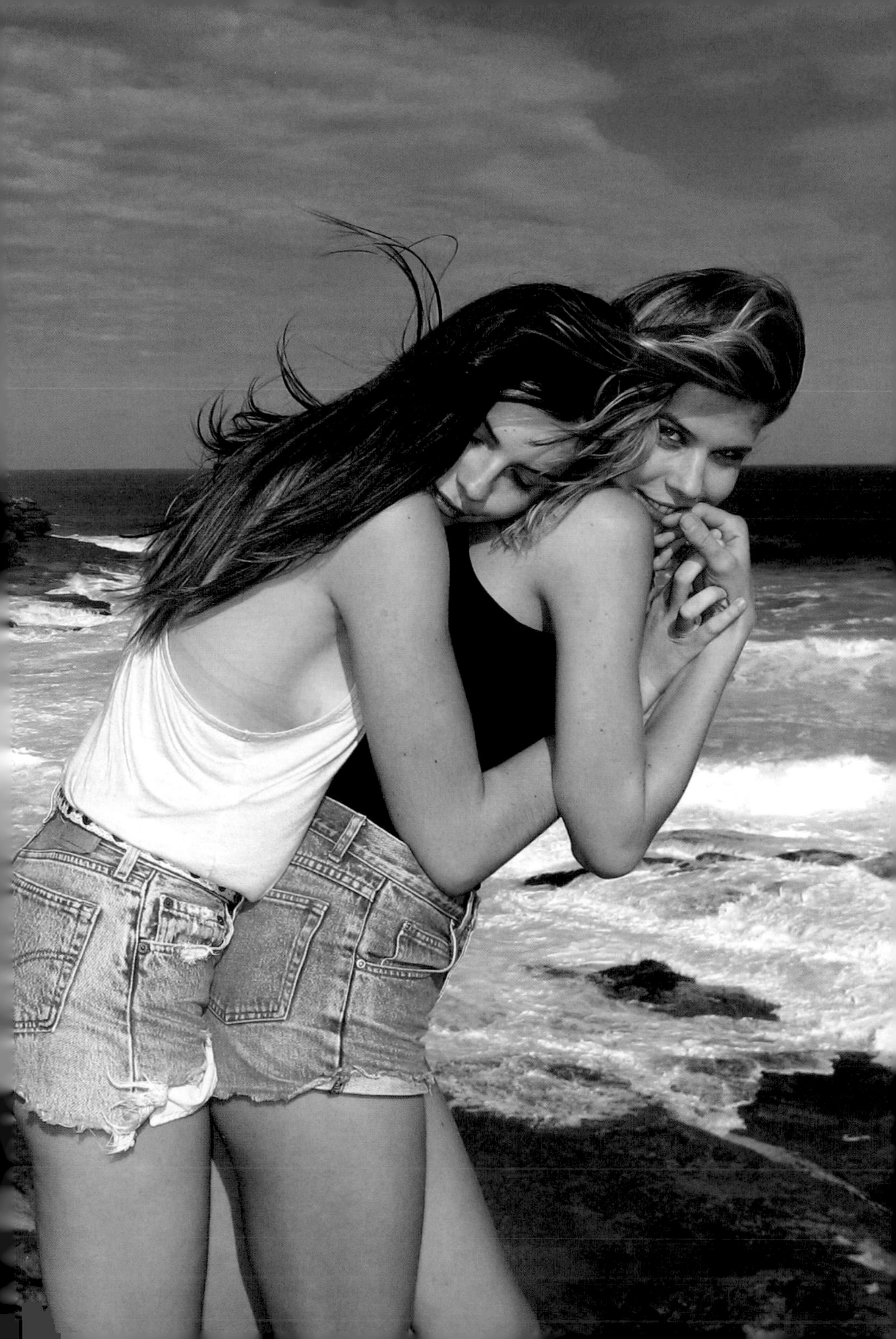

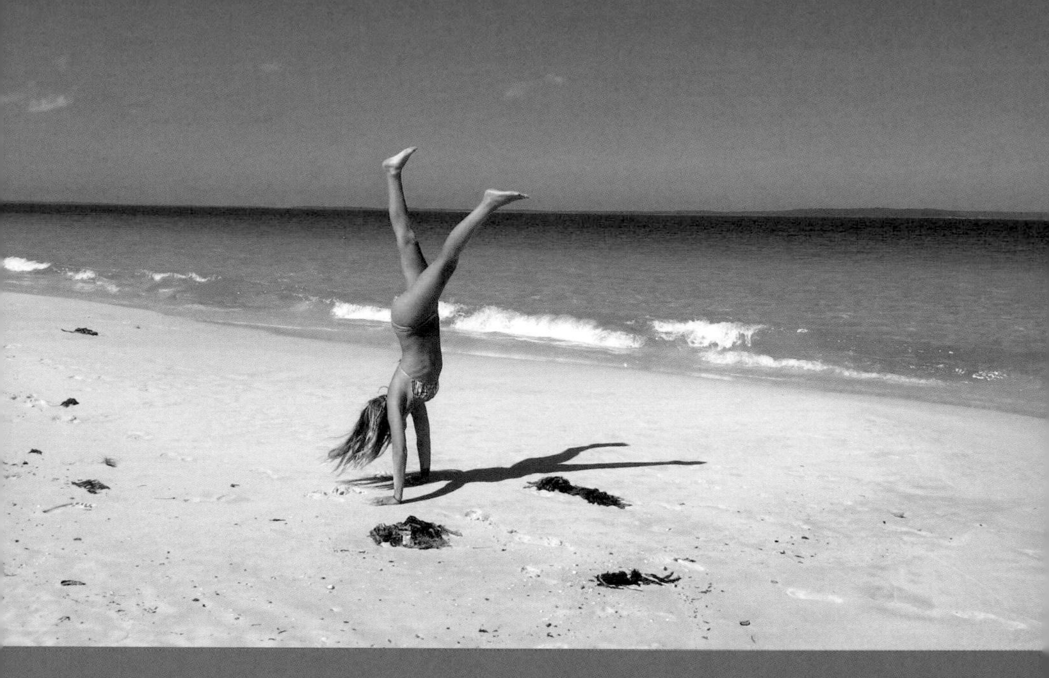

“I think Sydney is one of the most pleasant places on earth. It’s fun; it’s gorgeous; it has lots of space, good food and perfect weather – all the elements you need for a good lifestyle – but it’s also a city where there are a lot of things happening culturally. Sydney is definitely one of the new style capitals of the world. People tend to think of Australia generally and Sydney in particular mainly as surfers’ paradises, but actually the fashion scene is really booming, and in the last few years so many great designers have emerged. The catwalk is great, but so is the street, where you see so many well-dressed people. Normally people go to Australia for everything except its urban culture, but I think Sydney is really experiencing its fashion golden age at the moment.”

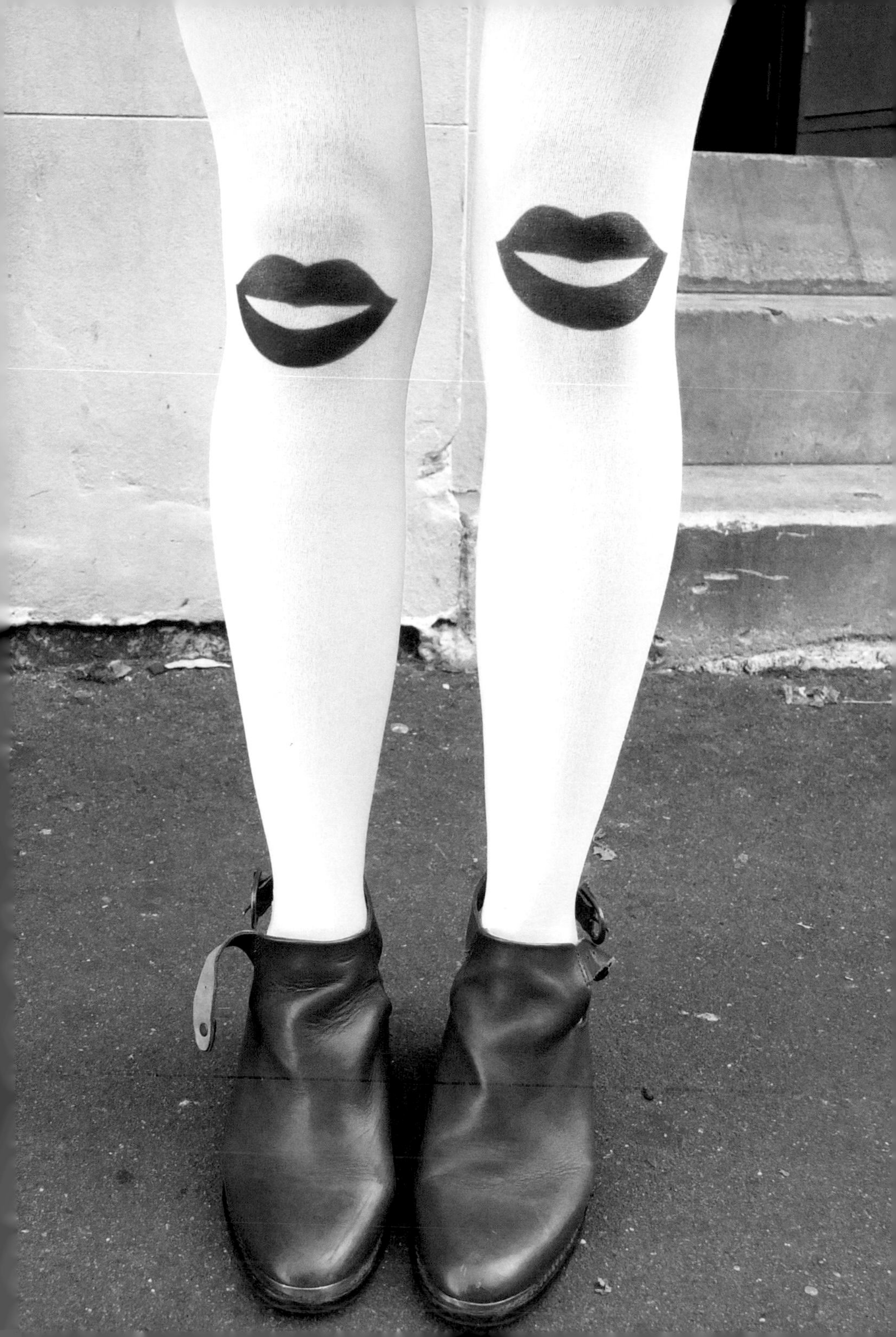

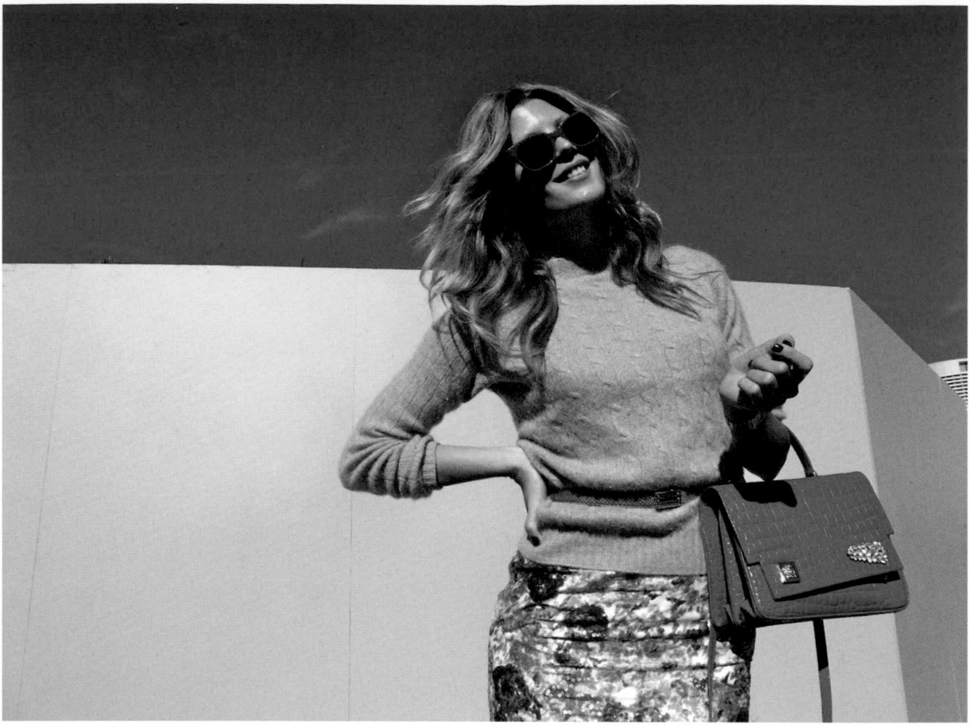

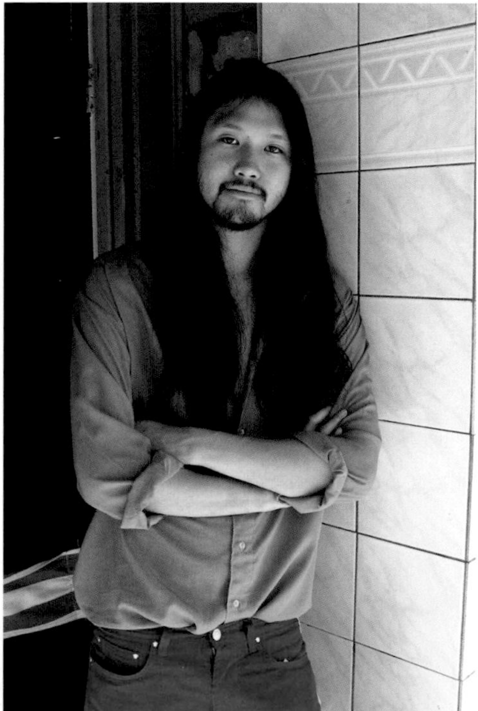

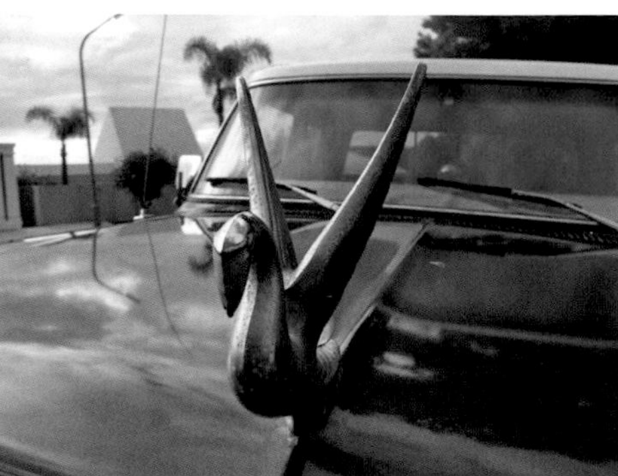

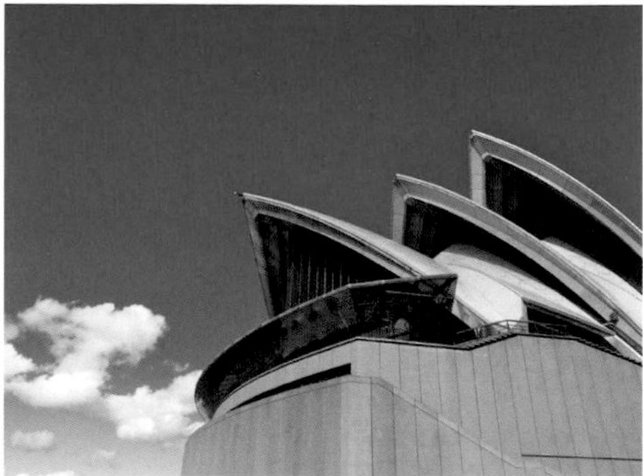

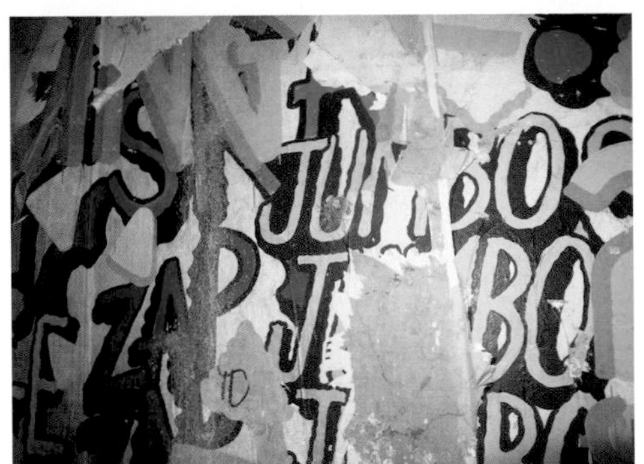

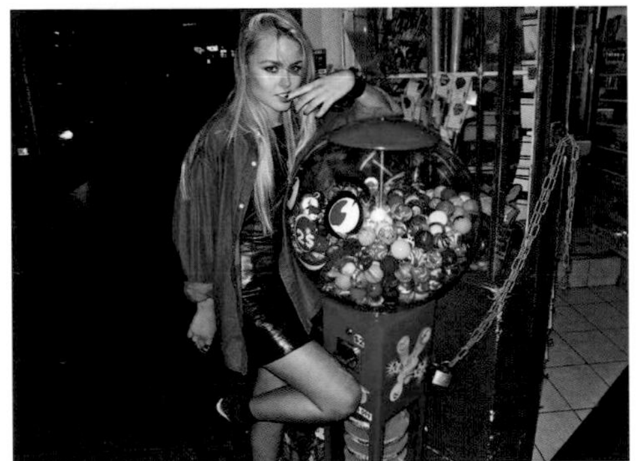

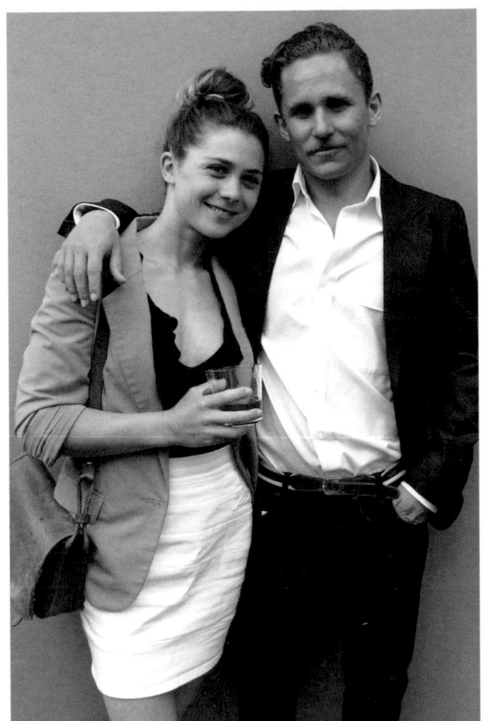

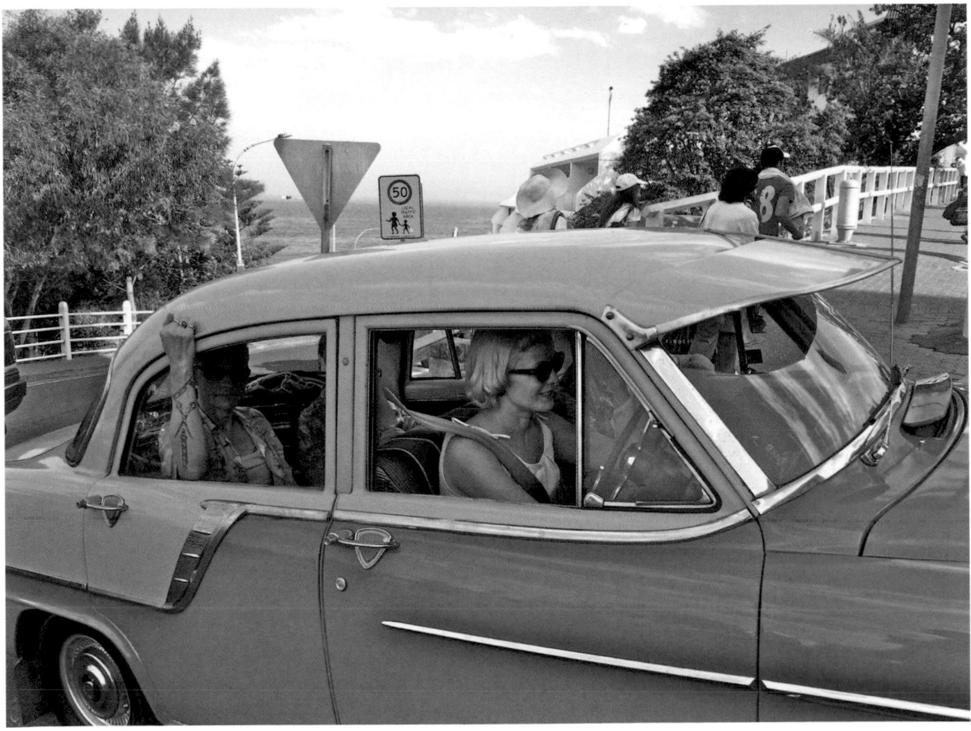

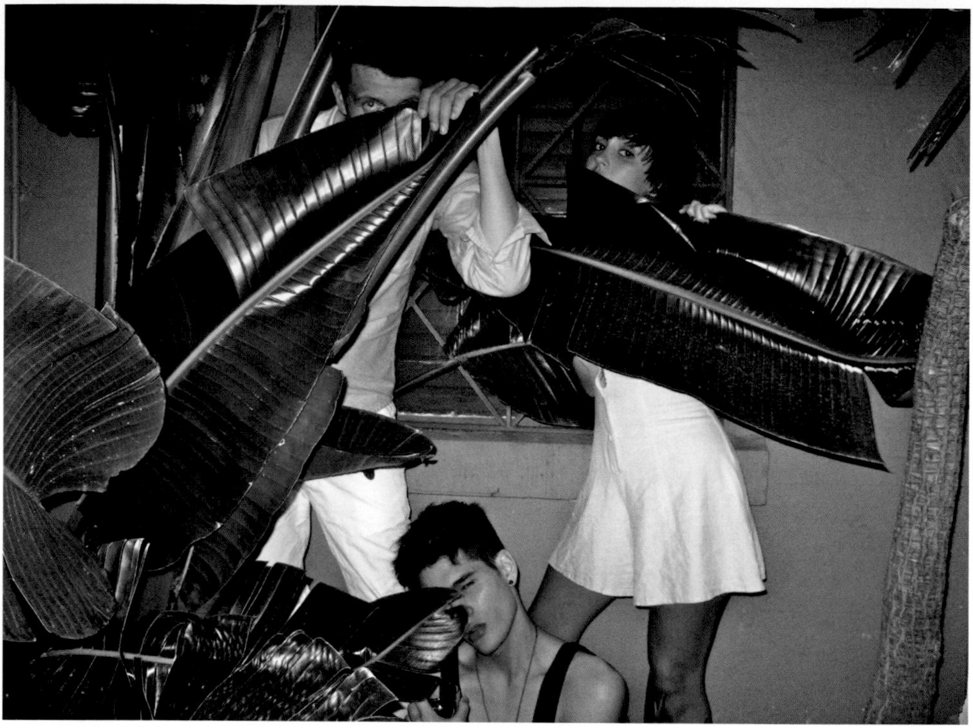

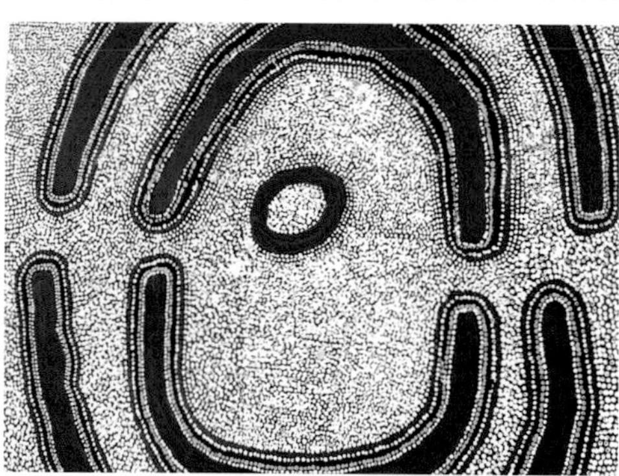

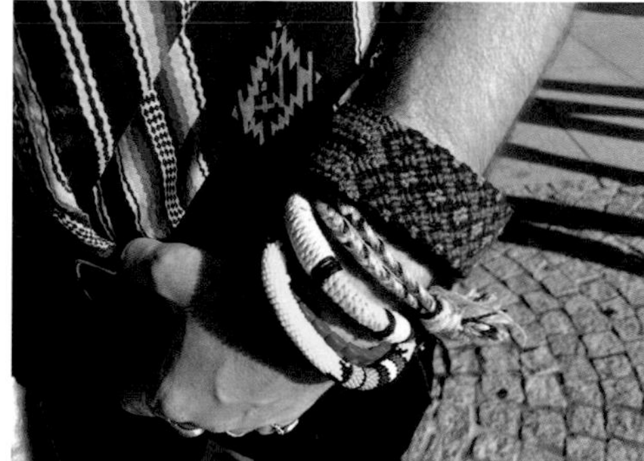

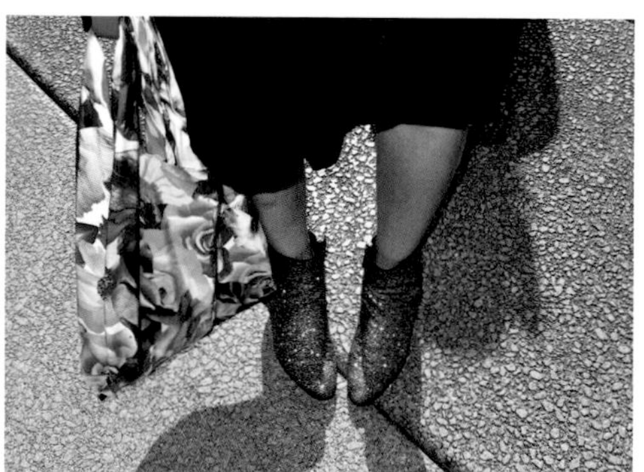

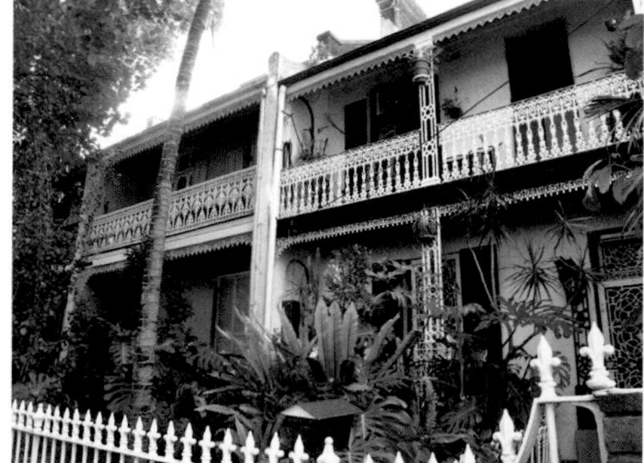

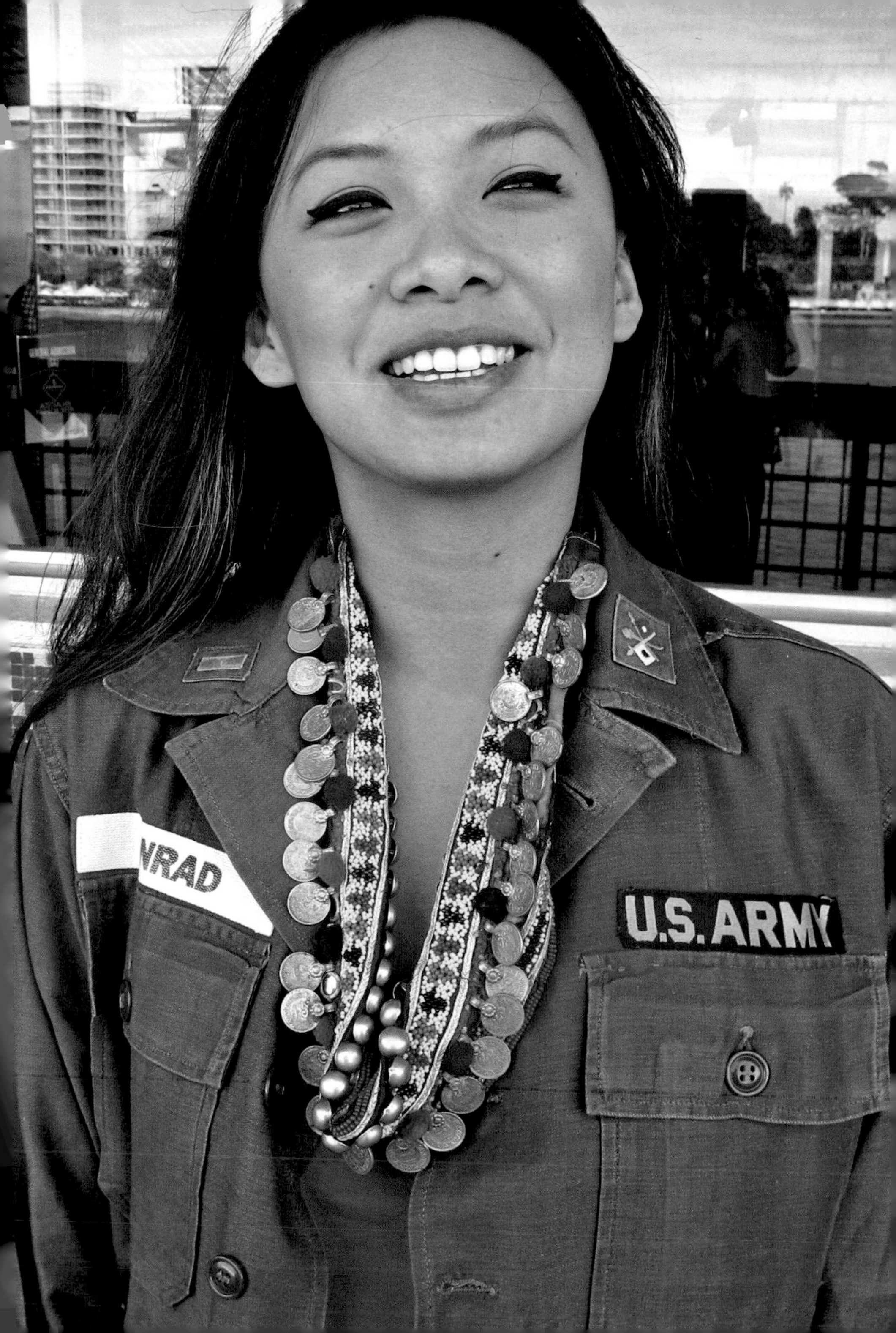
NRAD
U.S. ARMY

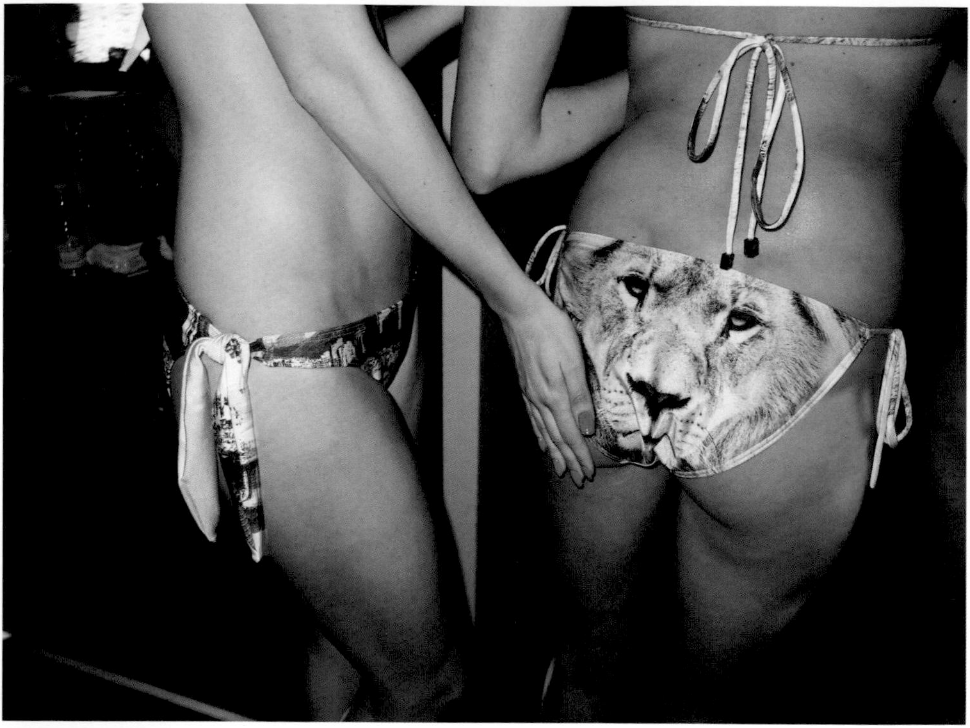

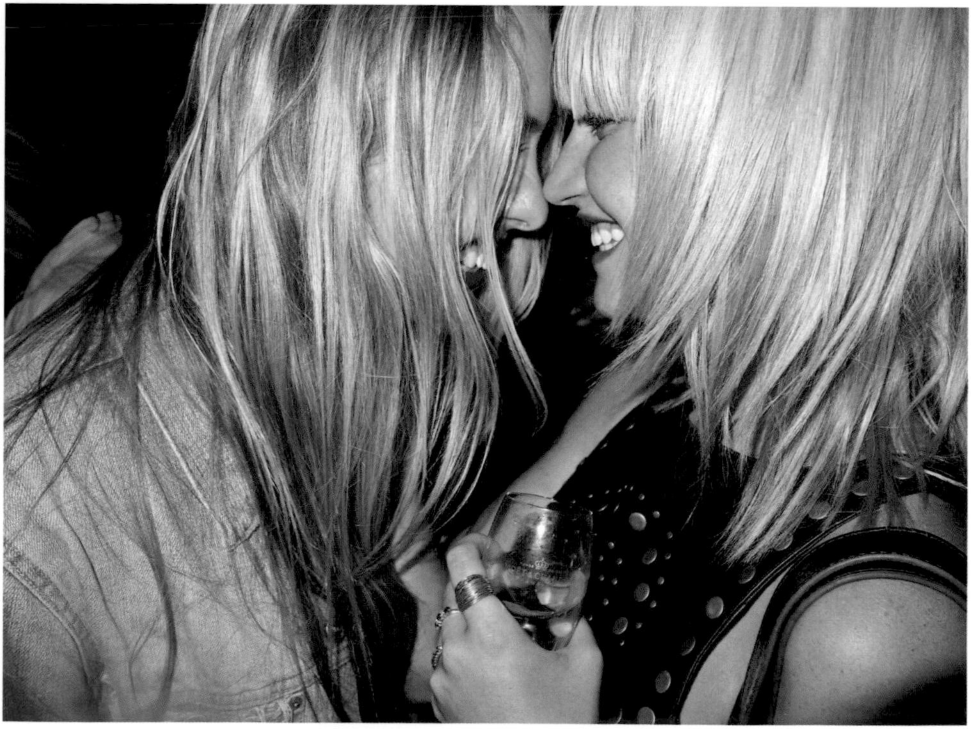

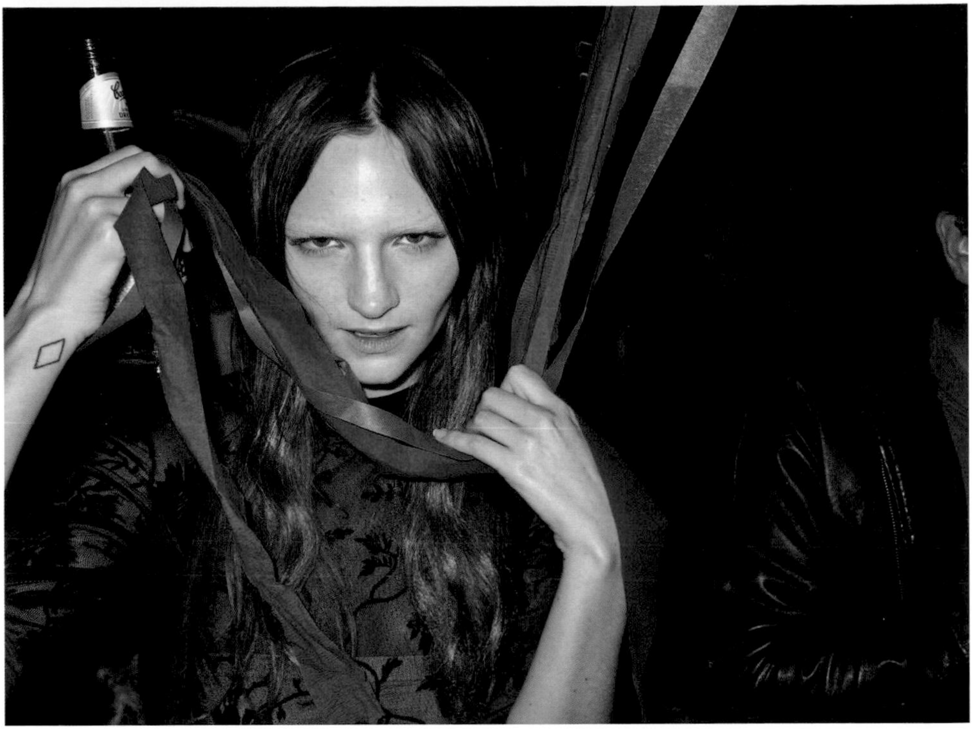

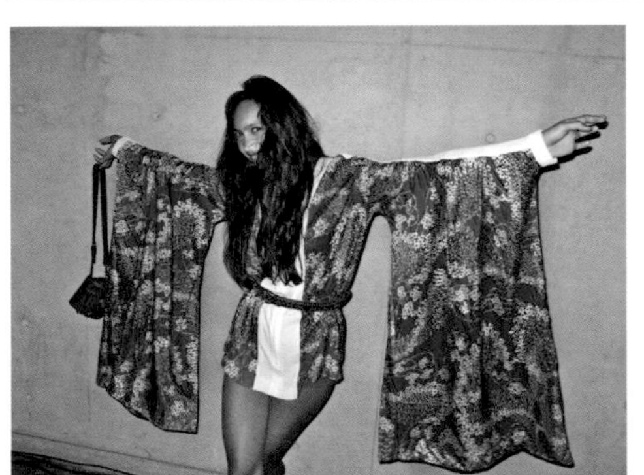

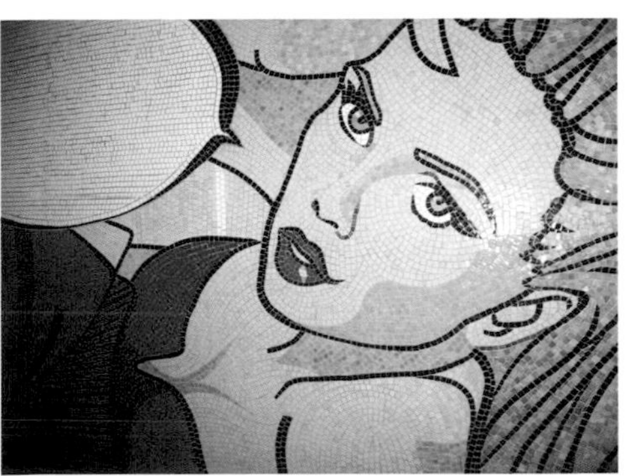

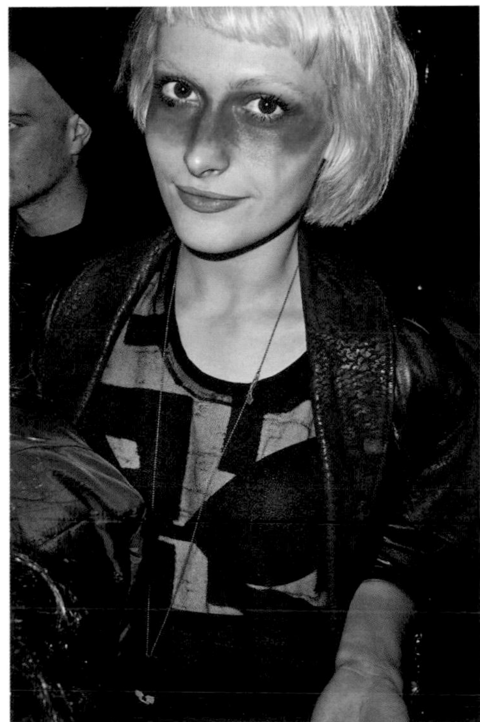

Kiev

Lat / 50° 27' 0" N

Lon / 30° 31' 0" E

25–27 Mar.; 21–23 Oct.

KIEV

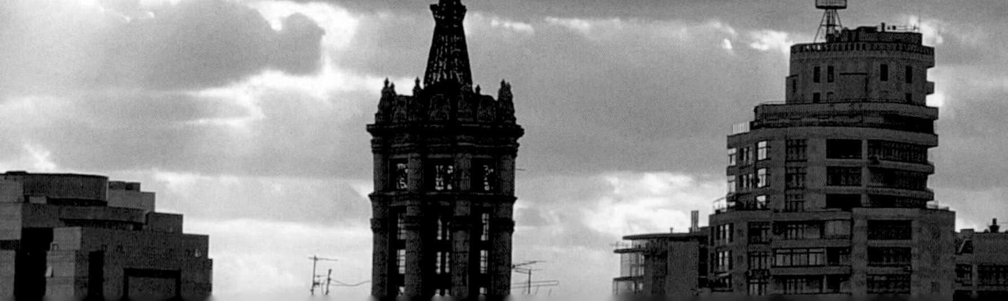

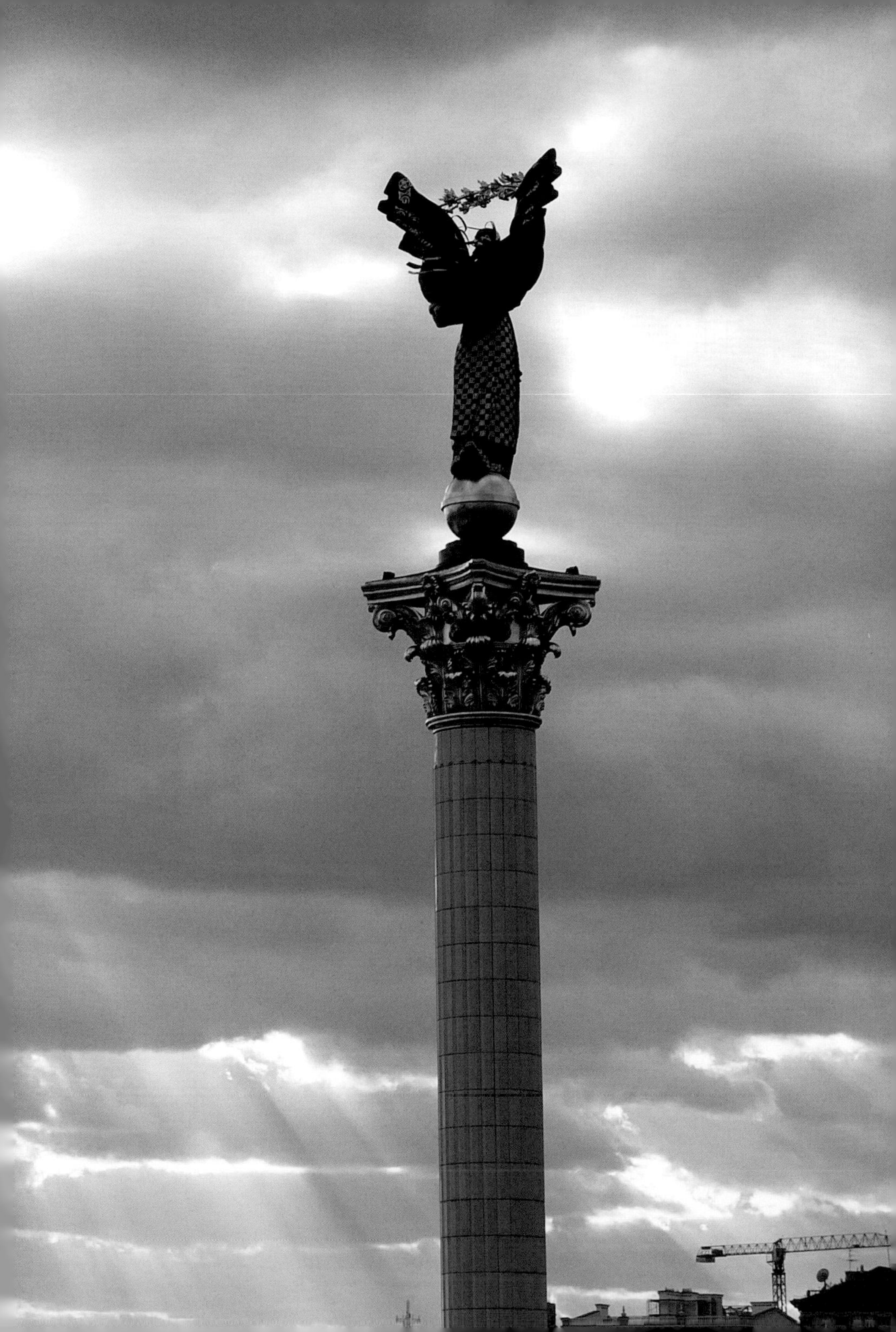

“I’ve been to Kiev quite a few times now. The biggest surprise when I first visited was how colourful the architecture is. I’d imagined a grey, gloomy place with a lot of concrete Soviet-era buildings, when in fact the city is incredibly pretty, full of brightly coloured churches and houses. When you see it you wonder why Kiev isn’t as big a tourist attraction as, say, Prague or Budapest, but at the same time it feels like it’s still a kind of undiscovered territory, and I like that. The people in Kiev are extremely welcoming – it’s sort of a softer version of Moscow (although the Ukrainians probably wouldn’t like that – they don’t like to be compared constantly to the Russians, except for the old cliché that Ukrainian girls are more beautiful than Russian girls!). Kiev does have a similar vibe to Moscow, but everything is smaller and less extreme. Thanks to the internet, people in Kiev are really connected to what’s happening in the West, but there are still plenty of visual clues to their Soviet past. They’re at a real transition point in their history.”

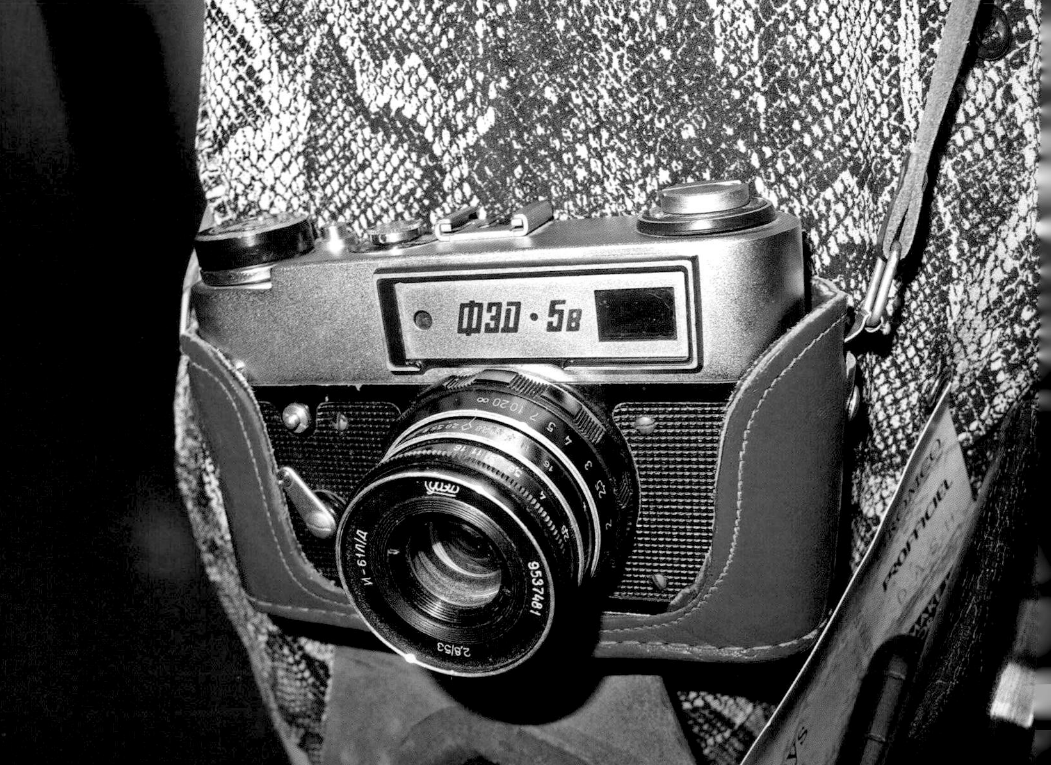

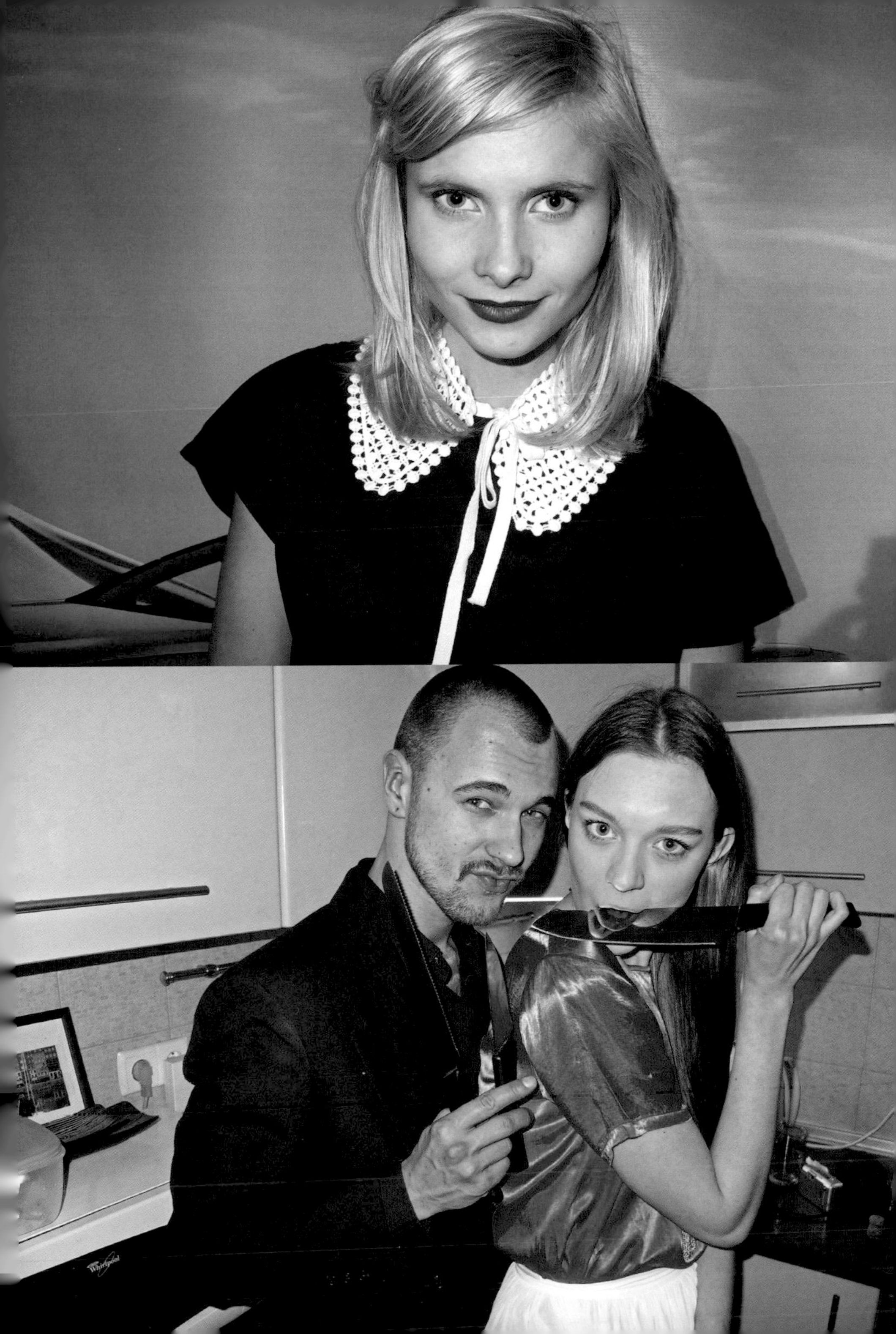
Whirlpool

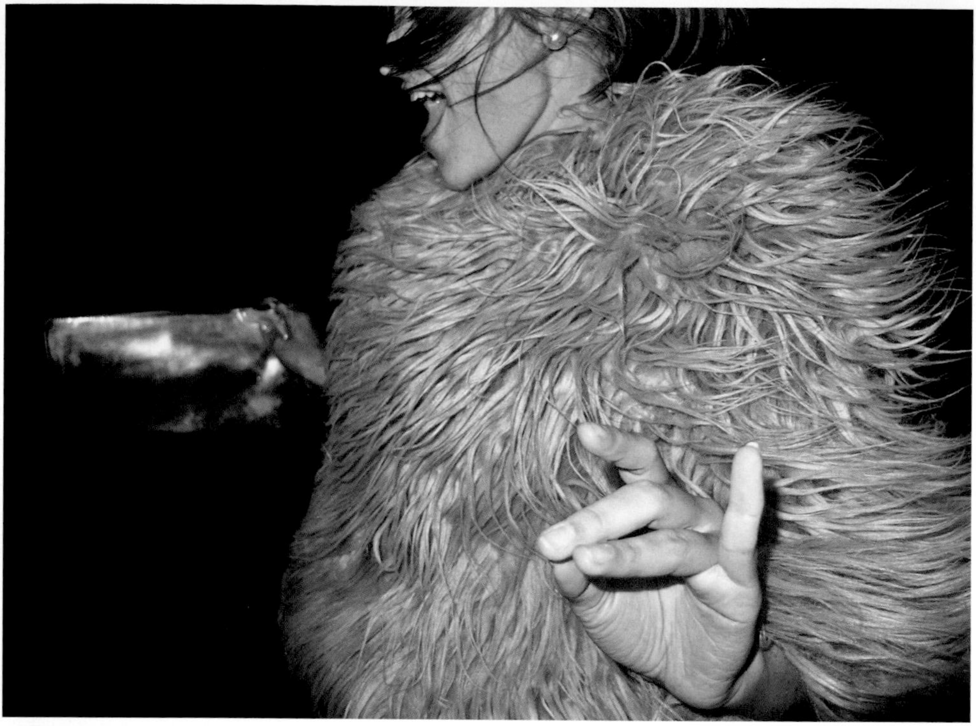

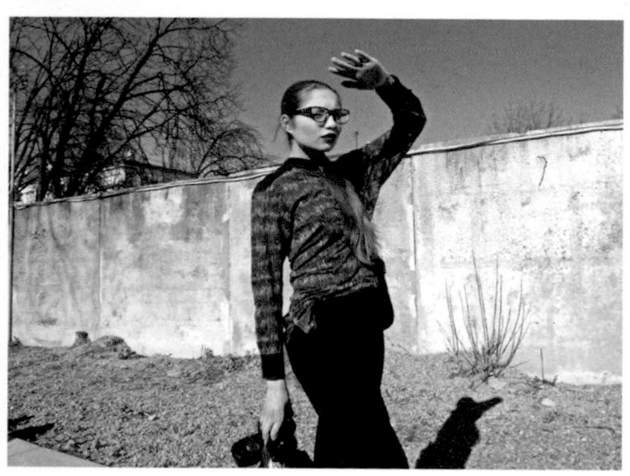

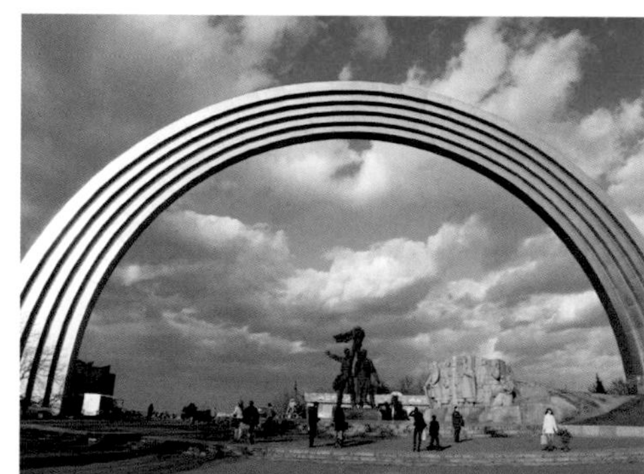

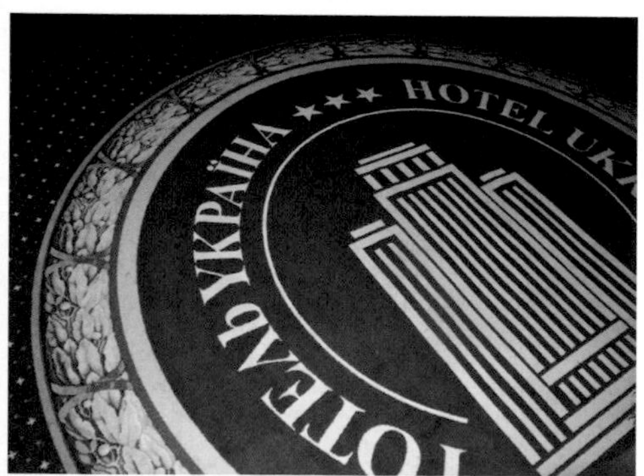
ГОТЕЛЬ УКРАЇНА
HOTEL

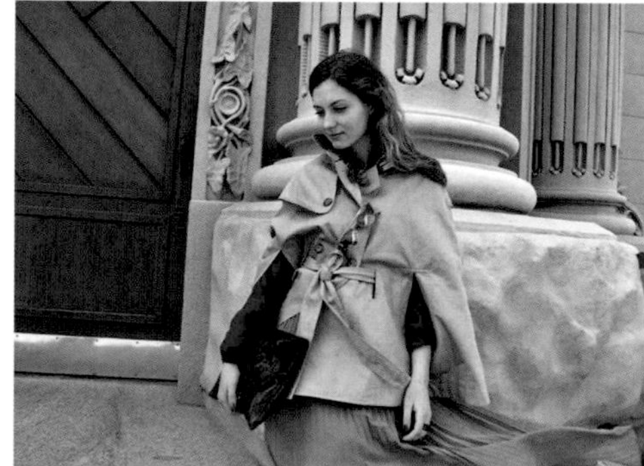

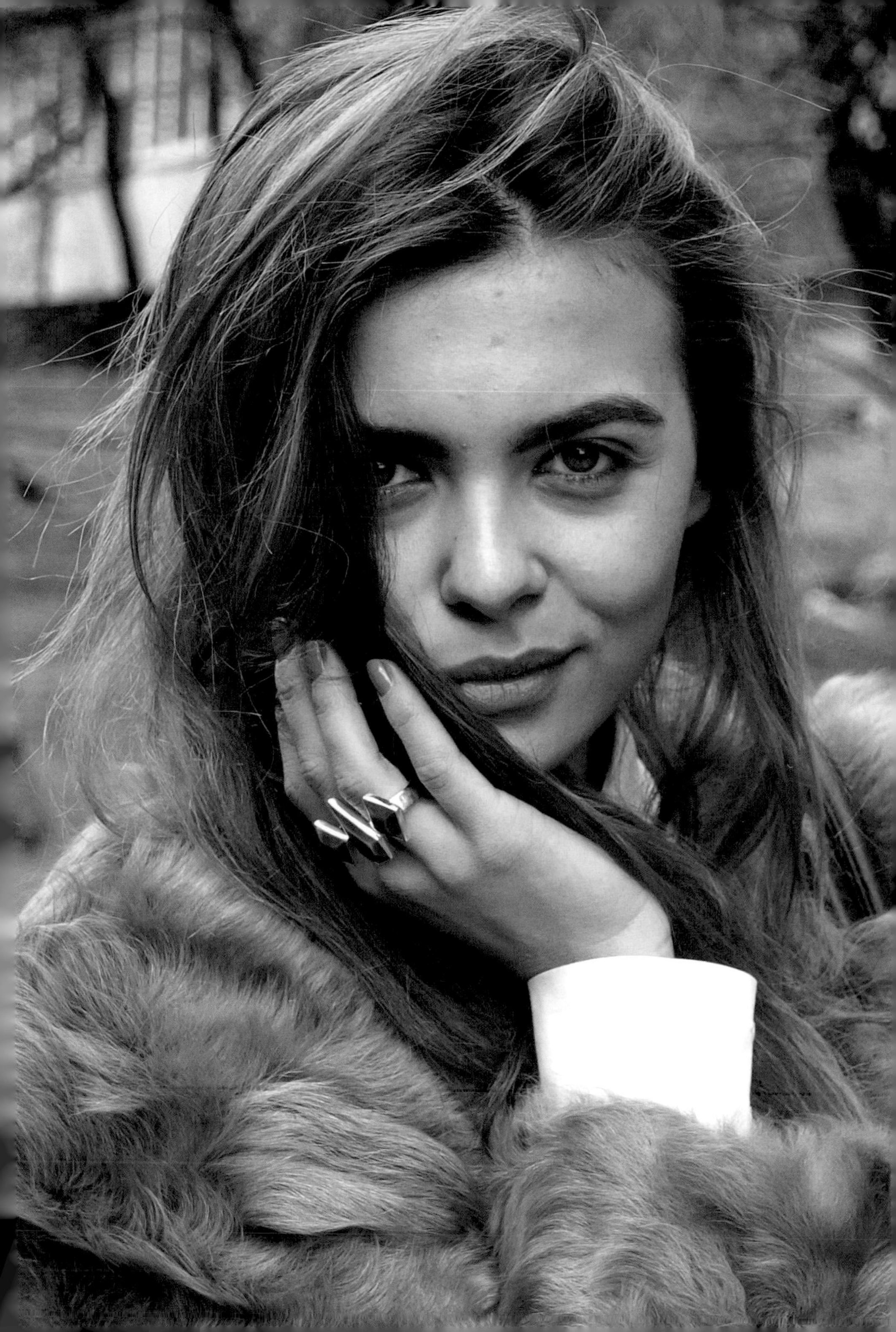

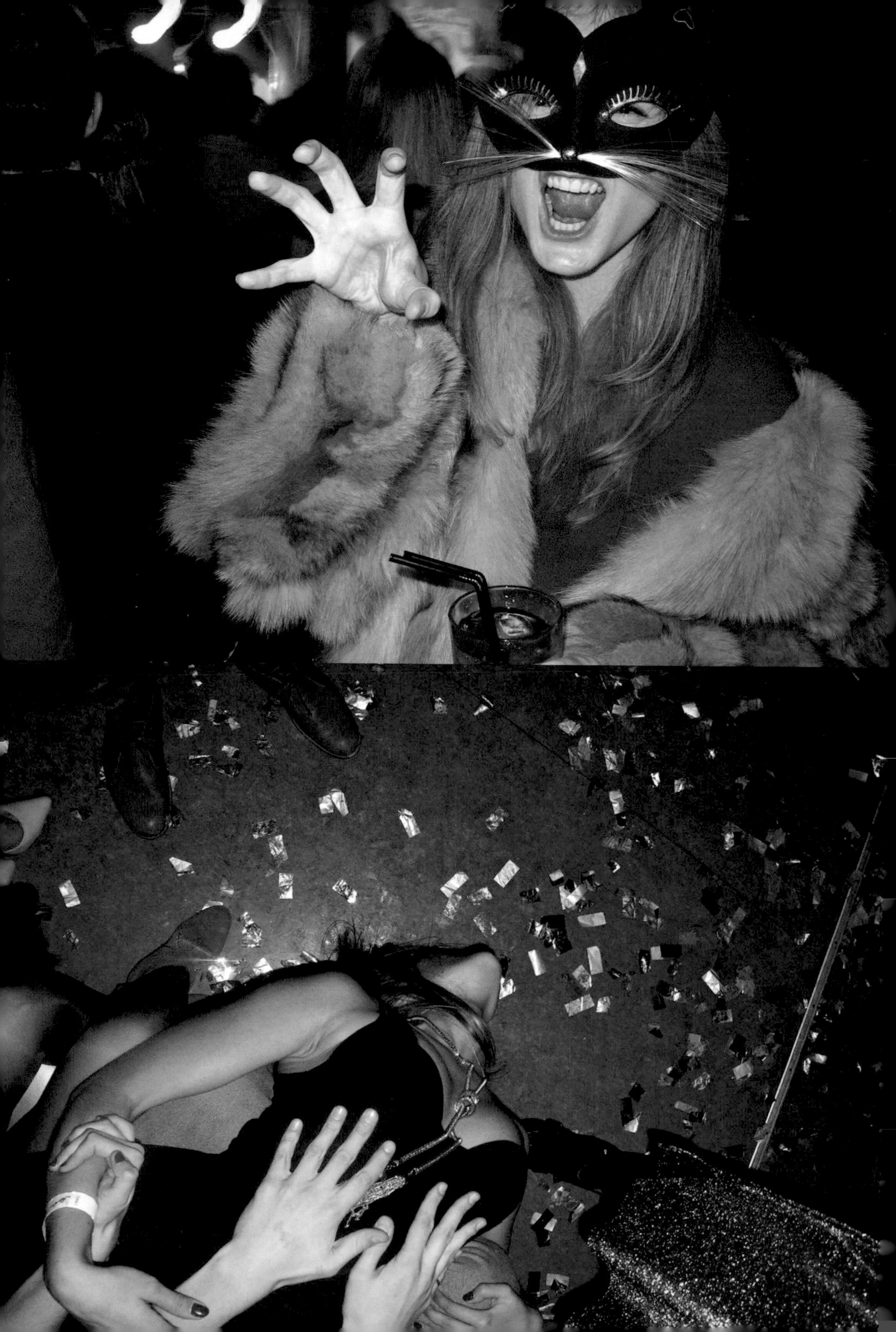

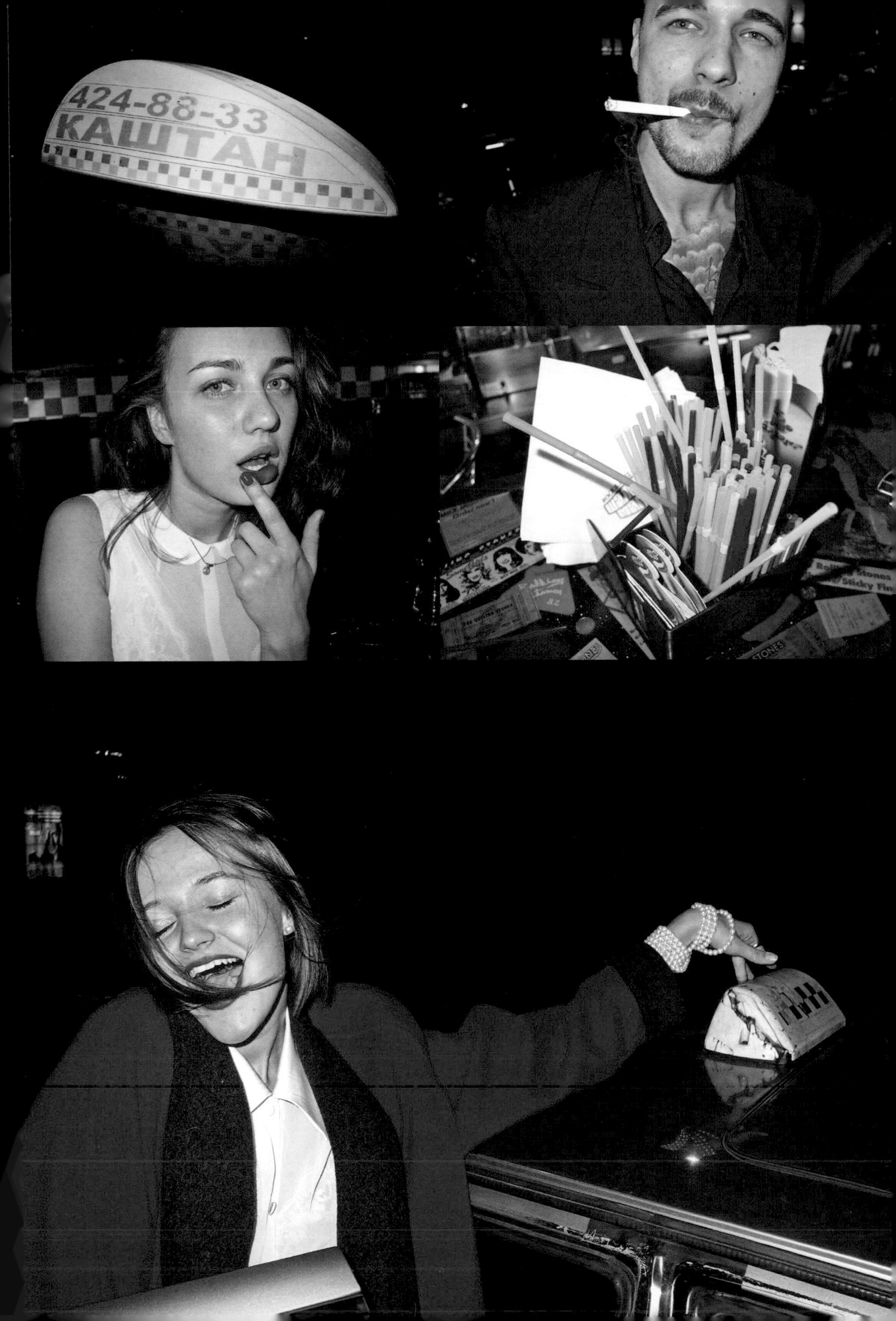
424-88-33
КАШТАН

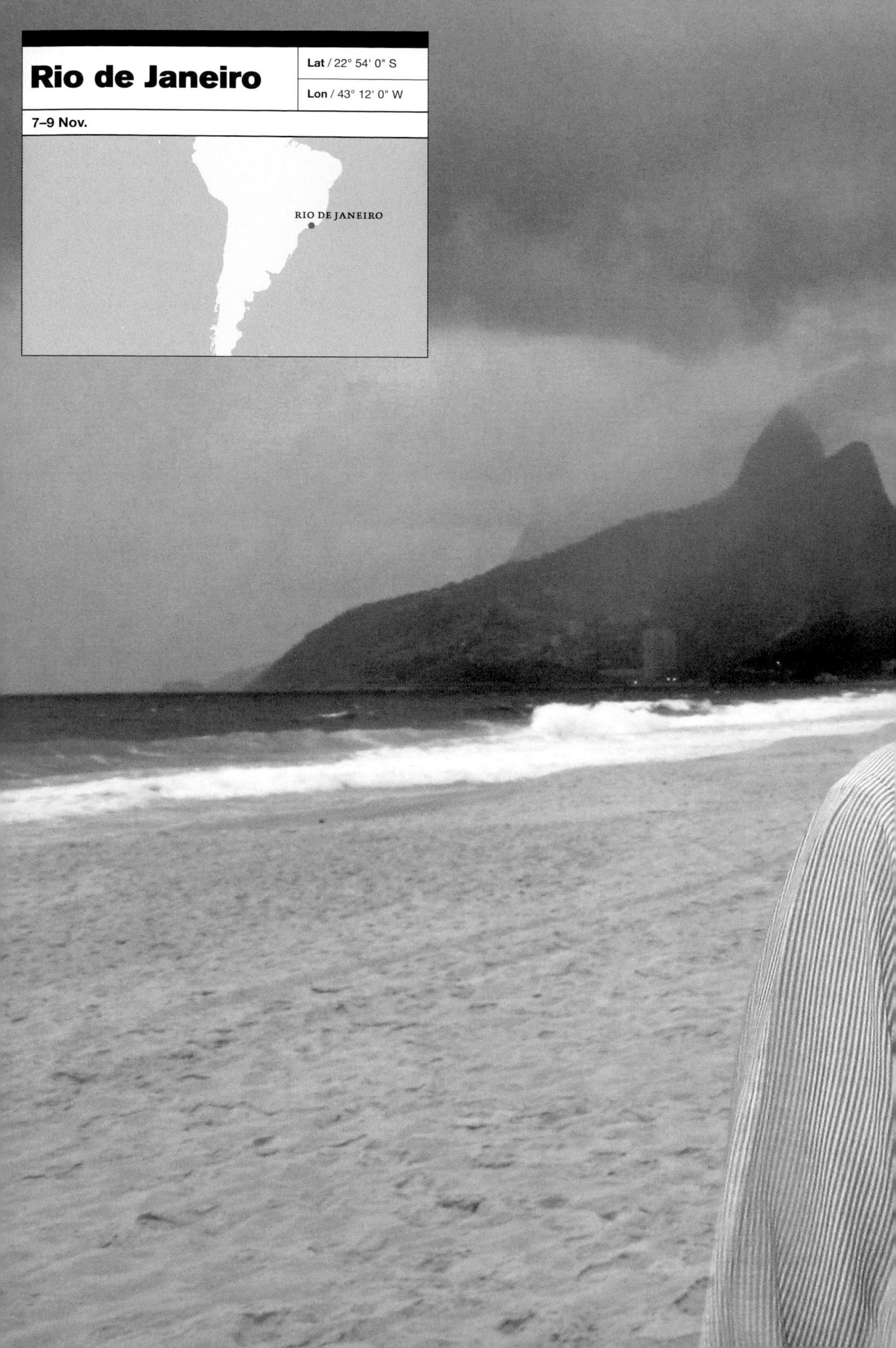
Rio de Janeiro
Lat / 22° 54' 0" S
Lon / 43° 12' 0" W
7–9 Nov.
RIO DE JANEIRO

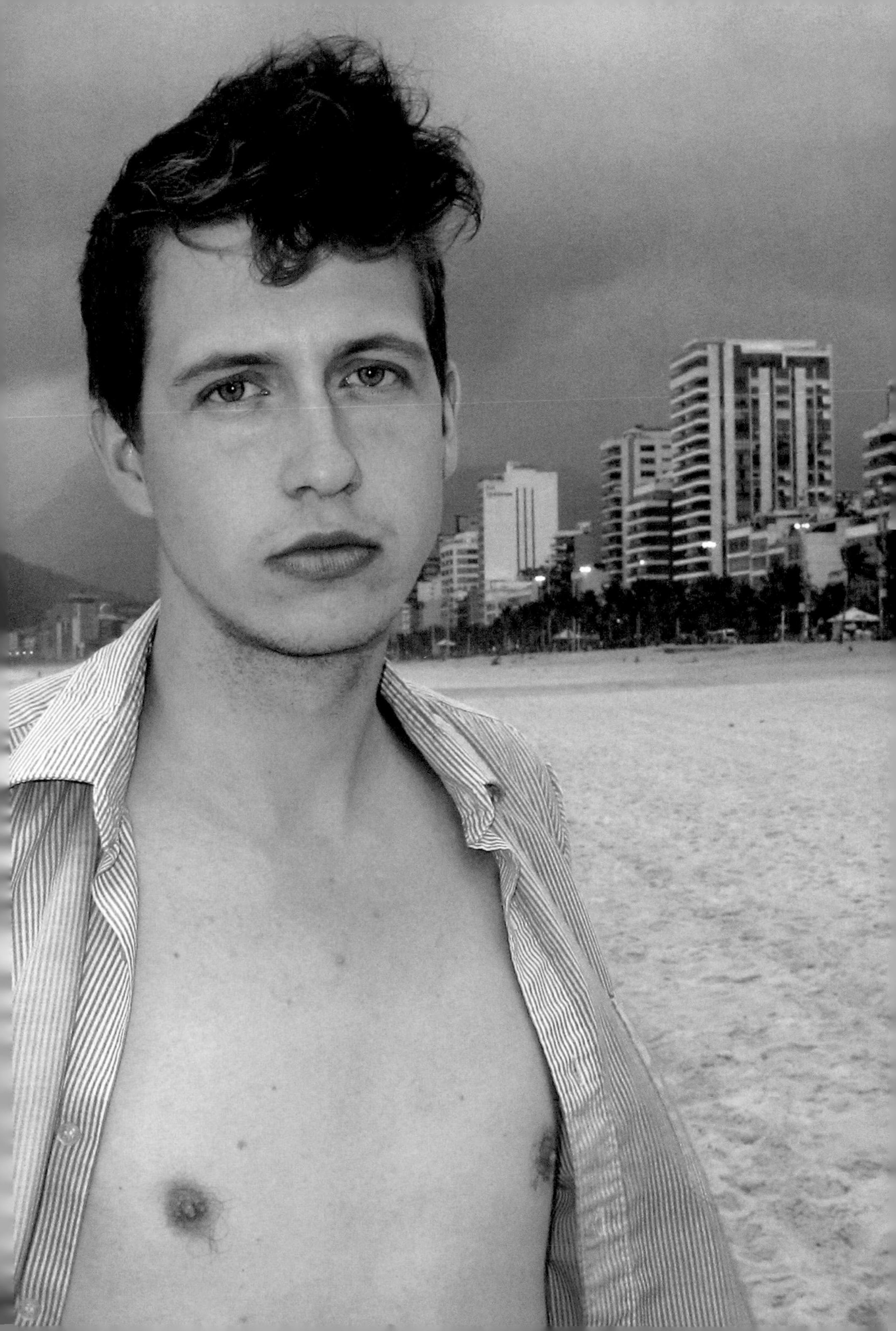

“Rio is one of the most sensual places I’ve been to. Even just looking at the people – the way that they move, how they show a lot of skin – you get the feeling that Brazilians have a very special relationship with the body, and with music and dance. Culturally it’s an interesting place because on one level it seems sexy and liberal but at the same time there’s a strong traditional Catholic conservatism, and this generates a strange tension in society. In Rio I had one of my most intense travel experiences – and one of the most intense experiences of my life. I had a friend who knew someone who was living in a *favela* (shanty town), which is how I ended up visiting Vidigal. It’s located right next to one of the wealthiest parts of Rio, LeBlon. You can’t really get there by car, and there’s only a single road that takes you in, so we ended up getting a ride on motorbikes (p. 245). I was given strict instructions by my friend not to take pictures of guns and to ask permission every time I wanted to take a photo of someone. My friend went on a bike with one guy; I was on a bike with another. The road we had to go up was very, very steep. Occasionally the guy driving my bike would put his hand across my camera to stop me shooting. And suddenly we were at the top of Vidigal, with the most incredible view across Rio. It gave me a bizarre feeling to realize that some of the poorest people in Rio live in this extraordinary place, right next to their super-rich neighbours, with the same stunning views. I was also surprised by how charming the *favela* was – even when people had no money they still found ways to make their homes visually distinctive. Vidigal was full of people trying to lead normal, pleasant lives despite gangs and desperate poverty. I got the sense that the feeling of community was so strong that the majority of people wouldn’t leave even if they could afford to do so.”

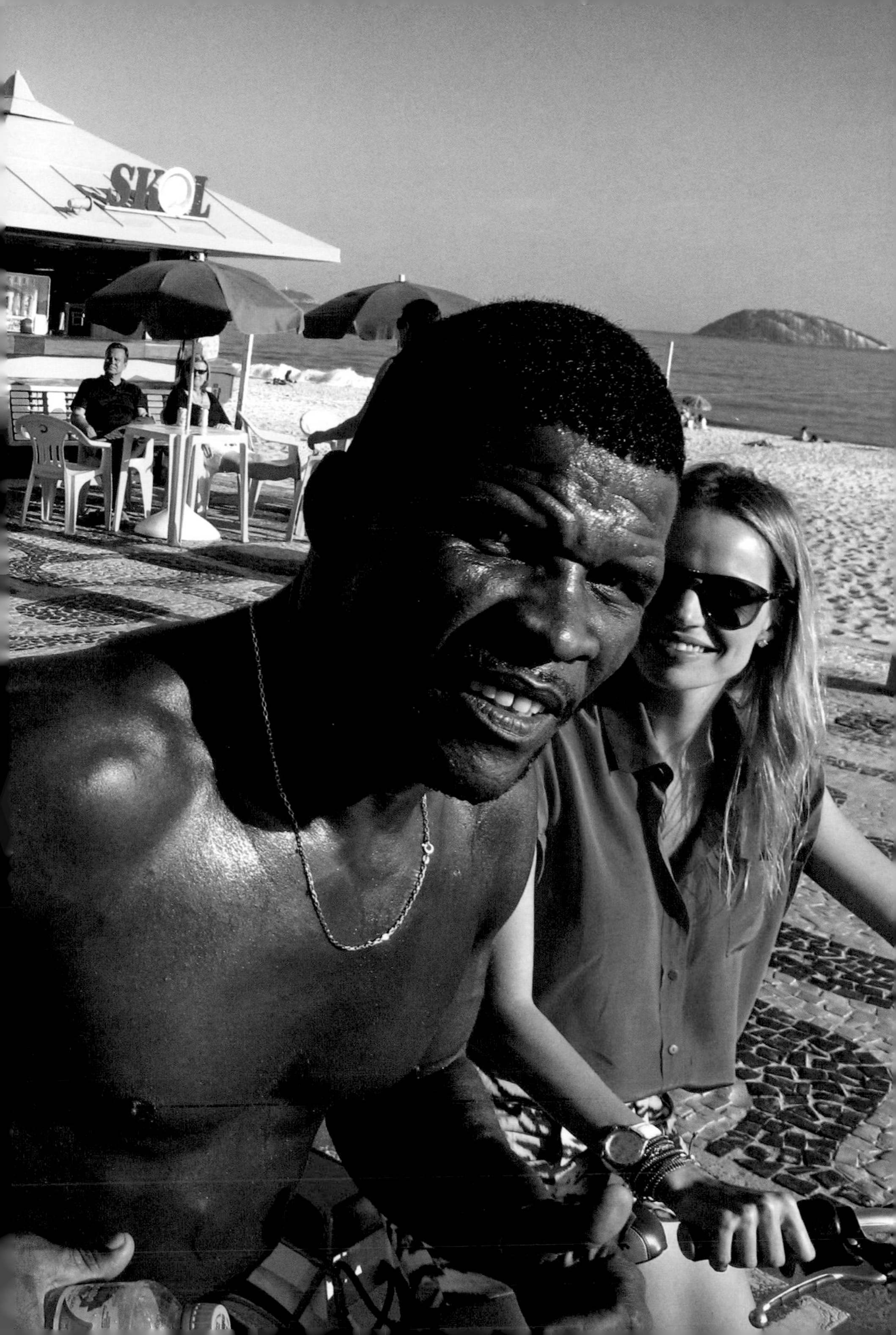
SKOL

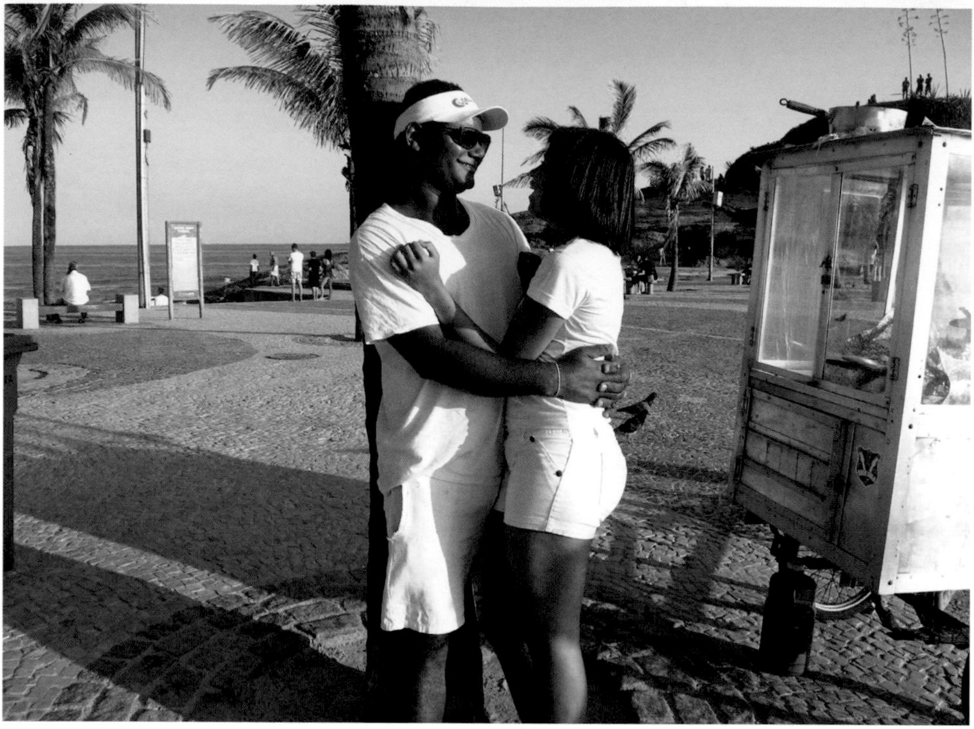

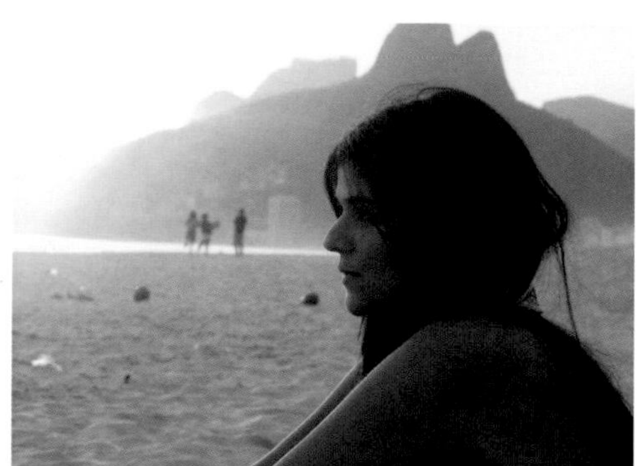

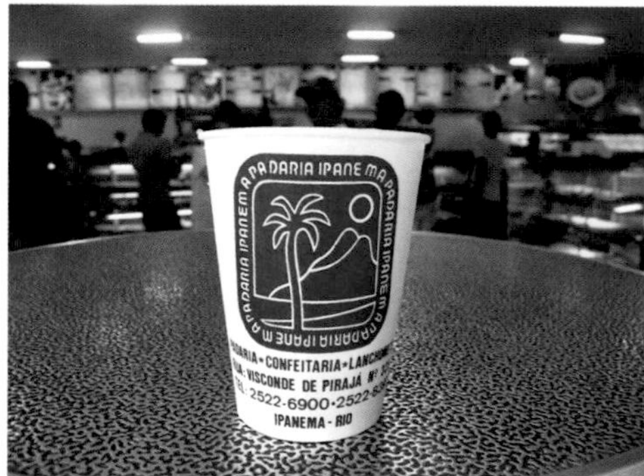
PADARIA IPANEMA
IPANEMA - RIO

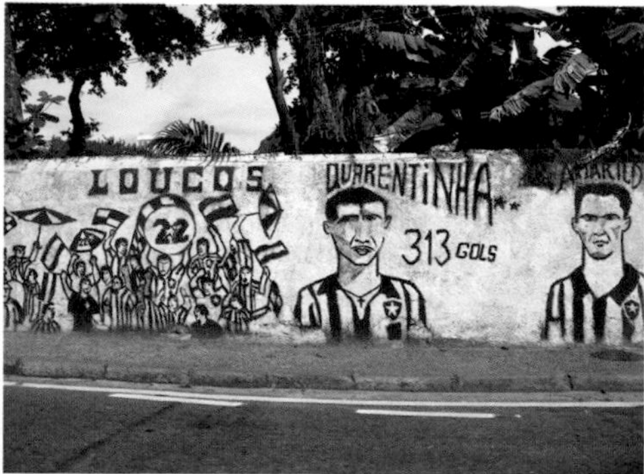
LOUCOS
22
QUARENTINHA
313 GOLS

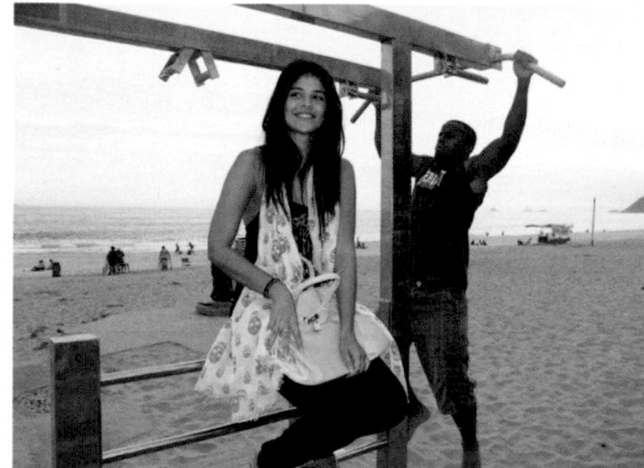

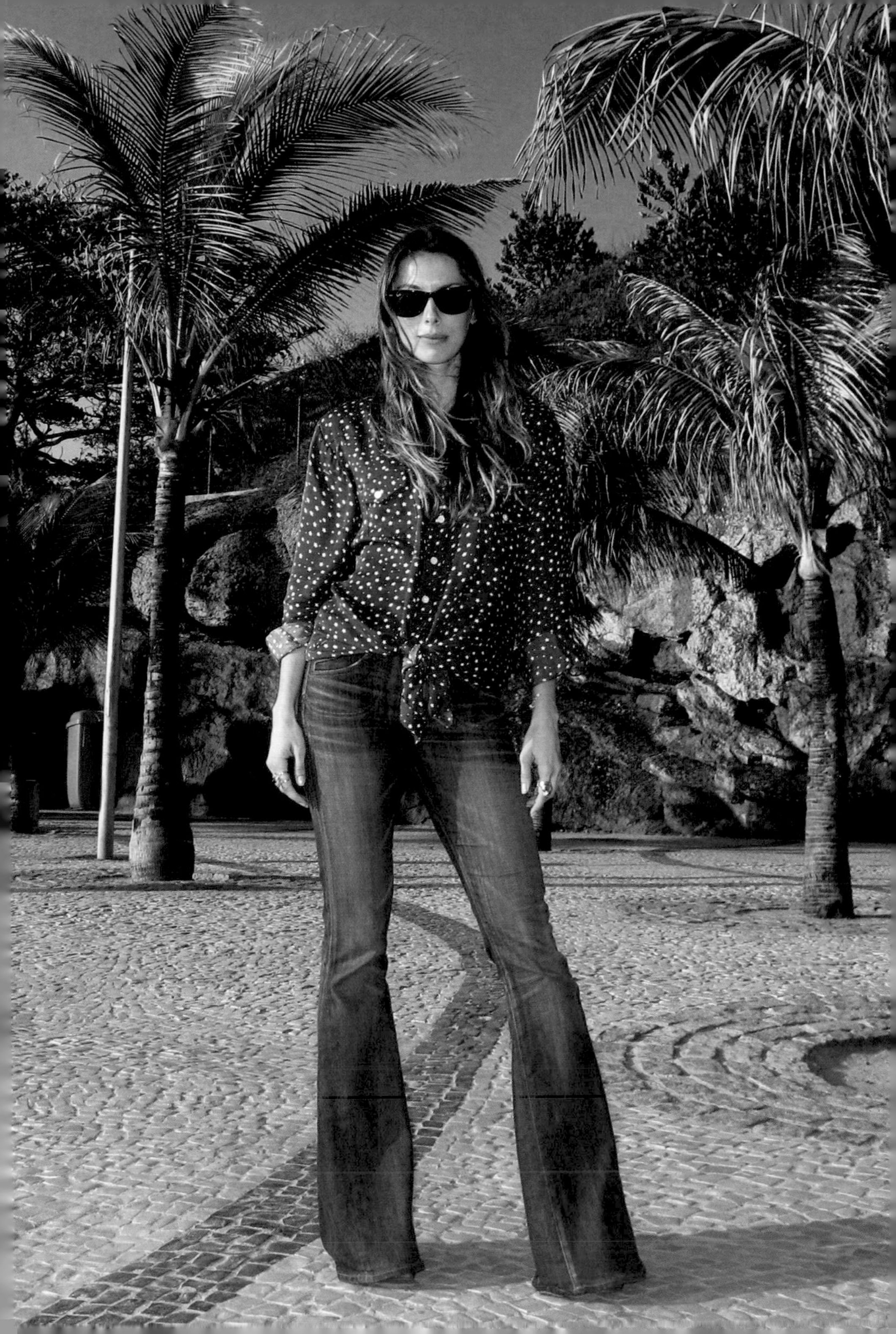

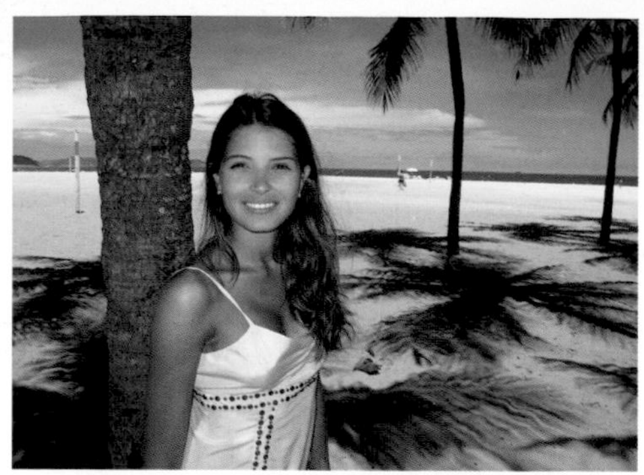

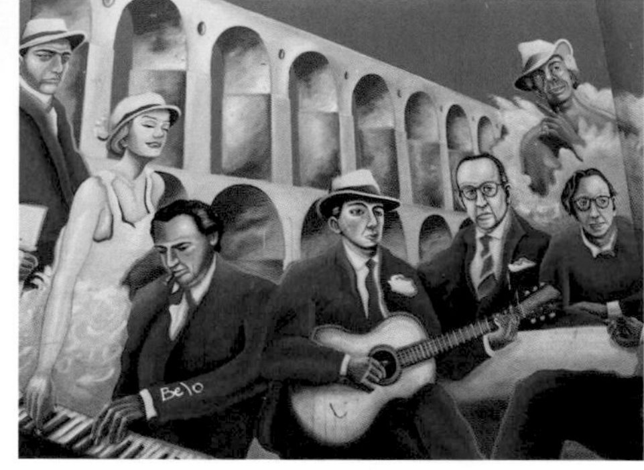
Belo

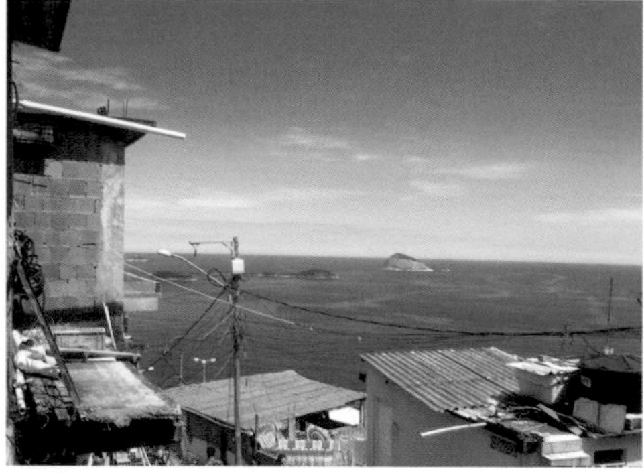

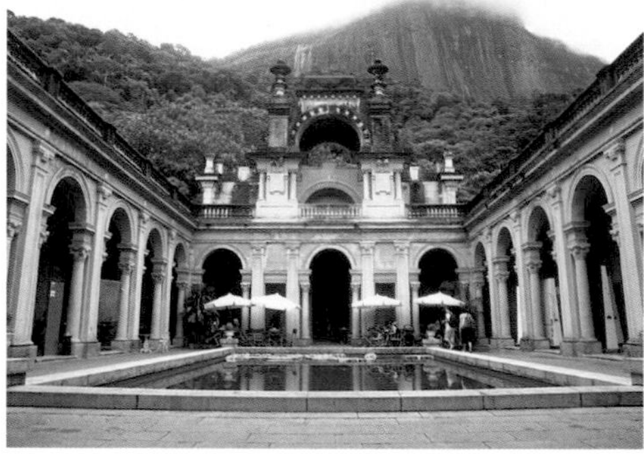

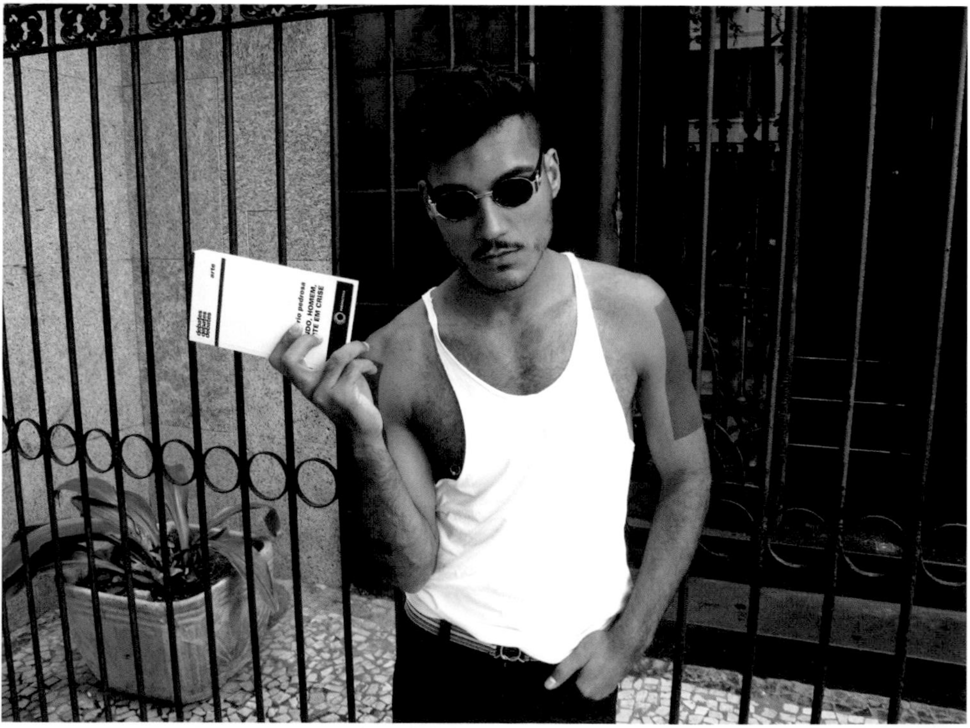

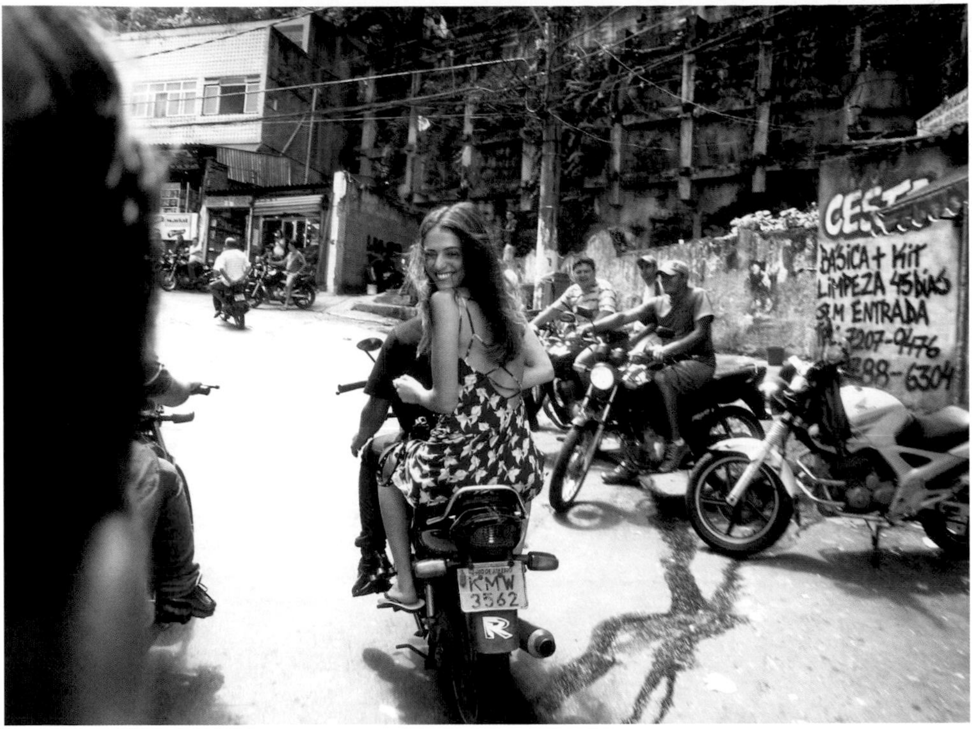

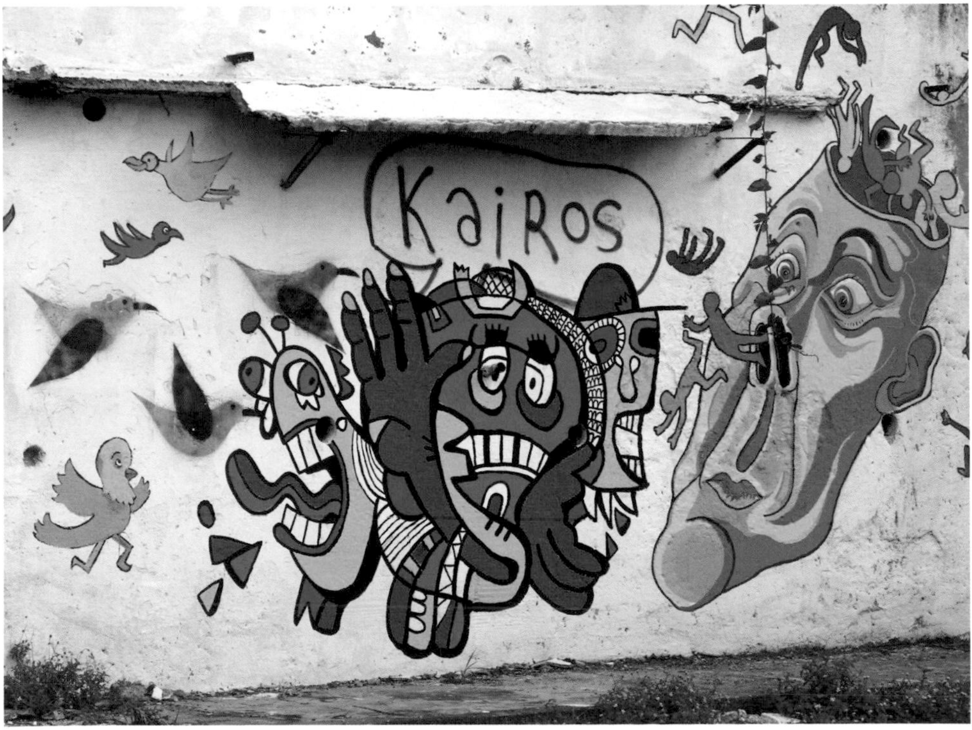

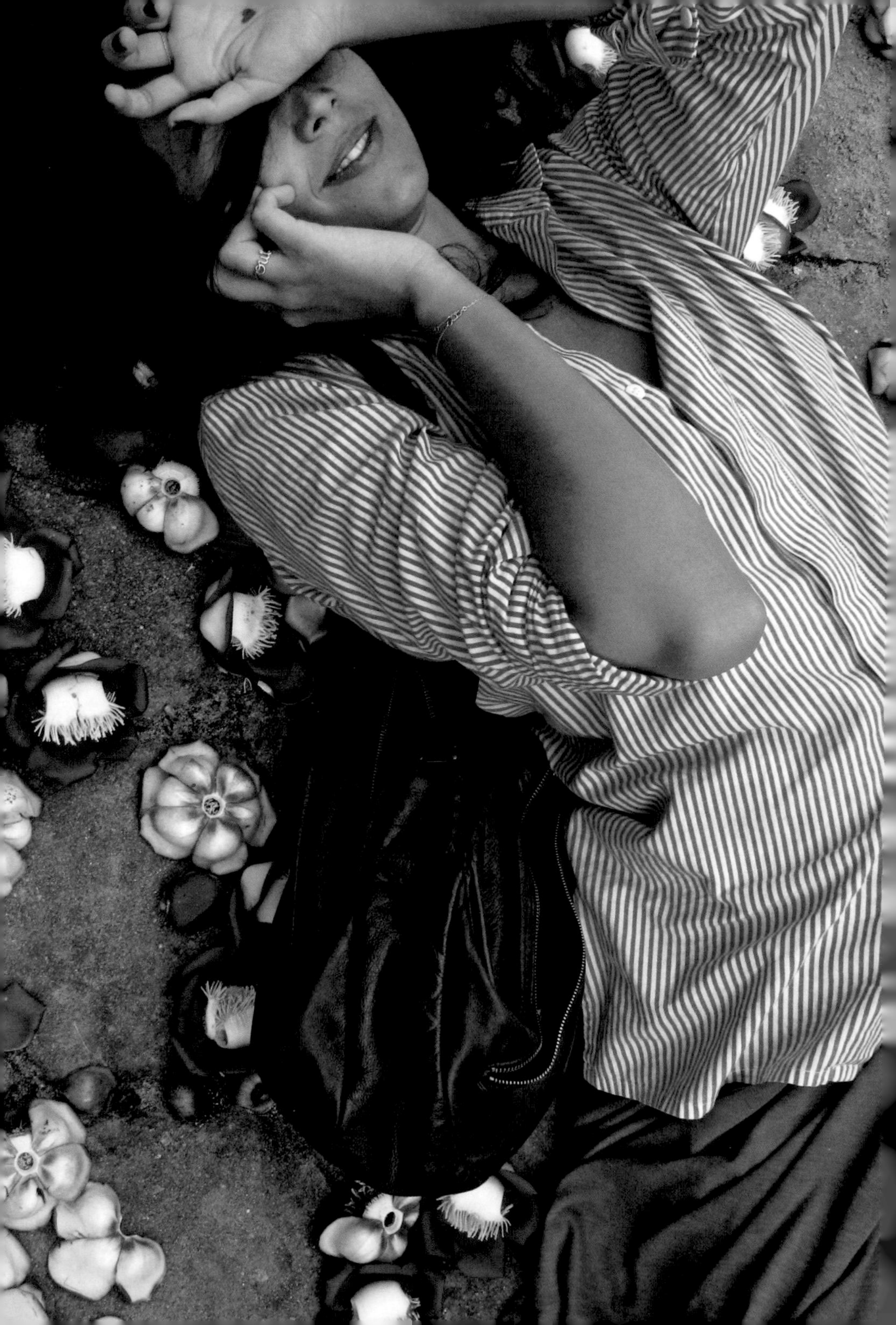

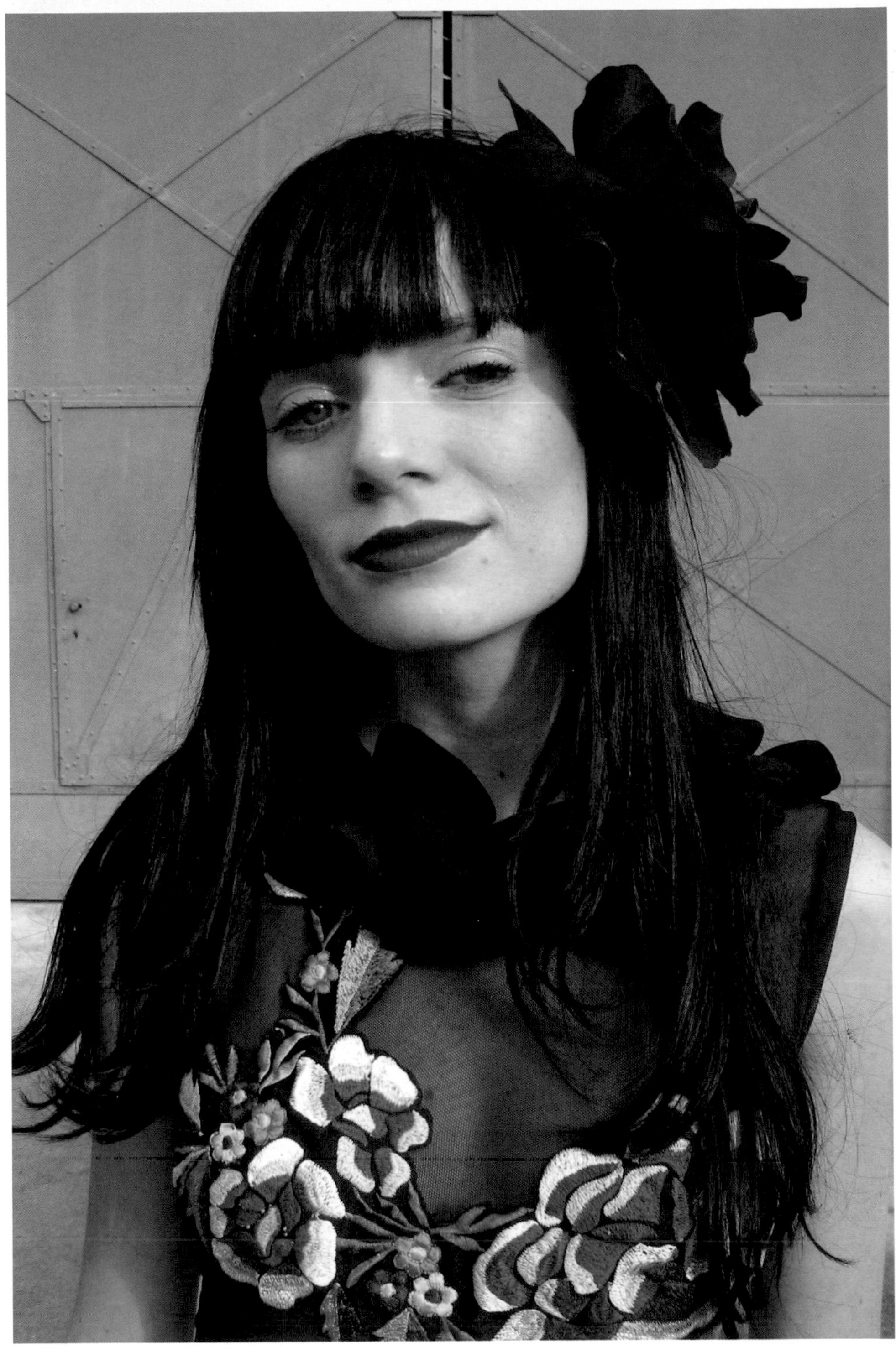

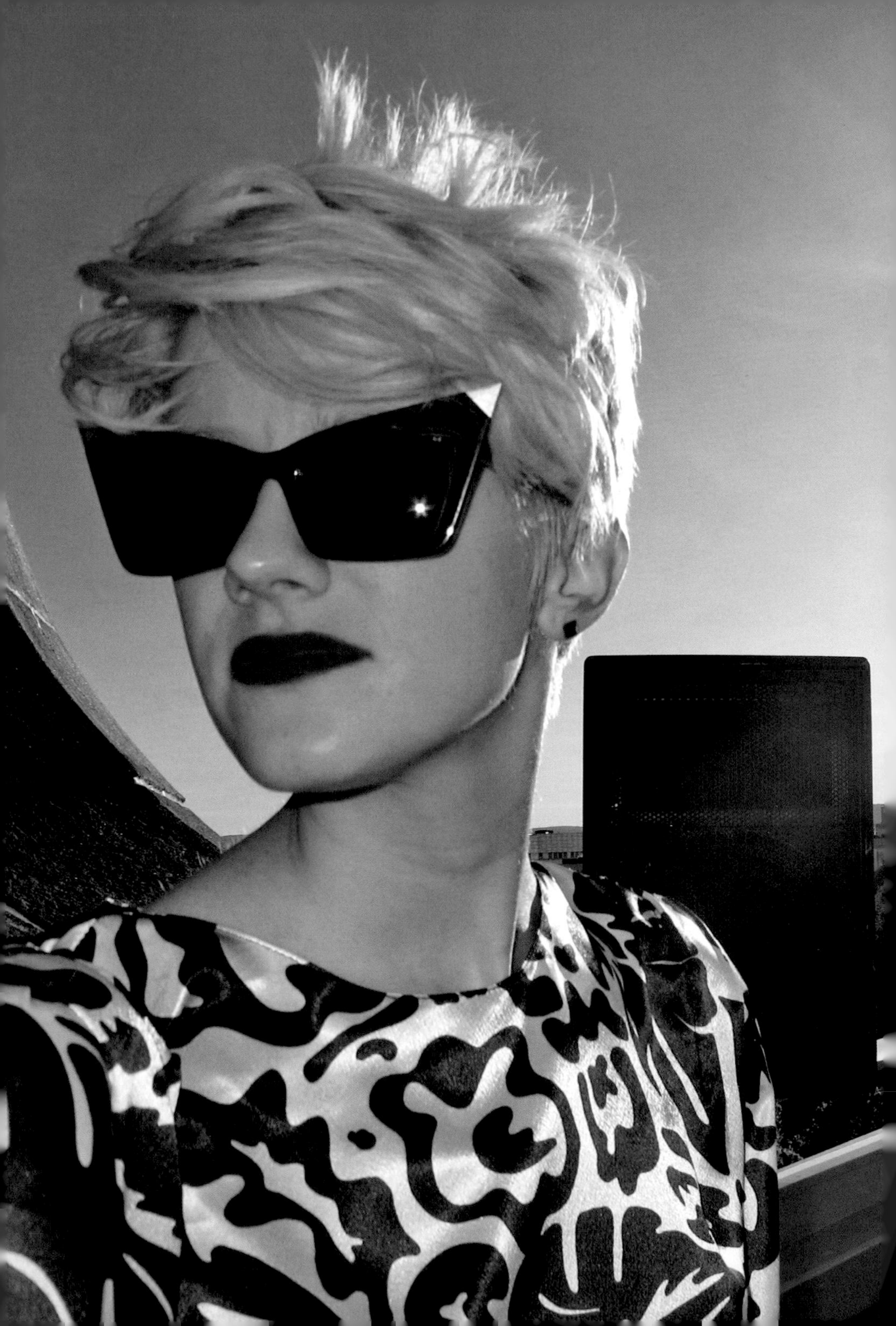

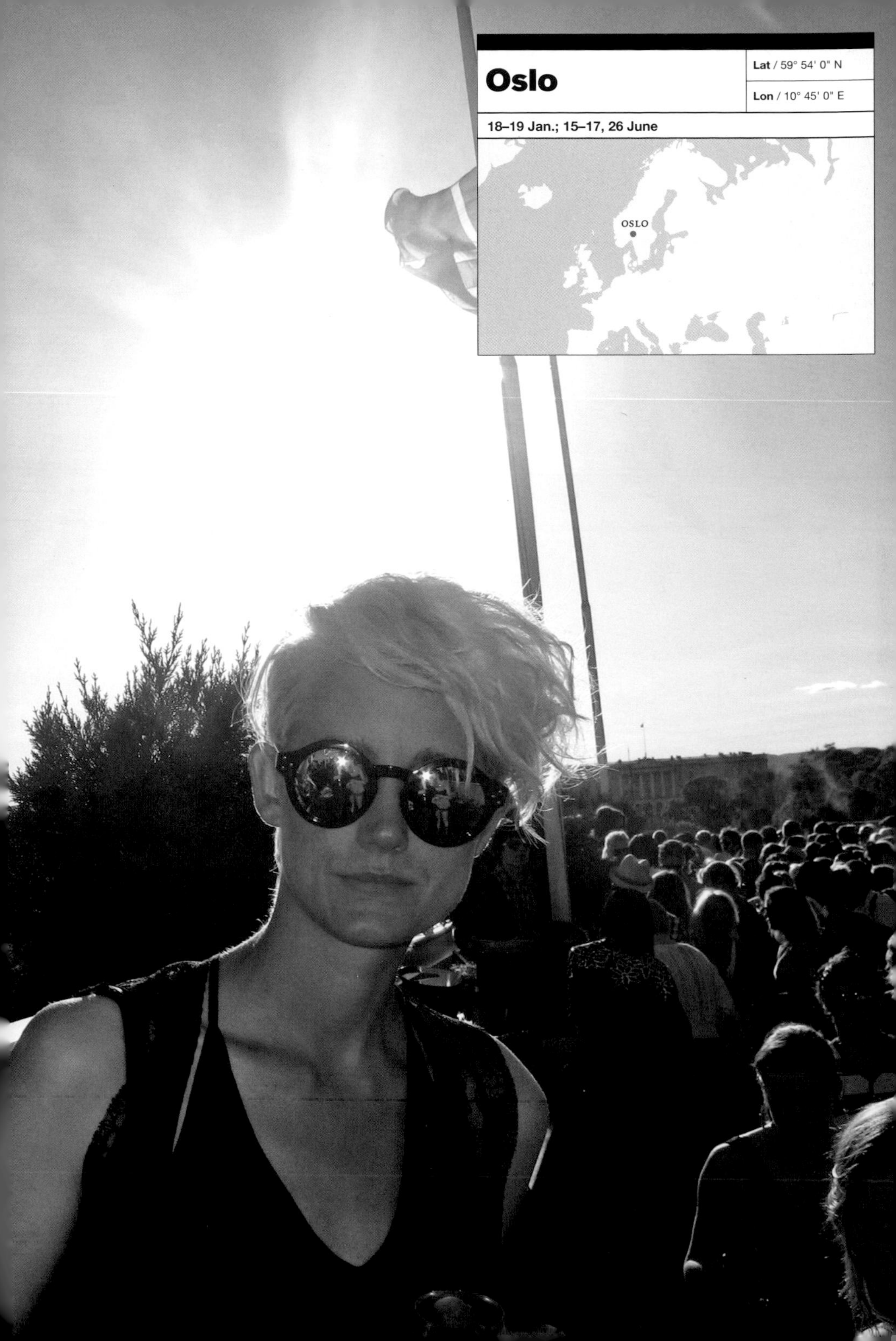
Oslo
Lat / 59° 54' 0" N
Lon / 10° 45' 0" E
18–19 Jan.; 15–17, 26 June
OSLO

“Oslo is like the little sister of Copenhagen. It's the smallest, quietest and least well-known of the Scandinavian capitals. It's like a village: it's very small and wherever you live you are close to the mountains and fjords that surround the city. Everyone seems to have a strong connection with nature because of this. In Oslo people seem very down-to-earth and dress in a simple way. It feels a bit less sophisticated than other big cities in Scandinavia, but it still has a lot of charm. One of my favourite places in Oslo is the opera house. The pavement outside it is white, and it feels like you're lying down in the snow when you get down to take a picture. In winter you can take a 10-minute bus ride from the city centre to one of the suburbs and when you open the door of the bus you find yourself at the beginning of a sledging slope. You can just jump on your sledge and slide away; no entrance fee, no long journey. On a sunny day, with all the kids running and playing in the snow without any sense of stress or fear, it feels completely idyllic.”

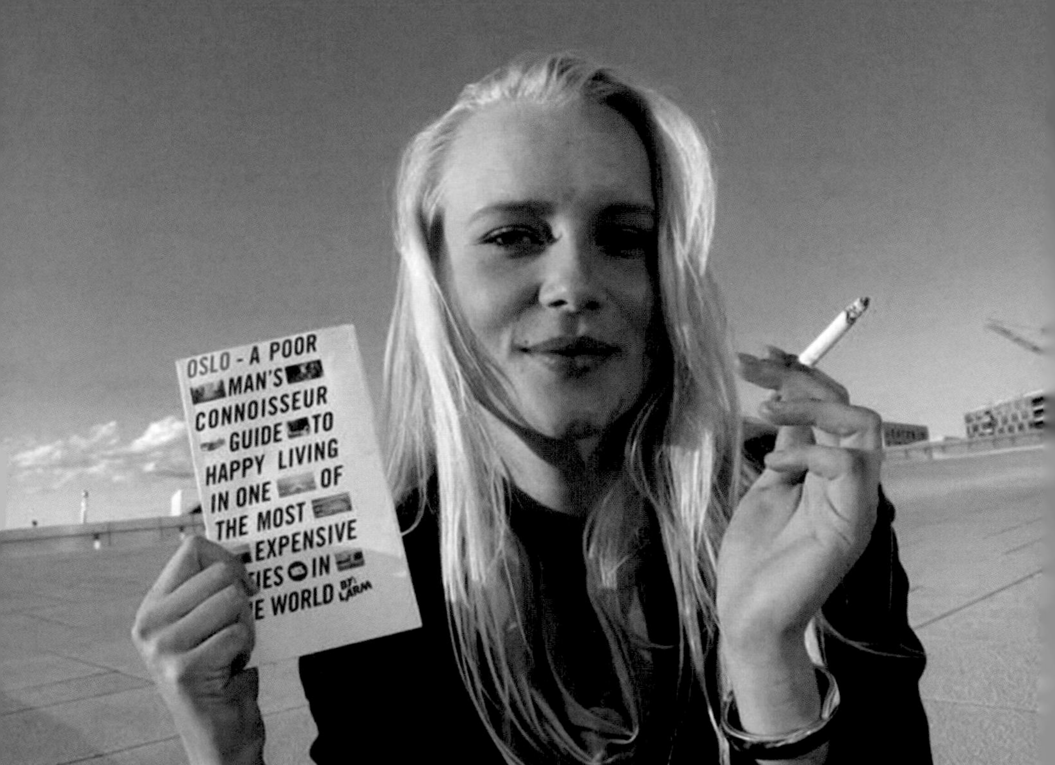

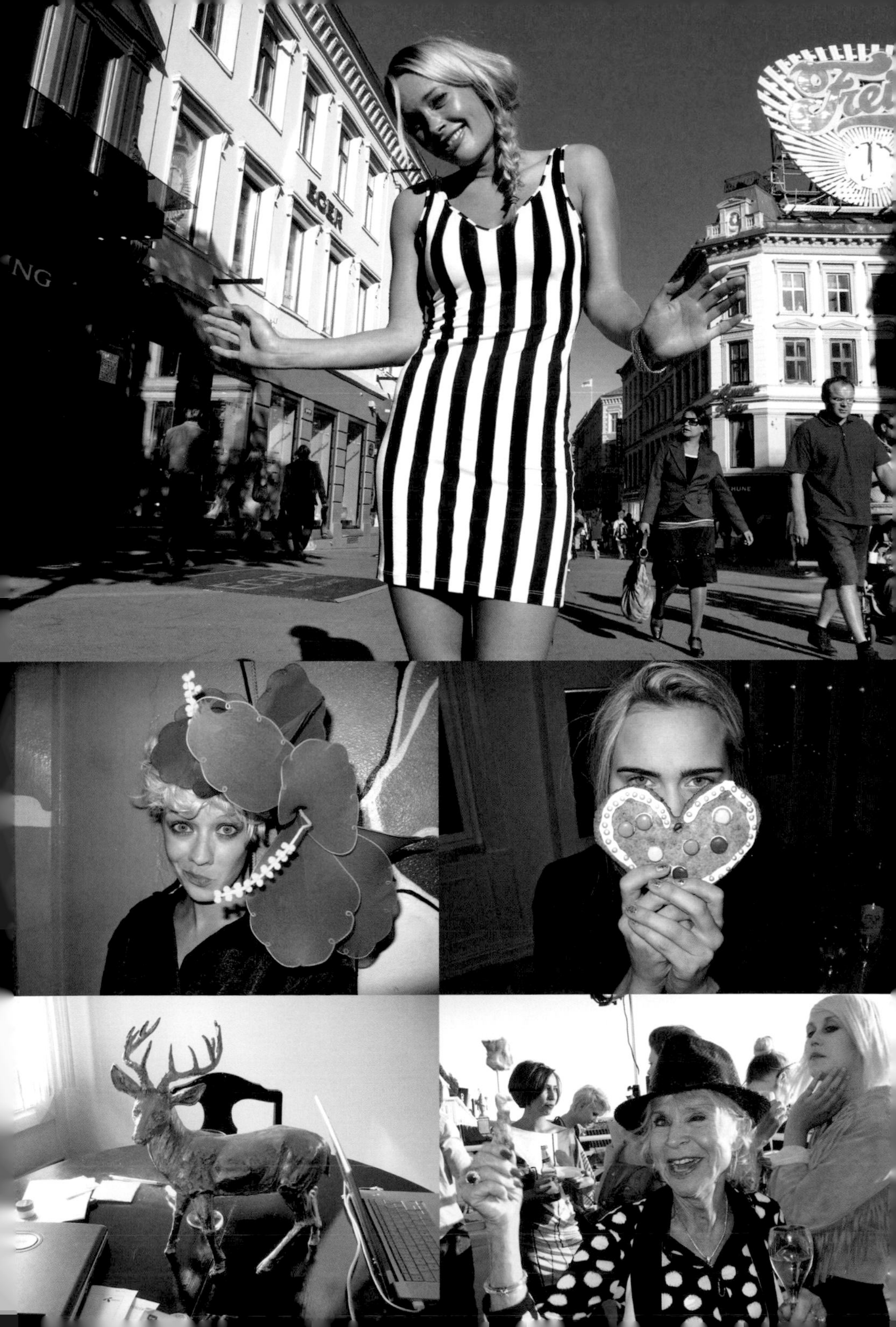
EGER

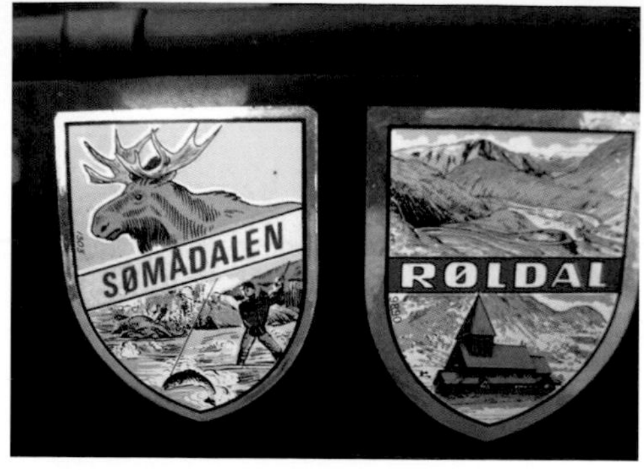
SØMADALEN
RØLDAL

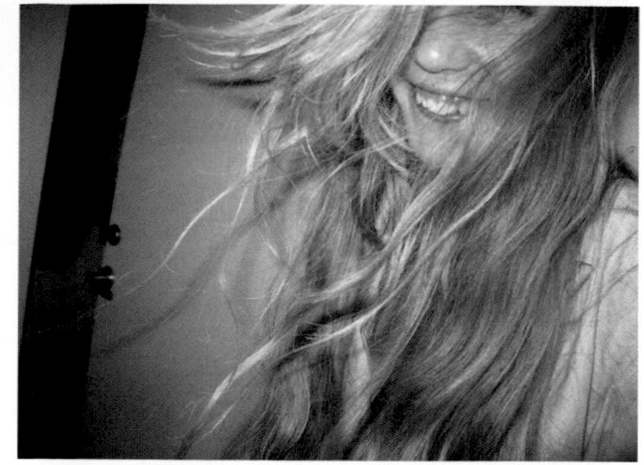

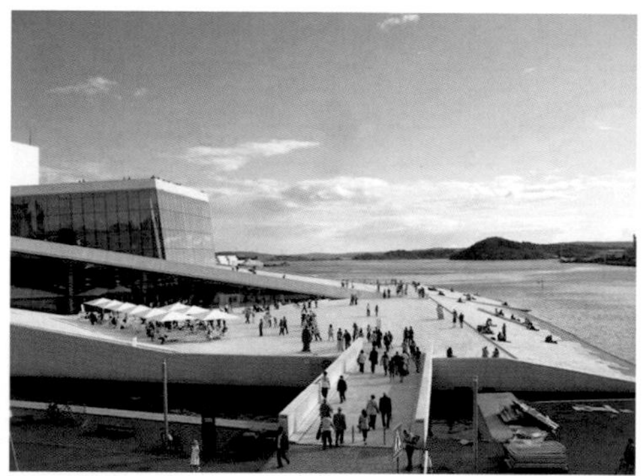

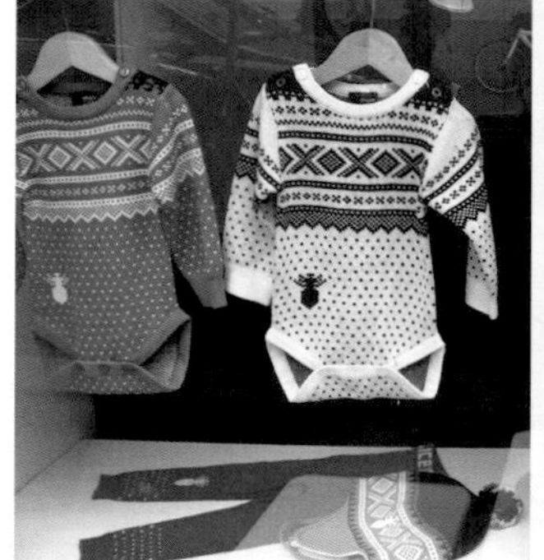

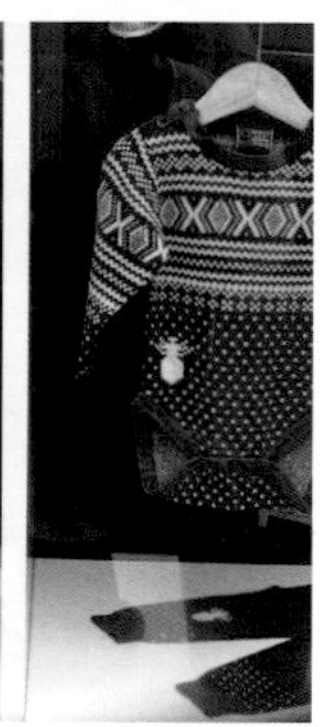

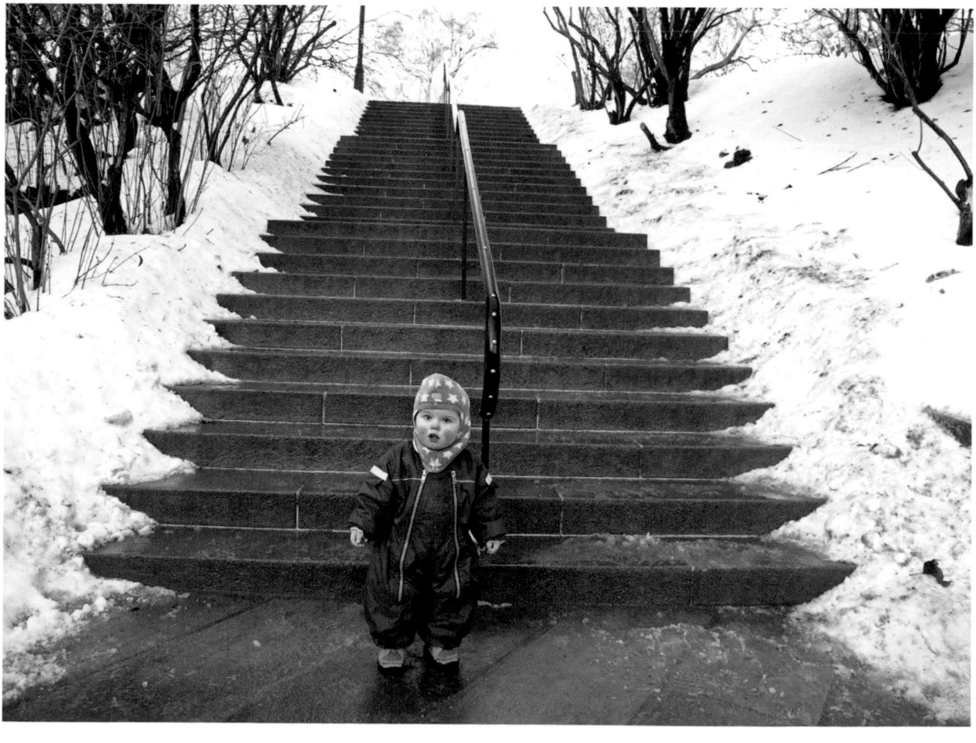

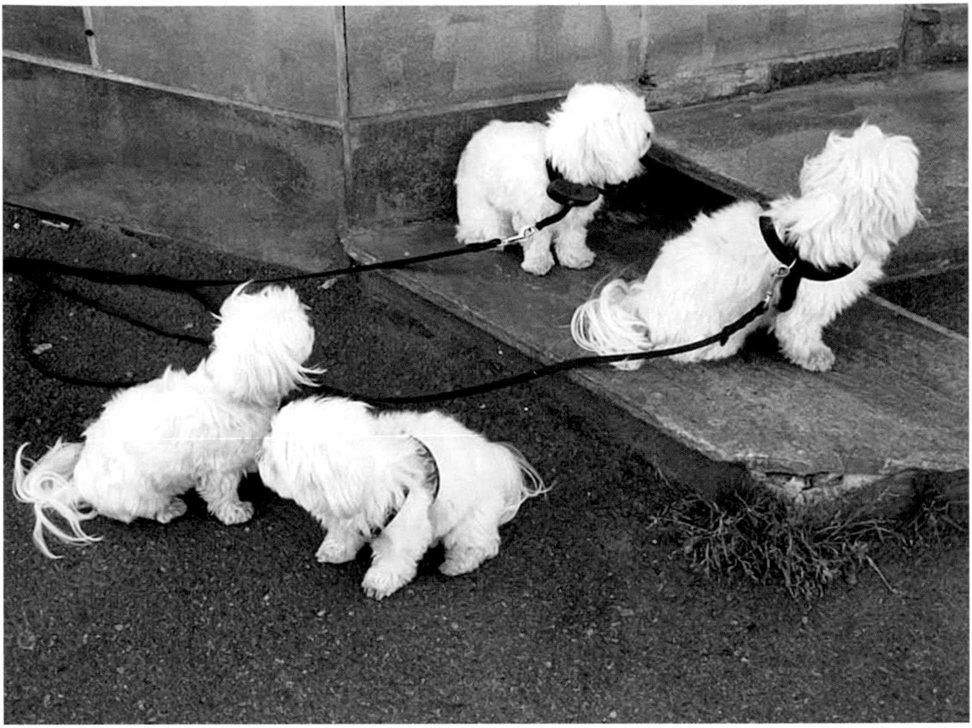

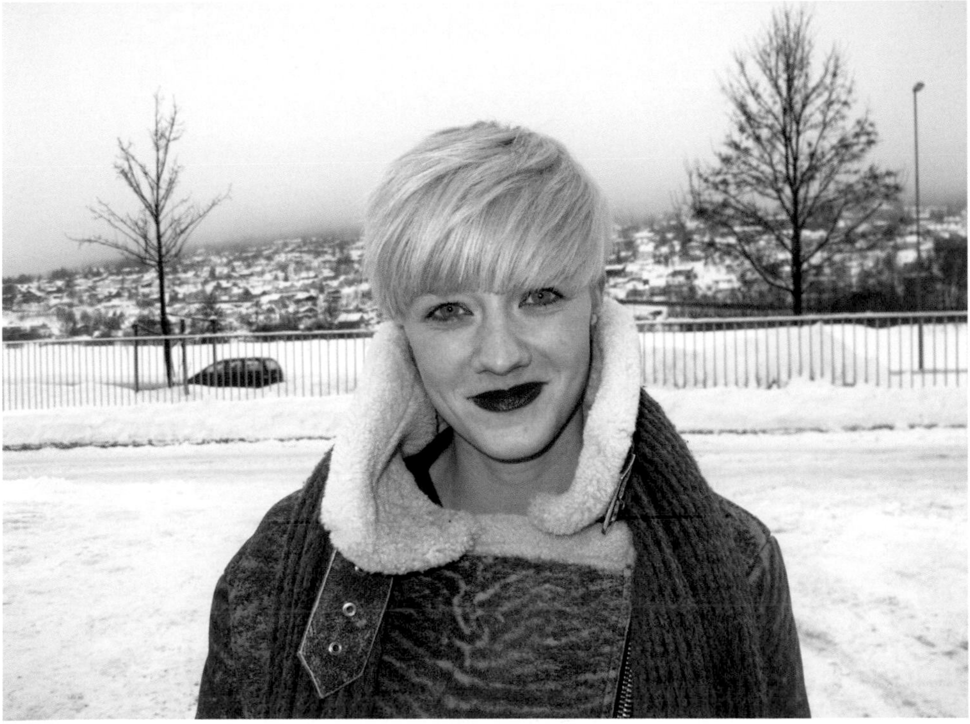

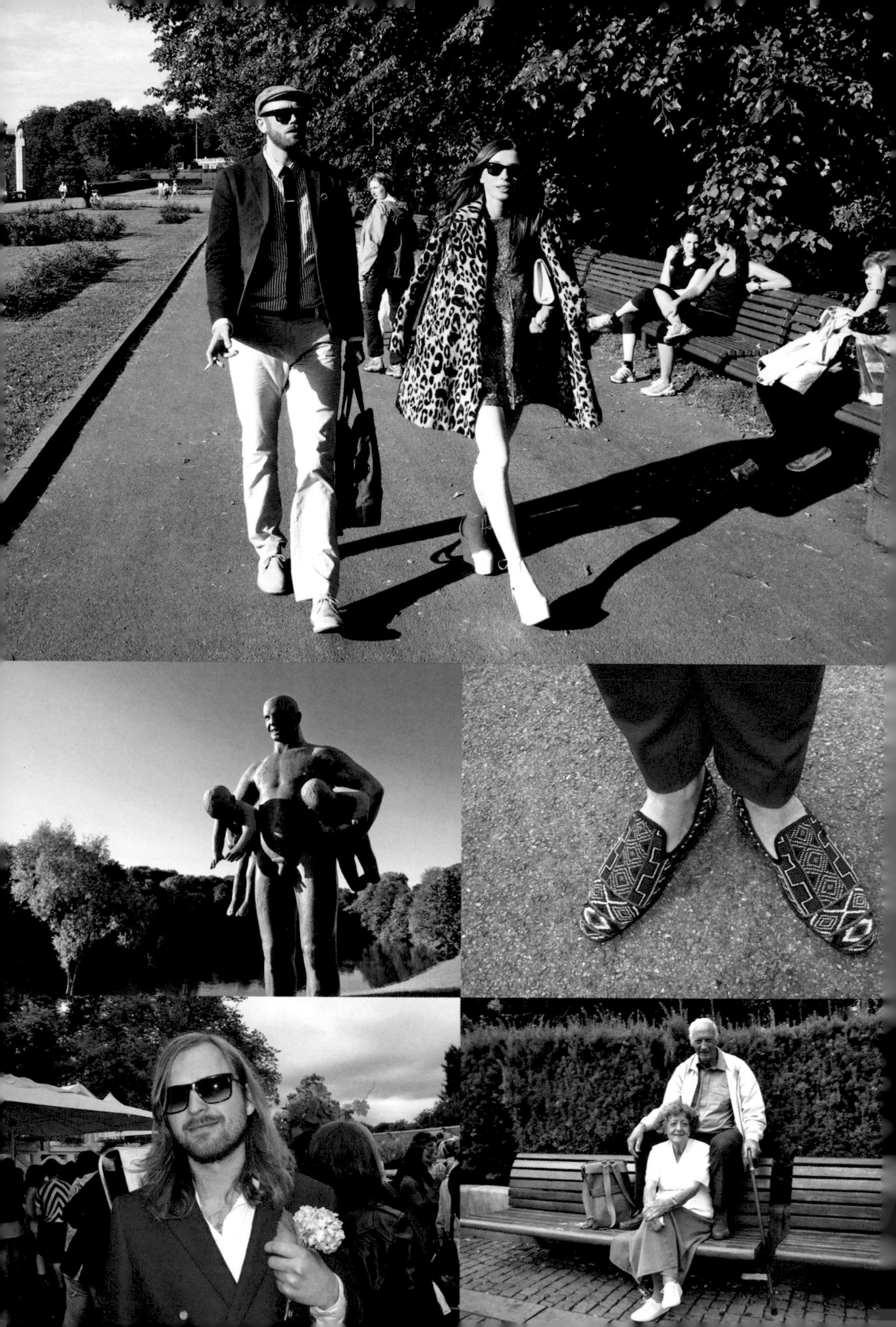

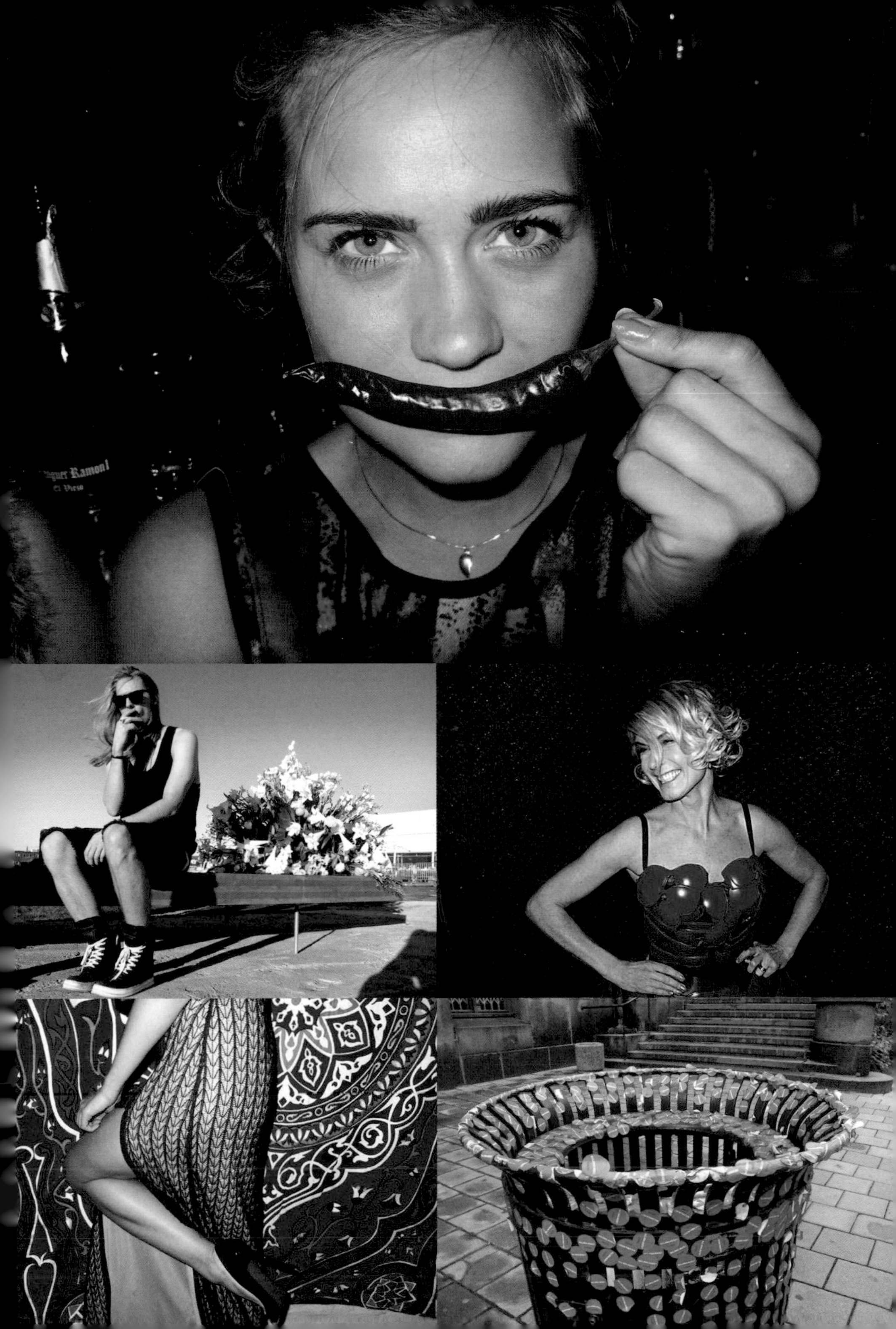

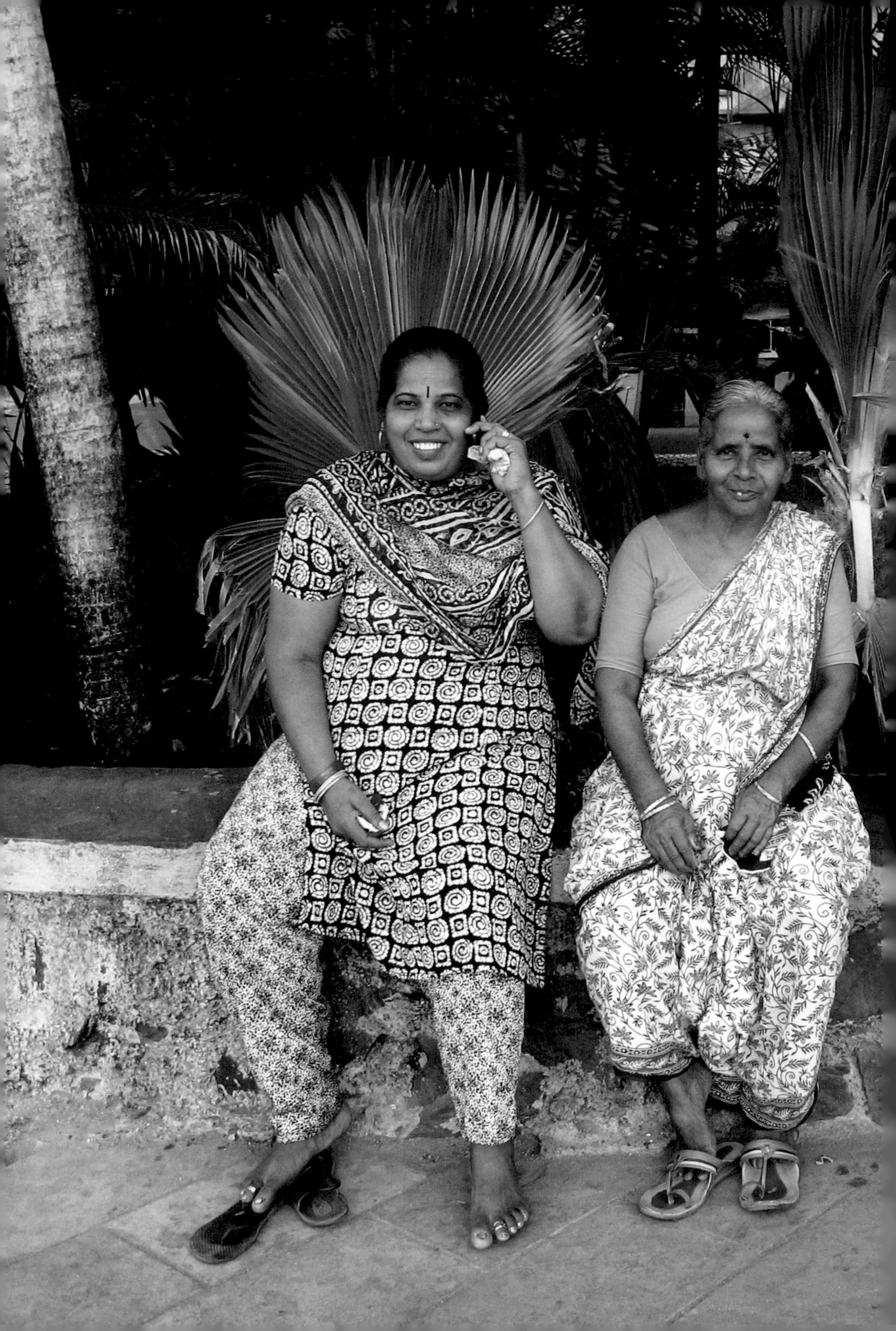

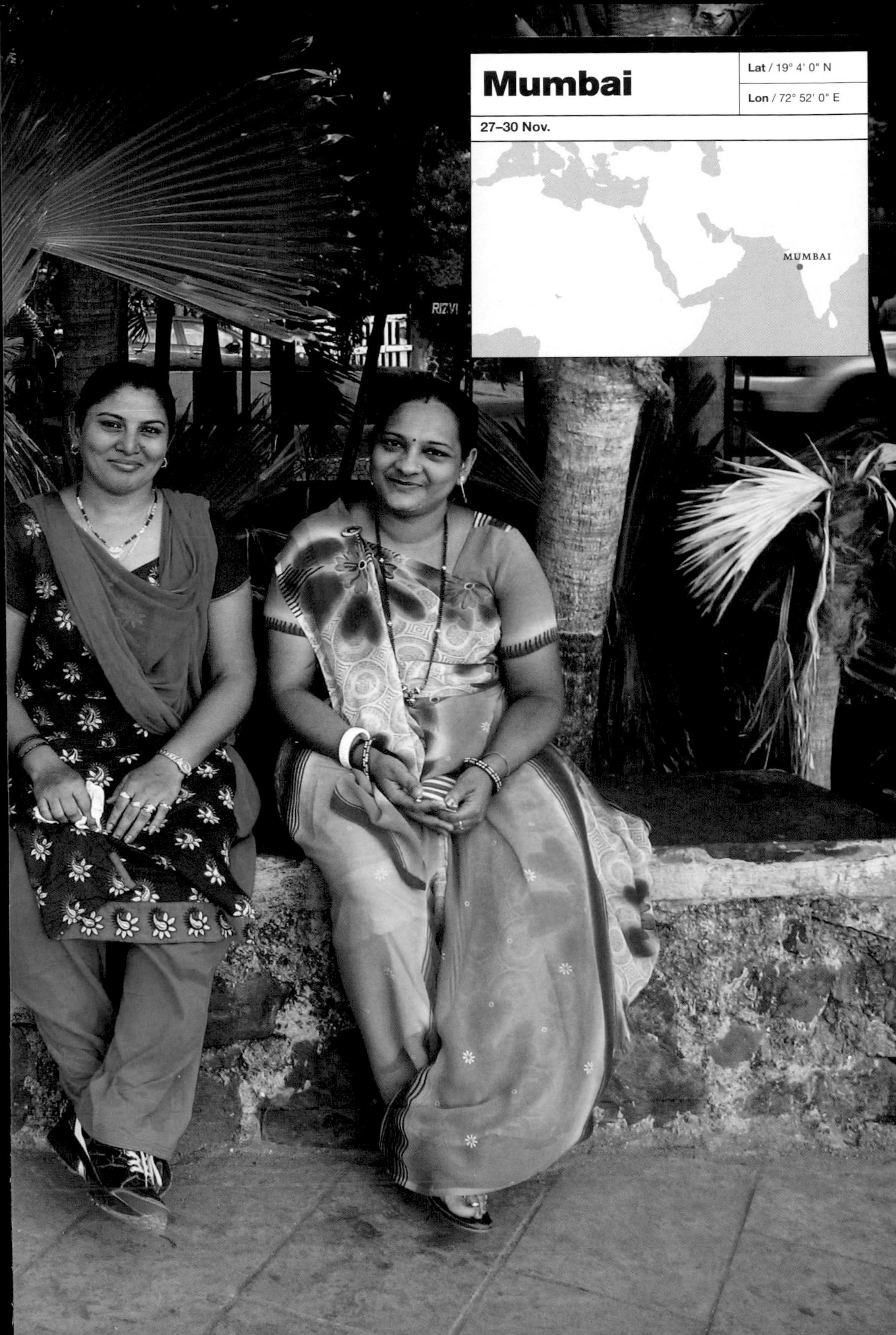
Mumbai
Lat / 19° 4' 0" N
Lon / 72° 52' 0" E
27–30 Nov.
MUMBAI

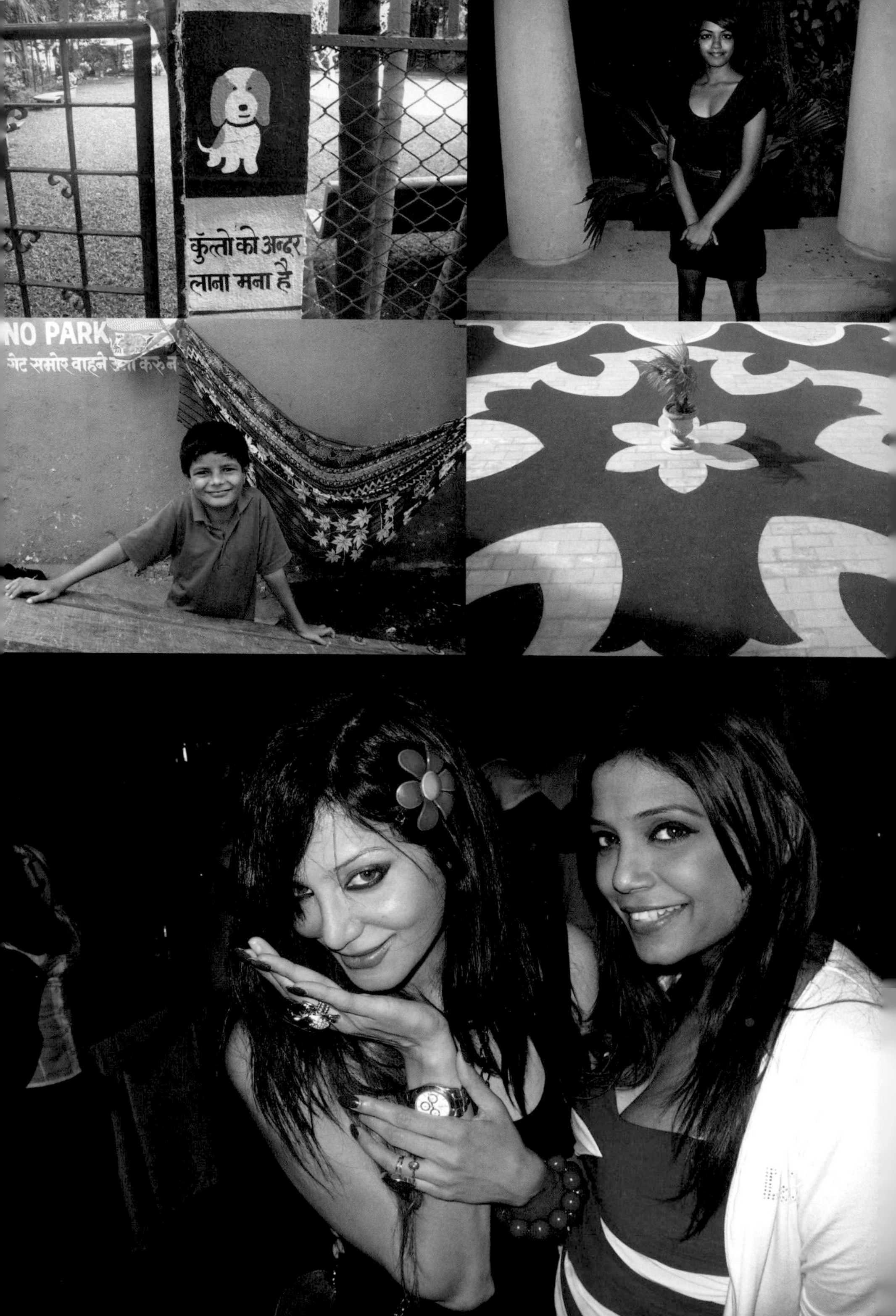
कुत्तो को अन्दर
लाना मना है
NO PARK

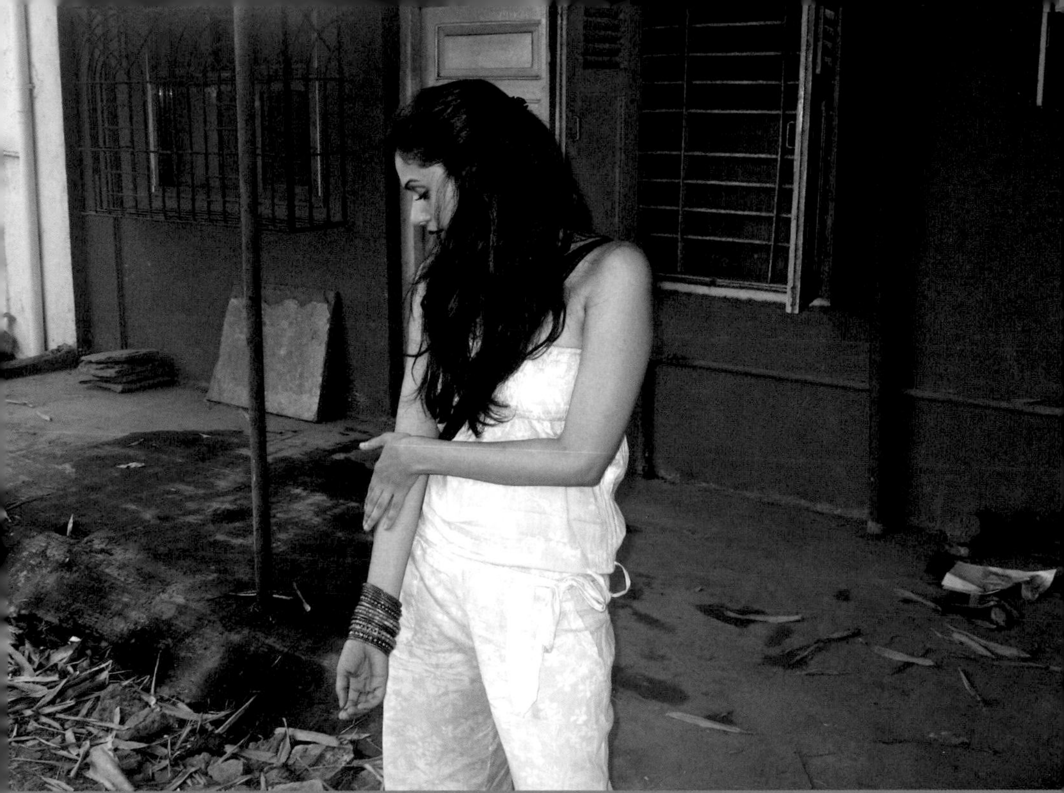

“Surprisingly, I found Mumbai one of the most challenging places to photograph. In Europe we grow up with exhibitions and books filled with amazing images of India – images so familiar that they're actually very difficult to transcend. It's hard to take a picture in Mumbai without it being a visual cliché. I got the chance to attend my first Indian wedding celebration – in India they celebrate for the entire week of the wedding, and one of my friends brought me along for part of it. It was a magical experience. I was impressed by the sheer size of the party – thousands of people, many of them dressed in fantastic traditional costumes. It was an incredible spectacle. There was also a stage where any member of the family could sing or dance for the bride and groom. I liked that everyone could be involved in the celebration, but it was surreal for me to be there, thrown into a completely different world.”

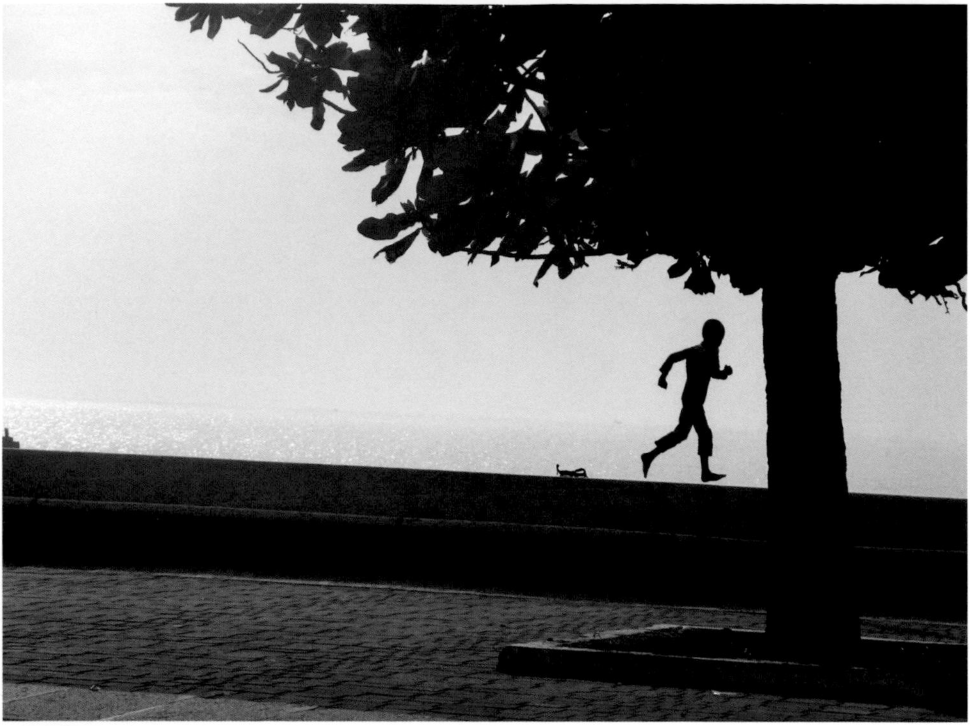

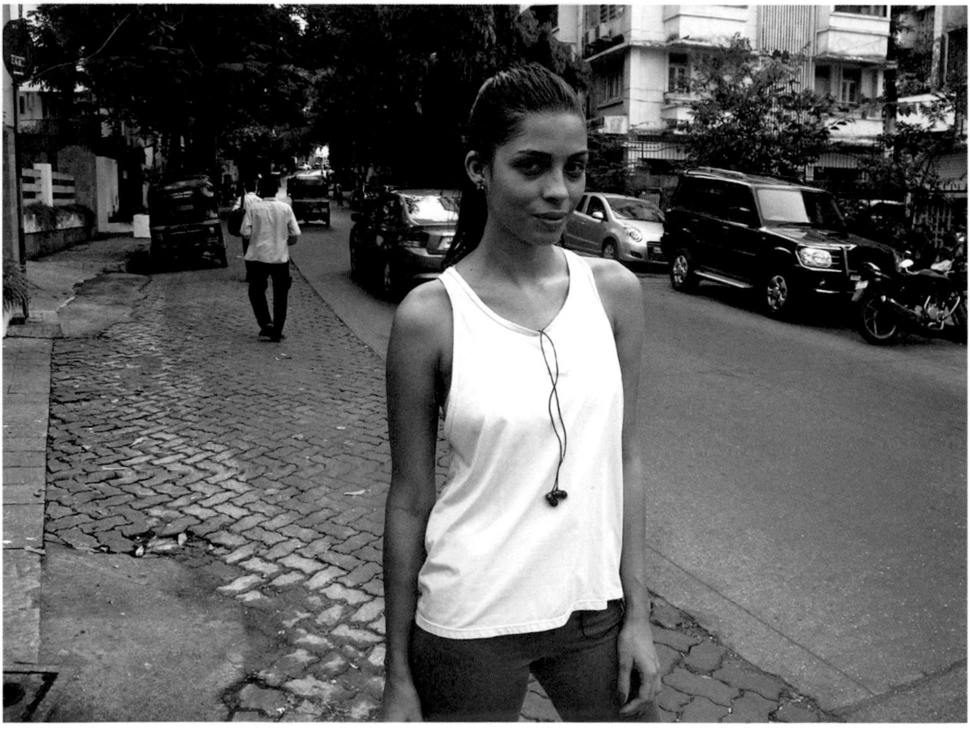

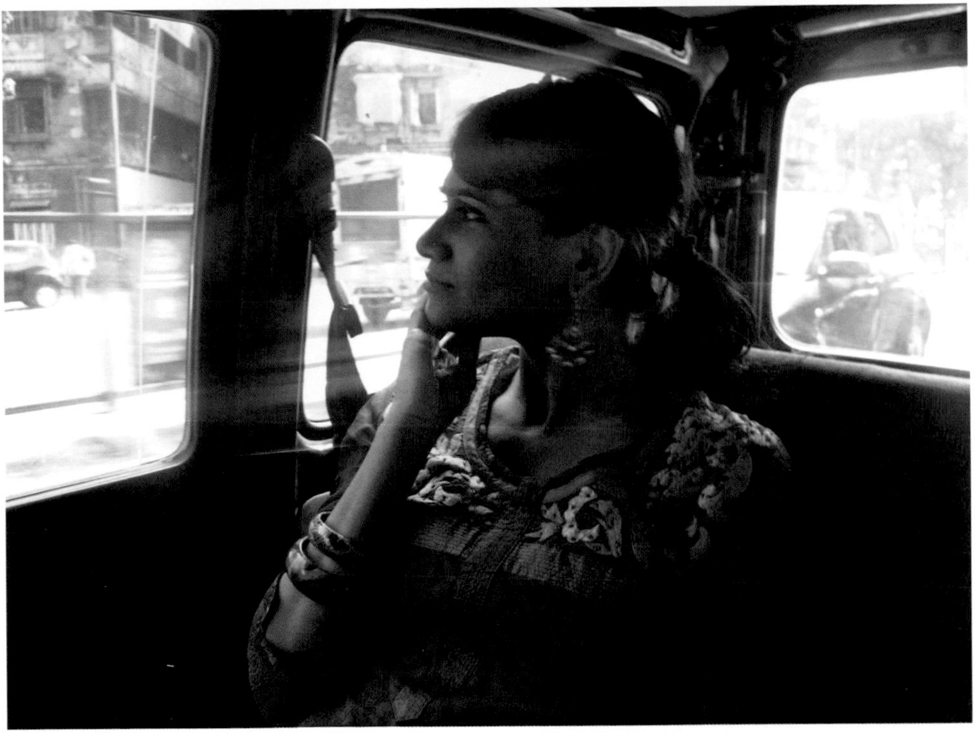

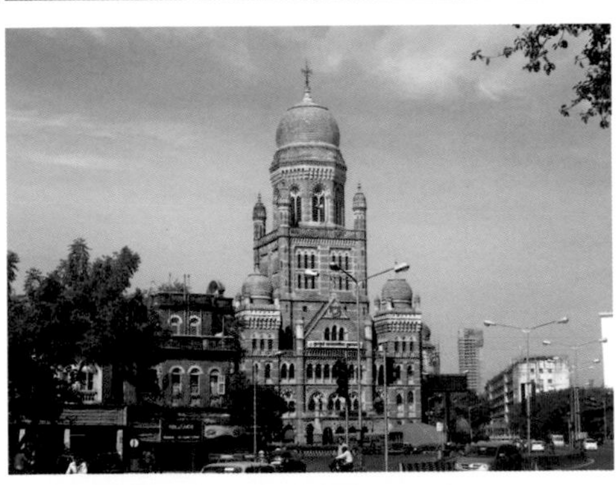

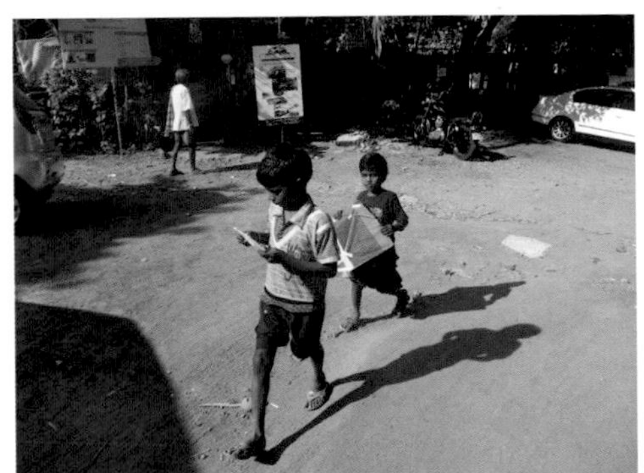

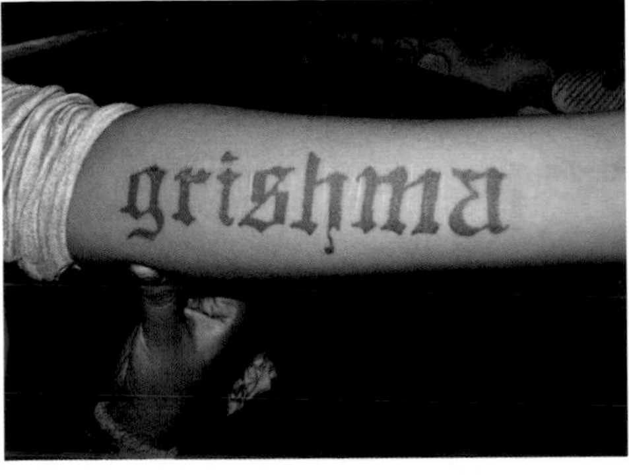
grishma

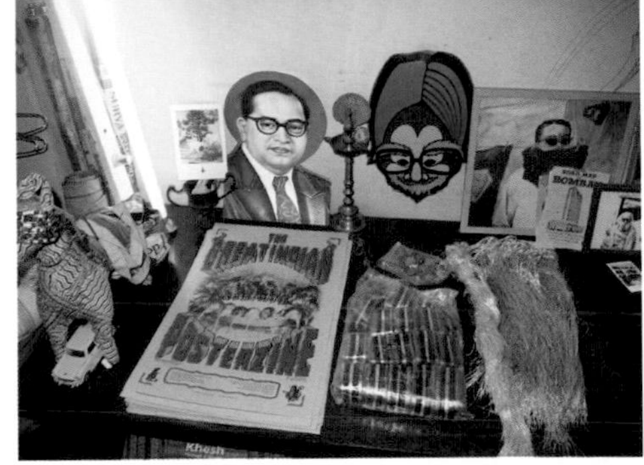
POSTERZINE

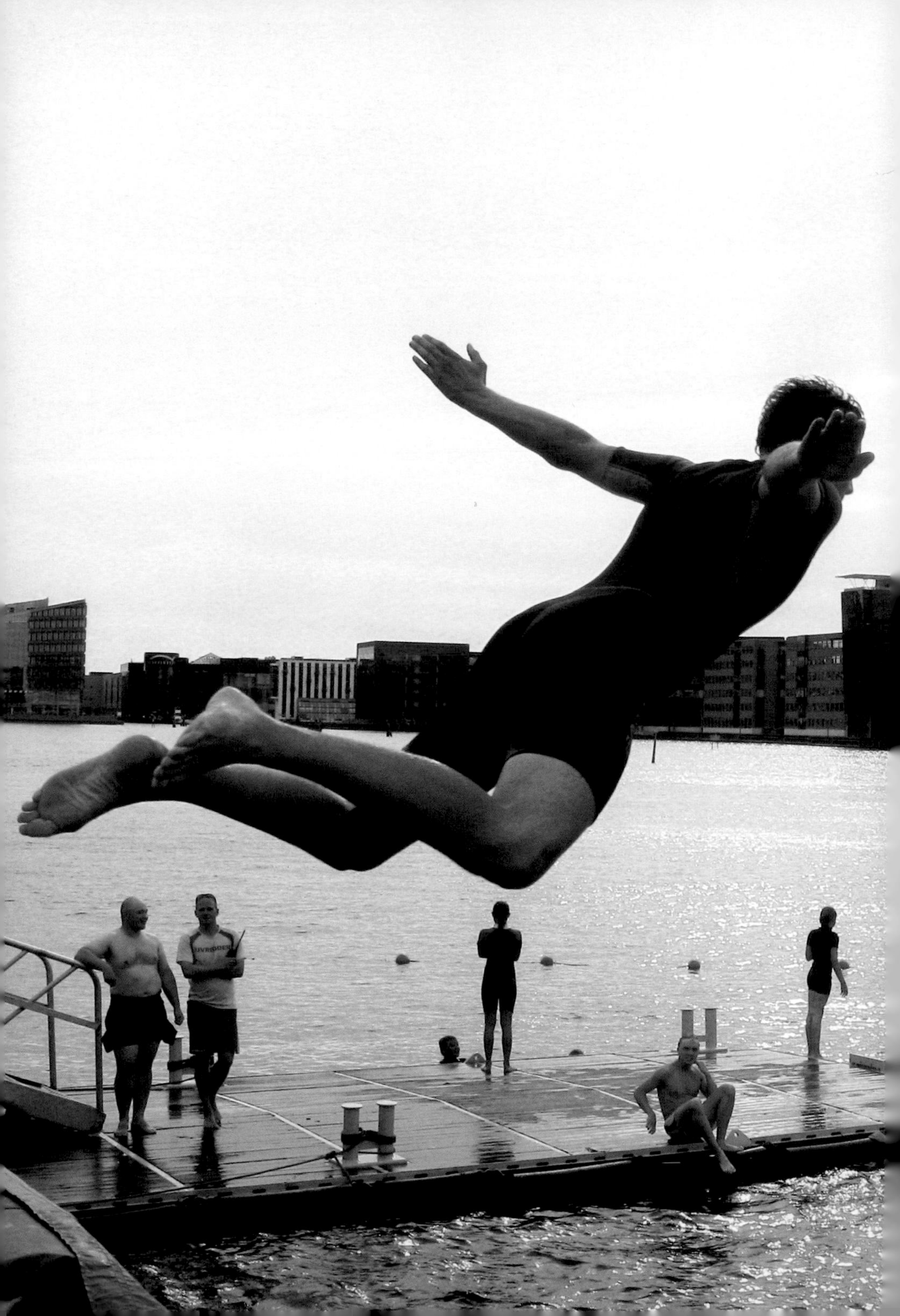

Copenhagen

Lat / 55° 67' 0" N

Lon / 12° 56' 0" E

1–4 June; 4–5 Aug.

COPENHAGEN

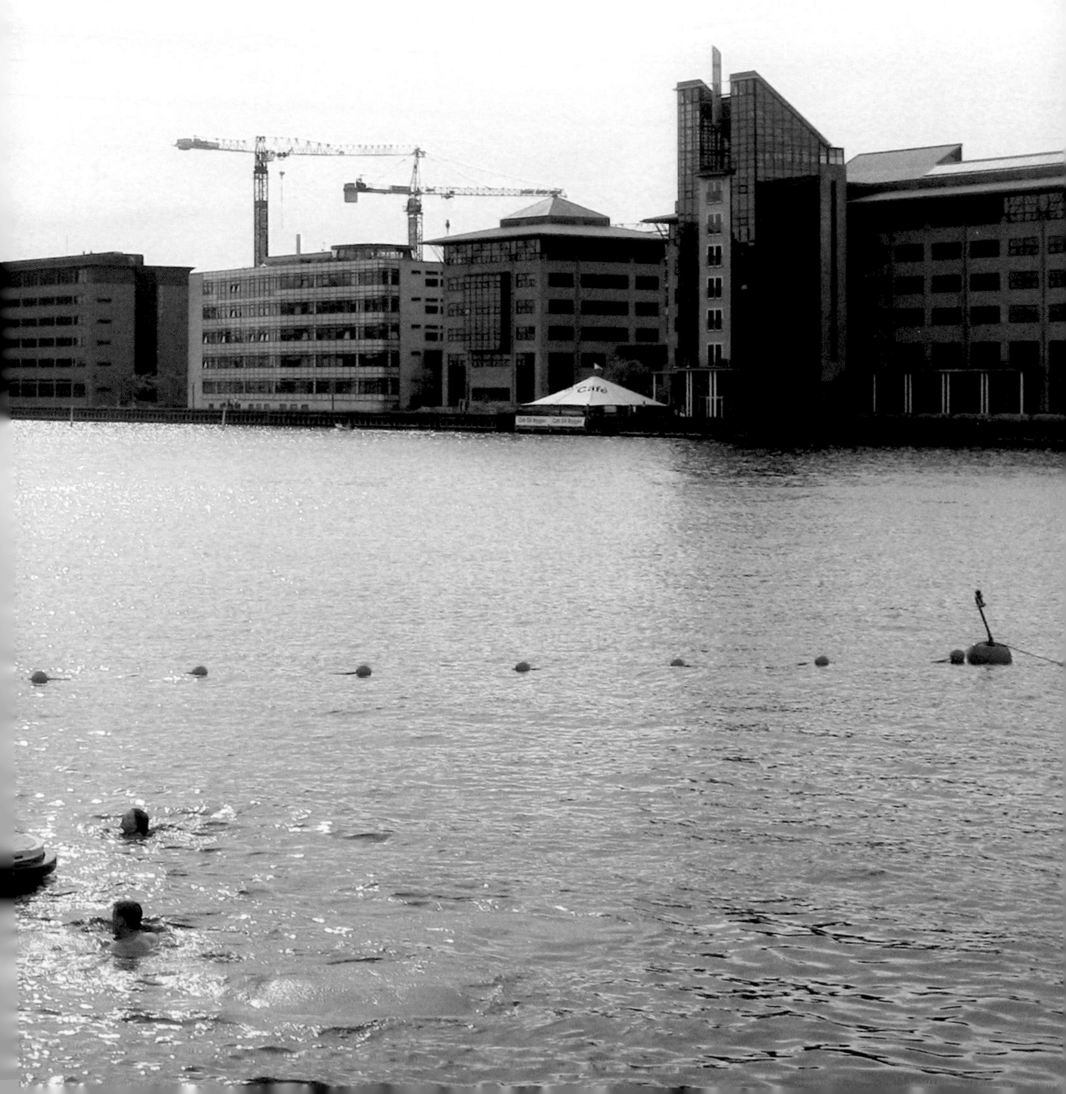

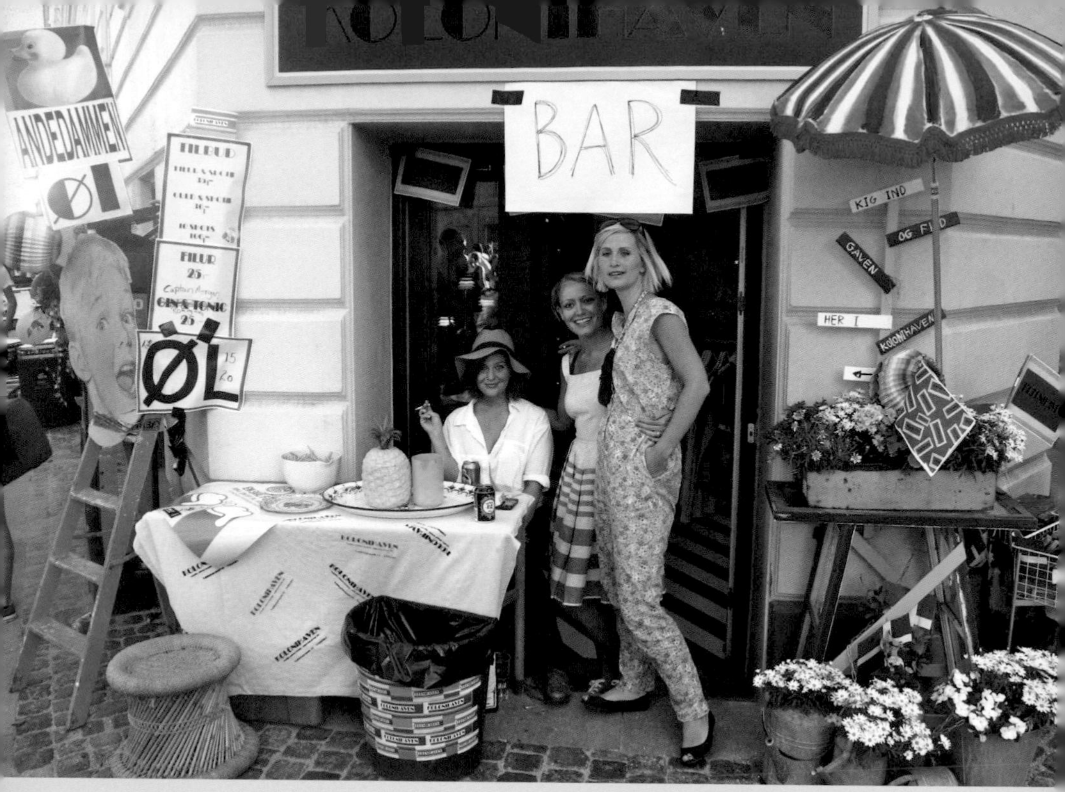

“People always think that Amsterdam is the capital of cycling, but I think that Copenhagen is even more bike-obsessed. The city planners have actually built cycle-highways that go above the main roads. The combination of this cycling culture and all the water surrounding the city gives Copenhagen such a romantic vibe. I like that Denmark – more than any other part of Scandinavia – has a certain roughness to its street-culture, set within the overall framework of Scandinavian perfection. There's a famous festival called Distortion that I think is essential to understanding Danish culture. It's like a huge street party with a DJ sitting on the street. Denmark is also an incredibly baby-friendly society – the amount of infrastructure and design intended to support family life makes the environment very playful and visually stimulating. Copenhagen is probably one of the best places in the world for raising children in a creative environment.”

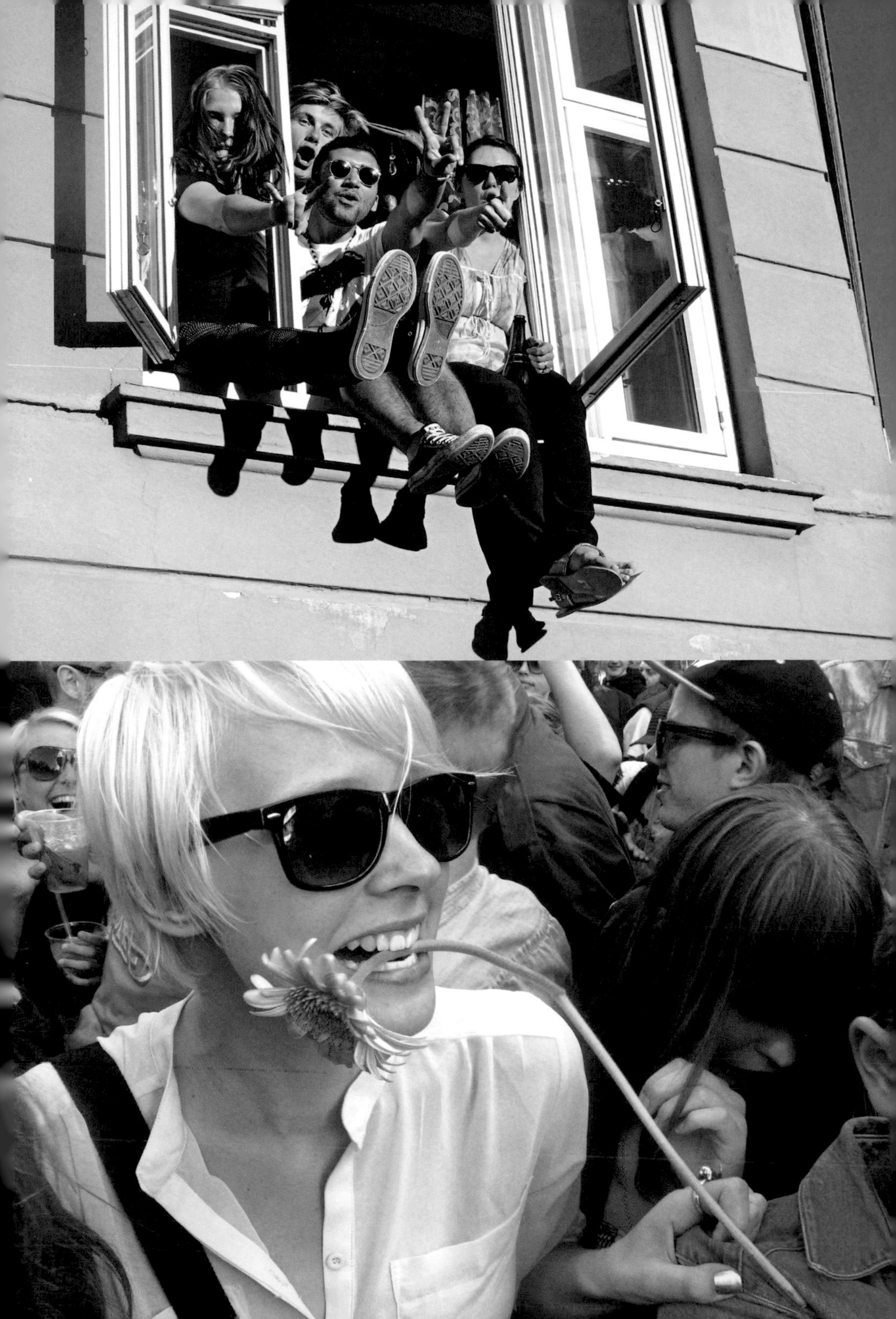

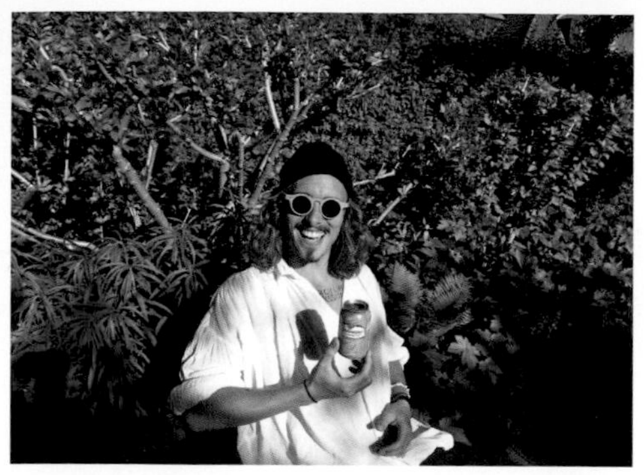

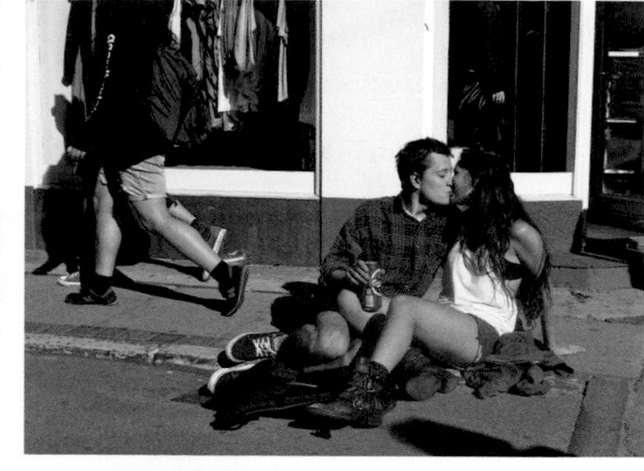

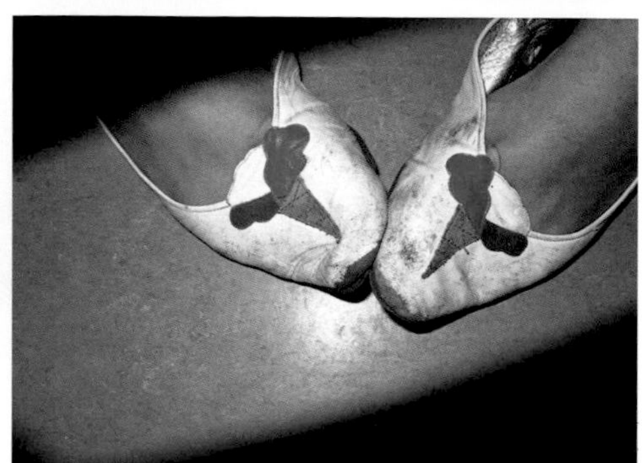

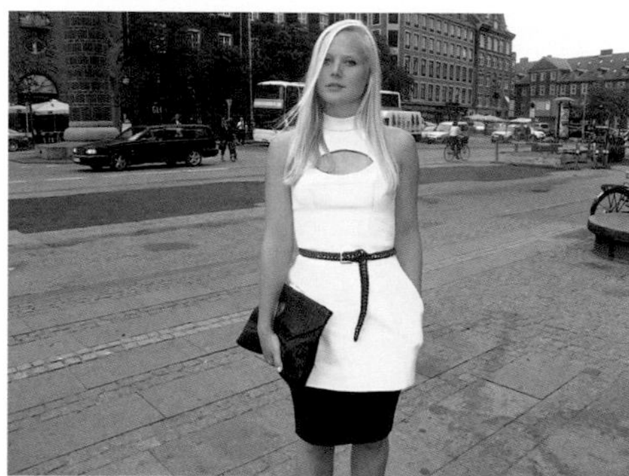

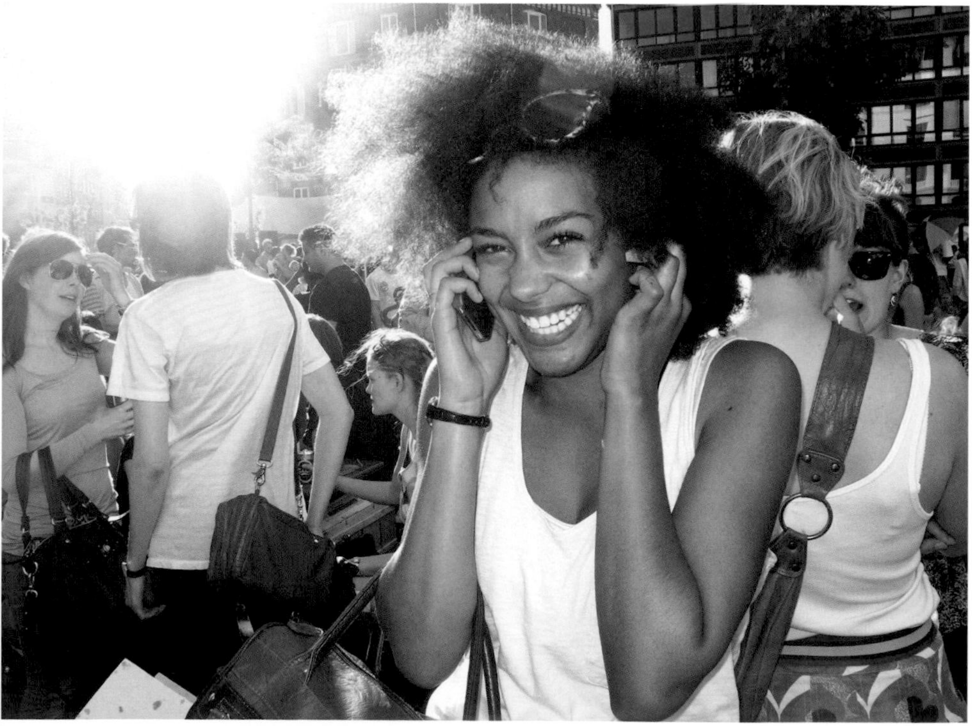

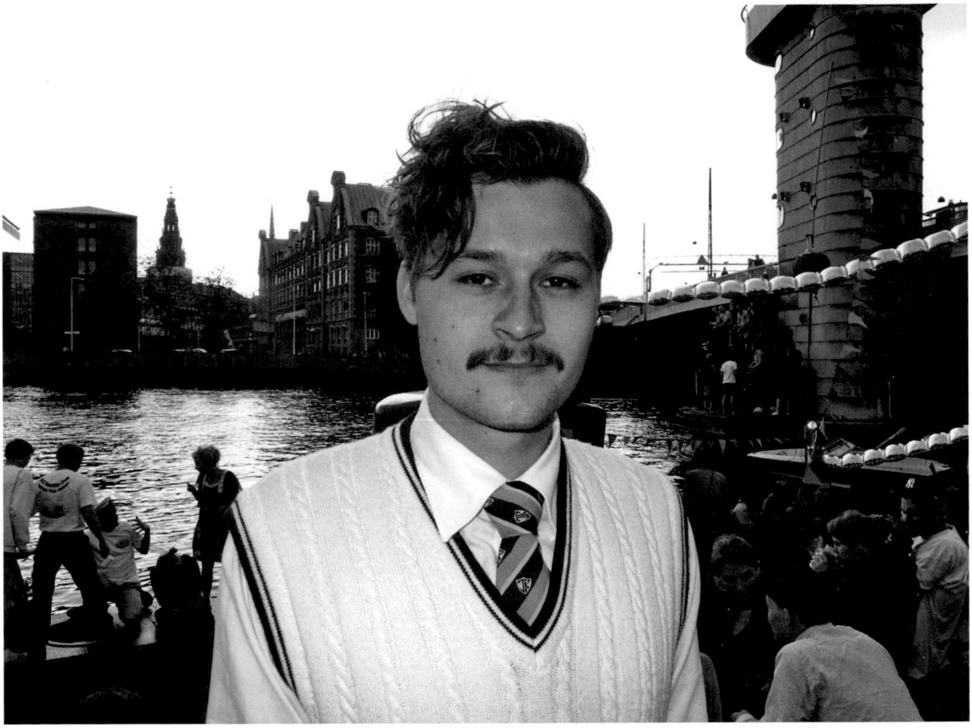

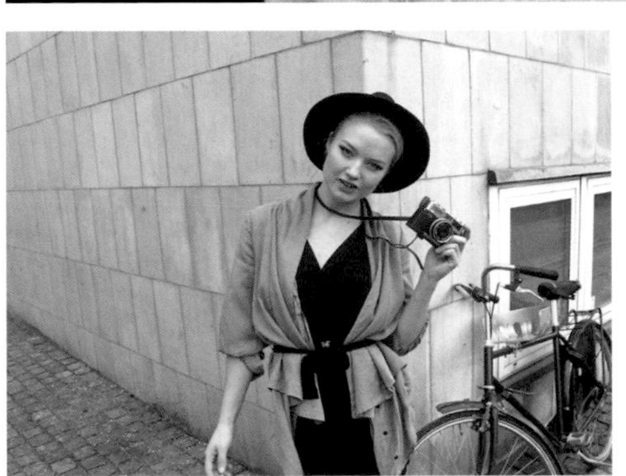

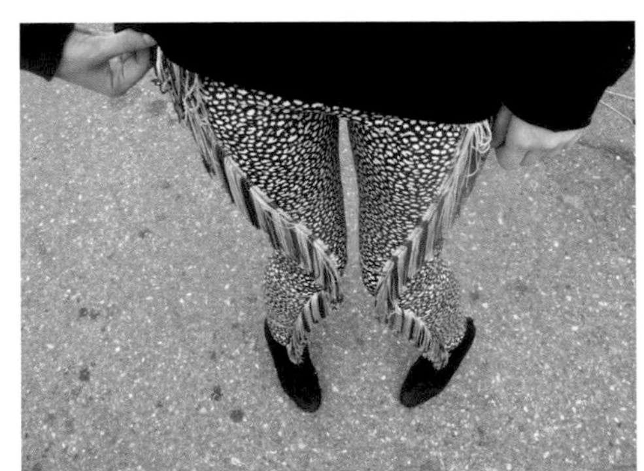

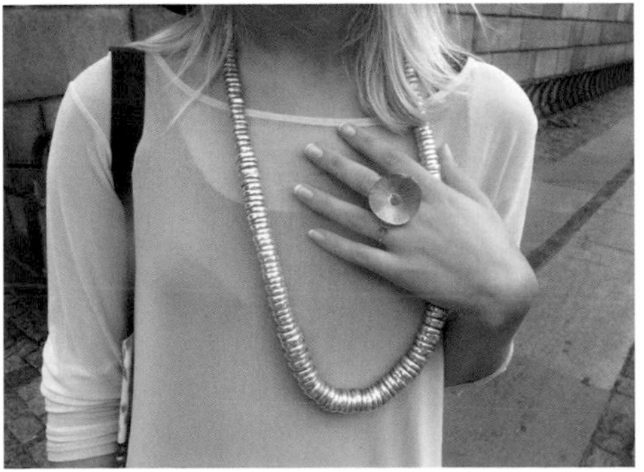

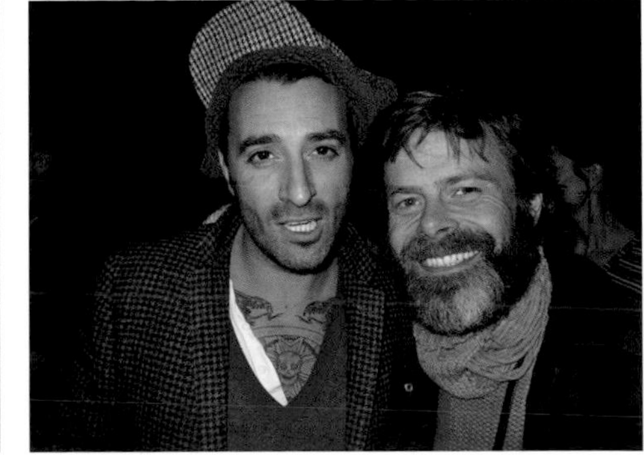

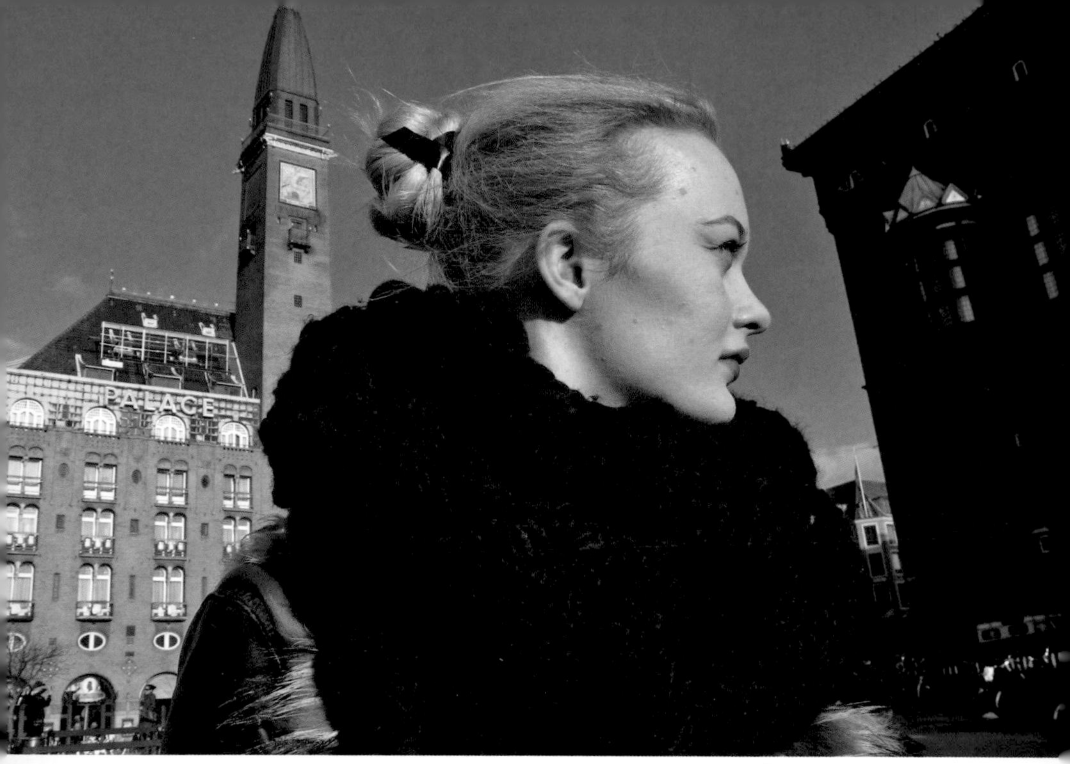

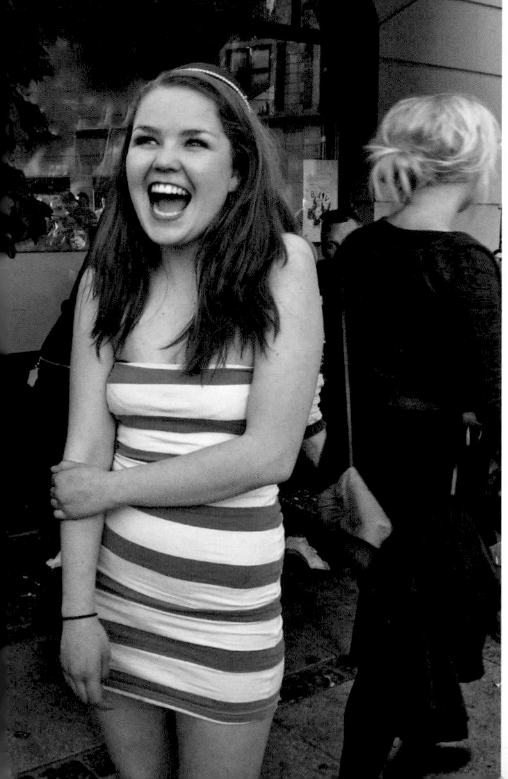

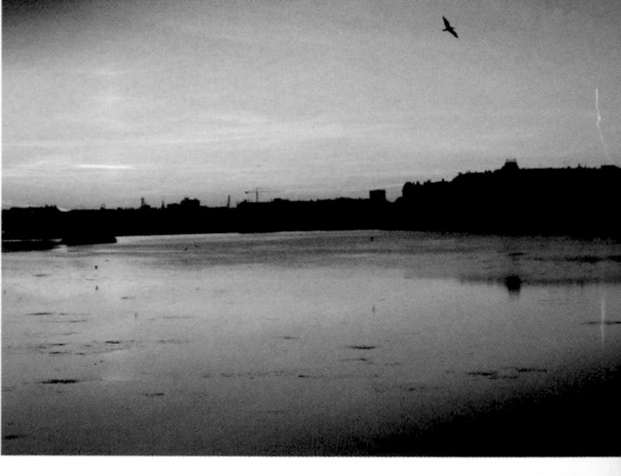

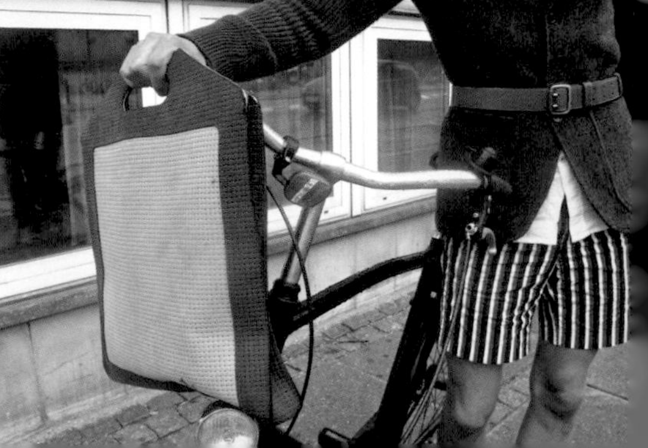

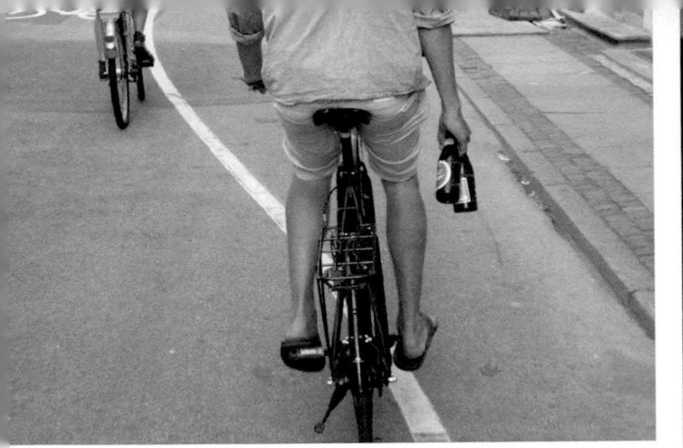

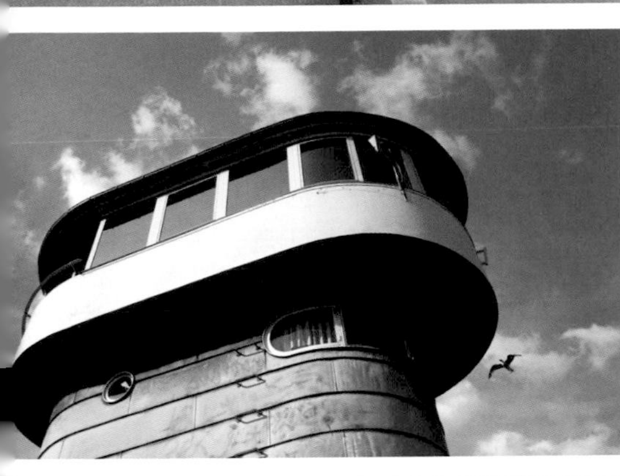

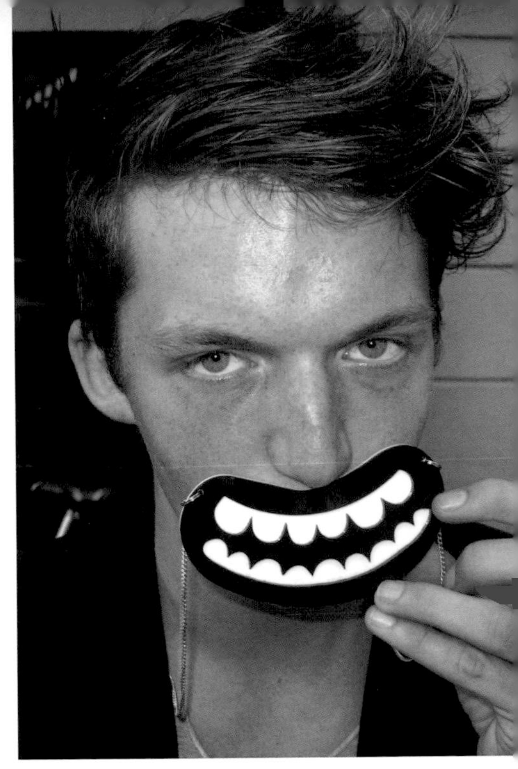

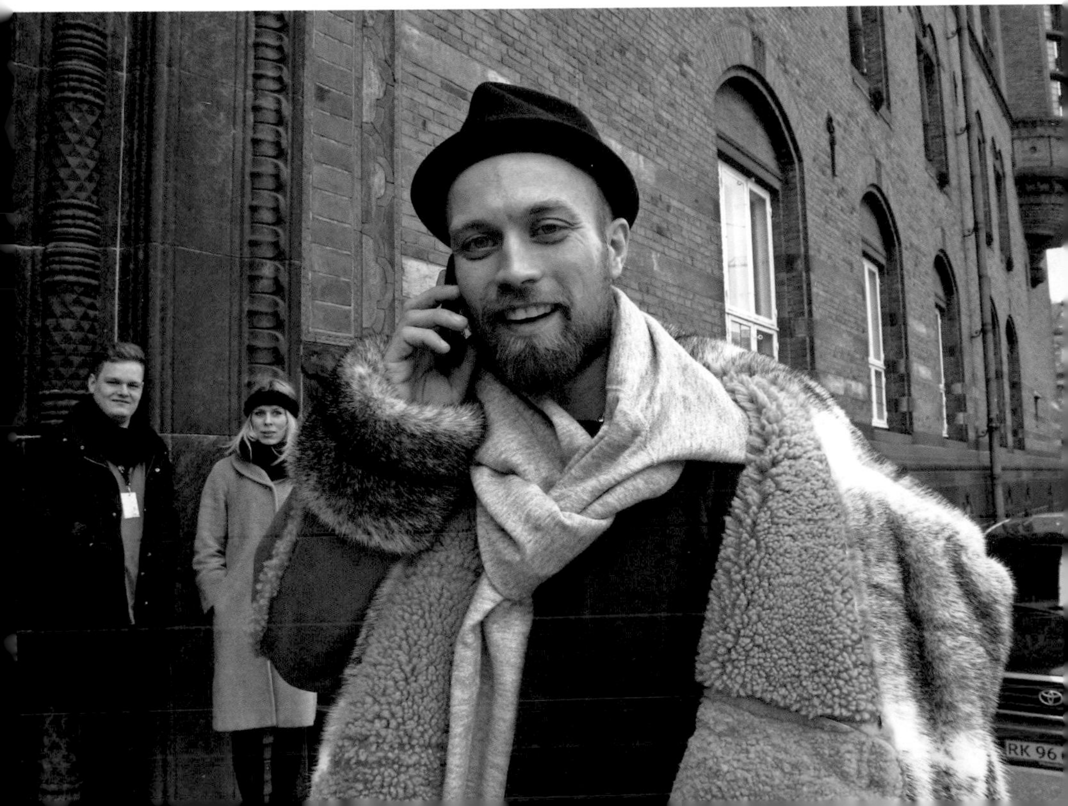

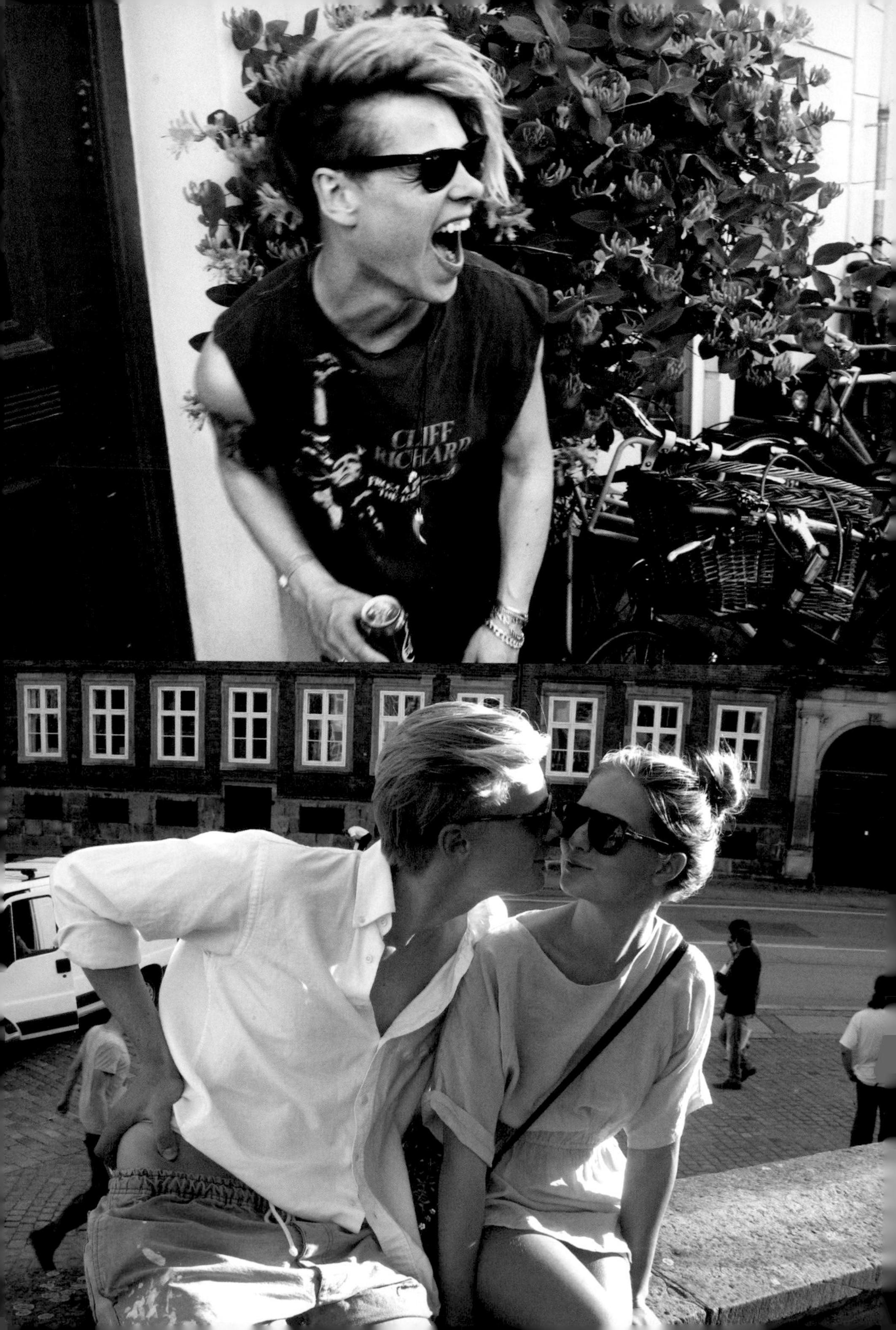
CLIFF
RICHARD

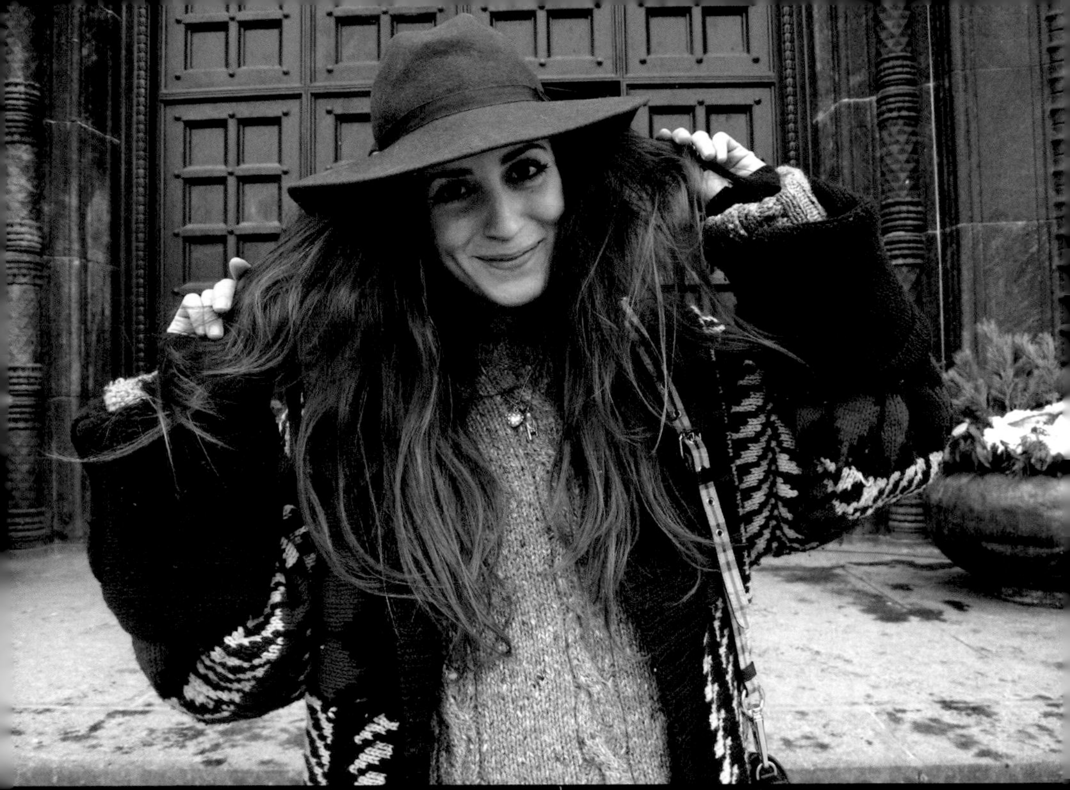

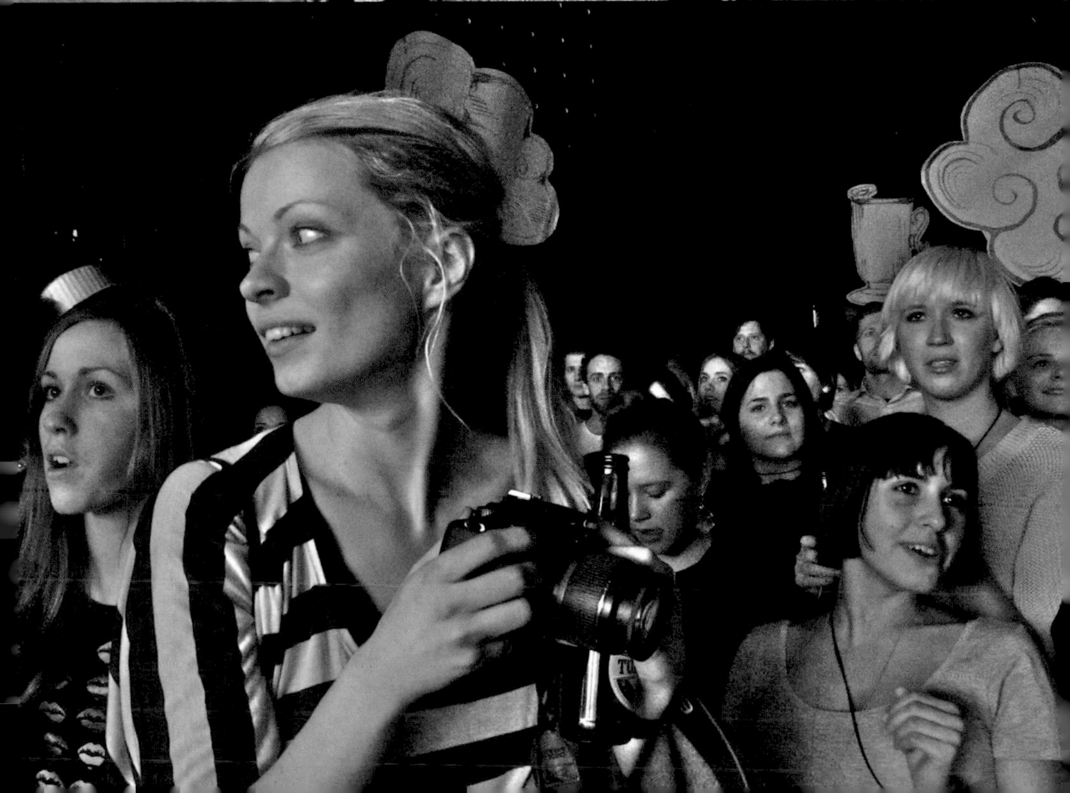

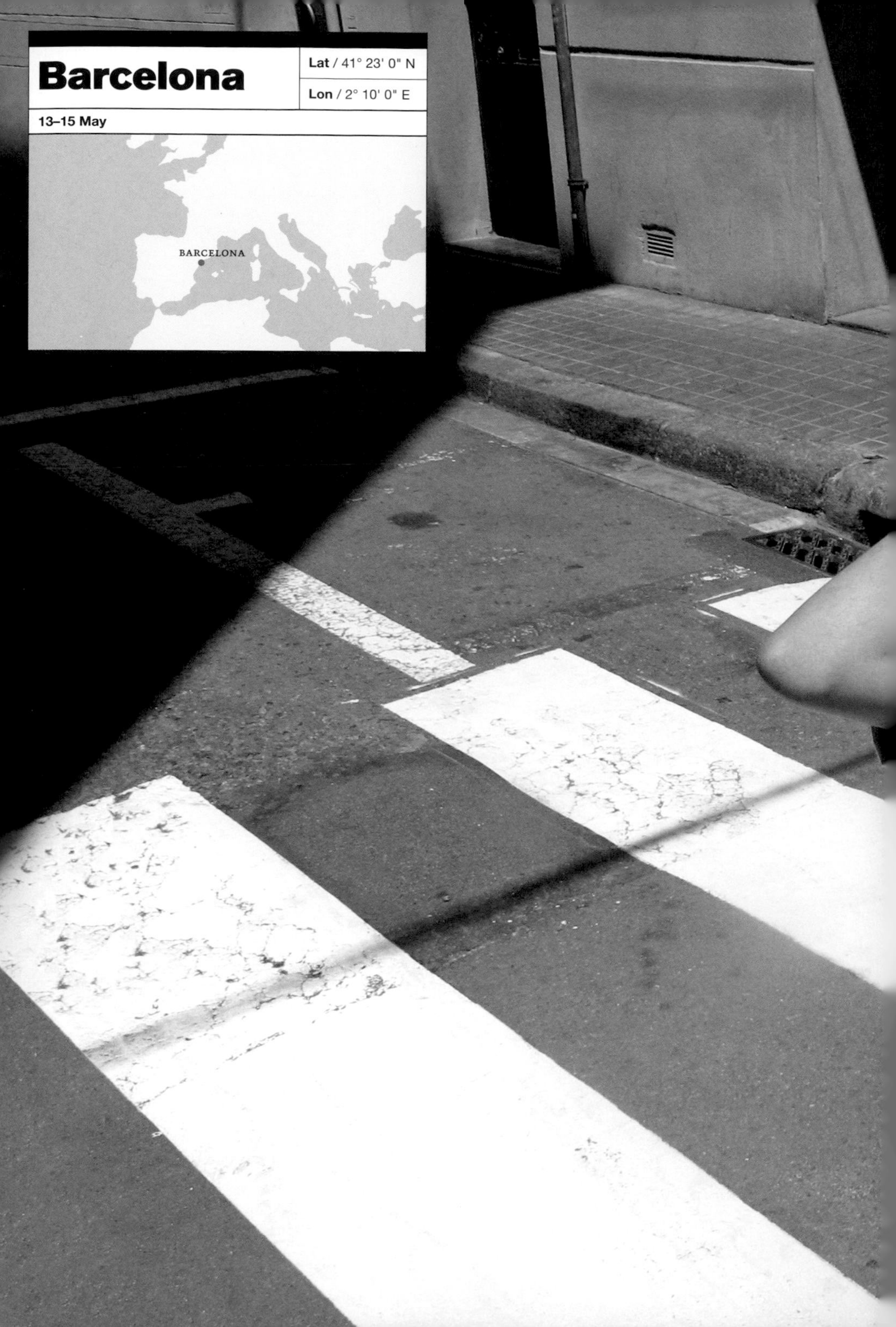
Barcelona
Lat / 41° 23' 0" N
Lon / 2° 10' 0" E
13–15 May
BARCELONA

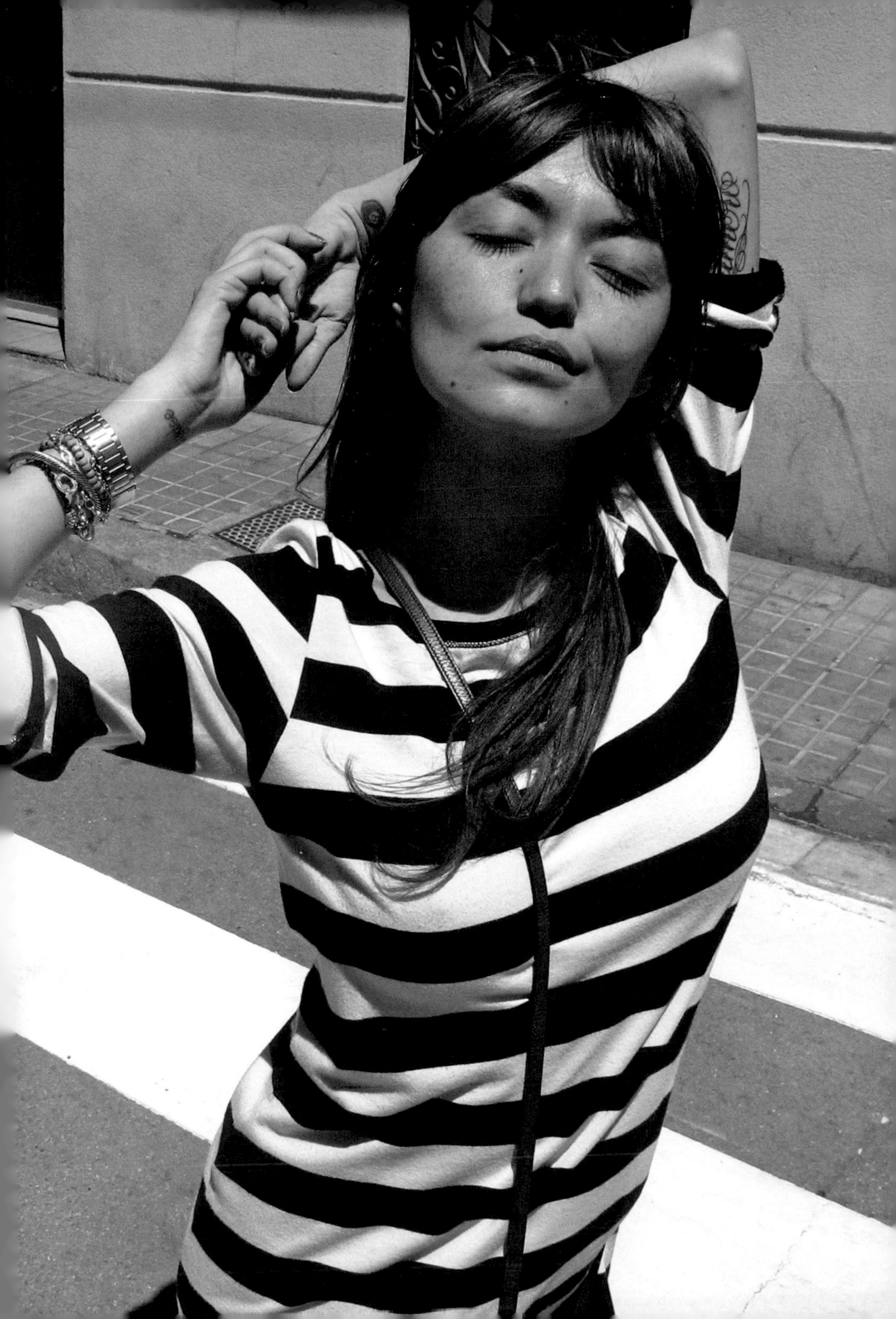

“Barcelona is both a bohemian paradise and a haven for refined architecture. It sounds like a strange mix, but that's the Catalan capital for you. At first glance, it looks as if the city is totally dedicated to the enjoyment of life's simple pleasures in low-key bars and home-style restaurants, but then you discover its more sophisticated side: Gaudí's Park Güell, Mies van der Rohe's Barcelona Pavilion, Jean Nouvel's Torre Agbar, Herzog & de Meuron's Forum Building and Ricardo Bofill's W Barcelona Hotel. So, even though Barcelona is a city by the sea, the beach is just something that happens to be there – Barcelona feels much more urban than places like Sydney and Rio, where the beach culture comes into the city. It's also one of my favourite places to go in Europe during the winter, since you can still enjoy lunch on a sunny terrace in January.”

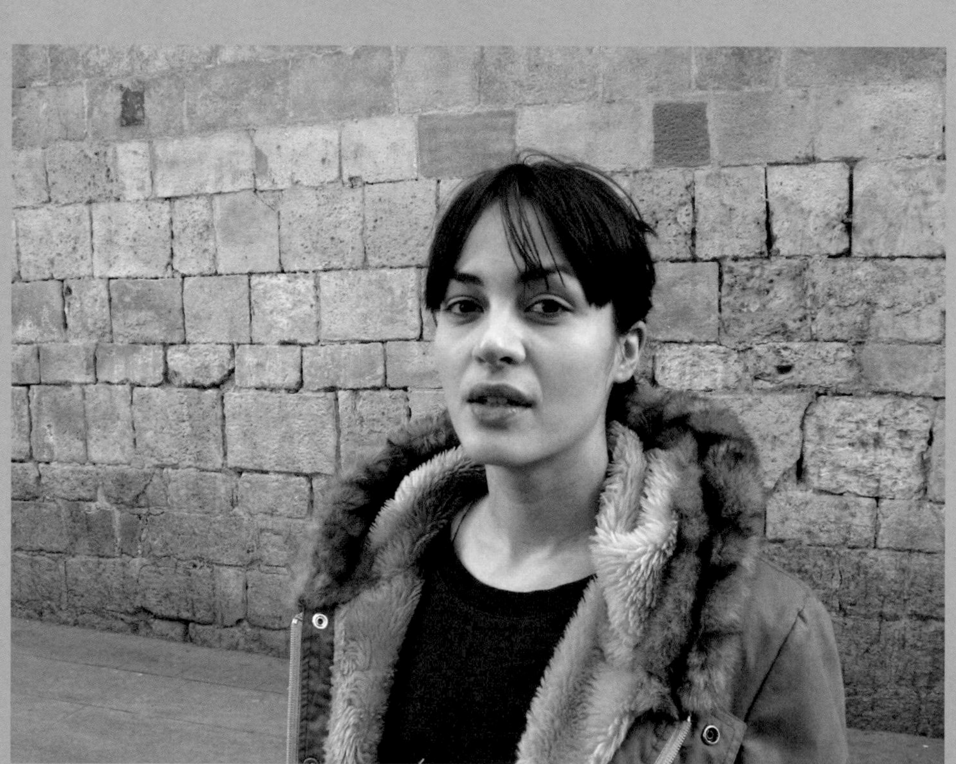

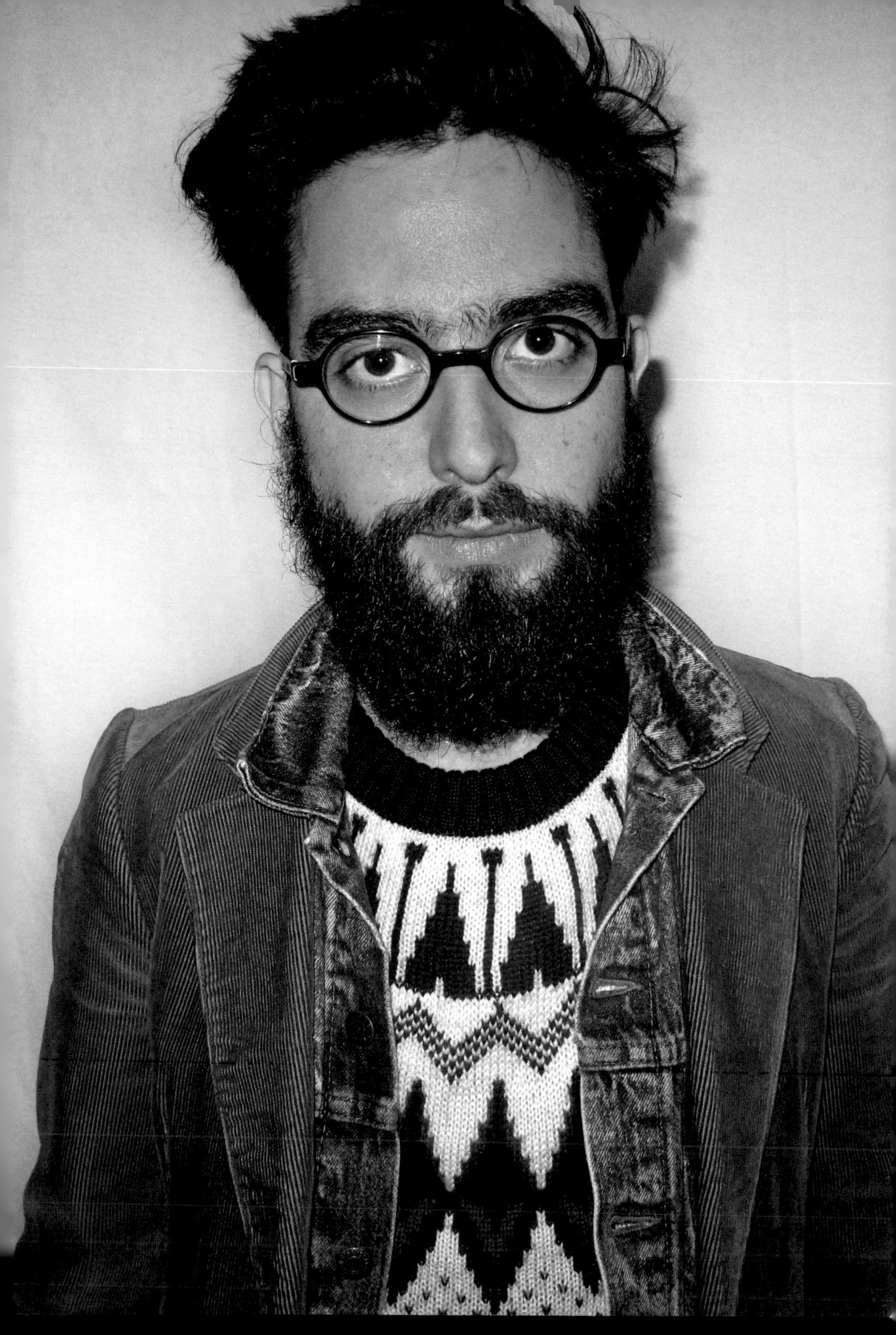

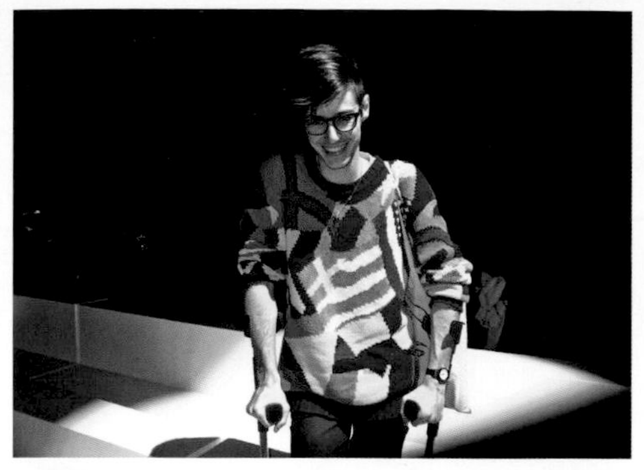

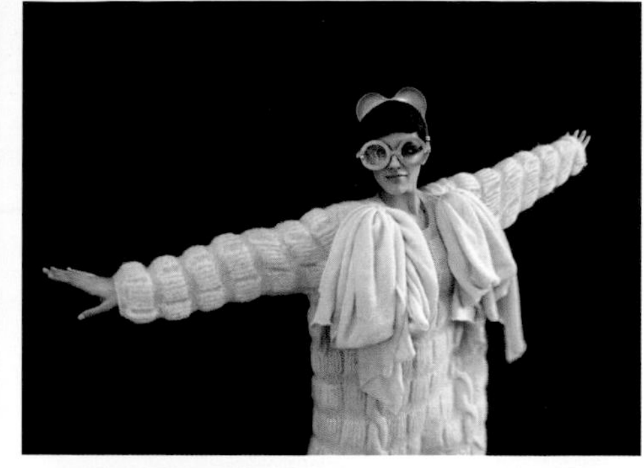

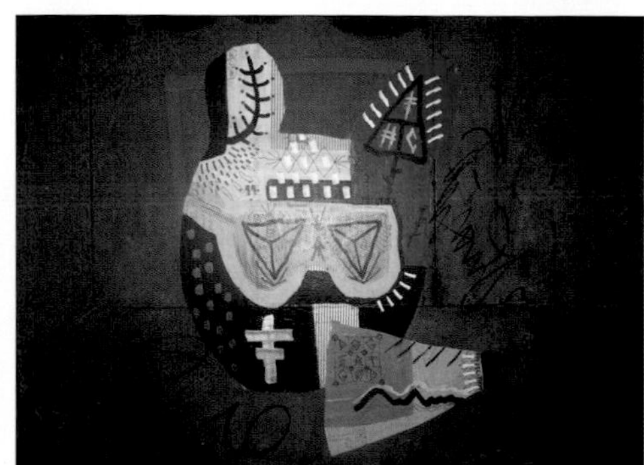

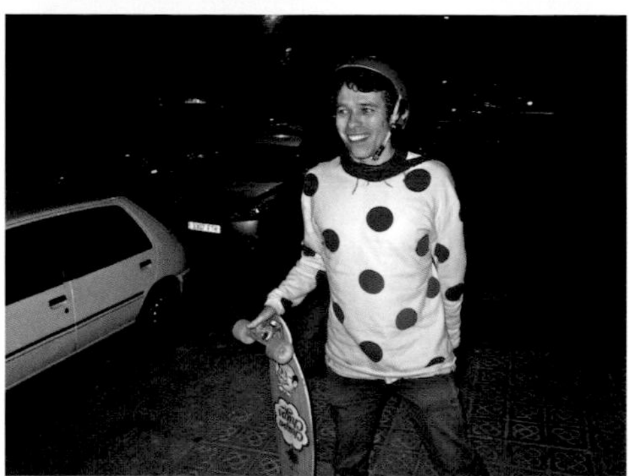

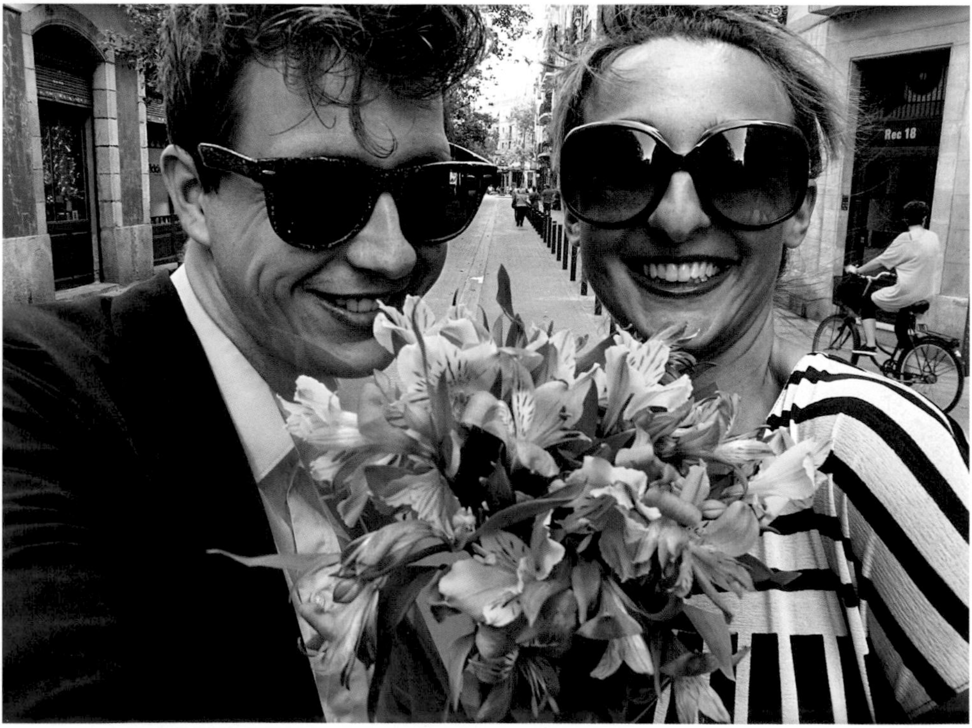

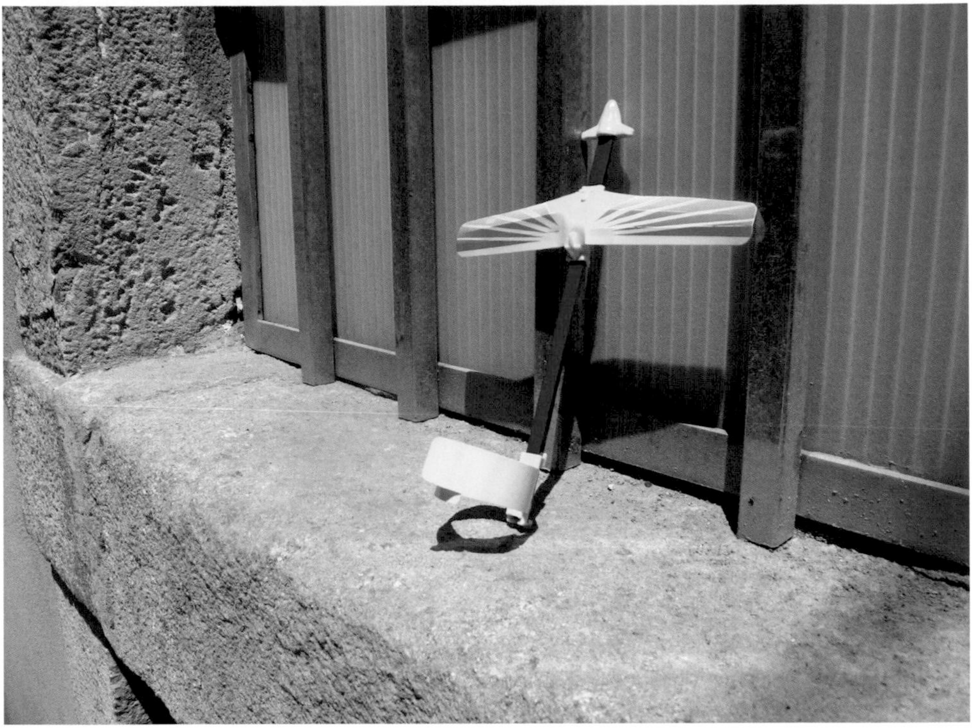

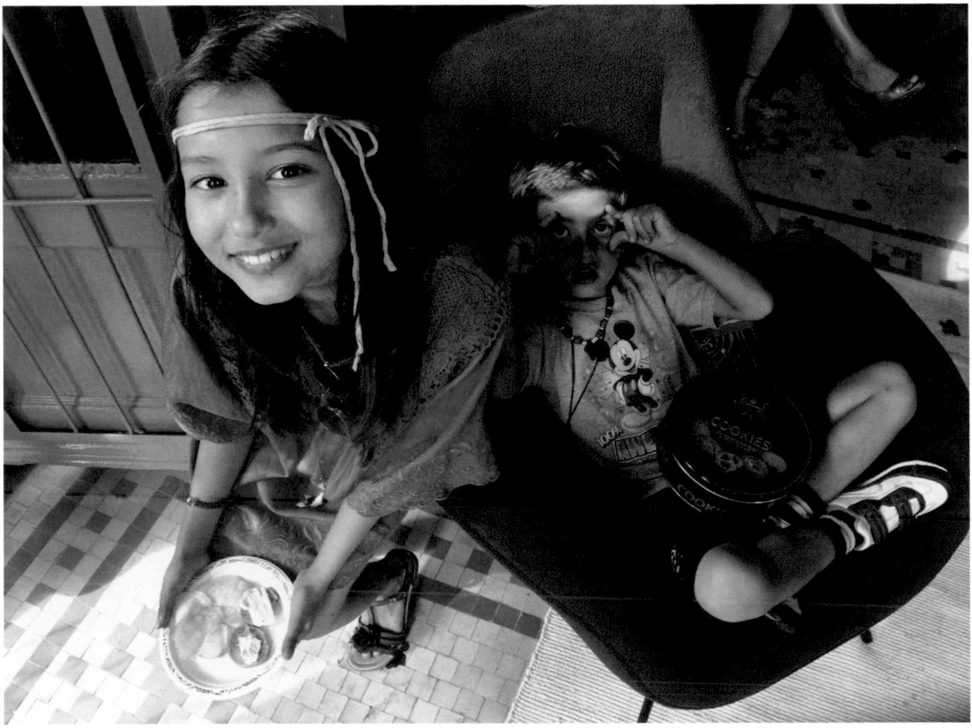

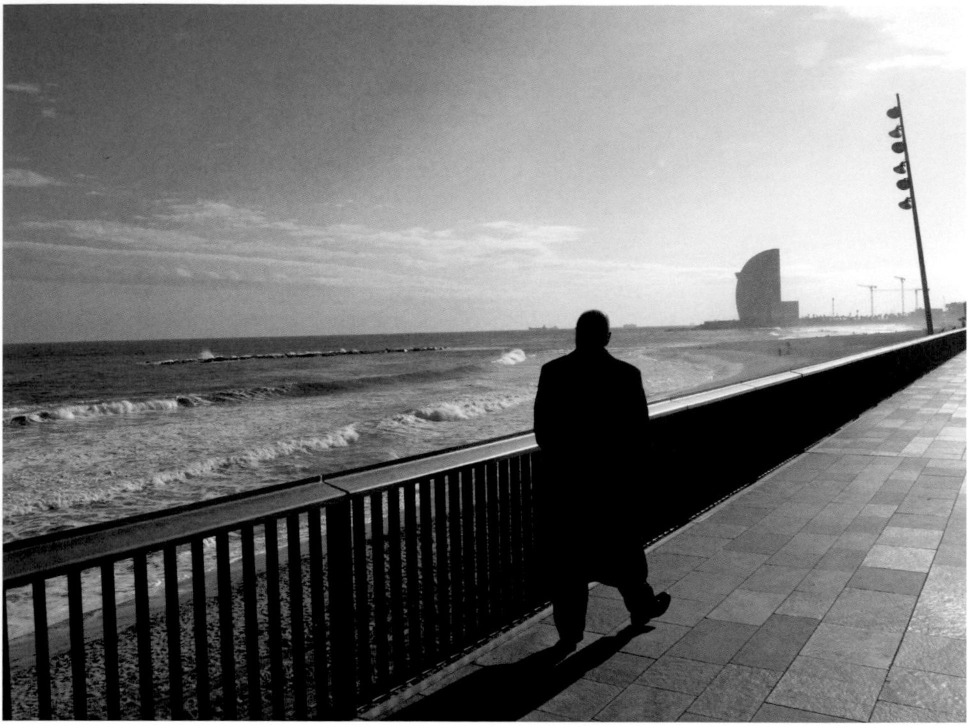

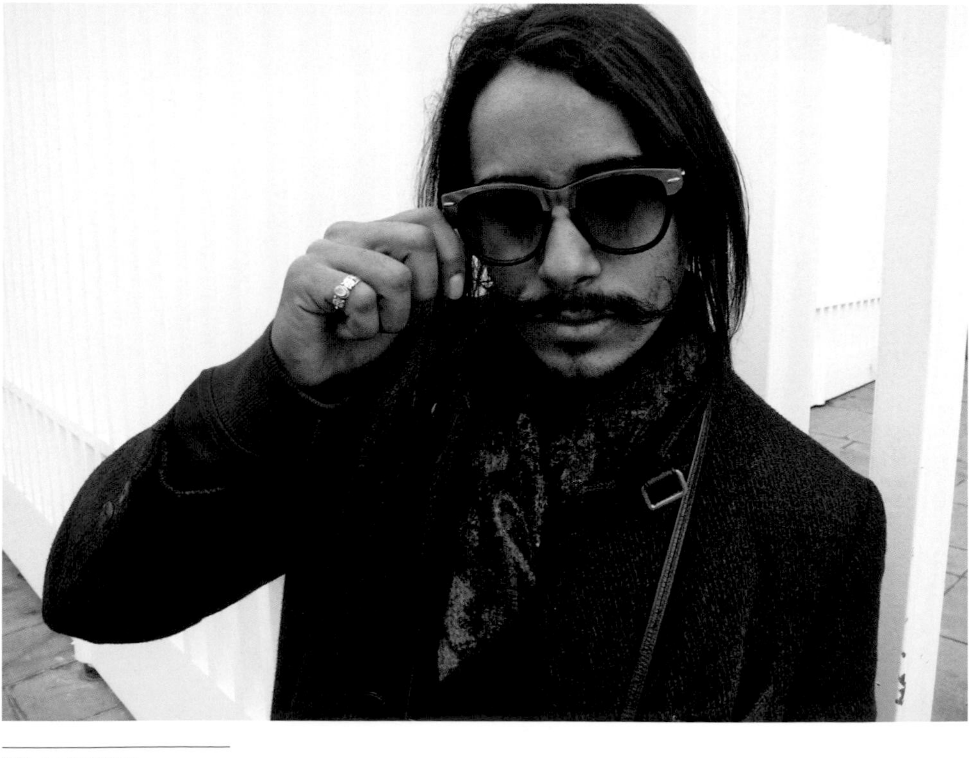

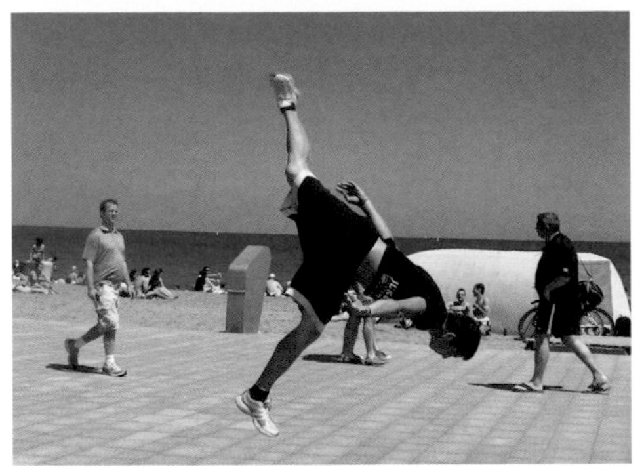

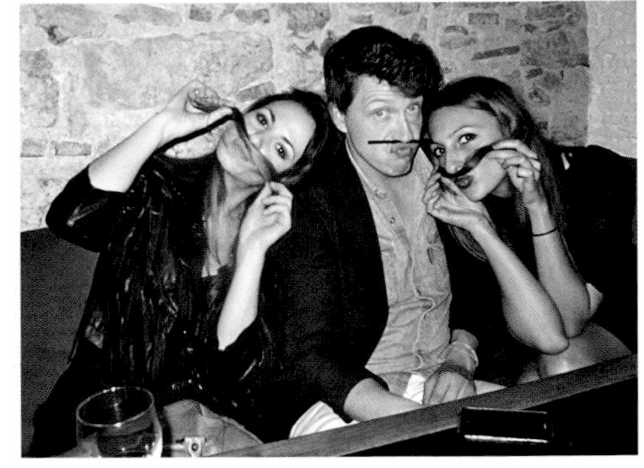

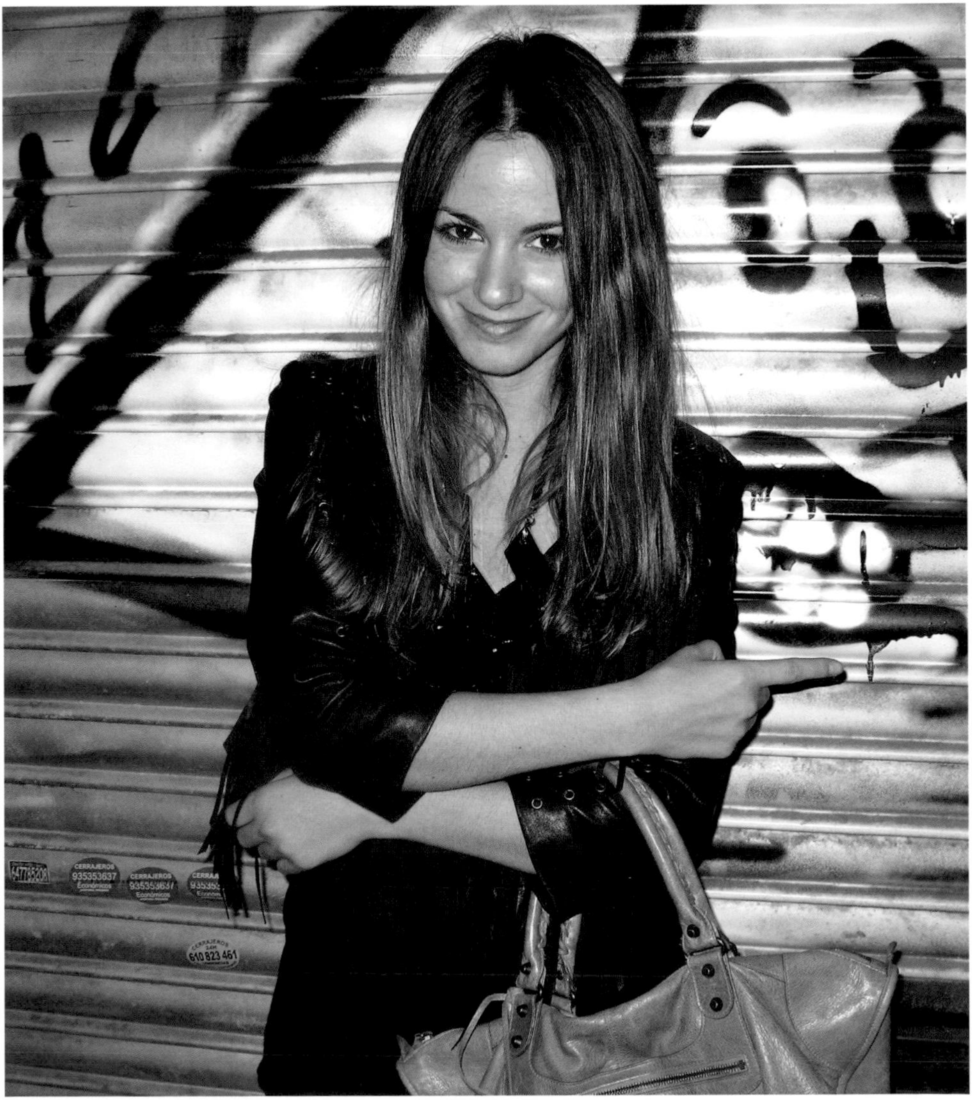

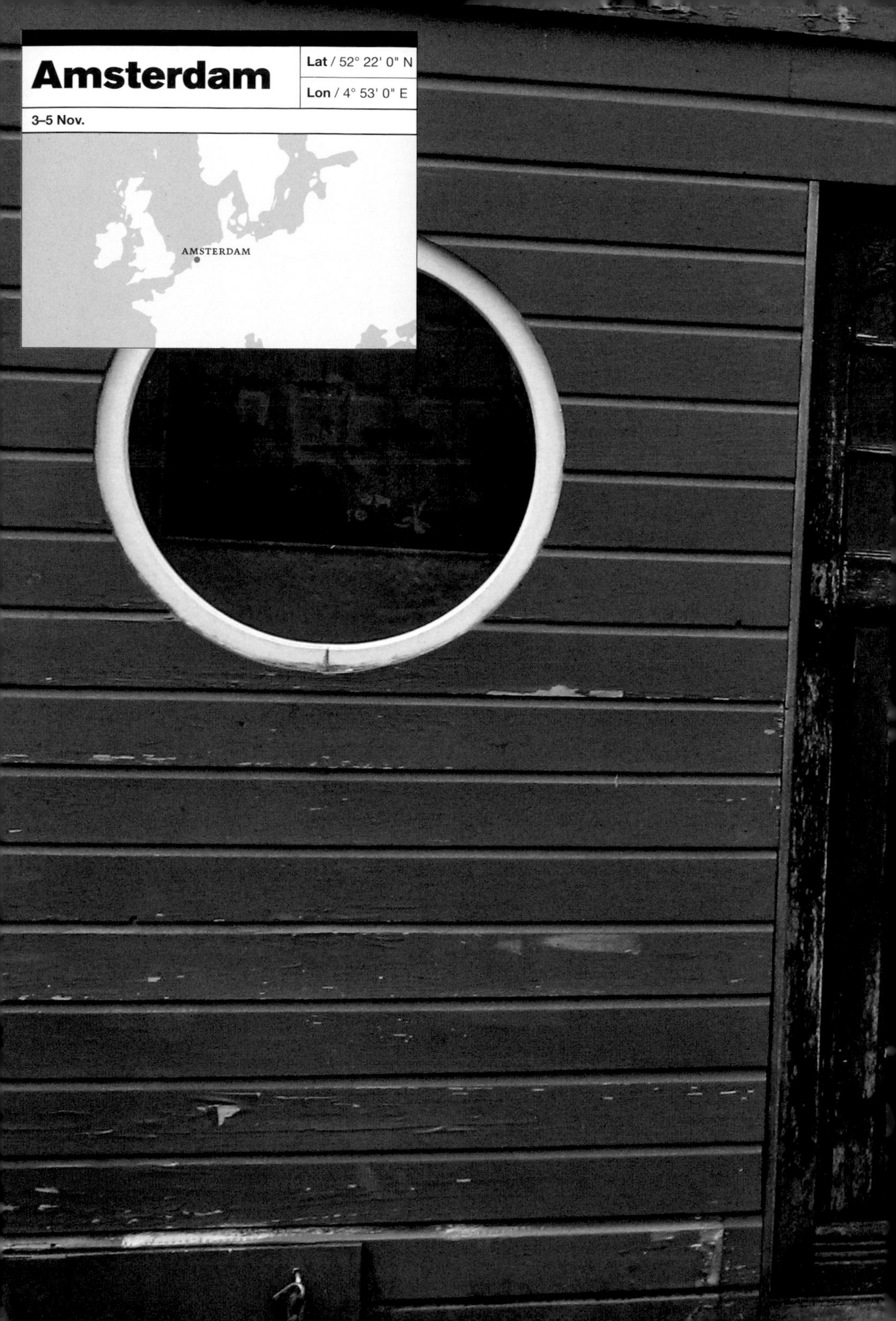
Amsterdam
Lat / 52° 22' 0" N
Lon / 4° 53' 0" E
3–5 Nov.
AMSTERDAM

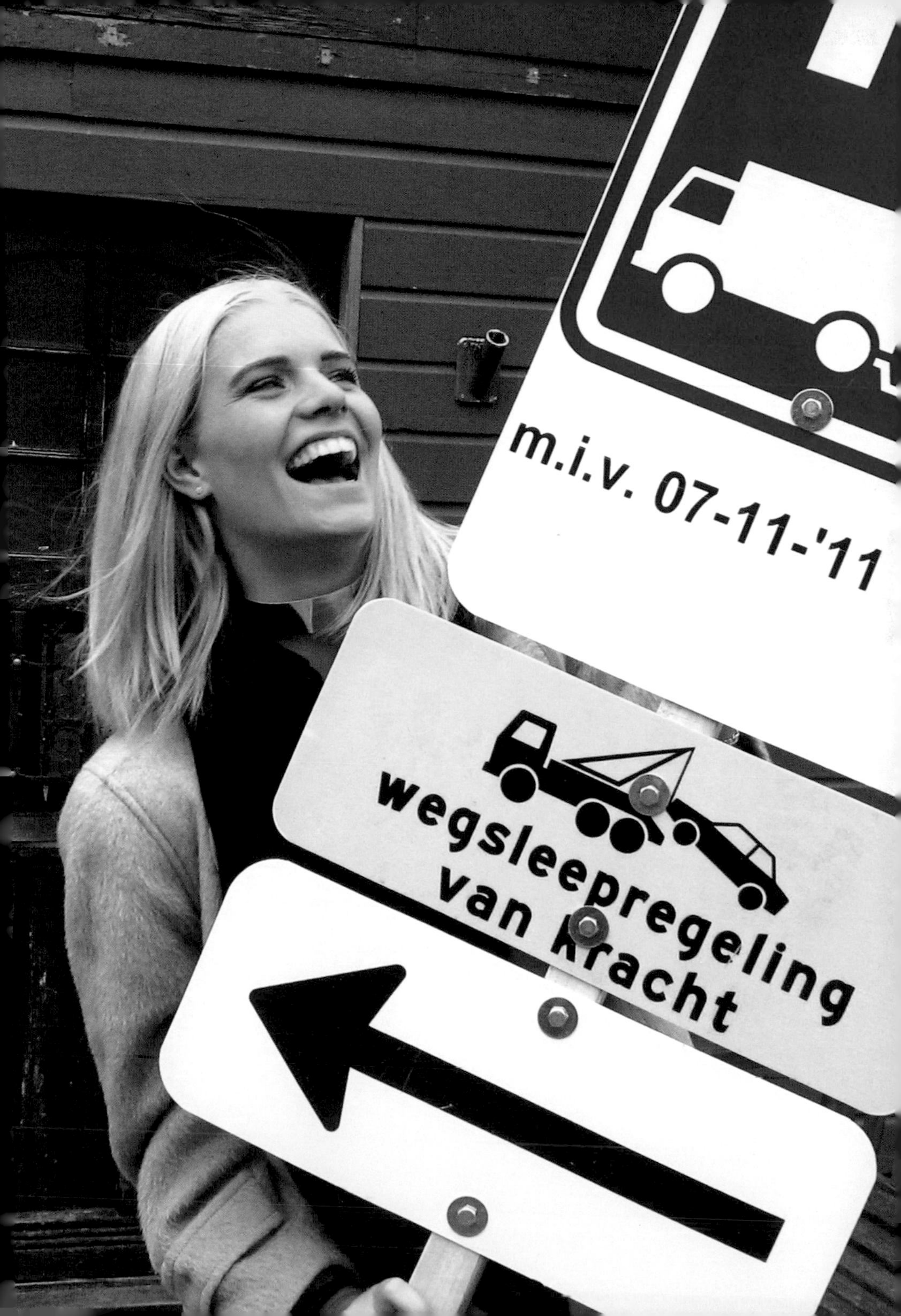
m.i.v. 07-11-'11
wegsleepregeling
van kracht

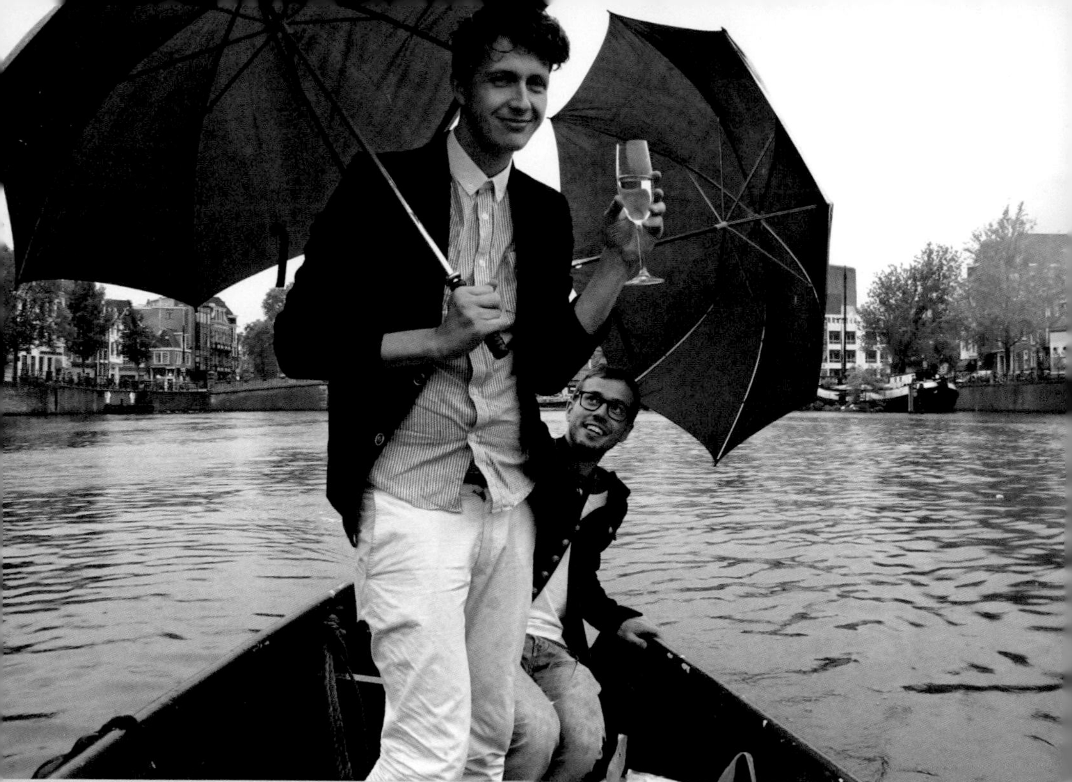

“ Amsterdam is charming, but do hordes of zombie-looking tourists really need to flock to coffee shops to get high on a daily basis and pollute the scenery? My absolute favourite place to stay in town is a guest house located on top of a fashion store in the Jordaan district, a real hidden gem with two corner rooms that feel like love nests. The store owners don't advertise the guest house, so you can only stay there if you've heard about it via word of mouth. Perfection. I like Dutch people because they are very down-to-earth and honest, and if they have something to tell you, they won't feel embarrassed to express it. ”

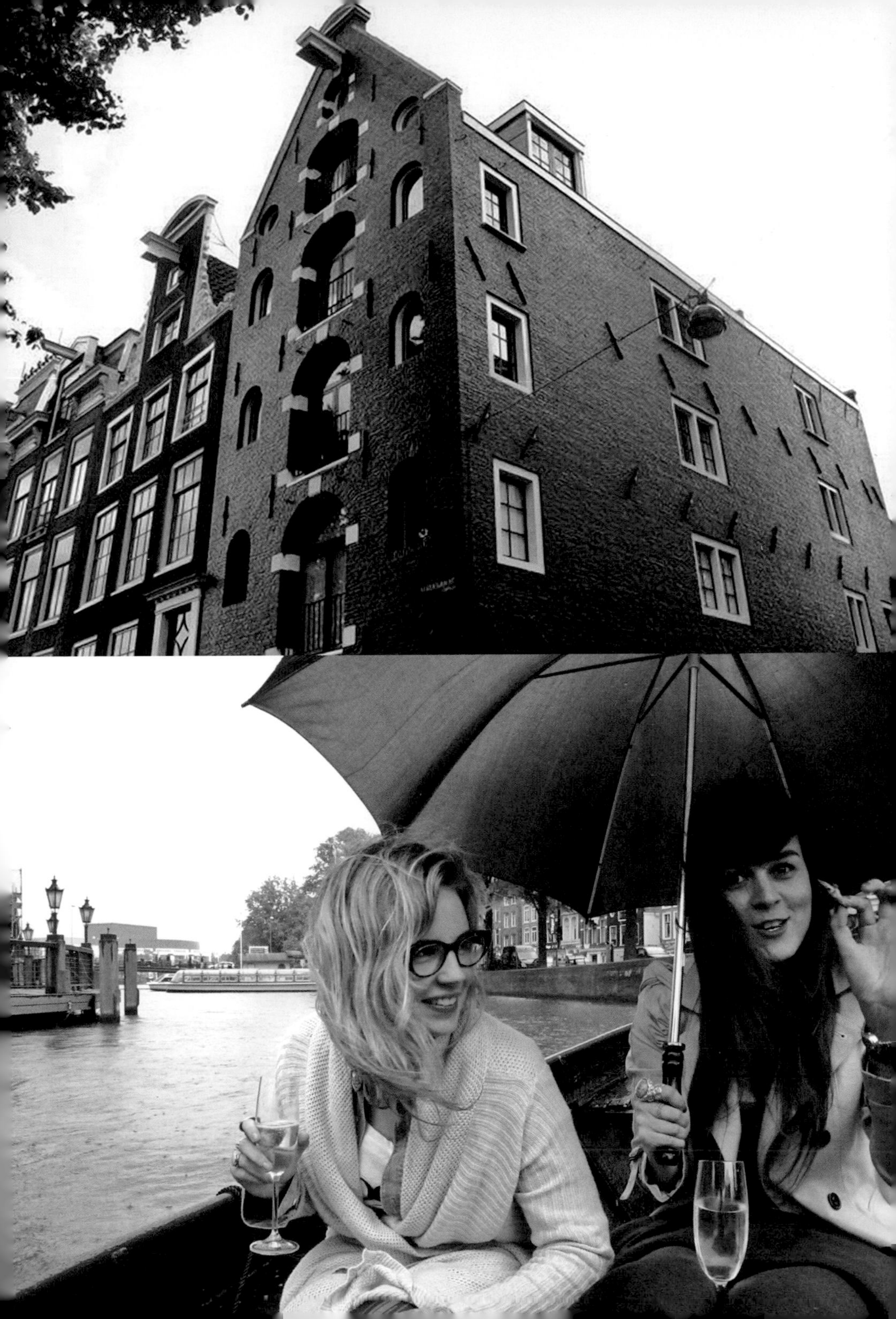

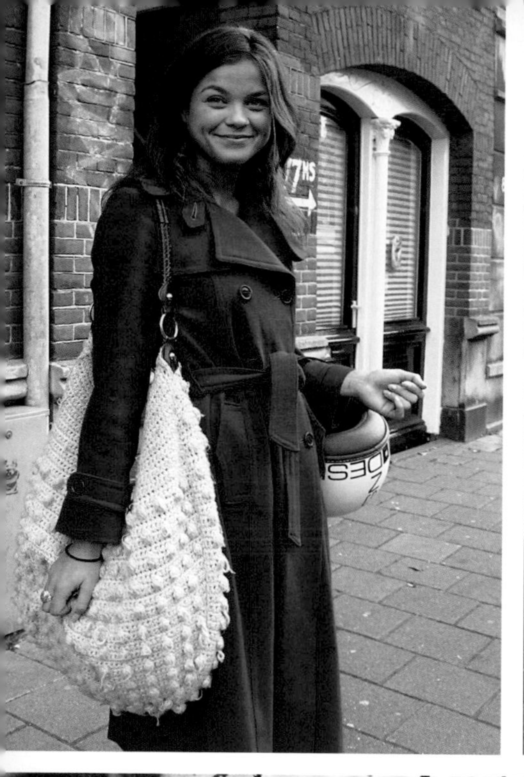

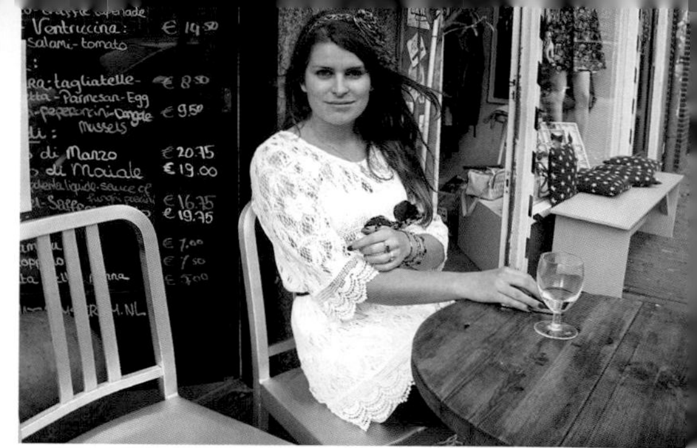

Ventruccina: € 14.50
salami - tomato
Parmesan - Egg
Mussels
di Manzo € 20.75
di Maiale € 19.00

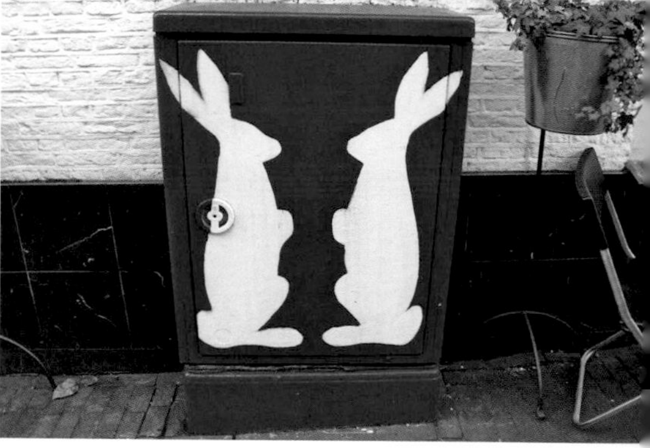

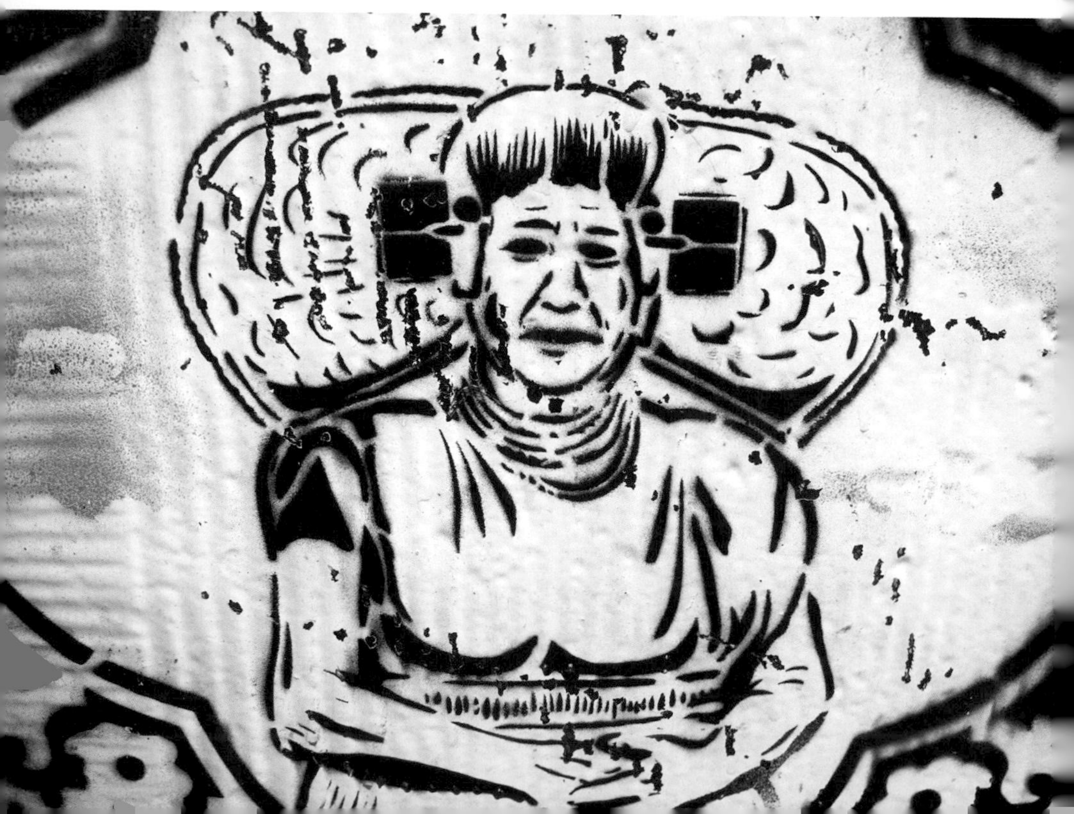

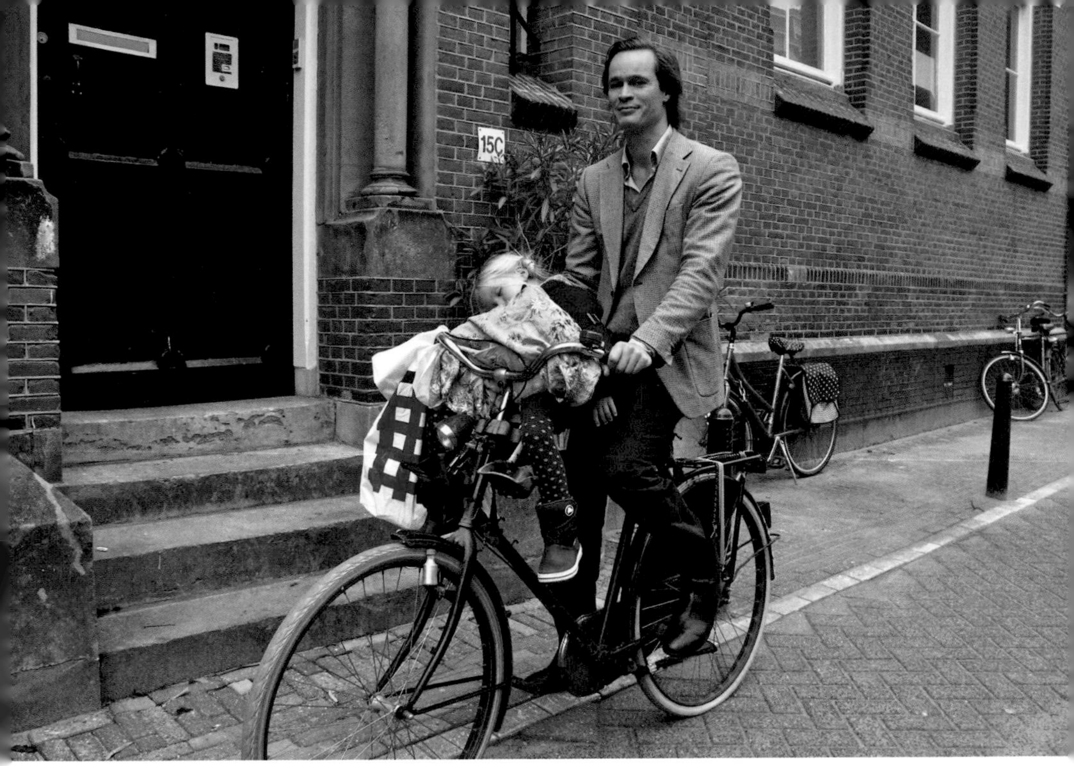

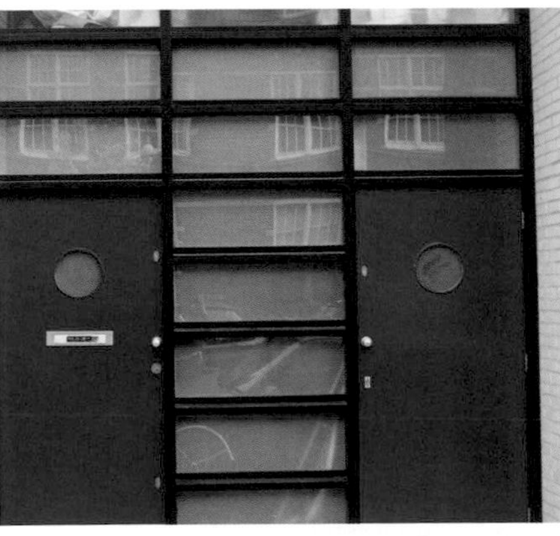

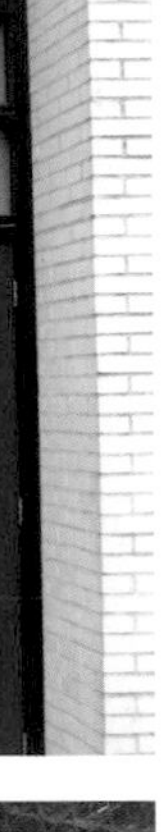

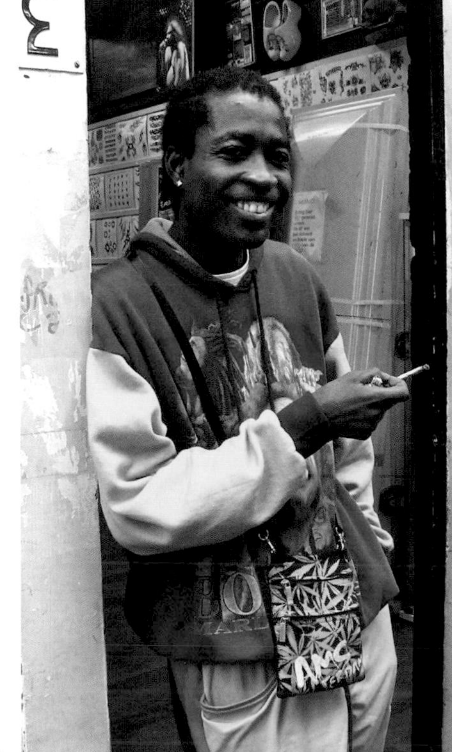

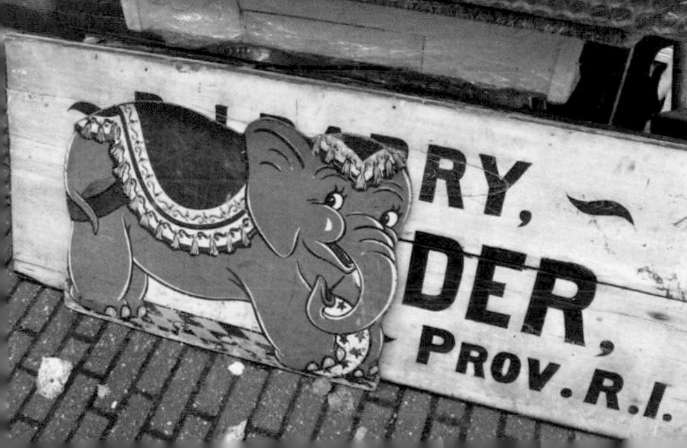
RY,
DER,
PROV.R.I.

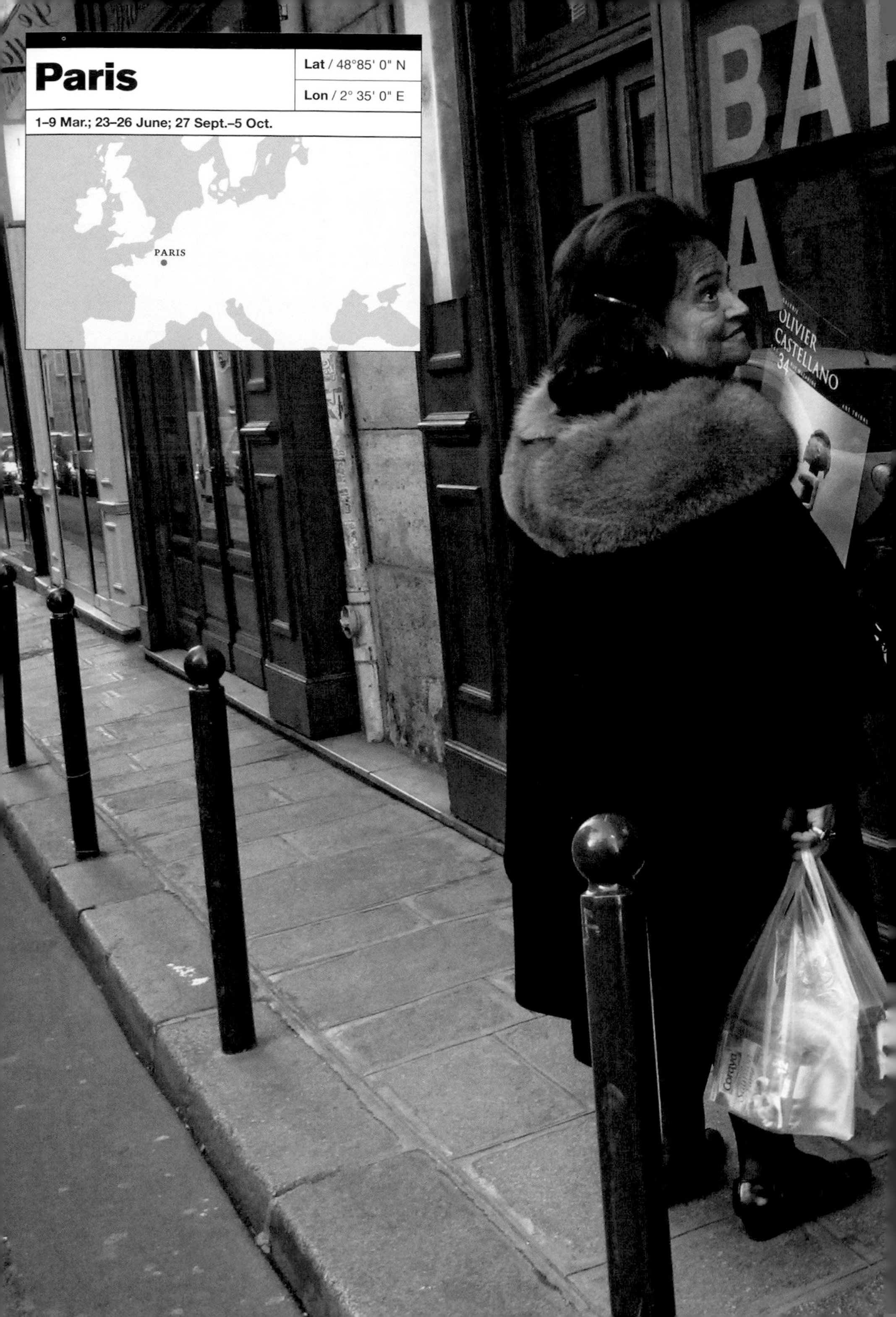

Paris

Lat / 48°85' 0" N

Lon / 2° 35' 0" E

1–9 Mar.; 23–26 June; 27 Sept.–5 Oct.

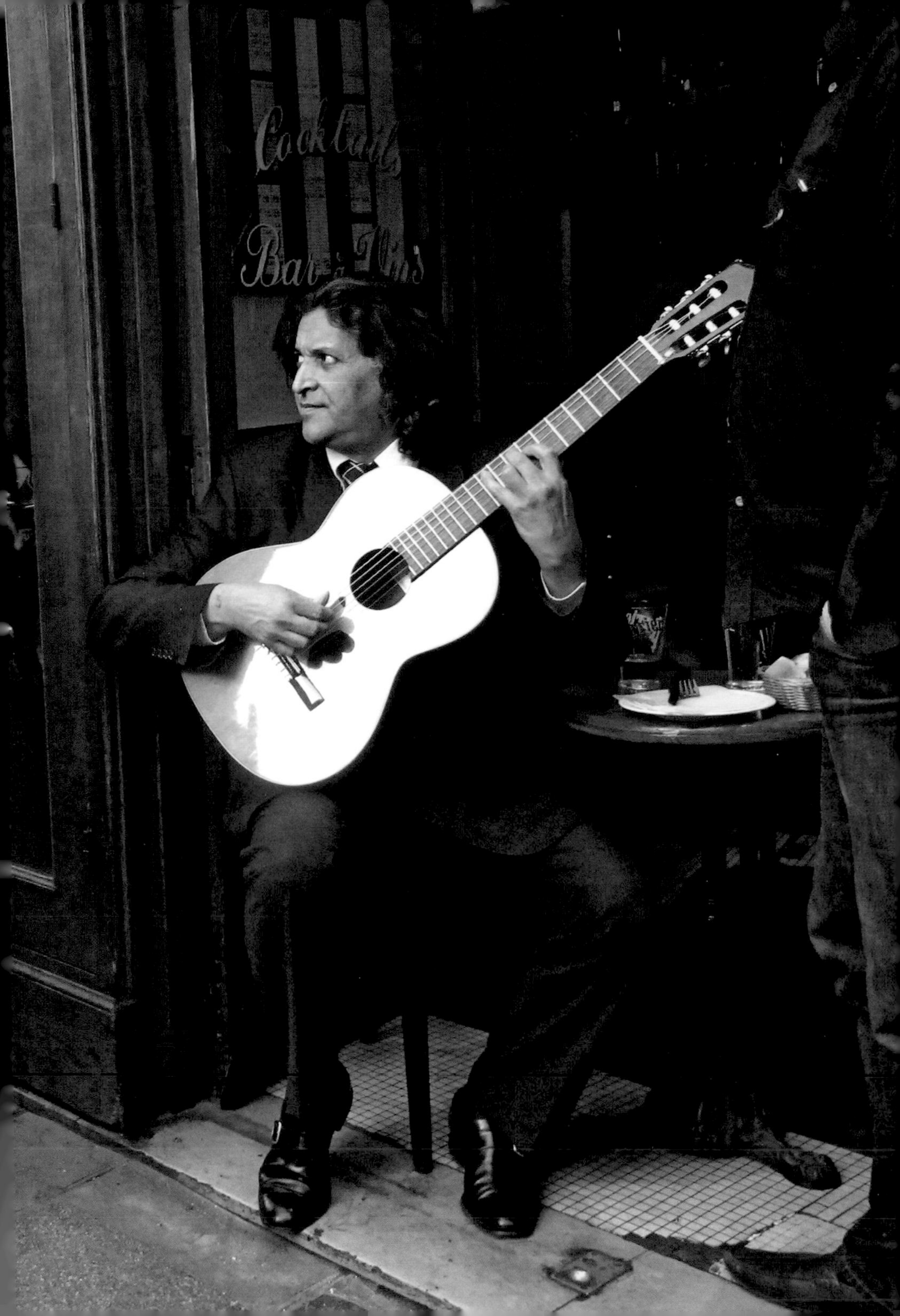

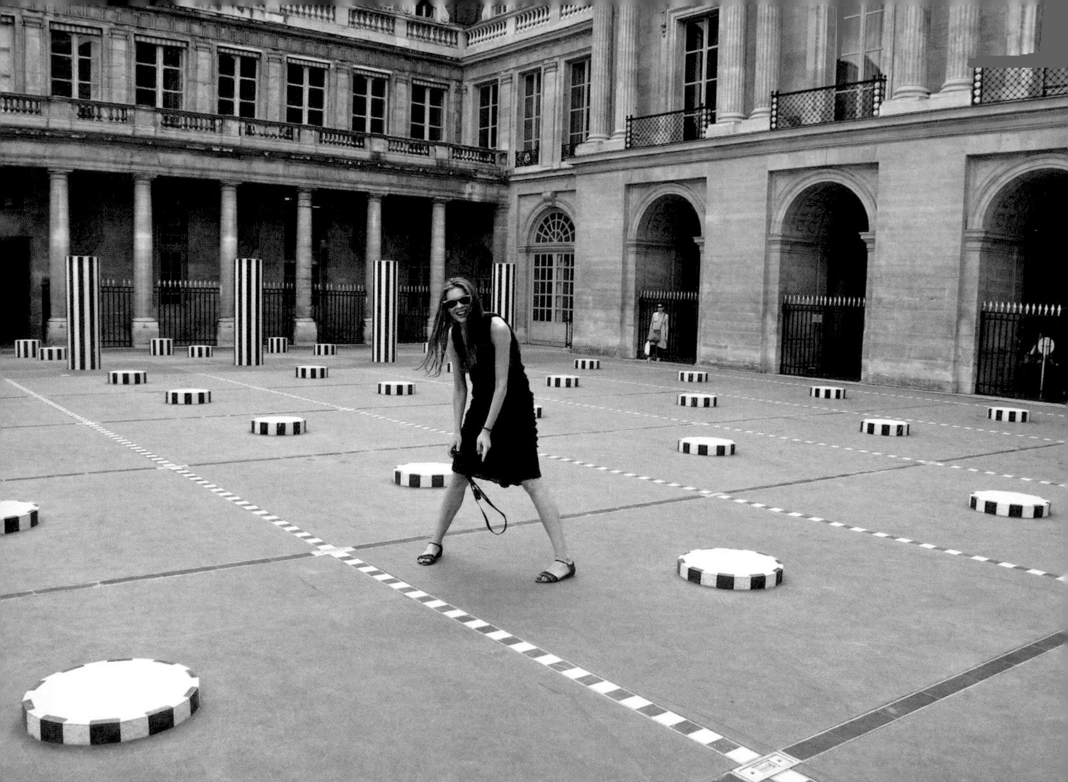

“The paradox is that in the country that invented the fashion industry as we know it, appearance is not actually that important. In a materialist world where appearance dictates status, France is one of the only places where your intellectual achievements are just as important – often even more so – than your personal style. Paris is such a great place for ideas: wherever you go, you can find someone willing to discuss any topic. But once Fashion Week arrives, it's another story: the fashion circus comes to town and Paris is not Paris anymore. It's a new phenomenon, fashion-week tourism, where socialites and wannabes come to be photographed by street-style bloggers. There are a lot of people who, when I meet them at Paris Fashion Week, are wearing the most amazing, daring outfits ever, but when I see them again in their own countries they say 'Oh no, I couldn't wear that here'. It's like the Olympic Games of fashion. The fashion industry is in Paris, and there are big fashion houses and great shows that people come from all over the world to see, but actually I'm not sure that the fashion on the street itself is really very inspiring. People live with the cliché of Paris being the 'fashion capital', and I think this gets in the way of them finding their own exciting style. I find places like Stockholm and Sydney more interesting. In a lot of countries people equate appearance with coolness, so it's nice that in France it's usually more important to show your intellectual abilities.”

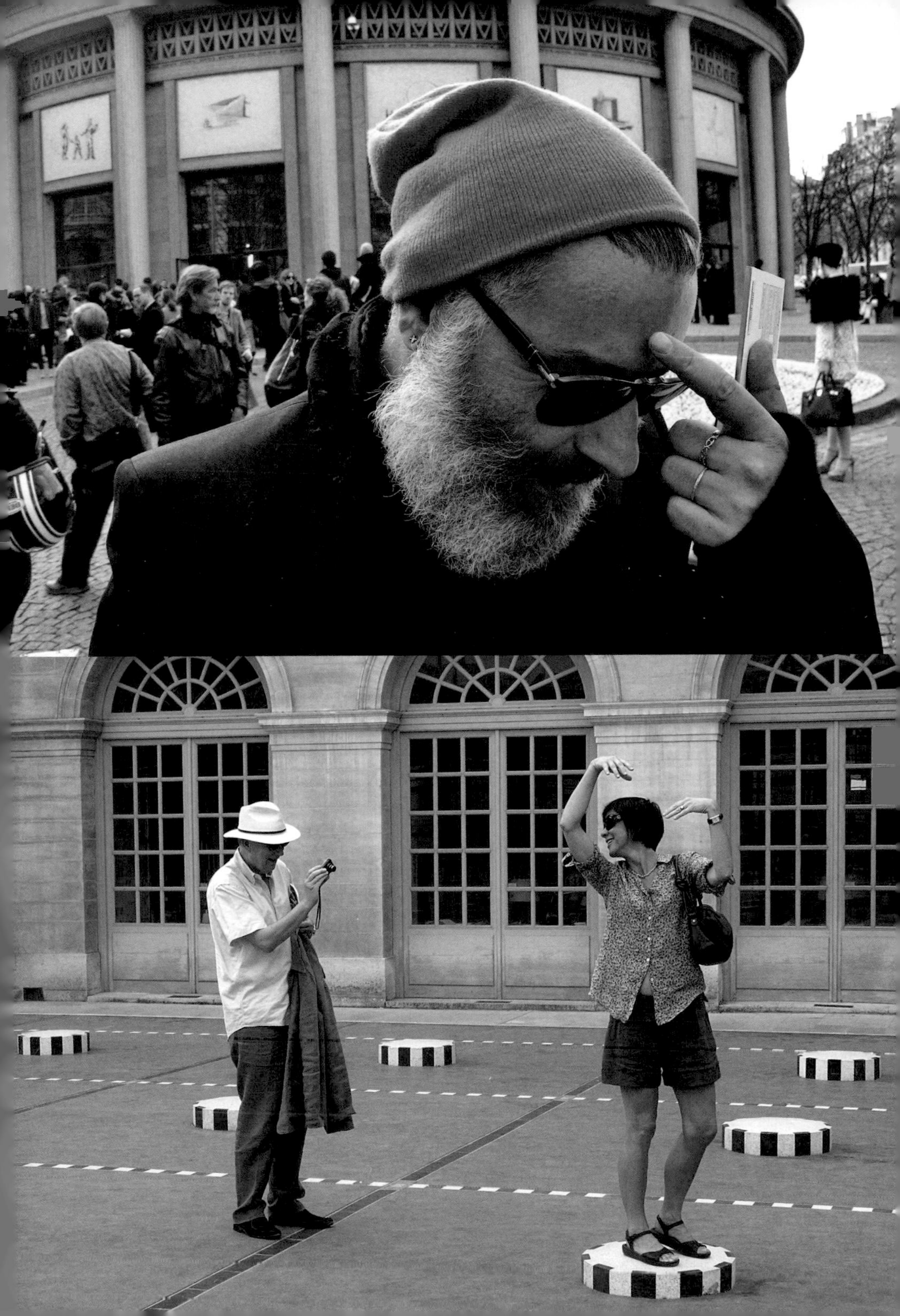

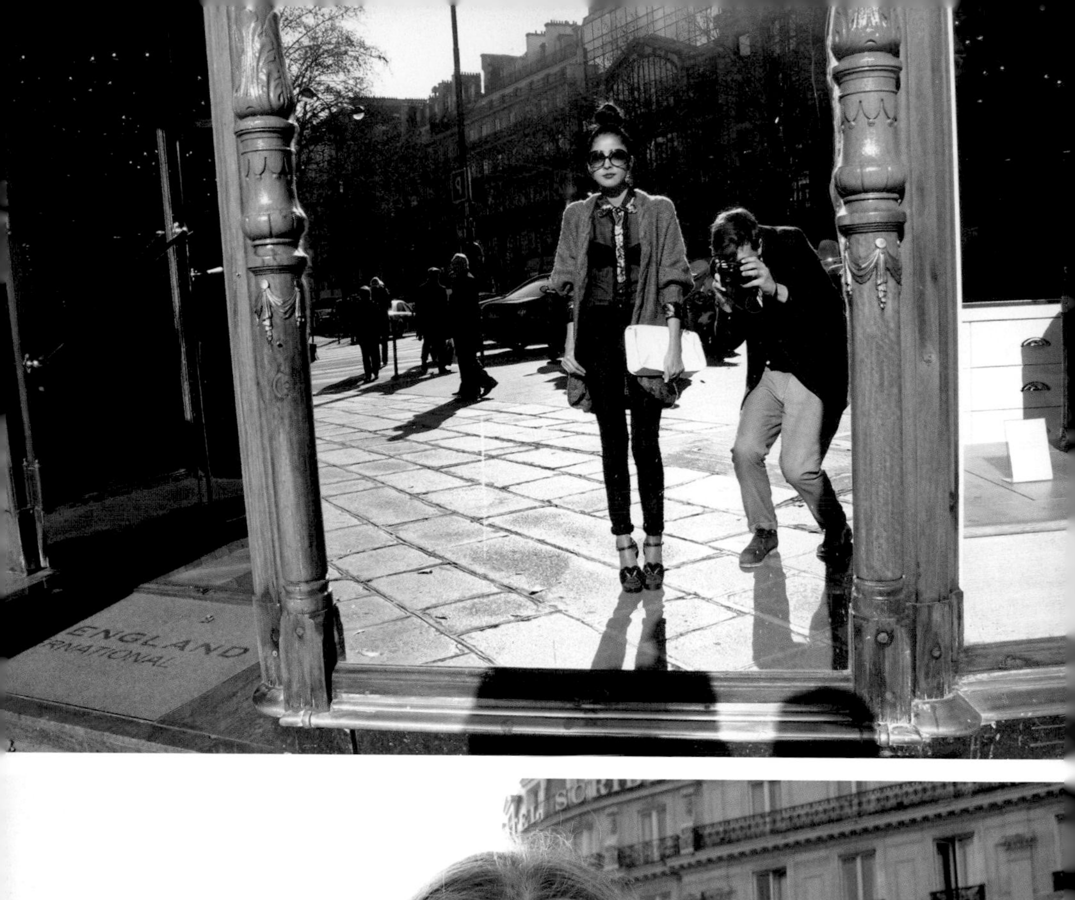
ENGLAND
RNATIONAL

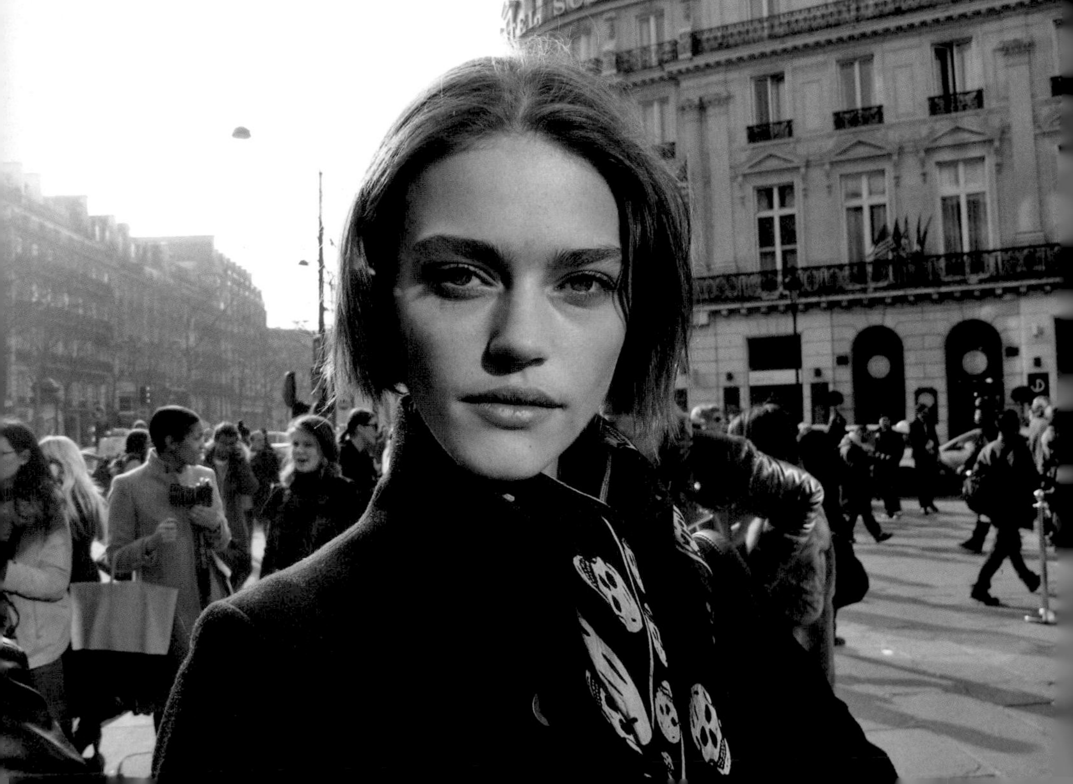

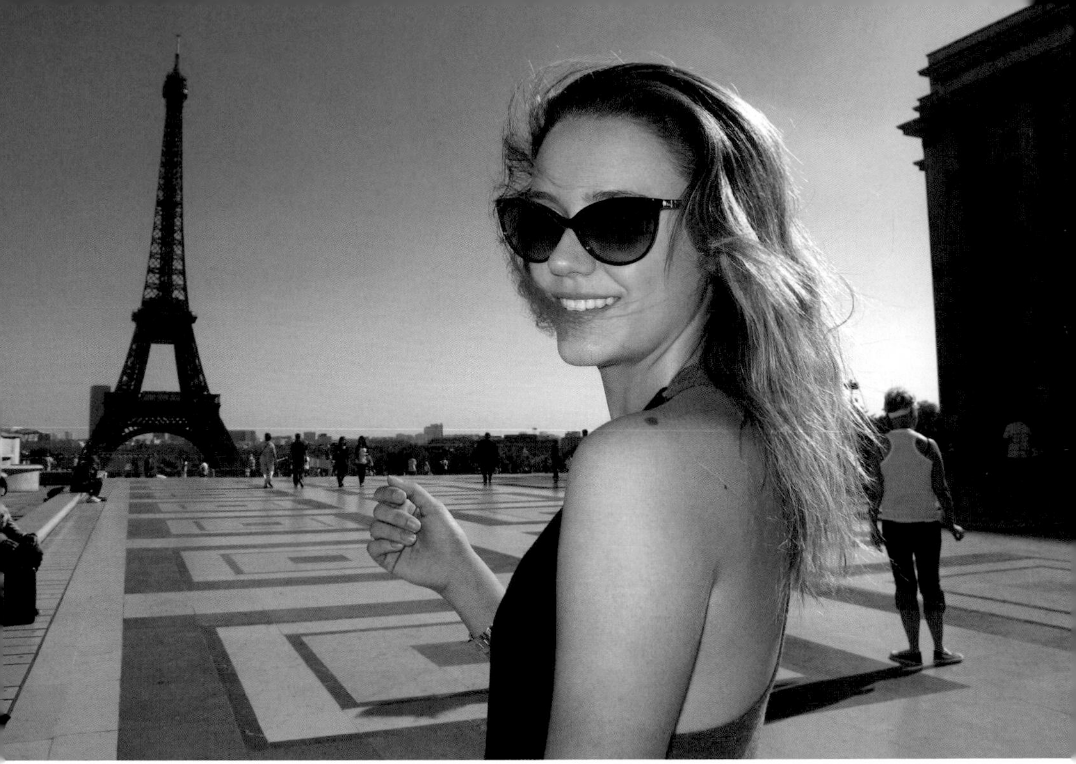

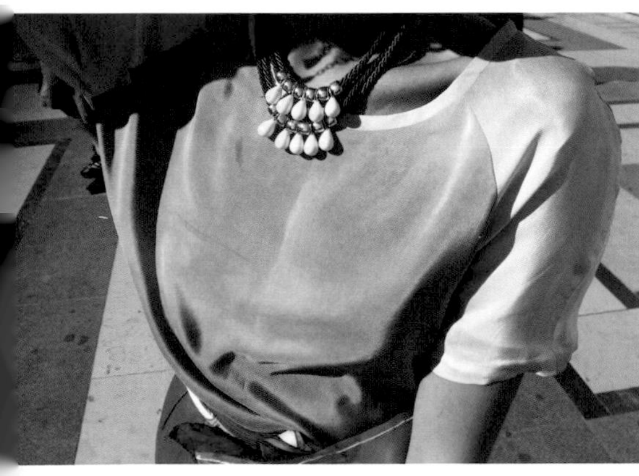

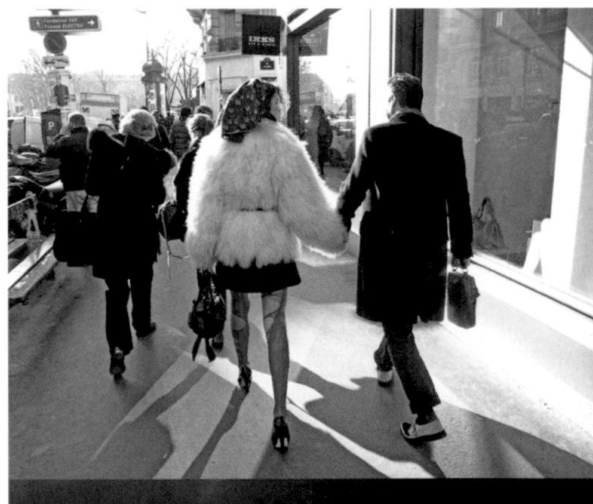

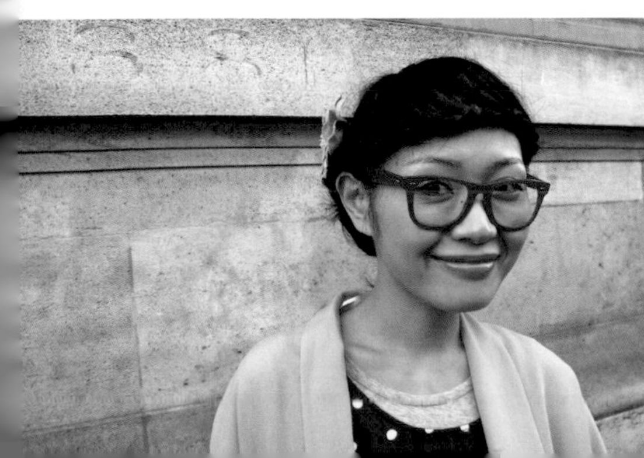

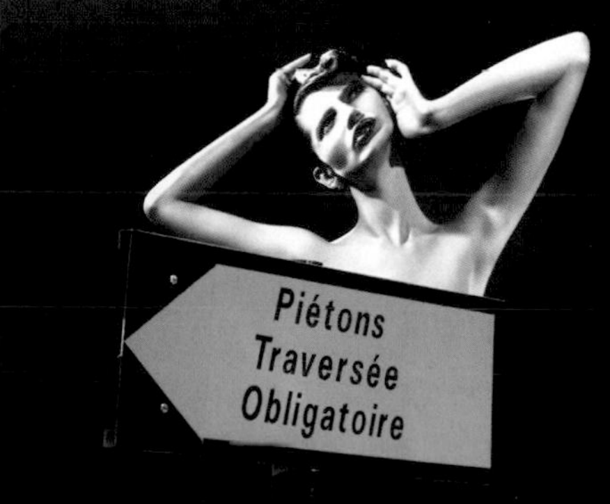
Piétons
Traversée
Obligatoire

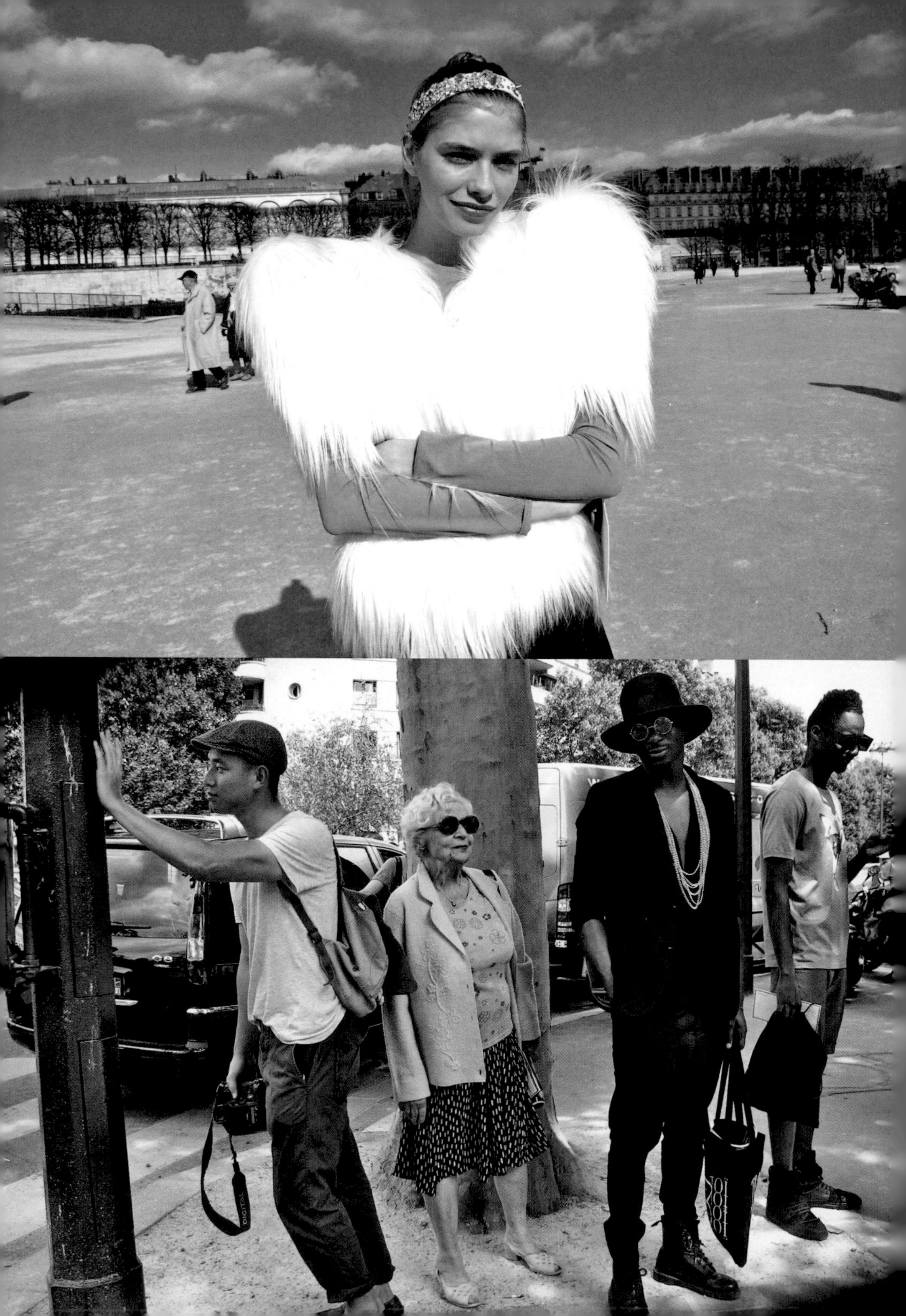
DIGITAL

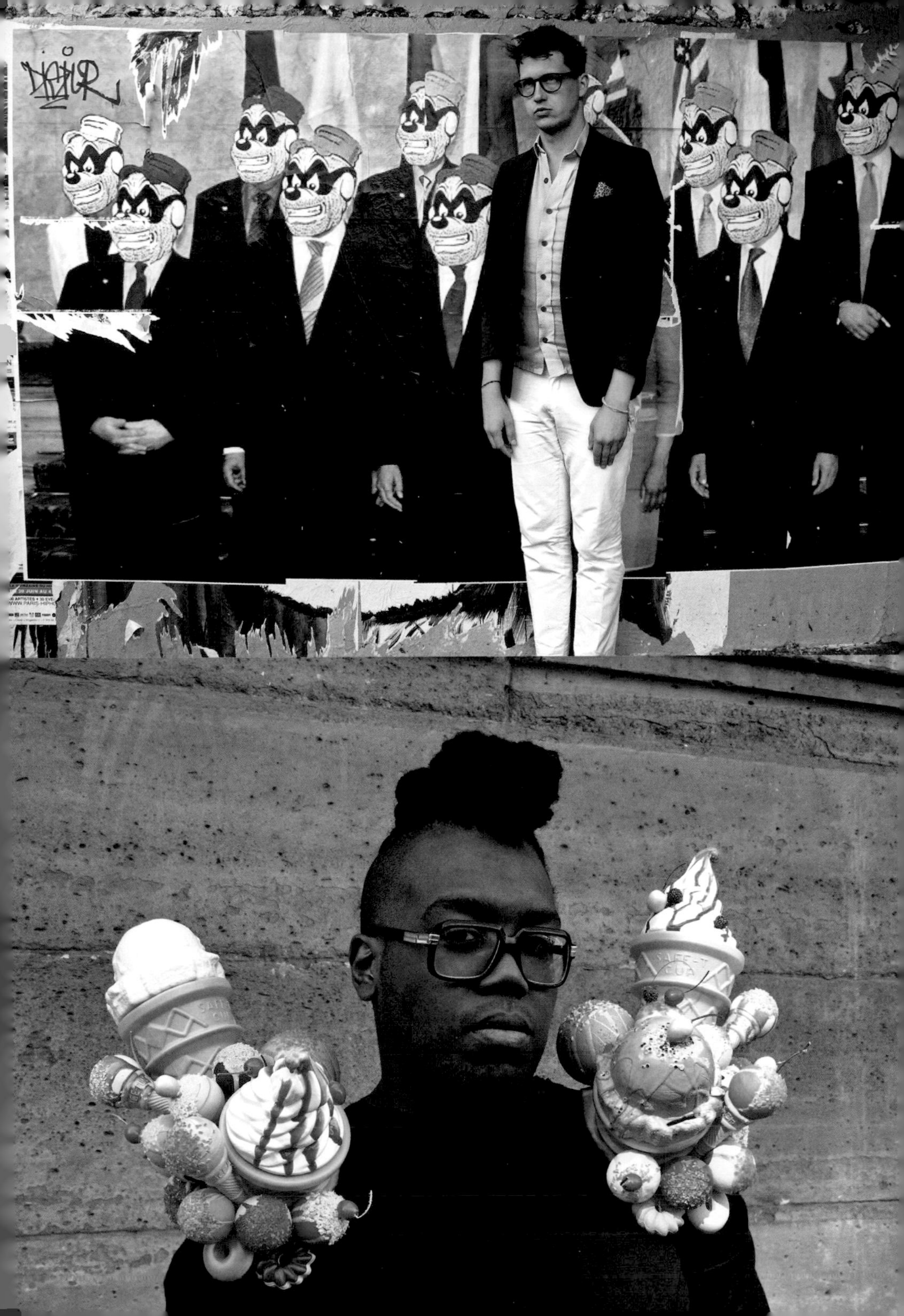

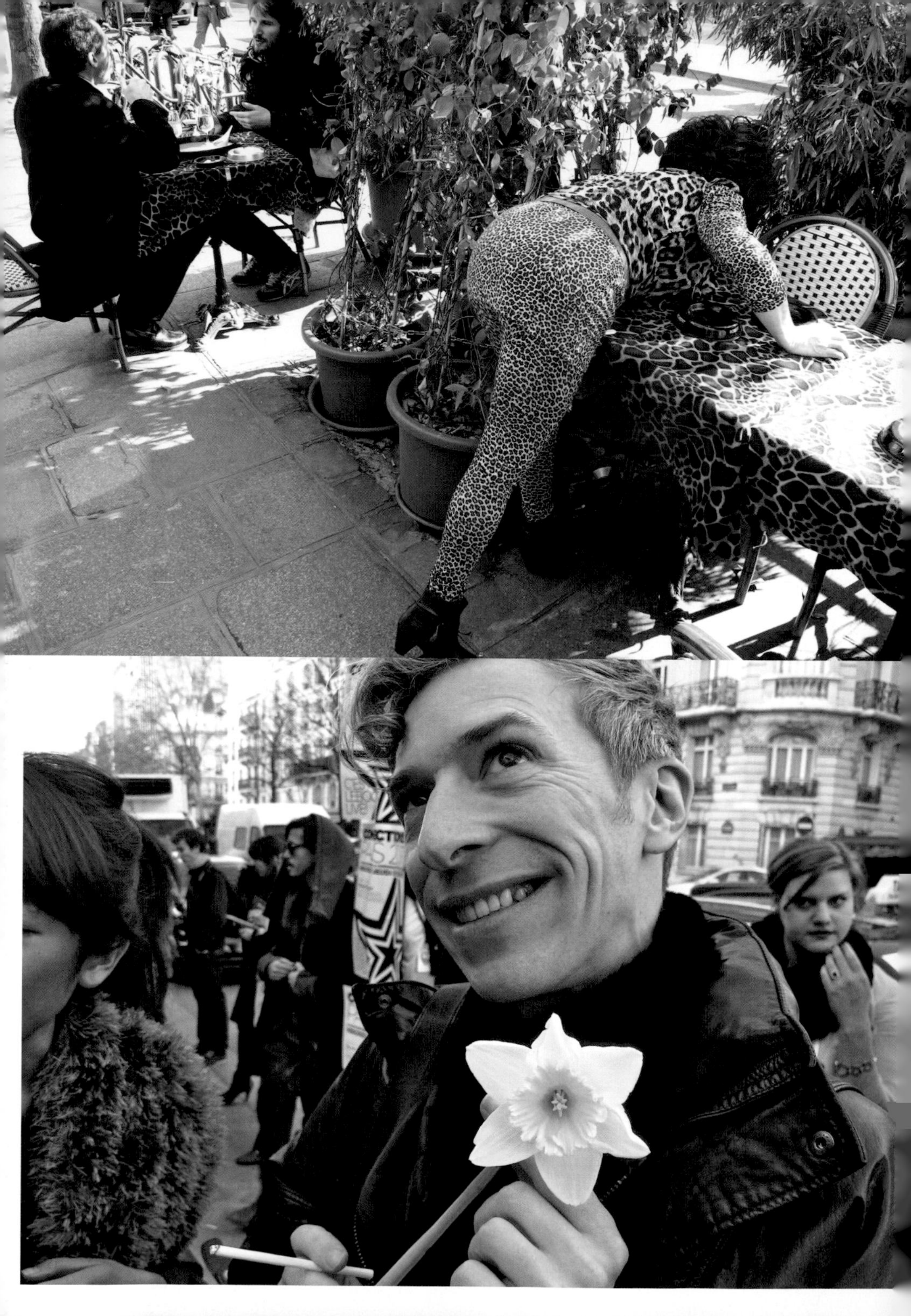

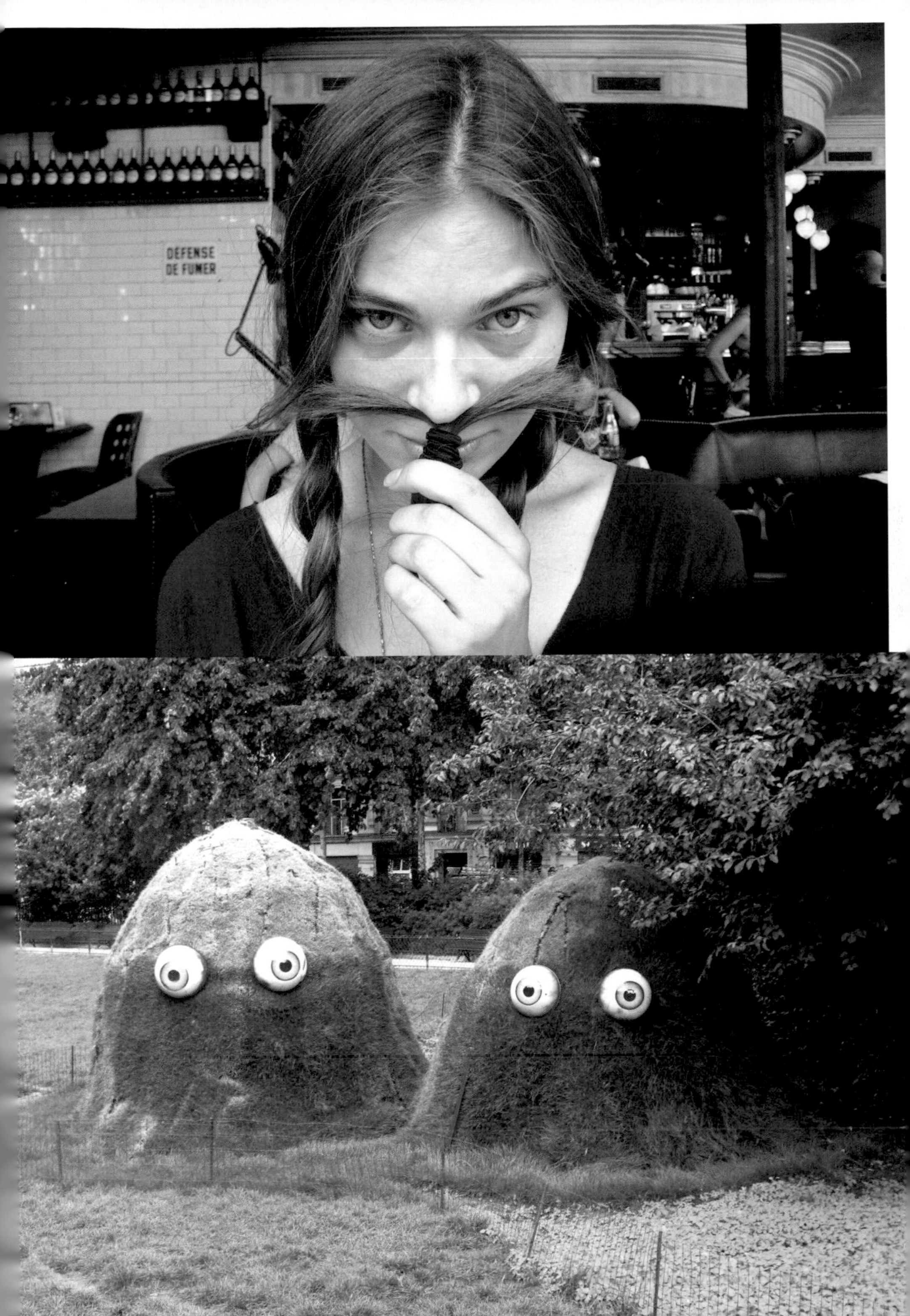
DÉFENSE
DE FUMER

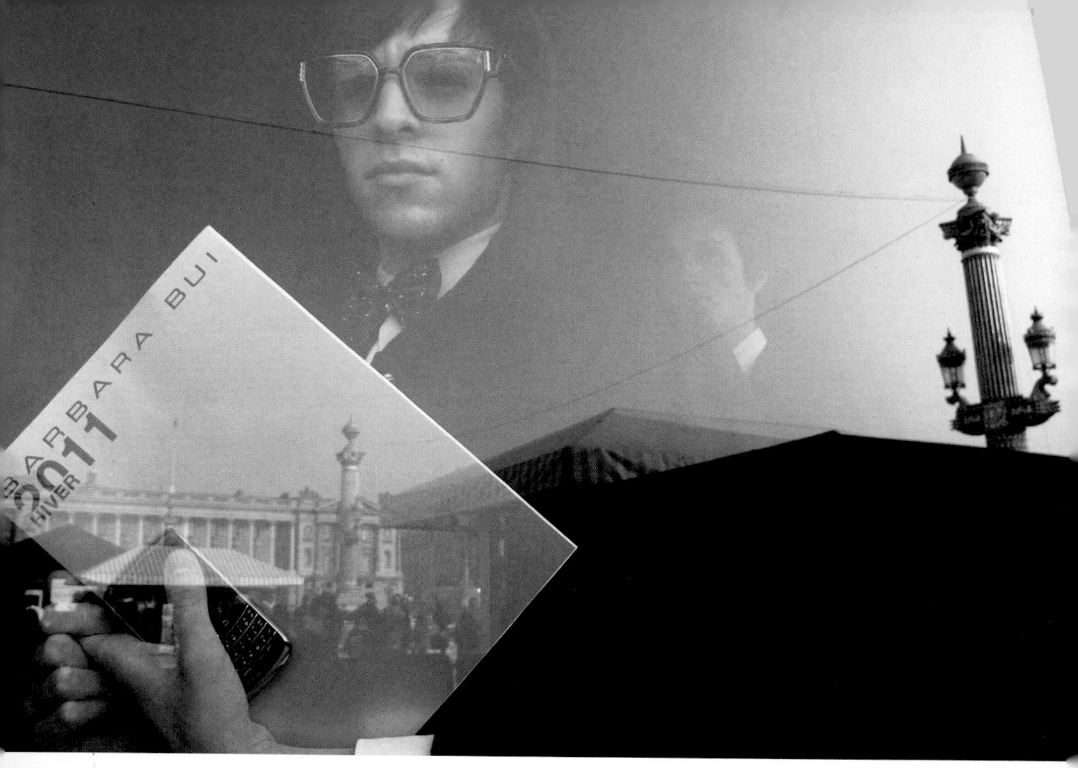

BARBARA BUI
2011
HIVER

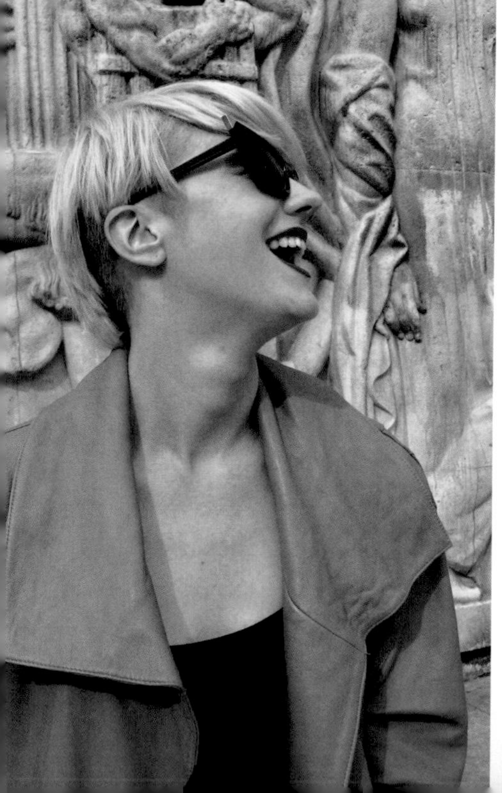

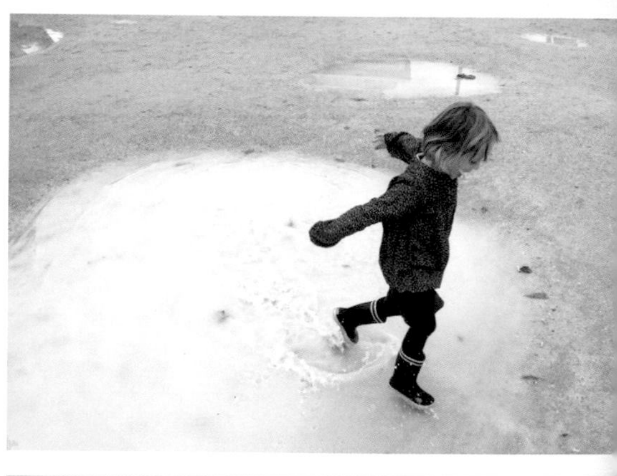

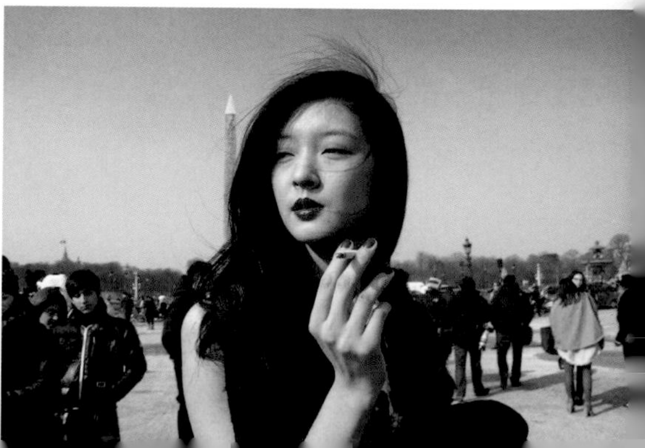

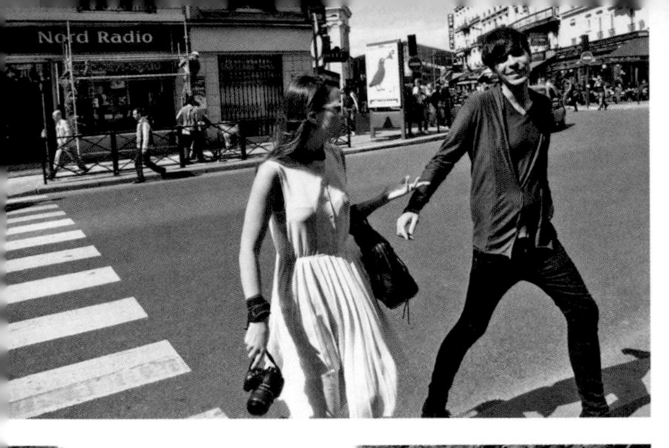
Nord Radio

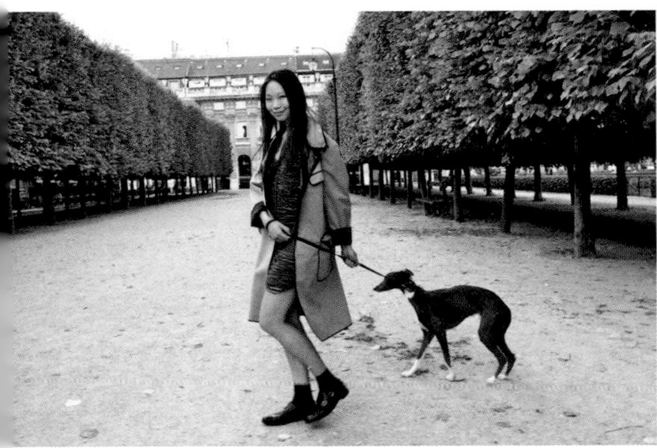

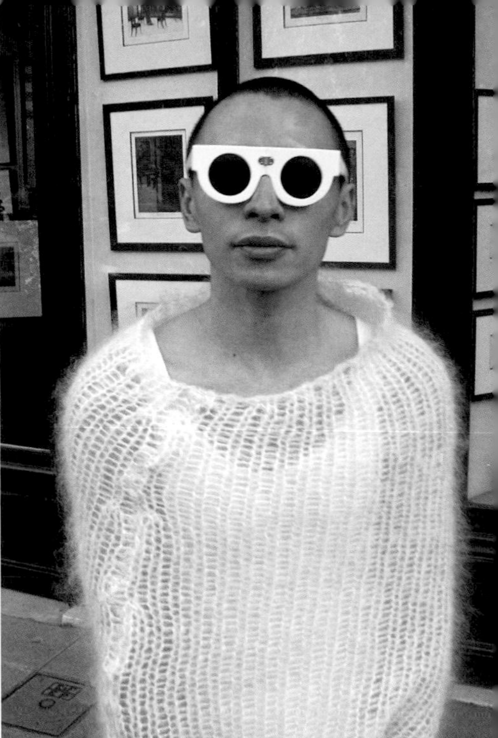

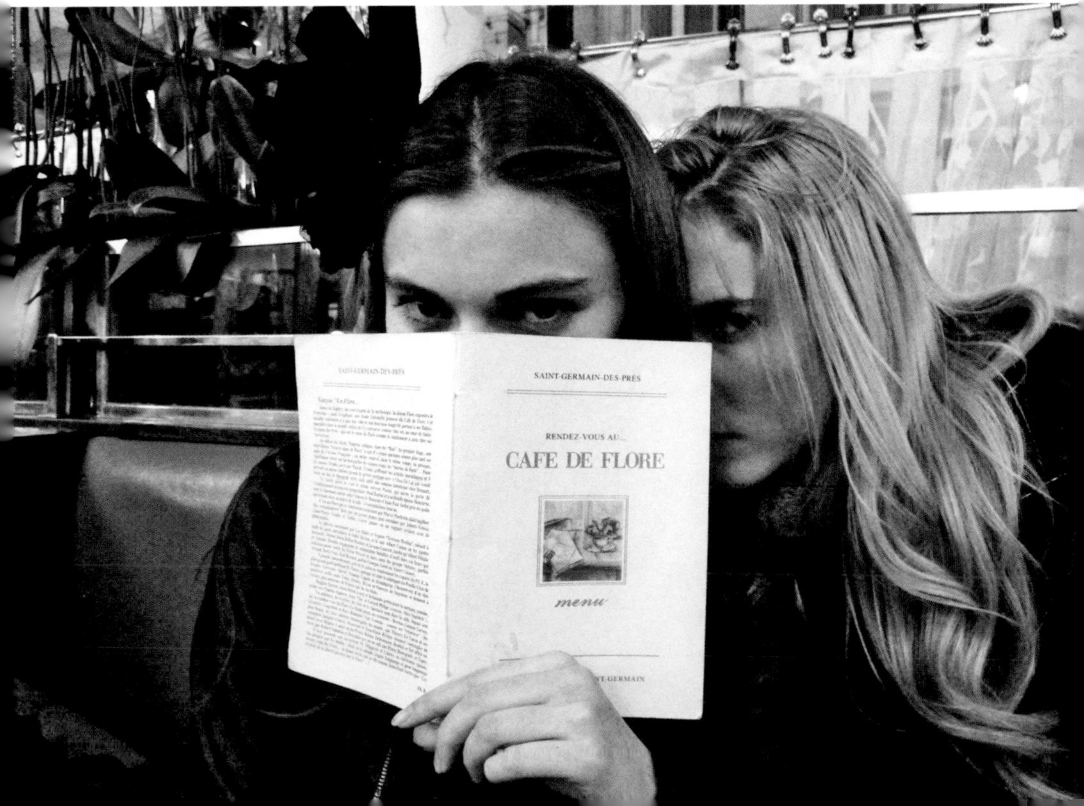

SAINT-GERMAIN-DES-PRÉS
RENDEZ-VOUS AU...
CAFE DE FLORE
menu

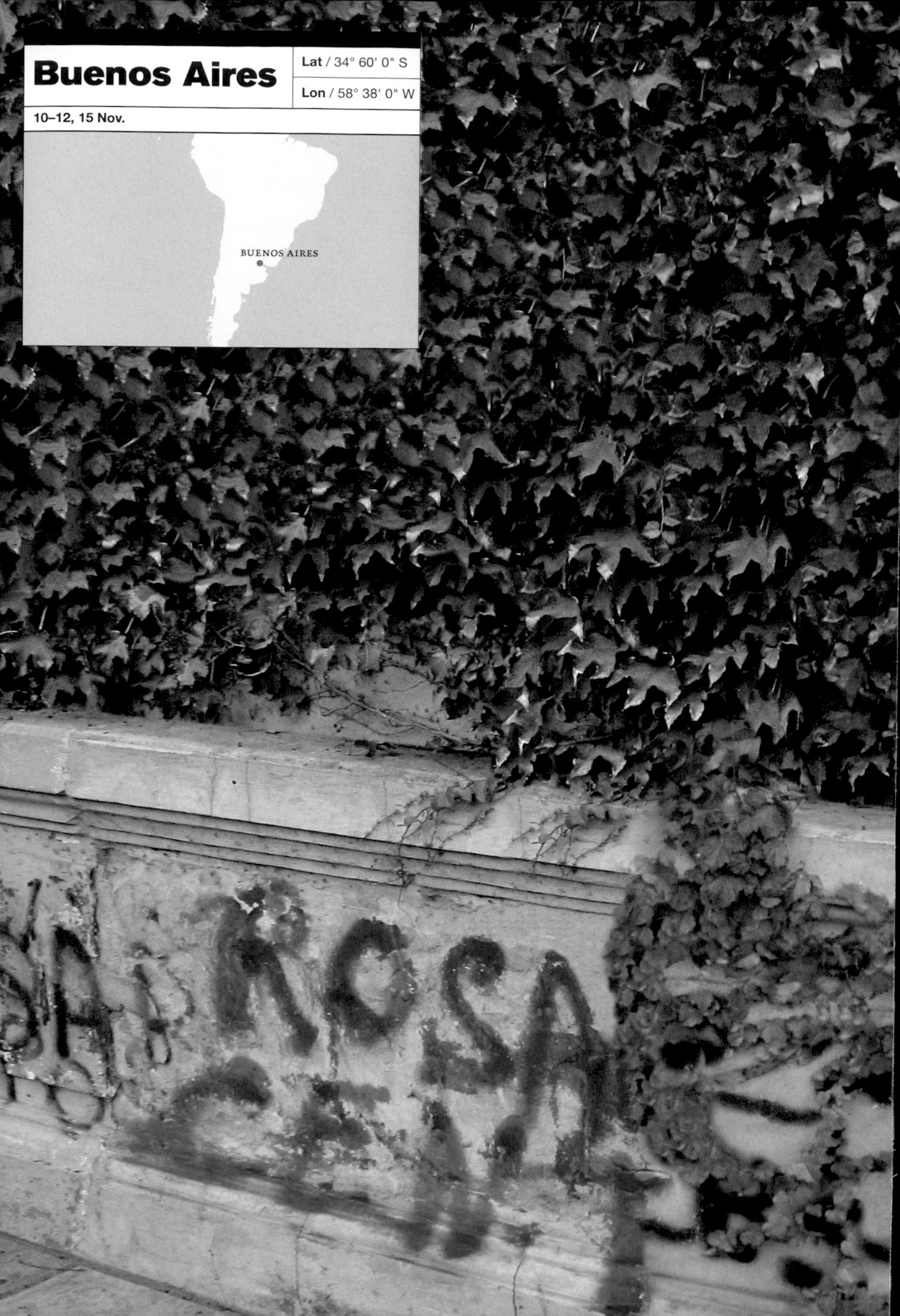
Buenos Aires
Lat / 34° 60' 0" S
Lon / 58° 38' 0" W
10–12, 15 Nov.
BUENOS AIRES
ROSA

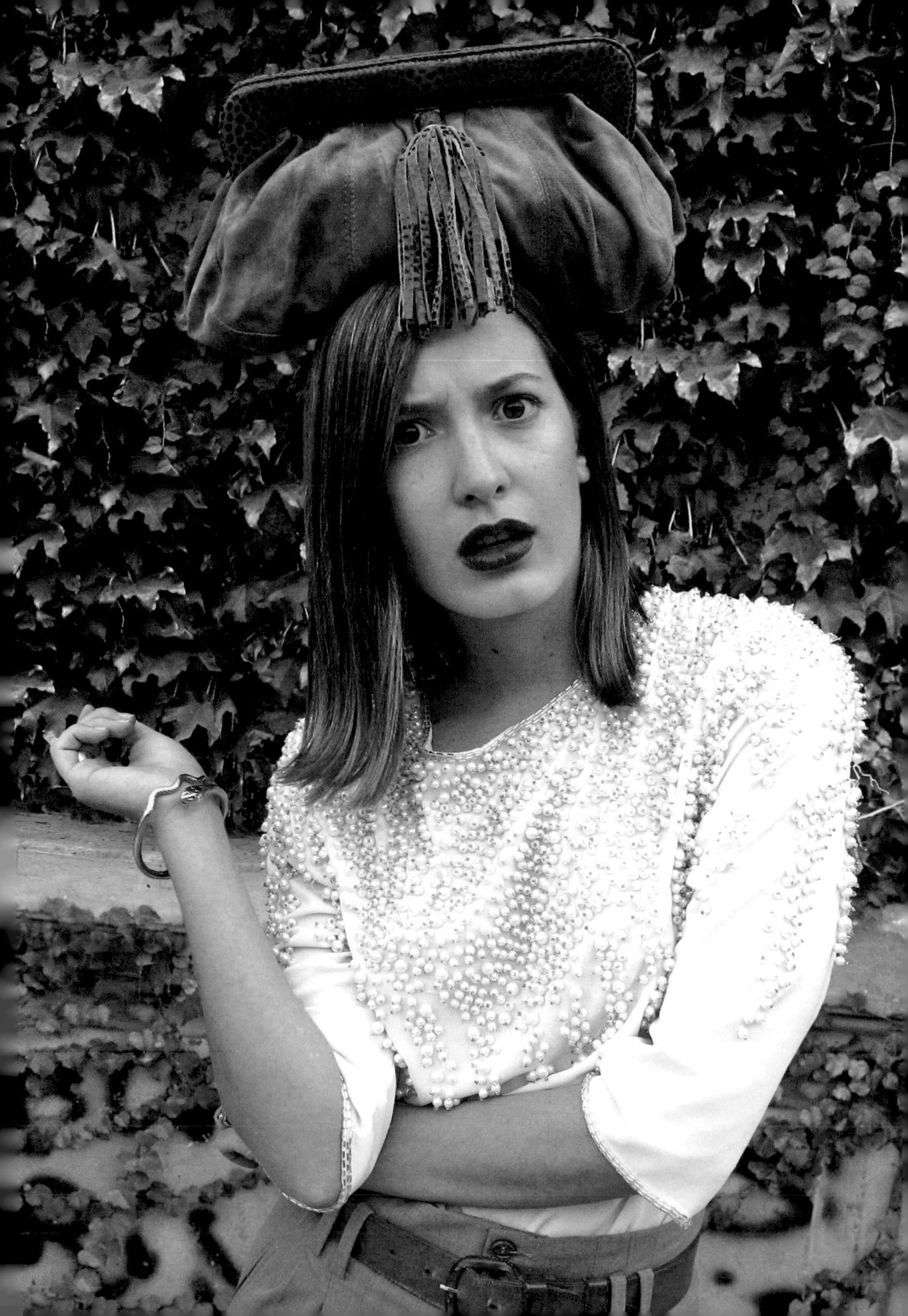

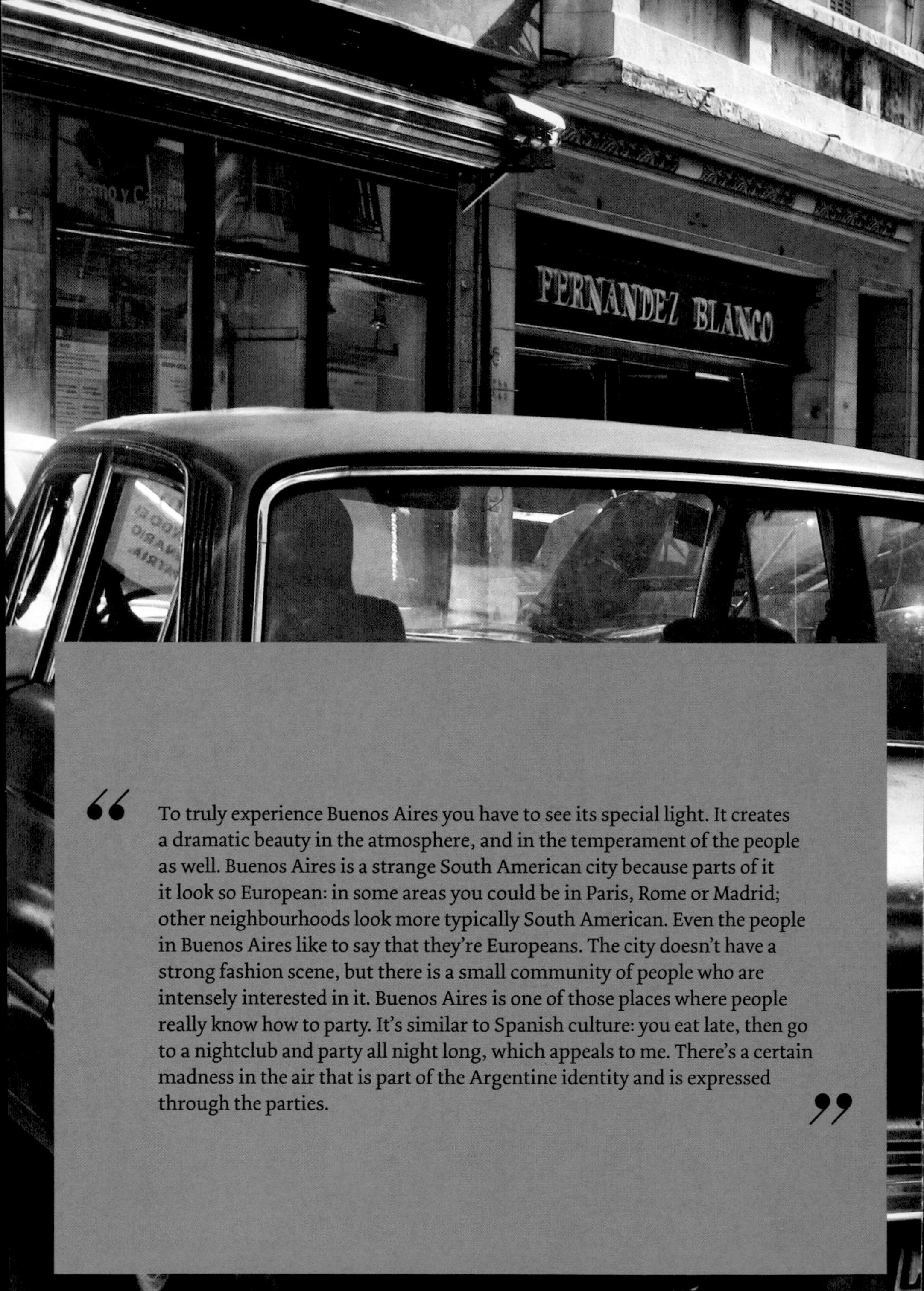

“To truly experience Buenos Aires you have to see its special light. It creates a dramatic beauty in the atmosphere, and in the temperament of the people as well. Buenos Aires is a strange South American city because parts of it it look so European: in some areas you could be in Paris, Rome or Madrid; other neighbourhoods look more typically South American. Even the people in Buenos Aires like to say that they’re Europeans. The city doesn’t have a strong fashion scene, but there is a small community of people who are intensely interested in it. Buenos Aires is one of those places where people really know how to party. It’s similar to Spanish culture: you eat late, then go to a nightclub and party all night long, which appeals to me. There’s a certain madness in the air that is part of the Argentine identity and is expressed through the parties.”

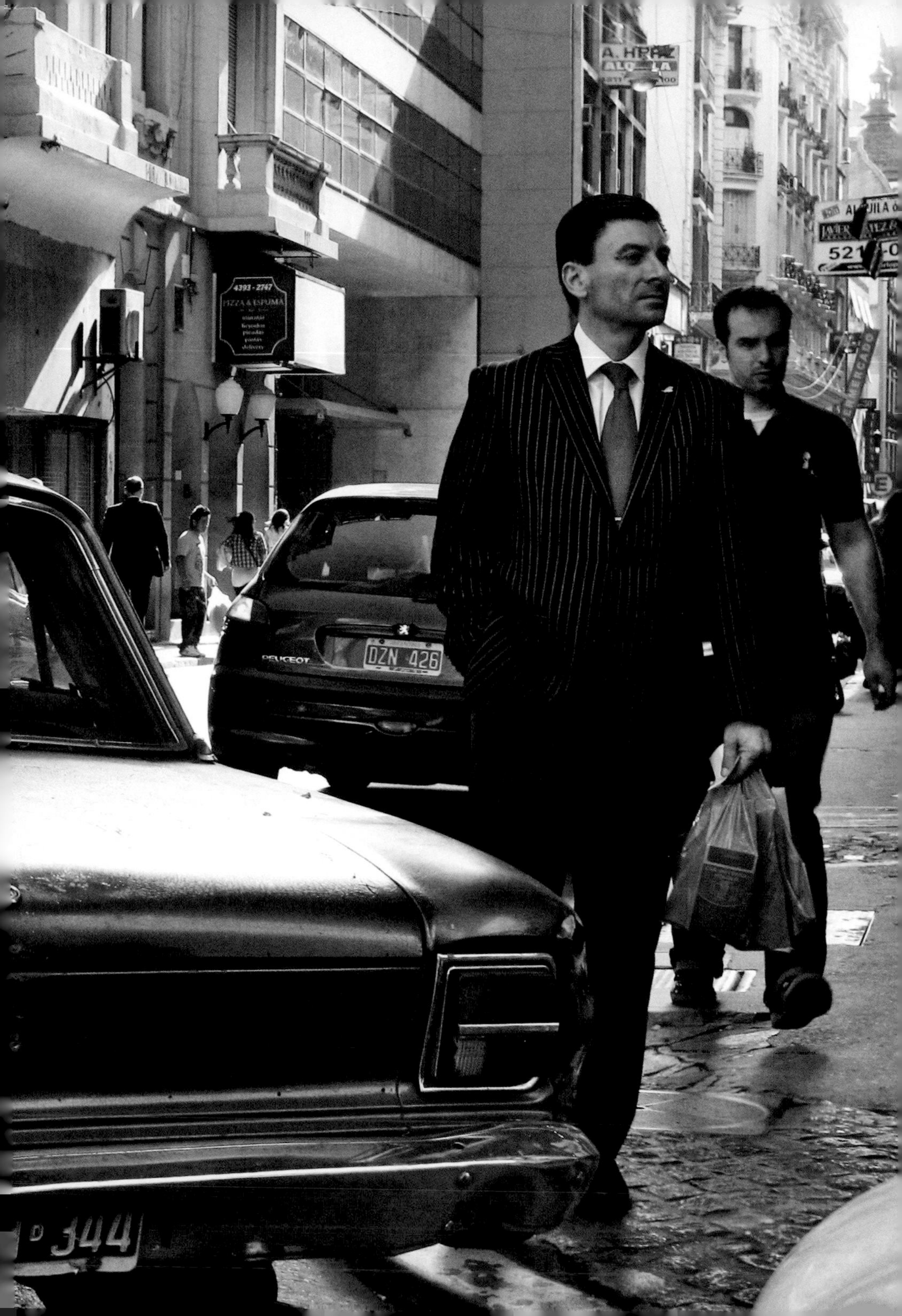
4393 - 2747
PIZZA & ESPUMA
PEUGEOT
DZN 426

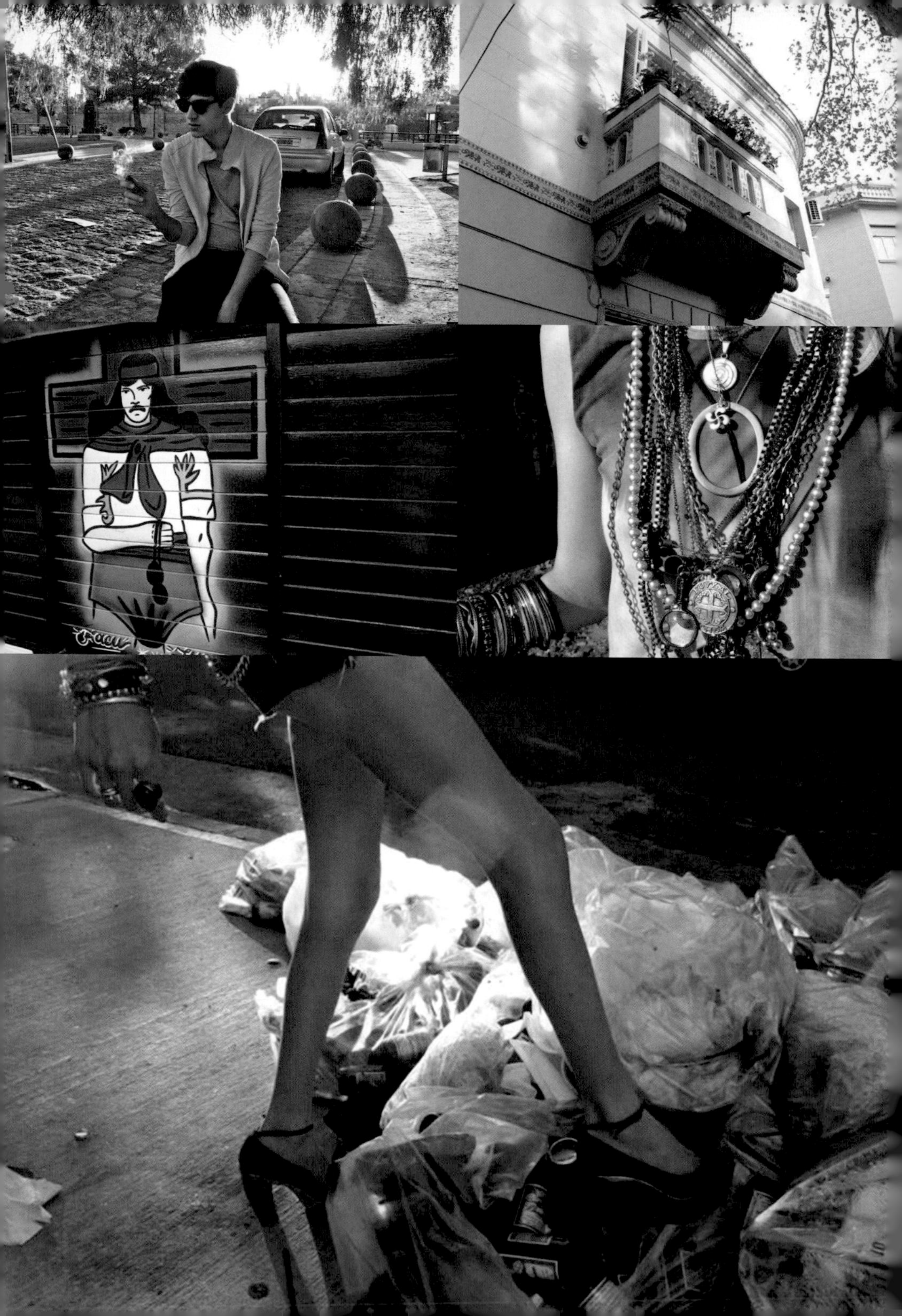

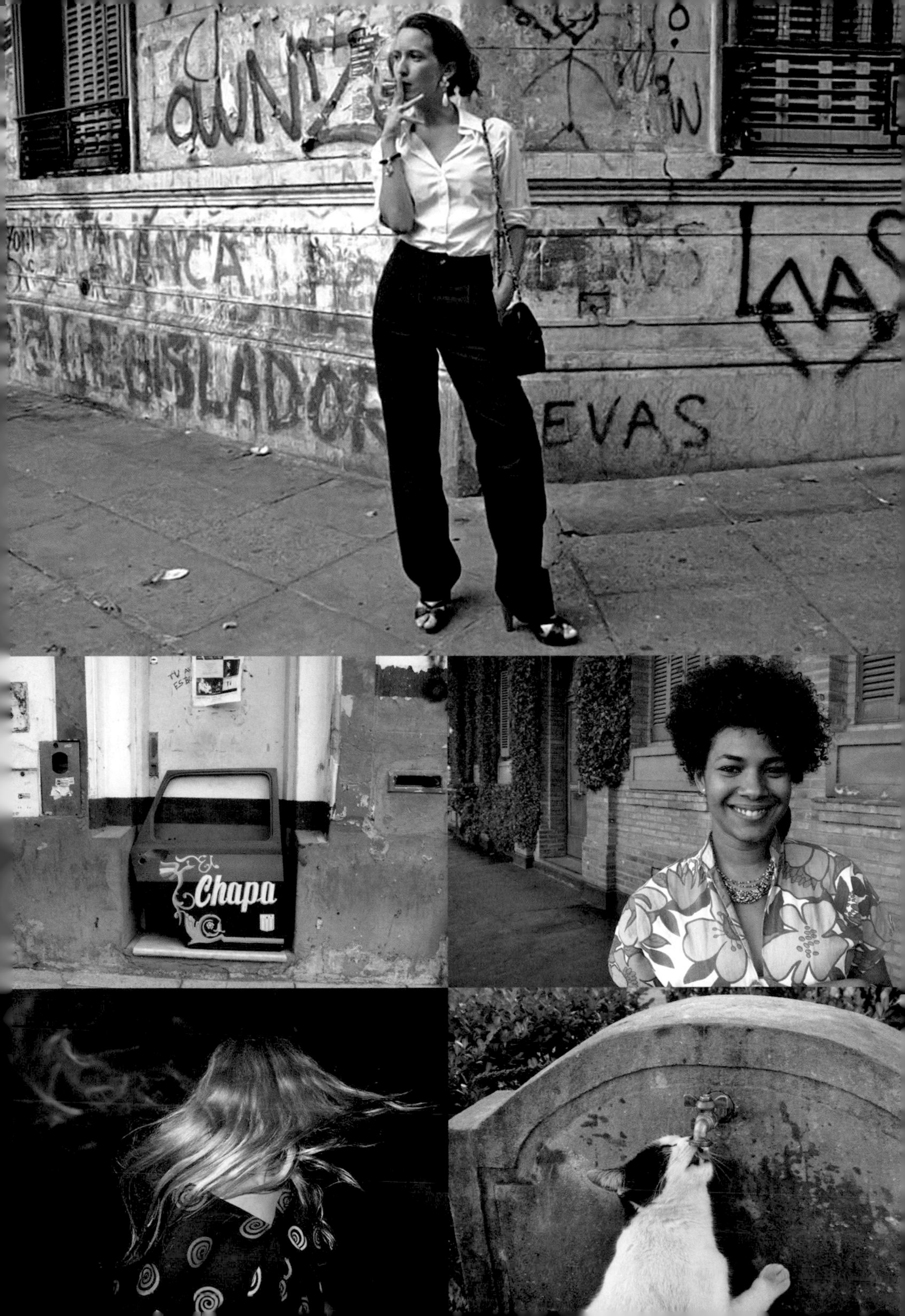
EVAS
El Chapa

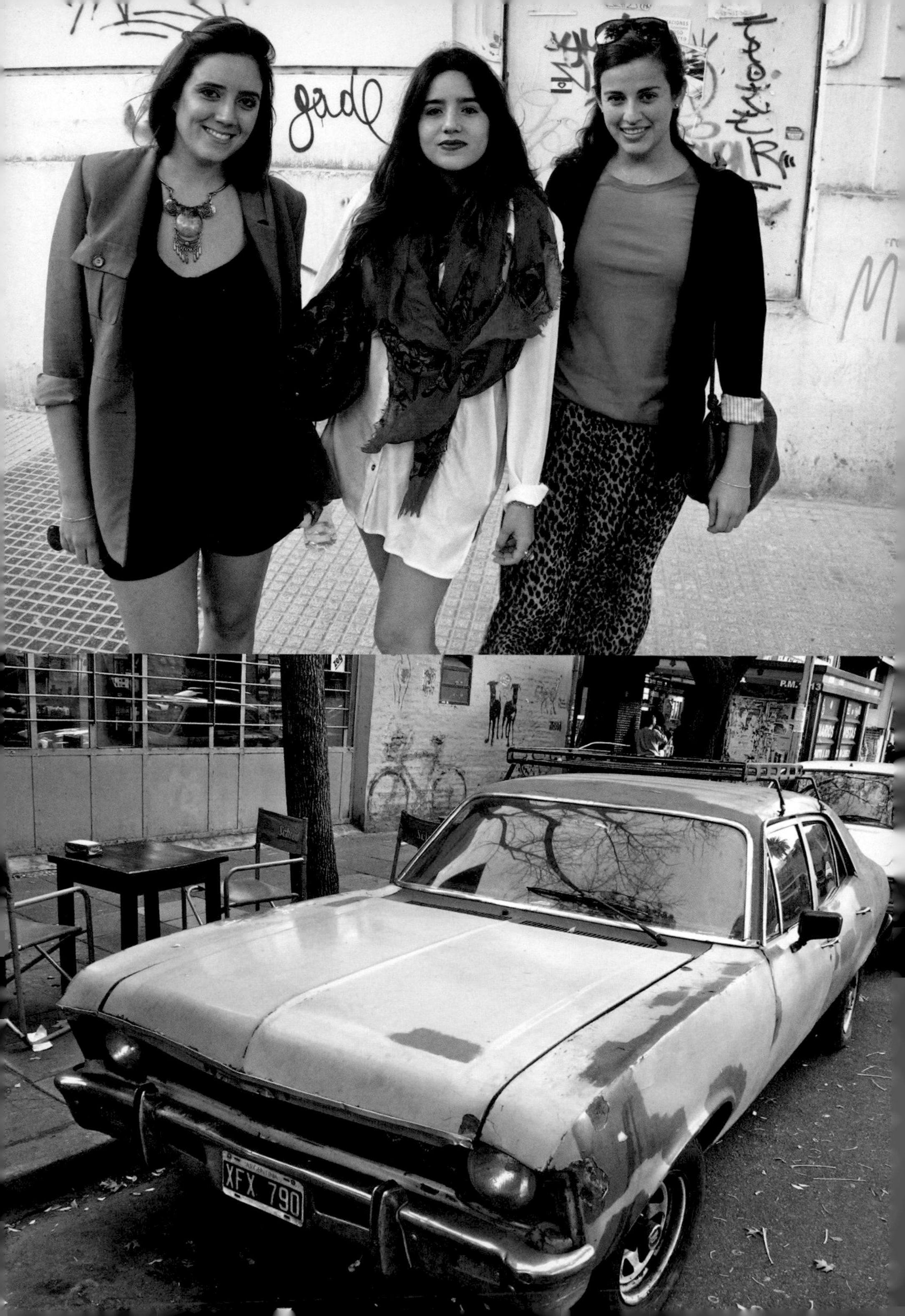
XFX 790

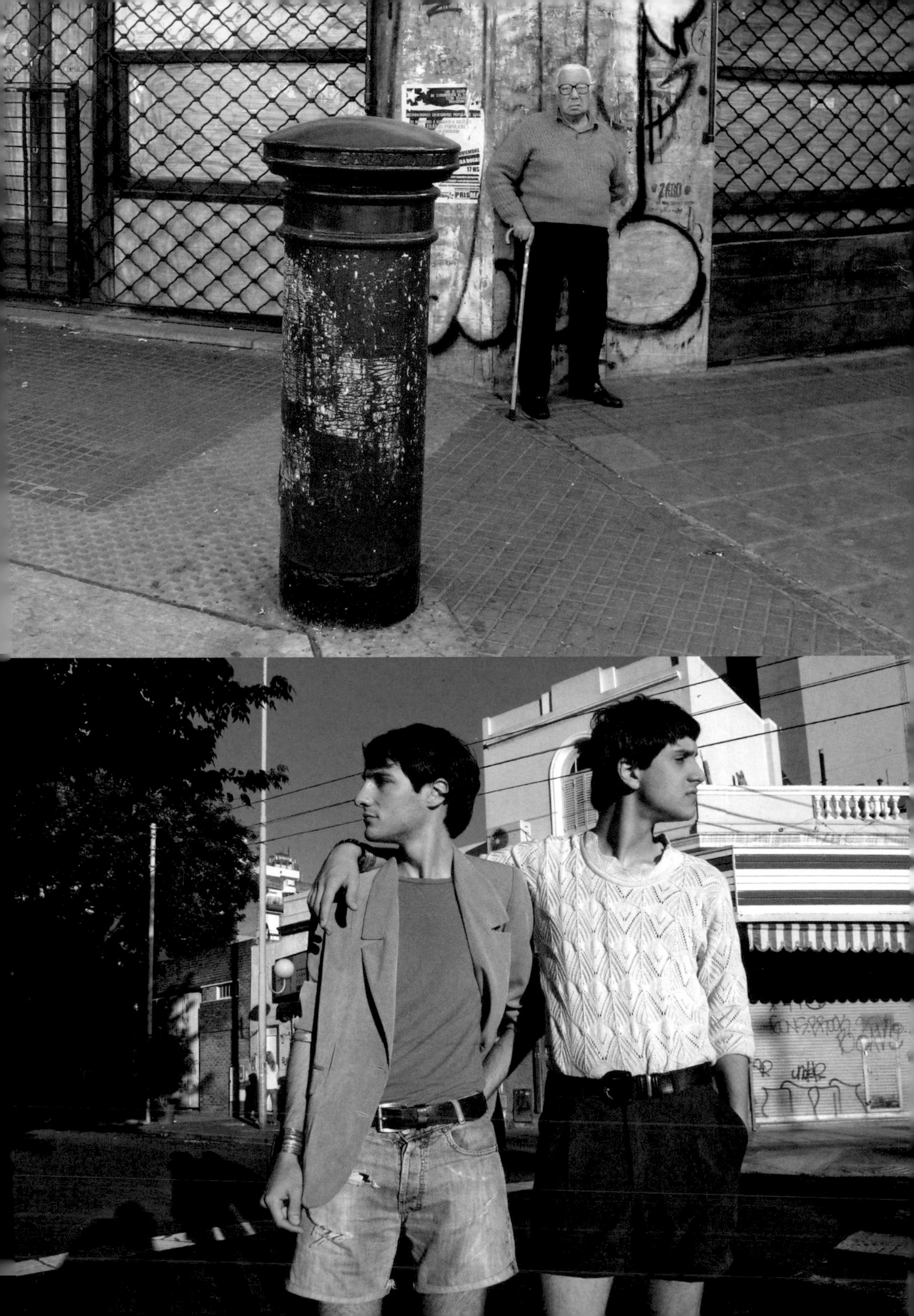

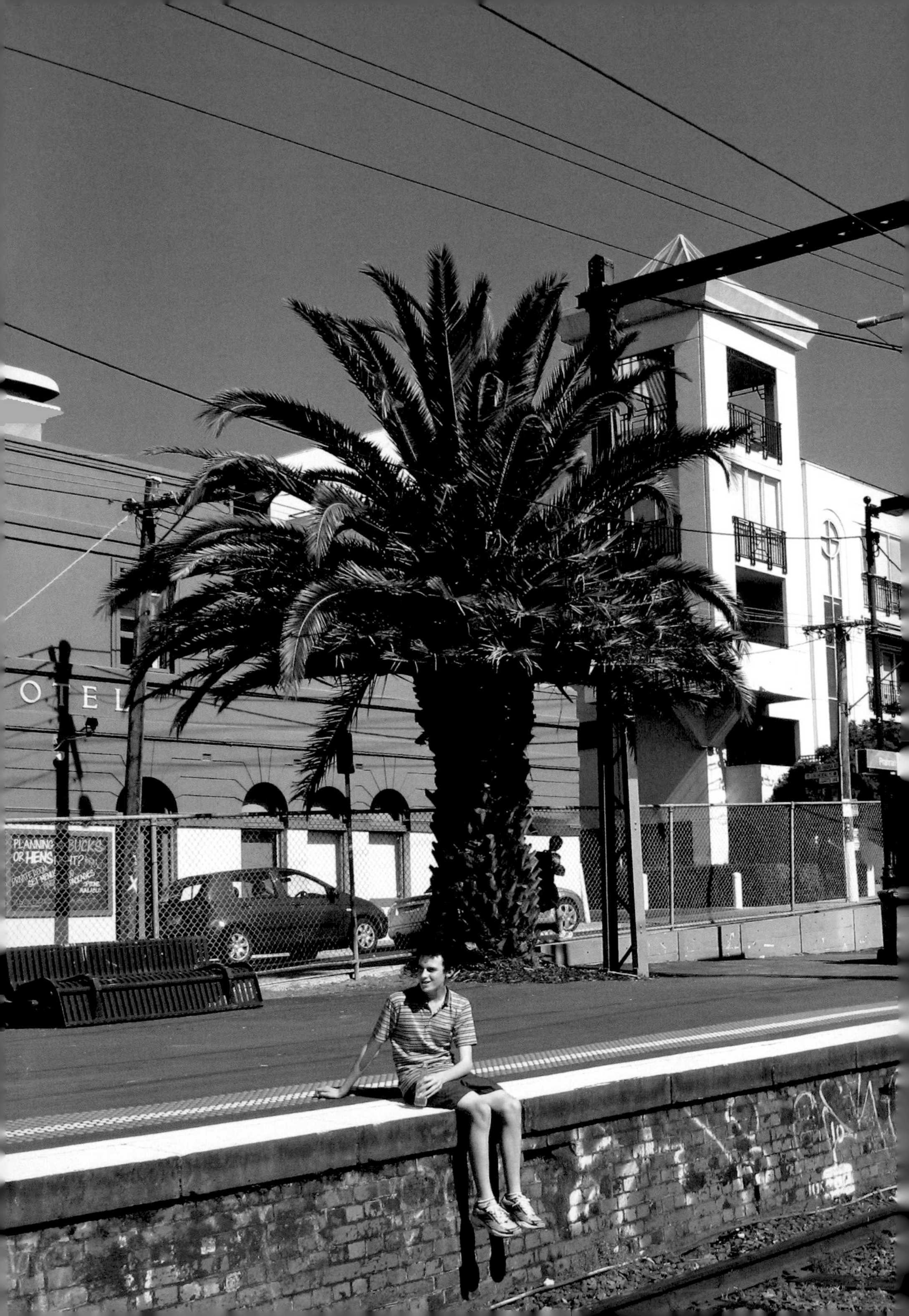
OTEL
PLANNING BUCKS
OR HENS
PACKAGES

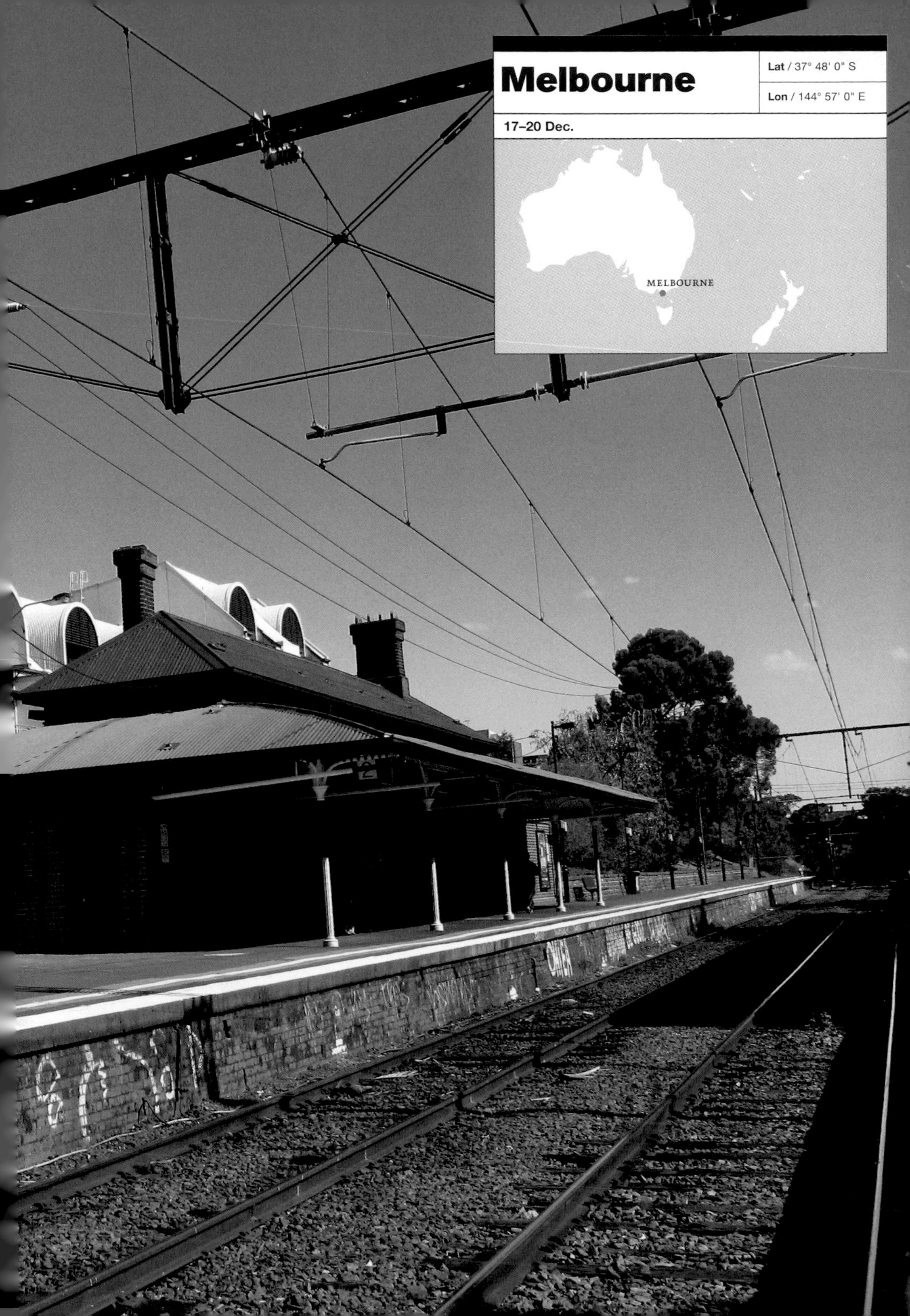
Melbourne
Lat / 37° 48' 0" S
Lon / 144° 57' 0" E
17–20 Dec.
MELBOURNE

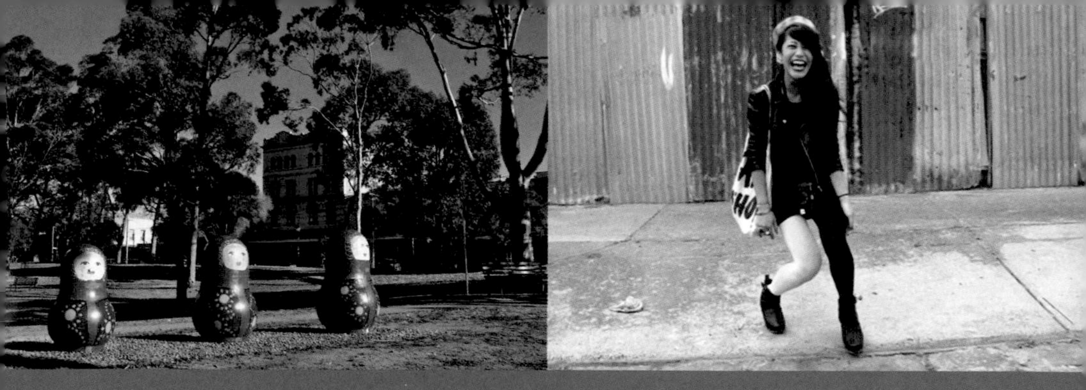

“When I visited Melbourne for the first time, I was shocked that after spending 24 hours on an aeroplane, I found myself in what on the surface looked like just another European city. The centre, especially, is filled with the same kind of Victorian buildings you see in London. But I quickly discovered the Australian twist. There is a relaxed New World vibe, lots of parks with stands of original bushland and exotic-looking animals everywhere. For me, the houses in the suburbs represent thc quintessence of aesthetically pleasant Melbourne more than its historic city centre. Melbourne is the capital of the state of Victoria and a major creative hub. Art, style and music are everyday obsessions for many locals. Melbourne counts hundreds of indie bands, and several of them have made it ‘overseas’ – one of my favourites is Cut Copy. The funny thing about people in Melbourne is that they’re constantly comparing their city to Sydney. As a visitor, you can easily be asked ‘Which city do you prefer?’ ten times a day, whereas in Sydney no one ever asks that. Melbourne, you are marvellous – there’s no need to ask me anymore!”

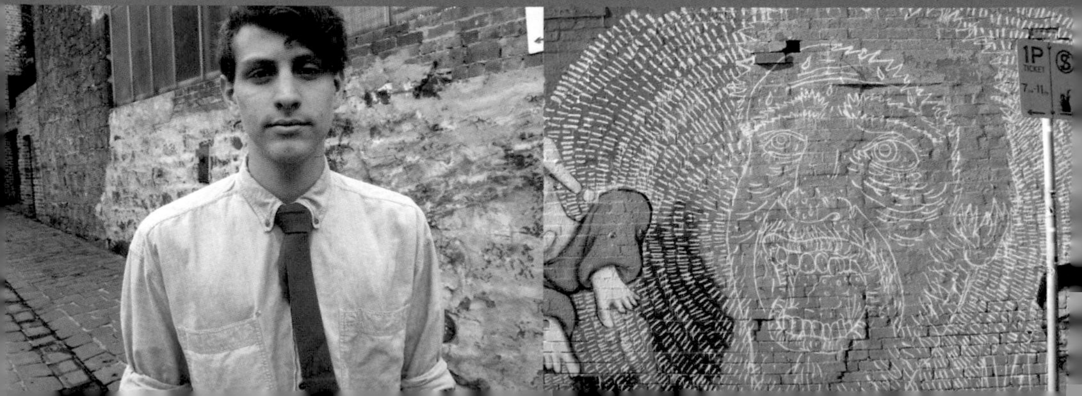

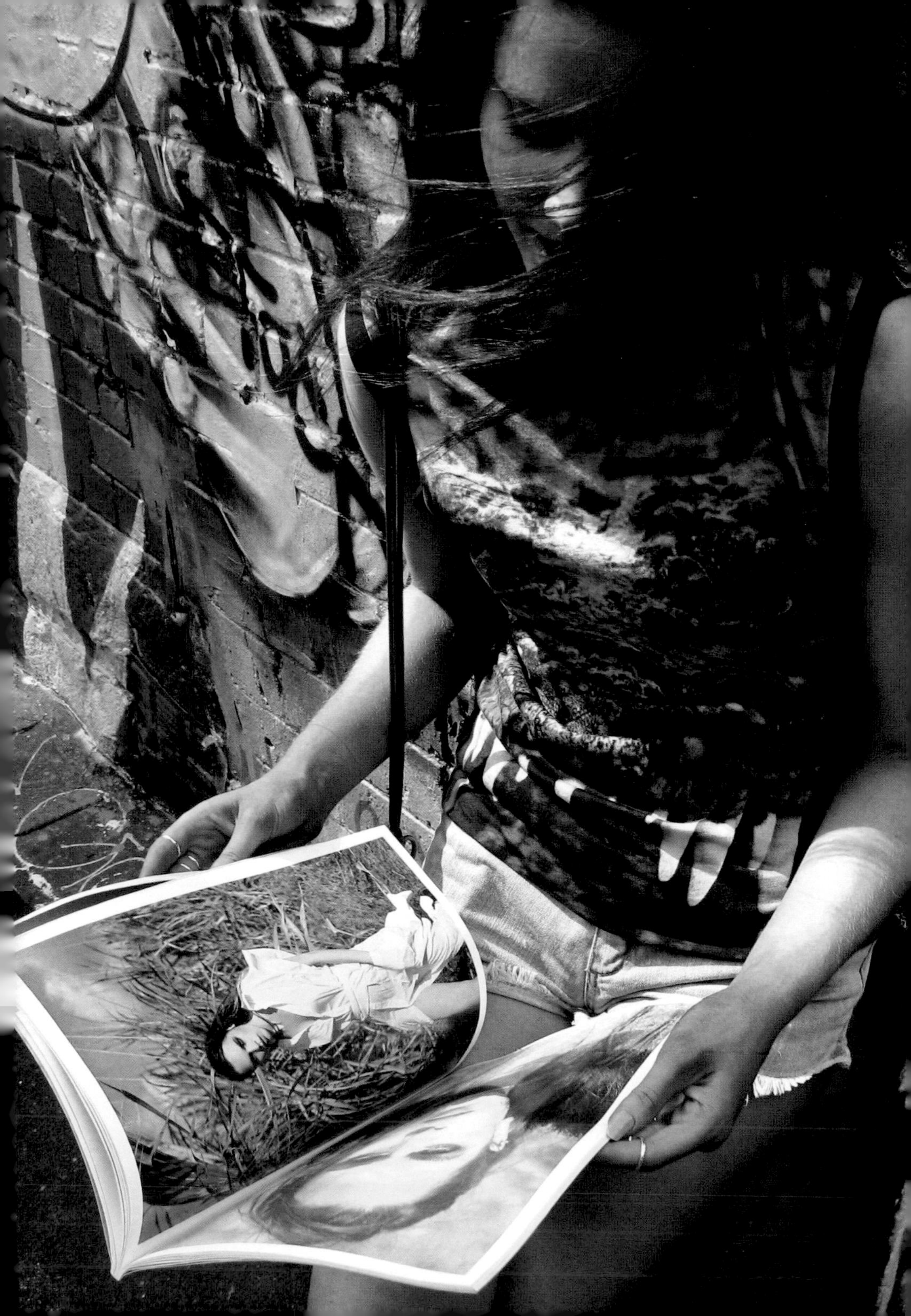

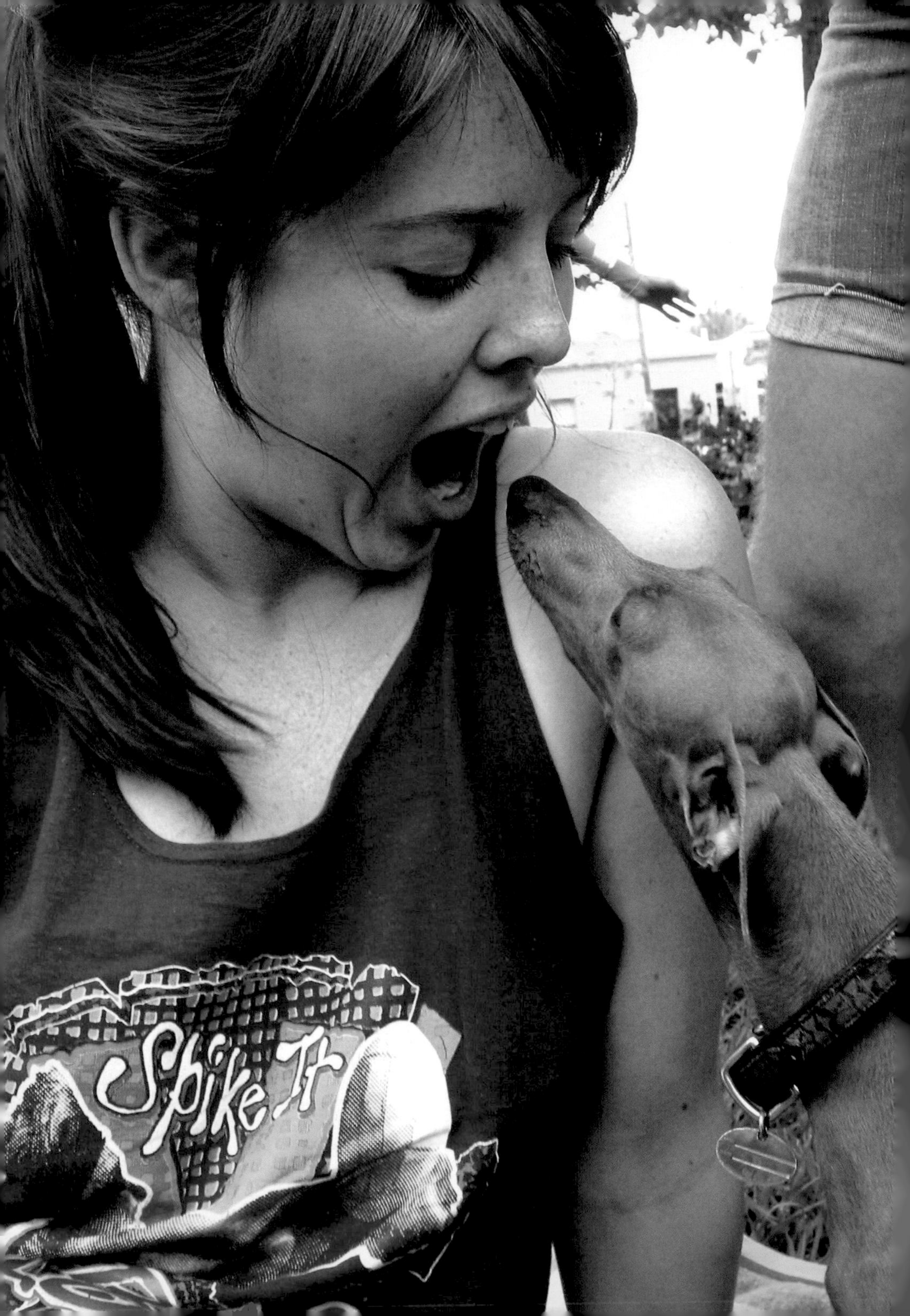
Spike It

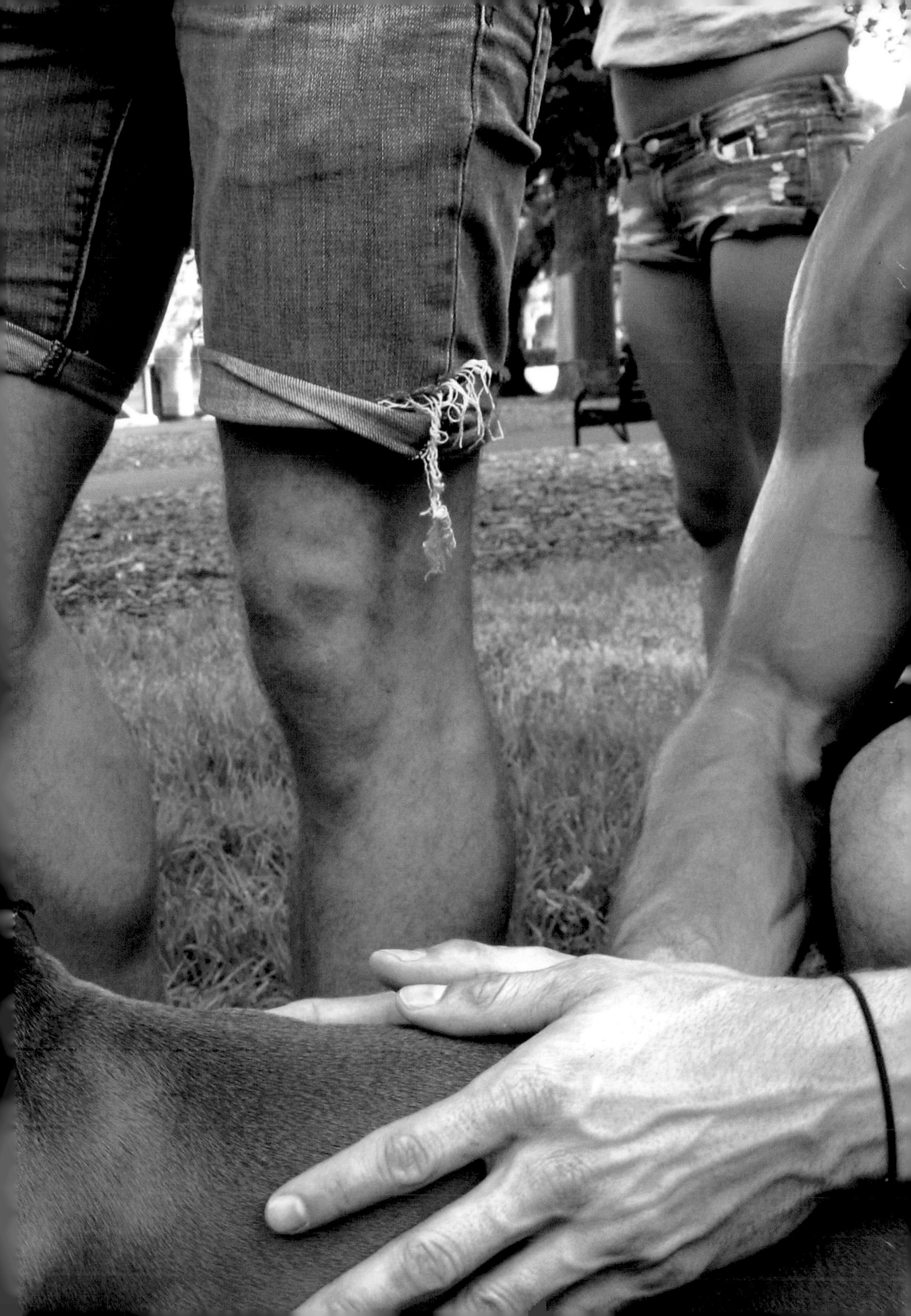

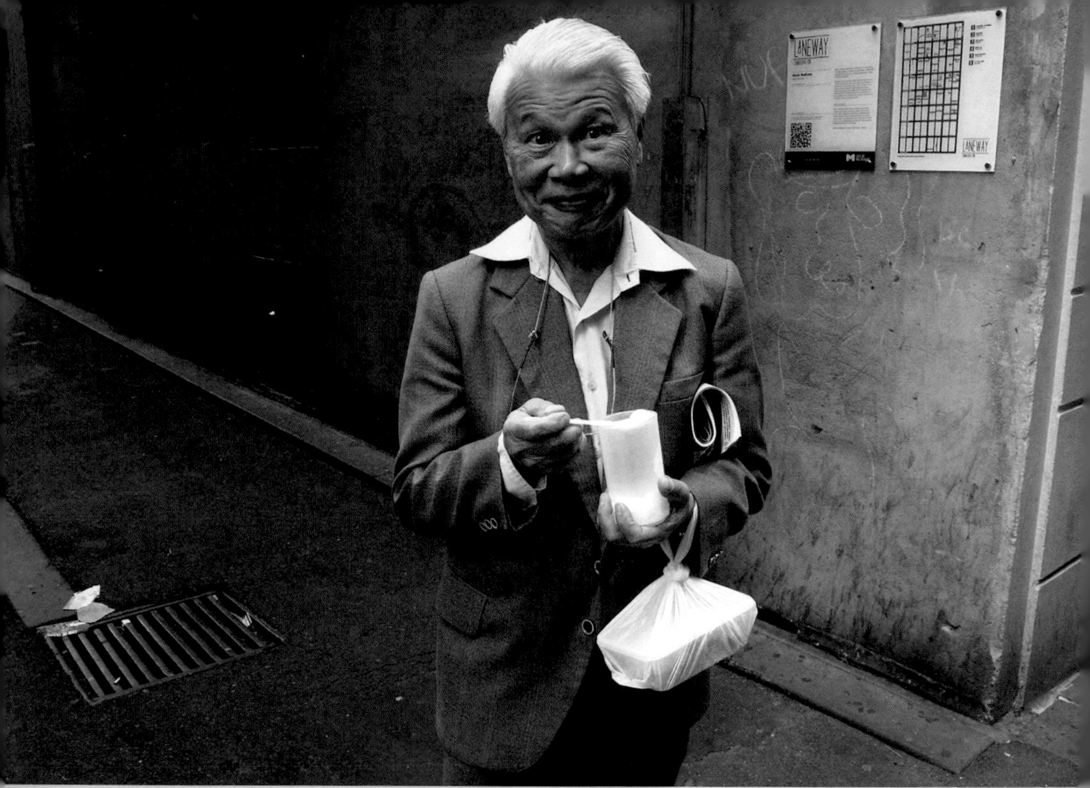

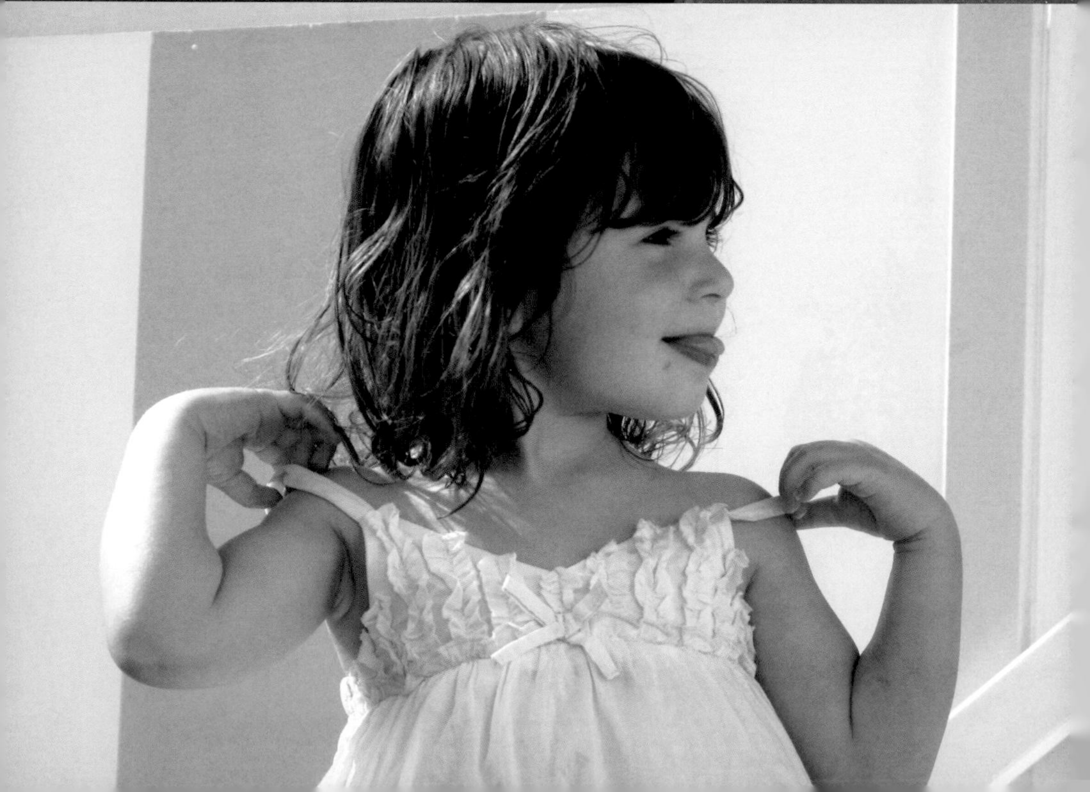

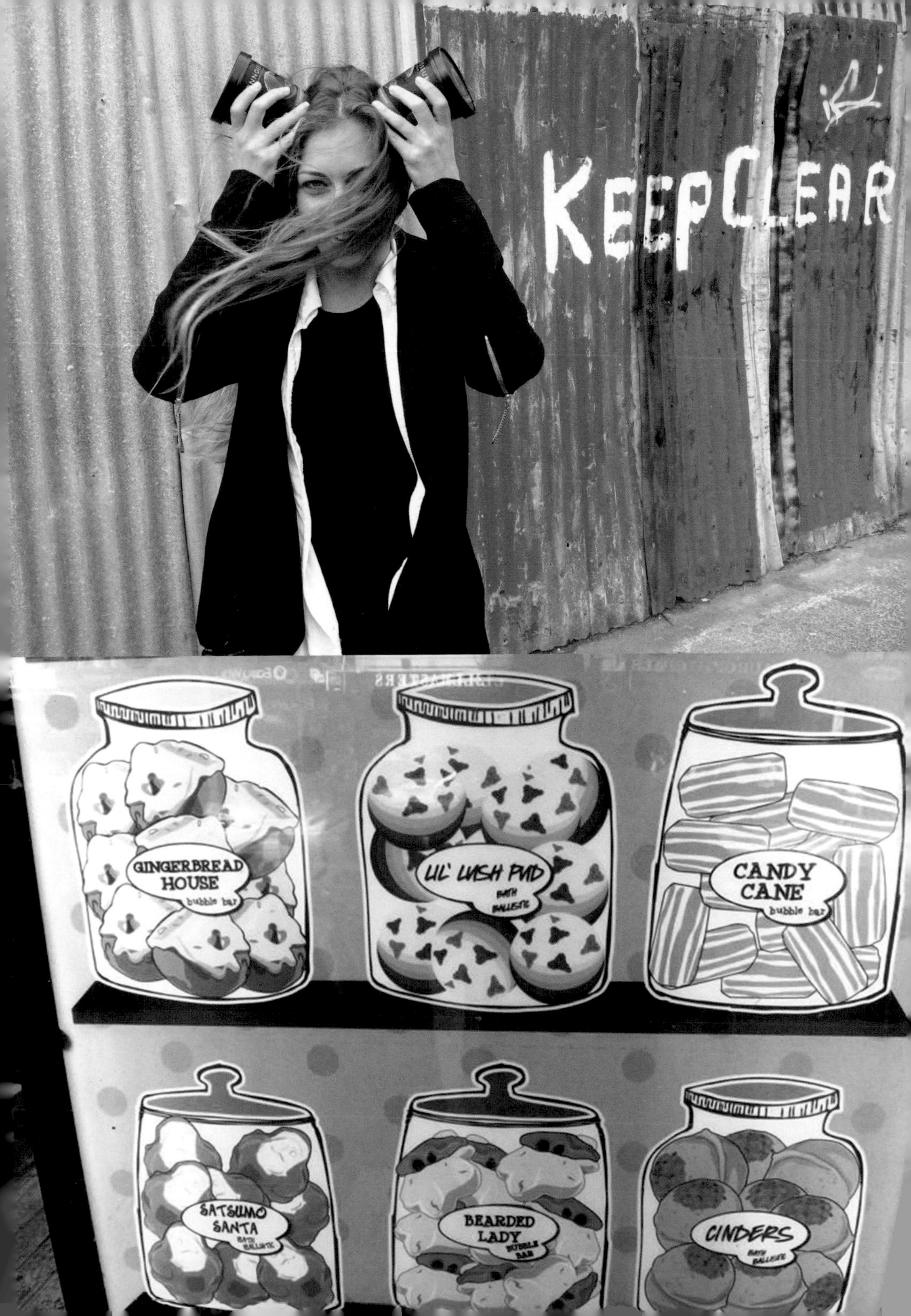
KEEP CLEAR
GINGERBREAD HOUSE
bubble bar
LIL' LUSH PUD
CANDY CANE
bubble bar
SATSUMO SANTA
BEARDED LADY
CINDERS

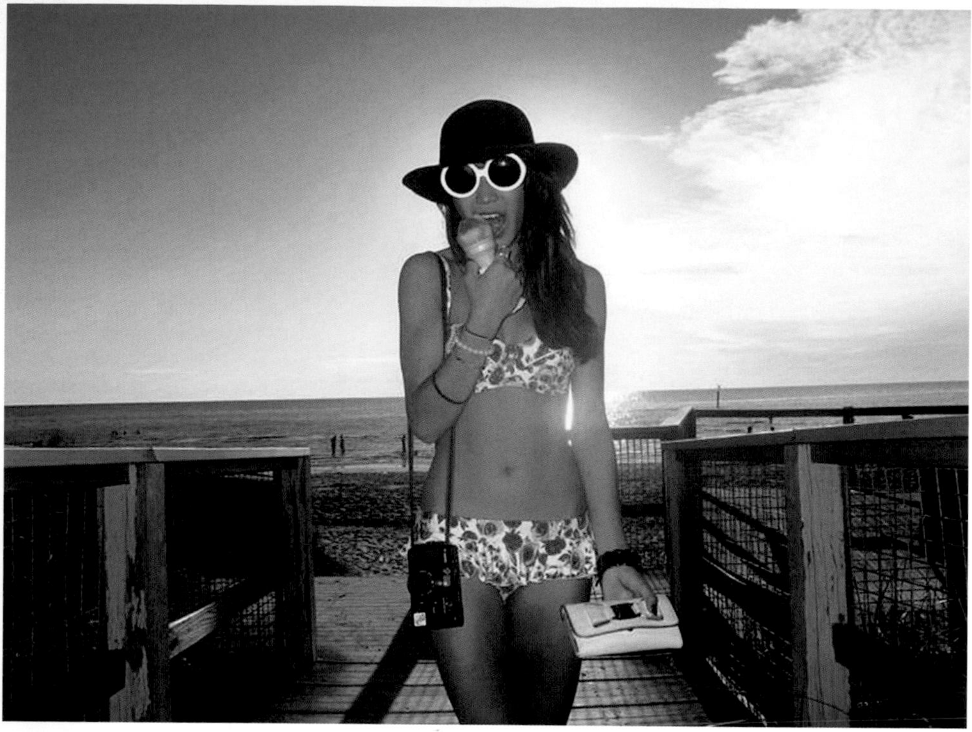

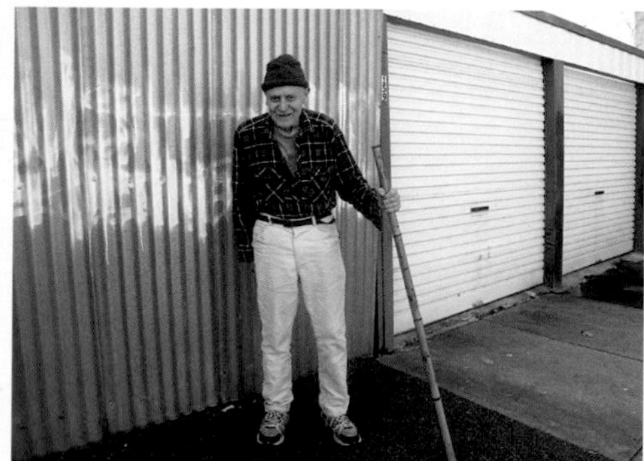

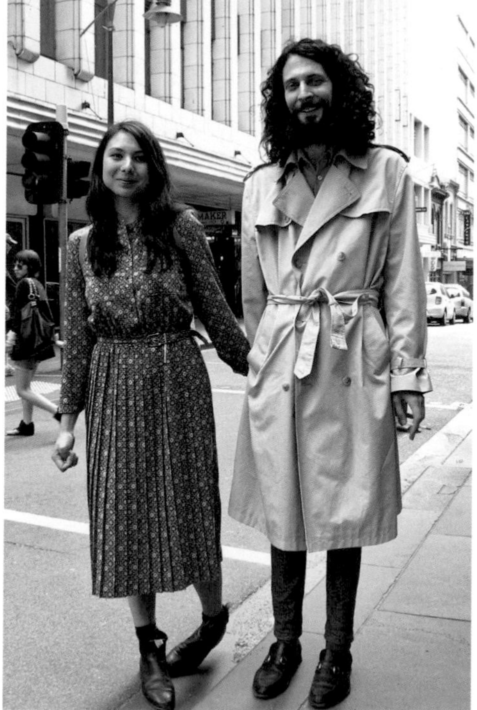

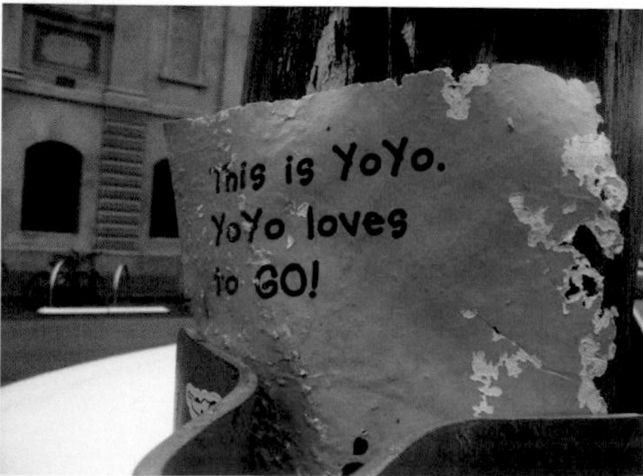
This is YoYo.
YoYo loves
to GO!

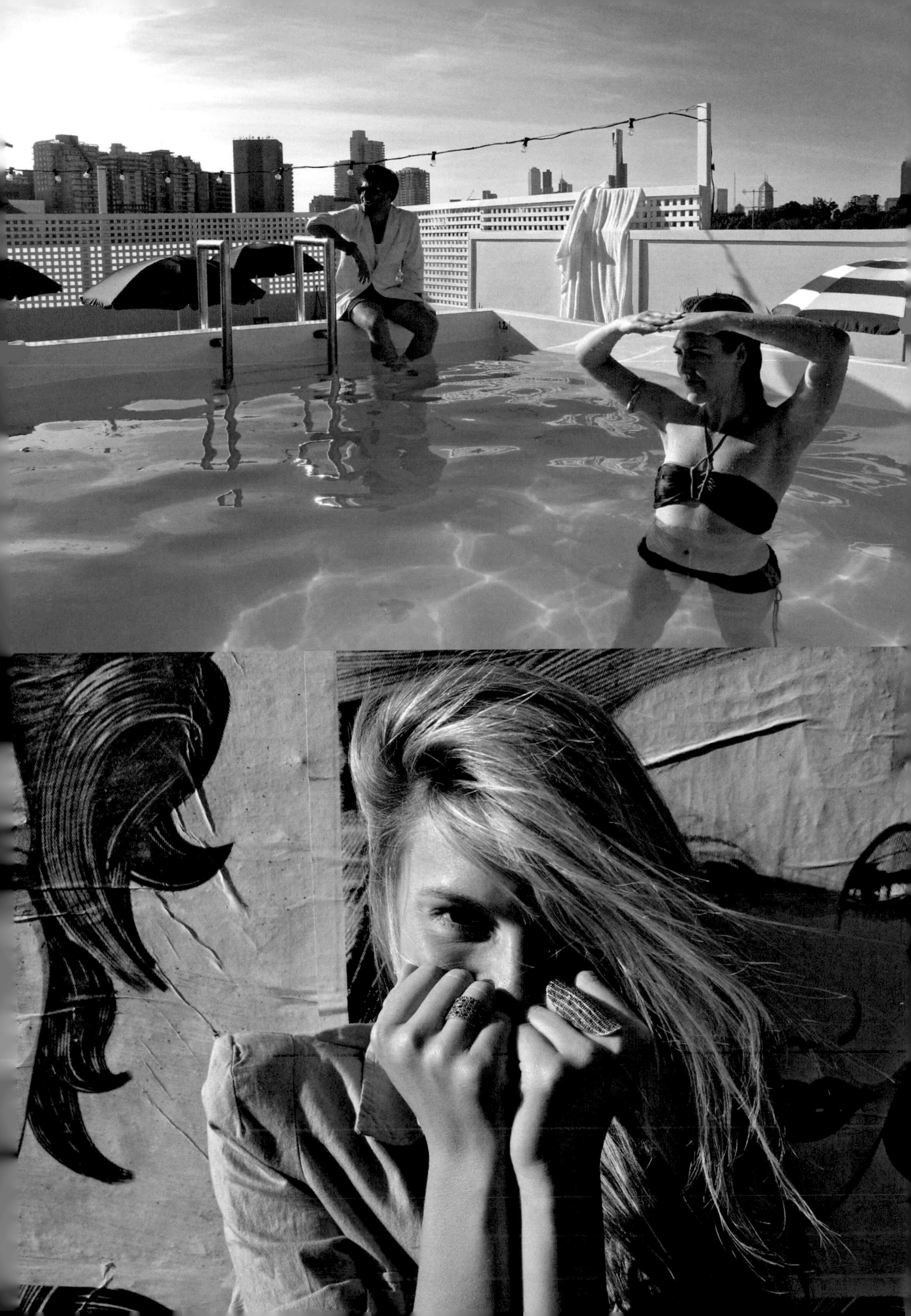

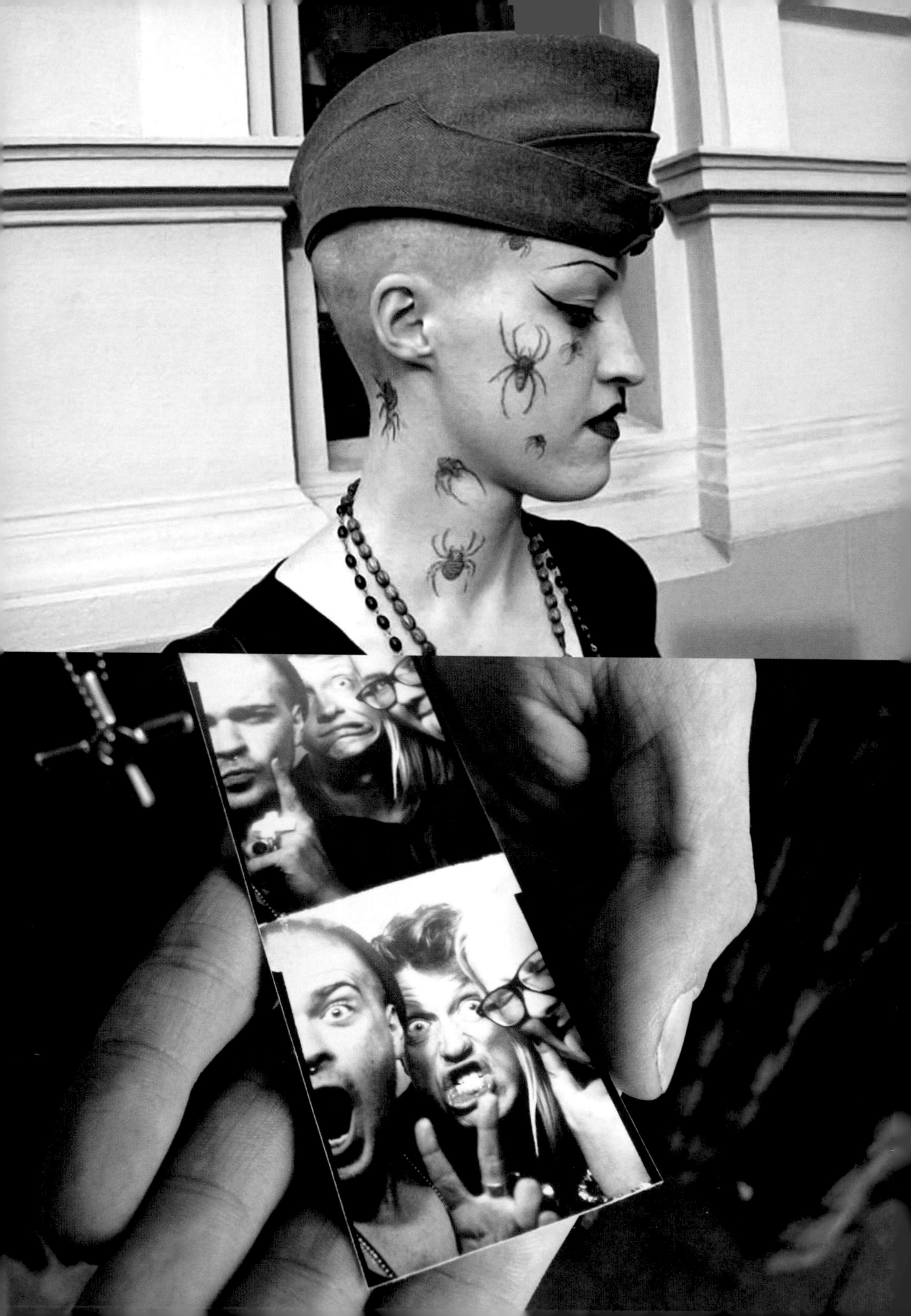

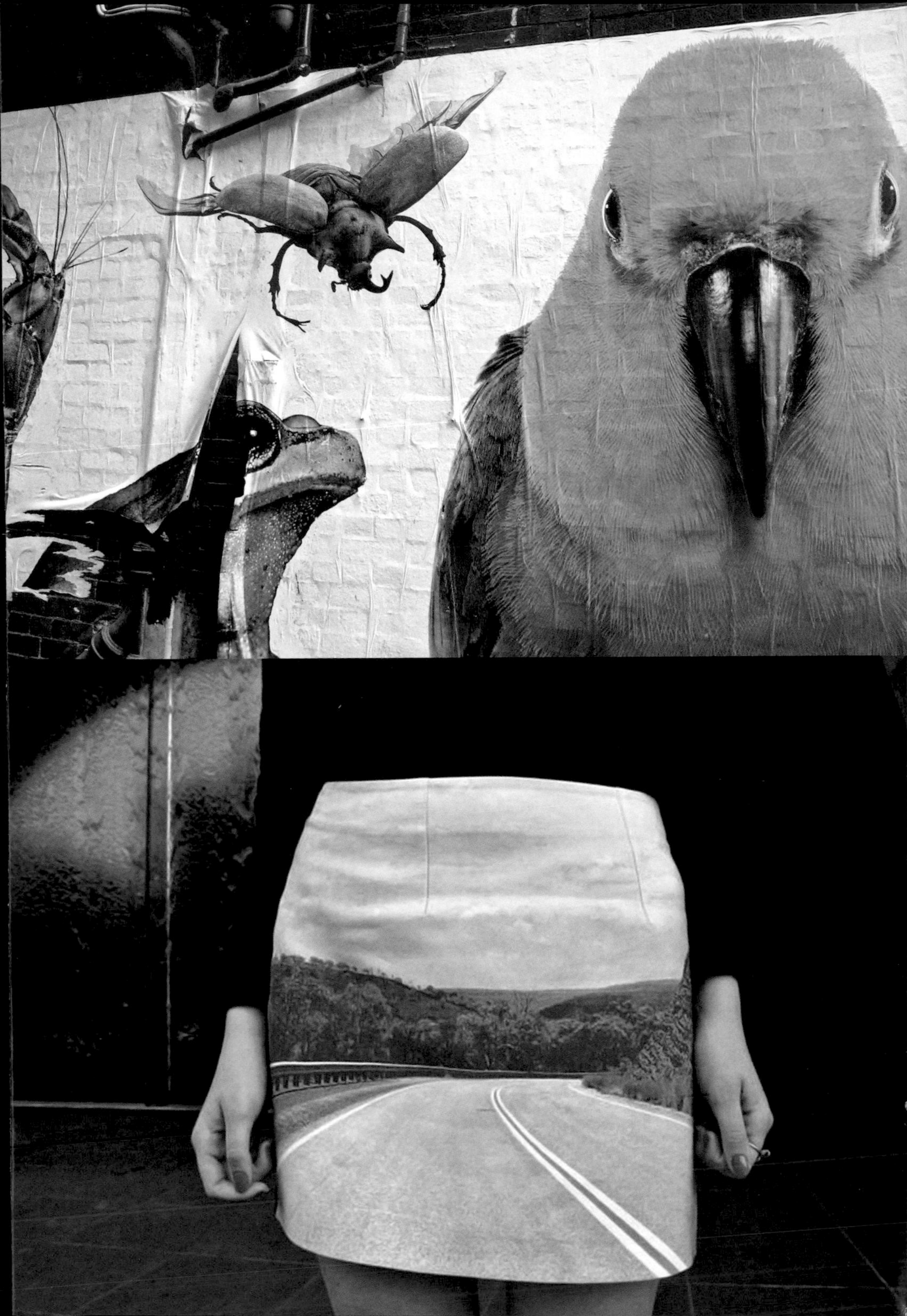

NUMBER OF FLIGHTS

146

10 DOMESTIC
136 INTERNATIONAL

DISTANCE TRAVELLED

268,460 miles
432,044 kilometres

NUMBER OF TIMES AROUND THE EARTH

10.8

TOP AIRCRAFT

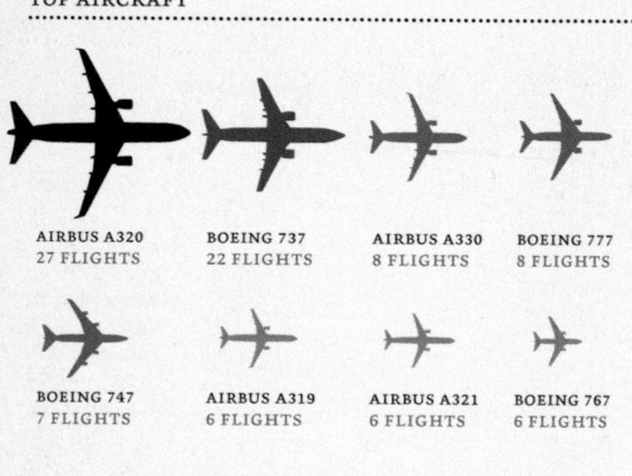

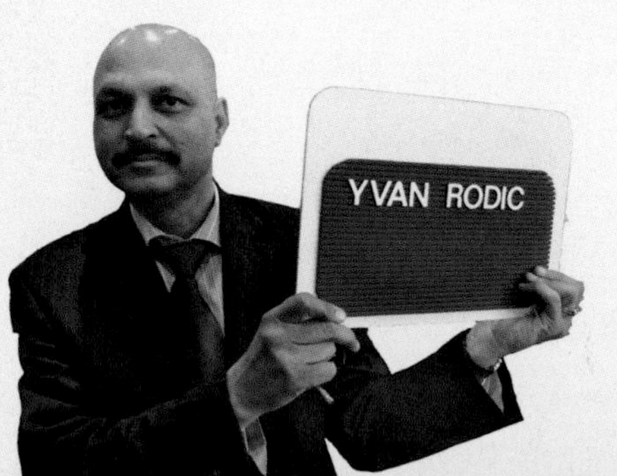

NUMBER OF AIRPORTS

80

MOST VISITED AIRPORTS

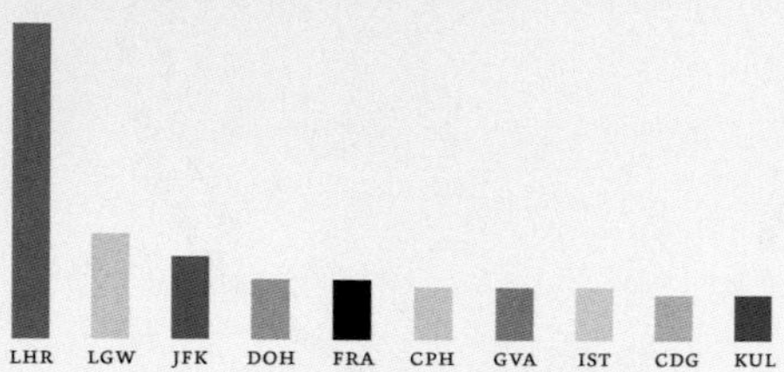

LONDON / HEATHROW (42); LONDON / GATWICK (14); NEW YORK / JFK (11); DOHA / DOHA (8); FRANKFURT AM MAIN / FRANKFURT (8); COPENHAGEN / KASTRUP (7); GENEVA / GENEVA (7); ISTANBUL / ATATÜRK (7); PARIS / CHARLES DE GAULLE (6); KUALA LUMPUR / KUALA LUMPUR (6)

OTHER AIRPORTS VISITED

SYDNEY / KINGSFORD SMITH (6); WARSAW / CHOPIN (6); STOCKHOLM / ARLANDA (5); SÃO PAULO / GUARULHOS (5); LONDON / LUTON (5); VIENNA / SCHWECHAT (5); KIEV / BORISPOL (4); REYKJAVÍK / KEFLAVÍK (4); KUWAIT / KUWAIT (4); LOS ANGELES / LAX (4); OSLO / GARDERMOEN (4); SHANGHAI / PUDONG (4); BERLIN / TEGEL (4); VANCOUVER / VANCOUVER (4); ZURICH / KLOTEN (4); AUCKLAND / MANGERE (3); RIO DE JANEIRO / GALEÃO (3); KATOWICE / KATOWICE (3); BUENOS AIRES / JORGE NEWBERY (3); AMSTERDAM / SCHIPHOL (2); ABU DHABI / ABU DHABI (2); BERGEN / FLESLAND (2); BANGKOK / SUVARNABHUMI (2); MUMBAI / CHHATRAPATI SHIVAJI (2); BRUSSELS / BRUSSELS (2); BUDAPEST / FERENC LISZT (2); CAIRO / CAIRO (2); JAKARTA / SOEKARNO-HATTA (2); NEWARK / LIBERTY (2); BUENOS AIRES / MINISTRO PISTARINI (2); ROME / LEONARDO DA VINCI-FIUMICINO (2); BAKU / HEYDAR ALIYEV (2); HANOI / NOI BAI (2); HELSINKI / VANTAA (2); HONG KONG / HONG KONG (2); HONOLULU / HONOLULU (2); SEOUL / INCHEON (2); IGUAZÚ / IGUAZÚ (2); KISHINEV / KISHINEV (2); LONDON / LONDON CITY (2); NEW YORK / LA GUARDIA (2); MILAN / LINATE (2); LISBON / PORTELA (2); MADRID / BARAJAS (2); MINSK / MINSK (2); MONTEVIDEO / CARRASCO (2); MILAN / MALPENSA (2); ODESSA / ODESSA (2); PORTO / FRANCISCO SÁ CARNEIRO (2); CHICAGO / O'HARE (2); PARIS / ORLY (2); BUCHAREST / HENRI COANDA (2); PORTO ALEGRE / SALGADO FILHO (2); PISA / GALILEO GALILEI (2); SANTIAGO / COMODORO ARTURO MERINO BENÍTEZ (2); SEATTLE / SEATTLE-TACOMA (2); TAIPEI / TAOYUAN (2); WELLINGTON / WELLINGTON (2); WROCLAW / COPERNICUS (2); BARCELONA / BARCELONA-EL PRAT (1); BEIRUT / BEIRUT-RAFIC HARIRI (1); BATUMI / BATUMI (1); SÃO PAULO / CONGONHAS (1); GIRONA / COSTA BRAVA (1); OSAKA / KANSAI (1); KRAKOW / JOHN PAUL II (1); NICE / NICE CÔTE D'AZUR (1); TOKYO / NARITA (1); RIO DE JANEIRO / SANTOS DUMONT (1); LONDON / STANSTED (1)

MOST FREQUENTED AIRLINES

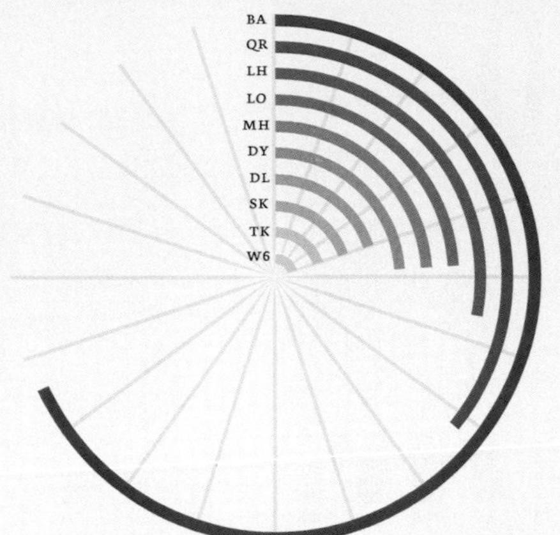

BRITISH AIRWAYS BA (17); QATAR AIRWAYS QR (9); LUFTHANSA LH (7); LOT LO (6); MALAYSIA AIRLINES MH (6); NORWEGIAN AIR SHUTTLE DY (6); DELTA AIRLINES DL (5); SCANDINAVIAN AIRLINES SK (5); TURKISH AIRLINES TK (5); WIZZ AIR W6 (5)

ROUTES MOST TRAVELLED

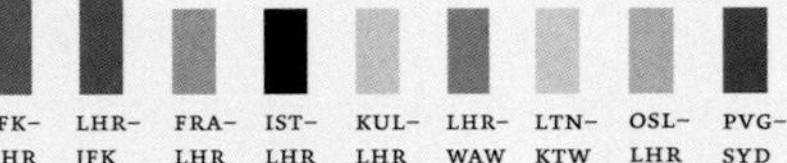

NEW YORK JFK–LONDON HEATHROW (4); LONDON HEATHROW–NEW YORK JFK (3); FRANKFURT FRANKFURT–LONDON HEATHROW (3); ISTANBUL ATATÜRK–LONDON HEATHROW (3); KUALA LUMPUR KUALA LUMPUR–LONDON HEATHROW (2); LONDON GATWICK–REYKJAVÍK KEFLAVÍK (2); LONDON HEATHROW–WARSAW CHOPIN (7); LONDON LUTON–KATOWICE KATOWICE (2); OSLO GARDERMOEN–LONDON HEATHROW (2); SHANGHAI PUDONG–SYDNEY KINGSFORD SMITH (2)

NUMBER OF HOURS IN THE AIR

616 hours 47 minutes

NUMBER OF UPGRADES

0

FLIGHTS PER WEEKDAY

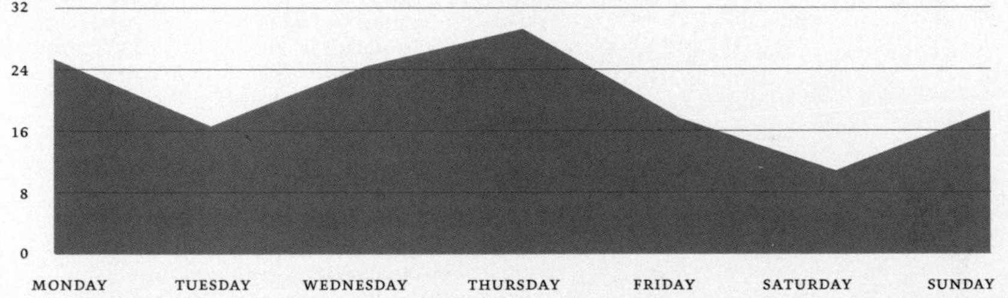

MONDAY 26
TUESDAY 17
WEDNESDAY 25
THURSDAY 30
FRIDAY 18
SATURDAY 11
SUNDAY 19

FLIGHTS PER MONTH

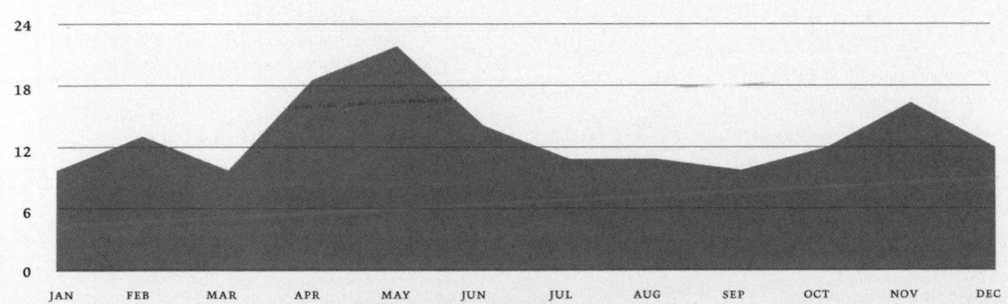

JANUARY 9
FEBRUARY 12
MARCH 9
APRIL 17
MAY 20
JUNE 13
JULY 10
AUGUST 10
SEPTEMBER 9
OCTOBER 11
NOVEMBER 15
DECEMBER 11

This book is dedicated to Mum and Dad

First published in the United Kingdom in 2013
by Thames & Hudson Ltd, 181A High Holborn, London WC1V 7QX

Design by Kate Slotover

British Library Cataloguing-in-Publication Data
A catalogue record for this book is available from the British Library

ISBN 978-0-500-29087-3

Printed and bound in China by C&C Offset Printing Co., Ltd

To find out about all our publications, please visit **www.thamesandhudson.com**. There you can subscribe to our e-newsletter, browse or download our current catalogue, and buy any titles that are in print.

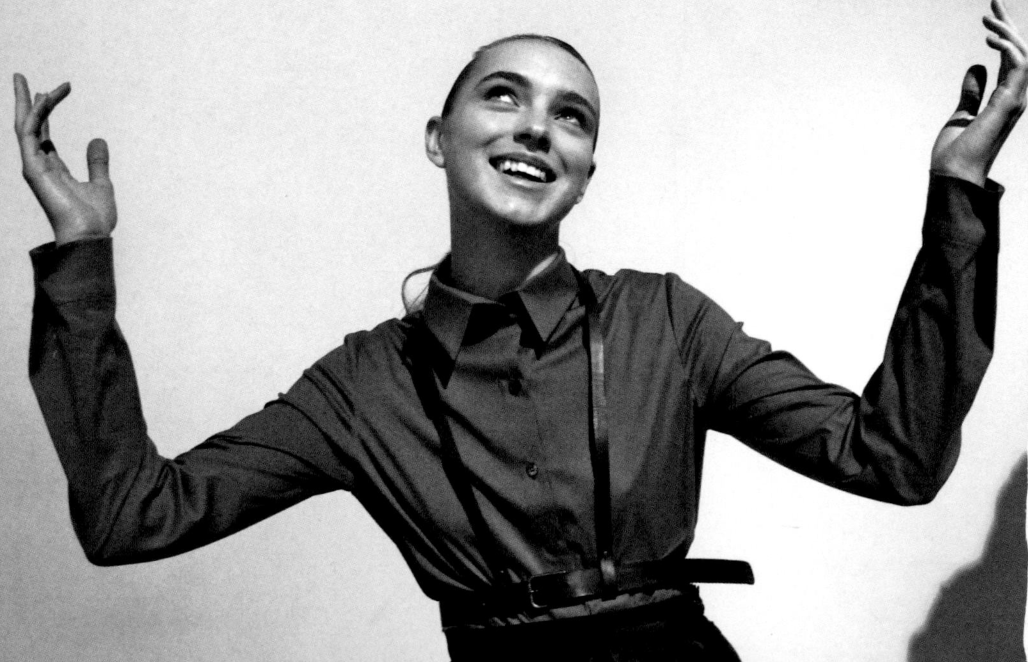

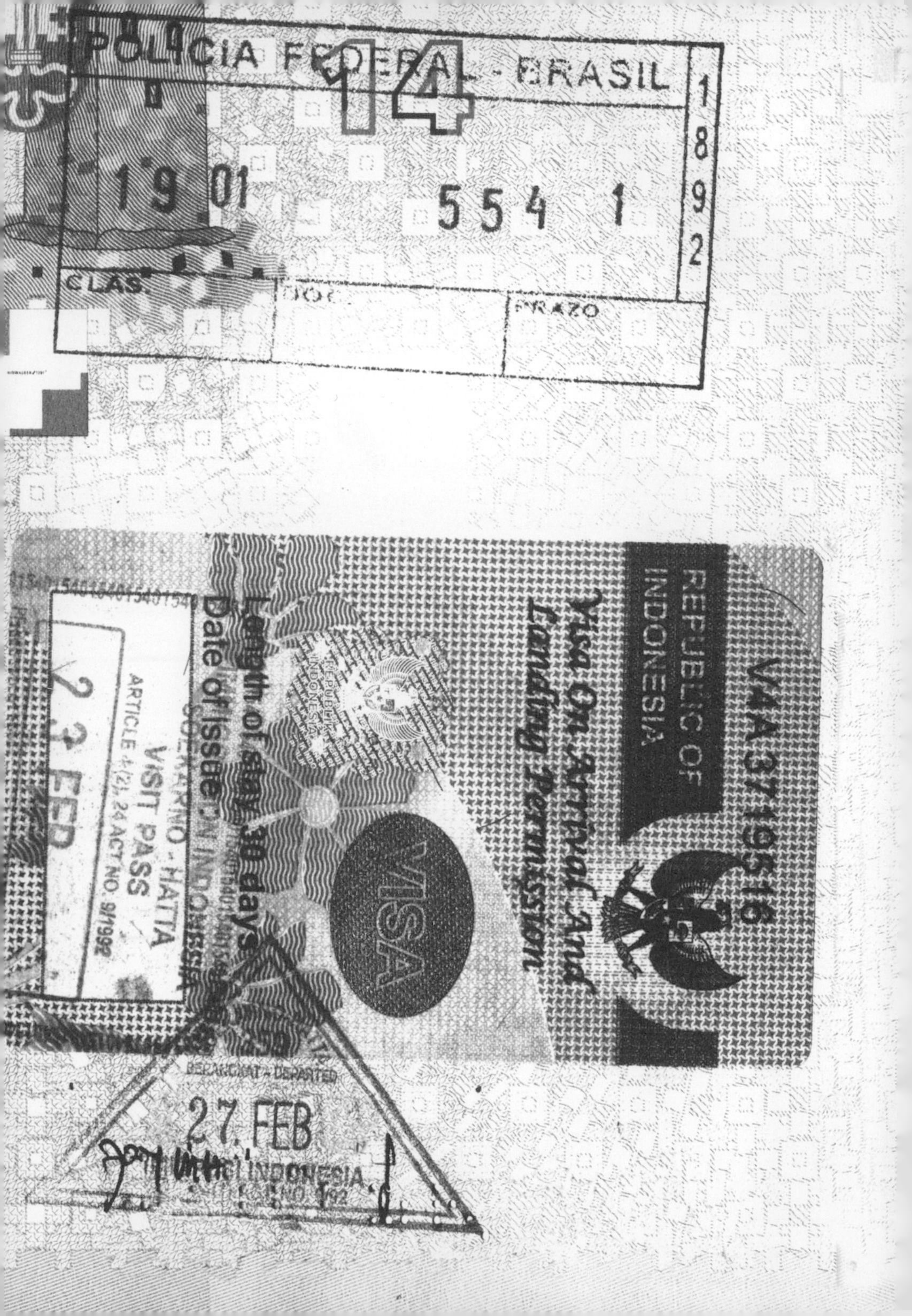

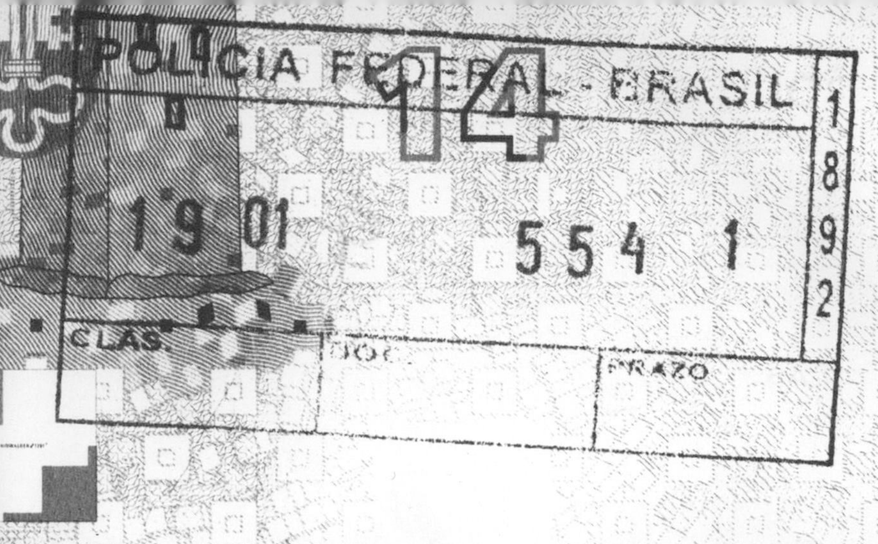

REPUBLIC OF INDONESIA

V4A3719516

Visa On Arrival And Landing Permission

VISA

Length of stay 30 days
Date of issue

SOEKARNO - HATTA
VISIT PASS
ARTICLE 4 (2), 24 ACT NO. 9/1992

23 FEB

BERANGKAT - DEPARTED
27. FEB
INDONESIA